The Psychology of Human Development

Under the General Editorship of
Jerome Kagan
Harvard University

The

of Human

Arlene S. Skolnick
Institute of Human Development
University of California, Berkeley

Psychology Development

HARCOURT BRACE JOVANOVICH, PUBLISHERS

San Diego   New York   Chicago   Atlanta   Washington, D.C.
London   Sydney   Toronto

To Jerry, Mike, and Alex

THE PSYCHOLOGY OF HUMAN DEVELOPMENT
Arlene S. Skolnick

ISBN: 0–15–572700–1

Library of Congress Catalog Card Number: 85–60812
Printed in the United States of America

Preface

*A*nyone who sets out to write a textbook on human development faces a challenge: how can one give a coherent, readable account of a science that covers an enormous array of topics, includes several major theoretical traditions, and produces new knowledge at an astonishing rate? In this book I have tried to achieve coherence in several ways. First, although the field seems fragmented, its pieces can all be fitted into one story—the ordinary course of life from birth to death. Thus, I define the task of a developmental textbook—if not the field itself—as making sense of a person's experience over the course of a lifetime. The organizing theme of the book is individuality and the development of self.

Second, while the study of human development is a rigorous science, it also touches on fundamental questions that have puzzled philosophers, poets, and ordinary people since the beginnings of human thought. Is there a human nature? If so, is it malleable or fixed, aggressive or altruistic, social or solitary? Are we governed by reason or passion? I have used these larger issues as another kind of thread linking the different aspects of developmental research.

Apart from the task of providing a coherent overview, a textbook is finally shaped by a number of other choices about what to include and what approach to take. After the first three chapters—an introduction and a chapter each on methods and theory—this book proceeds in chronological order through the life course, emphasizing development from infancy through adolescence. Each stage is examined in terms of its own unique characteristics and its place in the overall life course.

The multiplicity of influences on development is another major theme presented here. As Erikson once observed, the individual is at all times a biological organism, an ego, and a member of a particular society. I have tried to include all three aspects of development at every stage.

Despite the many influences that shape our lives, I have assumed that individuals at all stages, even infants, contribute to their own development. Moreover, change is possible at all stages of life, not just during childhood and adolescence.

While encouraging respect for disciplined, empirical inquiry, the book reflects the idea that science is a human enterprise which also develops. New questions are constantly being raised, new discoveries made, old facts reinterpreted.

Finally, I have taken an eclectic, pragmatic approach to theory. The era of opposing "schools" of psychology has faded; psychologists still carry on theoretical debates, but the ideological barricades that once divided behaviorists, Freudians, Piagetians, and others have largely been swept away by the cognitive revolution. Psychologists have not discarded the traditional theories; rather, they have assimilated their insights into the emerging cognitive framework. Each theory was once offered as an explanation for everything. Now each is recognized as contributing to our understanding of some particular aspect of behavior and development. Furthermore, some neglected theories are enjoying a renaissance. William James, for example, has been rediscovered as a founding father of contemporary psychology. His ideas are discussed in the chapter on the self.

All in all, these are exciting times in developmental psychology. Aside from the new theoretical ferment, the success of the cognitive paradigm has paradoxically opened the way for renewed scientific interest in feeling, emotion, personality, and social relationships. We have also witnessed remarkable advances in our understanding of infancy. I hope I have managed to convey some sense of the new intellectual excitement and achievement.

Special Acknowledgments

I am grateful to the many people who helped in the book's creation. Judith Greissman, now of Basic Books, originally encouraged me to write such a text and offered editorial help and enthusiasm through the whole first draft. Jerome Kagan, general editor in psychology for HBJ, read every chapter more than once and offered pointed criticism and welcome encouragement. I owe a particular debt to my colleagues at the Institute of Human Development for their intellectual companionship and commitment to developmental research.

I would also like to thank those at HBJ who helped turn the manuscript into a book, especially Marc Boggs, who had the difficult job of following Judy Greissman and succeeded admirably. Sarah Smith, more than a manuscript editor, often helped me to say what I thought I had said in the first place; it was Sarah who

suggested the Milne poem to open Chapter 9. Helen Triller, the production editor, was extremely helpful and reassuring.

Thanks are also due to Peter Martin of Design Office, who is responsible for the good looks of this book, and to Leslye Borden, the photo researcher, who somehow found the photos to illustrate what I had in mind. I would also like to thank Sarah Dorrell, who helped in numerous ways to cope with the task of getting the manuscript and its bibliography into final shape. I also appreciated the research assistance of Jane Bernzweig and David Peterzell; Donna Weston and Curt Samuels offered critical suggestions on some of the chapters.

I am indebted to those colleagues in the field who, along with Jerome Kagan, contributed to the book through their critical reviews. I owe a special debt of gratitude to John Wright of the University of Kansas at Lawrence, whose detailed comments and suggestions for each chapter provided important guidance throughout the final revision stage. I also owe special thanks to Gerald Gratch of the University of Houston, who offered, along with a careful review of the manuscript, enthusiasm and understanding of what I was trying to do which helped boost my morale through the last stages of writing. The reviewers listed in the Acknowledgments on the following page also offered careful readings.

Finally, I wish to thank my husband, Jerome H. Skolnick, for his support and encouragement throughout the long gestation of this book and my sons, Michael and Alex, who vividly brought to life many of the ideas presented here.

Arlene S. Skolnick

Acknowledgments

Clifford Butzin,
Duke University

Philip S. Dale,
University of Washington

Larry Fenson,
San Diego State University

John Gibbs,
Ohio State University

William J. Hoyer,
Syracuse University

Daniel P. Keating,
University of Maryland Baltimore County

Becky White Loewy,
San Francisco State University

Patricia H. Miller,
University of Florida

Barbara Rogoff,
University of Utah

Carol D. Ryff,
University of Wisconsin, Madison

Barbara Sommer,
University of California, Davis

Thomas D. Spencer,
San Francisco State University

Mark S. Strauss,
University of Pittsburgh

Katherine Van Giffen,
California State University

Malcolm W. Watson,
Brandeis University

Meredith West,
University of North Carolina

Robert Woodson,
University of Texas

Contents

6 Of Human Bonds: Social Development in Infancy 191

Part III Giant Step: The Transition to Childhood 234

7 The Origins of Identity 237

Part IV Middle Childhood: The School Years   350

10 The Age of Reason: Intellectual Development in Middle Childhood   353

11 The Social and Personal Worlds of Middle Childhood   387

The Psychology
of Human Development

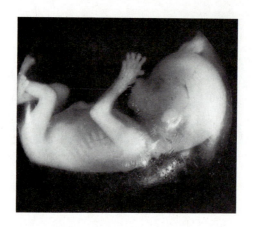

PART I

Human Development

THE RIDDLE OF THE SPHINX

*T*he Sphinx was a monster with the head of a woman and the body of a lion, who sat on a high rock outside of Thebes. She killed any passer-by who could not solve a riddle: "What creature walks on four feet in the morning, two feet at noon, and three feet in the evening?" No one could until Oedipus came and answered, "A human being in the different stages of life: an infant crawls on all fours, an adult walks on two feet, an old person uses a walking stick." As he finished, the Sphinx leaped from the rock and died, and Oedipus was made King of Thebes.

—Greek myth

CHAPTER 1

Introduction

Perspectives on Human Development

At Shanidar Cave in Iraq, in 1960, an archaeologist named Ralph Solecki made an amazing discovery. He found the fossilized remains of a funeral ceremony that had taken place some 60,000 years ago. A hunter with a badly crushed skull had been laid to rest on a woven straw mat, and masses of brightly colored flowers had been placed in his grave.

What was amazing about this discovery was that the hunter and his mourners were not fully evolved humans, but Neanderthals, a closely related but different subspecies which has been extinct for about 30,000 years. Neanderthals are usually depicted by cartoonists as bent over, heavy-browed, shuffling brutes, carrying big sticks and using them often to hit each other over the head. In contrast to this ape-man image, what is revealed at Shanidar and many other recent archaeological discoveries—some going back more than half a million years—is that our Neanderthal ancestors had an ability to use symbols, and to think and act in time and space, that was far beyond the ability of any ape.

Thus, the Neanderthals were the first prehistoric humans to display the chief characteristics that set us apart from all other animals: the anticipation of death, the belief in an afterlife, the care of the disabled and the elderly, the practice of magic to control the future, the beginnings of art.

If the Neanderthals were not apes, neither were they angels. They could care for the aged and handicapped and bury their dead with tenderness, but there is evidence of violence as well. Their behavior reveals the same two-sided human nature that has puzzled philosophers for thousands of years.

I have chosen to introduce a textbook on developmental psychology with this glimpse into prehistory because it reveals how early humans began to live in a world of cultural traditions and social obligations, with an awareness of self and of others as individuals and the realization that human lives unfold through time and end in death.

Funeral ceremonies like the one at Shanidar are probably only the best preserved of Nean-

derthal rituals. Like all known "primitive" peoples today, they must have had special beliefs and rituals marking all the key steps in the human life cycle: birth, the coming of sexual maturity, marriage, and death. Thus, the scientific study of human development may be seen as a modern version of humanity's ancient urge to understand its own essential nature and the ways that time transforms us from infancy through old age.

The Study of Human Development

Although an interest in human development is as old as humanity itself, as a field of scientific study it arose quite late in history, less than a hundred years ago. The field has undergone some dramatic transformations since its beginnings, with some of the most important ones taking place in the 1960s and 1970s.

The scientific roots of developmental psychology reach back to Charles Darwin and the publication of his *Origin of Species* in 1859. The theory of evolution transformed our society's conceptions of children and of human nature, and had a profound influence on all of psychology (Kessen, 1965). Above all, Darwin focused the attention of the intellectual world on the idea of development. Scholars looked for parallels between the development of species, the development of civilization, and the development of the child. Careful observation of children, it was widely believed, would reveal the steps taken by the human race in its evolution. Therefore, Darwin's work made the study of children scientifically valuable.

By the turn of the century, the study of the child was a thriving enterprise. It included not only child watchers looking for clues to the descent of man, but also those whose interests were often closely tied to clinical or practical issues; many child guidance clinics were set up to advise parents and teachers in how to deal with children. Child development research was funded to provide basic information on children's development and methods of childrearing. The development of standardized intelligence tests was another practical task that helped to make the study of children into a systematic science.

In recent years, the field has experienced some dramatic changes. It has changed its name to "developmental psychology," no longer concentrates on children, and has grown phenomenally. It has expanded to include the whole life span and deals with a vast range of topics. Many developmental psychologists now study such processes as perception, attention, or language development rather than the characteristics of people in particular life stages. Also, researchers from other disciplines have joined psychologists in studying the life course—sociologists, historians, demographers, economists, anthropologists. Thus, despite the diversity of their interests, developmental researchers share a common concern of change over time in how people think, feel, and act.

The size and diversity of developmental psychology today pose a challenge to both the student and the textbook writer. How can one grasp and organize an enormous body of information that includes physical, intellectual, emotional, and social development from womb to tomb, as well as a number of competing theories which differ in how they interpret the facts of developmental change?

This book tries to deal with the challenge by relating research findings to a set of central themes. These themes are outlined below.

Individuality and Development

Human development is the most universal process we know and at the same time the most personal. The basic story of any human life is always the same: we are born, we live for a time, we die. Many of the differences between us and other people can be predicted from the time and place we were born, the color of our skin, or whether we were born male or female, rich or poor, attractive or not, with or without defects—to mention only some of the more fateful contrasts among humans.

And yet, despite this regularity, no person is exactly like any other. No one grows and ages in the same way as any other, and no two people have the same biography; no one else was born to your particular parents at the exact moment you were—not even if you are a twin. Further, there is a great discrepancy between "the life course" viewed objectively and anybody's life viewed from the inside. We do not experience our own lives as the unfolding of some inevitable general pattern. Even the most detailed biography of our lives might not correspond to our lives as we live them—uncertain, full of small and large choices, not knowing in precise detail what will happen in the next hour, the next day, the next month (Olney, 1980).

This does not mean that human development cannot be studied scientifically. Modern physicists face a similar problem: they cannot make exact statements about the actions of subatomic particles, even though the laws of physics are well established for larger bodies of matter. This is the famous Principle of Indeterminacy.

Kurt Back (1980) has suggested that human development research can learn to deal with the indeterminacy of the individual life course just as physicists have come to terms with their scientific limitations. The solution is not to try to replace one vision with another, but to recognize that they are different aspects of the same complex reality.

The Centrality of the Self

In recent years, many researchers have concluded that some concept of "the self," however hard it may be to define, is necessary to understand human development. The self is the locus, or center, of developmental change across the life course, the "I" that experiences growth and change. One researcher defines the self as "the most fundamental process by which the individual organism comes to terms with the surrounding world, gives meaning to it, and ultimately adjusts to it" (Blasi, 1983, p. 190).

From infancy to death, individuals construct theories of themselves and of the world around them (Brim, 1976; Epstein, 1973; M. B. Smith, 1978). Like scientists, they do so in order to make sense of their experience, and then to act in the light of the sense they make.

In infancy, the discovery of the self is intertwined with the discovery of the world—what Piaget has termed "the construction of reality." With the discovery of language, self and world are recreated in symbolic terms. As experience accumulates with age, people become historians of their lives, making interpretations about what made them the kinds of persons they are—and what kinds of changes are possible in the future. Over the course of a lifetime, a person may reinterpret his or her life story many times as new happenings cast new light on the past. Always, these interpretations of self and world lead to actions and choices—or the choice not to act.

Multiple Influences

The course of anyone's development is influenced by a host of factors—physical characteristics, family, community, nutrition and health care, school, television, historical events, life events such as illness, divorce, an increase or decrease in the family income, and so on. No single cause can explain why a person's life turned out one way rather than another. Even developmental processes that seem to be largely biological, such as adolescence or the changes of old age, cannot be understood without taking social and psychological factors into account.

This book also tries to link areas of development that are often treated separately. Although intellectual and emotional development are usually studied as separate topics, in a living human being they are inextricably bound together. For example, the major intellectual milestone of the first year of life, as Piaget has found, is the infant's discovery of the permanence of objects—the realization that a ball still exists when it rolls under the sofa, that Mother still exists when she leaves the room.

This discovery is obviously important for the child's dawning awareness of self and the existence of other people. The major emotional development of the first year, the infant's attachment to its mother, cannot be understood

---

FIGURE 1.1
A Sea of Faces
Have you ever looked at the faces in a large crowd and wondered at how no two of them are exactly alike? As long ago as the first century A.D., the Roman writer Pliny marveled at the fact that "The human features and countenance, although composed of some ten parts or little more, are so fashioned that among so many thousands of men there are no two in existence who cannot be distinguished from one another."

apart from its growing intellectual skills. Similarly, the acquisition of language may be studied as a cognitive skill, but the ability to use language revolutionizes the child's emotional life and its relationships with other people.

It also seems to me that normal and abnormal development should be treated as two sides of the same coin, rather than as separate areas. Most psychological disorders can be viewed, at least in part, as normal developmental processes that have gone awry somehow. And looking at abnormal behavior can give important insights into normal development. For example, from autistic children and schizophrenic adults, we can learn part of what it means to have a self-concept by learning what it is like *not* to have a sense of oneself as a permanent object.

In a similar way, the assumption that there are multiple causes for behavior helps to resolve the old arguments about nature versus nurture, heredity versus environment, biology versus culture. There is no conflict between viewing humans as experiencing selves, as biological organisms, and as members of a particular society. To understand human development, we must understand the interplay between body, mind, and society (see Figure 1.1).

For example, even behavior that seems to belong to the realm of biology, such as sexual behavior, is strongly influenced by social and psychological factors. Yet, on the other hand, such seemingly psychological matters as the sense of self may be looked at in a biological perspective. Thus, self-awareness and symbolic communication are uniquely human traits that emerged as survival mechanisms in the course of human evolution. Although we may see the rudimentary forms of such capacities in other primates, the study of animal behavior enables us to understand both the similarities and differences between humans and other species. Our capacities for self-awareness and communication also depend on biological equipment, such as an intact brain.

Moreover, our individuality resides not only in our separate and distinct mind's unique set of life experiences, but in our biological nature

also. One of the most significant discoveries of twentieth-century biology is that every human being, except for identical twins, is an absolutely unique genetic entity. (Indeed, every living organism, down to the lowliest mosquito or microbe, is also unique.)

Our individuality is written not only on our faces and fingerprints, but in our hearts, stomachs, livers, bodily chemistry, and nerve endings as well. In short, "normal" people, from newborns to the aged, differ from one another in almost every conceivable way (Hamburger, 1978), as demonstrated in Figures 1.2 and 1.3 and in the box on Our Anatomic Individuality.

FIGURE 1.2
Anatomical Variations of Sinuses
The individual variations in these diagrams of "normal" 10-year-olds show that there is no average shape of sinuses. No wonder no two people's sneezes are alike.

Source: Adapted from studies by the Child Research Institute of Denver, Colorado, in "On your startling biochemical individuality" by R. J. Williams, 1976, *Executive Health, 12,* no. 8.

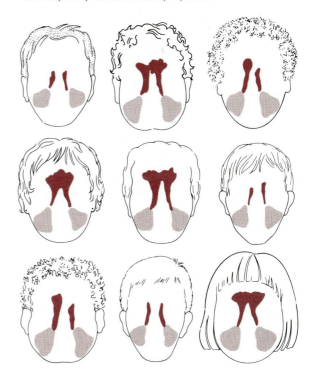

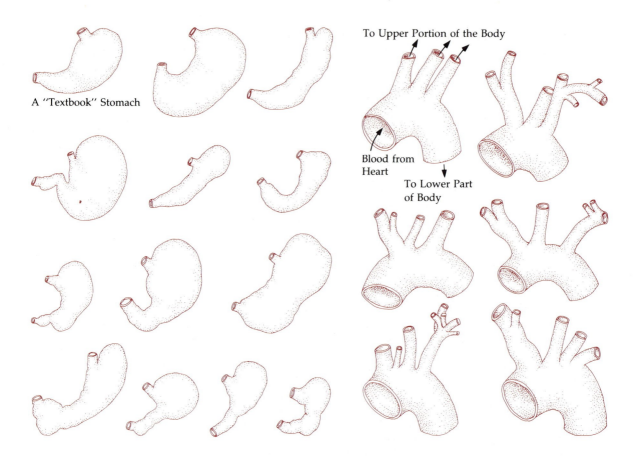

A "Textbook" Stomach

To Upper Portion of the Body

Blood from Heart

To Lower Part of Body

Individuals as Agents in Their Own Development

Until recently, much developmental research seemed to be based on an image of human beings as passive objects of powerful forces. Different researchers had different ideas about what these forces were, such as the environment, the family, inherited traits, instinctual drives. But they shared an image of children and adults as passive products of social or biological influence.

In the past decade or so, developmental researchers have recognized that individuals actively contribute to their own development. What happens to people across the life span is influenced by many factors, but we are not totally helpless in responding to the circumstances of our lives. Even very young infants have some degree of choice in what they will attend and respond to.

FIGURE 1.3
Anatomical Variations of Stomachs and Aortas
These illustrations of stomachs and branching aortas are also from organs that are considered to be "normal." Like the sinuses, the function of these organs is determined by their individual design.

Source: "On your startling biochemical individuality" by R. J. Williams, 1976, *Executive Health, 12,* no. 8. The stomach illustrations are from *An atlas of human anatomy,* 2nd ed., by B. J. Anson, 1963, Philadelphia: Saunders.

Psychologists and social scientists have sometimes assumed that it is unscientific to speak of humans as purposive beings who make choices and decisions. Yet economists, who can scarcely be accused of being less scientific or more tenderhearted than psychologists, consider individual choice as their basic unit of analysis. For the economist, life is a series of choices—small and large, hard and easy. This is not to say that these choices are unconstrained. A person without mathematical apti-

Our Anatomic Individuality

As the illustrations in Figures 1.2 and 1.3 show, the notion of an average stomach or heart, like the notion of an average body, is an abstraction. Bodies come in all sizes and shapes: short or tall; thin, fat, or muscular; with large or small eyes, noses, mouths, ears, hands, feet, and so forth. Our internal organs differ just as much, often in ways that have major implications for health and behavior.

Roger J. Williams is a biochemist who has devoted his career to the study of physiological differences between individuals. In his book, *Biochemical Individuality* (1956), as well as in his later work (Figure 1.2), Williams argues that variability is often overlooked by medical and behavioral researchers. In addition to describing differences in anatomy in humans and animals, Williams gives data on an extremely large number of biochemical features of the human body that vary enormously from one individual to another. These range from the composition of the blood and the amount of DNA in sperm to the output of hormones by the thyroid, adrenal, sex, and other glands. Williams concludes that if enough measures are taken on any individual, that person will be found to be "abnormal" in one way or another.

These variations affect psychological functioning as well as physical health. Everyone lives in a somewhat different world and responds to that world in an individual way. People react differently to temperature, tastes, and smells, as well as to stress and pain. When under stress, some people get headaches, others stomachaches, and still others high blood pressure. There is also evidence that such problems as schizophrenia, depression, and alcoholism may be related to biochemical differences.

As a result of these and many other findings about biological individuality, statements about "instincts"—supposedly common to everyone—are misguided, as are statements which assume that individuals are like blank slates on which the environment makes its mark. Beyond all the various kinds of biochemical variation described here, the most significant source of human individuality is the brain.

Our uniqueness derives not only from the brain's structure and metabolism, but also from its staggering capacity for learning and memory. It has been estimated that the human brain can store more bits of information than the number of elementary particles in the universe (Piel et al., 1979). This complex machinery makes it possible to record the particular experiences of our lives in great detail. Above all, the human cortex creates in each of us a unique and private consciousness.

Vernon Mountcastle, a neurophysiologist, has described how assemblies of cells in the cortex use sensations from the external world to create "neural replicas" of the world, which in turn help to create consciousness and a sense of self:

> We use them [sensory stimuli and their neural replicas] to form dynamic and continually updated maps of the external world, and of our place and orientation, and of events within it. At the level of sensation, your images and my images are virtually the same, and readily identified one to another by verbal description, or common reaction.

> Beyond that, each image is conjoined with genetic and stored experiential information that makes each of us uniquely private. From that complex integral each of us constructs at a higher level of perceptual experience his own, very personal, view of within. (Mountcastle, 1975, cited in Bloom, Lazerson, & Hofstader, 1985, p. 233)

tude does not really have the option of becoming a physicist or an engineer; the child of affluent parents has more choices than a poor child. Further, later choices are constrained by earlier ones. The decision to drop out of high school may severely limit a young person's later opportunities for education and work. But as one economist puts it, "The fact that choices are constrained . . . does not mean that all choice is eliminated. Individuals still choose, but within their constraints" (Fuchs, 1983, p. 7).

Multiple Pathways

William James once observed that it is impossible to write biographies in advance. But many developmental theorists and researchers have thought otherwise. Traditionally, they have assumed that if you know about a person's infancy and early childhood, you can predict at least the general outline of his or her life story.

Currently, there is a great debate about constancy and change across the life course. The traditional assumption about the special power of early experiences to shape later life has been challenged by many studies that fail to find such long-term effects. In a major statement challenging the traditional view, Brim and Kagan argue that "humans have a capacity for change across the entire life span . . . the experiences of the early years, which have a demonstrated contemporaneous effect, [do not] necessarily constrain the effects of adolescence and adulthood" (1980, p. 1).

The argument is far from settled at this point. But it is clear that there are many different pathways of development. Not every child from a deprived, broken, or unloving home becomes a maladjusted adult; not every child from a comfortable or kind home becomes a successful and happy adult. Many adults who succeed in our society have backgrounds that were less than ideal. Many of our leading authors, scientists, artists, and political leaders had difficult childhoods marked by family tension and traumatic loss (Rossi, 1968; Goertzel & Goertzel, 1962). Developmental researchers are just beginning to understand how some people manage to overcome adversity and stress. In the process, they are working out more complicated models of how people change across the life course. (See box on Multiple Pathways of Development.)

Multiple Pathways of Development

Sigmund Freud once observed that if we trace a troubled person's development backward from adulthood, "the chain of events appears continuous, and we feel we have gained an insight which is completely satisfactory or even exhaustive" (1920; 1955, pp. 167–68). In other words, we feel we can explain why this person is full of anxiety, that person is a child abuser, another is unable to form close relationships. But, he went on, if we proceed in the reverse way, starting at the beginning, and try to reconstruct the pathway the person took to reach the final outcome, "we no longer get the impression of an inevitable sequence of events—we notice at once that there might have been another result, and that we might

have been just as well able to understand and explain the latter."

Two main points Freud made are gaining increasing recognition in developmental psychology today:

1. Being able to *explain* adult outcomes by looking backward to childhood is very different from *predicting* how children will turn out as adults.
2. There are multiple pathways of development. Starting out from a set of similar circumstances, two children can end up very differently. And there are different routes to similar outcomes.

For example, consider the cases of two men, Lee Harvey Oswald, who killed President

Kennedy in 1963, and John Hinckley, Jr., who shot President Reagan and others in 1981. These two men certainly had very similar "adult outcomes" as presidential assassins, but they came from very different backgrounds. Oswald's story is a sorry tale of parental loss, economic insecurity, and emotional deprivation. Widowed two months after Oswald's birth, his mother was remarried and divorced twice while he was growing up, and they moved countless times from one state to another. She was described by social workers and others as a rejecting, neglecting, self-involved parent who failed to provide Oswald with any semblance of a family life. As a child and adolescent, Oswald had great difficulty

Lee Harvey Oswald

John Hinckley, Jr.

getting along with other children and got into serious trouble for truancy.

John Hinckley, by contrast, came from a respected upper-middle-class family. His parents have been described by those who know them as loving and devoted to their three children. According to one psychologist, David Elkind (1981), John's problem came from pressures to grow up fast and achieve early. His older brother and sister had succeeded in living up to the family's ideals: they were popular, good-looking, intelligent, and did well in school. John's older brother was a scholar and an athlete, as well as a social leader, and went on to become a successful engineering executive. According to Elkind, this brother fulfilled the family's expectations so well that John had difficulty following his footsteps. The brother had "preempted" all the identities his parents valued. So John adopted, in Erik Erikson's terms, a "negative identity"; he became the opposite of those values. If he could not be successful, he could at least be notorious.

Both of these accounts seem plausible. Yet both cases illustrate the difference between continuity and prediction. Hinckley's case is especially clear; we can understand what led up to his shooting spree, but we could not have predicted anything like that outcome from his childhood. The kinds of pressures John Hinckley experienced are rampant in the affluent suburbs of America. Many young people have trouble coping with them, but few get into serious trouble. Oswald's childhood seemed a more obvious prelude to a troubled adulthood. Yet many youngsters have troubled and unpromising childhoods and still manage to grow up as productive adults.

A single case history, studied backwards—or retrospectively—can yield only clues, not conclusions, about influences on development. What we need to know is the probability that a child with a particular characteristic or in a particular situation at time "A" will have a particular outcome at some later time "B." In other words, what is the frequency of different pathways of development? William Runyan (1982) has developed a method for answering such questions about different types of life courses and their distribution. A brief description of this method reveals how surprisingly many different pathways of development there can be.

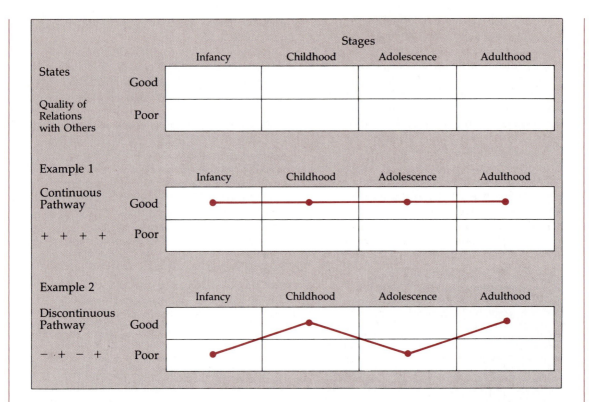

Runyan calls his approach the "stage-state" method. He divides the life course into a series of stages or periods, and each period into two or more states. For example, the life course could be divided into four stages, such as infancy, childhood, adolescence, and adulthood.

The stages do not have to be major life stages; they could be the four years of high school or college, or family background, education, or first and last job. The "states" could be differences in any characteristic or ability: height, intelligence, happiness, mental health. For example—using the four life periods of infancy, childhood, adolescence, and adulthood—we might consider how well the person was getting along with significant people at each stage of life. These stages and states might be illustrated as follows:

The number of possible life courses generated by such a table is 16 ($2 \times 2 \times 2 \times 2$). Thus, someone who was above average on the characteristic at all four stages could be described as $+ + + +$. Someone who was below average would be $- - - -$. In between would be people who varied on the trait at one

time or another. The 16 different pathways are as follows:

Path 1	$-$ $-$ $-$ $-$	Path 9	$+$ $-$ $-$ $-$
Path 2	$-$ $-$ $-$ $+$	Path 10	$+$ $-$ $-$ $+$
Path 3	$-$ $-$ $+$ $-$	Path 11	$+$ $-$ $+$ $-$
Path 4	$-$ $-$ $+$ $+$	Path 12	$+$ $-$ $+$ $+$
Path 5	$-$ $+$ $-$ $-$	Path 13	$+$ $+$ $-$ $-$
Path 6	$-$ $+$ $-$ $+$	Path 14	$+$ $+$ $-$ $+$
Path 7	$-$ $+$ $+$ $-$	Path 15	$+$ $+$ $+$ $-$
Path 8	$-$ $+$ $+$ $+$	Path 16	$+$ $+$ $+$ $+$

Looking at Oswald and Hinckley in terms of these different pathways, Oswald's life seems clearly to fall into path 1 ($- - - -$). Hinckley's case history seems to have been a path 13 ($+ + - -$); he apparently developed well in infancy and childhood, but started having trouble in adolescence.

The stage-state method is a useful reminder of how many possible patterns of development there are. Of course, not all pathways are equally likely. One of the uses of this method is to find out what the distribution of life courses actually is. For example, Runyan studied the occupational histories of 20,000

American men. He divided the life course into four stages consisting of family background, level of education, and first and last job.

There were four states within each stage, resulting in 256 possible life courses! (The possibilities multiply rapidly when you increase the number of stages or states.) But 99 of these possible life courses failed to occur in his sample of 614 men. For example, there was nobody who had an unskilled father and who himself had only an elementary school education, but who ended up as a professional or executive. The most frequent life courses were those in which the son's education and job level were similar to that of his father.

In my own research I am using this method to look at the quality of personal relationships across the life span—with parents in infancy, with peers in childhood and adolescence, and spouses in adulthood. I have examined the life histories of sixty-three people whose development was followed from infancy through middle age (Skolnick, in press). I found that about 25 percent of the people in my sample were in "continuous" pathways, either $+ + + +$ or $- - - -$; the remaining 75 percent showed discontinuity.

It was very common for infancy to be inconsistent with later stages; people could have poor relations with their parents in infancy, but get along with others in later life,

and vice versa. By contrast, it was unlikely for adolescence to be the one discrepant period; if someone got along well or poorly with peers in adolescence, it seems that he or she will do the same at some other period of life, if these preliminary results hold up.

Once we know what the distribution of life courses is, new questions arise that call for further research. Runyan's findings invite the question of why men who had unskilled fathers and an elementary education have unskilled first and last jobs. What was blocking their upward mobility? Was it their own lack of skills? Class bias on the part of schools or employers?

The study of relationships across the life span raises questions about why some people do continuously well or continuously poorly, while others manage to overcome difficult beginnings and still others do poorly after having had close and loving parents in infancy. There are probably many factors that influence a child's progress: temperament; intelligence; health; physical attractiveness; special talents such as artistic or athletic ability; relations with siblings, grandparents, and other relatives as well as with teachers and peers in school; and so on. A change in environment can also change a child's direction. Sometimes the course of a person's life can change in adulthood, even as late as middle age.

The Development of Developmental Theories

The study of human development is an enterprise that in itself is developing. Ideas in developmental psychology are born, grow, and die—and may be reborn at a later time. Many people, however, assume that any science is a vast collection of solid facts and unchanging laws. Yet this image does not describe how the sciences actually work. The conclusions scientists reach are far more tentative than most nonscientists realize. Lewis Thomas (1982) points out that the next issue of any journal in biology, chemistry, or physics can "turn a whole field upside down, shaking out any

number of immutable ideas and installing new bodies of dogma" which sooner or later may also be replaced. Further, he notes, every science is incomplete, no matter how great its achievements. There are still vast areas of mystery about the universe, the atom, the cell.

Finally, no matter how solid the facts of a science may be, they have little meaning outside of some framework of interpretation—that is, a theory. Jules-Henri Poincaré once observed, "Science is built up of facts, as a house is built of stones; but an accumulation of facts is no more a science than a heap of stones is a house" (1908, 1952). Thus, astronomers do not just describe the movements of planets and stars across the sky; they also develop theories to explain how the universe is organized, how it came to be, and what is likely to happen in the future.

The same set of facts can give rise to very different theories. For example, imagine you are standing on a hill looking at a sunset. You see a fiery circle of light gradually disappear below the horizon. But in itself, what you saw does not tell you whether the sun is sinking out of sight, or whether the earth is turning. For many centuries, people believed that the earth was at the center of the universe and that the sun and other heavenly bodies revolved around it.

The shift to the Copernican theory that the earth and other planets revolve around the sun is a major example of what Thomas Kuhn (1962) has called a scientific revolution. Kuhn argues that when one theory replaces another, it brings about a sudden change in the way the world looks to people. He compares this shift in perspective to the way an ambiguous picture can suddenly change from one thing to another—from a duck to a rabbit, from a young woman to an old one. (See Figure 1.4.) For example, the earth in the new Copernican theory was no longer the same earth as in the old theory. In the old theory, the earth was not something that could move; the new earth became a turning body, hurtling through space.

Similarly, different developmental theories are based on very different ways of looking at human beings. At various times and in different theories, the child has been portrayed as a seething cauldron of sex and aggression, a collection of learned reflexes, a young scientist exploring the nature of the world, an information processor. Psychology as a whole has also experienced two scientific revolutions in the twentieth century: a behaviorist revolution which proclaimed that behavior, not mind, was the proper subject matter for scientific study; and a cognitive revolution which once again made mental processes the focus of research.

In this book, I have tried to present ''the facts'' of development in the context of theoretical change and debate over what questions to ask, and how to go about answering them. I believe it is more interesting as well as more

FIGURE 1.4
Figure and Ground
Which do you see first: the profiles or the chalice? the young woman or the old woman? Initial perceptions of gestalt—or figure-ground—illustrations can vary widely from one person to the next.

accurate to present developmental psychology—or any field of science—as a human enterprise in which "the facts" change over time and are open to different interpretations.

The Importance of Social Context

The human organism does not live in a social vacuum, but rather as a member of a particular social group in a particular society at a particular time. While social scientists have often treated people as empty organisms, following scripts written for them by society, psychologists have tended to study an individual's development as if it were unfolding outside of any specific time and place. As Riegal and Meacham put it,

> For all too long, we have disregarded changes in the socio-historical conditions within which individual development takes place—changes in the conception of development, in the relationship between the individual and society, in the roles of the child, the adolescent, the adult, and the aged, and changes in the impact of education, communication, economics, and socio-political conditions. (1976, p. vii)

In the next section, we examine the major social and historical changes that have shaped human development and our conceptions of that development.

Social and Historical Backgrounds to Developmental Psychology

Beyond the biological facts of birth, growth, and death, the meaning of age and aging can vary a great deal. The basic facts of nature are "doctored," as Ruth Benedict (1938) puts it, in different ways by different cultures. In other times and places, the life cycle has been divided into different stages from the ones we recognize. And there have been great variations in how people have thought about the needs and capacities of different stages of life.

Let us look at several striking examples of this variation. Consider a newborn infant. We think of a baby as a precious, irreplaceable tiny person, full of unique possibilities. The death of an infant is cause for profound grief. Yet up until a few centuries ago in Europe, people could scarcely think of young infants as belonging to the same species as themselves; they seemed to be shapeless, animallike creatures, suspended between life and death (Ariès, 1962). The death of an infant was not nearly as deeply moving as it is to us today.

Indeed, shocking as it may seem, infanticide was a major means of population control in Europe, as it is in other societies lacking the means of controlling birth (Langer, 1972; Trexler, 1973). Plato, Aristotle, and other ancient writers advocated infanticide as a way of regulating population size, as well as ridding society of deformed and diseased infants. In later times, both church and state made infanticide a crime punishable by death. Nevertheless, until the middle of the nineteenth century it remained widespread and public attitudes toward it were remarkably lenient.

Historians have argued that infanticide was the outcome of an imbalance between fertility and the food supply. For people living at the margin of starvation, another mouth to feed could be a major burden. Parents often had to choose between the newborn and the survival of their older children and themselves. As historian Jean Flandrin put it, "The demographic system of past times, based on uncontrolled fertility, was murderous to the children" (1979, p. 216).

Some of the accepted childrearing practices of earlier times also seem incomprehensible now. The practice of wet nursing is symbolic of the gulf between modern and premodern infant care. Wet nursing is the breastfeeding of an infant by a woman other than the mother. An infant would be given to a stranger, often far from home, for the first year and a half or two of the child's life. Common in many European countries, in both upper- and lower-class families, wet nursing persisted for example in France until the onset of World War I (Meckel, 1984).

Historians disagree about whether wet nursing was part of traditional society's indifference to infants or a response to economic pressures—the need for mothers to work in the family's economic enterprise or outside the home (Sussman, 1982). Whatever the reasons, wet nursing was the central issue in what William Kessen (1965) has called "the war of the breast." He notes that the most persistent theme in the history of childhood is the reluctance of mothers to suckle their babies.

The children who survived the perils of premodern infancy entered directly into adult society. Adultlike behavior was expected of children long before the age modern adults expect it. Twentieth-century Americans take it for granted that children have special needs and interests, and that they are unable to take part in adult life until they have passed through many years of development and education. In the Middle Ages, however, children over the ages of five to seven were thought of, and treated in many ways, as small adults.

The French historian, Philippe Ariès, argues that in medieval Europe the idea of childhood did not exist:

> This is not to suggest that children were neglected, forsaken, or despised. The idea of childhood is not to be confused with affection for children; it corresponds to awareness of the peculiar nature of childhood, that particular nature which distinguishes the child from the adult, even the young adult. In medieval society, this awareness was lacking. That is why, as soon as the child could live without the constant solicitude of his mother, his nanny, his cradle-rocker, he belonged to adult society. (1962, p. 128)

Ariès's idea that premodern Europeans lacked a clearly distinguished concept of childhood is not entirely new. Anthropologists have often made the same point for non-Western cultures. Thus Ruth Benedict argues that our culture is unusual because it demands sharp contrasts between the behavior of children and adults: children play while adults work; children are supposed to be obedient, adults dom-

inant; children are supposed to be sexless while adults are expected to be sexually active and competent. In few other cultures, Benedict points out, do people have to learn one set of behaviors as children and then unlearn and reverse these patterns as they grow up.

Meyer Fortes observes that in many traditional African societies, "the social sphere of adult and child is unitary and undivided. . . . Nothing in the universe of adult behavior is hidden from children or barred to them. They are actively and responsibly part of the social structure, the economic system, the ritual and ideological system" (1970, pp. 13–14). Summarizing findings from many non-Western cultures, Stevens (1963) observes that children typically begin to work between the ages of 3 and 6. The load of duties gradually increases, and sometime between the ages of 9 and 15 the child becomes occupationally a fully functioning adult. Thus, the "small adult" concept of childhood is so common in other times and places that one is forced to the conclusion that, in worldwide and historical perspectives, our own concepts and practices are unusual.

Ideas about the other end of the life cycle have varied also. For example, we think of late old age as a time of weakness, uselessness, and mental deterioration. Yet, outside of modern

Even in developing countries today—in this case, Peru—rural children traditionally dress as adults.

Western society, people have thought of the aged as hardy survivors, full of wisdom and knowledge (Hareven, 1978).

The idea that age differences really matter is surprisingly modern. How old we are is almost as much a part of our identity as our name: parents teach their children to know their ages almost as soon as they learn to talk; newspapers regularly list the ages of people in the news along with their names. Yet this awareness of exact age is found only in modern technological societies. Some of us may have grandparents who do not know the exact date of their birth.

This preoccupation with age came about because modern technological society radically changed the conditions of growing up and the entire human life cycle. As modern societies developed age-graded institutions, age came to matter in new ways: our birthdates came to determine when we must go to school and when we can leave school, when we can vote, or work full time, drive, marry, buy liquor, enter into contracts, run for public office, retire, and receive Social Security.

Beyond this interest in chronological age, what is most unusual in historical and cross-cultural perspective is the modern focus on *psychological* change over time. People everywhere have taken note of the biological changes that occur as a person matures and ages; all societies categorize people to some degree by age. Some societies even have systems of age grading—people in certain age groups are assigned particular roles, such as warrior. But in modernized society, each era of life is believed to have its own special interests, capacities, and emotional concerns; we assume that knowing a person's age gives information not only about what the person's activities are, but also what his or her inner experience is like.

Socioeconomic Changes and the Discovery of Childhood

Child psychology is a twentieth-century luxury. For most of human history, the main issue has been survival. The most notable fact about children until quite late in Western history is that most of them would die before growing up. The question for parents was not *"How* will we bring up this child," but *"Will* we?" At the beginning of the twentieth century, about 140 out of every 1,000 infants died in the first year; now only about 14 in every 1,000 do—a tenfold decrease in infant mortality (Uhlenberg, 1980). People born in the early years of the twentieth century were much more likely than recent generations to have experienced the death of a brother or sister in childhood. And in many Third World countries today, survival is still the major issue in early childhood; in many countries parents can still expect one out of every three of their children to die before they reach the age of five (UNICEF, 1983). (See the box on Twentieth-century Infant Mortality.) However, even today the lowered infant mortality rates in the United States do not apply evenly to all social groups. On our Indian reservations and in inner-city ghettoes, the rates approach those in the Third World. The United States today is not first, but fifteenth among the nations of the world in infant survival rate (UNICEF, 1983). Finland, Japan, and Sweden have the lowest mortality rates.

The historical decline in infant mortality and in death rates across the life course had a

Twentieth-century Infant Mortality

The following is an excerpt from the 1983 United Nations Children's Fund (UNICEF) report entitled *The State of the World's Children, 1984.*

Less than a hundred years ago the infant mortality rate in Europe and North America was as high as it is in the developing world now. In New York City in the year 1900, for example, the IMR [infant mortality rate] was approximately 140 per 1,000—about the same as in Bangladesh today. In the city of Birmingham, England, a survey taken in 1906 revealed an IMR of almost 200 per 1,000—higher than almost any country in the world in the 1980s. A look behind these statistics also shows that the main causes of infant death in New York and Birmingham *then* were very much the same as in the developing world *now*—diarrheal diseases and malnutrition, respiratory infections, and whooping cough. . . . (P. 11)

The figures in this box illustrate how improved medical care, improved hygiene, and better nutrition have drastically cut back the infant mortality rates of industrialized societies in the twentieth century—and how the developing countries today are experiencing the same causes and rates of infant mortality that industrialized countries had at the beginning of the century.

Why Children Die: Percentages of Infant and Child (ages 0–4) Deaths Due to Preventable Diseases in Selected Countries

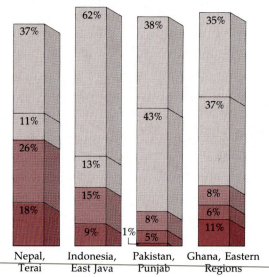

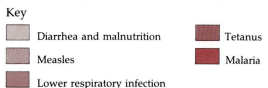

Infant Mortality and Its Causes: New York City, 1900–1930

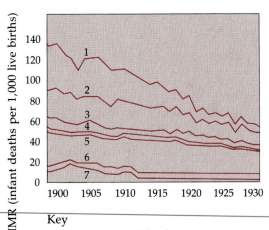

Key

1 Digestive system (diarrhea)
2 Respiratory infections, mostly pneumonias
3 Infectious diseases
4 Tuberculosis
5 Premature birth, injury at birth, other diseases peculiar to early infancy
6 Congenital malformations
7 All other causes

Source: New York City Department of Health, 1932, in UNICEF, 1983.

Key

Diarrhea and malnutrition   Tetanus

Measles   Malaria

Lower respiratory infection

Source: "Interrelation between health and population: Observations derived from field experiences" by R. N. Grosse, 1980, *Social Science and Medicine, 148,* no. 2, in UNICEF, 1983.

Infant Mortality Decline in Industrialized Countries, 1900–1980

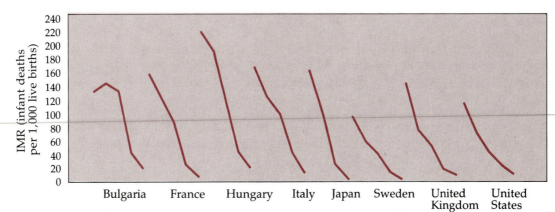

Sources: *UN demographic yearbook*, 1948, 1955, 1979 (supplement), 1981; *European statistics, 1750–1970*, abridged ed., by B. R. Mitchell, 1978; London: The McMillan Press; and "New estimates of child mortality in the U.S. in 1900" by M. Haines & S. Preston, 1981, Wayne Economic Papers, no. 141; in UNICEF, 1983.

Where Children Die: Countries with the Greatest Number of Infant Deaths

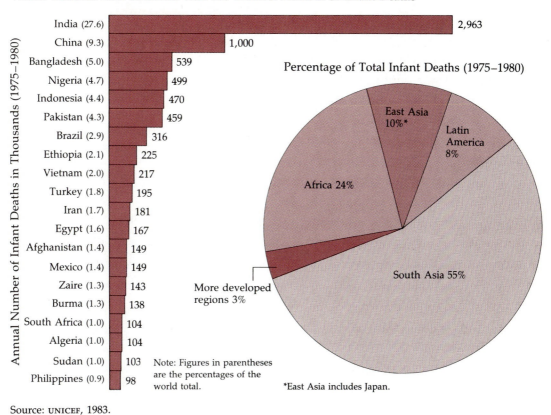

Percentage of Total Infant Deaths (1975–1980)

Note: Figures in parentheses are the percentages of the world total.

*East Asia includes Japan.

Source: UNICEF, 1983.

profound effect on children and family life (Uhlenberg, 1980). For example, historians generally agree that under conditions of high infant and child mortality, parents tend to be constrained in their feelings for their children. It is as if they cannot allow themselves to become too deeply attached to someone who might not be in this world for very long. Further, parents have felt that they have to have many children to make sure that a few survive until adulthood. Changed mortality rates made it possible for today's small, child-centered families to emerge.

But the declining rate of mortality was only one of many factors in the changing attitudes toward children. Over the last 300 years, European society was transformed by a set of economic, political, social, religious, and cultural changes which have generally been labeled "modernization." Although historians argue about the meaning of the term and its usefulness in describing other societies (see Stearns, 1980), there is general agreement that modernization is an apt description for the changes that occurred in Western society. There is also agreement that modernization involved pro-

---

FIGURE 1.5
"Traditionalism" versus "Modernism" in Family Form, Function, and Ideology

"Traditionalism"	"Modernism"
1. Kinship is organizing principle of society; almost everything a person does is done as a member of a kinship group.	Kinship is differentiated from economic, political, and social life; recruitment to jobs is independent of one's relatives.
2. Sons inherit father's status and occupation.	Individual mobility based on "merit."
3. Low geographic and social mobility.	High geographic and social mobility.
4. The extended or complex family may be basic unit of residence and domestic functions—e.g., meals and child care.	Conjugal or nuclear family is basic unit of residence and domestic functions.
5. Most adults work at home; the home is workshop as well as school, hospital, old-age home.	Separation of home and work; household consumes rather than produces.
6. Dominance of parents over children, men over women.	Relatively egalitarian relations within nuclear family in ideals and practice.
7. Kinship bonds override economic efficiency and maximization of individual gain.	Advancement and economic gain of individuals prevails over kin obligations.
8. Ideology of duty, tradition, individual submission to authority and to fate.	Ideology of individual rights, equality, freedom, self-realization.
9. Little emphasis on emotional involvement within nuclear family; marriage not based on love; predominant loyalty of individual is to blood kin, rather than spouse; children are economic rather than emotional assets, but subordination and dependency of children on parents may continue as long as parent lives—in Europe parent-child bonds may be reduced further by practice of apprenting children to other families at an early age.	Intense involvement of spouses, parents, and children with each other; ideologies of marital happiness and adjustment; great concern with child's development, current adjustment, and future potential, but sharp break with parental authority on attaining adulthood.
10. Little or no psychological separation between home and community; broad communal sociability; no large-scale institutions.	Sharp line of demarcation between home and outside world; home is a private retreat and outside world is impersonal, competitive, threatening.
11. High fertility and high death rates, especially in infancy; rapid population turnover—death a constant presence in families.	Low, controlled fertility and low death rates, especially low in infancy; death a phenomenon of old age.

Source: *The intimate environment: Exploring marriage and the family* by A. Skolnick, 1983, Boston: Little, Brown & Co.

found social and psychological change. Many of the ideas we take for granted about children emerged as part of this historical process. For example, the concept of childhood as a distinct stage of life; the emergence of the private, emotionally intense family; and the idea of school as a necessary part of the child's preparation for adult life were all part of the process of modernization. (See Figure 1.5.)

In most times and places, people have had no choice about the work they would do: they follow in the footsteps of their parents—and begin to do so at an early age. If children do the same things adults do, and if their individual interests and talents play no role in future occupation, there is little interest in child development.

In Europe, in early modern times, children were likely to enter such craft occupations as farming, baking, and shoemaking; they could also be apprenticed to lawyers, merchants, pharmacists, administrators, and clergymen. If children did go to school, they might share a grade with others who were much older as well as some who were much younger than they. Not only could 9- and 10-year-olds go to college, but children were taught the three Rs as early as age 2 or 3 through the first half of the nineteenth century. In 1840 in Massachusetts, for example, about 10 percent of all children under the age of four were enrolled as regular students in public schools (Kaestle &

Child labor was not abolished until 1936. Here (left), Addie Laird, 12 years old, is a spinner in a cotton mill in North Pownal, Vt., 1910. And boys like Johnny Clem (right), the "drummer boy of Shiloh," acted like men.

Vinovskis, 1978). "Precocious" children were not unusual. For a variety of reasons, however, the education of very young children and the practice of mixing children of different ages together came to be perceived as unhealthy. As a result, precocious children virtually disappeared from the social landscape.

The importance of the family in the development of children was not widely recognized until the nineteenth century. Indeed, as we saw earlier, the practice of wet nursing was extremely widespread in western Europe until the early twentieth century. Older children were apt to be away from home also. During the time when children above the age of seven worked, they were as likely to be apprentices or servants in other people's households as in their own. The practice of apprenticing children to other homes was found at all class levels.

The modern conception of childhood began in the aristocracy and upper-middle classes of seventeenth-century Europe. It did not spread to the working classes until the beginning of this century. Until that time, families outside of the middle classes still depended on the labor of their children. In Victorian London, Paris, and New York, many children were still dressing like adults, working, and taking part in adult leisure-time activities such as gambling. Eventually, legal and social change brought the concept of childhood to the working classes. Children of all ages had to go to school and so were excluded from the workplace and the rest of the adult world.

Images of Childhood

Paradoxically, one of the first results of the new attitudes toward children was a greater strictness. Ariès (1962) observes that the sexual treatment of children before the end of the seventeenth century provides the clearest evidence of a lack of the modern concept of childhood. Children were not only exposed to adult sexuality in talk and behavior, but were the objects of sexual teasing and horseplay. In the course of the seventeenth century, a great change in manners took place which was prompted by religious reformers; adult sexuality came to be more constrained, and the idea of childhood innocence came to be widely accepted. This new attitude was the first stage in the development of the modern concept of childhood.

At first, the new image of children emphasized their innocence and need to be shielded from adult corruption. Later, the image of childhood innocence was replaced by the idea that children were born sinners who had to have evil stamped out of them. Both the new Protestantism and the Catholic response to it brought about an increasing emphasis on the doctrine of original sin. As historian Lawrence Stone points out, parents in this period were both caring and repressive: "Puritans in particular, . . . were profoundly concerned about their children, loved them, cherished them, prayed over them, and subjected them to endless moral pressure. At the same time, they feared and even hated them as agents of sin within the household, and therefore beat them mercilessly" (1977, p. 175).

Toward the close of the eighteenth century the theme of childhood innocence was forcefully reasserted by Rousseau and the Romantic school of writers, most notably Blake and Wordsworth, and later by Dickens and others. The corrupt child was transformed into a "noble savage," whose "doors of perception" and capacity for joyful experience had not yet been deadened by society (Coveney, 1967).

The major English writers of the nineteenth century used the image of the child to criticize the emerging industrial order. The child became a protest symbol, representing Imagination, Sensibility, and Nature in a world coming to be dominated by the factory and the city. Toward the end of the Victorian era, the serious social criticism implicit in the works of Blake, Rousseau, and the others became trivialized and sentimentalized; the noble savage became an adorable innocent, and childhood a never-never land of fun and games.

Actually, the image of childhood innocence never entirely replaced the demonic child of the Puritans. At the end of the nineteenth century, Freud revived the image of the demonic child and made it the focus of a new psychology. Freud's theories of infantile sexuality attacked the image of childhood innocence and ushered in the first of the "developmental images" of the child which have dominated the twentieth century. Since that time the leading images of the child have been supplied by scientific experts—psychologists, psychiatrists, pediatricians—rather than by philosophers and poets. Thus, the child is defined by his place on a staircase of development—the child of ages and stages.

The Growth of Literacy

The new view of children was concerned with their minds as well as their morals. After 1500, an increasingly complex society began to need increasing numbers of educated people for commerce, law, and diplomacy. As towns and cities grew, the division of labor grew as did the need for literacy. Growth of an urban society and growth of schools and literacy were closely related. The areas that experienced higher rates of economic expansion and greater social change were also the areas in which schools and teachers were more numerous.

Imperialism and conquest—the growth of the French, British, Spanish, and Dutch empires—required diplomats and administrators. Nor was it only the gentlemanly arts of diplomacy and law that required education. In the sixteenth century one had to be literate to be a gunner, to navigate a ship on the open sea, to be a printer, or to be a maker of maps, clocks, and precision instruments. Schooling and literacy spread in response to social need, but they soon began to acquire an independent value. To be illiterate came to be a mark of social shame.

Although schools, as we noted earlier, began by mixing people of all ages, they gradually developed into private worlds of children, distinct from adult life. As a result, a culture of childhood developed, due in part to adult

A nineteenth-century, one-room schoolhouse. *The Country School* by Winslow Homer, 1871.

regulations of children's dress, reading, and deportment, and in part to the children themselves. Kept out of the adult world, children began to develop their own "lore and language" (Opie & Opie, 1959)—their own vocabulary, jokes, games, riddles, taunts, rituals.

The Discovery of Adolescence

The idea of adolescence as a separate stage of life between childhood and adulthood emerged even more recently. Adolescence became a kind of "second childhood" (Bakan, 1971), added on to childhood to meet the needs of twentieth-century urban industrial society.

The philosopher Rousseau is generally credited with introducing the concept into Western culture. Describing adolescence as a second birth, he was the first to list the emotional traits that have come to be the hallmark of adolescence: the frequent outbursts of temper, moodiness, and so on. Although Rousseau created his adolescent Emile in the eighteenth century,

G. Stanley Hall

the concept of adolescence did not become part of everyday social reality until the dawn of the twentieth century. The psychologist G. Stanley Hall helped to popularize the concept. His monumental two-volume work on adolescence, published in 1904, not only made the term a household word, but also stimulated a vast amount of scientific investigation. Hall was not the Dr. Spock of his times; his books did not find their way into most households. Rather, his influence was indirect—through teachers, ministers, pediatricians, judges, novelists, poets, and playwrights.

Rousseau and Hall, of course, did not create adolescence. Rather, their work reflected economic and social changes that were transforming human experience. The years between puberty and the achievement of adulthood were coming to have a significance they had not possessed in previous eras.

Like the concept of childhood, the concept of adolescence first took hold in the middle and upper classes, which could afford to provide longer educations for their teenaged children and to allow prolonged dependence. Adolescence became a mass phenomenon around the end of the nineteenth century for several reasons.

Throughout most of American history, a shortage of labor has existed, and anyone willing to work could do so. During most of the nineteenth century, a large proportion of young people left school and went to work at age 12 or 14. The introduction of new industrial machinery, however, reduced the need for children and other unskilled labor. Young people who had been mature enough to do manual labor in earlier times now found themselves immature and useless. The presence of large numbers of idle young people in the streets of American cities represented to many a dangerous threat to the social order. Drinking, gambling, and petty crimes seemed to be the major activities of the children of the streets; and the public was convinced that without some form of public action, these young people would grow up to be dangerous adults. Furthermore, parents, young people looking for jobs, and society in general were coming to see extended schooling as necessary preparation for work in an increasingly complex society.

Concern over such problems led to major social movements which produced important legislation setting up new institutions for youth. Child labor laws, compulsory education laws, and the creation of the juvenile court and the child guidance clinic were products of this ferment. These laws, with their precise age requirements, set a clear boundary for the end of adolescence. The period of adolescence was now clearly marked off as the time between puberty and the passing of legal milestones for the end of compulsory education, and thus the beginning of eligibility for work and treatment as an adult in the legal system.

These economic, familial, and cultural changes also transformed the inner experience of growing up; adolescence became an important stage of the individual's biography. The opening of a gap between physical and social maturity led to the psychological characteristics of the adolescent experience: the urge to be independent from the family; the discovery of the unique and private world of the self; the search for an identity; and the questioning of adult values and assumptions, which may take the form of idealism or cynicism—or both. Of course, some people had known this kind of experience in the past. St. Augustine, for example, who lived in the fifth century, described his identity crisis in his *Confessions*. But however universal the experience of adolescent change and growth has been over the centuries, only a few privileged individuals in past centuries were able to afford the luxury of reflecting on and making choices about their identity.

The Discovery of Adulthood

For about half a century, most psychologists as well as other people believed that adolescence was the last great stage of human development. After a person had left the upheavals of adolescence behind, and reached maturity in the eyes of the law, it was assumed that he or she would enter a period of changelessness which could last about fifty years. The person would age physically, but not psychologically, at least until old age began to cloud the mind. A few psychologists, most notably Erik Erikson, had theorized that adults do experience developmental change over the whole course of the life span. While Erikson's eight stages were often discussed in psychology textbooks, until recently there was very little interest in actually studying the "stages" of adult life. Developmental psychology meant the study of children, or of psychological processes in children, and most developmental psychology textbooks ended with adolescence. The 1968 edition of the *International Encyclopedia of Social Science*, for example, contained articles on adolescence and aging, but none on adulthood (Jordan, 1978).

As anyone who reads newspapers or magazines must know, all that has changed. Adulthood seems well on the way to becoming a preoccupation comparable to what Ariès described as our culture's "obsession" with childhood. Increasing numbers of social scientists are studying change across the life span. During the great ferment about children and social policy at the turn of the century, someone labeled the coming era as "the century of the child"; recently, it has been suggested we may be entering "the century of the adult" (Graubard, 1978, p. vii).

The emergence of an interest in adulthood sheds some light on the process by which new stages of life are recognized. As in the earlier discoveries of childhood and adolescence, there is a complicated interplay between psychological ideas and social realities.

Several steps in the process may be outlined (Hareven, 1978). First, people in different stages of life come to have different experiences from one another. For example, children go to school while adults work; or adults work until the age of 65, then retire and become eligible for Social Security.

The second step in the process is the discovery and labeling of the "new" segment of the life cycle and its popularization. We saw earlier how G. Stanley Hall and others helped to popularize the work on adolescence. Recently, the phenomenal success of Gail Sheehy's *Passages* helped to popularize the idea of the "mid-life crisis" as well as other stages of adult life originally described by psychologists and psychiatrists.

The third step in the process, which often goes along with the second, is the creation of special institutions and professional groups to deal with the problems of specific age groups—such as school psychologists and counselors, child psychiatrists, pediatricians, adolescent psychiatrists, geriatric specialists, and so on.

Thus, clinical psychologists and psychiatrists in recent years have found themselves spending increasing amounts of time with middle-aged and aged clients. Sociologists and demographers have become concerned with the effects of the increasing proportion of older people on the structure and functioning of society as a whole. For example, what will happen to the Social Security system when the number of retired people exceeds the number of younger people in the work force, as will happen by the end of the first decade of the twenty-first century?

The fourth step is the amplification and deepening of the stages of the life cycle. The growth of institutions for and knowledge about specific age groups creates still further differentiation among them. Thus, teenage culture was made possible when the high schools brought together large numbers of young people and segregated them from other age groups. Also, the popularization of developmental concepts makes people more aware of their own psychological processes. Countless numbers of people undoubtedly first learned about their own mid-life crises as a result of reading *Passages*, or magazine and newspaper articles.

Following the above scheme, we can see that one major reason adulthood has come to public attention recently is that the adult life course has been divided into distinct segments. As we mentioned earlier, in preindustrial society when work was done within the family, there were few distinctions between people in various stages of the life cycle. Children were seen

as small adults and began to take part in adult work as soon as they were able. At the other end of the life cycle, old people continued to work as long as they could and often exercised control over their children until they died.

The coming of advanced industrial society and the demographic changes it brought in its wake led to a greater differentiation between age groups. Sharper boundaries were drawn around the beginning and end of a person's working life. Such events as completing school, going to work, marrying, and having children came to be dramatic turning points in a person's life. They had not been such milestones in the past. For example, depending on the needs of their families, children could leave home in their early teens, or they could live with their families into adulthood—even after they were married. Before mandatory retirement and Social Security, the age of 65 was not the milestone it was later to become.

Moreover, because people are living longer and having fewer children, parenthood is no longer a lifelong career. In the past, when people married late, had many children, and died at an earlier age than now, parents rarely experienced an "empty nest" stage—the departure of all one's children from the home. Parents were likely to die while one or more of their children were still living at home, while today parents typically finish the active phase of childrearing with one-third or more of their

lives left to live. These demographic and social changes have had a profound effect on marriage; some sociologists (e.g., Davis, 1972) see rising divorce rates as compensating for declining death rates: the lower the probability of escaping a bad marriage by death, the greater is the willingness—and opportunity—to end it through divorce.

Social change also has a major impact on both the differentiation of age groups and the individual life cycle. When a society changes rapidly, parents can no longer use their own experience to guide their children; they become, as Margaret Mead once put it, "immigrants in time" (1970). Like all immigrants, they find themselves in a new land where their children may learn the language and the customs more quickly than they. The oldest generations find themselves even more obsolete, survivors of a world only they can remember. And the more differences there are between different segments of the life cycle, the greater the difficulty people will experience in moving from one stage to the next. Further, the glorification of youth and the denigration of age in American society add to the problems of moving from one life stage to the next.

While adulthood has become a more complicated terrain to cross, adults are becoming a larger proportion of the population than ever before. In preindustrial societies, the age distribution of the population, if shown visually,

Hypothetical and Actual Population Pyramids

The top two pyramids are abstract models of two stable populations with contrasting fertility and mortality rates. Model 1 shows a modern population with low fertility and mortality. Model 2 represents a typical developing or Third World country with high birth and death rates. The four pyramids in the second figure represent actual populations. Even though the populations of the four countries are changing, the contrasts in age distribution are as striking as in the models.

Differences in age structure have important implications. For example, how many schools will be needed to accommodate the changing number of children? How much of a country's resources will be needed to care for the aged? What is the ratio of those in their productive years to young and old dependents?

Age Pyramids of Stationary Populations

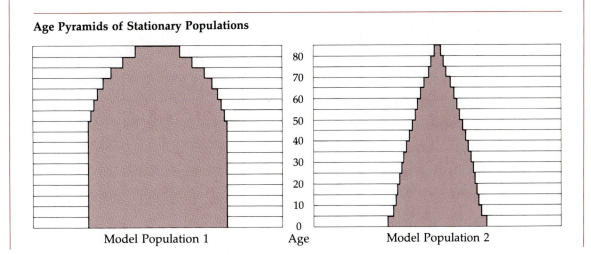

Model Population 1   Age   Model Population 2

Age Pyramids of Actual Populations

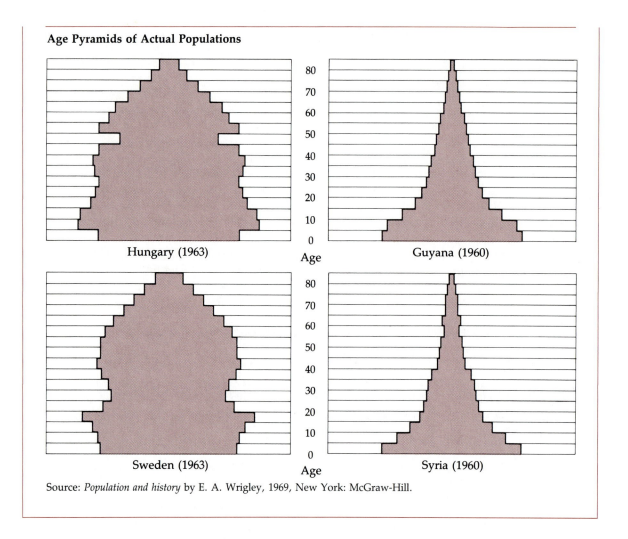

Hungary (1963)

Guyana (1960)

Sweden (1963)

Syria (1960)

Age

Source: *Population and history* by E. A. Wrigley, 1969, New York: McGraw-Hill.

tends to look like a Christmas tree. High birth rates form a wide base while high death rates reduce this base in each decade of life, leaving only a few to survive to old age. In contrast, the modern distribution of population looks like a house with a peaked roof on top: most children who are born survive their early years and live on through adulthood; death occurs mostly to old people. (See the box on Population Pyramids.)

In America and other technological societies in recent years, these demographic trends have increased to produce a population unlike any known before. At the turn of the century, only 40 percent of the population reached the age of 65, but now, 75 percent do. Once there, how-

ever, they live only 4.1 years longer than did their ancestors who reached that age in the past (*New York Times,* May 7, 1978). It is interesting that although many more people reach old age than did in the past, the life span itself has not been extended dramatically in recent years beyond the Biblical age of "three score and ten."

Paradoxically, while modern technological society has given people more years to live, it has deprived them of useful roles during those later years. The "young old" (Neugarten, 1974), still strong and healthy, must find new purposes in life; the "old old," often plagued by ill health and unable to provide for their needs, become dependent on a society that regards them as an irrelevant surplus population. In short, like adolescents at the turn of the century, people in the second half of life have become a problematic population.

The Origins of Developmental Psychology

The emergence of developmental psychology as a field of study was intimately involved with the whole complex of changes which made particular age groups into objects of public concern and social policy. Child psychology emerged as an academic discipline during an era of ferment and social reform involving children. Sheldon White (1975) has observed that psychology's subsidized existence as a field of scientific research has rested upon "promissory notes" laid down at the turn of the century.

The beginnings of modern academic psychology were closely tied to education and the growth of large public expenditures for the socialization of children. The first psychologists moved from philosophy departments to the newly forming education schools with the expectation that they would provide scientific methods of education and childrearing. The founding fathers of American psychology—John Watson, G. Stanley Hall, Lewis Terman, and others—accepted the challenge. Thus, learning has always been a central focus of psychologists, even though the rat eventually came to compete with the child as the favored experimental subject. And the promise of effective methods of social engineering has always remained an implicit, if not explicit, underlying justification for this research.

Psychologists have been enlisted to deal with more recently defined social problems. For example, when the Russians launched their first space vehicle in 1956, Americans were shocked by the expertise of what they had thought of as a relatively backward country. A race began to get to the moon before the Russians. Part of that race was an attempt to beef up the education of American children—not only to teach them more science and mathematics, but in

general to raise a generation of smarter kids. Psychologists were funded to help design new curricula and to study how scientific concepts were learned.

Later, during the 1960s, when President Johnson's War on Poverty was declared, psychologists were again enlisted to boost the cognitive capacities of poor children. Psychologists helped design and evaluate such programs as Head Start and others and also did basic research on the developmental issues involved. In the past several years, psychologists have been looking into the effects of divorce and parental unemployment on children.

Psychology is not the only field to be involved with its surrounding society. In recent years, scholars who study the development of the sciences have found that even "hard" sciences such as physics and chemistry are influenced by the social settings in which they are carried out. In psychology and the other human sciences, the impact of social context goes deeper. Unlike the atoms and molecules studied by the physicist, the people the psychologist studies are themselves affected by social and economic conditions and changes. These conditions influence not only how people think about human development, but development itself. Psychology, in turn, both reflects the society around it and influences it as well.

Although the growth of psychology as an academic field was influenced by social needs, these did not determine how psychologists would go about solving the problems they had been called upon to deal with. The history of psychology is also the story of the growth of scientific ideas. Historians have found that various sciences typically undergo a series of shifts in the way they look at the world. The history of any science is not just the accumulation of facts, but changes in the kinds of questions asked, the range of data considered relevant, and in the methods used to study this data. More importantly, there are fundamental changes in the way scientists think and talk about the field.

The field of psychology has undergone several of these shifts. For example, when psychology as a science took hold toward the end of the nineteenth century, it was defined as the study of the mind; its chief goal was to understand how people think. Later there was a "behavioral revolution" which redefined psychology as the study of behavior; thinking and consciousness were regarded as unimportant or not even real, and not proper subjects for scientific investigation.

In the past few years, there has been a cognitive revolution. "Mind" is no longer a taboo word. Once again psychologists are studying topics that had been put aside for half a century: perception, memory, imagery, language development, and many others. Studies based on the developmental theories of Jean Piaget, neglected for decades by American psychologists, came to crowd the pages of developmental psychology journals in the 1960s and 1970s.

These changes in the definition of psychology are what Thomas Kuhn (1962) has labeled "paradigm shifts." A paradigm is a set of assumptions about what the world is like, what should be studied, what kinds of questions should be asked, and what methods should be used to answer them. All of the sciences and arts have been marked by a succession of paradigms. Major examples of paradigm changes are the scientific revolutions that resulted from the theories of Copernicus, Darwin, and Einstein. Paradigm shifts come about because of problems in the older paradigm.

Behaviorism, for example, was a reaction against difficulties in psychology around the turn of the century. Defining psychology as the study of immediate conscious experience, psychologists at that time relied on the introspection of specially trained, educated adult subjects. They could not easily study infants or young children, the mentally disturbed, or animals. The early behaviorists pointed a way out of this impasse by redefining psychology as the study of overt behavior, not conscious states. The cognitive revolution arose, in turn, because of problems in the behaviorist paradigm; it was hard to explain behavior without invoking some notion of inner psychological states—expectations, attention, and so forth.

The development of the computer and other complex machines has also contributed to the cognitive revolution. By imitating human mental processes such as memorizing, manipulating symbols, recognizing patterns, and solving problems, the computer helped make it respectable once more for psychologists to use mentalistic terms.

Evolution and Psychological Development

Developmental psychology, as a part of the science of psychology, has experienced the same shifts as the field as a whole. But its ways of thinking have also been shaped by its special mission to study children and changes in behavior over time. Because of this focus on growth and change, developmental psychology was greatly influenced by Darwin's theory of evolution. Although developmental psychology has outgrown its historical origins, evolutionary doctrines continue, in subtle ways, to influence the study of the child.

The idea of mental development as a natural progression of stages, unfolding from within the child like the growth of a plant or insect, had existed before Darwin. The eighteenth-century philosopher Rousseau introduced the idea of developmental stages in his *Emile.* But the theory of evolution in the following century gave powerful support to this image of development. "Development" became the guiding metaphor for thinking about children. As Kessen (1965) puts it, there was a "riot of parallel-drawing" between the mind of the child and what was presumed to be earlier historical stages of the human species.

One of the most influential ideas to emerge from Darwin's work was the recapitulation hypothesis, the notion that the development of the individual repeats the history of the species ("ontogeny recapitulates phylogeny"). The recapitulation hypothesis was based on the development of embryos. The human embryo starts out as a single-celled organism, becomes a multicelled organism, then resembles a fish, and so on. Extending this idea, some psychologists assumed that the mental development of the growing child repeated the mental development of the human race, reaching its highest point in the adult rational mind of Western man.

G. Stanley Hall's work is the prime example of how Darwin's biological concepts were translated into psychological ones. Hall, widely recognized as the "father" of child study in America, divided child development into stages corresponding to prehistoric eras in the development of the human race. Thus, infancy, the first four years of life, corresponded to the animal stage of the human species when it was still using four legs. The period of childhood—from 4 to 8—was supposedly a recapitulation of an earlier cultural era of hunting and fishing; while 8 to 12, a period Hall called "youth," was a reenactment of the "humdrum life of savagery" before the higher human traits emerged. Hall's conceptions of childhood seem to have influenced the founding of the Boy Scouts. Scouting was thought to provide a means of satisfying the various prehistoric instincts such as hunting, fishing, and gathering (McCullers, 1969). Adolescence, in Hall's scheme, represents a turbulent, transitional stage in the history of the race after which the highest levels of civilization were attained: "The child comes from and harks back to a remoter past; the adolescent is neo-atavistic, and in him the later acquisitions of the race slowly become prepotent. Development is less gradual and more saltatory, suggestive of some ancient period of storm and stress when old moorings were broken and a higher level attained" (1904, p. xiii).

Hall's ideas sound rather farfetched to modern ears. Indeed, his highly literal version of the recapitulation theory was based on the inheritance of acquired characteristics and is no longer acceptable scientifically. Yet in some basic ways, Hall's views of human development are very much alive in current developmental psychology.

Developmental psychology has been dominated by two models, or images, of development: the organismic and the mechanistic. The organismic model (Reese & Overton, 1970) sees development as a biological process; the mech-

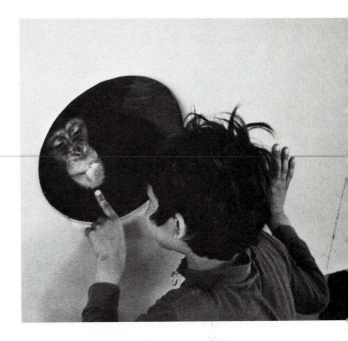

anistic model assumes that learning is the fundamental explanation for all behavior and changes in behavior. In fact, psychologists who hold to this model do not call themselves "mechanists," but rather, "learning theorists." The learning theorists' legacy from Darwin may be seen in the great influence animal psychology has in the study of the child and psychology generally. Cats, rats, monkeys, pigeons, and other animals are studied with the assumption that their learning processes do not differ in any essential way from those of humans.

Although the two models disagree about many things, they both reflect, in different ways, the evolutionary frame of reference inherited from Darwin. Almost every major organismic theorist has been influenced by the assumptions of recapitulation doctrine. In a review of Hall's influence on developmental psychology, McCullers (1969) has pointed to important parallels between Hall's ideas and those of several eminent developmental psychologists: Freud, Jung, Werner, Vygotsky, and Piaget. Although most of these men rejected aspects of Hall's thinking and did not consider themselves his followers, Hall was

their senior and had many opportunities to influence them both directly and indirectly. As a
group, McCullers observes, these men had a
surprising number of things in common. They
all believed development consists of a succession of predetermined stages, that each stage
in the sequence is necessary for the emergence
of the next, that there are direct parallels between child development and cultural development, and that at the apex of each developmental sequence stands Western adult man.
Thus, both the development of the individual
and the development of the species follow a
unilinear progression from lower, simpler, and
more primitive functioning to higher, more
complex, more advanced functioning.

There is no doubt that the evolutionary, biological point of view provides indispensable insights into human development. And the
study of animal behavior can provide clues to
understanding human behavior. But the biological frame of reference, and the use of animal behavior, acts as a set of lenses for looking
at the world. It leads us to look at certain
things and ignore others, to ask certain questions and fail to ask others.

Traditionally, developmental psychology has
tended to view development as an individual
process unfolding from within. It has paid little
attention to the influence of social and cultural
context on children and concepts of childhood,
and it has emphasized grand theories and lab-

oratory experiments rather than empirical studies of children in their ordinary environments.
In the past decade, however, developmental
researchers have come to recognize the necessity for studying development in the real
world.

Overview of this Book

The five parts of this book are designed to give
the reader a basic understanding of psychological development across the life span. The first
three chapters introduce the field and some of
the issues confronting it, the methods used to
study development, and the major theories
that have been advanced to explain it. The following chapters proceed chronologically
through the life course from infancy through
adulthood. Two topics, however, are discussed
in separate chapters: the development of the
self and the development of language. For each
stage of life, the themes outlined above—those
of individuality and development, centrality of
the self, multiple influences, individuals as
agents in their own development, multiple
pathways, developmental theories, and the importance of social context—are used as the
framework for presenting research and conclusions.

SUMMARY

This chapter has briefly introduced developmental psychology and how this book
will present human development as a science. It has also provided a brief look at
how ideas about the stages of life, and the life cycle itself, have differed historically
and cross-culturally. In short, human development does not take place in a social
vacuum and cannot be understood apart from specific social, cultural, and
historical settings.

The concept of childhood as a separate stage of life, having its own psychology
and requiring separate institutions, is an invention of modern times. In premodern
societies, including Western society a few centuries ago, children did not live in a
separate world from adults. In the premodern pattern, children after the age of
infancy participated in the economic life of society. The new concept of childhood
seems to be a product of the process of modernization: a complex occupational
structure calls for an educated population.

During the medieval era and early modern times, schools were not age graded. There was no sequence of courses and no notion that a person could be too young or too old to study a subject. Precocious children were common in school as well as in the professions, arts, and trades.

During this period there was less emphasis than there is now on love as the essential ingredient in parent-child relationships. These relationships were weakened further by the practice of apprenticeship, with children often residing and working in other homes by the age of seven.

Over several centuries, definitions of childhood, school, and family changed. Childhood came to include adolescence, which has been defined as the preparatory stage of life for the not fully socialized. Accordingly, schools became instruments of discipline and character training. The home became a place to nurture children and prepare them for later life. Precocity came to be seen as unwholesome.

Adulthood is the most recent stage of life to have been "discovered." Over the course of the twentieth century, the adult life cycle has changed in a number of ways. People are not only living longer than previous generations, but the adult years are segmented into distinct eras in ways that were not recognized in the past. Before improved health care and social reforms, most people spent all or most of their adult years working and rearing children. Today people finish both their childrearing and occupational careers with many years left to live. The necessity to make transitions into the empty nest stage and retirement calls for adaptations and redefinitions of self that were unknown to earlier times. Modern societies also face a new situation in that their populations are containing increasingly larger proportions of aged and dependent people.

Since the turn of the century, psychology has been called upon by the larger society to deal with the problems of various age groups. Child development emerged as an academic field when children and adolescents were the problematic populations. The recent interest in adult development has been stimulated in part by the fact that middle-aged and older adults are also emerging as populations with distinct sets of problems.

But psychology has never been a purely practical field, devoted to social engineering. Developmental psychologists have also pursued the theoretical understanding of age changes in physical, intellectual, and emotional behavior. Following these scientific goals, the ideas of developmental psychology have changed over time. For example, developmental psychology took part in the behavioristic revolution of the early decades of the century, when mental processes were defined as inappropriate topics for scientific investigation. It was also influenced by the cognitive revolution in psychology, when mind once again became an important focus of research. Throughout its history, developmental psychology has been influenced by biological frames of reference, especially Darwin's theory of evolution.

CHAPTER 2

The
Research Enterprise
Developing a Science of Human Development

What the research attitude presumes is that the first look—and every other look—may be prone to error, so that one must look again and again, differently and thoroughly each time. Each method of investigation may have its own particular limits. We must try to make ourselves aware of these limits so that we can transcend them or at least not be taken in by them. As the nineteenth century American humorist Artemus Ward once said, "It ain't the things we don't know that get us in trouble. It's the things we know that ain't so."

—Sellitz, Wrightsman, & Cook,
Research Methods in Social Relations

Contemporary Americans are avid consumers of psychological findings, especially about human development. An ever-growing flood of information and misinformation in the form of books, magazine and newspaper articles, and television programs tells people how to improve their marriages, raise smarter and happier children, deal with their own mid-life and other crises. Millions of parents consider a copy of Dr. Spock and other books on childrearing as essential as cribs and diapers in preparing for the arrival of a child.

Although vast numbers of people are involved in presenting this material and in advising and educating the public about human development, the entire enterprise ultimately rests on the much smaller number of people actually doing research in development. It is the findings and theories brought forth by researchers that serve as the scientific gold backing up the soft currency of popular and applied writing on human development. Often the pop psychology presented in the media is not backed up by good research at all.

As consumers who are bombarded by scientific findings every day, we need to be able to have some ability to judge the adequacy of the methods used. Students who take human development courses have a need for a more detailed understanding of how to evaluate and use research. While this chapter is not a substitute for a more thorough analysis of research techniques, it does attempt to provide the student with an overview of the major methods used in the study of human development and the virtues and limitations of each.

Until about a century ago, there was no systematic research on human development. Instead, people relied on common sense, traditional wisdom, and the opinions of various authorities. Since the human race obviously succeeded in raising countless generations of children before the science of human development emerged, we might ask, is scientific research necessary? Common sense and other traditional ideas must have been right often enough, or else humans would not have survived long enough or developed societies affluent enough to produce a science of development.

But common sense is often contradictory and philosophers often disagree with one another. "Spare the rod and spoil the child" offered one prescription for childrearing; while in the sixteenth century, essayist Montaigne wrote, "I have never observed other effects of whipping than to render boys more cowardly, or more willfully obstinant" (1952, p. 185).

For a variety of reasons, as we saw in the last chapter, traditional speculations about human development no longer seemed to be enough. The empirical approach is the essence of the scientific method: it assumes that statements about the world must be based on observations. Thus, some of the early researchers interviewed children about their knowledge and attitudes; others observed children systematically in their natural environments; some collected records of physical and mental growth; others began to observe children in special laboratory environments. They produced papers with titles such as the following: "On the observation of mental abnormalities in school children"; "A study of children's rights as seen by themselves"; "The study of the boyhood of great men"; "Influence of school life on curvature of the spine" (S. White, 1976). Much of the work of these pioneers in child study seems quaint and outdated because the early researchers had little to guide their work.

The essential difference between scientific explanations and those of philosophers of the past is the use the scientist makes of observation. It's not that the philosophers and ordinary people of prescientific times did not rely on observation; for example, Aristotle, who believed that homosexuality was caused by parental abuse, may have come to this conclusion by hearing some homosexual friends talk about their abusive parents. But in science, such observations are only the starting point for a long chain of observations. Conclusions are not called conclusions, but **hypotheses,** indicating that the explanation is tentative, pending further study. Ways must be found to test the hypothesis, to see if the new observations support it, to change the hypothesis if they do not;

to see if the hypothesis holds in different samples, under different circumstances.

Perhaps, if Aristotle had interviewed a representative sample of homosexuals on the streets of fourth-century B.C. Athens—of which there was a large population, by the way, since homosexual love was highly regarded—his idea may have been confirmed. More likely, though, according to modern researchers, it would not have been (Bell & Weinberg, 1978). Oddly enough, the idea of making an observation to test a hypothesis never occurred to Aristotle.

Ideally, research is supposed to be a constant interplay between facts and theories. Observations lead to a theory, the theory suggests new observations, the new research confirms, disconfirms, or modifies the theory, further research is done, and so forth. As we shall see later, there are complications in this picture of how scientific research is carried out. Yet the ideal of open-mindedness, of skepticism, is the essence of science.

In short, science at its core is not white coats and complicated laboratory instruments or computers, but rather a more systematic and skeptical kind of common sense. Above all, science is, as B. F. Skinner points out, a set of attitudes: "It is a disposition to deal with the facts rather than what someone has said about them . . . a willingness to accept facts even when they are opposed to wishes. . . . Scientists have also discovered the value of remaining without an answer until a satisfactory one can be found" (1953, pp. 12–13).

As with most ideals, there is sometimes a gap between the scientific ideal of open-mindedness and real life. For one thing, scientists are not likely to reject a well-supported theory on account of one or several observations that do not agree with it. They are more likely to conclude that there was something wrong with the observations. Many times in the history of science, scientists have clung to "erroneous" theories until they were overturned by new theories that could incorporate the new observations (Kuhn, 1962).

Further, research in real life does not always follow the ideal image set forth in textbooks or the neat steps from hypothesis to method to results set forth in journal articles. As many leading researchers have pointed out, scientific investigation can often be a frustrating, disorderly enterprise, involving false starts, inconclusive outcomes, faulty hunches, and unexpected insights.

The idealized image of research does not reveal the difficulty of deciding on a topic to investigate or the disappointment of research that fails to produce any findings and is never published. Published articles usually do not

Piaget observing children in their natural habitat (top), and clinical researchers observing in a controlled setting (bottom).

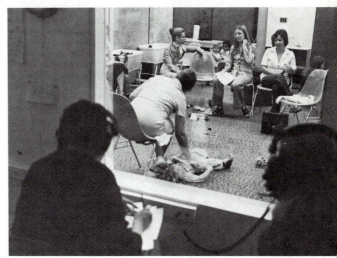

reveal how or why one method was chosen rather than another. Sometimes the hypothesis that appears in the journal article was not the one the researcher had in mind when he or she began the study, but rather emerged as the data began coming in.

As John Flavell puts it, the field of cognitive development looks very different to a professional in that field, an insider, than it does to an outsider:

> The insider continually lives with its numerous questions, problems, ambiguities, and uncertainties. He becomes used to, although never unconcerned about, its untidy, openended, no-problem-ever-seems-to-get-solved character. He knows how incredibly difficult it is even to think up a research study that will tell us something we really want to know. (1977, p. 219)

In none of this does psychology differ from the other "harder" sciences, such as physics or chemistry; George Miller, a psychologist of language, argues that science is not "an inevitable march forward from rational insight to established truth," but rather, it is "hard work, carried on with normal human passions and confusions, intended to reduce the number of alternative views of the universe and its inhabitants that a rational person might subscribe to" (1977, p. xxiv).

A Sample of Current Research in Developmental Psychology

The best way to understand the sorts of issues studied by developmental psychologists is to look at a sample of studies that can be found in recent journals dealing with developmental psychology. The following studies were selected to illustrate some of the questions contemporary researchers are investigating and some of the methods they use to answer them.

1. Does memory deteriorate with age? People in their twenties or sixties were compared on a variety of memory tasks. While older peo-

ple did more poorly than younger ones on many tasks, they did better than the younger people on certain ones. The authors conclude that the idea that a person's overall memory capacity deteriorates with age is too simple a notion (Perlmutter, 1978).

2. Are preschool children egocentric, or can they adapt to the perspective of another person? Children from one to three years of age were given a variety of simple tasks, in their homes, with the aid of their mothers. They were asked to make another person see something, to hide something from the other person, and to infer what someone else was looking at or pointing to. For example, in one task, the child was handed pictures and asked to show them to an observer seated across a table—usually, the observer was the child's mother.

If the children were egocentric, they should have held up the pictures so that the picture itself was facing themselves and the back was to the observer. All 2½-year-old children showed the picture side to the observer, and most of them showed the picture right side up when it had been presented to them upside down. Even the very youngest children failed to use the egocentric strategy of looking at the picture themselves while showing the blank side to the observer. Rather, they tended to lay the picture out flat so both they and the observer could see it. Thus, even the youngest subjects were able to produce a percept that another person could see. The researchers concluded that young children are not as totally egocentric as had previously been believed (Lempers, Flavell, & Flavell, 1977).

3. Can young infants recognize people in photographs? A study by Dirks and Gibson (1977) followed the "habituation paradigm" which has been used to study perception in infants. This method is based on the observation that if you show something to a baby, say a picture, he or she will look at it (or make some other response) for a while, and then lose interest—as indicated by looking away. If you then present a new picture, the baby is likely to pay attention again. If, however, the baby cannot tell the difference between the two pic-

tures, he or she will not look more at the new one. In this study, five-month-old babies repeatedly saw a live person smile at them through an opening in a screen. Then they saw a life-sized color photograph of either the same person or a different one. The babies did not look more at the photograph of the original face, but their response to the new person's picture rose dramatically. This result showed that young infants do not regard a photograph as a patchwork of shapes and colors, as some earlier research has suggested; rather, they can recognize what is being portrayed in the picture. A second experiment, also using the habituation method, showed that babies of this age cannot tell the difference between two people who look somewhat alike—for example, two men with beards of a similar hair color and style.

4. Are racial differences in IQ scores based on environment or on heredity? Scarr and Weinberg (1976) looked at the IQ scores of black children who had been adopted by middle-class white families during the first two years of life. They found that these children's average IQ scores were 106, rather than 90, the typical score of black children raised by their biological parents. Also, black and white children placed in white adoptive homes since the age of two or three have similar IQ scores. Finally, they found that the more education the adoptive mother had, the higher was her adopted child's IQ. These findings suggest that racial differences in IQ reflect differences in the social environment in which black and white children grow up, rather than genetic differences between the races.

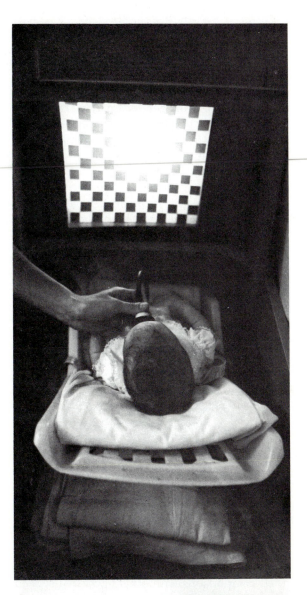

Siqueland and Delucia experiment with learning in young infants. The 14-month-old is shown a pattern on a screen. He can keep the pattern in sharp focus by sucking on a pacifier hooked up to the projector (top). Eventually he becomes bored with the pattern and decreases his sucking, which makes the picture fade (bottom). When the infant is shown another pattern, his interest will increase again, as shown by his reactivated sucking.

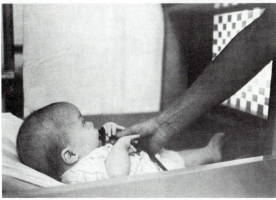

5. Are young children's perceptions of social reality influenced by cultural stereotypes about male and female roles? Drabman and his associates (1979, 1981) showed preschool and school-aged children a film in which doctors and nurses of both genders played important roles. Later, the children "remembered" that all the doctors had been men, and all the nurses women. The authors concluded that culturally established expectations distort perception and memory in both younger and older children.

6. How do children of different ages interpret storytelling devices used in films? Saloman (1979) showed children video clips showing a distant shot of a complex scene, followed by a cut to a close-up shot of a small detail from the scene. Older, school-age children understood that the close-up had been part of the larger scene, but preschoolers did not. Then he tried a long, slow transitional zoom in from the wide shot to the close-up; the preschoolers could now understand the relationship between the part and the whole, but the older children were confused because they tried to attach extra meaning to the zoom.

Looking at the studies described above, and the hundreds of others that appear in the journals, we can see that several different kinds of information are being gathered. First, there are descriptions of the psychological characteristics of people at particular ages or stages of the life cycle. For example, a study might look at the abilities of the newborn to perceive shapes, colors, or sounds, or at the egocentricity of the preschooler. In this kind of study, there are implied comparisons with other ages. In a second type of study, the behavior of different age groups is actually compared and contrasted.

A third kind of study examines the environmental factors that influence behavior—for example, the effects of television violence on children's aggressiveness, or the effects of different kinds of rewards or instructions on children's learning, or the effects of day care on children's emotional development.

Another study looks at the interaction between age and experimental conditions. For example, in the Saloman study cited above, younger and older children differed in the

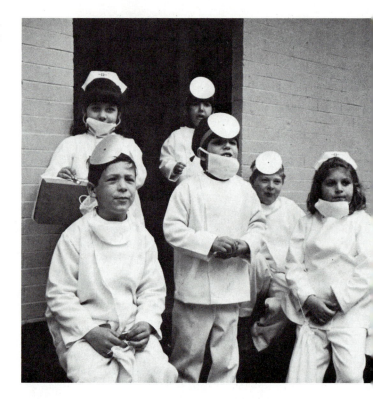

kinds of television filming techniques they found easy and hard to understand. Older children understood the relation between the distant shot and the close-up, but the younger ones did not. Younger children found the slow zoom easy to understand, but the older ones were confused by it.

Still other studies analyze the relation between two different processes or aspects of behavior. For example, a researcher might look at the relationship between children's intellectual development and their thinking about moral issues. Finally, some studies research individual differences in particular traits, such as intelligence, creativity, problem-solving styles, personality traits, and so forth.

Another way of looking at the kinds of research being done in developmental psychology is suggested by the observation that every person is like all other people, some other people, and no other person (Kluckholn & Murray, 1948, p. 35). Thus, some research tries to describe the general process of development as it applies to all people, ignoring individual differences. This approach emphasizes stages and transitions that all people go through and has been called the *classical developmental* approach (Emmerich, 1968). For example, Jean Piaget's theory and research describe how thinking changes from the first days of life through adulthood; Sigmund Freud describes how the pattern of a person's emotional concerns changes from infancy through adulthood. Similarly, researchers in language try to describe the various stages all children go through in learning to speak, as well as the underlying processes that explain linguistic development. Most experimental work also tries to establish general laws that apply to all people.

Some research looks at how some kinds of people differ from other kinds in their psychological development, thereby taking a *differential* approach (Emmerich, 1968). Such research might compare children's development or the aging process in different cultures, classes, or races, or in the two sexes. Other kinds of research in this vein might study individual differences in temperament, personality, or problem-solving style in school children.

Still other studies examine unique individuals. Although the differential type of research mentioned above deals with individual differences, it does not deal with the ways in which a person is *un*like any other individual. This kind of study is found most often in clinical psychiatric writings, usually in the form of case histories of maladjusted people. There are, however, some studies where "normal" personalities have been intensively studied over a long part of the life cycle.

In real life, of course, all three approaches are intertwined; development never occurs in the abstract, but in particular individuals, and every individual is a mixture of likenesses and differences from others. Research in any of the three styles is a matter of focus; in any experimental or classical developmental study, individuals respond differently, but individual differences are not what the researcher is interested in looking at. Similarly, when writing a life history, the author is aware that the individual being written about is like everyone else in some ways, and also like others of his or her age, sex, or social class.

Most research in developmental psychology is of the general kind, which ignores individual differences. The differential kind of research, which looks at group differences, is the next most common, while studies that deal with unique individuals are rarely found. Textbooks, this one included, usually reflect the work going on in the field itself. Thus, in the chapters that follow, there will be a heavy emphasis on general developmental changes and the contrasting theories that have been put forth to explain these changes. Although individual variation may not always be emphasized, it should remain constantly at the back of the reader's mind.

Individual differences occur in almost all behavior, and most research findings represent statistical trends, not iron laws producing an inevitable outcome. For example, if one or a series of studies shows that first-born children are more anxious or ambitious than later-born children, or that showing children violent television programs leads to aggression, this does not mean that every first-born child is anxious and ambitious, or that every child responds to television violence in the same way. In fact, there can be many individual exceptions to a research finding, and yet the finding will still be statistically *significant*. In psychological research, the term **significance** has a special meaning, that a particular finding is unlikely to have happened by chance. The term does *not* mean that the effect is large or that the finding is significant in the sense of important.

Research Methods in Developmental Psychology

Like all psychologists, the researcher in human development must decide which of several strategies to use. One decision is whether to use experimental or nonexperimental procedures. If the researcher decides not to do an experiment, he or she must choose between correlational and observational techniques.

In contrast to other psychologists, the developmental researcher usually wants to find out how behavior changes over time. The time dimension may be approached in two different ways: first, using a **cross-sectional** design, the researcher may study people of several different ages. For example, a study of values over the life span might examine teenagers, young adults, and people in their fifties and seventies; or a study of language development in childhood might select groups of children who are 2, 3, 4, and 5 years of age. The second option for studying development over time would be to start with a group of children or adults and gather information about them repeatedly over a long period of time. This is the **longitudinal** method. For example, a researcher might study the same group of people at age 5, 10, 15, 20, and 25. Each of the approaches to research has advantages and disadvantages, which we will examine in more detail later in this chapter.

The Experiment

Experiments have traditionally been the preferred way of doing research in all branches of psychology. They provide the researcher with the greatest amount of control over the **variables** under study. Like a playwright and director combined, the researcher writes the script for the experiment and assigns the actors—the subjects—to their parts. This random assignment of subjects is a key difference between **experimental** and **nonexperimental** methods. It means that the researcher can manipulate variables while everything else is held constant or randomized so it cannot have systematic effects on the outcome.

Suppose, for example, that the researcher wants to look at the effects of failure on children's problem solving. The hypothesis of such a study would be that the experience of failure will lead children to perform less well on problem-solving tasks than they otherwise would. In this example the experience of failure would be the **independent** or *causal variable,* and the later problem-solving performance would be the **dependent** or *outcome variable.* To test the hypothesis, the researcher would take a number of children and randomly assign them to two subgroups. One group of children would be given a set of very hard or impossible problems. This would be the **experimental group.** The other group, the **control group,** would not receive the impossible problems, hence would not have the experience of failure. The researcher would make sure that the two groups were comparable in age, intelligence, health, or any other possible influence on their performance.

In the second part of the experiment, both groups would be given the same set of problems to solve, and their performance would be compared. If the group that had been given the impossible problems did worse on the second set, the hypothesis that failure interferes with problem solving would be supported. Since the groups had been randomly assigned to the failure or no-failure condition, the researcher could be fairly certain that the difference between the two groups, assuming there was one, was due to the independent variable, the experience of failure. (See the box on Significance Tests.)

The experimental method has an elegance and certainty about it which other methods lack. A good experiment can provide a convincing demonstration of cause and effect relationships. It permits a refined examination of both the independent and dependent variable. For example, in the hypothetical study mentioned here, the experience of failure could have been varied in a number of ways—to see, for example, the effect of degree of failure. Perhaps failing one or two problems might motivate children to improve their performance on the second set of problems. Instead of just two groups, the researcher could have several experimental and control groups, each exploring a different facet of the problem.

Despite its seeming elegance, however, the experimental method has limitations as well, particularly in the study of human development. The experiment is ideally suited to short-term studies of variables that can be readily isolated and manipulated in laboratories. Human development, by contrast, is a slow process

On the Significance of Significance Tests

Studies in developmental psychology and other fields of research that use statistics usually report their findings in terms of "significant" results, or "significant" differences between the groups. Used in this way, as explained earlier, the term "significant" does not mean that the results are important, or even that there are very large differences between the groups. Rather, a significant finding is one that is not likely to have happened by chance. In other words, a significant finding permits the researcher to generalize from the specific individuals studied to larger populations.

Consider the following example: A psychologist working for a toy company is trying to find out which of two toys babies will prefer to play with—its own jack-in-the-box or Brand X's. On the first day of the study, she observes five babies. Four out of the five show a preference for the company's toy. Can the psychologist assume that babies *in general* prefer her company's toy and that another sample of babies would show the same preference? Can the company claim that "4 out of 5 babies prefer our toy to Brand X's"?

Before our psychologist can come to that conclusion, she has to find out whether she could have obtained her results by chance alone. She begins by making the assumption that there is *no* difference in infants' preferences for the two toys. This is known as the *null hypothesis.* That is, she assumes that if she could actually go out and test every baby in America, she would find that they liked the toys equally well. She then asks, what is the probability that, of any five babies picked at random, four of them would pick one of the two toys?

Computing the probability of this happening, she discovers that it is three chances in eight— so high that the result could be due to chance. She cannot assume that babies in general really do prefer one toy over the other. Usually, researchers require that there be only one or five chances out of a hundred to obtain a result before they assume that their findings reflect a true difference in the population. Thus, our toy tester's finding was not statistically significant

because it could have occurred by chance.

Two types of errors can be made in trying to determine whether a research finding is valid. The researcher may infer that there is a real difference in the population when in fact there is none. For example, a particular finding could represent the one in a hundred chance occurrence. This is known as a Type 1 error. Tests of significance are aimed at preventing Type 1 errors—that is, preventing researchers from leaping to the conclusion that their hypotheses are true when the differences they obtained could have been due to chance.

On the other hand, it is possible to go astray in the other direction, rejecting a hypothesis when it really is true—the Type 2 error. In the toy example cited above, it is possible that four out of five babies in the general population would have preferred the company's toy to Brand X's. However, with such a small sample, the possibility of this outcome could not be tested in an adequate manner. The larger the sample used in a study, the more likely the results will reflect the true state of affairs in the general population. This is the **law of large numbers.**

Here are some points to remember about statistical significance:

1. Statistical inference is based on the assumption that the sample actually studied is representative of the population it is drawn from. For example, a survey of "American voters" would assume that every member of the American voting population has an equal chance of being included in the sample. If a sample is biased, it is hard to draw valid conclusions from it.

2. A significant difference does not explain *why* the differences exist. Any finding can usually be explained in a variety of ways. For example, if a researcher found that boys and girls differ on a test of mathematical skill, this does not in itself tell you whether the result is due to biological sex differences or to differences in skill, motivation, or the encouragement of parents and others.

3. As mentioned above, statistical significance does not mean psychological

significance. If the toy researcher tested 1,000 babies, she could find that a slight preference for one of the toys was statistically significant. Such a finding would have little practical use. For example, somebody trying to choose which jack-in-the-box to buy for a child could not assume that the child in question would definitely prefer one to the other.

4. Psychology is a science like meteorology or pharmacology in that the phenomena it studies are small in relation to uncontrolled variability; the messages psychologists receive from nature have a low "signal-to-noise ratio,"

like a staticky radio or a poor connection on a telephone (Tversky & Kahneman, 1971). This means that even strong, significant findings do not allow for complete predictability. While the physical sciences such as physics and chemistry can make firmer predictions about the behavior of matter, modern philosophers of science tell us that absolute certainty can never be achieved. A recent book on statistical analysis put it this way: "As the ancient Hebrews felt about their God, the scientist should never speak the words truth or proof, but always keep them in mind" (Kenney, 1979, p. 2).

involving a complicated array of interacting factors, most of which are, for ethical or practical reasons, impossible for a researcher to control. It is possible to think of certain experiments that would provide valuable information but which should not be done because they would be ethically wrong.

For example, an experiment in which boy and girl infants were raised as members of the opposite sex might provide valuable insights into the innateness of sex differences, but ethically could never be done. Similarly, children cannot be subjected to severe stress, deprivation, or isolation. Nor can questions about the effects of childrearing methods be answered by randomly assigning parents to raise their children in prescribed ways. (See the box on Ethical Principles.)

Because of these limitations, psychologists have turned to nonexperimental methods and have also taken advantage of so-called **natural experiments**—situations in which children have been exposed to conditions that could not be manipulated. Thus, for example, there have been studies of children raised in extreme isolation, in concentration camps, or in severely deprived institutional environments. There have also been studies of children who, because they were born with malformed genitals, were raised as members of the other sex.

Of course, the natural experiment does not parallel the laboratory experiment; the researcher here does not control the independent variable or assign subjects to the experimental condition, but merely investigates the outcome. Therefore, it is hard to be sure exactly what factor is responsible for any differences that are found.

Nonexperimental Research

In situations where experimental manipulation is difficult or impossible, researchers can study relationships among variables in a variety of ways. Many studies involve comparisons among groups differing in a particular characteristic. Some of the best-known studies take this form, such as those that compare smokers and nonsmokers on rates of lung cancer. Experiments with animals have confirmed that the chemicals in cigarette smoke cause cancer, but the studies of cancer and smoking in humans are based on observed variation rather than manipulation.

Sometimes the term **correlational** is applied to any study that examines relationships among nonmanipulated variables. Correlation, however, is also a specific statistical technique which indicates whether having high (or low) scores on one variable, say height, are likely to go along with high (or low) scores on another variable, such as weight. For example, although researchers cannot randomly assign children to different social classes, or control the childrearing methods parents use, they can look at the relationship between, say, childrearing methods and children's behavior or social class and grades in school.

Correlation research is also done as an alternative to, or in conjunction with, experiments. The effects of television violence could be studied by setting up an experiment in which children were shown violent programs and their later behavior assessed. The same issue could also be studied through the use of correlation: parents—or children—could be asked about the children's television viewing habits, and then the children could be rated by classmates or teachers on their aggressiveness in real life.

The outcome of a correlational study is a correlation coefficient, "r," which indicates the relationship between the two variables. If two variables are perfectly correlated, so that either can be predicted from the other with perfect accuracy, the correlation coefficient would be +1.00. An "r" of −1.00 would mean that high scores on one variable could be perfectly predicted from low scores on the other. In other words, one varies inversely as the other. (An "r" of 0, or close to 0, means the variables are unrelated.) (See Figure 2.1.) Most correlations in real life are not as high; variables that correlate highly, such as height and weight, or IQ scores and school performance, typically yield correlations ranging around .70 to .80.

It is interesting and important to note that a correlation of .70 does not mean that it is possible to predict one variable from the other with 70 percent accuracy. The appropriate measure of the accuracy of prediction is "r^2." Thus, an "r" of .70 means that one variable can be predicted with .49 accuracy, or that about half the observed variation in one factor can be accounted for by the other.

A Note on Ethical Principles in Research

In recent years, organizations such as the American Psychological Association and the Society of Research in Child Development have formulated ethical guidelines for carrying out research with children. These guidelines apply to all kinds of research, not just experiments.

In general, the basic principle underlying the guidelines is that the rights and well-being of the child supersede the rights of the researcher. Thus, the researcher can use no procedure that may harm the child physically or psychologically. The researcher must inform parents and other responsible adults in detail about the research and obtain their consent before the study is carried out; the child and the parents must be allowed to refuse to participate and to drop out of the study at any time without penalty.

Applying these rules to specific research projects can often be complex. Universities, for example, have review committees, consisting of professors from many fields, that examine all proposed studies involving human subjects. No such research can be done without the approval of these review committees.

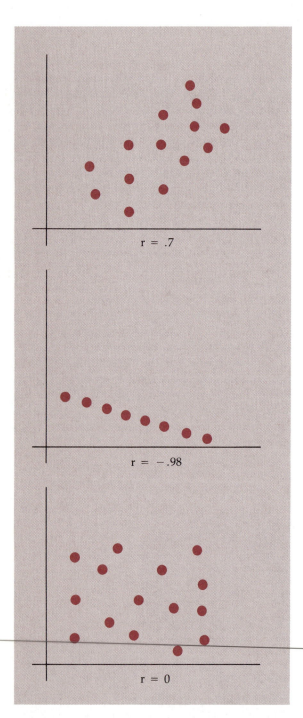

FIGURE 2.1
Scatter Plots
The outcome of a correlational study is a correlational coefficient "r," which can be positive (shown here as .7), negative (−.98), or unrelated (0).

The major difference between experiments and correlational studies has to do with what one can conclude about cause and effect relationships. In an experiment, it is possible to be fairly certain that the independent variable, say watching a violent television show, is the cause of the experimental group's more aggressive behavior, such as hitting a large doll. This is so because the experimenter has made sure that watching a particular program was the only difference between the experimental and the control group. But in the correlational study, the researcher cannot be certain that the variable under study is the only thing influencing the outcome behavior. Nor can he or she be certain which way causality is working. For example, suppose a study of television viewing habits showed that children who watch a lot of violent programs, such as "Miami Vice" and the "A-Team," tend to fight with other children more than those who do not watch as much television violence. Can we conclude that TV violence leads to aggressive behavior? The answer, of course, is no, because it may be that children who are aggressive in the first place like to watch violent television programs and also are more likely to fight with their classmates.

Although every psychologist learns in basic statistics that correlations do not imply causal statements, in practice such inferences are often made. Thus, many correlational studies of parent-child relationships assume that the parents' behavior is the cause, and the child's behavior is the effect. For example, suppose a study finds that parents who use physical punishment have aggressive children, and that parents who use reasoning and avoid punishment have well-behaved children. The researcher may conclude that physical punishment causes aggression in children, and that reasoning is a much more effective disciplinary technique. Or a researcher might observe that the parents of schizophrenics speak to them in confusing ways and therefore conclude that the family's peculiar communication style drove the young people out of their minds. In these instances, the researcher seems to be assuming that because the parents are older, bigger, stronger, and supposedly wiser than their children, that they are the dominant parties in parent-child interaction. They also seem to be assuming that how the parents act at the time of the study precedes the behavior it is assumed to have caused—that the parent behavior always came first and was stable over time.

But it is just as reasonable to make the opposite interpretation of parent-child correlations. Children can influence parents as much as parents influence children. It may be that punishment and aggression go together because aggressive children are disobedient and provoke their parents to punish them, while children who are temperamentally more easy-going are more likely to do what their parents ask them to do, thus encouraging parents to reason with them in a calm way. Similarly, the parents of schizophrenics may be responding to the peculiarities of their offspring; or else, the behavior of both parents and children might be explainable by a third variable, such as vulnerability to anxiety.

Naturalistic Observation

Although correlational research does not permit the degree of control that the laboratory experiment does, it brings the researcher close to "real life." Laboratory experiments set up artificial conditions which may not reflect how people behave in the natural environment. For example, a study showing that children can be made to act aggressively after watching a violent television program does not necessarily mean that television violence is the cause of the aggressive behavior we see in the streets and on the playgrounds. As Robert McCall (1977) puts it, the experiment answers "Can" questions rather than "Does" questions. That is, an experiment asks the question, "Can factor 'X' produce Factor 'Y,' under laboratory circumstances?" It does not ask whether factor "X" *is* the major cause of factor "Y" in real life.

McCall is one of a number of developmental psychologists in recent years who have challenged the heavy reliance on experimental methods in developmental psychology. While

recognizing the value of experiments, they point out that the process of development as it takes place in real life has been largely ignored. Urie Bronfenbrenner (1974) has argued that much experimental research is "ecologically invalid"—that is, not generalizable to real-life circumstances. This is so, he contends, because it deals with children interacting with strangers—the experimenters—in strange environments, such as the laboratory.

The natural settings children grow up in differ in several crucial ways from the laboratory. In families, schools, and day-care centers, there are individuals who have enduring relations with the child; and the interaction that goes on between the child and others is reciprocal—the child influences those who influence him or her. In addition, the behavior of the child and others is affected by the social and physical environment—for example, the neighborhood, the nature of the parents' work, and the wider society itself in the form of the economic system, the mass media, and so on. Finally, all of these environmental circumstances can have different meanings to the different people in them. In other words, we need to know not only about the everyday world of the child or adult, but how it is perceived by that person.

Recently, perhaps partly in response to the criticisms by Bronfenbrenner and others, there have been an increasing number of studies using **naturalistic** methods. Such studies usually involve the observation and description of behavior in its natural context, such as the home, school, street, or playground. For example, a researcher might observe the interaction of a family around the dinner table, or how fights begin and end on school playgrounds, or how friendship cliques and a leadership hierarchy emerge in a summer camp.

Actually, observation was once the main method used by the early developmental psychologists. At the beginning of the twentieth century, researchers devoted themselves to describing children's behavior at particular ages and to tracing in precise detail the sequence of steps in the development of such behaviors as walking and talking, grasping and manipulating objects. Usually these researchers did not

Most psychologists recognize that the environments in which children spend their time have profound effects on their behavior and development. Ecological psychologists pay special attention to the various dimensions and impact of environment. Affluent or poor, urban, rural, or suburban, school or home, local or regional are only a few of the distinctions that can be made.

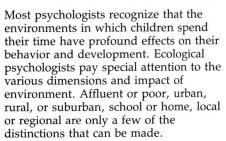

have any particular theory in mind to guide their observations: they aimed at a complete description of behavior. One major—and later—work in this tradition was *One Boy's Day* by Roger Barker and associates (1966), which was an attempt to describe everything that happened to one midwestern boy over the course of a day. In the 1950s, observation and description fell out of favor as developmental researchers turned to experimental methods and lost interest in questions that could not be answered in the laboratory. Observational methods were also disparaged because they

were not theoretical and did not explain how and why behavior changed.

The revival of naturalistic observation in recent years was encouraged by the accomplishments of the **ethologists** in their studies of animal behavior. Ethologists such as Konrad Lorenz and Niko Tinbergen argued that the first step in understanding the behavior of a particular animal is systematic observation in the natural habitat. Observations made in the laboratory, or even in the zoo, they claimed, are premature until the more naturalistic studies are done. Ethologists study the relationship

Konrad Lorenz and his imprinted graylag geese.

between an animal species and its total environment—how it gets its food, the enemies that prey on it, its social organization—in order to identify what is uniquely characteristic of that particular species. Using the method of simple but patient and detailed observation, researchers in the ethological tradition have studied birds, fish, wolves, gorillas, chimpanzees, and other primates, as well as human beings. Because the ethologists study nonverbal behavior—animals obviously cannot talk—their methods have been most useful when applied to human infants.

Ethologists have made numerous important discoveries. Probably the best-known example is **imprinting** in birds, the process by which birds learn to follow whatever object is close to them at a critical time shortly after they hatch. Since the nearest object to a baby bird is usually an adult bird, imprinting helps to ensure the survival of the baby birds. Another major discovery arising out of naturalistic observation in the wild is Jane Goodall's (Lawick-Goodall, 1971) finding that chimpanzees make and use tools and eat meat. This discovery challenged the previous beliefs that humans were the only tool-making and -using animals, and that primates were herbivores.

The ethologists differ from the earlier researchers who used observation because the new method has been guided by a theory: the theory of evolution. Their hypothesis has been that much of the social behavior seen in animals has evolved because it has survival value for the individual and the species. Thus, ethologists focus on the adaptive behavior of the species under study. One particularly important concept is that of **releasor** or *releasing* **stimulus**—the event that evokes a particular behavior in all members of a species. For example the sight of a large, moving object is what releases the imprinting response in the baby bird. In applying their approach to humans, ethologists have looked at the behavior of infants from the point of view of its adaptive functions. For example, human infants cannot follow their parents, but they do cry to attract the attention of adults. Human ethologists argue that crying is a releasor stimulus which makes adults respond by attending to the infant's needs. If crying were the only adaptive mechanism, however, adults might lose interest in infants and stop paying attention to them. Therefore, they argue, babies are also "cute": They smile and coo and have relatively large heads and

eyes. Ethologists have argued that "cuteness" is a releasing stimulus which leads to caretaking behavior in both animals and humans (Lorenz, 1943).

Despite the successes of ethology, its methods are controversial. Ethologists tend to study humans as if people were no different from other animals, and they freely compare human and animal behavior. Some critics have pointed out that by ignoring what is unique to human beings—namely language, learning, and culture—they violate their own rules about studying species-specific behavior. As Washburn points out, "Human ethology might be defined as the science that pretends humans cannot speak" (1978, p. 414). The issues in human behavior that can be studied through the use of observation alone are limited. We need to know the psychological and cultural meaning of behavior, as well as to have detailed descriptions of behavioral sequences. In spite of these limitations, the ethological approach has contributed important insights and has stimulated thought in significant new directions in the study of human development. Above all, its emphasis on the observation and description of

behavior in its natural settings has brought developmental research closer to real life.

Other kinds of psychologists, in addition to the ethologists, have also helped to revive observation as a research method. Students of language development have observed children in their everyday environments learning how to speak. And behavior modifiers have gone into the homes of problem children to observe the everyday family interaction. For example, Gerald Patterson (1982) and his associates closely observe the events leading up to and following children's aggressive acts. They might find, for instance, that a boy typically hits his younger brother before dinner. The boy's mild efforts to gain his parents' attention are ignored because the parents are busy making dinner, and they only give him their full attention when he starts hitting his little brother. Thus, the parents seem to reward unintentionally the very behavior they want to change.

As a research method, naturalistic observation has drawbacks as well as unique advantages. For one thing, observing how people behave does not reveal what they are thinking. Bronfenbrenner and others have pointed out the need to know what situations mean to the participants, but most observational studies present only an outsider's view. Further, there is a real dilemma in observational research: the method aims at getting very close to natural, everyday, real-life behavior, but doesn't the presence of the observer influence what is going on? Researchers disagree about how serious a problem this actually is.

One study (Graves & Glick, 1978) compared the interaction of mothers and their preschool children in a playground under two conditions: in one the mothers were aware that their behavior was being observed and recorded; in the second, they thought they were not being observed when they actually were.

It turned out that the mothers behaved very differently when they thought they were being watched. In the observed condition, the mothers, who were all middle-class, seemed to be displaying behavior likely to be regarded by the experimenters as "good mothering": they spoke a lot to their children, played with them, tried to get them to display various skills. In contrast, in the unobserved condition, the same mothers were much less attentive to the children; they often seemed preoccupied with their own thoughts or busy with projects of their own. In short, when they thought they were unobserved, these middle-class mothers behaved much the way lower-class mothers had been described as acting. The study raises the possibility that some of the class differences found in previous research may be due in part to middle-class mothers behaving in a particular manner for the benefit of psychological observers.

The only solution to the dilemma would be an invisible cloak for researchers to wear while observing interaction in the home and elsewhere. Even if such a cloak were not a fantasy, however, it would be ethically impermissible to use it. As it is, observing real-life interaction in the family raises serious problems of confidentiality and intrusion in people's private lives.

Field Experiments

Field experiments combine real-life settings with experimental methods. In a field experiment, the researcher enters into an ongoing social situation and gives contrasting experiences to two or more groups of individuals or to the same people at different times. For example, in one study (Klaus & Kennell, 1976) one group of new mothers was given skin-to-skin contact with their babies immediately after birth, while other new mothers experienced the usual hospital procedures. The outcome or dependent variable was the mother's "bonding" or attachment to the child. (Bonding is discussed in detail in a box in Chapter 6.)

In another example, Stein and Frederick (1975) studied the effects of different television "diets" on nursery school children. They observed the play behavior of children in matched Head Start centers before, during, and after assigning children to one of three experimental conditions: watching violent programs such as "Batman" and cartoons; watch-

ing prosocial programs like "Mr. Rogers' Neighborhood"; and watching neutral programs such as nature films. There was also a no-TV condition. The outcome measures were differences observed between the children's play behavior over several weeks. The results showed that children who were aggressive before the experiment became more aggressive after watching the violent cartoons, while the prosocial cartoons led to more prosocial behavior.

One advantage of the field experiment over the correlational method is that it permits causal inferences to be drawn. For example, suppose a correlational study found that aggressive children watch more television. You could not tell from a correlational study whether television viewing caused the aggression, whether aggressive children like to watch more television, or whether some other factor—such as the child's family background—is contributing to both high viewing and high aggression.

Some of the questions are the same ones that can be asked about any experimental study—for example, how representative of the general population is the sample used in the study? The original sample in the bonding study was poor, black, young, and unmarried, so the finding of greater bonding after skin-to-skin contact did not apply to other populations (Svejda, Pannabecker, & Emde, 1982).

Further, field experiments generally have more **ecological validity** than laboratory experiments. That is, they are more directly relevant to real life. However, questions may still be raised about how findings of field experiments should be interpreted. Do the children know there is an experiment going on? Are they aware of being observed or of being treated differently? Are they aware of the different treatments being given to other children? Also, is this knowledge affecting the outcome in any way? In the bonding studies mentioned above, the mothers in the experimental group seem to have been responding as much to the extra attention they were getting from the doctors and nurses as from the early contact with their babies.

Also, field experiments raise certain ethical questions in that the people who are participating often do not know they are research subjects. For example, in some field experiments with adults, researchers have staged epileptic fits on the street and heart attacks on subway trains in order to study helping behavior. The less field experiments interfere with ongoing activities or expose participants to stress, the less severe these ethical questions are (Sellitz, Wrightsman, & Cooke, 1976).

The Case Study

The **case study** method is an intensive study of one individual. Actually, this method, in the form of baby biography—a diary of an infant's first days and months—was the first step in the development of the systematic observation of children. In seventeenth-century France, the court doctor recorded the infancy of the future King Louis XIII. During the nineteenth century, baby biographies became popular among scholarly fathers. Charles Darwin's biography of his son is probably the best-known example. Baby biographies have the advantage of describing development in the minute daily detail that only a parent living with a child can provide, but the method has its limitations as well. As William Kessen points out, "no one can distort as convincingly as a loving parent" (1965, p. 117). Each biographer, including Darwin, tended to see in his child the living proof of his theoretical notions.

Although baby biographies are no longer in vogue, one of the major figures in contemporary developmental psychology, Jean Piaget, used observations of his own children as the starting place for research and theorizing. Piaget, however, not only watched the child's own behavior as it changed over time, he also devised little gamelike experiments to clarify the nature of the child's concepts.

For example, one of Piaget's main interests was the child's realization that objects are permanent—that they exist when they are out of sight. At first he observed that infants stopped looking for a toy or bottle as soon as it vanished from sight. Piaget explored this situation further by hiding a toy under a blanket just as the child was about to reach for it. He rattled the toy under the blanket, but still the child did not try to lift it. When Piaget left part of the toy sticking out, the child was able to remove the blanket and grasp the toy. Eventually, the child was able to find an object even when it was hidden. At this stage, Piaget introduced a new experimental game: he hid a toy and the child found it; next he hid the toy in a different place, but still within the sight of the child. The child looked for the object at the first place it had been hidden—as if it could mysteriously return to the place it had first been found. Piaget's observations, intervention by means of playful experiments, speculations, and explanations of the child's thinking continued throughout the infancy of his three children and resulted in two major contributions to developmental psychology: *The Origins of Intelligence* (1952) and *The Construction of Reality in the Child* (1954).

The case method was also used in another major psychological theory of the twentieth century: psychoanalysis. Sigmund Freud made his momentous discoveries about the hidden workings of the mind in the course of his clinical work with disturbed patients; he presented many of his theoretical ideas in the course of describing individual cases. The case of "Little Hans," for example, was a study of phobias in a small boy. It was also a major presentation of Freud's theory of the Oedipus complex—the notion that all little boys pass through a phase of romantic attraction for their mothers and hostility toward their fathers.

Hans was a five-year-old boy who was so afraid a horse would bite him that he would not leave the house. Freud conducted the analysis through the boy's father, one of Freud's students. After amassing many details about Hans's life, his dreams, and his responses to questions, Freud concluded that the horse symbolized Hans's father. The biting symbolized the punishment—castration—that Hans and other boys that age fear is due them because of their rivalry for their mother's love. The story of Little Hans is one of Freud's most readable and persuasive case histories (see Brown, 1965).

The case method is also used to study children and adults who are unusual in some way or who have grown up in extraordinary circumstances. For example, there have been several studies of so-called wild or feral children, that is, children who have lived in isolation from their parents and other human beings and have grown up in the wilderness (Davis, 1947). The best-known instance of this kind was the wild boy of Aveyron, a boy of about 12, seemingly deaf and mute, who in 1799 was found running wild in the forest. The story of this boy, Victor, and of the efforts of a dedicated doctor, Jean-Marc Itard, to educate him inspired numerous case studies, several novels and plays, a film by François Truffaut—"The Wild Child"—a hit song of the 1950s, and most recently a detailed history and psychological analysis of Victor and the methods of Dr. Itard (Lane, 1976). (See the box on Wild Children in Chapter 6.)

In the past few years, there have been case studies of a girl with unusual drawing ability, a girl who was kept chained to a potty in a closet from infancy to adolescence, and a little boy of three who was born without any immunity to disease and so spent his life in a plastic bubble in a hospital. Although the case method is most often used to study individuals who are deviant in some way, it has also been used to study ordinary people intensively (e.g., Vaillant, 1977; White, 1966).

The Life History Method When a case study covers a good deal of someone's life course, it becomes a **life history.** Life histories have been of interest to sociologists, political scientists, anthropologists, and historians as well as to psychologists. The life history method was popular during the first part of the twentieth century, particularly through the 1920s to the 1940s (Runyan, 1982). In the 1950s and 1960s, social scientists turned to experiments and other quantitative methods and expressed little interest in life histories.

Beginning in the 1970s, however, interest in the course of lives has been renewed for several reasons: psychologists were becoming disillusioned with experiments as the only way of gathering data; there was a growing interest in development across the whole life span and in transitions at various points across the life cycle; and there has been a growing recognition that development cannot be studied as if it took place in a social vacuum, but rather that it is necessary to look at the impact of the social and cultural environment in which people grow. At the same time, clinical researchers have become interested in studying how biological, psychological, and social factors work together in the lives of people who become schizophrenic, neurotic, and so on. Finally, the new—and controversial—field of psychohistory has stimulated interest in the life course and psychological development of historical figures, ranging from Martin Luther and Mohandas Gandhi to Lyndon Johnson and Richard Nixon.

There is a significant difference between a life course approach and life span development. Developmental changes are general, applying to all people; the life course or life history approach deals with group and individual differences in experience. As Runyan (1978) points out, not all life changes are developmental: going to a therapist, getting a new job, taking heroin, or having a serious accident can be important events that can alter the course of a person's life, but they have little to do with maturation or systematic developmental change.

Longitudinal versus Cross-sectional Studies
A life history usually looks backward through time. It starts with an adult or child at a particular point in life and tries to understand how he or she got there. A study of individuals that goes forward in time is a longitudinal study, which begins at a particular moment and continues for weeks, months, or years. The longitudinal approach is one of two major ways of studying psychological change through time. The other is the cross-sectional method, which compares people all at one time who represent different age groups. Each method has unique advantages and disadvantages.

Longitudinal studies observe the same person over a long period of time.

The major advantage of the cross-sectional method is that the investigator does not have to wait for the subjects to grow up or become older. If, for example, the researcher wants to study the course of language development or reasoning or intelligence, all he or she has to do is to find people at varying ages and compare their behavior.

Despite its simplicity, this method has its drawbacks. It provides no information about how individuals change or about the stability of their traits. The process of development gets lost. For example, a cross-sectional study of the physical growth of children would reveal how height increases on the average, year by year. It would not indicate how individual children grew over the years, nor would it tell whether children who were taller or shorter than their peers in elementary school would maintain their relative heights as adolescents or adults. Cross-sectional studies cannot answer questions like these, but longitudinal studies can. Thus, it was one of the major longitudinal studies at the University of California which discovered the adolescent growth spurt: until the physical growth of individual children was tracked, it was believed that individual growth followed the curve representing the average growth of children over the years. Observation by these researchers of individual children through time revealed that they did not reach adult height in regular steps, but rather experienced periods of rapid growth, gaining several inches in the course of one or two years. Further, the growth spurt occurred at different times in different individuals (Stolz & Stolz, 1951).

In the longitudinal method, a group of subjects is selected and is given a series of interviews, questionnaires, tests, and so forth periodically over several years. For example, several major longitudinal studies were begun in the 1920s and 1930s, such as Lewis Terman's study of the entire life span of children with very high IQ scores, which will not be concluded until 2010 (Sears, 1977); The Guidance Study and the Oakland Growth Study at the University of California at Berkeley, which began observing children, respectively, in their infancy and late childhood and continue to this day, when the subjects are in their fifties and sixties; the Fels Institute study of children from birth to maturity; and the Grant study of adult development, which began with freshmen at one of America's leading universities and charted their lives over forty years (Vaillant, 1977).

The longitudinal method is ideally suited to looking at how individuals change or remain the same over time—indeed, it is the only way to answer such questions. It is also the only valid way to examine the effects of early experiences on later development. For example, many personality psychologists believed that painful experiences early in life, such as the loss of a parent, the lack of parental love, or family tension, must lead to psychological damage and maladjustment later in life.

This theory about the impact of early "trauma" on later experience arose from clinical studies which started with troubled adults and worked backward toward childhood conditions. It is only recently that longitudinal studies have persisted long enough to provide useful information about normal development from childhood to maturity. Such forward-looking studies have challenged widely held assumptions. One of the University of California studies, for instance, found that not only was there no necessary cause and effect relationship between having a troubled childhood and being a maladjusted adult, but growing up under seemingly excellent circumstances was no guarantee of adult happiness or competence (MacFarlane, 1964): take, for example, the comparison in Chapter 1 of the childhoods of John Hinckley, Jr., and Lee Harvey Oswald.

Similarly, the Grant study found many surprises in its survey of the lives of its participants. Although this study began when the subjects were in college, information was obtained about their early childhoods. This information did not predict adult outcomes very well: "When identified in advance, fingernail biting, early toilet training, the 'tainted family tree,' even that old standby—the cold rejecting mother—failed to predict emotionally ill adults" (Vaillant, 1977, p. 283). Note that the findings of these studies do *not* mean that the events of childhood have no impact on children, but rather that these effects are not simple and direct responses to environmental events. Later in this book, I will be discussing more appropriate models of how external realities affect the inner, psychological world of the child.

Despite its virtues, the longitudinal method is plagued by numerous problems. It is expensive and time-consuming. In addition, the longer a study lasts, the more participants will drop out: people move, get sick, lose interest. This subject loss may bias the outcome, since the people who remain may not be similar to those who drop out. Perhaps those who remain are those who have less accomplished professional lives than those who drop out, biasing the findings toward the less successful. Or perhaps, if intelligence is being studied, those people who have a harder time taking IQ tests may drop out, making the average intelligence scores of the sample higher and distorting any age trends that might emerge.

Another problem is that ideas and methods in psychology change over time. It is difficult to choose tests and devise observations that will be of major importance twenty or thirty years hence. Sometimes, however, it is possible to re-analyze old data using more up-to-date concepts and measures (see Block & Haan, 1971).

Recently, the short-term longitudinal study has been used as an alternative to the longitudinal study designed to cover decades. Such a study might focus on a key developmental process and be tied to some particular theoretical question. For example, the researcher might start with a group of one-year-olds and follow their social behavior over the next two or three years. Or the language development of a group of children could be followed over several months or years. Adult subjects could be studied for a few years before and after they experience a turning point in the life course, such as marriage, the birth of the first child, the departure of all the children from the "nest," retirement, and so forth. This method provides a way of resolving some of the problems of long-term longitudinal studies; it does not, however, provide information about entire life histories.

Lifetime and Historical Time: Age and Cohort Effects   Over the past few years, students of human development have realized that they are dealing with at least two kinds of time, not just one. Although they are mainly interested in changes over time in individuals, it is clear that individual change is inextricably mixed up with historical change. No one ever develops in a vacuum. Every person is born and lives out his or her life at some particular time and place.

What this means is that the three-year-olds of today may be different from the three-year-olds of the 1950s and both may be unlike the three-year-olds of the 1920s or the 1820s. Today's three-year-old, for example, is more likely than those a decade or two ago to come from a single parent family, to have a working mother, to have few or no brothers and sisters, to have experienced group care early in life, and so on. Similarly, today's 70-year-olds differ in many ways from what today's 40-year-olds will be like in thirty years. Future generations

of old people will have more years of education and will have enjoyed better health, as well as be less likely to be foreign born or to have had working-class jobs, than old people today. The technical term for people who were born at any particular time is **cohort.**

In addition to being influenced by changes in health, education, and other general social and cultural changes, cohorts differ in their experiences of historical events such as wars, economic depressions and booms, and so on. Cohorts differ not only in whether they live through such events, but also the age at which they encounter them.

Although cohort differences are most striking in modern industrial societies which change rapidly, they can exist even in seemingly changeless traditional societies due to wars, epidemics, crop failures, increases or declines in the number of children born in a particular year. These cohort differences limit the conclusions that may be drawn from both longitudinal and cross-sectional studies.

The cohort effect can be seen most clearly in the longitudinal studies that follow the development of a group of people of one age. Does the course of their lives represent development in general, or is it specific to that particular cohort? Consider for example the members of the Oakland Growth Study, one of the longitudinal studies at the University of California (Elder, 1974, 1975). These men and women were born in 1920–21 and grew up in Oakland, California. During the worst years of the Great Depression—the early 1930s—they were just entering their teens, which, it turned out, was the luckiest age to be during a time of economic collapse. Younger people, such as those born in 1927 or 1929, were in their most dependent state of development and were most vulnerable to family misfortune precisely when their families were most likely to be in economic trouble. Older cohorts, say those born around 1910, were entering the age of marriage when economic conditions were at their worst. Even though the Oakland men experienced economic hardship, it did not handicap their occupational futures. They were at the right age to take advantage of the economic boom that followed World War II and achieved a striking degree of economic success and mobility. The women of the Oakland study, many of whom had heavy household responsibilities during the depression, made early and strong commitments to home and family; they were the generation that created the baby boom and were the objects of the "feminine mystique."

A comparison of the Oakland cohort with today's young adults reveals some striking changes in the economy and society. Such a comparison also reveals how historical factors work together with developmental changes in individuals. While the Oakland cohort knew economic deprivation as children and became

Cohort studies observe different groups of people at a given age or stage.

adults in the affluent society, their children's generation, the babies from the postwar baby boom, grew up in a time of seemingly limitless economic growth, only to reach adulthood in a time of scarcity, limitations, high unemployment, and inflation. Values also changed. The sexual revolution transformed the sexual morality that had prevailed in the 1950s, and the sex role revolution offered a new definition of what it means to be a man or woman. New definitions of self-fulfillment challenged formerly unquestioned values with regard to work, family, and the larger society.

All of these changes affected the psychological development of young people making the transition from adolescence to adulthood. The developmental "tasks" of early adulthood—the commitments to work and marriage—that were accomplished so early and so decisively for their parents were delayed, resulting in a lengthening transition to adulthood and the creation of a "new" stage of psychological development, that is, youth (Keniston, 1971).

Not everyone, of course, experiences being a member of a cohort in the same way. There is great individual variation in the way the historical events and central tendencies of a generation are woven into the fabric of individual lives. Some people live their lives much like people in earlier cohorts; other people live out life patterns that may be deviant in their own day, but anticipate the way large numbers of people in future generations may live. Nevertheless, the cohort concept points to an important source of systematic variation in the study of human development.

The cohort problem affects cross-sectional studies also. For example, for many years there seemed to be strong evidence that intelligence test scores decline with age. Thus, when the Wechsler Adult Intelligence Scale was given to people ranging in age from 15 to 65, test scores rose until about age 25, leveled off between 25 and 30, and continued to decline steeply until age 65 (Wechsler, 1955). As a result of this and many similar findings, there was speculation about the possible physical reasons for such mental deterioration; perhaps it was because brain cells began to die off after the age of 30.

In recent years, however, results from the first longitudinal studies of adult intelligence have begun to appear. Surprisingly, when individuals were tracked through time, it turned out that IQ scores did not decline sharply after all (Botwinick, 1977). Why then did earlier studies find a sharp drop in IQ scores between age 30 and 65? A major reason seems to be that older cohorts had less education than younger ones (Kimmel, 1974). The increasing "smartness" of younger cohorts was also found through comparing the scores of succeeding generations of 17-year-olds on army intelligence tests (Riegel, 1976).

One way of controlling for cohort effects is the **cross-sequential** research design (Schaie, 1965), which combines cross-sectional and longitudinal approaches. The researcher starts with a cross-section of ages and follows them over time. For example, a study could start out by testing a sample of people aged 10, 20, and 30. Every decade for the next thirty years, the sample would be tested again and younger groups would be added. Thus, a sample of 10-year-olds would be added at the second testing; 10- and 20-year-olds at the third, and so forth. Each individual's scores could be traced over time, and different cohorts could be compared. Although this method yields information about age differences (across ages) and age changes (within individuals) as well as cohort effects (looking at different generations at the same age), it is expensive and requires a long time to carry out.

In Search of Knowledge: Science and Certainty

There is no one best research method in developmental psychology. All of the ways of gathering information discussed above have advantages as well as disadvantages. Laboratory experiments give precise measurements and convincing evidence about cause and effect relationships, but they may have little relevance for what goes on in real life. Correlational studies do not manipulate variables, but they do abstract them from real life, possibly overlooking other important variables in the process. Naturalistic observation deals with real-life development firsthand, but cannot in itself offer final answers about cause and effect, or tell us about the conscious reasons or unconscious processes that lie beyond the behavior we can see with our eyes.

Beyond all these problems of particular research methods, developmental psychology shares some difficulties which face all the sciences that deal with human beings. Ethical conditions limit the kinds of research that can be done. Research may change the behavior being studied; any research involving conscious, self-aware individuals—whether a laboratory study using complicated apparatus, an interview in an office, an observation in someone's home—runs the risk that the people involved may not behave the way they normally do. Researchers themselves are human beings with their own complex personalities and values; they may have strong feelings about the issues and people they are investigating, which may distort their interpretations. Thus, no particular method or individual study can provide that last word on an issue. Generalizations must be built up from many different sources and yet, by the time the various pieces of evidence are put together, social and cultural change may have made them out of date.

All of this means that psychology has its own *indeterminacy principle*. It would be strange indeed if absolute knowledge and perfect prediction could be achieved in the study of human beings, when twentieth-century physics has shown that such certainty is unattainable in the physical world (Bronowski, 1973). Since parallels are drawn so often between the natural sciences and psychology, it is worth spending a little time discussing what kind of model of knowledge the so-called hard sciences actually provide.

In the early years of the twentieth century, at the same time psychology was becoming a scientific enterprise, the physical sciences were making some of the greatest advances in history. Basic discoveries were being made about the inner core of matter—the structure of the atom. Einstein's theory of relativity, first published in 1905, revolutionized ideas about time and space, matter and energy. These advances overturned the view of the universe that had prevailed through the nineteenth century. Ironically, as the new field of psychology emerged, it embraced a model of the physical sciences that physics itself was abandoning.

For 200 years, since the time of Newton, scientists had viewed the universe as a giant clockwork. The universe, from stars and planets to human beings and atoms, consisted of particles moving in determined courses like the parts of a watch. In principle, if the location and speed of all the particles in the universe were known, one could calculate the past and future course of all events. Time and space were absolute, the same throughout the universe. This image of the physical world was overthrown by the theory of relativity and the uncertainty principle.

The theory of relativity holds that time and space are not absolute, that they are relative to an observer's position and speed. For example, a question about whether an object is moving or standing still cannot be answered with a simple yes or no. It is necessary to ask, "In relation to what?" A person sitting on a moving train is motionless in relation to the train, but to someone standing on a station platform watching the train whiz by, he or she is obviously in motion. From the point of view of physics, it is as valid to say that the person on the platform is moving as it is to say that the person on the train is. Even more startling, the theory of relativity states that the size of an object and the duration of an event are also relative. As Bronowski points out, Newton's view of the universe is a god's eye view: it looks the same no matter where you are or what you are doing. Einstein's view, by contrast,

> is a man's eye view, in which what you see and what I see is relative to each of us, that is, to our place and speed. And this relativity cannot be removed. We cannot know what the world is like in itself, we can only compare what it looks

like to each of us, by the practical procedure of exchanging messages. (1973, p. 249)

The indeterminacy or uncertainty principle was also devastating to the image of the universe as a giant clock. In 1927, Heisenberg proved that it was impossible to determine at the same time both the position and the speed of an electron. This was a revolutionary discovery. Until then, scientists had believed that if instruments were calibrated more precisely, a more exact picture of physical reality was possible. Heisenberg showed that perfect accuracy is unattainable no matter how fine the measuring instrument. There is some uncertainty in every observation, not only because measuring instruments are imperfect, but because of the inevitable interaction between the observer and the thing observed. Paradoxically, an increase in the fineness and precision of measuring instruments can lead to a greater inaccuracy in measurement prediction.

This paradox of knowledge is not confined to the scale of atoms and electrons, it also exists at the human level and even that of the stars; the positions of stars cannot be determined precisely, but can only be estimated, statistically, to lie in an area of uncertainty. Other fields of knowledge were also overturning the belief in the possibility of absolute knowledge. In 1931, Godel proved the existence of an area of uncertainty at the heart of mathematics: he made the startling discovery that it is impossible to create a unitary system in which all mathematical truths can be deduced from a handful of axioms (Nagel & Newman, 1958).

Oddly enough, although psychologists were trying to model their field on the harder sciences, they paid little attention to the intellectual upheavals that were going on in physics and the other sciences. In 1934, Shuey pointed out the serious implications that the concepts of relativism and indeterminism had for psychology, but his message was ignored. He argued that the new physics had shown that instruments had to conform to the system being measured. A static instrument could not be used to measure a moving system. Yet psy-

chologists were using static measures on constantly changing organisms that are influenced by many variables. Shuey summed up his argument by noting that

> the idea that measurements are not yet fine enough for prediction is erroneous, since with an increase in their fineness will go a decrease in the ability to predict. This peculiar situation arose in physics and it is now facing the psychologists with the same paradoxical force. . . . The long dream of psychologists to perfect instruments of measurement as fine as those of natural sciences has finally led to an increased ignorance of the very thing they want to know. (1934, pp. 215–16)

In recent years, however, psychology seems to be more open to relativism and to the idea that knowledge is never absolute (Allred, Harper, & Wadham, 1984). Jerome Kagan (1967) sums up the arguments for a more relativistic view in psychology in general and developmental psychology in particular. He also points to research and theory in psychology which support relativism—that it is impossible to describe a stimulus in absolute physical terms, but only in relation to a particular point of view. For example, consider the concept of "parental rejection." The traditional view is that there are fixed sets of behaviors that reveal parents' attitudes toward their children. If the parents love and accept their children, they will praise them and show them love. If they reject their children, they will ignore them, criticize them, and use physical punishment to discipline them. The children in turn will respond to this treatment in fixed ways; a child whose parents do not act in accepting ways will feel rejected and come to have a poor self image.

This traditional interpretation parental rejection confounds three points of view: the parent's, the observer's, and the child's. Thus, from the point of view of a middle-class American professional psychological observer, a mother's slapping her young child across the face for misbehaving, or not talking to the child for five hours, would be considered an act of

the child's point of view. We cannot tell whether or not a parent is rejecting simply by looking at what the parent is doing. We need to know how the child perceives the parent's behavior. As Jerome Kagan observes, like pleasure, pain, or beauty, "rejection is in the mind of the rejectee" (1978, p. 48).

Although the new physics of the twentieth century overturned previous assumptions about absolute knowledge, the advances that were made were among the greatest achievements in the history of sciences. Indeed, the new ideas about the limits of knowledge were embodied in the new advances. In applying the concepts of relativism and indeterminism, psychology need not thereby become less scientific or forfeit the possibility of significant advances in knowledge and theory. Bronowski points out that the Principle of Uncertainty would be more aptly named the Principle of Tolerance. The principle does not imply complete uncertainty, but only that knowledge is confined within a certain tolerance or area of uncertainty.

Many people believe there is an inherent opposition between science and more humanistic approaches to knowledge, such as art and literature. But one lesson of twentieth-century physics is this: giving up the hope of perfect prediction and measurement does not mean abandoning scientific method or careful observation and theorization. The other lesson is that the methods of the artist and writer are not as far apart as they were once believed to be. Bronowski sums it up best: "There is no absolute knowledge. And those who claim it, whether they are scientists or dogmatists, open the door to tragedy. All information is imperfect; that is the human condition; and that is what quantum physics says. I mean that literally" (1973, p. 353).

rejection. A middle-class American mother who has been influenced by modern psychology is likely to share the view that such behaviors are rejecting and probably would not behave in such ways—at least while a psychologist is watching (Graves & Glick, 1978). But for a mother who belongs to another ethnic and cultural tradition, such behavior may not mean that she is indifferent or hostile to her child. From the mother's point of view these acts may simply be the normal ways a loving mother acts toward her child.

Finally, and most important of all, there is

SUMMARY

1. The scientific study of human development differs from earlier, more philosophical approaches in the methods it uses, not in the conclusions it reaches. Scientific research is an endless cycle of observation and explanation. The key is willingness to keep an open mind and to revise one's conclusions if the evidence contradicts them.

2. Broadly speaking, there are three approaches to developmental research. One, the classical developmental approach, looks at development in general as it applies to all people. The second approach is differential. It examines development in some kinds of people as opposed to other kinds. The third is the individual approach, which examines the unique qualities of people and their pattern of change over time.

3. Major methods of gathering data in developmental psychology are the experiment, the correlational study, behavioral observation, and the case study.

   A. In an experimental study, the experimenter manipulates one variable, the independent variable, to determine its effects on some form of behavior, the dependent variable. By randomly assigning subjects to experimental and control groups, the researcher makes sure that the groups are alike before the manipulation. Thus, the experiment allows for clear-cut inferences about cause and effect.

   B. The correlational method is often used when conditions cannot be manipulated. It is also used to study variables in real life, rather than the more artificial setting of the research laboratory. In a correlational study, the researcher asks whether two variables are related to one another; that is, having information about the person's score on variable X, can his or her standing on variable Y be predicted also? The degree of relationship between the two variables is indicated by the correlation coefficient, "r." Because the variables are not under the control of the researcher, correlational studies do not lead to definitive statements about cause and effect relationships.

   C. Observational studies bring the researcher directly into ongoing, real-life situations. They have been used by ethologists studying animal and infant behavior, by behavior modifiers in the course of doing therapy with problem children, as well as by researchers interested in infant behavior and parent-child interaction. One drawback of the observational method is the possibility that the presence of the observer may influence the behavior of the people being observed; another is the tendency to give only an outside, objective view of social behavior, without regard to its meaning to the participants.

   D. The case study method involves the detailed investigation of one or several individuals. While this method has been used to study normal development, usually it describes people who have had unusual developmental histories. Two of the major theories of human development, Freud's and Piaget's, grew out of intensive use of the case study method.

4. Regardless of the particular method used, most developmental studies deal with change over time. There are two ways of introducing the time dimension. In a cross-sectional study, developmental change is assessed by comparing people of different ages. In a longitudinal study, the same individuals are studied at different ages. The cross-sectional study provides a general picture of development across time, but it does not reveal the course of individual development or the stability of individual traits. The longitudinal method does supply answers to these questions, but has its own drawbacks as a research method. It is expensive and subjects may drop out as the study goes on.

5. The problem of both cross-sectional and longitudinal studies is that they must distinguish individual change from historical change. A longitudinal study may follow the development of one cohort—a group of people of a similar age—but its findings may not be applicable to cohorts who grew up under different circumstances. In the cross-sectional study, the people who are of different ages are also members of different cohorts. Thus, the 70-year-old of today may not represent what today's 20-year-olds will be like in fifty years.

6. Every research method has its weaknesses as well as its particular advantages. Developmental psychology bases its conclusions on long chains of observations, and on different kinds of evidence, based on different research methods. Still, no conclusions can be regarded as the final word. Knowledge is never absolute. This uncertainty does not mean that psychology is unscientific. In fact, the key concepts of twentieth-century physics are indeterminism and relativity. These concepts have led to some of the greatest advances in the history of science at the same time as they have pointed to limits to precise description and prediction.

Key Terms

case study **54**
cohort **58**
control group **44**
correlation **46**
cross-sectional **44**
cross-sequential **60**
dependent variable **44**
ecological validity **53**
ethologist **50**
experimental group **44**
experimental method **44**
field experiment **53**

hypothesis **38**
imprinting **51**
independent variable **44**
law of large numbers **45**
life history **55**
longitudinal **44**
natural experiment **46**
naturalistic **49**
nonexperimental method **44**
releasor stimulus **51**
significance **43**
variables **44**

CHAPTER 3

Theories of Human Development

There is nothing so practical as a good theory.

—Kurt Lewin

The great tragedy of Science—the slaying of
a beautiful hypothesis by an ugly fact.

—Thomas Henry Huxley,
Biogensis and Abiogenesis

We are all in a sense psychological theorists. Simply to get through an ordinary day we must interpret other people's behavior and predict the effect our own words and actions will have on others. Every parent uses some theory of child development to get children to learn and to do the right thing. Psychological theorizing, in short, is not some abstract, ivory tower enterprise, far removed from the practical matters of everyday life.

A number of influential psychologists and philosophers have pointed to similarities between commonsense theories and scientific theories (Heider, 1958; Kelly, 1955). Thus, the ordinary person constructs theories about human behavior in the same way scientists construct their formal theories. They derive concepts and make predictions on the basis of their observations. Conversely, all scientific theories grow out of the glimmerings of common sense—the scientific theory simply refines and elaborates on the commonsense notions. For example, before there was a science of physics there was a commonsense physics that worked to solve practical problems such as pumping water. Yet commonsense ideas may simply be wrong.

As Alfred Baldwin (1968) points out, commonsense theories have had a profound influence on scholarly theorists even—or especially—if they see common sense as a source of erroneous ideas which must be uprooted. Some of the leading theories in psychology can be viewed as denials of one or another widespread naive psychological assumption. For example, B. F. Skinner and other behaviorists have tried to scrap all of commonsense psychology. In particular, they have attacked the assumption that people's behavior is guided by thoughts, feelings, and intentions; Skinner argues that we can understand human behavior from the *outside*, just as we examine machines, chemical reactions, or electrical currents. Similarly, Sigmund Freud attacked the commonsense notion that people have conscious, rational reasons for the things they do; he argued that much, if not all, behavior is guided by unconscious thoughts and intentions.

One major difference between commonsense theories and scientific ones is in their explicitness. Few people bother to put their psychological theories into words, and fewer still put them onto paper. In addition, psychologists' theories are usually tied to a series of observations. Also, explicit theories try to specify limiting conditions, that is, the circumstances under which the theory does and does not apply. Finally, while scientists are aware that their theories may be proved wrong, commonsense theories are taken for granted as the truth—the way things really are.

The purpose of any theory is to explain some set of observations. The most powerful theories are those that can explain a great deal using a small number of principles. The best example of this ideal kind of theory is Newton's. By using three simple principles, which any school child can learn, Isaac Newton could explain the movements of the planets, the tides of the ocean, the paths of billiard balls, and the falling of apples. In contrast, as we noted earlier, there is no overarching, agreed-upon theory of behavior that explains human actions in the way that Newton explained the workings of the physical universe. Psychological theorists do not state universal laws and deduce mathematically precise predictions from them as do theories in physics and the other natural sciences. Rather, they use approaches or perspectives, ways of thinking about human thought and behavior.

Approaches to Human Development

The number of general explanations of why people turn out the way they do is limited. Indeed, the reasons that have been advanced through history are remarkably similar to those current today. They can, in fact, be counted on fewer than the fingers of one hand:

- A child's future is set at birth, determined by inborn temperament and capacities.
- Children come into the world like blank sheets of paper or unformed lumps of clay. Their early experience determines the whole course of their development.

- Children are essentially wild beasts. Their animal nature has to be tamed to make them civilized. Some of them are harder to tame than others.
- Ultimately people choose what they will become; they do not choose the circumstances of their lives, but they do decide, within limits, how they will respond to those circumstances.

These ideas have taken various forms throughout history and have existed side by side in the same time and place. Thus, in ancient Greece, Hippocrates advanced a theory of inborn temperament to explain both physical health and personality. He suggested that people have four bodily humors or fluids: blood, black bile, yellow bile, and phlegm. The proportion of these humors determined physical and mental health—for example, depression and several other disorders were attributed to an excess of black bile. While the notion of bodily humors seems farfetched today, Hippocrates' concepts may be viewed as the ancestor of more modern biological and physiological theories which explain behavior in terms of hormones or biochemistry.

The environmental molding, or socialization, explanation of human development was also current in ancient Greece. Plato's *Republic* gives a detailed explanation of how the future leaders of the ideal state would be removed from their families in infancy and trained for their roles. Aristotle anticipated later psychological explanations of homosexuality when, as we saw in Chapter 2, he suggested that homosexual preferences were the result of parental abuse.

Finally, during the same cultural era, and for the first time in history, Greek drama was presenting the vision of human beings as free agents, making genuine moral decisions. In earlier Greek literature, the gods had been the sources of human action and people merely puppets. The major Greek dramatists, however, presented human beings as "independent agents, acting upon the bidding of their own hearts, instead of merely reacting to external stimuli" (Snell, 1960, p. 103).

The Nature of Human Nature: Underlying Theoretical Issues

Every theory of human behavior, naive or formal, is based on a set of assumptions about human nature and human society. Often these underlying ideas are not part of the theory itself, and they are usually unstated. In constructing a theory, one must make a number of choices among alternative positions concerning philosophical dilemmas which have been debated for centuries. This necessity for choice puts the psychologist in the uncomfortable position of having to come to conclusions about problems philosophers have not been able to resolve.

For example, when psychologists try to explain some aspect of behavior, say language learning or sex role development—that is, the child's learning to identify with one sex and prefer the other as a sexual partner—they must come to grips with the ancient dilemma of the *mind-body* problem. They would ask: Can mental states, such as intentions, thoughts, feelings, ideas, images, and so forth, be used as explanations of why people do things the way they do? Can mind move matter?

Psychologists in the *behavioristic* tradition argue that it is as unscientific to use such mentalistic description to explain human behavior as it is to speak of ghosts and spirits causing events in the physical world. Behaviorists prefer to use *mechanistic* explanations of human behavior. In effect, behaviorism is based on a model of humans as machines—complicated, robotlike machines, but machines nonetheless.

The *cognitive* psychologists' view of human nature contrasts sharply with that of the behaviorists. Cognitive psychologists, following the philosopher Descartes' first premise—"I think, therefore I am"—argue that thought is the essence of human nature. They believe that humans do not simply react passively to external stimuli; they actively construct their own experience. People attend to some stimuli and ignore others; they interpret information from the external world.

Cognitive psychologists deny there is any contradiction between the concept of mind and the demands of scientific method; for example, Piaget showed that objective methods can be applied to the study of mental processes. His experiments with the hiding of toys demonstrated that mental processes, such as the concept of the permanent object, can be inferred from the child's outward behavior. Although the cognitive approach has come to dominate both general and developmental psychology, behaviorism is also alive and well. Modern behaviorists, particularly those of the social learning theory, incorporate mental processes into their theories, but strict or radical behaviorists still insist they can explain all behavior on the basis of stimulus and reward.

Active versus Passive Models of Human Nature

Several other related philosophical issues divide psychological theorists. For example, are human beings active agents in their own development, or are they helpless pawns in the grip of environmental conditions or biological forces? The philosophic version of this question is the dilemma of determinism versus free will.

Many psychologists have traditionally assumed that science "requires" a deterministic view of human nature: science deals with cause and effect relationships; you press a switch and the light goes on; you put two chemicals together and a chemical reaction takes place. The deterministic view assumes that every event in the universe is predictable, if only we had enough facts. Causality pervades the universe, which includes human beings.

Psychological experiments that manipulate behavior, and clinical studies that show how character is molded by early experience, seem to provide strong evidence for the determinists' claim. They seem to show that whether or not we think we can make choices, our behavior is determined by forces beyond our control. A development psychology based on the assumption of determinism would, in principle, be able to write the biography of a newborn infant's life before he or she lived it!

Although determinism seems at first glance to be the only position a hardheaded scientist could take, it quickly leads to an absurd kind of fatalism. It implies that a newborn baby's biography has already *been* written in the Book of Destiny. If determinism is true, the world is a perfectly running clock, in which everything that happens *had* to happen and could not fail to happen (Popper, 1962). All our thoughts, feelings, and actions have been determined since the beginning of time and can have no effect on the world whatever; they are simply illusions or byproducts of physical events.

Thus, if determinism is true, your reading of these words at this particular moment was predetermined thousands, even millions, of years ago, and could not have been otherwise. It must also have been predetermined that you would be born, and therefore that your parents would meet and conceive you, that their parents would meet and conceive them, and so on back through prehistory to the primordial ooze.

There is still another kind of logical impasse in the deterministic argument. Psychologists or other scientists who write articles in favor of determinism are in a peculiar position; they are doomed to present themselves as living contradictions of their own theories (Chein, 1972); they are in fact caught up in a classical paradox—the statement by Epimenides the Cretan that all Cretans are liars.

Thus, when psychologists such as Skinner and Freud put forth their theories, they tacitly assumed that they themselves, and the reader, were different from the people being written about. "The writings of psychologists are typically filled with allusions to their own active intellectual pursuit of knowledge about people," Wegner and Wallacher remark. "Psychologists clearly see themselves as active agents in their environs. Yet these same theorists persist in characterizing the individual as a pawn, a puppet or a robot" (1977, p. 301).

Although both Freud and Skinner attempted to apply their mechanistic theories to themselves, these efforts did not reconcile the robot-like model of the theories with their own active and constructive behavior as theorists, or to

Conflict or cooperation. Which is the true face of human nature?

their faith that their readers could be persuaded of the truth of their theories through reason. It is possible to be a scientific psychologist without believing that people are nothing more than complicated machines. It is also possible to be a scientist without believing in strict determinism. As we saw in the last chapter, physical scientists have been living with indeterminacy and relativity for most of the twentieth century. The notion of indeterminacy does not rule out predictability and regularity in the universe. It simply means, according to Popper, that "*not all* events in the physical world are predetermined with absolute precision, in all their infinitesimal details" (1972, p. 220).

Indeterminacy makes it possible to construct psychological theories with the assumption that people are active and constructive agents rather than passive objects. Psychological research would explain *why* people do what they do, but not necessarily what *makes* them do what they do.

What would a developmental psychology based on indeterminacy be like? Leona Tyler (1978) argues that it would be a psychology of individuality and possibilities. Instead of assuming that people's biographies can be written at birth or in early childhood, we can view development as a process of selection from multiple alternatives. It is true that our heredity and environment place limits on these possibilities; we cannot choose who our parents will be, the social class or historical era we are born into, our genetic structure, or our basic body type. But within these limits people can and do make choices. Each of us could have been different from the way we are, and the key question is, how did we choose to become ourselves, and not the other selves we could have been? At each of the many choice points in our life, why did we choose the path we took and thus give up the other possibilities? As Tyler sums it up, "To understand a person completely, we would need to trace the road he or she has taken on one occasion after another. It is development we must study, but the development of the shaper rather than the shaped" (1978, p. 234).

Beast or Angel?

Theories of human development reflect their formulators' intuitions about human nature. Human behavior presents an amazingly varied spectacle. On the one hand, there are concentration camps, torture, wars, murder, cruelty, and selfishness. On the other hand, there is heroism, self-sacrifice, altruism, love, empathy, and kindness. Which is humankind's true face? Philosophers and others differ as to which kind of behavior is the rule and which the exception. But they agree that truth about human nature is likely to reveal itself in infancy and childhood.

Throughout Western history, as we saw in Chapter 1, the child has symbolized both good and evil. The child has represented innocence, the impulsive side of human nature, and subordination to authority. Attitudes toward childhood have varied depending on whether impulse and authority were viewed positively or negatively. Contrary attitudes have often coexisted. In his history of child study, William Kessen observes that, particularly in England and America, there has been a "curious conflict between childhood as innocence and the grim portrait of an evil being who must be scourged to his salvation . . ." (1965, p. 33).

Calvinist theory, which influenced many Protestant sects, had as a prime tenet of childrearing the doctrine of "infant depravity," that is, the infant was doomed to be evil unless controlled by parents. Good parents were supposed to "break the child's will." "Will" was defined as any defiance of the parents' wishes. Even the crying and thrashing of tiny infants was seen as a sign of rebellious will (Sunley, 1955).

The doctrine of infant depravity was one aspect of the extreme asceticism and antisensuousness of early Protestantism. Toward the close of the eighteenth century, however, the theme of childhood innocence was forcefully asserted by Jean-Jacques Rousseau and the Romantic school of writers, most notably Blake and Wordsworth, and later, by Dickens and others. As explained earlier, Rousseau's views of childhood were revolutionary in several respects. Rather than treat the child as a small adult, to be trained out of its childish ways into adult morality and reason, he argued that childhood was important and natural in itself. In contrast to the doctrine that the child was innately depraved and needed vigilant adult guidance to develop properly, Rousseau argued that the child would develop naturally toward virtue with a minimum of adult training.

Rousseau's notions of development also were at odds with philosophers such as Locke and Hume who argued that the child's mind was a *tabula rasa*—a blank slate to be filled in by experience and education. These philosophical views of children are the direct ancestors of views prevailing today. Thus, Rousseau is the ancestor of certain schools of contemporary developmental psychology, as well as of much of "progressive" education, while Locke's point of view is maintained by the behaviorists, who argue that growth is shaped by the push and pull of environmental forces. The Calvinist view also still persists in something close to its original version in large segments of the population.

There are also many parallels between the Calvinist idea of infant depravity and the Freudian concept of the unconscious mind as a seething cauldron of lustful and murderous impulses. Like the Calvinists, Freud emphasized the role of parents as tamers of the child's animal nature and agents of civilization. The modern demonic view of the child has been forcefully represented in such literary works as William Golding's *The Lord of the Flies,* a work that not only attained wide popularity, but sometimes is cited by psychologists as a valid representation of the nature of childhood. But like Rousseau's, the Freudian message about the child also contained a plea for the recognition and protection of the special qualities of childhood and of the naturalness of development.

The Concept of Development

All developmental theories try to explain the changes that transform newborn infants into adults. Yet they differ in how they conceive of

A scene from the movie made from Golding's novel, *Lord of the Flies.*

these changes. Thus, the term "development" has several different meanings according to which theory the speaker is using. At the most basic level, "development" simply means the changes that take place as the child grows older. Used in this way, it is not abstract or theoretical, but merely describes the changes that go along with chronological age. Thus, the term refers to changes anyone can observe, such as the sequence of a baby sitting, then crawling, then standing, then walking; or the sequence of children babbling, then using one word at a time, then two words, then sentences, and so forth.

Beyond simply describing such changes, however, the term "development" usually implies other things. It suggests that the changes occur in a regular order, that they are predictable, and that changes bring improvement: development brings greater complexity, skill, efficiency, competence. Thus, the concept of development is infused with value judgments.

The value problem becomes acute when a theory tries to describe some sort of final state toward which the child is growing. Most people would agree that the change from being a nonspeaking, nonwalking infant to a walking, talking child is a change toward a better, more complex form of living. But is there a particular kind of adult who represents the mature end-state of development? Is this superior end point somehow built into development from the beginning, just as the human form is implicit in the fertilized egg?

Some of the major developmental theorists—Sigmund Freud, Jean Piaget, Heinz Werner, and Erik Erikson—have assumed that "development" does imply a single, ideal adult goal. Werner expressed this view most explicitly in his "orthogenetic principle." The principle states that "wherever development occurs it proceeds from a state of relative globality and lack of differentiation to a state of increasing differentiation, articulation, and hierarchic integration" (1957, p. 126). Werner tried to arrange all forms of thought along a developmental continuum. Like other developmental theorists who applied Darwin's notions of evolution to psychology, he believed that children, schizophrenics, and "primitive" peoples represent the low end of the sequence, while the educated, middle-class, Western adult represents the highest developmental stage.

Freud and Piaget also assumed that development is directed toward specific forms of adult competence. Freud defined this goal as "working and loving." By this he meant the mature adult would have resolved childhood conflicts, be stably married, have children, and be committed to a career. Piaget, who was more concerned with the development of thought than the development of personality, described the end point of development as the ability to think like a scientist—a graduate physicist, in fact (Kessen, 1966).

Not all developmental psychologists agree that development is directed toward any specific goal. Behaviorists describe how children change through learning, but they do not assume that this learning must lead in any particular direction. Researchers who have studied other cultures are especially critical of the idea that development inevitably follows a particular course. In this view the development of middle-class Western children represents only one of many possible ways of growing up, not some built-in human nature.

The Idea of Stages

Another important issue is whether development is continuous or divided into distinct stages. People often use the term "stage" in a descriptive way to talk about some particularly notable behavior in children of a specified age. Thus, parents often talk of "the terrible two's" to describe rebellious toddlers. Or they talk

about children—or adults—"going through a difficult stage," meaning they are struggling with a particular developmental task or theme.

Developmental theorists use the term in a more precise way. Freud, Piaget, and Werner are *stage-developmental* theorists in this restricted sense. They all view development as a series of *qualitatively* different stages. Each stage depends on the previous one, and no stage can be skipped. Further, each developmental stage has its own structure or form: the child's mental functioning at any one stage is all or a piece, and a change from one stage to the next means a complete reorganization of many aspects of thought and behavior. Stage theories of development are modeled on such examples of biological development as the change of an insect from egg to caterpillar to butterfly, or the development of the fetus from a fertilized egg to a collection of dividing cells, to an embryo, and finally to a human infant.

There is a great deal of skepticism among developmental psychologists about the usefulness of the strict concept of stages. Behaviorists have always believed that the child progresses toward maturity through gradual, continuous change. Many cognitive psychologists also believe that thought develops continuously, and that the child's mental functioning does not change in an abrupt way. As Flavell sums it up, the current evidence suggests that cognitive development is "more like a three-ring circus than a chamber-music trio" (1977, p. 249). Nevertheless, the stage concepts of Freud, Piaget, and Werner do have many adherents. And psychologists generally find the notion of developmental sequences useful. The idea of qualitative change also seems a useful way of thinking about such changes as the shift from having no language to knowing how to talk, or from being illiterate to knowing how to read and write.

Nature versus Nurture

The nature versus nurture debate is one of the perennial issues that divide psychologists. Is our behavior determined by our innate biology, or does the environment make us what we are? The argument about heredity and environment reaches back to the ancient Greeks. Nativists, or biological determinists, have argued that biology makes all humans similar and also accounts for group and individual differences. Although the idea of hereditary influence is an ancient one, Darwin's theory of evolution led to an emphasis on the biological basis of human nature and development.

During most of the twentieth century, however, environmentalists have dominated psychology. Behaviorists such as Watson and Skinner argued that human nature was completely malleable; early training could take any child and turn him or her into any kind of adult. This is the nurture side of the debate. In recent years, however, biological determinism has been revived in a variety of forms, ranging from sociobiology to pop ethology to genetic explanations of class and race differences. (We cover these issues in greater detail in later chapters.)

Today, practically every writer in the field of human development claims that both heredity and environment interact to shape development, and that the distinction between nature and nurture is artificial. Yet the debate goes on because most researchers emphasize one sort of influence more than the other. As William Kessen points out, all psychologists claim to occupy the middle ground on the nature-nurture issue, "pointing the finger at their extremist opponents who are not as balanced as they" (1965, p. 211).

Arnold Gesell (1880–1961) was the leading proponent of the "nature" side of the debate in twentieth-century American psychology. Gesell was one of the first developmental psychologists in America, and yet his work continues to have influence. A pioneer in the use of sophisticated observational techniques, he was one of the first psychologists to use a movie camera to record behavior. Gesell's detailed and systematic observations have held up well over the years. Parents still turn to such works as his *Infant and Child in the Culture of Today* (1943) to compare their own children's progress with the detailed schedules of development they contain. Here, for example, is an excerpt from a "behavior profile" of the 15-month-old infant:

> At about Fifteen Months of age the American baby becomes something more than a "mere" infant. He is discarding creeping for toddling. He is discarding his nursing bottle. . . . He says "ta-ta" on more or less suitable occasions; by gesture language he calls attention to wetted pants; he makes an imitative stroke with a crayon; he helps to turn the pages of a picture book, albeit several leaves at one swift swoop. (1943, p. 131)

All of Gesell's observations were designed to demonstrate his theory that maturation is the key to understanding development. A student of G. Stanley Hall, one of the founding fathers of developmental psychology around the turn of the century, Gesell believed that development was determined mainly by biology. Learning and experience contributed something, but their influence was minor compared to the biological growth tendencies built into every human and the individual differences based on heredity.

A physician as well as a psychologist, Gesell was impressed by the orderliness of development. For example, he noted that all normal infants learn to grasp, sit, stand, and walk at approximately the same time and in the same order. Further, they all go through similar stages in mastering these skills.

Gesell was also impressed by what he saw as the toughness and resilience of children. He felt that the tendency to grow is the strongest force in the child and cannot be diverted by different childrearing practices, or even parental mishandling. Gesell pointed to the paradox of the human nervous system—it is, he wrote, both highly impressionable and remarkably resistant to adversity: "All things considered, the inevitableness and surety of maturation are the most impressive characteristics of early development . . . [the child] benefits liberally from what is good in our practice, and suffers less than he logically should from our unenlightenment" (1928, p. 116).

Gesell's career lasted until his retirement in 1948, but his work and views had long been overshadowed by behaviorism. For behaviorists concerned with children, Gesell became the leading example of the misguided hereditarian views they opposed. Ironically, Gesell's work is no longer as out of step with the rest of the field as it once was. Fewer psychologists now view the child as a blank slate on which the environment writes. Naturalistic observation has become a respectable research technique once again, thanks largely to the ethologists and their work with animals. There is also renewed interest in mapping out stages in the development of particular skills, especially cognitive ones, such as language development.

Further, most psychologists would now agree with Gesell about the "surety of maturation." There is mounting evidence that young children are more resilient in the face of bad experiences or parental mishandling than had formerly been believed. Some researchers use the term "canalization," borrowed from the embryologist Waddington (1940), to describe the self-righting tendencies in early development. In the course of evolution, the human organism seems to have been programmed to produce normal development in all but the most adverse circumstances.

Finally, the field as a whole is now more willing than it had been to accept the idea that some differences between individuals are innate. However, current theories are much less simplistic than Gesell's. To Gesell, individual development was like the blooming of a plant; the environment, like soil, was merely the setting in which this blooming takes place. To current theorists, whatever temperamental or other potential characteristics a child may be born with, the eventual outcome is shaped by life experiences as well as the child's own perceptions of self and others. The child is no longer viewed as the passive object of either heredity or environment.

John B. Watson

Behaviorism

For approximately fifty years, the field of psychology was dominated by the theoretical approach known as **behaviorism,** learning theory, or **stimulus-response** (S-R) psychology. Its direct influence began to wane in the 1960s and is no longer the mainstream theory.

In 1913 the publication of John B. Watson's "Behaviorist Manifesto" was the opening gun of the behaviorist revolution. When Watson strode onto the psychological scene, he overthrew the two dominant approaches of the time—nativism and introspectionism. In developmental psychology, the **nativist** or nature side of the nature-nurture debate was prevalent. Most psychologists believed, along with Gesell, that individual differences in children were due to constitutional and genetic factors. If one child was fearful and shy and another bold and outgoing, it was because their innate temperaments had made them so.

In contrast, Watson argued that children come into the world as blank slates or unformed lumps of clay. They develop their particular personalities and skills through learning. If Jimmy is frightened of dogs, it is because he has had frightening experiences with dogs. If Mary hits other children, it is because she has been rewarded for behaving aggressively.

Thus, Watson attributed to the environment or society an enormous power to shape a child's development. One of his most startling and yet influential ideas was that parents could make of their children whatever they willed. "Give me a dozen healthy infants, well-formed, and my own specified world to bring them up in," he wrote, "and I'll guarantee to take any one at random and train him to be any type of specialist I might—doctor, lawyer, artist, merchant, chief, and yes, even beggar man and thief!" (1950, p. 104).

Watson not only rejected biological explanations of behavior, he threw out the concept of mind. Henceforth, psychologists were to look at overt, observable behavior. To explain behavior, they could only use such terms as stimulus, response, and reinforcement. It was not permissible to use such mentalistic terms as thoughts, feelings, images, intentions, purpose.

His approach quickly transformed the definition of psychology from a science of mind to the science of behavior. Like all revolutions, the behaviorist revolution succeeded because of discontent with existing conditions. Psychology had seemed to reach a dead end in the early years of the twentieth century. The psychology journals were filled with armchair speculations and hair-splitting discussions about small psychological distinctions. Psychologists did carry out experiments, but the chief method they used was a special kind of introspection in which highly trained observers reported on the contents of their own minds. The brand of psychology practiced by the introspectionists was narrow and applied only to laboratory situations. It did not deal with everyday experience, the emotions, or mental illness; nor did it deal with the development of children's minds. Behaviorists promised not only to explain all of these aspects of psychological reality, but to predict and change behavior as well. Behaviorism aimed at both relevance and scientific truth.

The Essence of Behaviorism

Although behaviorism has changed over the years, and there are several different kinds of behaviorism, there is a core of beliefs and practices common to all varieties. First, behaviorists assume that practically all human behavior is learned. Second, behavior is learned in small bits rather than structured wholes. Just as a complex machine such as a locomotive consists of many separate parts joined together, a complicated act such as talking or playing the piano is thought to consist of many small responses strung together; learning to talk is a matter of learning individual words, then stringing them together into sentences; learning to play the piano is a matter of learning how to strike the right notes one after the other.

Further, behaviorists have traditionally assumed that even studies carried out with animals are applicable to humans. Thus, behaviorists study rats learning to run mazes and pigeons learning to peck at lighted disks, not to make statements merely about rats or pigeons, but about human learning. The basic principles of learning are assumed to apply across species.

Still another assumption of behaviorism is that the psychological mechanisms that can be demonstrated in the laboratory are widely applicable to real life. In a famous experiment, Watson showed that a child could be taught to be afraid of something. An 11-month-old called "Little Albert" was made to fear a white rat when Watson made a loud clanging noise each time the child reached out to touch the animal (Watson & Raynor, 1920). Although the child was not afraid of the rat at first, he eventually began to cry at the sight of it. Watson assumed that he had demonstrated how all childhood fears—and adult phobias—were learned. In his later work, he showed that fears could be reduced by exposing a child to a feared object under pleasant circumstances.

Classical and Instrumental Conditioning

Traditionally, behaviorists have recognized two main principles of learning: classical (or respondent) and instrumental (or operant) conditioning. **Classical conditioning** is the principle followed by Watson in his experiment with Little Albert: two different stimuli—the sight of a white rat and the sound of a loud clang—repeatedly occur together. Eventually, the response to one stimulus, the noise, was transferred to the other, the rat. Classical conditioning always involves a natural or unlearned reflex response, such as blinking when a puff of air strikes the eye or salivating at the taste of food. In instrumental conditioning, a particular behavior is rewarded, and the likelihood of repeating that response is increased. Thus, a rat who presses a bar and receives a pellet of food is likely to make that response to the bar again.

The distinction between the two kinds of conditioning corresponds roughly to the distinction between voluntary and involuntary behavior. We can't help blinking as the eyedropper approaches our eye, but a voluntary action is one we carry out because we know what the result will be and value it.

Classical Conditioning Watson did not invent the method of classical conditioning he used with Little Albert and in other experiments; the original work on conditioning was done by the Russian physiologist Ivan Pavlov. In Pavlov's most famous experiment, he taught a dog to salivate at the sound of a buzzer. Salivation, in the vocabulary of classical conditioning, is called the unconditioned response (or UCR) to the unconditioned stimulus (UCS)—food. The buzzer is the conditioned stimulus (CS). By ringing the buzzer just before the dog was given the food, Pavlov was able to produce a conditioned response (CR)—salivation—in response to the buzzer.

He believed that the dog started salivating to the sound of the buzzer because it formed an association between the buzzer and the food; salivation is part of the dog's unlearned response to food. When the experimenter delivers food after sounding the buzzer, the dog begins to associate the sound with the food—the buzzer calls up a representation of the food. The dog then salivates to this representation just as it would to real food. Similarly, we automatically salivate if we think of sucking on a lemon, and our hearts beat faster if we think of a frightening event (see Mackintosh, 1983).

While unconditioned reflexes are involuntary, it is possible to bring them under voluntary control. Biofeedback is one example of controlling such involuntary processes as heart rate, skin temperature, and blood pressure. Conditioned reflex therapy (Salter, 1949) attempts to deal with neurotic fears and anxieties using the ideas of Pavlov and Watson. Thus, a person who is terrified of flying is taught to relax while *thinking* of going to an airport and getting on a plane, and then will gradually work his way up to getting on a real plane and flying somewhere. This procedure is called *desensitization*. Another form of conditioned reflex therapy is based on negative imagery; a person

A classical conditioning experiment by Pavlov.

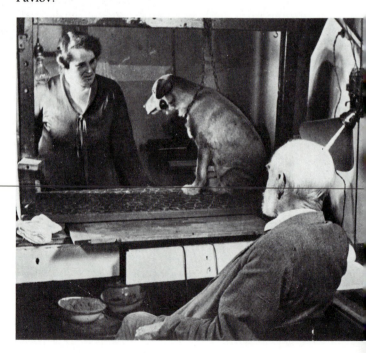

trying to lose weight might be taught to think of disgusting images when tempted by forbidden foods—to imagine, for example, that a piece of chocolate cake has just come out of a garbage can and is covered with filth and crawling with insects.

Pavlov also showed that conditioned responses could spread to stimuli similar to, for example, the buzzer or another conditioned stimulus in a process called *generalization.* In Watson's experiment with Albert, the child's fear of the rat generalized to other fuzzy white objects, such as his mother's muff and Santa Claus's beard.

Instrumental Conditioning   The second major learning mechanism in the behaviorist tradition, **Instrumental conditioning,** can also be represented by a vivid example. Instead of the salivating dog of classical conditioning, the image of instrumental conditioning is of a rat or a pigeon in a box. A Skinner box, named after its inventor is a simple piece of apparatus: a box containing a bar which automatically releases a pellet of food or a drop of water (Figure 3.1).

An animal placed in the box will move about in a random way, and sooner or later will press the bar and receive a pellet of food. Eventually, the animal will learn to press the bar repeatedly for pellets of food. This example illustrates the major features of instrumental or operant conditioning: first, the behavior is a voluntary movement rather than a built-in reflex; second, the food serves as a *reinforcement* or reward for the bar-pressing behavior.

The basic assumption of instrumental conditioning is that behavior followed by a reward tends to be repeated, while unrewarded behavior will fade away or *extinguish,* to use the technical term. One seemingly paradoxical principle discovered by Skinner is that a response reinforced only some of the time will take longer to extinguish than one that is rewarded all the time. Gamblers, especially slot machine players, reveal the persistence of behavior that is only partially reinforced. Partial reinforcement may also help to explain why children persist in certain annoying behaviors such as whining: parents who do not want to give in

to the child when he or she whines sometimes break down and do so. This creates a reinforcement schedule most likely to result in the persistence of the obnoxious habit.

The process of shaping illustrates instrumental conditioning in action. Through the careful application of reinforcements, the experimenter can shape animal behavior in remarkable ways. For example, Skinner trained pigeons seemingly to play a game of ping pong, and turn pirouettes; animal trainers using the technique of shaping teach dolphins to jump through hoops and bears to play musical instruments. Shaping involves leading an animal step by step to desired behavior. Thus, to teach a pigeon to do a pirouette, the experimenter would wait for it to turn itself around slightly, then give it a reward. Bigger turns would then be rewarded, which would shape the pigeon's behavior as a sculptor shapes a lump of clay.

The principle of instrumental conditioning has been applied to many different kinds of human behavior—from teaching basic skills to retarded or autistic children, to changing children's aggressive behavior in the home, and even helping people to change their own eating, smoking, and working patterns. It also

FIGURE 3.1
A Skinner Box
Rat pressing bar in a Skinner box.

seems applicable to childrearing in real life. Parents actually do reward children's behavior they approve of. As the child grows older, parents increase their standards for performance, which shapes the child's behavior toward more mature forms.

The Limits of Behaviorism

Given that reinforcement techniques seem to work in the laboratory, in the clinic, and elsewhere, and that they seem to describe what goes on in daily life between parents and children, can we assume, as Skinner does, that we have the key to the understanding and control of all of human behavior? Need we fear that skillful behaviorists can shape the behavior of other people to their will?

Pavlov and his salivating dog have come to symbolize the power of psychologists and those who hire them to manipulate human behavior on a large scale. Books such as Aldous Huxley's *Brave New World* and George Orwell's *1984*, and films such as *Clockwork Orange*, show conditioning techniques being used to brainwash people.

These fears are based on misunderstanding. Classical conditioning in itself is not an all-powerful technique that can bend people's minds against their wills. Conditioned responses tend to fade quickly, and behavior modification techniques in humans require the active cooperation of the subject. For example, a homosexual who is given electric shocks while being shown homosexual images can sabotage the procedure by imagining heterosexual scenes while being shocked (Davison, 1973).

Further, classical conditioning does not seem to be a major influence on child development; it is difficult to achieve in infants even under ideal laboratory conditions. Even Little Albert, the baby John Watson taught to fear a white rat, was not a case of pure classical conditioning. It turns out that some of the time Watson made the loud noise only after Albert reached out to touch the rat, thus mixing classical and instrumental conditioning. Further, although the Little Albert study is often cited as an example of how a phobia can be conditioned, a close reading of the original study reveals that the child did not display a great and consistent level of fear (Harris, 1979).

In recent years, many psychologists have come to believe not only that conditioning fails to explain much about human behavior, but that it does not even explain what happens in experiments with animals. There is experimental evidence to show Pavlov's dogs and Skinner's rats were not learning simple connections between stimulus, response, and reinforcement. Rather, it seems what they were learning was *information*. Pavlov's dog was learning to expect the buzzer to be followed by food, while Skinner's rats were learning that pressing the bar would be followed by food. Thus, in one experiment (Solomon & Turner, 1962) a dog learned which of two tones would lead to shock, even though it was paralyzed by a drug and could not respond during the learning phase of the experiment. The outcome cannot be explained as a stimulus response connection since there was no response. Other experiments show that animals can learn even without rewards.

Finally, there is evidence that shaping through reinforcement is not the all-powerful technique it seems to be at first glance. Contrary to Skinnerian doctrine, it is not possible to teach an animal to do almost anything. Perhaps you have seen an animal act where the "performer" failed to do what the trainer expected. According to Breland and Breland (1961), what you saw may have been a case of "instinctive drift." The Brelands are two psychologists who trained a variety of performing animals over the years, including pigs, raccoons, cockatoos, chickens, whales, and reindeer. They found that the inborn behavioral tendencies of different species of animals limited the ability of a trainer to shape behavior.

For example, one of the Brelands' tricks was to have an animal pick up coins and drop them into a piggy bank; when the animal performed correctly, it would be given food. But after training the animals would often revert to their instinctive ways, rather than carry out the act of putting the coins in the bank. Thus, the pigs would drop the coins, root at them, pick them up, toss them, drop them, and so forth; raccoons would rub the coins together, going through their natural washing motions. Each species would do what came instinctively to it, even to the point of delaying the receipt of the food, or even failing to get it altogether.

Even if conditioning did explain animal behavior, it would still be reasonable to ask whether the same principles could explain behavior and development in human beings. The idea that reinforcement directly strengthens human actions has been made obsolete by a large number of experiments showing that humans respond to the *information* provided by a reward, not the reinforcement itself (Estes, 1977; Nutting & Greenwald, 1968).

Pavlov himself did not believe conditioning could explain all of human behavior, or that animals and humans could be understood in the same terms. He thought that language, which he called "the second signal system," introduced an entirely new principle into human psychology. Since Pavlov's time, a great deal more has been learned about the nature of language and its complexity. The prospect of reducing language to a stimulus-response behavior has grown increasingly remote. As we shall see in more detail in Chapter 8, learning a language is not learning a set of verbal responses, but rather learning a set of rules for transforming thoughts into sentences, and vice versa.

The basic trouble with using stimulus-response, or S-R, theory as a complete explanation of human behavior lies in the premise that people can be understood from the outside, as a camera would see them. To say, for example, that a boy rapidly contracted his right eyelid is a good Skinnerian description of a response. But, as Gilbert Ryle (1971) has pointed out, it is only a "thin" description: just from the movement alone, we cannot tell whether we have witnessed a twitch or a wink. The difference between the two is immense, but not observable. (It is significant that the camera can perceive what the naked eye cannot. High-speed photography can distinguish between voluntary and involuntary eye blinks and can even tell the difference between a conditioned and an unconditioned eye blink.)

A twitch is of course involuntary and a wink voluntary. But beyond this a wink is a secret signal, to a particular person, of a definite message according to an already understood code. The wink could have still other meanings. Maybe the boy was mimicking somebody else's wink—or twitch. Or perhaps the boy, not sure of his ability to wink, is rehearsing a wink. Or perhaps he is only fake-winking to make outsiders think there is a conspiracy going on. To a radical behaviorist, all these eyelid contractions are alike. Between the "thin" or physical description of what the eyelid is doing and the "thick description" or meaning of what the boy is doing—signaling, mimicking, rehearsing— lies the world of human thought and social life: a world of intentions, motives, feelings, signals, symbols, and rules in which these different kinds of eyelid contractions are produced and interpreted.

Social Learning Theory

Not all S-R theorists are radical behaviorists in the style of Watson and Skinner. Modern or **social learning theory** differs from the more extreme form in two ways: by rejecting the idea of shaping through reinforcement as the basic principle of learning, and by allowing for inner psychological mechanisms which *mediate* between stimulus and response.

Social learning theorists argue that traditional conditioning theory fails to explain how new behavior is acquired in the first place. Recall that Skinner's shaping methods require that subjects begin to do the thing the experimenter wants them to before reinforcement can begin. Bandura and Walters argue that it is doubtful that "many of the responses that almost all members of our society exhibit would ever be acquired if social training proceeded solely by the method of successive approximation. This is particularly true of behavior for which there is no reliable eliciting stimulus apart from the cues provided by others as they exhibit the behavior" (1963, p. 3).

Instead of the step-by-step shaping of behavior, Bandura and other social learning theorists argue that children learn a great deal simply by observing what their parents and others do and then imitating them. By modeling themselves on the people around them, children learn to speak and take on the ways of their culture.

Although social learning theorists disagree with Skinner about the development of responses, they agree with his emphasis on reinforcement. Thus, they argue, children will persist in imitating their parents only if they are rewarded for doing so. Usually, according to the theory, when children do imitate their parents, they are rewarded, which not only reinforces the particular behavior of the moment, but also the general tendency to imitate. Imitation comes to be rewarding in itself. Some social learning theorists argue that it is not necessary for children themselves to be rewarded for imitating a model; they will copy the model's behavior if the model is rewarded.

In sum then, according to social learning theorists, imitation and its reinforcement form the basis of socialization. The social environment rewards behavior it regards as good or appropriate, and it punishes or fails to reward behavior it regards as inappropriate. Thus, a boy will be rewarded for imitating his father and acting in masculine ways, and a girl will be rewarded for imitating her mother and acting in feminine ways.

How then does the theory explain children who do bad or inappropriate things—a child who acts aggressively or adopts a deviant sex role? The theory has a ready explanation—the parents must have been rewarding the deviant behavior somehow, whether or not they realized it. An aggressive child must have been rewarded with parental attention when he or she was acting up, and the tomboyish girl and the effeminate boy must have been reinforced for those behaviors.

Bandura and his associates have carried out a large number of experiments dealing with imitation. Typically, children are presented with real or filmed models performing some action. Next, children are given the opportunity to im-

An aggressive behavior being learned.

itate the model, and their tendency to do so is assessed. Probably the best-known imitation experiments are those dealing with aggression in which children observe a model hitting a large inflated clown doll (Bandura, Ross, & Ross, 1963). These and other experiments have revealed some of the conditions under which children are more or less likely to imitate a model. For example, they are more likely to imitate models that are high rather than low in prestige, that are like rather than unlike themselves, and models who are rewarded rather than those who are punished or unrewarded.

Limitations of Social Learning Theory The model of mind used by social learning theorists is not quite the mechanistic one of Watson and Skinner, and yet not a cognitive model either. Observational learning and imitation do involve a great deal of mental activity. Imitating another person's behavior involves such cognitive processes as perception, imagery, short-term memory, long-term memory, and recall, as well as figuring out how to translate the observed behavior into one's own actions.

Yet social learning theorists do not analyze these cognitive processes in any great detail. They regard cognition mainly as a mediator of external events; in other words, the mind mirrors the environment. The individual is still responding to the pushes and pulls of the environment, and perceptions and thoughts are only "mental way stations" (Skinner, 1953) between stimulus and response.

Social learning theory does not use the concept of stages of development. It sees growth as a continuous process; new kinds of behavior learned through imitation do not imply new kinds of psychological functioning. This view is disputed by other developmental psychologists, who argue that imitation reflects the child's stage of cognitive functioning—it is the child's growing understanding that makes imitation possible. For example, children are unable to imitate sentences that are much beyond their own level of competence. A young child may imitate the sentence, "The cat bit the dog," but not, "The dog was bitten by the cat," which has a more advanced grammatical structure.

In fact, language development, which at first glance seems to provide strong evidence for imitation as the key to socialization, does not really do so at all. The imitation theory seems to be supported by the fact that children do learn to speak exactly the way the people around them do. But it is not true that language is a collection of words and sentences that children learn through imitation. Learning a language is learning how to say and understand things you have never said or heard before, in a form that others can understand. It involves cracking the complicated code of adult speech, figuring out how to convert sounds into thought, and thoughts into sound.

Research in psycholinguistics shows that imitation and reinforcement play a surprisingly small role in the growth of language. For example, one of the common kinds of language mistakes made by young children involves verbs: "He goed" instead of "He went"; "It breaked" instead of "It broke"; "It ringed" for "It rang." Slobin (1979) and other researchers have observed that children actually learn the correct forms of these troublesome verbs *before* they use the wrong ones.

The important thing about these errors is that in one sense they are not really errors. If English were a perfectly regular language, we would all use constructions like "He goed." In making these mistakes, the child is simply overextending the rules that do exist in English and apply most of the time. If language were learned by imitation, however, then normal children would not regularly make errors they have never heard. These "mistakes" show that the child is learning rules about how to construct words and sentences, not a collection of sayings to be imitated.

There is one example in the psychological literature of a child who did conform to the imitation theory of language learning. Roger Brown reports on the sad case of John, an autistic 10-year-old boy. John's every sentence exactly duplicated the one he had just heard spoken to him. Of the many peculiarities this resulted in, one stands out: John used the word "you" to refer to himself, because other people had used the word when referring to him, and "I" when talking about his mother, imitating the way she talked about herself. A short time with John convinced Brown that normal language cannot be learned by imitation: "[John's] speech is unlike normal children's speech in all kinds of ways that are implied by the collection-imitation theory, but we had never actually worked out the implications. When they are worked out, and one sees them in performance, it is clear that the theory generating them is untenable" (1975, p. 449).

The Contributions of Behaviorism

Behaviorism no longer dominates psychology, but it remains alive and well as one theoretical approach among others. The rigorous experimental methods introduced by the behaviorists have had a lasting impact on all psychologists. Even critics of behaviorism acknowledge that their "intellectual puritanism" (Bruner, 1983, p. 33) had a beneficial effect on the field. Behaviorists have always insisted that terms be defined precisely, that hypotheses be tested, and conclusions be supported by data. This research model put an end to the armchair speculation that typified much of psychology around the turn of the century.

Another lasting contribution of behaviorism is the focus on what people actually do and the circumstances in which they do it. Arguing against the notion that people's actions are caused only by deep-rooted character traits, behaviorists insist on searching for the causes of behavior in the immediate environment. For example, Gerald Patterson's (1976) work with aggressive boys as well as research by others on children's behavior problems suggest that parents may be rewarding the very behaviors they would like to eliminate in their children—by ignoring children's "good" behavior and giving in to aggressive acts. Most psychologists now agree that the sources of behavior are not to be sought only within the individual, but also in his or her environment. As we noted earlier, emphasis on the situations surrounding problem behavior led to new forms of therapy

based on behavior modification. These methods have often been successful in relieving a person's problems without prolonged and deep exploration of the reasons why the individual came to have the problem in the first place.

As we approach the end of the century, the debate that began in its earliest decades is fading away. John Watson's insistence that psychology could study only observable behavior, not thoughts and feelings, has been made obsolete by new technology. The advent of the computer—a machine that can solve problems—made the study of human thought scientifically respectable once again. New technologies also made it possible to study the physiological correlates of mental processes, such as brain waves and blood flow in the cortex. Looking back on the debate, Albert Bandura summed it up this way:

> Man is a thinking organism possessing capabilities that provide him with some power of self-direction. To the extent that traditional behavior theories could be faulted it was for providing an incomplete rather than an inaccurate account of human behavior. (1977)

Sigmund Freud

Freud and His Followers: Psychoanalytic Theory

Sigmund Freud is undoubtedly the most influential psychological theorist of all time. He was not, however, a psychologist but a neurophysiologist and a medical doctor. Freud revolutionized the way our culture thinks of childhood, but he did not systematically study children; the patients he analyzed were adults. Freud attacked the commonsense notion that people are rational beings who know the reasons for the things they do. His ideas about hidden sexual and aggressive motives changed the way we think about ourselves and have become part of the common sense of modern time.

Because so many of Freud's notions have

come to be taken for granted, it is hard to assess his influence. It is difficult to imagine a time when people did not know that children have an interest in sex and strong feelings about their parents, or that an outwardly prim and proper individual can harbor seething passions within.

We are all in some sense Freudians, even if we have never heard of Freud or studied his writings. If we make a slip of the tongue, or forget a name or appointment, we wonder what our motive could have been. We talk about Oedipus complexes and about people treating their bosses or teachers as father and mother figures. Parents worry if a mistaken word or deed will turn their children into adult neurotics. We see sexual satisfaction as a key element in good living and so strive to overcome our sexual hang-ups. Television and movie writers make up dreams to show us the inner lives of their characters, and they tell us about the characters' childhood traumas to explain their current dilemmas. Psychotherapy has spread from being a treatment for severely troubled upper-class people to a treatment for millions seeking "growth" and "awareness" as well as help with life's problems.

Freud is not to blame for the fact that his once unbelievable and disreputable ideas have become popular clichés. Many of the notions attributed to Freud, in fact, are distorted or totally erroneous. Far from being an advocate of sexual freedom, Freud himself was a proper Victorian. While his theory asserted that repressed sexual desires were the cause of neurotic symptoms, he believed that the cure lay in consciously recognizing such wishes, not acting them out. There are many ironies in the story of Freud and his work.

He would undoubtedly have been shocked by the new psychotherapies promising happiness and self-fulfillment. The purpose of psychoanalysis, according to Freud, was not to bring permanent bliss; it was to replace neurotic misery with normal human unhappiness. Freud was a hard-nosed determinist who grew ever more pessimistic in his later years. He came to believe that inborn human urges toward cruelty and aggression were stronger

than the sexual instincts. Little wonder that on his way to America to introduce psychoanalysis to the New World, he said, "I am bringing them a curse."

Despite the excesses of pop psychology, and although his theories contained serious flaws, Freud remains a monumental figure in psychology. All students of human development are followers of the trail he blazed. Freud's concern with the evolution of the human organism from infancy to adulthood, and his belief that early experience shapes later personality helped lead to the emergence of developmental psychology as a field of study.

Freud's theories have had an enormous impact on academic developmental psychology, even though he worked in a very different professional tradition, and even though most developmental psychologists would not label themselves as Freudians. For example, many social learning theorists borrowed Freudian concepts, translated them into S-R language, and studied them either in the laboratory or in interviews with parents. Studies of dependency, frustration, aggression, anxiety, resistance to temptation, sex role learning, and other topics are examples of this borrowing from Freud.

Aside from his contribution to psychology, Freud was instrumental in what Fromm has called "the revolution of the child" (1970). Traditionally, young children had been regarded as blank insensitive creatures; they lacked adult reasoning and were assumed not to think very much at all. Freud was the most influential and systematic of a number of nineteenth-century theorists who articulated a new view of young children as passionately emotional beings with complicated thought processes.

Problems in Understanding Freud

It is extremely hard to offer a brief summary of Freudian theory. Freud lived a very long and productive life. He had many different ideas and changed his mind many times, sometimes without acknowledging that he was doing so. Thus, although Freud's writings are fairly easy and enjoyable to read, to understand what he is saying it is necessary to know something about the evolution of the topic or concept one is reading about. In addition, his concepts have been revised and reinterpreted by his followers as well as by dissenters up until the present day. Indeed, just in the past few years there have been several major reinterpretations of Freud that have become part of the development of psychoanalytic theory (see Eagle, 1984; Greenberg & Mitchell, 1983).

Language poses another set of difficulties facing anyone who wants to get acquainted with Freudian ideas. For one thing, psychoanalytic writing bristles with jargon—technical terms used by Freudians to communicate with one another. Thus, the reader will be confronted by such terms as *id, ego, superego, libido, cathexis, reaction formation,* and a host of others. (See the box on Some Key Freudian Terms.) Some of these words refer to abstract concepts that would be difficult to discuss in other terms, but they are used where plain English often would do as well—for instance, talking about the ages from 6 to 12 as the "latency period."

Another linguistic problem arises from the translation of Freud's original German into English. For example, the German word for "I" is *ich;* and the word for the abstract concept of

Some Key Freudian Terms

Freud's fertile mind generated a large number of new terms and concepts—which in turn have generated several dictionaries of psychoanalytic terms. Among the most essential terms are those describing what Freud conceived to be the three major components of personality: the **id,** the **ego,** and the **superego.** With what Jerome Bruner once called "the eye of the tragic dramatist," Freud saw the human mind as a battleground—the scene of a never-ending struggle between these opposing forces.

The id is what Freud referred to in his earlier writing as "the unconscious." It represents blind impulse and energy and operates according to the pleasure principle. Freud likened the id to a cauldron full of seething excitations.

The ego represents reason and common sense; it is also the part of the personality that the person recognizes as "I." In relation to the id, Freud compared the ego to a man riding on a spirited horse, trying to control its superior strength.

The superego is the part of the personality that watches and judges the ego. It represents the rules and standards of adult society as they are transmitted by the parents. The superego is often described as the conscience, but it is often much more punitive, unforgiving, and irrational than the term "conscience" implies.

Many present-day analysts reject this division of the mind into three warring entities, although they do not reject the clinical observations on which the entities are based. Rather, they interpret desire, reason, and guilt as aspects of the self.

Another important set of concepts in Freudian theory refers to various mechanisms of defense—that is, the ways a person uses to ward off anxiety. Some of the major mechanisms are as follows: *repression,* or "forgetting" some painful past or current event; *isolation,* remembering a painful event but without any emotion; *projection,* attributing one's own emotion to another person, such as being angry with someone and thinking that person is angry with you; *reaction formation,* mastering an unacceptable impulse by doing the opposite, such as being exaggeratedly kind when the impulse is to be cruel, or being excessively clean when the impulse is to be dirty; *regression,* returning to an earlier pattern of behavior under stress, such as when young children lose their toilet training after a separation from the parents or the birth of a baby in the family.

Freud's office. He called himself an "archaeologist of the mind" and liked to collect archaeological relics.

the self is *das Ich*. The term *das Ich*, however, has been translated into English as the "ego," rather than "the I." This makes it easy to think of the ego as an abstract, impersonal agency in the mind, or as a sort of miniperson inside a person's head. Actually, "the ego" is simply a term for the person, that is, for herself or himself (Rycroft, 1973; Schafer, 1976, 1978).

Finally, the method psychoanalysts use to gather their data puts another obstacle in the path of trying to understand Freud's ideas. Freud invented a special kind of therapeutic relationship. He did not discuss his patients' problems with them in a conversational way, nor did he interview patients, asking them a series of questions. Rather, he invented the method known as "free association" in which the patient is supposed to talk about whatever comes into his or her mind, no matter how illogical, obscene, or outrageous the thought might be. The psychoanalyst also violates the everyday rules of conversational politeness by remaining silent much of the time. The therapist is supposed to be a "blank screen" so that the personality of the patient will emerge of its own accord, without being influenced by the therapist as a particular individual.

This special kind of human relationship is the major source of psychoanalytic observations and ideas. Freud's explorations in this inner world have been compared to the discoveries of Columbus and the conquistadors in the outer world. He explored large areas of inner life that had previously been felt too meaningless or too disturbing to study: dreams, fantasies, childhood memories, seemingly irrelevant and irreverent thoughts. In these explorations, Freud discovered that the impact of early experience in the family was more lasting than anyone had suspected. He found that his patients regularly began to treat him as one or another of their parents; although his patients were adults, the little children they had once been seemed to spring into life again in the analytic situation. The wishes and fears they had had as little children came vividly alive, revealing a world more like Grimm's fairy tales than the mundane reality of everyday adult life.

From these observations, Freud derived some of his major concepts: the unconscious, fixation, and infantile sexuality. Thus, the wishes and fears expressed in the therapy usually came as a surprise to the patients; they were ordinarily **unconscious** of having such thoughts and feelings. The freshness and vividness of the early memories and feelings suggested the concept of *fixation*; it was as if early experience had been frozen and preserved, like a prehistoric animal in the arctic ice. The concept of *infantile sexuality* arose because the childhood recollections of patients suggested they had been preoccupied with their mouths, bowel functions, and genitals.

In evaluating Freudian theory, it is important to remember that the clinical situation described above is the major source of Freud's observations. This means that it is difficult either to prove or disprove the theory using the usual psychological methods of experiment, interviews, or behavioral observation. It is also important to remember that Freud's ideas about children were derived from adults. In recent years, analysts have observed and treated children, but the basic concepts of emotional development were derived from the analytic treatment of adults.

Freud's Developmental Theory

Freud's developmental theory is a **psychosexual** one. It states that the driving force in the child's emotional development is sexual energy or **libido.** In Freud's definition, sexuality is really sensuality—pleasurable feelings that can arise from various areas of the body. He postulated a developmental sequence in which sexual gratification centers first in the mouth, then in the anus, then the genitals. During the oral stage, which occurs in the first year of life, the infant's main satisfaction comes from sucking and feeding. The oral zone is also the major point of contact with the world. If the infant is deprived during the oral stage, the theory states, he or she may forever be dependent and depressed or aggressive and distrustful.

During the second year of life, sexual energy moves to the anal area. The child's emotional life centers around passing and retaining bowel movements and struggles over toilet training. The child who is frustrated during this period may develop in either of two ways: into a messy and wasteful adult; or into one who is excessively neat, stubborn, and stingy.

In the third stage of psychosexual development, the genital organs become the main center of satisfaction. Freud called this the phallic stage (phallus is Latin for penis), and his account of the period is centered on the development of boys rather than girls. Between the ages of three and five, the little boy manipulates his genitals, falls in love with his mother, and wishes he were rid of his father. Assuming the competitive feelings between his father and himself to be mutual, he unconsciously views his father as a dangerous ogre who may castrate him. This is, of course, the famous Oedipus complex, which is based on the Greek myth about King Oedipus who unknowingly and by coincidence killed his father and married his mother. Freud postulated a direct counterpart in girls—the Electra complex.

Freud thought of the Oedipus crisis and its resolution as the key to later personality development. The boy must learn to give up his Oedipal wishes and identify with his father. Instead of wanting to replace his father, he should want to be like him. This identification brings about two major developments in the child's personality: he takes on the sex role he will follow through life, and he acquires a conscience, or *superego*. In other words, the child comes to accept not only the prohibition against sex within the family, but also the rest of the moral code of society.

Freud traced the origins of many different forms of neurosis to the Oedipal period. For example, a man might remain excessively close to his mother, unable to find happiness in love or marriage. Or, he might remain permanently hostile to his father and other older men, and thus be unable to deal with authorities such as bosses or police officers. Failure to identify with the father, Freud thought, could result in homosexuality or in the lack of a superego.

Freud postulated two developmental stages after the Oedipus period: latency and adolescence. The *latency* period lasts from about age 6 to 12. During this time between the phallic stage and sexual awakening at adolescence, Freud thought that sexual energies declined or became latent, hence the term "latency period." During adolescence, sexuality revives in a greatly strengthened form. The old Oedipal feelings are reawakened and are resolved when the person becomes sexually adult in love and marriage. Freud has relatively little to say about these two latter stages of development. He believed that once a child passes through the emotional crisis of the Oedipal period, his personality is set for life. The events of later childhood and adulthood will be a reenactment of the way the child had originally dealt with the Oedipus complex.

Although Freud's psychosexual stages are the core of his developmental theory, some of his other concepts also describe developmental trends. For example, as we saw earlier, *id, ego,* and *superego* are the major divisions of personality in psychoanalytic theory, and they develop in sequence. The id—which means "it" in Latin—is the biological core of the personality, the sexual and aggressive instincts. At first, the infant is only an id, blindly seeking gratification. The id operates according to the "pleasure principle."

Later, the ego develops to take account of reality. The child develops the ability to take account of facts, to avoid danger, and to find ways to satisfy the id. If development stopped with the ego, the child would be a small criminal, the fulfillment of his sexual and aggressive wishes limited only by the "reality principle." However, the amoral ego comes to be limited by the superego. The child takes the parents' moral standards into his or her own personality. The superego is experienced as a kind of "overself," a part of the self that watches over what we do, and tells us when we step over the bounds of morality.

The other developmental scheme in Freud's writing involves two different ways of thinking: primary and secondary process. **Primary process** thinking is the kind found in dreams and hallucinations. Freud thought it the normal mode of thought of the infant. It is visual and blurs the distinction between real and not real, self and not self, past and present, logic and illogic. **Secondary process** thinking makes all these distinctions and becomes the normal, waking mode of thought after infancy. But the primary process is always there, ready to emerge in dreams, mental illness, stress, fatigue, or drug-induced states of consciousness.

Unresolved Issues

Certain fundamental questions about Freudian theory were never resolved by Freud, or by his successors. To this day, there is debate about which side of the following issues Freud was really on. Psychoanalysts may also be found on both sides, and each side can quote chapter and verse from Freud supporting his or her own position.

1. Was Freud trying to explain *all* of human behavior or only behavior that seemed disturbed or irrational? In other words, was Freud trying to understand commonplace behavior or just supply explanations for such deviant behavior as phobias, compulsions, schizophrenic delusions, slips of the tongue, and so forth?

2. Did he believe that deep and unconscious instinctual drives are the *only* causes of all behavior? Or did he agree that people often engage in ordinary behavior for reasons that require no "deeper" explanations: shopping for groceries, meeting a friend, going for a walk?

3. Did Freud believe that parents determine their children's personalities? In other words, did Freud believe children are blank slates, shaped by the family environment? Or did he believe that the child's biological drives determine the child's future? Or are the child's perceptions and interpretations of parental behavior the crucial factors?

This last issue is, obviously, an important one for both theoretical and practical reasons. If we know that the parents' behavior can cause their children to be neurotic, schizophrenic, criminal, or mentally healthy, successful, and moral, then we have a theory about the causes of important social problems—and a possible means of eliminating them.

The issue of whether parents have a major or minor influence on the psychological development of their children is a long-standing controversy among psychoanalysts themselves. To the outside world, however, Freud and his followers were almost always assumed to be arguing for parental determinism—that parents were to blame for their children's personalities. To this day, the leading theories of juvenile delinquency, mental illness, homosexuality, and so forth are parental cause theories—or more precisely, maternal cause theories; it is all the mother's fault.

Within academic psychology, the Freudian message was taken to imply that early child training practices—feeding, weaning, toilet training, and so on—were the crucibles in which the child's character was formed. Child development researchers in the 1940s and 1950s spent an enormous amount of time and energy looking into the effects of variations in such practices on later behavior. By and large, these studies failed to find that such practices in and of themselves have any demonstrable effects (Caldwell, 1964).

Ironically, psychoanalysis was never as clearly a theory of parental determinism as many had assumed. Freud himself acknowledged that although he could trace symptoms *backward* in time to childhood origins, he could not predict *in advance* that a particular event would have a specific outcome in adulthood.

Further, Freud took a major turn away from explaining his patients' problems in terms of external reality when he abandoned what he called "the seduction theory." In his early writings, Freud argued that hysteria in his women patients was caused by sexual abuse, mainly by fathers. Later, Freud blamed the patients' Oedipal wishes for their problems. The incidents of sexual experience with the father were imagined, he said, not real, and the unresolved wishes were also responsible for the patient's current symptoms. Recently, a major controversy has erupted over Freud's apparent denial of the reality of widespread sexual abuse of children (Masson, 1984).

In general, whatever the incidence of sexual and other forms of child abuse, psychoanalysts today believe that the actual events in childhood are only the raw material for the child's experience. What the child makes of this raw material is the product of his or her conscious and unconscious interpretations. As one psychoanalyst puts it, "given an unfavorable home situation, one child might grow into adulthood correcting the frustrating influences. Another, starting with an ideal home situation, could magnify small incidents into 'injustices' and later, as a neurotic adult, continue to feel that he has been wronged" (Bergler, 1964, p. 9).

The Limits of the Psychosexual Theory

When Freud's writings on infantile sexuality were first published, most people were horrified. Freud's ideas were announced to a Victorian world that sentimentalized children as innocent angels. Sex was something that reared its ugly head at adolescence and after that was to be kept as much out of sight and mind as possible.

Partly as a result of this fierce opposition, Freud's early followers turned the psychosexual theory into a test of orthodoxy. Such prominent analysts as Adler and Jung, who disagreed with the central role Freud assigned to sex, were cast out of the psychoanalytic movement. In recent years, however, many psychoanalytic writers within the Freudian community have been revising his ideas, trying to bring his concepts in line with recent knowledge and eliminate inconsistencies. For example, Freud's theories are based on an antiquated concept of the nervous system. Following nineteenth-century physiology and physics, he believed that the nervous system was in a state of rest unless it was jolted into activity by stimulation. Freud saw sexual energy as the force that made the mental apparatus work. Today we know that the nervous system is in a state of constant activity. It is the patterning of activity that needs to be explained, not its onset or level.

Another legacy of nineteenth-century physiology in Freudian theory is the idea that psychology had to be based on physical and chemical forces. In other words, like the behaviorists, Freud believed that only a mechanistic model of human behavior was scientific. In some of Freud's more abstract writings, where he describes the clash of opposing mental forces or the flow and blocking of sexual energy, it seems as if he is not writing about people at all.

On the other hand, in his dealings with patients, and in his clinical writings, Freud used a very different conception of human behavior. He did not treat his patients as complicated robots. Rather he treated them as active agents who chose or arranged their fate intentionally but unconsciously—and who could act differently in the future. He tried to explain the *reasons why* the patient dreamed about his grandfather, forgot a friend's name, made a slip of the tongue, or accidentally broke his wife's favorite vase, not necessarily the *causes* that *made* him do these things.

Erikson's Psychosocial Theory Freud's developmental concepts have also been reworked by

Erik Erikson

later theorists. Erik Erikson (1960), for instance, reworked Freud's *psychosexual* theory into a **psychosocial theory.** Erikson kept Freud's emphasis on bodily zones but redefined the developmental crisis for each stage. Erikson sees development as the process of social interaction between the child and his parents, as well as between the child and other emotionally significant people. For example, during the oral stage the central issue is not so much whether the child will get enough sucking, but rather whether the child will come to feel that his caretakers can be depended on for consistent, good care. In Erikson's terms, this issue is one of basic trust versus mistrust.

Similarly, the central issue in the anal stage is not whether or not anal urges are gratified or frustrated. Rather, it is the clash between parental authority and the child's growing sense of his or her own power and autonomy. The outcome of the crisis at this stage is either a

Old Age								Integrity vs. Despair. WISDOM
Adulthood							Generativity vs. Stagnation. CARE	
Young Adulthood						Intimacy vs. Isolation. LOVE		
Adolescence					Identity vs. Confusion. FIDELITY			
School Age				Industry vs. Inferiority. COMPETENCE				
Play Age			Initiative vs. Guilt. PURPOSE					
Early Childhood		Autonomy vs. Shame, Doubt. WILL						
Infancy	Basic Trust vs. Basic Mistrust. HOPE							

FIGURE 3.2
Erikson's Chart of Psychosocial Stages
The horizontals designate the different stages of life from infancy through old age. Along the diagonal are the basic psychosocial crises which, according to Erikson, dominate each stage. The terms in capital letters illustrate the basic strength that emerges when each crisis is successfully resolved, from *hope* in infancy to *wisdom* in old age. Erikson believes that the issues that dominate a particular stage continue to be relevant at later ones, hence the diagonal progress of the stages.

Source: "Reflections on the last stage—and the first" by E. H. Erikson (1984) in A. J. Solnit et al., eds., *The psychoanalytic study of the child*, vol. 39, New Haven: Yale University Press.

sense of autonomy or a sense of shame and self-doubt. Erikson does not define this as an Oedipal crisis; rather, he writes about a conflict between self-assertion and guilt. Erikson also extended the idea of development for the first time to ages later than young adulthood. He postulated eight stages of development covering the entire life span, which are outlined in the box opposite and in Figure 3.2.

Further Modifications on Freud Other developmental theorists such as Harry Stack Sullivan (1953) and Robert White (1960) went still further than Erikson in their modification of Freud's theories. Sullivan was a psychiatrist who worked mainly with schizophrenics. He saw the driving force in human behavior as the

search for security and the avoidance of severe anxiety. Sullivan was impressed by the amount of change for good or ill that can occur throughout childhood and adolescence. Rather than being doomed forever by a problem at one stage of development, Sullivan believed later stages could correct defects of earlier ones. On the other hand, a child could successfully pass through early childhood only to run into developmental difficulties later on.

For example, Sullivan made the juvenile era (ages 6 to 12) a major developmental stage. He believed the school-aged child's experiences outside the family are extremely important for future development. During this time the limitations and peculiarities of the child's home can be remedied by his social adjustment at school. A child from a troubled home might find social approval and self-esteem through success on the playground or in the classroom. Or on the other hand, the child coming from a secure early family life might find his or her self-esteem battered by the tough, competitive, unaffectionate world outside the home. Failure in school or rejection by peers can create painful feelings of inferiority. Sullivan believed that

Erikson's Eight Stages

Trust versus Mistrust (birth to one year)

Babies learn either to trust or mistrust that their needs will be met and that the world is a friendly or hostile place. The strength that emerges from this stage is *hope.*

Autonomy versus Shame and Doubt (first to third year)

Children learn to exercise their will and to become self-sufficient in walking, talking, feeding, and toileting. Or, they come to doubt their abilities and feel ashamed of themselves. *Will* is the positive product of this stage.

Initiative versus Guilt (third to sixth year)

Children learn about adult roles and want to be like adults in many ways. If the child's self-assertion leads to a great deal of conflict with the parents, guilt and lack of initiative can result. The trait of *purpose* emerges from this third stage.

Industry versus Inferiority (sixth to twelfth year)

Children learn that they are competent and productive, or they feel inferior and unable to do any task well. *Competence* is the result of this period.

Identity versus Role Confusion (adolescence)

Adolescents try to find out who they are, to find an identity that will integrate various aspects of themselves: sexual, moral, ethnic, work interests, etc. Or, they remain confused about what to do with their lives. The positive product of this stage is *fidelity.*

Intimacy versus Isolation (early adulthood)

Young adults commit themselves to a love relationship, or they develop a sense of isolation. *Love* is the strength of this stage.

Generativity versus Stagnation (middle adulthood)

Adults commit themselves to productive work and to raising and teaching the next generation, or they become stagnant and self-centered. The basic result is *care* for this seventh stage.

Integrity versus Despair (old age)

Older people try to make sense out of their lives and to feel that the choices they made were reasonable ones. Or, they despair at the wrong turns they took and the goals they never reached. *Wisdom* is the strength that results from this final stage.

Harry Stack Sullivan

patients analysts see are people who have become "stuck" at one point of their development. The theory can explain why a person treats his teachers, employers, and business rivals like his father, but it has little to say about the person who treats all of them realistically.

Freud did not attempt to explain how the child adapts to physical and social reality. As White notes, while the id is shifting from oral to anal, the child is learning how to manipulate objects, walk, and talk—and learning about categories such as space, time, and causality. It is not clear how a child who is primarily an id, emotive and irrational, can carry out the enormous amount of learning necessary to be able to understand the world and act in it.

White proposes a *competence* model of development to supplement Freud's stages. Unlike Erikson, however, he does not tie his developmental stages to libido. By "competence," White means all the kinds of learned behavior whereby the child comes to deal with the social and physical environment. He borrows freely from other theorists, such as Sullivan and Piaget, and from empirical research to describe what else is going on in the child's life besides orality, anality, and other bodily issues. Thus, during the first year, the child is learning to separate self and not-self and to develop the concept of permanent objects. During the second and third year of life, the child engages in a battle of wills with his or her parents that goes far beyond the bathroom. The child learns the word "no" and can also give commands. The toddler's increased ability to move around, manipulate objects, and think of new things to do opens up new worlds to explore and sets the stage for conflicts with parents. The developmental stages of Freud, Erikson, White, and Piaget are charted in Figure 3.3.

Summing Up Freud

Despite the errors and inconsistencies in Freud's work—and the controversy many of his theories have stirred—it remains a monumental contribution to psychology. Apart from his influence in the field of psychology, Freud's ideas became part of everyday modern culture

only the most assertive children are likely to find a sense of security in juvenile society. His emphasis on the importance of what happens outside the home, and after age six, stands in sharp contrast to Freud, who believed personality was firmly set for life in early childhood.

Robert White (1960, 1963) formulated another major critique of Freud's developmental theory. Unlike Sullivan, White does not ignore the sexual and aggressive urges that Freud emphasized. Also, he does not share Sullivan's emphasis on security as the major theme in development. White argues that Freud's psychosexual scheme gives an incomplete view of development: the very young infant does not spend all its time being "oral," and toilet training does not occupy most of the toddler's days. Rather, from infancy on, children are curious, active, playful creatures who avidly explore and seek to master the world around them.

White points out that psychoanalytic theory does not study the normal course of life; the

FIGURE 3.3
Stages of Development According to Four Theorists

	Infancy	Early Childhood	Middle & Late Childhood	Early & Late Adolescence	Early	Middle Adulthood	Late
Piaget's Cognitive Developmental Stages	Sensori-motor	Preoperations (growth of symbolic function)	Concrete operations	Formal operations →			
White's Competence Stages	Active exploration of environment	Experimentation with adult roles	Growth of social competence with peers {Competition & compromise / Group membership & close friendship}	Development of heterosexual relationships & capacity for work →			
Erikson's Psychosocial Stages	Trust vs. mistrust	Autonomy vs. shame / Initiative vs. guilt	Industry vs. inferiority	Identity vs. role confusion	Intimacy vs. isolation	Generativity vs. stagnation	Ego integrity vs. despair
Freud's Psychosexual or Libidinal Stages	Oral	Anal / Phallic or Oedipal	Latency	Genital →			
Age	0 2	4	6 8 10	12 14 16 18	20		Late →

because they rang true to the inner experience of large numbers of people. Freud's mapping of the inner landscape of wishes, dreams, and childhood terror is persuasive because each of us has been there.

Ironically, what Freud valued most in his own work—his grand, overarching theory; his electromechanical model of the mind—has stood the test of time less well than any other of his ideas. What remains of lasting value in Freud's work are the observations and discoveries he made in his clinical studies. He revealed a part of reality that other writers before him had hinted at, but only he was able to describe it in such systematic detail: the emotional sensitivity of young children and their complicated thought processes; the persistence of childhood memory and fantasy; the hidden meanings in dreams, slips of the tongue, mistakes, and neurotic symptoms.

Above all, Freud's work profoundly changed our culture's views of human nature. Many observers have compared Freud to Newton, Darwin, and Einstein—individuals who introduced a new way of looking at the world and mankind's place in it. Because Freud lived and wrote, our habits of thought—and our experience of ourselves—are different from those of our ancestors. When Freud died in 1939, the poet W. H. Auden (1940) wrote:

> To us he is no more a person
> Now but a whole climate of opinion.

Jean Piaget

Piaget and Cognitive Development

In recent years developmental psychology, along with the rest of the field of psychology, has experienced a revolutionary change. The study of mind is once again the central topic of research and theory. A Rip Van Winkle psychologist who went to sleep in the 1950s and woke up in the 1980s would be astonished at the transformation. The white rat is no longer the prime experimental subject for finding out how humans learn. Few if any developmental psychologists now talk about stimulus generalization or goal responses. Instead, our newly awakened psychologist would find his colleagues talking shamelessly about cognitive structures, moral development, emotional states, memory strategies, and—most shocking of all—the self.

At the center of these changes, he would find the work of Jean Piaget (1896–1980), a Swiss theorist and researcher who had already produced most of his life's work before American psychology discovered him. The interest in Piaget, and the cognitive revolution in general, came about because of discontent with behaviorism. Traditionally, behaviorism had been built on the model of a passive organism—the child as a blank slate. But the experiments of

the behaviorists themselves brought forth more and more evidence that humans are active organisms who have purposes, who direct their attention, reason, and choose whether they will accept, modify, or reject environmental influences (S. White, 1976).

Meanwhile, advances in technology were making certain behavioristic claims obsolete; the behaviorists had said it was meaningless to talk about mentalistic things such as memory, purpose, knowledge. But after engineers began to build machines with memory, purpose, information processing capacity, and even artificial intelligence, it no longer seemed softheaded for psychologists to use such terms.

In short, thought has come to be seen as a central factor in all aspects of psychological functioning. Cognitive psychologists hold that it is artificial and misleading to divide the mind into separate realms such as thinking and feeling. Knowledge and thought permeate all psychological activities—including such seemingly noncognitive aspects as personality, emotion, sexuality, and aggression. In short, as John Flavell observes, "We have only a single head, after all, and it is firmly attached to the rest of the body" (1977, p. 3).

Cognitive theories come in a variety of forms, all with different images of the mind. There are modern cognitive versions of both psychoanalysis and behaviorism. There is an "information processing" approach which views the mind as a highly elaborate computer with complicated programs for taking in, processing, and storing information. As Baldwin (1969) sums it up, the central assumption of any cognitive theory is this: people respond to the environment by first forming some sort of image or interpretation which becomes the first step in the chain of events leading from the stimulus to the response. In other words, the person does not respond to the external event itself, but to an internal representation of it. This inner image of the world also includes a representation of the self.

Piaget has provided the most influential and detailed account of cognitive development. Like Freud, Piaget is a towering figure in developmental psychology. Where Freud revealed the irrationality of the mature adult, Piaget's work revealed the rationality of little children. Ironically, like Freud, Piaget became a major figure in developmental psychology without having started out as a developmental psychologist. Rather, he came to a study of the child through biology and philosophy.

Piaget started his scientific career at a remarkably young age; he was particularly interested in birds and snails and published his first scientific paper when he was 10. Although it seems a very long way from the study of snails to the growth of thought in humans, Piaget's underlying interests remained the same. Human intelligence to Piaget is a different form of adaptation. The same processes—**assimilation** and **accommodation**—can be seen at all levels of biological functioning, from the cell to the animal to the human. In assimilation, the organism behaves in a familiar way to a new situation. For example, babies are born with a sucking reflex; touch a baby's lips and he or she will suck. The baby will *assimilate* almost anything to the sucking reflex—nipples, fingers, blanket. But babies also *accommodate* their sucking to different objects; they will not suck a large rattle in the same way they suck a nipple. Through experience with different objects, the sucking reflex is modified. Thus, in accommodation the child is adapting to external reality by changing the self.

Assimilation and accommodation persist throughout life as basic ways of dealing with reality. For example, the make-believe play of the preschool child consists largely of assimilation. Consider a little boy straddling a broom, pretending to ride a horse. The child must accommodate somewhat to the broom in order to "ride" it, but he is disregarding most of the broom's qualities as a broom. Suppose, however, the boy were to use the broom to imitate somebody sweeping the floor; that would be an example of accommodation.

At a later age, assimilation and accommodation can be seen in anyone trying to learn a new concept or set of ideas, such as a person trying to learn about developmental theories. At first we try to interpret new information and experience in terms of patterns of action and thought we have already established. Then we alter our existing understandings. However, this is more than the passive acceptance of external inputs. It is the active construction of understandings—or, in Piaget's terms, "schemes" —whose discrepancy from experienced reality is carefully minimized.

As the above examples show, assimilation and accommodation go on simultaneously, even though one may dominate at a given moment. Piaget based these concepts on biological processes such as digestion; the body accommodates to food by secreting enzymes, and it assimilates the food by breaking it down into substances that can be absorbed. The processing of information not only takes a similar form, but is just as necessary as eating. On biological grounds, Piaget assumed that living things require constant interaction with their environments in order to survive.

Piaget's commitment to biology was as deep as Freud's. But where Freud saw our biological selves at war with our higher, thinking selves, Piaget denied such opposition. Piaget believed that our higher mental abilities—our capacity to reason, to use symbols—emerge from our biological nature. Mind is the evolutionary adaptation that enables human beings to respond to and survive in the physical environment.

Piaget's biological interests later merged with philosophical ones. His career was devoted to answering one of the questions that has puzzled philosophers for centuries—the nature of reality, and how we come to know about it. In commonsense psychology, it is taken for granted that the world we see all around us— the world of buildings, trees, chairs, stones, and other people—is really there.

For philosophers, and psychologists, things are not as simple. There have been two opposing opinions on the matter. One view, the empirical, is close to the commonsense position. It argues for a copy theory of reality: the mind is like a blank tape or slate, and the things and events of the world impress themselves on the mind. In ancient times, some philosophers believed that faint copies of objects actually entered into the mind directly; you looked at an apple, and a faint little picture of the apple was

inscribed on the brain. Thus, the child's task in learning about the world is to build up images of reality through repeated experiences.

The opposing point of view is called nativism, or idealism, and is in fact an older philosophical tradition, derived from Plato. This view assumes that the mind already comes furnished with a copy of reality or with categories such as object, space, and time that it will impose on reality. For the nativists, it seems impossible that the child could come to know of the world without having some built-in categories or organizing principles. The nativist tradition is very much alive today in developmental psychology, although it remains a minority view. The leading exponent is Noam Chomsky (1975), who asserts that children possess at birth the basic rules of language, needing only to hear speech for this knowledge to emerge.

Piaget's career was devoted to working out a reconciliation between these two points of view. His view of knowledge was an interactional one: knowledge is neither inborn in a child, nor is it a copy of external reality. For Piaget, there is a real world of objects and events occurring in time. But anyone's knowledge of this world is a construction or interpretation.

Piaget made two key points about the child's interpretation of reality. First, it is an active process: the child does not simply allow reality to stamp itself into the mind; nor does the child simply wait for innate knowledge to unfold over time. Rather, Piaget's child is created in the image of the scientist. The child creates theories about the world, tests them empirically, and revises them in the light of later evidence.

The second major point Piaget made is that the same reality can give rise to very different views of the world. The child's ways of knowing, or mental structures, change radically in the course of development. For example, babies do not realize that objects are permanent. Show five-month-old infants a toy, and they will reach for it. Cover the toy with a cloth, and they will not reach or search for it.

Piaget has also shown that the preschool child gives surprising answers to simple questions. Consider the following experiment, which can easily be carried out by anyone who knows a three- or four-year-old. Show the child two rows of objects lying on a table, say a row of ten toy bears and ten toy chairs. Arrange the two rows so that each bear is directly adjacent to a chair. Then ask the child if there are the same number of bears and chairs. Not surprisingly, the child usually answers yes. Next, with the child looking on, spread out one of the rows, say the bears, so that it is longer than the other. Again, ask the child whether there are the same number of bears as chairs. Almost without exception, the child will answer no, there are more bears than chairs. If the experiment is varied, say by pushing the bears closer together, the child will usually say there are fewer bears. The child apparently thinks it is possible to increase the number of objects in an array simply by spreading them out over a larger area, or reduce the number by pushing them into a smaller space.

Piaget's Developmental Stages

Piaget's theory is developmental in the strict sense of the term: it is divided into distinctly different stages; there is an invariable order; no stage can be skipped; each stage is more complicated or advanced than the previous one. Further, the theory assumes that development is heading in a direction that is built in from the beginning.

Piaget postulated four main stages of cognitive development. Within each stage are several substages. Here we will give only a brief overview of the four main stages, saving the details for discussion later in the text.

1. The first is called the **sensorimotor** stage, which lasts from birth to approximately a year and a half, or the beginnings of language use (the term *infant* means "someone who does not speak").

Although infants in the first year or so of life cannot be said to think or have knowledge in the same way that adults or older children do, they do exhibit intelligent-appearing behavior. They have the same kind of nonsymbolic, prac-

tical intelligence as animals. Piaget used the word **scheme** to refer to the action patterns of this period. A scheme is both the action pattern itself, such as sucking, grasping, looking, hitting, and so on, as well as the inner, mental basis for the action. Thus, a scheme is the wordless counterpart of what would be a concept in an adult. Piaget's notion of *schemes* is his own version of the *schema* concept widely used in psychology today. (See the box on Schemas.)

An important part of development in Piaget's theory is the combination and coordination of schemes. For example, the infant gradually learns to combine sucking and grasping, bringing objects in its hand to its mouth. Later the infant learns to push aside one object to reach for another. Through the combination of elementary schemes, the child's behavior comes to be increasingly organized, purposeful, and intelligent. (See Chapter 5.)

2. The next major stage is referred to as the **preoperational** period and lasts from around the age of 18 months to 6 or 7 years. During this period the child learns to use language, symbols, and mental imagery. Thus, the child comes to have images of absent objects, can imitate an action that happened in the past, and can engage in make-believe play in which one object stands for something else—for instance, a broom can be a horse, or a stick a gun. During this period, the child is building up a picture of the way the world works. At first children do not make the kinds of interpretations of physical reality that adults do. For example, they think that the objects and characters in their dreams are really in the room, that all things that move are alive.

3. The **concrete operational** stage lasts from about 7 years of age to around 11. During this period the child acquires a mental ability Piaget called "operations." It is the ability to perform certain actions mentally. For example, in the bears and chairs problem mentioned earlier, the operational child can mentally line up the rearranged bears and chairs. The preoperational child judges by appearances and does not think of rearranging the objects to solve the problem. Piaget used the word "operations" to

Schemas

Think of a flower, a door, a bird, a melody. Think of the face of a friend, the smell of a rose, the route from your home to the nearest airport. To think any of these thoughts, or to recognize the real things, you made use of what cognitive psychologists call **schemas**. (Some writers use *schemata* as the plural of schema.) The schema is the basic unit of cognition. Different researchers use the term in slightly different ways, but it always refers to a mental representation of experience.

Kagan (1984) compares the idea of schemas in psychology to the idea of the atomic nucleus in physics: neither can be seen directly. The existence of the nucleus was originally inferred from the patterns of light flashes emitted when a sheet of zinc sulfide was struck by radiation. In a similar way, psychologists infer the existence of schemas from the responses of children and adults. For example, if one-year-old babies are shown pairs of dog pictures, each picture showing a different kind of dog, they will look equally long at each one of the pair. If, however, after a series of such pictures, the infants are shown a picture of a bird along with a picture of a dog they have never seen before, they will look much longer at the bird. It seems reasonable to assume that the babies recognize that a new dog is not as different from what they have already seen than a member of an entirely new category of animal. In other words, the infants seem to have formed a concept or schema about what a dog is.

There are several important points to be made about schemas:

1. A schema is not a carbon copy of an experience. For example, if you think of a room in your home, say your bedroom, what you see in your ''mind's eye'' is not the same as what a camera would record—unless you are one of the extremely rare individuals with a ''photographic memory.''

Schemas can take the form of images, but more generally they are abstract mental patterns. A schema of a table is not an image of a specific table, but rather the *idea* of a table—that is, flat surface with four legs, which is the right size for a person to sit at. It would be difficult if not impossible for schemas to be exact copies of reality because events are so complicated and varied. Consider, for example, your schema for your mother's face. It would be a composite of all the different occasions you looked at your mother, in all her moods, states of health, dress, and so on. Schemas can also take the form of *scripts*—representations of complex events such as going into a restaurant and ordering a meal (Shrank & Abelson, 1977).

2. Schemas organize our experience and direct our behavior. For example, they permit us to recognize what we have experienced in the past, and to know what to expect from particular objects, people, and situations. Recognition memory begins in a rudimentary way in the first days of life; newborns can perceive the difference between a checkerboard pattern that has just been shown and a new one. As infants become more familiar with the world, events that are discrepant from existing schemas capture their attention. For example, four-month-old infants, who are familiar with human faces, will look a long time at pictures of faces in which the eyes have been rearranged. Events that are extremely discrepant from existing schemas will receive less attention. Thus, babies will not look very long at faces without eyes or a mouth. This curvilinear relation between attention and discrepancy—the tendency to pay the least attention to both the very familiar and the incomprehensible—persists throughout life.

3. There is constant interaction between schemas and the environment. They are part of a highly plastic, informationally sensitive system. We are constantly using our schemas to make sense of ongoing events in the world, and our experience in the world is constantly changing our schemas. This is the process that Piaget refers to as assimilation and accommodation. As he and others have stated, the human capacity for forming mental representations of the world must have evolved because it helped our species to survive.

Piaget, as part of his clinical method of observation, engaging a child in conversation.

express his view that intelligence consists of motor activity carried out in the head—that is, of mental transformations of experience.

4. The period of **formal operations** begins at around age 11. During this period, reasoning is completely freed from dependence on actual objects. Reasoning can be based on abstract statements, and the adolescent can think about thinking. Formal operations give the child the capacity to think like a scientist or philosopher.

Why does the child move from one stage to the next? Piaget's answer involved the concept of *equilibration*. He assumed that in children's transactions with the world, they are con-stantly testing their notions of reality. Thus, erroneous notions such as the idea that dreams are real will be corrected eventually through the accumulation of experience. A little boy who thinks the moon follows him will be in a state of *disequilibration* when he realizes that other people think the moon follows *them*. He resolves the discrepancy when he comes to the conclusion that the moon actually follows no one.

Implications of the Theory

Piaget's image of the child is as revolutionary in its way as Freud's was. His work challenges both the behavioristic and psychoanalytic views which have dominated American psychology. But Piaget has not had the popular impact that Freud or even Skinner has had.

Part of the reason is that Piaget's writing and concepts are hard to understand; another is that, unlike the high-voltage emotional world of Freudian writings, Piaget's domain is the cool world of logic and physics. It is hard to imagine Piaget's work giving rise to a pop psychology.

The implications of Piaget's ideas for social and personality development have yet to be realized (Cowan, 1978). Piaget himself was unconcerned about individual development; he was interested only in the typical, not in the range of variation. Nor was he concerned with personality and emotion. Piaget did not deny the emotional side of life; he saw feelings and thought as "opposite sides of the same coin" and looked forward to the eventual theory that would integrate his discoveries with those of Freud. But he focused his work on cognition, leaving to others the task of extending his ideas to the study of individual differences, personality, and disturbances in development.

Although Piaget's ideas are limited in their application, they have profoundly important implications for evaluating other theories and therapies involving socialization, particularly socialization within the family. For example, behaviorists and some Freudians believe that the child is at the mercy of his parents. The behaviorists cast parents in the role of Pygmalions, sculptors who mold the child's character. In one version of Freudian theory, the child is helpless and vulnerable in the face of powerful parents. Piaget's work challenges this overemphasis on the parents as all powerful. His work reveals that children acquire important knowledge about the world without any explicit instruction. As we have seen, Piaget assigned children a crucial role in their own cognitive development. If Piaget was correct, then by implication children also play an active role in their own social and emotional development.

Reactions to Piaget

Over the years, Piaget's theories have been criticized from a number of perspectives. Traditional behaviorists have mistrusted his use of clinical interviews with children and his mentalistic approach to psychology. Other critics have disagreed with Piaget's age norms, arguing that he placed certain developments too early or too late.

More serious criticisms challenge Piaget's concept of developmental stages. There is evidence that young children are not as egocentric as Piaget portrayed them, as shown in Chapter 2 (Borke, 1978; Gelman, 1978). In addition, research has shown that very young children do have more skills in handling number concepts than his theory assumes (Gelman, 1972). These findings also suggest that cognitive abilities are not as discontinuous as Piaget states.

Further, while Piaget may have underestimated the cognitive abilities of young children, he may have overestimated those of adolescents and adults. Formal operational thinking is far from universal in our culture—only about 30 to 40 percent of adolescents and adults seem to show this form of thought (Grinder, 1975). And it may be rarer still outside of Western culture.

This last point is part of a more general criticism of Piaget's work, that is, that he ignores social and cultural variation. Some critics argue that what Piaget is describing is the process of intellectual socialization in modern, Western society, and not the built-in tendencies of the human mind.

There is still another way in which Piaget may be said to ignore the social environments in which children grow up. He saw all of cognitive development taking place within the mind of the individual. The theory discounts the role of language, social interaction, and education; so that, according to Piaget, each child is a little Robinson Crusoe, an isolated individual reinventing the concepts of physics, logic, and mathematics on his own. The world is a physical world of objects, space, and time. As one critic put it, "The principal failure of . . . [Piaget's] organism/environment model is its refusal to accept the fact that individuals are immersed in a non-natural world, in an environment of ideas, meanings, intentions, history, symbols, within a matrix of social influence and cooperation" (Rotman, 1977, p. 181).

Yet Piaget's achievements are not diminished by these criticisms. Again, as in Freud's work, what counts most in Piaget's writings is not the grand theoretical system, but rather his discovery of important phenomena no one had noticed before. No one has ever so daringly, painstakingly, and brilliantly illuminated the growth of human intelligence from the first gropings of the newborn infant to the most abstract forms of logic and mathematics. (See the comparison of Piaget's stages with those of Freud, Erikson, and White in Figure 3.3 on p. 95.) Piaget's ideas dominate research into early mental life and have fundamentally changed the way psychology views infants.

Social Psychological Approaches to Development: Mind, Self, and Society

Mead and the Social Self

Piaget's theory of development has very little to say about language and communication. He did not think that the exchange of ideas plays a very significant role in cognitive development. To him, it was the real world of physical objects and space and time that forms the child's mind, not the social world of human interaction.

In contrast to Piaget, several important theorists place language and social interaction at the center of mental development. These theorists were active around the turn of the twentieth century, or in the early decades of it, and their interpretations have recently been undergoing a revival. Some developmental psychologists are moving Piagetian research and ideas in a more social direction and are returning to the concepts developed by George Herbert Mead and others (Flavell, 1968; Kohlberg, 1969; Selman, 1976).

Mead, who was a philosopher at the University of Chicago, was a member of a group of scholars which included William James, John Dewey, and others. His major claim was that "mind" and "self" are products of social interaction. According to Mead, the sense of self is not present at birth, but is a process that is continually developing and changing. The child comes to be aware of herself as she becomes aware of other people. The infant's consciousness is not much different from that of an animal. But humans have evolved the ability to communicate with one another through the use of *significant symbols*.

The self arises out of this process of symbolic interaction, he felt, and consists of two parts, the I and the Me. The I is the spontaneous, subjective aspect of self: the thinker of our thoughts, and the agent of our actions. The Me according to Mead is the image of ourselves as others see us. Unlike animals, the human child takes a pivotal step toward self-consciousness by being able to take the role of the other person. This "taking the role of the other" is the central concept in Mead's thinking. Paradoxically, the ability to see an event from the perspective of another not only makes us into socialized human beings, able to take part in social life, but it also makes us realize our unique individuality. Mead saw people as active agents, who define their own situations and choose their own actions.

While Mead's work has been important in the field of sociology, it is only in recent years that his ideas have been taken up by developmental psychologists. Recent studies of the development of self-awareness, empathy, and role playing have taken Mead's concepts out of the philosopher's armchair and into the experimental laboratory and observational settings. We will review this work in detail in later chapters.

Vygotsky: The Growth of the Mind in Society

Lev Vygotsky was a Russian psychologist who died in 1934 at the age of 37. He has been recognized for many years as a pioneer in developmental psychology, but recently he has been rediscovered as someone with important things to say about many issues psychologists are dealing with today. Vygotsky's ideas seem remarkably contemporary; psychologists now researching cognitive development, languages, cultural differences in problem solving, and other matters are finding his writings a rich source of ideas (Laboratory of Comparative Human Cognition, 1983).

Like Mead, Vygotsky emphasized the central role of language in human development. He believed that the moment the child discovers that speech sounds have meaning is the greatest discovery in the child's life. But where Mead focused on face-to-face social interaction, Vygotsky emphasized the importance of the wider culture and society in the child's mental development.

Vygotsky believed that culture—the body of knowledge, tools, and skills that humans have built up throughout history—plays a major role in individual development. Unlike Piaget, Vygotsky saw language and other cultural inventions as tools that change children's inner worlds. Thus, language, arithmetic, and such aids to memory as tying a string around one's finger provide the individual with technologies that shape the private workings of the mind at the same time as they help to solve practical problems.

Like Piaget, however, Vygotsky saw the child as an active contributor to his own development. Vygotsky felt play was the main way the child learns the rules of his culture, although, again in contrast to Piaget, he did not think that development could be studied in isolation from the surrounding society. While Piaget emphasized universal stages of development, Vygotsky believed that "If one changes the tools of thinking available to a child, his mind will have a radically different structure" (1978, p. 126).

Vygotsky's work appeals to contemporary psychologists partly because his interests were very broad. He tried to integrate a number of different aspects of human experience. Not only was he interested in cultural influences on cognitive development, he was also interested in the brain changes that permit the higher forms of mental functioning to emerge. Although he emphasized the social sources of human thought, he also stressed the private and personal uses of cultural tools. To Vygotsky, as to Mead, language provided the best example of this duality. The child acquires language from her culture, and knowing it enables the child to participate in society. Yet language also enables the child to develop her own unique consciousness: language comes to be internalized in the form of inner speech; children talk to themselves to control and direct their behavior and to reflect on and elaborate their individual experience.

Vygotsky also tried to integrate the concepts of learning and development. Like the behaviorists, he believed that much of the child's mental growth occurs from the outside in; the child learns from the surrounding cultural environment. But unlike the behaviorists, Vygotsky did not believe that the mind is merely a mirror of the external world. He saw learning as only the first step in the process of development. Once a cultural tool such as speech, written language, or mathematics is learned, it changes many psychological processes. Thus, once the child learns to speak, speech changes the child's perception, memory, and problem solving.

Vygotsky's ideas that tools and symbols have shaped human development—both individually and historically—fit in with recent archaeological findings. According to Washburn and other scholars of human evolution, it was the use of simple tools that set human evolution in motion. It used to be thought that our prehuman ancestors developed large brains which resulted in tool use. It now seems that it was the use of tools in the first place that ultimately led to the development of the human brain. Tools, fire, food sharing, complex social speech, and the human brain evolved together; and advances in one area led to advances in others (Isaac, 1978; Leakey & Lewin, 1978; Washburn, 1960). Human social interaction and technological inventiveness appear to have stimulated further evolution. As the earliest humans began to shape the world around them, they became cultural animals. Culture in turn provided an environment that shaped the human mind as we know it today.

Toward a Synthesis of Developmental Theories

For many years, developmental psychology was divided into competing schools. One was either a behaviorist, or a Freudian, a Piagetian, a Wernerian, a maturationist, or a gestaltist, and so on. Each school tended to regard its own methods and particular findings as the core of scientific psychology and paid little attention to the work of the others. Each tended to see its own approach as the key to unlocking the secret of human behavior.

In recent years, psychologists have become more open-minded and have begun to realize that different approaches can be complementary rather than contradictory. For example, learning theorists have been recognizing the importance of thought in human development. Cognitive psychologists are paying increased attention to social knowledge and to the physical and social environments in which development takes place. Freudian psychologists are paying greater attention to thinking and language, as well as to social and cultural factors. Many psychologists have recognized that while a theory may explain some people some of the time, it is not necessarily valid for all of the people all of the time (Gergen, 1977).

Thus, different theories may not necessarily represent irreconcilable views of the world, but rather different ways of looking at the same phenomena. For example, consider the rebelliousness and emotional upheavals of the teenage years. To the Freudian, adolescence is a crisis because of the reawakening of the sexual drives and the resulting need to get free of incestuous entanglements with one's parents. To Piaget, adolescence is a time of questioning and conflict with family because the growing capacities for thought during the teen years make the young person aware of discrepancies between the ideals preached by the older generation and social reality. The learning theorist might explain teenage problems in terms of the growing importance of the peer group as a source of reward. Someone with a cultural-historical approach would argue that adolescence as we know it today is a product of a specific set of social conditions and cultural beliefs, and that it was very different in other times and places.

Is it necessary to choose one of these explanations and discard the rest? Or can they all contribute to understanding a complex and variable part of the life cycle? It seems to me that the second approach is much more useful.

This does not mean, however, that we must mindlessly accept every aspect of every point of view. Thus, we can accept the behaviorists' emphasis on the immediate environment and its pushes and pulls without accepting the extreme view that all behavior is simply a matter of S-R connections. As we have seen, this view is no longer tenable even to many behaviorists. Similarly, the idea of Freud and others that all behavior results from a few primary drives such as sex, aggression, and hunger does not stand up in the light of contrary evidence. On the other hand, we can accept Freud's insight that emotional experience and ties to other people and early experience play an important role in development.

In the following chapters, as we trace development through the life span, we will use the contrasting approaches as different lenses to look through. We will look at the interplay between contrasting aspects of growth; that is, the biological versus the cultural, the cognitive versus the emotional, the uniqueness of the individual versus environmental circumstance and universal trend.

SUMMARY

1. Theories of development try to integrate diverse facts and explain why behavior and thinking change over the life span. There are several different types of explanations, some dating back to ancient times: one attributes development to innate, biological factors; a second views the environment as the determining influence; a third views development as a process of taming animal instincts;

while a fourth view looks at development as the growth of purposive behavior and of selection from multiple possibilities.

2. Theories of development are based on contrasting assumptions about nature: psychology is deeply embroiled in a number of dilemmas which philosophers have not been able to resolve. Are people complicated machines, governed by external forces? Is all of our behavior determined by causes outside of our control? Do children play an active role in their own development, or is a child's fate completely determined by heredity or environment? Is human nature basically good or evil?

3. Aside from different concepts about human nature, developmental theories also differ in their view of development. Some theories hold that there is a built-in direction in human development, that from the beginning of a child's life, development is heading toward some final end point. Others do not believe that development tends in a particular direction. Some theories maintain that development proceeds through a series of distinct changes. Piaget, Freud, Erikson, and White have presented different versions of stage theories. Such theories propound that the stages follow an invariant sequence, that each stage involves a total, qualitative change in mental functioning, and that each stage is better or more complex than the preceding one. Other developmental psychologists dispute the assumptions of stage theories and the evidence backing them up.

4. Behaviorism or learning theory has been the dominant theory of both developmental and general psychology in America for most of the twentieth century. It uses a mechanistic model of human beings—that is, it assumes that people are complicated machines whose behavior is under the control of environmental factors and the stimulus-response (S-R) connections that have been built up by previous experience. The two major forms of learning in behaviorism are classical conditioning and instrumental conditioning. More recently, social learning theories have emphasized the role of imitation and its reinforcement in human development.

5. Freudian theory emphasizes the role of emotional forces in behavior, especially unconscious sexual and aggressive drives. Freud's developmental theory sees the sexual energy in its changing forms as the force behind psychological growth. The Oedipal period, at around age 4 to 6, is the time when the child falls in love with the parent of the opposite sex and fears and feels hostile toward the same-sex parent. This is the crucial stage according to Freud. Later life is merely a reenactment of the child's modes of coping with the Oedipal period.

Later theorists modified Freud's view in various ways. Erikson changed Freud's *psychosexual* theory into a *psychosocial* one: the child's relationships become the central factor in development, not the sexual drives themselves. Erikson also extended the concept of development and stages across the entire life span. Sullivan emphasized the drive for security and interpersonal relationships within and outside of the family as crucial factors in development. White proposed a competence model of development to describe the child's growing abilities to understand and act upon the physical and social environment.

6. Piaget's theory differs from behaviorism in its emphasis on internal mental processes; it differs from Freudian theory in its focus on the child's rational understanding of the external world. Piaget saw the child as an active agent in the construction of reality; knowledge does not come only from experience in the environment, nor is it built into the child's mind at birth. It emerges, according to Piaget, from the interaction between the external world and the child's mental and physical actions. Assimilation and accommodation are the two processes by which the child adapts to new experience.

7. Social psychological theories of development emphasize the role of the social and cultural environment. Like Piaget, they view the child as an active agent in his own development. But unlike Piaget, they believe that social interaction and cultural learning play an important role in intellectual development. George Herbert Mead argued that language is centrally involved in the uniquely human capacities for self-awareness and symbolic communication. Language enables us to "take the role of the other"—look at ourselves through other people's eyes. Vygotsky, like Mead, believed that language is a tool that makes it possible for us to take part in organized social life and also enables us to develop our individuality and inner experience. Vygotsky also stressed the importance of other cultural tools in shaping inner experience, such as writing, number systems, devices to aid memory. Mental growth occurs from the outside in, he felt, as well as through complicated internal processes.

8. Although for many decades developmental psychologists were divided into competing schools, they are beginning to recognize that the different theories are complementary, rather than contradictory. They look at different aspects of experience and can all contribute something to our understanding of human development.

Key Terms

accommodation   97
assimilation   97
behaviorism   76
classical conditioning   78
concrete operational   99
ego   86
formal operations   101
id   86
instrumental conditioning   79
libido   88
nativist   76
preoperational   99

primary process   89
psychosexual theory   88
psychosocial theory   91
schema   100
scheme   99
secondary process   89
sensorimotor   99
social learning theory   81
stimulus-response   76
superego   86
unconscious   88

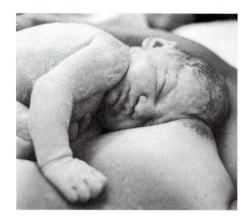

PART II

Infancy
From Organism to Person

The human being, at all times, from the first kick *in utero* to the last breath, is organized into groupings of geographic and historic coherence: family, class, community, nation. A human being, thus, is at all times an organism, an ego, and a member of society.

—Erik Erikson,
Childhood and Society

*A*fter dealing with the history, methods, and theories of human development, we begin to look at the life course itself. Many of the themes dealt with earlier will reappear in different contexts—the nature-nurture problem, the interplay of theory and observation, the relationship of individuals to the biological and social forces that act on them. Two points should be kept in mind. First, as we study each period of development in detail, we should not lose sight of the fact that human development covers the entire life span. There has been a tendency for the study of human development to be child-centered—to focus on childhood as the key to later life, and to assume that adulthood is just a reenactment or fulfillment of childhood. More recently, as adults have been studied in greater depth and across greater spans of time, we have learned that the child is not as much "father of the man" as we used to believe. Changes and plasticity are as much part of the story of human development across the life span as continuity. And if we do find that certain traits remain constant over different periods of a person's life, we need to ask why, just as much as we do if we find change.

Second, it is important to remember that human development is also a multidimensional process. In looking at the biological aspects of genetics and prenatal development, we should remind ourselves that physical development does not take place in a social vacuum. It is itself influenced by the social and psychological context in which it occurs. For example, whether a fetus is growing in an affluent middle-class woman, a ghetto teenager, a heroin addict, or a starving refugee from a war zone makes a difference not only to its life chances after birth, but to its development in the womb. As Erikson reminds us in the quotation on the opposite page, we are always, from very early on, bodies, minds, and members of societies.

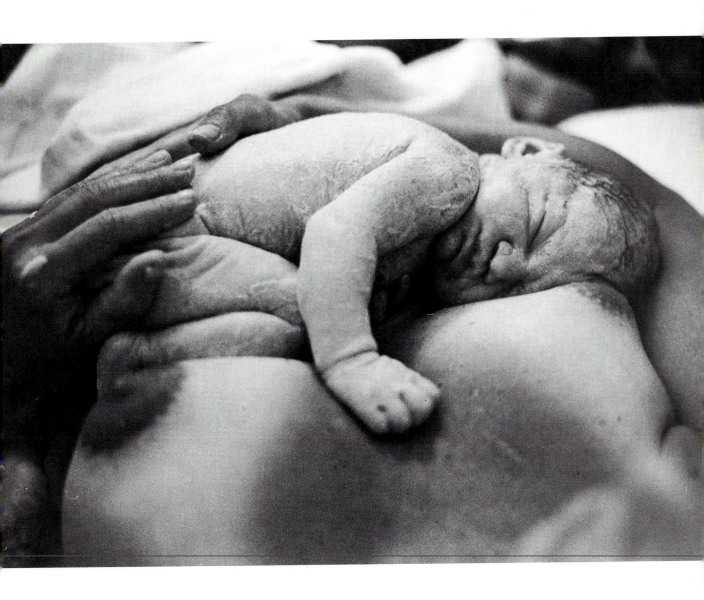

CHAPTER 4

Beginnings
Genetics, Prenatal Development, and Birth

A baby is the most complicated object made by unskilled labor.

—Anonymous wit

The truth is that the beginning of anything and its end are alike touching.

—Yoshida Kenko,
"Life (Frail and Fleeting)"

The Museum of Science and Industry in Chicago is a sprawling building with an enormous array of fascinating exhibits. A visitor can go down into a coal mine or walk through a thumping model of a human heart. There are many buttons to press which produce sights and sounds that illustrate the wonders of technology. The most popular display at the museum, however, does not deal with any of these examples of human ingenuity. Rather, it is a glass-enclosed incubator containing eggs and live, hatching chicks (Webb, Campbell, & Schwartz, 1966). Despite the advances of technology, people continue to marvel at the creation of new life: how can something so lively and complicated as a little chick emerge from something so simple and inert as an egg?

Genetics and Human Development

The creation of a new human being is a complicated drama with many acts. Out of the millions of sperm released in one act of intercourse, only one will fertilize the egg. Of the close to half a million egg cells in a woman's body, only one or two will be in the right place, at the right time, to be fertilized. Before conception, the odds were very much against any of us ever being created.

It is only fairly recently that scientists have come to understand the mystery of reproduction—for example, how does an egg "know" how to produce a complete organism? Why does a chicken's egg always produce another chicken, and not, say, a snake, a dog, or a human? We now know that the egg cell contains information—coded instructions—that tells it how to form the proteins which create the cells which compose the organs which make up the organism.

This information is contained in a complex chemical called *deoxyribonucleic* acid—or **DNA** for short. DNA is the basic unit of heredity, the blueprint or the determinant of growth and development of all living things, from single-celled organisms like bacteria to human beings. In 1953, Watson and Crick published their findings that the DNA molecule was structured in the form of a double helix: two strands, wound around one another like two spiral staircases or a twisted ladder (Figure 4.1).

Even more stunning than their discovery of the architecture of DNA was their cracking of the genetic code. They recognized that the genetic code consists of four "letters"—four different chemicals known as "building blocks": adenine (A), thymine (T), cytosine (C), and guanine (G). (See the box on DNA.) These substances are combined along the strands of DNA into three-letter "words." Each "word" tells how to make one of the twenty-odd amino acids that form protein. A string of these

---

FIGURE 4.1
The DNA Double Helix
The four "building blocks"—adenine (A), thymine (T), cytosine (C), and guanine (G)—combine along the strands of DNA to make "words" (left), which direct the formation of amino acids. The twisted ladder (right) shows the physical arrangement of the DNA molecule.

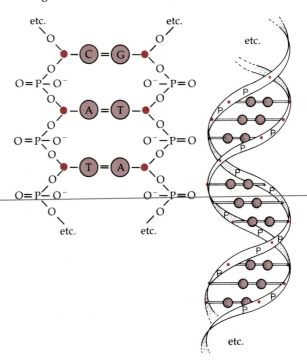

The Brain at Work

In recent years, researchers have developed new techniques to "see" the brain at work as it carries out different mental tasks. Among these new methods of observing brain function are studies of blood flow to different parts of the cortex and *positron emission tomography* (PET), which measures glucose uptake in various parts of the brain as they become activated. The illustrations show the brain activity of normal individuals under various conditions. Complex mental activities involve many different parts of the brain; these and other methods of studying brain function have laid to rest the doctrine that science can say nothing about what goes on inside the mind and must speak only of stimulus and response.

The red indicates the most active areas, yellow the next most active, deep purple the least active (see the rainbow scale). Photos were scanned from above, and the heads face the top of the page.

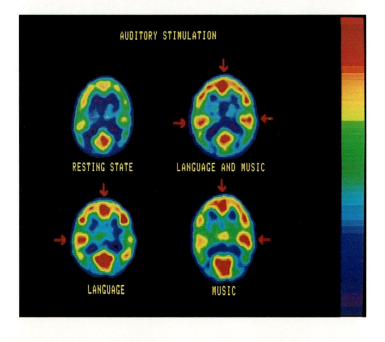

Illustration A

Checkerboard pattern activates the *visual* areas of the cortex.

Sounds stimulate the *auditory* areas.

A complex auditory problem activates *cognitive* areas where problems are solved, not just areas where stimuli are passively perceived.

A *memory* task involves the temporal cortex (near the temple).

A task involving moving the finger of the right hand activates the left *motor* strip and other parts of the motor cortex.

Illustration B

Brain in *resting state*—ears plugged, eyes open—shows both sides of the brain equally active.

Language and music activate both hemispheres.

Language stimulates more of the left hemisphere than the right (in a right-handed person).

Music alone activates more of the right hemisphere than the left (in a right-handed person).

Prenatal Development

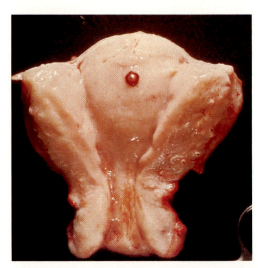

The early weeks. The blastocyst
—a hollow ball of cells—
implants itself in the wall
of the uterus.

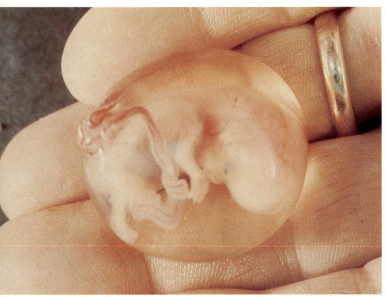

8 weeks

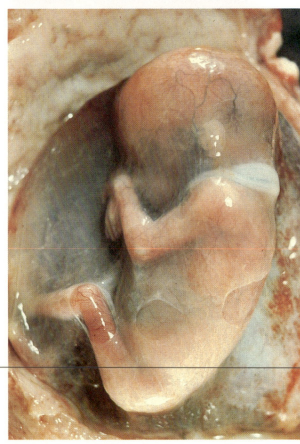

10 weeks

12 weeks

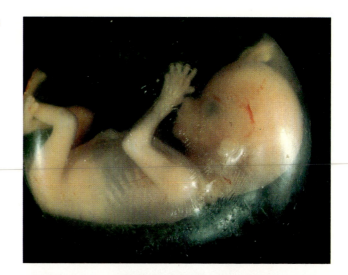

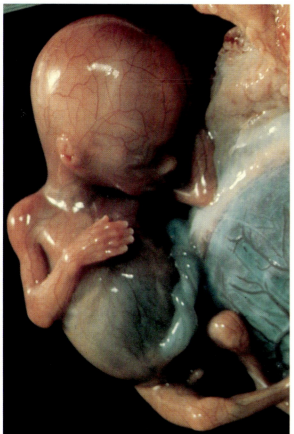

4 months

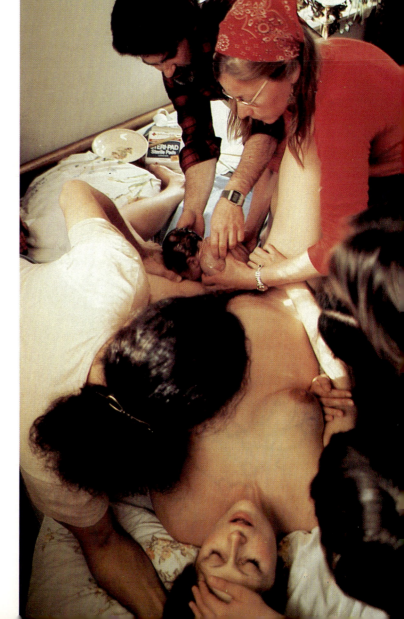

Birth

A newborn
and its
mother

In just a few months,
a helpless newborn grows
into an eager explorer.

DNA

Before Watson and Crick solved the puzzle of DNA in 1953, people knew that genetic information was somehow encoded in its long, complicated molecules. They knew that the composition of DNA varied from one species to another, particularly in the amounts of the four components, A, T, C, and G. They also knew that the number of As always equaled the number of Ts, and the Cs were equal to the Gs. Rosalind Franklin, who had studied x-ray pictures of DNA, had found that the DNA molecule probably was shaped like a corkscrew.

But the exact structure was still a mystery. Nor did scientists know how the molecules of DNA held genetic information, or how the information was used to manufacture the thousands of different proteins. Watson and Crick's discovery made it possible to answer these questions. By playing with scale models of atoms, they discovered that A and T fit one another, and G and C were also attracted. A did not fit with C, nor G with T. So they put together pairs of molecules, A and T, C and G, stacked them on top of one another like stairs, and wound two strands of sugar phosphate around the outside (see Figure 4.1). They realized that the order in which the four elements appear along the double helix contains the key to the genetic code. The only difference between human DNA and that of other living things is the arrangement of A, T, C, and G.

The structure of the double helix also explained how cells reproduce themselves. Organisms grow by cell division: one cell divides into two exact replicas of itself, two divide into four, and so on. The process is called mitosis, which is explained in detail later in this chapter.

After they had built their model of DNA, Watson and Crick observed that each strand of the double helix contained the information necessary to make the opposite strand and thus create a new double helix. They had discovered the mechanism by which the fertilized cell divides and divides until it is an embryo and then a fetus.

Watson and Crick's research not only answered many scientific questions about the mechanisms of genetics and functioning of cells, but it has important practical implications for the control of disease. For example, genetic engineering may soon make it possible to cure hereditary diseases by splicing good genes into human chromosomes.

Yet, like other scientific advances, Watson and Crick's discovery and the genetic engineering that is based on it also have disturbing implications. They have placed awesome power in human hands—the power to alter the genetic makeup of the human species as well as that of the other species on the planet.

"words" forms "sentences" which tell how to manufacture particular proteins. In other words, all the variations in species and individuals are based on differences in amino acid sequences. Along with the theory of evolution, these discoveries have been the most important ever made in biology (Bronowski, 1973).

The idea that the egg contains coded instructions for making a chicken did not occur to biologists in previous centuries. There seemed to

be only two possible explanations of how chickens emerge from eggs. Either the chicken is somehow in the egg from the beginning, or it is not. To the naked eye, it certainly *looks* as if the chicken is not there. If it is not there, then some outside force must be at work to mold the head, the body, and all the rest from the formless matter of the egg. This is the theory known as **epigenesis**. Aristotle, who put forth one version of epigenetic theory, thought that the soul or spirit of the father was the shaping influence which molded the fetus out of the formless substance supplied by the mother.

The other theory of development was **preformationism**. Preformationists believed that miniature replicas of the adult organism were contained in the germ cells. There was a great debate between homunculists, who believed that the sperm contained the tiny baby which could grow only in the womb, and the ovists, who believed that a woman's egg cell was the locus of new life, needing only to be activated by the sperm. When Antonie van Leeuwenhoek, in the eighteenth century, was the first to look at human sperm cells under the microscope, which he invented, he—and others—thought they saw miniature people, complete with heads, arms, legs, and other parts, huddled in the heads of the cells.

The preformationists avoided the problem of explaining how unknown forces enter the egg cell to make the parts of the body appear. But they opened themselves up to another problem. If a complete miniature human is contained in the egg or sperm, then the egg or sperm cells of this miniperson must also contain miniature people. These in turn presumably contain the preformed adults of the next generation and so on. Going backward, preformationism implies that all the generations of the human race were already present in the Garden of Eden in Eve's ovaries, nested inside one another like a set of Russian dolls.

Although preformationism sounds absurd to us today, it seemed more reasonable to scientists of the eighteenth century than a theory that relied on spirits or other mysterious forces. Actually, the truth contains elements of both theories. The epigeneticists were right that the chicken is not inside the egg from the beginning. But the preformationists were right in saying that *something* is there and that form does not arise from formless matter. They thought this "something" was the organism itself.

By the beginning of the nineteenth century, accurate information began to replace the misconceptions of earlier times. The contribution of both parents was recognized, and by the

Meiosis and Mitosis

As we noted earlier, chromosomes are the carriers of genetic information; they appear under the microscope as short, stringy objects in the nucleus of the cell. Each human cell contains twenty-three pairs of chromosomes, along which genes are arranged, like beads on a string. Each chromosome contains thousands of genes, and one chromosome of each pair comes from each parent.

Every cell in the body contains a complete set of chromosomes; it is theoretically possible to make a copy of a person by implanting a nucleus from a body cell into an egg whose own nucleus has been removed. This process is called "cloning," and scientists have already succeeded in cloning mice and frogs.

The more usual form of reproduction involves two kinds of cell division. **Mitosis** is the process in which the cell divides into two exact replicas of itself. In mitosis, the 23 pairs of human chromosomes duplicate themselves (see Figure 4.2). **Meiosis** is a special kind of cell division just for making sperm and egg cells. These reproductive cells—or *gametes*—are single cells with only half the usual number of chromosomes. If the parent cells did not have half the usual number, the fertilized egg would end up with ninety-two chromosomes. Once the egg has been fertilized, it divides by mitosis to develop into the embryo.

During meiosis, the chromosomes line up side by side in pairs. Sometimes the chromosomes cross over one another, break apart, and rejoin. This process of *crossing-over* greatly increases the range of individual variation. In other words, the chromosomes you get from your mother and father are not exactly their own; each passes along a reshuffled combination of genes.

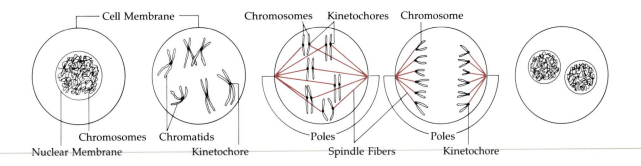

FIGURE 4.2
A Close-up of Cell Division
Diagrams show how chromosomes align themselves and divide during mitosis to form a duplicate cell.

middle of the century, the union of egg and sperm could be observed under the microscope. Improvements in microscopes also made it possible to observe the internal structures of the cell. First the nucleus was discovered, and then *chromosomes*—short, stringy objects that appeared at the time of cell division. Biologists recognized that the chromosomes somehow governed heredity, but exactly how they did it was not clear.

The idea of coded information was not readily understood before the machine age. As Jonathan Miller (1978) observes, advances in the scientific understanding of biological processes have often been speeded by images based on machines. For example, the idea that the heart pumps blood through the body did not exist before the mechanical pump was invented. In the same way, in the age of handmade objects—before the invention of player pianos, carpet looms, and computers—it seemed that the instructions for making an object had to resemble the object, like a mold or a picture. A visual image seemed necessary to guide the craftsman. Reproduction had to be carried out by means of a shaping spirit, or the growth of preexisting form.

As a theory, the idea of coded instructions introduced by Watson and Crick may be as fantastic as the idea of nested organisms or shaping spirits. As Stephen Gould puts it,

> What could be more fantastic than the claim that an egg contains thousands of instructions, written on molecules that tell the cell to turn on and off the production of certain substances that regulate the speed of chemical processes? . . . The only thing going for coded instructions is that they seem to be there. (1977, p. 206)

Genotype and Phenotype

In human beings, the genetic information is contained in twenty-three pairs of **chromosomes**—ribbons of DNA in the nucleus of the cell on which genes are strung like beads. Every cell of the body, except for the egg and sperm cells, contains the same twenty-three pairs of chromosomes. The sex cells contain only half the usual number, so that when they link up at conception, the fertilized egg will have one set of twenty-three chromosomes from each parent. The box on Meiosis and Mitosis explains this further.

After fertilization, the egg is called a **zygote**. Although it is only about 1/200 of an inch in diameter, or smaller than the period at the end of this sentence, the zygote contains all the information needed to make a complete human being. The total genetic makeup of an individual is called the **genotype**; the observed characteristics of the person are called the **phenotype**. For several different reasons, to be explained later in this chapter, there is not a direct correlation between genotype and phenotype.

Every individual, except for identical twins, has a unique genotype. The source of this genetic uniqueness is the reshuffling of the parents' genes in the process of reproduction. Each child represents a random combination of countless parental features. When the parents' cells divide to become germ cells—the egg and sperm—the chromosomes of each parent split up in random ways. In other words, each egg or sperm cell contains a different assortment of parental characteristics.

There is still another source of variation. Because DNA is both breakable and sticky, when the parental cells split apart to form the sex cells, some of the chromosomes break apart and unite with other chromosomes. This interchange between homologous chromosomes is known as *crossing over*. (The term is not to be confused with the cross-over of nerve impulses in the brain explained in Chapter 10.)

Thus, the number of different individuals that could be created out of the human gene pool is almost infinite. A set of forty-six chromosomes contains 3 to 5 million genes. Genes may exist in several different forms, or *alleles*. The creation of an individual genotype may be compared to writing a paragraph containing about 10,000 letters—the length, for example, of the Preamble to the Constitution (Hamburger, 1978). Like the paragraph, the uniqueness of the individual is not in the words and letters, but in the way these are combined. Even though our alphabet is based on only 26 letters, it might take a computer almost forever to duplicate randomly a 10,000-letter paragraph just by successive random selection of letters, spaces, and punctuation marks.

In a human genotype, the alphabet is made up of millions of characters. The number of possibilities is so large that there is practically no chance that anyone's genotype will be exactly the same as anyone else's who ever lived or will live. What was once said of a famous man at his death could be said of anyone—"We shall not see his like again."

A major point to remember about the genotype is that it does not directly produce the observed characteristics of an individual. Genes are not little models of the traits they influence. The only instructions in the genetic code are for assembling proteins. This means that genes for blue eyes or tallness do not exist in a literal sense: these traits are the result of a genotype that contains recipes for proteins whose actions and interactions may influence eye color and height, among other things. The same trait can be due to a variety of genetic and nongenetic causes. For example, a group of mentally retarded people of the same intellectual level may seem to be similar. Some may be genetically defective: there are seventy different genes that can cause mental retardation. Others may owe their retardation to nutritional deficiencies. In short, they may be *phenotypically* alike, but genetically different, and vice versa.

The pathway from gene to behavior is complicated. Consider the example of sex determination. Whether the infant is going to be male or female is determined at the moment of conception. One pair of chromosomes out of the twenty-three determines sex. Female cells contain two X chromosomes (XX), while male cells contain an X and a Y (XY). Since all of the mother's egg cells contain X chromosomes, it is the father's sperm cell that determines the sex of the child. The sperm cell contains either an X or a Y chromosome; thus an X-bearing sperm will produce a girl, while a Y-bearing sperm will produce a boy (Figure 4.3).

Genes and chromosomes, as noted earlier, do not automatically produce male and female infants. Rather, they direct the production of the chemicals that influence the formation of bodily structures. Occasionally, this complicated chain of events goes awry somewhere along the line. For example, the hormones that result in the formation of the genitals may not function properly. A genetically male infant may be born with female-appearing genitals; or a genetically female infant may be masculinized in the womb and emerge looking like a boy.

There is still another genetic principle involved in the distinction between the genetic makeup (genotypes) and personal characteristics (phenotypes): the principle of **dominance** and **recessiveness**. Certain traits come in pairs, and one trait is dominant over the other. Thus, in humans, brown eyes are dominant over blue eyes, which means that a person who has one blue-eyed gene and one-brown-eyed gene will have brown eyes. Two brown-eyed people can produce a blue-eyed child, if each has a recessive gene for blue eyes. Recessive genes such as blue eyes emerge only if the person has two similar genes. Thus, two blue-eyed people should have only blue-eyed children, since neither of them can be carrying the dominant brown-eyed gene.

Because of dominance and recessiveness, people who appear to have the same traits may have different genotypes. It is possible for normal individuals to harbor recessive genes for genetic diseases such as phenylketonuria, (PKU) a metabolic disorder that can result in mental retardation if not treated. Some conditions such as hemophilia—the lack of a clotting factor in the blood—or color blindness are sex-linked. That is, they are carried by recessive genes on the X chromosome. Because the Y chromosome is smaller than the X, certain

genes on the X are not matched by corresponding genes on the Y. A girl will show hemophilia or one of the other sex-linked traits only if she gets recessive genes both from her father and her mother. But a boy will show the trait if it occurs on the X chromosome, which he inherits from his mother.

The effect or result of genes can be seen not only during prenatal development, but across the life span. Genetic differences play a role in how long people live, and what diseases they will succumb to. And genetic "birth defects" may not appear until later in life. For example, Huntington's chorea is a degenerative nerve disease caused by a dominant gene. People afflicted with the disease may show no signs of it until their forties. The well-known singer Woody Guthrie died of Huntington's chorea and his son Arlo stands a 50–50 chance of having it also. (See the box Common Genetic Diseases and Conditions.)

It has been estimated that the average person carries from three to eight harmful recessive genes (Annis, 1978). Intermarriage between close relatives is more likely to result in the appearance of these recessive trait defects, sex-linked and otherwise, than matings between unrelated men and women. As shown in Figure 4.4, royal families, which tend to inbreed more than other people, have been plagued by genetic diseases such as hemophilia.

FIGURE 4.3
Human Chromosomes

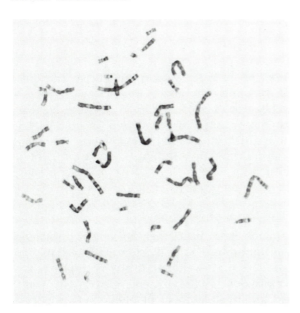

Mendel and Models of Genetic Transmission

The discovery of dominant and recessive genes was one of the achievements of the Austrian botanist Gregor Mendel (1822–1884), the founder of the science of genetics. Mendel discovered the basic principles governing genetic transmission and published his results in 1866. His findings were ignored until their rediscovery in 1900, when scientific research on heredity gained momentum as a field of study. Mendel had the brilliant insight that the hereditary material took the form of particles that came in pairs. Other biologists, including Darwin, took it for granted that the hereditary material was

Some Common Genetic Diseases and Conditions

Disease	Description
Cystic Fibrosis	Mucous glands produce obstructions in lungs and stomach. Incidence: about 1 baby in every 1,000; usually fatal before adulthood.
Down's syndrome* (mongolism)	Severe mental and physical retardation. Caused by extra chromosome. Incidence: about 1 out of 600; increases with age of mother.
Hemophilia*	Blood cannot clot because of lack of clotting factor. Caused by recessive gene; runs in royal families of England, Germany, Russia.
Huntington's chorea	Deterioration of brain and nervous system in middle age. Caused by dominant gene, so child of victim has 50% chance of being afflicted.
Phenylketonuria* (PKU)	Abnormal digestion of protein, leading to mental retardation and death if untreated by special diet. Incidence: about 1 in 15,000 births.
Sickle cell anemia*	Blood cells cannot carry oxygen; painful crises and death by age 40 in severe cases. Incidence: about 1 in 400 black babies; smaller number of Latin Americans.
Spina bifida* (open spine)	The lower portion of the spine is open; may cause death soon after birth or paralysis of the legs and lack of bowel and bladder control. Incidence: 3 in 1,000 births.
Tay-Sachs disease*	Enzyme deficiency causes progressive brain deterioration and death by the age of 3 to 5. Caused by a recessive gene. Eastern European Jews most susceptible.
Thalassemia*	A fatal anemia similar to sickle cell disorder. Greeks and Italians most susceptible.

*Disease can be detected prenatally through amniocentesis or other procedure.

like a fluid—that father's and mother's traits would blend like two kinds of paint to produce an intermediate result in the child. Some traits do in fact work this way—skin color, for example—but that is because such traits depend on many genes. Individual genes work in an all or none way (see box on Mendel).

Although Mendel's basic insight was confirmed by later research, his model of heredity turned out to be too simple. Only a small number of human traits are under the control of a single pair of genes, and most of these have to do with some abnormality such as PKU. Most human traits result from the joint action of several genes, each making a contribution to the total phenotype. Modern geneticists have also discovered that genes interact with one another, that some traits are influenced by three or more genes, not just two as Mendel had thought. For example, human blood groups are based on multiple alleles.

The Norm of Reaction

Finally, there is another concept of fundamental importance to understanding the impact of genetics on development: the norm, or range, of reaction. The same genotype can give rise to an unlimited number of phenotypes, depend-

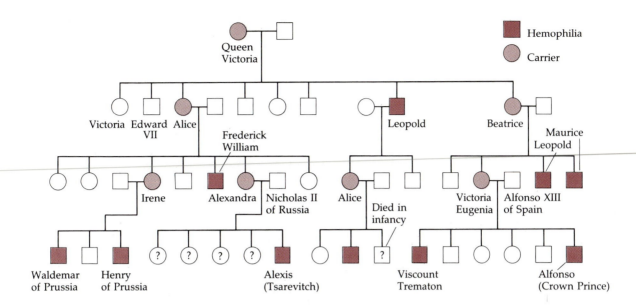

Hemophilia

Carrier

Queen Victoria

Victoria · Edward VII · Alice · Frederick William · Leopold · Beatrice · Maurice Leopold

Irene · Alexandra · Nicholas II of Russia · Alice · Died in infancy · Victoria Eugenia · Alfonso XIII of Spain

Waldemar of Prussia · Henry of Prussia · ? · ? · ? · ? · Alexis (Tsarevitch) · Viscount Trematon · ? · Alfonso (Crown Prince)

ing on the environment in which it develops. Observing how an individual develops in one environment provides no basis for predicting how that same person might have developed in a different environment. Indeed, it is not possible to predict with 100 percent accuracy how the same individual or an identical twin would develop in the same environment (McGuire & Hirsh, 1977).

The norm of reaction may be thought of as a list or graph of different environments that a particular genotype might encounter, and the corresponding phenotype that would result (Lewontin, 1982). For example, consider a person's tendency to be fat. To say that John has a genetic tendency to be fat implies that on a normal diet John is likely to be fatter than other people. But what is a normal diet? In some places, a normal diet might be 2,000 calories a day, in others, 5,000. John might not be fatter than other people if he lived in a place where the average intake was 2,000 calories. Rather than describe John as having a single tendency to be fat, we should chart what his steady body weight would be for each level of caloric intake. This would be John's norm of reaction.

Using the same list of caloric intakes, we could chart another person's steady body weights. A different person is likely to have a different norm of reaction. Thus, while John

FIGURE 4.4
Hemophilia as Pedigree in the Royal Families of Europe
Because Queen Victoria was a carrier of hemophilia, the marriage of her children into the other royal families of Europe spread the recessive gene to each family.

The characteristic Hapsburg lip as family trait.

Mendel

Mendel was an Austrian monk who in his spare time bred pea plants in the monastery gardens. But he was not an ordinary amateur gardener. He studied his plants with the care and precision of a scientist.

Before Mendel, farmers and stockbreeders had carried out a great deal of practical work in genetics. They knew, for example, that some kinds of plants and animals always produced offspring that resembled the parents— Macintosh apples, Arabian horses, people with blue eyes, to name a few. Other kinds showed great variation in their offspring. They also knew that it was possible sometimes to mate two different kinds of parents to produce hybrids—a mule, for instance, is a cross between a horse and a donkey—although the offspring of hybrids were hard to predict. Finally, they had learned that all varieties, even stable ones, occasionally produce "sports"— offspring different from either parent. But the farmers worked by trial and error and often failed to produce the qualities they wanted.

Scientific investigators before Mendel also failed to come up with general principles of inheritance. Some had crossed breeds that varied in too many characteristics. Others failed to keep precise records of the results of each crossing and the characteristics of succeeding generations. In contrast, Mendel was a meticulous observer and recordkeeper, and happened to select a plant ideally suited for genetic research. Peas have a number of stable varieties that can form hybrids—tall or short, green or yellow, smooth or wrinkled, white flowers or purple flowers, and so on.

Mendel's first discovery was dominance. What happened when a tall plant was crossed with a short one, or a smooth one with a wrinkled, or one with yellow flowers and one with purple? He found that rather than producing intermediate results, all of the first generation of hybrids resembled one of the parents. A tall plant crossed with a short plant did not yield medium plants, but all tall plants. However, when these tall hybrids were mated

with one another, one quarter of their offspring were short. Continuing to breed one generation after another, he found that about a third of tall plants produced only tall plants, while the others produced talls and shorts in a ratio of 3 to 1. The short plants produced only short offspring. The other traits worked the same way.

Mendel concluded that there is something in the parent cells that determines the height and other characteristics of the plants. Further, he deduced that this "something"—which we now call genes—comes in two distinct types, (which we now call *alleles*), one of which is dominant over the other. Mendel also believed that genes sorted out independently of one another—that genes for height were transmitted independently of genes for smoothness. Geneticists now know there is more linkage between genes than Mendel suspected. Nevertheless, he had "discovered" the existence of genes and the basic principles of genetics.

Gregor Mendel

might be fatter than Jack at 3,000 calories, he might be thinner than Jack on 1,500 calories a day. In short, the phenotype—the observed trait—is the unique outcome of a particular genotype developing in a particular environment. The genotype does not provide a single "tendency" that appears in all environments, and a given environment will not have the same effect on all genotypes (see Figure 4.5).

Another common but misleading idea about genetics is the cliché that the genes set the limits on a person's development, but the environment determines the extent of development within those limits. The problem with this idea is that the genetic limit or the norm of reaction in humans is unknown. Even in plants and animals, only estimates can be obtained. Knowing how an organism develops in ten environments does not tell you how it will develop in the eleventh. The more varied the conditions, the greater the number of phenotypes that can develop.

The norm of reaction means that there are a multiplicity of developmental outcomes for any genotype. Although the individual's unique genotype is fixed at the moment of conception, the development of the person is not predetermined. The concept of innate and fixed intelligence, or height, is no longer tenable. The idea of the genes as a blueprint is also somewhat misleading, since the organism develops differently according to the context in which it grows. Genes are never expressed directly in a trait. There is a long chain of events that occurs between the information coded into the gene, the physiological processes, the impact of the environment, and the actual trait itself. Even during prenatal development, the environment inside the mother as well as the maturing organism itself influence the chemical events originating in the genes (Gottlieb, 1976).

Developmental Noise

Apart from the influence of genes and environment, there is a third source of individual variation—what geneticist Richard Lewontin calls "developmental noise" (1982, p. 26). De-

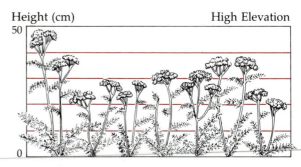
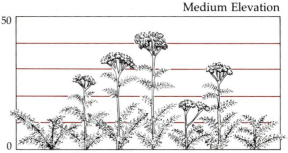
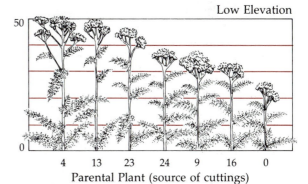

FIGURE 4.5
The Norm of Reaction
Growth of cuttings from seven different individual plants of Achillea when planted at three different elevations.

Source: *Human diversity* by R. Lewontin, 1982, San Francisco: W. H. Freeman.

velopmental noise refers to random events that occur in the complicated process of building an organism from the genetic blueprint. Lewontin gives the example of an asymmetry in fruitflies (drosophila). Many of these flies have more bristles on one side or the other. The two sides of the fly are genetically identical, and there is no reason to assume that the environment differs for each side. Rather, the asymmetry results from developmental noise. The formation of a bristle requires that certain cells grow, divide, and migrate to just the right places at just the right time. Small variations in the molecular structure of these cells will influence the process and can result in great variation in the number of bristles on each side.

Because of developmental noise, differences between individuals may be present at birth and thus "inborn," and yet not be a result of genetic differences. Two children, for example, may possess the genetic capacity to become virtuoso violinists, but in one of them the necessary neural connections might not develop. The interconnections among the billions of neurons in the nervous system are not specified precisely by the genotype.

The development of an organism from its genotype is often compared to the building of a house. The architect prepares the plans in the form of a blueprint, and the carpenter has to use these plans to make the house. In translating the plans into an actual structure, the carpenter must adapt the architect's specifications to the materials at hand. Also, he must sometimes interpret what the architect was trying to say, because not every detail is specified. As a result, two carpenters working with the same set of blueprints may produce somewhat different houses. As a psychologist once put it, "God is a great architect, but a sloppy workman" (quoted in Rosenzweig & Leiman, 1982, p. 127).

The Concept of Heritability

The study of genetics is not merely a scientific issue of interest only to geneticists. The issue of heredity versus environment, or nature versus nurture, is a highly charged question which continues to be debated despite many claims that it has been resolved or fizzled out. (See the discussion in Chapter 3.) It is deeply enmeshed with politics, social policy, and, in some times and places, life and death.

Recently there has been a new interest in genetic explanations of both individual and group differences. Speculation on the role of genes in problematic individual behavior from schizophrenia to criminality to homosexuality has become fashionable in the 1970s and 1980s. As E. O. Wilson argues in his *Sociobiology* (1978), human behavior in general is determined by genes developed in the course of our evolution as a species.

There is no disagreement that many physical traits are strongly influenced by the genes, but the inheritance of *behavior* is a much more controversial issue (Lewontin, 1982). Genes do influence behavior, but in complex ways. Extreme hereditarians have argued that if genes influence a trait, that means environment plays little role. They have assumed that if a trait is heritable, it must be fixed and unchangeable. And extreme environmentalists have resisted the idea of any genetic influence, assuming that individuals are blank slates affected by the environment in uniform ways.

Today, most researchers agree that nature and nurture are inextricably intertwined. As Donald Hebb (1980) puts it, behavior is determined 100 percent by heredity and 100 percent by the environment. Ann Anastasi (1958) argues that we have been asking the wrong questions about heredity and environment. Instead of asking *which one* determines a trait, or *how much* each contributes, we should ask *how* and *in what way* do heredity and environment interact.

Modern geneticists recognize that there is a constant interplay between environment and genes, even within the egg cells. Further, they recognize that the plasticity of behavior, such as the ability to learn and change, can be as "biological" as any alleged fixedness of behavior (Michel & Moore, 1978). In short, while modern genetics does not support the belief of early behaviorists in the basic similarity of all humans (and animals), it also does not support the extreme hereditarian position that the most significant differences between individuals and groups are determined by the genes.

The critical distinction between genotype and phenotype should always be kept in mind when hearing assertions that we are "ruled" by our genes. The genotype is inherited, while the

Fraternal twins

Identical twins

phenotype develops and changes constantly. As Lewontin and his colleagues put it, "At every instant in development (and development goes on until death) the next step is a consequence of the organism's present biological state, which includes both its genes and the physical and social environment in which it finds itself" (Lewontin, Rose, & Kamin, 1984, p. 95). The interaction of heredity and environment is a textbook principle in biology, but it is often ignored by extreme determinists.

Although there is evidence that some behavioral traits run in families, and are therefore influenced to some degree by heredity—intelligence, musical ability, vulnerability to certain mental illness, temperamental traits such as sociability (see the discussion on the heritability coefficient, p. 126)—no one has yet identified a particular gene that accounts for a significant amount of variation of a particular trait in human behaviors.

The concept of **heritability** was originally used by animal breeders. If high rates of milk production in cows was a largely hereditary trait, then the breeders could develop high-producing cows through selective mating. Geneticists, on the other hand, study smaller animals such as rats and mice.

Behavior geneticists typically work with animals to try to determine just which traits are hereditary. They mate brothers and sisters for twenty or thirty generations and thus produce a strain of rats or mice as similar as identical twins. Then they vary the environments in which these inbred animals are raised; any differences in the animals' scores on some tests can then be attributed to environmental influences. By comparing the variation of scores in inbred strains with those of a normal, randomly bred population, investigators can obtain a numerical estimate of heritability of a particular trait, such as fighting in mice.

The concept of heritability is often misunderstood and erroneously applied to human behavior, such as performance on intelligence tests. For obvious moral reasons, researchers cannot create inbred strains of human beings, nor can they manipulate the human environment. It is for these reasons that some geneticists insist that there cannot be an adequate science of human behavior genetics (Cavalli-Sforza & Bodmer, 1978; Lewontin, Rose, & Kamin, 1984).

Nevertheless, the attempt to develop a science of human behavior genetics has been made. As a substitute for the more rigorous methods used by geneticists who study animals, investigators of human genetics have compared people with different degrees of relatedness on various traits. For example, the IQs of identical twins raised together are compared with the IQs of those raised apart. Or the IQs of adopted children are compared with those of both their biological mothers and their adopted mothers. In general, researchers have found support for a genetic component in intelligence, although the size and significance of these findings is the subject of great debate. (We will look at the IQ controversy in greater detail in a later chapter.) However, some serious problems have been raised in connection with the twin studies. One researcher, Cyril Burt, turns out to have published fraudulent data (Hearnshaw, 1979). It has also been pointed out that separated twins are often raised in similar environments, sometimes by a close relative living in the same neighborhood

(Bronfenbrenner, 1972). (See the box on Uncanny Resemblances.)

Assume for the moment that we could get valid heritability estimates for various human traits. There is a great deal of misunderstanding about what such a figure would tell us. Heritability is a population statistic, like divorce or infant mortality rates. It does not tell us about inheritance in a particular individual. For example, if we know that Tom is a foot taller than Dick, can we say that Tom's genes are the reason? Even though height is a highly heritable trait we could not be sure how much of the difference between the two is due to genetics. Dick may have been malnourished or had a growth hormone deficiency. Tom may have had growth hormone injections. If Tom and Dick were identical twins, the difference between them would be entirely environmental.

Heritability is also a fluctuating statistic, based on particular populations in particular

Uncanny Resemblances: Identical Twins Reared Apart

> Any of us could be the man who encounters his double.
> —Friedrich Dürenmatt

You have undoubtedly seen stories about them in the newspapers. Identical twins are separated in infancy and reared by different families. Decades later, they meet. The similarities between them are astonishing.

The twins have similar jobs. They have been married and divorced the same number of times. They both smoke and drink too much and bite their nails. They have the same interests in music, food, and sports. Perhaps the most extreme example is the case of Oskar Stohr and Jack Yuhl. Separated at the age of six months, they were raised on different continents—Yuhl with his father, and Stohr with his mother. They spoke different languages and had different religions. But there were striking similarities. Both were poor in math and good in sports. They had similar tempers. They both tended to fiddle with rubber bands and paper clips; they both had

the habit of flushing the toilet before and after using it (Chen, 1979).

What are we to make of these stories? Quite apart from their relevance to the issue of heredity versus environment, they have a peculiar fascination. The theme of the double—of meeting a second self—is common in literature and mythology. Oscar Wilde's *The Picture of Dorian Gray* is one example, Dostoyevski's early novel *The Double* is another.

The psychoanalyst Otto Rank (1971), one of Freud's original followers, argued that the theme of the double raises issues central to the core of human existence—issues of identity and the fear of death. Rank points to certain features that all tales of the double have in common: the double always resembles the main character down to the smallest details—as if he (it almost always is a he) has stepped out of a mirror. The hero is at first perplexed, but may develop a close friendship with his double. However, catastrophe always follows. The double eventually conspires against the hero. The hero, seeking revenge, tries to kill the double, but ends up destroying himself.

Returning to the issue of heredity and environment, do separated twins provide evidence of the overwhelming power of heredity to shape us as individuals? Some researchers seem to think so. Others remain skeptical. For Lewontin and his associates, stories about amazing resemblances and coincidences between separated identical twins should be considered on a par with reports of ESP, UFOs, and Urie Geller bending spoons with his mental powers. "Scientific research and explanation," they argue, "are concerned above all with the understanding of regularities and repeatable phenomena, not exceptions and flukes, many of which, like the apparent coincidence of behavior of long separated identical twins, simply disappear on close analysis." (Lewontin, Rose, & Kamin, 1984, p. 56).

But do all such similarities disappear on close analysis? Undoubtedly many do. Further, many similarities become less mysterious when we realize that being "reared apart" has been very loosely defined in the twin literature. Many "separated" twins, although living in different families, have had contact with one another in childhood or adolescence. Others, who may have lived in different places, always knew they had a twin somewhere. A further complication is that most separated twins had discovered and come to know one another before they were studied.

Susan Farber (1981) has attempted to sort out the data of what she terms "reputable" separated twin studies to see how much, and in what ways, identical twins do or do not resemble each other. Her findings are complex and at times paradoxical. She concludes that the available data on twins is highly questionable. None of the studies she reviews resolves troublesome questions about how much heredity or environment contributes to any particular trait. In general, her reanalysis raises new questions about these issues.

Farber's findings are complicated and intriguing. On the question of IQ, she concludes that while there may be a genetic component, it is lower than previous studies have estimated. The hypothesis that IQ is determined mainly by heredity appears untenable (p. 208). Nor was their much similarity in attitudes, values, overall personality, or psychopathological symptoms. On the other hand, there were some "eerie" resemblances in such traits as smoking, nail biting, laughing, gestures, and mannerisms such as finger tapping—even in twins raised apart. Twins also resemble one another in physical traits such as the onset of menstruation and menopause and susceptibility to diseases ranging from dental cavities to heart disease to types of psychosis.

Paradoxically, Farber found that twins who had the least contact seemed most alike in their basic styles of personality. She suggests that the very experience of being a twin has a profound psychological effect. Identical twins, she speculates, share basic temperamental predispositions, such as proneness to anxiety, fearfulness, and depression. Raised alone as a single child, the separated twin somehow creates or experiences an environment in tune with his or her basic temperament. When identical twins are raised together, the childrearing scenario gets complicated. The parents and others, confronted by two seemingly indistinguishable children, tend to seek out and exaggerate slight differences between them. For example, if one twin walks slightly earlier than the other, he or she may be labeled "the active one" or "the athlete." The twins themselves are likely to seesaw back and forth between identifying with and differentiating themselves from one another.

Farber concludes that the most forceful theme in her findings concerns individuality as it is revealed in the pattern of similarities and differences between identical twins.

> If separated twins remain similar in many ways despite different homes and social milieus, how must each of us also be unique in our perceptions, our feelings, and our way of shaping the world? If twins, consciously or unconsciously, make themselves different . . . what more do we need to underscore the need of each individual to be an individual? (1981, p. xiv)

environments at particular times. A heritability estimate, whether high or low, is not valid for other populations, or the same population in other circumstances. For example, the heritability of tuberculosis was once high, but now it is low. The reason is that when germs for TB were everywhere, whether or not a person got the disease depended on his or her constitutional susceptibility. Now, the germ is so rare that only people who live in the worst slums are exposed to it. Most people who are susceptible to TB never come into contact with the germ, so the heritability of TB is low.

Technically, the heritability of a trait is the proportion of all the variation of that trait in a population that is accounted for by the genotype. It may be represented in the following way:

$$\text{Heritability or } H^2 = \frac{\text{genetic variance}}{\text{genetic variance} + \text{environmental variance}}$$

In order to use this formula, there has to be variability in the trait being considered. Thus, even though all human beings inherit five fingers, the heritability estimate of that trait would be zero since there is no variation. A lack of heritability in one population does not mean that the trait would show a similar lack of heritability in other populations at other times. Some human traits with high heritability are height, arm length, and foot length.

An important fact about heritability is that knowing how heritable a trait is tells us nothing about how much it can be changed. Many people believe, fallaciously, that "heritable" means resistant to environmental change. However, several inherited diseases are curable. For example, Wilson's disease, which is a defect in copper metabolism, is caused by a single gene disorder. Although it is fatal if untreated, it can be cured by one of the penicillin drugs. Similarly, PKU is an inherited disorder of amino acid metabolism. Infants born with PKU are unable to digest phenalalanine, an amino acid found in milk and other foods. If these infants eat a common diet, brain damage

will result. But this effect can be prevented if the child is placed on a special diet for the first six years.

Turning to more common traits, while height is relatively heritable, it is also strongly influenced by environmental conditions, especially diet. In Japan, in the years following the Second World War, the average height of young people came to exceed their parents' average height by several inches. The height of parents and children was still correlated—but the overall *level* of height increased. The same is true of adopted children's IQs. Adoption studies, as we shall see in more detail in a later chapter, are often cited as evidence for the heritability of IQ. Whatever the correlations may be between the IQs of children and their adopted parents—and there is a great deal of controversy as to the degree of correlation—adoption raises children's IQs significantly (Skodak & Skeels, 1949; Tizard, 1974). This is not surprising when the social characteristics of adopting parents are considered. They are generally solid middle- or upper-class citizens whose personalities and lifestyles have been inspected and approved by adoption agencies.

Finally, it is important to distinguish between heritability and family resemblance. Members of the same family share many characteristics, but not all of them are passed along genetically. For example, parents and children usually belong to the same political party and the same religion, but no one argues that there are Democratic and Republican genes. What about traits such as musical ability, which is often said to run in families and thereby "inherited"? We do not have a great deal of evidence that would allow us to determine how much of this family resemblance is due to growing up in a musical environment and how much is innate in a child.

Genetic Individuality

Although we often think about genetics as the science that explains why certain traits run in families, the other principle of genetics is equally significant: the principle of individual uniqueness.

As we have seen, except for twins, no two individuals are genetically identical. (And even identical twins have slight facial differences which enable their parents to tell them apart.) Individual variation is not confined to human beings. All animal species that reproduce sexually produce uniquely different offspring. As Darwin first pointed out, this individuality is essential to species survival. For example, a new pesticide may kill 999 out of 1,000 mosquitos. But if the thousandth mosquito survives because it is genetically different, the future of the species may be assured (Hamburger, 1978).

Thus, the genetic information in the genotype makes us in some ways like all other people, in some ways like some other people, and in many ways unlike anyone else. Our genes determine that we will be human beings, not dogs or chickens or gorillas. We inherit not only the bodily form of homo sapiens—that is, "intelligent man"—but also certain capacities that are the most highly developed of all primates, if not unique to our species: capacities for self-awareness, the ability to use symbols and vocalize, and the depth of social interaction.

Our genes also make us like some people and unlike others. Family members are apt to resemble each other, and one group of people will be distinguishable from another group in outward physical characteristics such as skin color, hair color, the shape of eyes and noses. These features have been used to characterize races; but although racial differences are striking to the eye, and have important social consequences, they are based on only a small number of genes. The biggest differences are between individuals, and these individual differences overshadow those between population groups (Cavalli-Sforza & Bodmer, 1978).

The outward signs of individuality are familiar—faces, signatures, and fingerprints. The individuality of our internal organs is less well known, but even more striking. As we saw in Chapter 1, there is no such thing as an average or typical body part: stomach, heart, liver, nasal passages, muscles, and nerves show wide variations in size and shape.

The full extent of genetic individuality has been realized only in recent years, and its discovery is one of the landmarks of modern biology (Hamburger, 1978). Researchers trying to transplant organs from one person to another, or from one animal to another, discovered that somehow the body is able to identify the transplanted organ as foreign and reject it. Yet tissue from one part of an individual's body to another is not rejected, nor are transplants from one twin to another. It became clear that within the same species—human, dog, goat, or mouse—no two individuals are alike, and each is able to "recognize" another individual from the same species as different. The countless enzymes that make up any animal vary in structure and function. In the past few years, this *polymorphism*—this existence of a species in different forms—has been found in organisms lower and lower down the evolutionary scale, down to the level of microbes.

This inborn individuality has profound implications for psychological development as well as for the health of the individual. Consider its implications for health. The doctor's job is complicated by the fact that individuals do not respond to drugs in a uniform way. For example, while aspirin, penicillin, antihistamines, or other drugs may be beneficial to most people, they produce a variety of responses. Some people may not be helped by the drug, some may have mild side effects, some may have reactions severe enough to result in death—as in penicillin shock, for example. Unlike the chemist describing the effects of adding one chemical to another, the doctor, trying to describe the effects of a drug on a person, is faced with a certain amount of unpredictability and indeterminacy.

For similar reasons, the job of the psychologist is immensely complicated by the fact of individual uniqueness. The hope of Watson and other behaviorists that it would be possible to write general laws of behavior that would apply not only across all peoples but across all species turned out to be naive (Hinde & Stevenson-Hinde, 1973; Seligman, 1970).

Describing human development is especially complicated by individual differences. If every newborn infant comes into the world with a unique physiology, the idea of "normality," or the concept of the child as a blank slate, becomes meaningless. Not all individual differences at birth are genetic. Some can be due to influences in the uterine environment, such as the mother's use of drugs, or to the birth process itself. Nevertheless, we are unique individuals before the external world can affect us, and our uniqueness makes us respond to that world in our own ways.

For example, each of us has a distinct number of nerve endings in our skin and sensory organs. This makes us differentially sensitive to the environment. As one researcher put it, "People live in different worlds so far as their sensory reactions are concerned" (Williams, 1976, p. 3). Thus, people have different reactions to temperature: the same room may be too hot for one person, too cold for another. One person can be extremely sensitive to smells, others may be oblivious to all but the strongest. Many of the little differences between husbands and wives, parents and children that can lead to annoyance or irritation may derive from these quirks of physiological individuality.

People not only vary in reaction to the everyday world of sensory experience, but to pain as well. Doctors and nurses have often observed that individuals differ a great deal in their responses to the pain of injuries, disease, and medical procedures. In the past, they assumed that the same kind of injury, say an ulcer or a broken leg, would cause everyone the same amount of pain, but that some people could "take" it better than others. Recent evidence suggests, however, that a great deal of the difference in response to pain lies in an individual's neurological sensitivity, rather than in self-control or bravery. Given the same injury, some people will actually feel acute pain, some mild pain, and some none at all (Petrie, 1978).

Finally, there is evidence that each individual has a distinct pattern of response to stress. The **autonomic nervous system** produces bodily response to emotional arousal such as sweaty palms, a faster heart rate, the dilation and constriction of blood vessels, stomach contractions, and other changes. John and Beatrice Lacey (1970) have found that individuals have distinct patterns of autonomic response. What they term "autonomic response specificity" emerged from longitudinal studies extending from early childhood to adulthood. In their studies, the Laceys provoked autonomic responses by such stressful conditions as plunging hands into ice cold water, applying intense stimuli to the skin, and presenting people with rapidly paced arithmetic calculations. Individuals reveal distinct patterns of response across these situations which are evident even in newborns. Some babies responded with marked heart rate changes, others with changes in stomach motility, still others with increases in blood pressure. These patterns remained remarkably consistent over time and may help to explain what diseases a person may be susceptible to later in life. Thus, some of us may develop ulcers in response to stress, and others high blood pressure.

Even though our society supposedly values the individual, individual differences are often regarded as abnormal deviance. Families, schools, and communities often expect children to respond to events and situations in similar ways and to follow a uniform timetable of development. Children who vary from the norm may be labeled as sick or bad or "atypical." We are highly sensitive to age differences—we do not expect two-year-olds to act like three-year-olds—but we are not as sensitive to individual variations *within* developmental stages.

Prenatal Development

The earliest stages of human development unfold in darkness and are still the least understood. Prenatal development has been enveloped in myth and superstition. For example, it took human beings a long while to discover that men have a role to play in the making of babies; anthropologists tell us there are still some societies that do not understand this. In some times and places, people have believed many acts of intercourse, not just one, are necessary to create and nourish a new life.

Our own Western society has had its share of superstitious beliefs about prenatal development. Perhaps the most widespread one concerns prenatal influences on the child: almost anything the pregnant mother did or even thought was at one time believed to affect the child. Birth defects in particular were attributed to the mother's experiences during pregnancy: if a child was born with a "strawberry mark," it might be because the mother had crushed a strawberry; if the child was born with a harelip, it might be because the mother saw, or dreamed about, a rabbit.

As scientists learned more about prenatal development, they overthrew many of the old superstitions. They learned that the fetus is far more independent of the mother than had been assumed. The blood systems of mother and child do not mix directly, and there are no direct nerve connections between them. For some time, scientists assumed that the opposite of the old superstition was true: they thought the unborn child was perfectly insulated from the environment; the only direct effect the mother had on the fetus was the food she ate and the oxygen she supplied to the fetus by her blood.

In recent years ideas of prenatal influence have changed once again. Superstitions about maternal impressions have not been revived, but the thalidomide tragedy of the early 1960s revealed that the unborn child is affected by more than just what the mother eats. As explained later in this chapter, we have learned that drinking, smoking, taking drugs—or medications—as well as the mother's general health and her emotional state can influence the environment in which the unborn baby develops.

There is still much that is unknown about prenatal development. At the beginning of the process, we do not know why it is that one sperm cell out of many millions is selected to fertilize an egg. And, although the structure of DNA has been worked out, and the genetic code has been cracked, scientists still do not understand how cells join together to form tissues and organs, or how all the various parts of the body are joined to form whole organisms. Francis Crick, one of the discoverers of the structure of DNA, points to the paradox of developmental biology:

> We understand how an organism can build molecules (even very large molecules) in great variety and with great precision, although the largest of them is far too minute for us to see, even with a high-powered microscope; yet we do not understand how it builds a flower, or a hand, or an eye, all of which are plainly visible to us. (1977, p. 300)

The Stages of Prenatal Development

By the end of the second month after fertilization, the embryo for the first time resembles a miniature human being—and is at this stage called a fetus. The basic components of every essential body part are in place. From this time until birth, the fetus grows in size and the body parts become more finely sculpted. The entire process of transformation from fertilized egg to newborn baby takes about nine months or thirty-eight weeks.

The growth of normal, healthy fetuses is difficult to follow. Scientists have had to rely on the study of spontaneously aborted embryos, medically aborted fetuses, and prematurely born infants. They have had to assume that these babies have grown in the same way as infants who develop in the uterus for the normal length of time.

Scientists have divided prenatal development into three periods. The first, the **germinal stage,** lasts from fertilization until the time the egg is implanted in the uterus—about one week. Fertilization usually takes place in one of the fallopian tubes leading from the ovaries to the uterus (Figure 4.6). During the journey to the uterus, the zygote divides steadily. By the time of implantation, the original cell has multiplied to about 150 cells, which take the form of a hollow ball called the **blastocyst** (Tanner, 1978).

FIGURE 4.6
Fertilization, Cell Division, and Implantation
Once the ovum is fertilized by the sperm, the newly formed zygote begins to divide and passes down the fallopian tube. By the time the zygote reaches the uterus, it has developed into a fluid-filled blastocyst which then implants itself in the endometrium of the uterus.

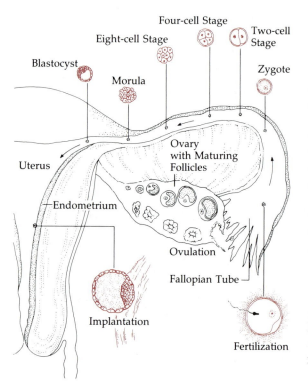

It is possible to remove a blastocyst and implant it in the womb of a foster mother. This is done routinely in the breeding of certain animals. Recently, doctors have succeeded in fertilizing human egg cells in test tubes and implanting the fertilized ovum in a woman's uterus. The process has resulted in many famous babies—the first of whom was Louise Brown—and a number of serious ethical issues. (See the box on New Ways of Creating Babies.)

The **embryonic stage** is the second period of fetal development. It lasts about six weeks, from the time the blastocyst is implanted in the uterus—at which time it is called an **embryo**—until the embryo takes on a recognizable human form. From the outer layer of the blastocyst, the **placenta**—the fleshy disc that is an organ in itself, which connects the unborn child to the mother—is formed. The embryo itself takes form from the inner area of the blastocyst (Tanner, 1978).

The third stage of prenatal development, the **fetal stage,** lasts from the beginning of the third month until birth. The dividing line between the embryonic and the fetal stages is the appearance of the first bone cells. The skeleton of the embryo is made of cartilage, the material, for example, in the soft part of our noses (Annis, 1978). The **fetus** at this stage also has a heart that beats and a nervous system able to show reflex responses to touch. It is about an inch long.

The earliest stages of development are the

New Ways of Creating Babies

In recent years, science has developed a large array of artificial methods for creating life. The age of the test tube baby is well under way, raising a host of legal, moral, and social problems. Among the various techniques are the following: (1) Artificial insemination by donor: A married woman is inseminated by a male donor's sperm. This method has been widely practiced since the 1960s and has led to an estimated 250,000 births in the United States alone. (2) Surrogate motherhood: A couple pays a woman to be artificially inseminated by the husband's sperm. She gives birth to the child and gives it up for adoption by the couple. The legal status of surrogate motherhood is highly uncertain. Some states are considering legalizing it, others are considering measures that would ban the practice. (3) In vitro fertilization: An egg is removed from a woman's ovary, is fertilized by her husband's sperm, and is transferred to the woman's womb. The complete array of techniques is shown in the diagram.

The reason for all the new techniques is infertility. About one in six American couples is infertile, a large increase over previous decades. Part of the increase is due to higher rates of genital infections; another reason is

that couples are postponing having children until their thirties when fertility is somewhat lower than in the twenties. Further, the possibilities of adoption have been drastically reduced in recent years because of the availability of abortion and the growing social acceptance of single motherhood.

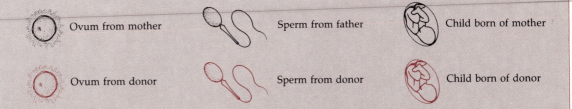

| Ovum from mother | Sperm from father | Child born of mother |
| Ovum from donor | Sperm from donor | Child born of donor |

AID: Artificial Insemination by Donor

1. Father infertile

2. Mother infertile and unable to carry child

3. Both parents infertile, but mother able to carry child

4. Mother infertile but able to carry child

IVF: In-vitro Fertilization

1. Mother fertile but unable to conceive

2. Father infertile, mother fertile but unable to conceive

3. Mother infertile but able to carry child

4. Both parents infertile, but mother able to carry child

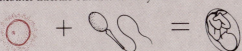

5. Mother infertile and unable to carry child

6. Both parents infertile, mother unable to carry child

7. Mother unable to carry child, but both parents fertile

8. Mother fertile but unable to carry child, father infertile

Source: "The new origins of life," *Time*, 124, September 10, 1984.

Louise Brown, the first test tube baby

most hazardous. In fact, most fertilized ova fail to develop into newborn infants. About 10 percent fail to implant themselves in the uterus, and about 50 percent are spontaneously aborted, even before the mother is certain she is pregnant. Usually these aborted embryos are defective in some way (Tanner, 1978).

It is also during these earliest stages of development that the unborn child is most vulnerable to environmental damage. The times when body parts such as eyes, ears, hearts, arms, and legs are forming are critical periods. Thus, if a woman has German measles during the first three months of pregnancy, her baby may be born with deafness, eye defects, and heart disease. The drug thalidomide, which

mothers took in this early period as a sleeping pill, took its horrendous toll by causing babies to develop without any arms or legs, but with hands and feet attached directly to the body. (It seems hard to believe now, but before the thalidomide tragedy, people were generally unaware of how vulnerable the fetus is to drugs taken by the mother. I recall that period very well because I was pregnant then, just as the terrible effects of the drug were being discovered. Thanks to a vigilant federal Drug Administration doctor, thalidomide was never allowed to be prescribed in this country.)

Although the most dramatic changes take place during the germinal and embryonic periods, the fetal stage lasts the longest. The infant grows in size and its body parts become more elaborate and differentiated. During the third month, the external genitals develop, and the sex of the fetus can be observed.

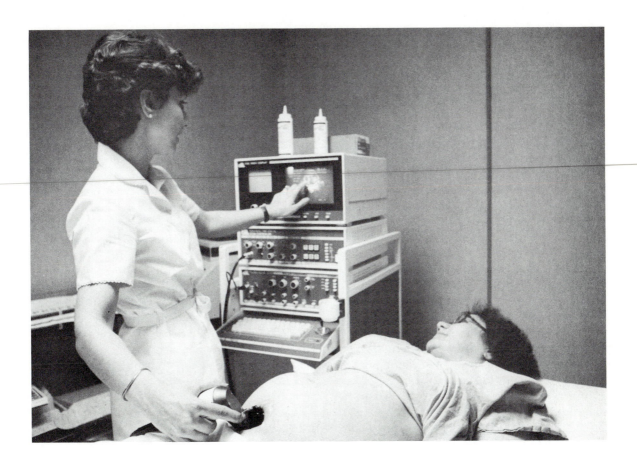

Ultrasound technician using a Real Time Digital Ultrasound Scanner on a woman in her seventeenth week of pregnancy.

By the end of the fourth month, the fetus is about six inches long and weighs approximately six ounces. Around this time, there are two changes that make the mother aware that there is a child growing inside her. The fetal heartbeat can be heard through a stethoscope, and the fetus's movements can be felt—an experience known as quickening. The fetus not only can move its arms and legs, but can suck, swallow, hiccup, blink its eyes, and turn its head. Some fetuses of this age can even suck their thumbs (Annis, 1978). There is growing evidence that the activities of the fetus are a kind of exercise of its sensory and motor systems in preparation for later life outside the womb. Further, these activities may be necessary for the maturation of the nervous system during prenatal development (Gottlieb, 1976).

Despite this repertoire of activities, the fetus is not ready for survival outside the womb until the last three months of pregnancy. Although the fetus can breathe on its own by the sixth month, and it sometimes inhales the amniotic fluid—resulting in hiccups—its respiratory system is too weak to sustain breathing movements outside the womb. Also, the brain and nervous system are too immature to coordinate activities necessary to sustain life. Recent medical advances, however, have made it possible to keep alive many babies born during the sixth month. Sustaining such an infant requires careful attention in intensive-care nurseries. These advances have raised serious ethical problems, since these very premature infants may suffer from serious defects: should doctors use their technological abilities to sustain life without regard for the quality of life the child is capable of living, or the impact on the parents and their other children?

Seven months or twenty-eight weeks is the age of viability—the first time the baby is able to survive on its own if born prematurely. A child born during the seventh month has about a 50 percent chance of surviving, if kept in a heated incubator and protected from infection and temperature change. During the eighth month it has a 90 percent chance, and at the end of the ninth month it has a 99 percent chance of surviving (Guttmacher, 1973). Recent technological advances in intensive care have made it possible to increase the survival rate of premature infants. The premature infant is vulnerable to infection because the mother's antibodies are not transmitted to the fetus until the ninth month of pregnancy. If a fetus is born earlier, it will not have its own immunities. It needs an incubator to keep it warm and protect it from germs. Low birth weight is another complication of prematurity (see p. 140). During the final two to four weeks of pregnancy, the fetus gains a significant amount of weight (Tanner, 1974).

Psychological Development of the Fetus

When does the unborn baby make the leap from being a biological organism to a psychological being? Does the fetus perceive and feel anything? Does it have conscious experience? These questions have both fascinated and perplexed psychologists for a long time.

Determining the beginning point of psychological experience is a thorny problem. Philosophers have been debating for centuries whether it is possible to prove consciousness in a full-grown adult, and behavioristic psychologists traditionally denied the existence of conscious experience. Recently, there has been a great resurgence of interest in consciousness; neuropsychologists have shown that different patterns of electrical activity in the brain ac-company different mental activities and states of consciousness (Uttal, 1978).

However, as mentioned above, it is difficult to study behavior in the uterus. Most of the data on fetal behavior are from observations made on fetuses that had to be removed prematurely from the mothers. Such fetuses suffer from lack of oxygen, changes in temperature and pressure, and the anesthetics that may have been given to the mother.

Some psychologists believe that before birth the fetus is simply a biological entity, somewhat like a patient in a coma who is attached to life-sustaining machines. In this view, fetal movements are physiological, not psychological, events: they exercise muscles and limbs, increase circulation, and prevent the fetus from adhering to the membranes which surround it. Other psychologists suggest that the beginning of psychological behavior is the point at which the central nervous system is activated (Carmichael, 1970), or when the fetus begins to respond to environmental events in a unified manner.

Given these conflicts of interpretation, how can we answer the question of whether the fetus is a psychological being? Perhaps the best way to deal with the issue is to start with the newborn and work backward. If we regard the newborn as a psychological being, it seems appropriate to ask, When does the fetus's central nervous system and/or its behavioral capabilities attain the level of the newborn's? One possible answer might be at about twenty-eight weeks—the beginning of the age of viability. At this age, the nervous system as well as other major systems are far enough along in their development so that the infant born at this time has a fair chance of surviving. The preterm infant can cry, suck, and swallow, although weakly, and turn away from bright light and loud sound.

However, this kind of behavior does not mean that the fetus is experiencing anything; people who are unconscious—in a stupor or a coma—also show such responsiveness. Indeed, the lack of response to external stimuli is what doctors use to tell the difference between deep coma and death (Smith, 1984).

One recent study concluded that it is not until thirty-eight or forty weeks—the ninth month—that the fetus develops the behavioral capabilities shown by a full-term newborn. J. G. Nijhuis and his associates (1982) studied fourteen fetuses (in utero) from thirty-two weeks of gestation onward. They were looking for the age of onset of what they termed "organized behavioral states"; they considered such a state to occur when fetal body and eye movements and heart rate patterns were coordinated. Before thirty-eight to forty weeks, they found, "true" behavioral states did not occur.

Apart from the issue of the fetus's psychological capabilities, there is probably not much to experience in the womb. There is no light, no hunger, no heat, no cold, and no pain. There are no objects to touch, and although sounds can pass through the watery environment, the fetus may not hear them because its outer ears are closed and its middle ears are filled with liquid. Some researchers have tried experimentally to condition fetuses in the eighth and ninth month of pregnancy using classical conditioning—the kind used by Pavlov and in the early work of Watson and of Spelt (1948). Spelt used a loud noise as the unconditioned stimulus, while the conditioned stimulus was a mild vibration. Although he reported successful results, his findings have not been replicated by others. More recent research has shown that classical conditioning probably does not occur even in newborns (Sameroff & Cavanaugh, 1979).

Further evidence that prenatal experience, if any, is dim and muted is the fetus's relative insensitivity to pain. Neither fetuses nor newborns show very much response to pain for several hours or even days after birth. Their sensitivity to pain, as measured by the number of pinpricks needed to cause withdrawal of the stimulated area, increases rapidly within the first few days after birth (Annis, 1978).

Finally, newborns themselves are neurologically immature organisms. Although at the time of birth the child has a complete set of nerve cells, the so-called higher parts of the brain, such as the various lobes of the cerebral cortex or gray matter, are not fully developed. In fact, the brain of the human infant, unlike that of any other animal, triples in size during the first year. The cerebral cortex is the area of the brain that distinguishes humans from our primate relatives (Figure 4.7).

There is a correlation between the proportion of cerebral cortex in an organism's brain and its rank on the evolutionary scale. Rats, for example, have very little. All complex kinds of psychological functioning, such as memory, thought, and language, as well as sensory perception and voluntary movement, take place in the cerebral cortex. Although newborn babies are competent in many ways, according to several criteria of brain development they are essentially precortical organisms and remain so for several months (Conel, 1954; Woodruff, 1978). The association areas of the brain—the areas which integrate perceptions from the various senses and thus are responsible for conceptual thought—develop more slowly than the areas directly concerned with the senses, such as hearing and sight, or with movement. (See Figure 4.8 and the box on Prenatal Brain Development.)

Birth

The climax of the drama of prenatal development is, of course, the moment of birth. Birth has been thought of as both triumph and tragedy—an awakening to freedom and life, or an expulsion from Paradise. Freud saw birth as the primal anxiety state, the model for all our later terrors. Here is Dr. Frederick Leboyer, the French obstetrician, describing his view of the birth process:

> Hell exists, and is white hot. It is not a fable. But we go through it at the beginning of our lives, not the end. Hell is what the child goes through to reach us. Its flames assail the child from every side; they burn its eyes, its skin, they sear its flesh, they devour. This fire is what the baby feels when the air rushes into the lungs. (1975, p. 20)

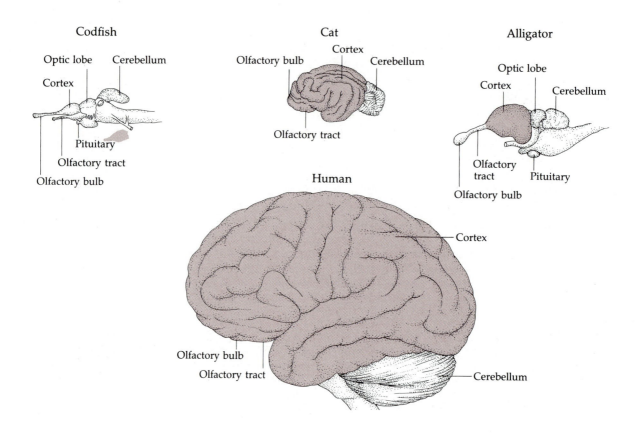

FIGURE 4.7
A Comparison of Vertebrate Brains
The brains are not drawn to scale, but notice the proportionally different sizes of the cerebral cortex that have evolved.

Source: *Human neuroanatomy* by R. C. Truex & M. B. Carpenter, 1964, Baltimore: Williams & Wilkins.

Leboyer's method has babies born in darkened, silent rooms, rather than the brightly lit and noisy atmosphere of the usual delivery room. Immediately after birth, the baby is placed on its mother's stomach and gently massaged. After several minutes of soothing, the umbilical cord is cut and the baby is bathed in warm, body-temperature water. The baby is placed in water to reduce the trauma of the transition from uterine weightlessness to the feel of gravitational pull on the body. Leboyer claims that babies delivered in this way are healthier, happier, and less anxious than those subject to the more common birth procedures which he considers "cruel."

We will never know exactly what babies experience during birth, but other obstetricians who have watched babies closely after delivery do not agree that they are traumatized. After the first cry, most babies seem to calm down and adjust to their new environment. Babies whose mothers have received no drugs are often remarkably alert (Macfarlane, 1977).

It is true, as Leboyer points out, that passing through the birth canal puts great physical pressure on the child; hemorrhages are fairly common, and even bones can be broken. Babies who are delivered by cesarean section—removed through an incision in the mother's abdomen—do not experience this crushing passage. Yet there is no evidence that such individuals grow up to be any different from people born the usual way.

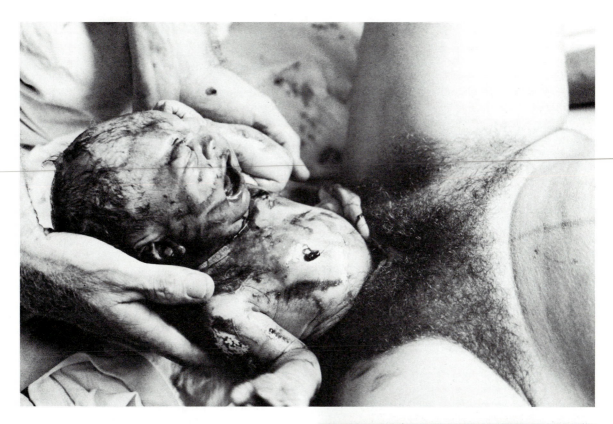

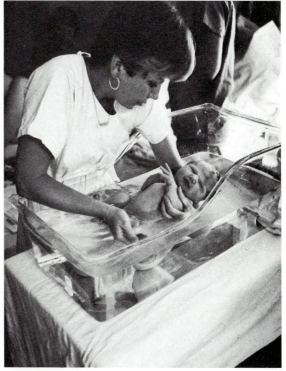

Many researchers are skeptical about the assumptions underlying Leboyer's ideas. At best, they feel, gentle birthing merely postpones the newborn's inevitable contact with the cold, noisy world for a half hour or so. From a medical standpoint, other obstetricians have also been skeptical of Leboyer's methods; many feel that his ideas may actually be dangerous. For example, delay in cutting the umbilical cord may increase chances of infection or other complications. Still, "gentle" birth has an intuitive appeal to many parents.

Birth Complications

Although most babies are born without any complications, and most of those with birth complications grow up normally anyhow, the perinatal period—which includes the time before and shortly after birth—is the most hazardous stage of a baby's new life outside of the womb. We saw earlier that about half of all

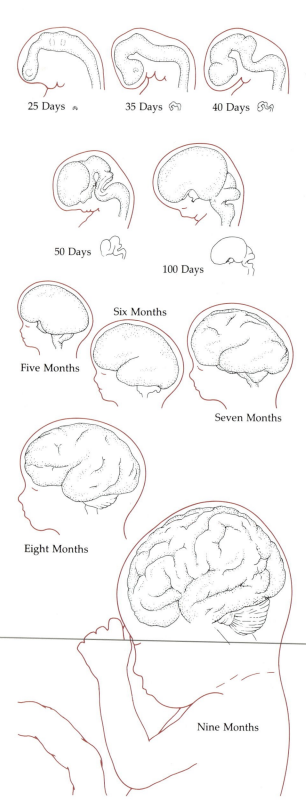

25 Days

35 Days

40 Days

50 Days

100 Days

Five Months

Six Months

Seven Months

Eight Months

Nine Months

FIGURE 4.8
Prenatal Brain Development
The development of the prenatal brain is shown here from the embryonic stage—during which the brain end of the neural tube differentiates into the hindbrain, midbrain, and forebrain—to full term, when many of the secondary folds of the brain which make the brain distinctly human have been created. The smaller illustrations directly below the top row show the embryonic brain in proportion to that of the later months.

Source: "The development of the brain" by W. M. Cowan, 1979, in Scientific American, *The brain: A Scientific American book,* San Francisco: W. H. Freeman & Co.

embryos are spontaneously aborted. While the later stages of pregnancy do not have such high casualty rates, it has been estimated that of the approximately 3.5 million fetuses that reach twenty weeks of gestational age in the United States in any year, 50,000 die before birth, another 50,000 die in the first month after birth, 50,000 have severe congenital defects, and another 30,000 have learning disabilities or are mildly or severely retarded (Babson & Benson, 1971). This range of deviant pregnancy outcomes has been labeled as the "continuum of reproductive casualty" (Pasamanick & Knobloch, 1961, 1966).

Four factors in the perinatal period that have been related to developmental difficulties are anoxia (or lack of oxygen), other complications of delivery, low birth weight, and the socioeconomic status of the mother. The social factor turns out to be the most important of all, as we shall see shortly.

Anoxia occurs when the supply of oxygen available to an organism falls below its requirements. At any age the nervous system and brain are highly vulnerable to anoxia: a drop in oxygen levels can destroy brain tissue. Anoxia during birth can result from pressure on the baby's head as he emerges from his mother, or from a delay in breathing. About 5 percent of newborns experience some anoxia. Despite the

A Calendar of Prenatal Brain Development

Day 1½   First division of fertilized cell. Two-cell stage.

Day 4   Ball of 60–70 cells.

Day 5   Blastocyst enters uterus from fallopian tube. Ball becomes hollow with a mass of cells at one end.

Day 6–9   Cells separate into 3 layers. Embryo ⅟₁₀₀ of inch long.

Day 10–13   Primitive streak is formed: a bulge in the outside layer (ectoderm) that is the origin of the spinal cord.

Day 18   Nervous system starts to form. This is sometimes called the neurola stage because focus of development is on this system.

Day 20   Neural tube now formed along length of the primitive streak.

End of Week 3   Brain end of neural tube swells out. The 3 major divisions of the brain—hindbrain, midbrain, and forebrain—begin to differentiate.

End of Week 4   Nervous system arches over to resemble a cane.

End of Week 6   Brain begins to lose simple canelike form. The 3 main parts of the brain are distinct bulges.

End of Week 7   Forward swelling of the brain is very large. This will become the cerebral hemisphere—the folded gray matter on the outside of the brain, as well as some of the internal structures. After this point, the brain folds over as the cerebral hemispheres eventually envelop most of the rest of the brain. The brain is less than ½ inch in diameter. Neurons are developing at the rate of thousands per minute.

End of Month 3   The brain now looks like a small, smooth boxing glove with wrinkles at the wrist end. The size is still little more than ½ inch. Fetus capable of reflex responses to touch, first on the face, then on the body.

End of Month 4   The division between two halves of the brain becomes visible. More reflexes are possible, including swallowing and sucking.

End of Month 5   Brain almost 2 inches from front to rear. Other divisions or fissures of the brain become apparent. Heartbeat can be heard. Fetus less than 1 pound. Full quota of nerve cells—12–15 billion—are present. Myelinization, the sheathing of the nerve fibers, has begun but will not be completed for several years after birth.

End of Month 6   Brain surface is still smooth, but the sylvian fissure between the two sides of the brain is very marked. Reflexes include gripping with hands, opening and closing eyelids.

End of Month 7   Boxing glove smoothness begins to disappear. Brain 3 inches from front to rear. Retinal layers of the eye are completed, and the eye can respond to light.

End of Month 8   All of the primary folds of the brain are present, but many secondary ones will continue to form after birth.

Month 9   The fetus adds 50% to its weight in the last month. Brain becomes considerably more convoluted. At 8 months, it looked like the brain of a primitive mammal. At 9 months, it is clearly human. Although the fetus is very active at this point, and has many reflexes, there is no evidence that the "higher" portion of the brain, the cerebral cortex, has any influence on behavior now or in the first few weeks after birth.

Birth   Although the baby's head takes a considerable battering during birth, there is little evidence of damage in the normal run of births. Parents are often alarmed at the misshapen heads of their newborns, but the vast majority of them have nothing to worry about.

Source: *The mind* by A. Smith, 1984, New York: Viking.

seeming vulnerability of the newborn to the effects of oxygen deprivation, however, very few anoxic infants seem to suffer long-lasting developmental deficits later on. Anoxia affects behavior during infancy and even the preschool period, but by school age these differences tend to disappear. The same is true of other complications, such as long labor (Sameroff & Chandler, 1975).

More lasting complications may arise from low birth weight or prematurity. At birth, the average American middle-class baby weighs a little over seven pounds and is twenty inches long. Girls and babies from low income groups are usually shorter and lighter. Pregnancy commonly lasts 266 days from conception, or 280 days from the last menstrual period, but babies have been known to survive birth as few as 180 days and as long as 334 days after conception. Babies born between thirty-seven and forty-two weeks are called **term** babies. Those born earlier are called **preterm** babies (or ''preemies''), and those born later, **postterm**.

The weight of a baby at birth is more significant than the precise length of time it remained within the womb. In the past, all babies who weighed less than 5½ pounds at birth were called ''premature.'' Recently, the word ''prematurity'' has dropped from scientific usage and has been replaced by the term ''low birth weight.'' Low birth weight can be due to a baby being born too early or being pathologically small for its actual age.

The distinction is important, because leaving the uterus too early may not in itself be harmful, but growing at less than a normal rate suggests that something has gone wrong during prenatal development. Premature babies eventually ''catch up'' to what their weight would have been had they been born at the normal time. But small-for-term babies do not usually catch up to normals. Unless treated, they may grow to be abnormally small children and adults, and their mental abilities may be impaired.

Malnutrition is one of the leading causes of low birth weight. Poor countries and poor people in well-off countries have the highest incidence of low birth weight babies. In the

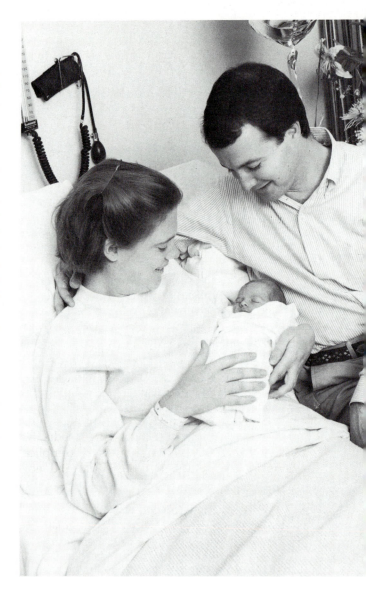

United States, for example, the incidence among nonwhites is about twice the rate among whites—13 percent versus 7 percent (Niswander & Gordon, 1972).

Another factor in low birth weight is smoking. Women who smoke tend to have lighter babies and greater rates of perinatal mortality (Frazier et al., 1961). Substances in cigarettes, especially nicotine and carbon monoxide, impair fetal development by reducing the amount of oxygen and nutrients that pass through the placenta. It is also possible that the link between smoking and perinatal problems is the mother's emotional state. Women who smoke do so because they may experience more stress and anxiety than nonsmokers. There is evidence that prolonged emotional stress—not the "normal" stresses of daily life—can have negative effects on the child, including low birth weight and irritability (Sontag, 1966). Although there are no direct connections between the mother's nervous system and the fetus's, when strong rage, fear, or anxiety is felt, certain hormones such as adrenalin are released into the blood stream. These chemicals can cross the placental barrier and affect the fetus.

Drinking alcohol also affects the weight of the fetus. If the mother drinks a great deal, the baby may be born with fetal alcohol syndrome, which was first identified in 1973 (K. L. Jones & D. W. Smith, 1973). A baby whose mother consumed a great deal of alcohol will have a face of a distinct appearance; it will show insufficient development around the eyes, nose, and upper lip. Other drugs and environmental factors can also influence the fetus.

The most important factor in reproductive casualty, however, is not medical complications in themselves, but the social and economic situation of the mother. Lower-income mothers are three to four times more likely to experience problems in pregnancy and delivery than middle-class mothers. Poor nutrition, poor health, and greater exposure to disease, emotional stress, and a lack of adequate medical care are some of the reasons why perinatal problems are high among low-income mothers. When good prenatal care is available, socioeconomic differences in birth complications tend to disappear. In other industrial countries, access to good medical care for pregnant women and infants is not limited to the middle class. The United States is the only advanced industrial country without such care, and our infant mortality rates, which are comparatively high, reflect this.

Infants born into poor environments are not only more likely to suffer from perinatal complications, but they are more likely to suffer lasting effects from them. Social and economic factors seem to reduce or amplify the effects of birth complications. Thus, in middle-class families, children with birth complications tend to show few or no effects later on, while children from poor homes, with the same complications, often show retardation or physical or emotional problems. (See the box on the Baby Doe Dilemma.)

The Baby Doe Dilemma

"I don't care if it's a boy or a girl as long as it's healthy." That has been the standard response of expectant parents to equally standard questions about what sex they prefer. Unfortunately, some babies come into this world who are far from healthy. The birth of a deformed and retarded infant has always been a family tragedy. In the past, the parents endured their pain in privacy; with their doctor, they would review the options, if any, and come to a quiet decision. But today, parents must make difficult and complex decisions in the glare of public controversy. The treatment of handicapped newborns has been radically transformed by medical technology, government intervention, and political agitation.

Consider the case of the infant called "Baby Jane Doe." Born on October 11, 1983, to a couple in Long Island, New York, she had spina bifida, which caused an open spine, an abnormally small skull, "water on the brain," and other deformities. Without an operation, the doctors said, the infant could live from 6 weeks to 2 years. With surgery, she might be able to live until she is 20, but she would remain profoundly retarded, epileptic, bedridden, and paralyzed from the waist

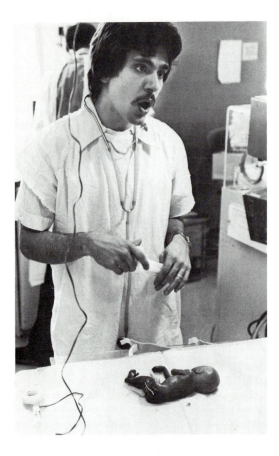

As the babies they treat get smaller and smaller, doctors are faced with more difficult choices about when to let nature "take its course." The 22-week-old fetus on the *left* was brought into the hospital weighing only 14 oz. No life-intervening measures were taken. In the *right*-hand picture, at the same hospital, a father touches his son who was born premature, weighing only 1 lb., 14 oz. Although he was critically ill at birth, he gained weight, and in this picture weighs 2 lbs., 5 oz. Eventually, the baby recovered and went home.

down. It also seemed likely that she would never be aware of herself or the world. After consulting with their doctors, social workers, and clergy, Baby Jane's parents decided to forego the surgery and let nature take its course.

If Baby Jane had been born a decade or more ago, her story would have remained a quiet family tragedy. Instead, she became the focus of a heated national controversy. Three days after her birth, a lawyer with no connection to the family or the case took Baby Jane's parents to court. Contacted by an anonymous informant, he had filed a suit to order the doctors to operate. A New York State Supreme Court justice ordered the surgery, but was later overruled. The appeals court found that the parents had chosen a reasonable option and denounced the lawsuit as "offensive and distressing."

Meanwhile, the United States government entered the case. At the urging of right-to-life and handicapped advocacy groups, the surgeon general asked to see the baby's medical records. The government argued that it wanted to find out if the baby was being denied surgery because she was so handicapped her life wasn't considered worth saving. If so, the government argued, the hospital could be in violation of a federal law prohibiting discrimination against handicapped individuals by any institution that receives federal funds. The hospital refused to turn over the records and a prolonged legal battle ensued.

Earlier, the Reagan administration had become involved in another Baby Doe case. In 1982, after the death of a severely handicapped infant boy whose parents had refused corrective surgery, the White House set up a twenty-four-hour hotline and "Baby Doe squads" to investigate complaints about the treatment of severely handicapped infants. Doctors and hospitals challenged the rulings as government intrusion into the practice of medicine. Various courts have ruled in favor of parents and doctors, but the government has continued to appeal.

Repeated attempts were made to work out a compromise. One idea was that hospitals would voluntarily set up infant care review committees to oversee treatment. But the opposing sides could not agree about the rules that should guide such committees. At the heart of the matter are profound disagreements as to who should make such decisions and about the ethics of alternative courses of action. Should the parents, who will have to raise the child, and who are the usual decision makers in matters of medical care for their children, be permitted to make life-and-death decisions about severely handicapped newborns? Or should the law, as the intervening lawyer in the Baby Jane Doe case put it, be "blind and deaf" to the wishes of parents, and consider only the child's right to life? Should the doctors decide? The government? Should the possibly devastating emotional and financial impact on the family of caring for a Baby Doe be considered? Should the quality of the child's own future life be a consideration in the decision? That is, should treatment be allowed to be withheld on grounds that the child would be brain damaged, severely retarded, handicapped, or bedridden? Complicating matters is the fact that it is very hard to make predictions about how an individual child will turn out.

Eventually, the government and hospital administrators came to an agreement. The treatment of handicapped newborns would be determined only on medical grounds; quality of life considerations would play no role. The American Medical Association objected. In January 1984, a court ruling upheld this decision: hospitals are required to intervene to maintain life, regardless of the condition of the newborn or the parents' wishes.

The Baby Doe dilemma came about because of recent advances in medical technology which have made it possible to prolong life indefinitely, not just for handicapped newborns, but for people at all ages who would otherwise die from injury, disease, or the infirmities of extreme old age. Increasingly, the most difficult and controversial problems facing families and doctors are ethical, not medical. Such problems rarely have clear-cut solutions. When doctors "pull the plug" on patients in deep coma who will never awaken, or refuse to make heroic efforts with respirators, incubators, or surgery for severely disabled newborns, they are cast in the uncomfortable role of "playing God." But they have no choice. Making the heroic efforts is also playing God.

Some doctors, in particular those in the new specialty of neonatology, have been criticized for intervening too aggressively. They are able to keep tinier and tinier babies alive, yet unable to predict the infant's outcome. Consider the story told in *The Long Dying of Baby Andrew*, by the baby's parents, Robert and Peggy Stinson. Born nearly four months premature, Andrew weighed only one pound, twelve ounces, and was critically ill. He was placed on a respirator against the wishes of his parents that they be notified before such a step was taken. There he lingered for six months, becoming progressively weaker as every vital organ began to fail. No one could turn off the respirator because that would cause his death. Eventually, a doctor noticed that the baby was breathing, haltingly, on his own. Then it became possible to take him off the respirator and decide not to put him back on when his breathing failed.

In the end, the Stinsons felt that Andrew's agony and their own emotional pain had been prolonged for no good reason. They felt that Andrew had been little more than an experimental animal to some of the doctors who treated him. At the same time, they felt that they had been treated as "bad parents" by some of the staff. On the other hand, the Stinsons' ordeal ended relatively quickly. Some babies like Andrew live on for many years at the edge of life.

The high-technology medical care such as what Andrew received also involves significant risks. The very techniques that keep babies alive often create new problems. For example, the oxygen needed to keep a premature baby alive is often damaging to the blood vessels in the retinas of premature eyes. Compounding the difficulties of choice are the staggering costs of the new medical technology. No one argues against saving a baby with a fair chance of leading a normal life, no matter what the cost; but extraordinary measures have been taken to extend the lives of babies for just a few extra days. In one Baby Doe case in which the government intervened, the medical bills amounted to $400,000 for a baby that doctors said had "zero chance for a normal life expectancy" (Peracchio, 1983, p. 10).

The problems and controversies surrounding the new technology will not be resolved any time soon and in fact are likely to grow worse. The latest advance is in fetal surgery, which will deepen the ethical quagmire. We are approaching the time when the ability to save fetuses will collide with parental rights to choose an abortion. While doctors have the ability to maintain fetal life, they will not know whether the fetuses they save will be healthy normal children who would otherwise have died, or if they will be profoundly retarded or otherwise handicapped, or whether they would have survived anyway. Should parents, unwilling to face a lifetime with a retarded and severely handicapped child, be allowed to stop the proceedings?

One issue that does seem close to resolution is the matter of government intervention in Baby Doe cases. In the course of pursuing the Baby Jane Doe case through the courts, the administration has not only lost that particular battle, but has had most of its actions, including hotlines and "Baby Doe squads," declared illegal. Future Baby Doe parents may be spared the court battles and legal fees endured by Baby Jane's parents. Meanwhile, her parents are struggling to raise their disabled child, vindicated in court but thousands of dollars in debt. A Republican senator has introduced a bill into Congress to have the government pay their legal expenses. But in general, those inside and outside of government who have proclaimed the rights of severely disabled newborns have not proposed ways of paying for their early treatment or for the lifelong care they will require. These proponents have not suggested raising taxes to support handicapped newborns, nor have private insurance companies offered policies to ease the burden on families.

Apart from the issue of government intervention, the ethical issues remain. The advocates of increased rights for the disabled have raised some significant and troubling issues. They argue that including the handicapped in the mainstream of society is part of the same process that has extended rights to other formerly excluded minorities. The disabled have successfully demanded access to schools, streets, jobs, and transportation. Just as American society is no longer only for white males, they argue, it is no longer only for the physically and mentally fit. Now the advocates of the disabled are extending their claims to argue that the wishes and interests of parents, and the quality of life issue, have no place in decision making about handicapped newborns. For some time to come the intensive care nursery is likely to remain a battleground between competing ethical principles.

Thus, rather than the birth complications themselves being responsible for later problems, the evidence suggests that socioeconomic factors affect both of these outcomes. It seems likely that having a newborn with birth problems may overtax the limited resources of low-income families; the intense care such infants need may lead their parents to perceive and treat them as difficult, different, sick, retarded, and generally unrewarding. Difficulties in the parent-child relationship resulting from birth complications, rather than the physical complications themselves, may be responsible for later developmental problems (Sameroff & Chandler, 1975).

Despite the variety of things that can go wrong in prenatal development, most babies are born without any complications. And, as we have seen, most complications need not inevitably lead to deficits later on. In fact, normal development seems to occur under all but the most adverse circumstances. The prenatal organism is vulnerable in many ways, but there are also self-righting tendencies built into development. As Sameroff has observed,

Evolution appears to have built into the human organism regulative mechanisms to produce normal developmental outcomes under all but the most adverse of circumstances. . . . Any understanding of deviancies in outcome must be interpreted in the light of this self-righting and self-organizing tendency, which appears to move children toward normality in the face of pressure towards deviation. (1975, p. 282)

SUMMARY

1. The development of a complete human being from a fertilized egg is guided by information coded in the DNA, the blueprint for growth for all living things.

2. In human beings, the genetic information is contained in twenty-three pairs of chromosomes—ribbons of DNA in the nucleus of the cell. The total genetic makeup of an individual is called the *genotype*. The observable characteristics of the person are called the *phenotype*. Genes do not lead directly to observable traits; rather, they direct the production of chemicals which influence the formation of bodily structures. Individuals can be phenotypically alike, but genetically different, and vice versa.

3. Genes for certain traits such as eye color come in pairs, one of which is dominant over the other. Thus, a person with one gene for blue eyes and one for brown will have brown eyes. Blue eyes and other recessive traits require two blue-eye genes. Certain genetic diseases are caused by recessive genes which may be carried by normal individuals.

4. Gregor Mendel discovered the basic principles of genetics. He hypothesized that the "hereditary material" comes in paired particles that work in an all or none fashion—producing for example either blue eyes or brown eyes, but not a blending of the two. Mendel's hypothesis was confirmed by the discovery of genes. However, only a small number of traits are controlled by single genes.

5. The "norm of reaction" is the term geneticists use to refer to the fact that a particular genotype can give rise to a variety of phenotypes. Although the genotype is fixed at the moment of conception, the development and characteristics of the individual are influenced by the environment. The environment includes the prenatal environment as well as growth processes taking place inside the new organism.

6. The concept of heritability is an extremely controversial subject, deeply enmeshed with political and social values. Some researchers claim that major human traits such as intelligence are largely determined by heredity. Others hold that there is no firm evidence for genetic influences on such traits. Many geneticists argue that there can be no adequate science of behavior genetics because researchers cannot experiment with people as they can with animals. In general, most developmental researchers believe that heredity and environment interact to produce development.

7. Except for twins, no two individuals have the same genetic makeup. This individuality or *polymorphism* has been found in all organisms down to the level of microbes. It has profound implications for psychological development, since it means that individuals differ in their reactions to the same stimulus or situation and experience the world in different ways.

8. Prenatal development is divided into stages. The germinal stage lasts from fertilization to the time of implantation in the womb. The embryonic stage lasts from implantation to the time when the embryo takes on human form, at the beginning of the third month of gestation. The fetal stage lasts from this point until birth. During the earliest months, when the parts of the body are forming, developing organisms are most vulnerable to environmental damage. Late in the seventh month is the point at which the fetus has an even chance of surviving, given intensive medical care.

9. The fetus does not develop psychological attributes until quite close to the time of birth, about thirty-eight to forty weeks. It is not until this time that organized behavior states occur. Before that, fetal movements and responses appear to be reflexes rather than "behavior."

10. Some theorists have speculated that birth is highly traumatic for the child, but there is little evidence to support this claim. However, the perinatal period—the time before and shortly after birth—is the most hazardous stage of life. Lack of oxygen and low birth weight (prematurity) are two of the leading complications of birth. The social and economic situation of the mother is the most important correlate of birth complications. Poor and ill-nourished women are more likely to have birth complications and their infants are more likely to suffer lasting effects than middle-class infants with similar birth problems. Most babies, however, are born without complications.

Key Terms

autonomic nervous system **128**

blastocyst **129**

chromosomes **115**

DNA **112**

dominance **116**

embryo **130**

embryonic stage **130**

epigenesis **113**

fetal stage **130**

fetus **130**

genotype **115**

germinal stage **129**

heritability **123**

meiosis **114**

mitosis **114**

phenotype **115**

placenta **130**

postterm **140**

preformationism **114**

preterm **140**

recessiveness **117**

term **140**

zygote **115**

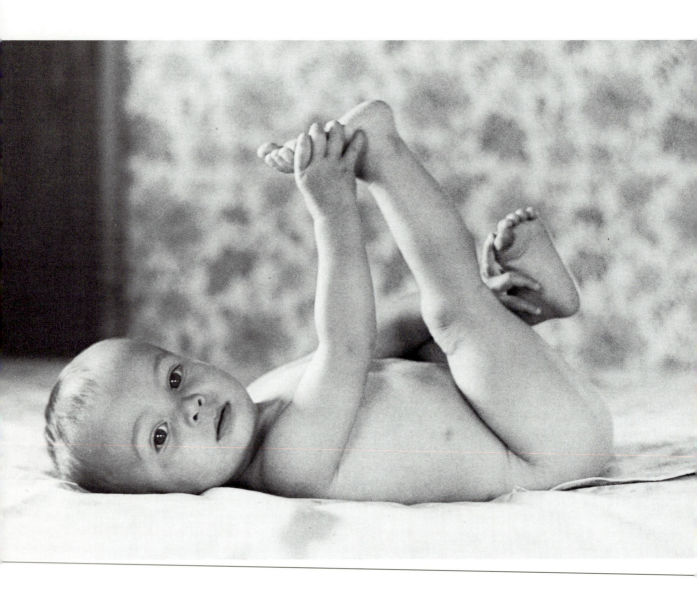

Infancy

Reflexes to Intentions

In every child who is born, under no matter what circumstances, and of no matter what parents, the potentiality of the human race is born again.

—James Agee

My mother groan'd! My father wept
Into the dangerous world I leapt.
Helpless, naked, piping loud:
Like a fiend hid in a cloud.
                          —William Blake,
                          "Songs of Experience"

*I*nfancy is usually defined as the first year and a half or two of life after birth. The end of infancy is marked by the child's beginning use of language. The name for this period of development comes from the Latin term *infantia*, which means inability to speak.

No other two years of life are so full of change. During this wordless time, before the beginnings of conscious memory, the child is transformed both physically and mentally. The newborn and the two-year-old seem almost as different from one another as a caterpillar and the butterfly it will later become. Little wonder that all societies regard the first two years as a special time of life.

Newborn infants, however, have been viewed quite differently by different people at various times and places. (See the box on The Social Birth of the Human Infant.) To modern American parents, the newborn is likely to be an adorable, miraculous being, although some new parents may be surprised that their baby does not resemble the chubby, rosy-cheeked infants that appear in advertisements. Other people may be less entranced by new babies. One of the founders of developmental psychology, G. Stanley Hall, wrote of the newborn as "squinting, cross-eyed, pot bellied and bowlegged", with a "monotonous and dismal cry" (1891).

When infant mortality rates were high in premodern Europe, people saw very young infants as existing in a sort of limbo between life and death, more animal than human, without mental activities or recognizable bodily shape. The historical literature contains many statements from preindustrial Europe that sound unbelievably callous to modern ears:

> As late as the seventeenth century, in *Le Caquet de l'accouchée*, we have a neighbour, standing at the bedside of a woman who has just given birth, the mother of five "little brats," and calming her fears with these words: "Before they are old enough to bother you, you will have lost half of them, or perhaps all of them." . . . People could not allow themselves to become too attached to

> something that was regarded as a probable loss. (Ariès, 1962, pp. 38–39)

Throughout most of history, and in much of the world today, parents are mainly concerned with the physical survival of their children. Concern about a child's psychological development is a luxury that comes only with relative affluence and low infant mortality rates.

Since the beginning of scientific child study, research on infancy has accumulated at an astonishing rate. In 1970 the leading reference work in child development contained one chapter on infancy which listed in its bibliography more than 2,000 titles (Mussen, 1970). Since then, research has continued its explosive growth. The 1983 version of the Mussen handbook, for instance, contains an entire volume on infancy. It is obviously impossible to summarize this literature in any detail. Instead, in this chapter and the next, we attempt to deal with some of the most general and basic issues: the ideas that have guided research and thought about infancy; the impact of early experience on later life; and most important of all, the organizing principles that govern the child's changing ways of thinking and acting.

In this chapter, we trace the major landmarks in infant perceptual and cognitive development. Chapter 6 will discuss in more detail the social and emotional development and individual differences. Although these divisions are useful for organizing knowledge about infancy, they are artificial. Personality and social development depend in crucial ways on the child's changing cognitive abilities. And yet thought processes are also influenced by emotions. The autistic child or the schizophrenic adult are tragic examples of the way thought, emotions, and social behavior are intertwined.

Moreover, psychological development is not about the growth of a disembodied mind. Cognitive growth depends on the maturation of the brain and body. It is through bodily experience—seeing, hearing, touching, manipulating objects, moving through space—that the child builds up knowledge of the world. One of the major tasks facing the infant is to take possession of its body, to recognize its body as

The Social Birth of the Human Infant

People in modern, "civilized" societies believe that parental love for newborn infants is a universal instinct. In fact, the idea of infants as unique and precious beings right from the moment of birth is a product of modernization. Under conditions of scarcity, when there were no reliable birth control techniques, parents often had to choose between survival of a new infant and the survival of themselves and their older children.

In most times and places where such conditions prevailed, infanticide has been one of the major ways of limiting population. As we saw in Chapter 1, infanticide was one of the leading means of population control in Europe as late as the nineteenth century, although it was considered a crime by church and state. Infanticide had not been a crime in earlier times. In fact, in ancient Rome, it was customary to take the newborn child "still red from its mother's blood" and place it on the ground at the father's feet (Belmont, 1976, p. 1). If the father recognized the child and decided to take care of it, he would raise the child up from the ground and hold it in his arms. But if he thought the child was illegitimate, or deformed, or if there had been bad omens at the time of the birth, he would not pick it up. Servants would put the child into a basket and take it to a special place where it could be adopted by a stranger, brought up to be a slave, or else simply left to die.

These practices seem unbelievably cruel now, because we think of a newborn child as a person with human rights from the moment of birth. But in most times and places, the *biological* fact of birth does not coincide with the *social* birth of a person and a member of a society. The practice of raising up the newborn child to declare its acceptance into the family is found across cultures and time (Belmont, 1976). In all cultures, birth rituals are the first rite of passage in the human life cycle, and it is only after passing through these ceremonies that the child is recognized as both an individual and a member of the group (Van Gennep, 1960). Before the rites are performed, the child is thought to be in a state of limbo, often the world of the dead. In fact, there is often some resemblance between birth and funeral rites.

Birth rituals express two things: the separation and purification of the child after its former state—as in baptism—and rites of inclusion. Often there must be some public expression of willingness to receive the child into the community, and thus someone, usually not the parents, must come forward to receive the child. In our own culture we see the remnants of this custom in the presence of godparents in Christian and Jewish birth ceremonies. The naming of a child is another universal part of birth ceremonies; when a child is named, it is recognized both as a member of a social group and as a unique individual.

belonging to itself, and to distinguish self from not-self (Figure 5.1).

The Great Transformation

Although we now know that newborn infants are not as incompetent as they seem, they are enormously less competent than an 18-month- or a 2-year-old. Newborns are totally dependent, helpless beings, with no knowledge of themselves, the world, or other people. To understand the momentous transformation that takes place in a relatively short span of time, let us look at some examples of 18-month-old behavior.

The first example comes from the work of Arnold Gesell, who systematically observed and plotted the month-by-month changes of children's everyday behavior during the first five years. The child who at birth could scarcely lift

FIGURE 5.1
The First Year of Life

Motor Behavior

1 Month

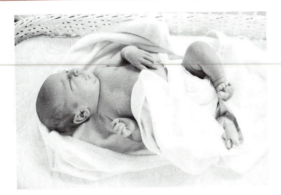

- Baby prefers to lie on back, with face to one side.
- If placed on stomach, may draw both legs up under body.
- Cannot hold head erect; head sags forward.
- Hands usually tightly fisted.

2–3 Months

- Baby still prefers to lie on back with face to one side; sometimes brings head to center.
- When lying on stomach, will lift head 45° and extend legs.
- Head-bobbing gradually disappears; may hold head erect.

4 Months

- Baby prefers to lie on stomach.
- Can roll from back to side.
- When lying on stomach, head lifts 90°, arms and legs lift and extend.
- Can sit propped up for 10–15 minutes.

5–6 Months

- Lying on stomach is often the favorite position, but baby can sit leaning forward on hands.
- Can roll from lying on back to lying on stomach.
- May "bounce" when held standing.

7–8 Months

- When lying on back, may extend legs and lift feet to mouth.
- Prefers sitting and can sit erect for 5–10 minutes or longer.
- May crawl.
- Can stand supporting full body weight on feet if held up.

9–10 Months

- Creeps on hands and knees.
- Can sit indefinitely.
- Can pull self to standing position using crib rails and may "cruise" by moving feet.
- By 10 months may be able to sit down from standing position.

Hand-Eye Coordination	Language Behavior	Personal-Social Behavior
<ul><li>Looks at object held directly in line of vision.</li><li>Will grasp reflexively if rattle or other object is placed in hand.</li><li>Eyes begin to coordinate.</li></ul>	<ul><li>Baby startles easily to sudden sounds or movements.</li><li>Makes small, throaty sounds, but primary means of communication is crying.</li></ul>	<ul><li>Facial expression is generally remote and impassive.</li><li>May smile at other people.</li><li>May quiet activity when held or approached socially.</li><li>Response to world is primarily visual.</li></ul>
<ul><li>When lying on back, follows objects visually within limited range.</li><li>Looks at object but can grasp only by reflex.</li></ul>	<ul><li>Exhibits interest in sounds and voices.</li><li>Makes cooing and chuckling sounds when happy; cries when unhappy.</li><li>Responds vocally when mother approaches.</li></ul>	<ul><li>Exhibits interest in people within sight.</li><li>Responds vocally to others.</li><li>Shows interest in food.</li><li>Regards own hands with great interest and fingers one hand with the other.</li></ul>
<ul><li>When lying on back, follows objects with eyes through an arc of 180°.</li><li>When presented with object, may touch or grasp it.</li><li>Brings any object grasped to mouth.</li></ul>	<ul><li>Makes many different kinds of sounds—squeals, gurgles, laughs out loud.</li><li>"Talks" to people or objects, using punctuated vocalizations.</li><li>Smiles, squeals and coos when spoken to.</li></ul>	<ul><li>Smiles when smiled at; sometimes smiles spontaneously.</li><li>Often vocalizes when smiling.</li><li>Continues play with hands and fingers.</li><li>May begin to have a schedule of waking and sleeping.</li></ul>
<ul><li>Grasps small block using "palmar" grasp; little use of thumb or forefingers.</li><li>Scratches at tiny objects but cannot pick them up.</li><li>May hold own bottle with one or two hands</li></ul>	<ul><li>Turns head toward sounds produced out of line of vision.</li><li>May express displeasure by making sounds other than crying (like shrieks or howls).</li><li>Utters vowel sounds.</li></ul>	<ul><li>May initiate social approach (asking to be picked up).</li><li>May seem shy or fearful with strangers.</li><li>Touches and shakes objects.</li><li>May imitate sounds and movements.</li></ul>
<ul><li>Can grasp a small block in each hand, or may transfer a single block from hand to hand.</li><li>Likes banging blocks or other objects vigorously on table top or floor and playing with noise-making toys.</li></ul>	<ul><li>Vocalization now includes vowels (ah-ah, oh-oh) and initial consonant sounds (Mum-mum, Da-da).</li><li>May respond to "No-no."</li><li>May use gestures to communicate.</li></ul>	<ul><li>Reaches for toys out of reach.</li><li>Can hold and manipulate spoon or cup (but awkwardly).</li><li>Bites or chews on toys; shakes them to make noise.</li><li>Nap patterns vary, but usually 2–3 naps a day.</li></ul>
<ul><li>Pokes at objects with forefinger.</li><li>Bangs two blocks together in "pat-a-cakes" gesture.</li><li>May uncover toy he or she has seen hidden.</li></ul>	<ul><li>Can say "Ma-ma" as a sound; says and understands "Da-da."</li><li>May use two other words.</li><li>May respond to "No-no."</li><li>May imitate cough, tongue clicks, kisses.</li></ul>	<ul><li>Waves "Bye-bye" and plays "pat-a-cakes" and "peek-a-boo."</li><li>Hands toy on request but does not release from grasp.</li><li>Takes liquids well from cup.</li><li>Takes two daily naps; may sleep soundly through night.</li></ul>

Figure 5.1 continues on page 154.

Motor Behavior

11 Months

- Baby pulls self actively to feet and "cruises," using side rail of crib or playpen.
- May stand momentarily without support.
- Can walk if one hand is held; may take a few steps alone.

12 Months

- Can get up without help and may take several steps alone.
- Can creep upstairs on hands and knees.
- May be able to squat or stoop without losing balance.
- Can throw ball.

Source: "The changing baby" by Louise Bates Ames, May 1983, *Ladies' Home Journal.*

his or her head, and at 6 months was just beginning to sit unaided, now, at 18 months, prefers running to walking. He or she can use about a dozen words, along with a large vocabulary of expressive gestures. "Thank you," "all gone," and "bye-bye" are among the favorites; these terms express an interest in completions which many children show at this period: closing a door, handing over a dish when finished, mopping up a spill (Gesell & Ilg, 1949).

The next description was written by the mother of an 18-month-old girl as part of a psychological research project:

> Debbie is good company these days—eager to cooperate or help in anything we do. . . . She helps put weeds in the basket, and works along with either of us at yard chores. In the house, she helps push the vacuum or mop, finds a sponge and "dusts" furniture, anticipates her father's needs in dressing or in building a fire in the fireplace. . . .
>
> She has begun to take great pleasure in bedecking herself with beads, hats, work gloves, father's jacket, mother's slippers, etc. . . .

The addition of a full-length mirror in the parental bedroom two weeks ago has interested Debbie. She goes to see herself in various costumes and in various moods, either mugging extravagantly or eyeing herself detachedly with extreme casualness. (Church, 1968, p. 72)

Hand-Eye Coordination	Language Behavior	Personal-Social Behavior
■ Can grasp small objects in a pincer grasp; can grasp larger objects using thumb opposition. ■ May try to make a tower of two blocks. ■ Explores surroundings: crumples paper, shakes rattle.	■ Says "Ma-ma" and "Da-da" with meaning. ■ Says "No" and shakes head; may say "Bye-bye" and wave; uses four additional words (besides "Ma-ma" and "Da-da"). ■ Follows simple commands.	■ Is becoming aware of social approval and disapproval. ■ May give away a toy or object on request.
■ Helps turn pages of book. ■ May succeed in building tower of two blocks. ■ Can find toy under box, cup, or cloth. ■ Enjoys putting objects into containers and taking them out.	■ Uses six or more words besides "Ma-ma" and "Da-da." ■ May pat pictured object in book on request. ■ May point to desired object.	■ May show increasing preference for certain people. ■ Hugs and "loves" doll or stuffed animal. ■ Holds cup to drink and may succeed in using spoon. ■ Only takes one nap.

Of course, not all children of a particular age behave in the same way, nor do they develop at the same rate. But in general, in only eighteen months, the average child will have acquired the basic skills that set humans apart from other animals and make human culture and society possible. During infancy, each child repeats the achievements of the human race in its evolution, such as the ability to stand upright and walk on two feet and the ability to shape the hands to an infinite number of tasks, from wielding a hammer, to picking up a tiny speck of dust, to drawing a fine line.

Above all, the child has acquired the most important human skill, the ability to use and understand symbols. During the later part of infancy, the child shows increasing skill at various forms of symbolic behavior—make-believe play, for example, or remembering absent objects and events. But learning language, a symbol system that is shared with others, makes it possible for the baby to break out of its own private world, to communicate with others, and to begin to learn their ways of looking at the world. Complicated joint activities become possible. Moreover, language makes it possible

for the child to develop a more self-conscious self-awareness—the ability to see the self through the eyes of others.

Conceptions of Infancy

How does the child learn all that it does in such a short amount of time? For centuries, philosophers have debated about how the child comes to know what it knows at the end of infancy. Perhaps we should note here that to those closest to the development of a particular baby—its parents—infancy may not seem so short a time. When infancy is measured in sleepless nights and dirty diapers, the distance between developmental milestones can seem very long indeed. But the philosopher's or scientist's view of infancy is different from the parental one.

The growth of scientific study of child development did not resolve the issues that had been raised by the philosophers. Although an enormous amount has been learned, scientific theories continue to be guided by images of infancy rooted in philosophical assumptions. There are so many different views of infancy reflected in the scientific literature that, as Kessen and associates have observed, a visitor from another planet would have a hard time understanding that a single species was being examined (Kessen, Haith, & Salapatek, 1970, p. 311).

To the behaviorists, who emphasize the role of environment, infants are empty vessels waiting to be filled by experience, or mirrors reflecting the world around them. To those who emphasize maturation, infant development is the unfolding of preprogrammed capacities. To traditional Freudians, the child is a seething cauldron of lustful and aggressive instincts. To John Bowlby and others, the story of infant development is essentially a love story: the infant is a young animal programmed to form a passionate attachment to a one and only love—mother—and all of its future development rests on being able to do so.

As we saw in Chapter 3, some observers argued that the child could not possibly learn all it does in infancy if the mind at birth were not already furnished with knowledge of what the world is like. Others argued that everything the child learns comes from experience. Until the dawn of the twentieth century, these debates were carried on without systematic observation or experiment.

However, because science does make use of empirical observations, new findings can enter the argument which make certain views of the child seem more or less in agreement with the facts. Although there are still disagreements between different theoretical approaches, recent research has led to several major changes in the way psychologists view infants. For example, there has been a change from viewing babies as passive organisms to seeing them as active agents in their own development. Second, psychologists no longer think of infants, even newborns, as total incompetents, unaware of their surroundings, and without any influence on their own experience. Third, the Freudian image of the infant as a sensual, aggressive little animal, interested only in the release of powerful impulses, has not stood up to empirical scrutiny, the observed realities of babies' everyday behavior, or what is now known about cognitive development.

Even very young babies are interested observers of the world around them.

Observation does not always correct erroneous preconceptions, however. Although we now know that newborns can see and hear, several generations of pediatricians and psychologists assumed that they were functionally blind and deaf—and some still do. As Thomas Bower has pointed out, scientists are as likely as anyone else to be blinded by preconceived notions of what babies—or other creatures—can or cannot do. They look for what they expect to see, rather than what actually is happening. He gives himself as an example. In the process of doing research on very young infants, many new mothers told him that their babies could reach out and touch things. Bower was politely skeptical about such statements:

I was so convinced that the textbooks were right and that reaching began at about five months—not five days—that I simply paid no attention to such reports. I was finally convinced that they had some substance when I saw my own nephew display this behavior at three weeks of age; and again when a child of a colleague who was not about to be put off by polite skepticism did so at the age of only one week. It was only after these parents had alerted me to this behavior that I even noticed it, despite the fact that I had been working intensively with babies in this age range for several years. (1977, p. 27)

The Importance of Infancy

Another reason why infants have been so fascinating to psychologists and others is the notion that the earliest months and years determine what kind of person the infant will be for the rest of its life. The idea that the child is "father of the man" is an old one. In centuries past, the idea was usually based on some concept of heredity. The child was assumed to have an inherited nature that would reveal itself sooner or later. Thus, there were many tales of little princes or princesses who had been stolen by gypsies: their sensitive natures would emerge in spite of growing up in rough circumstances.

With the growth of scientific psychology and the child study movement around the turn of the century, ideas about the importance of infancy played a major role in theory and research. Freud and Watson differed enormously from one another in their views of the human mind, but they agreed on one central point: the experiences of the first few years of life determine the kind of person the child will be for the rest of its life. The Freudians postulated an image of the vulnerable infant: babies are sensitive beings who can be damaged for life not only by traumatic events and emotional neglect, but also by overdoses of affection. The behaviorists postulated an image of the malleable infant: parents could shape their infants however they wished if they were consistent and began early enough to teach good habits and eliminate bad ones. Both models agree that

if the parents made any mistakes, the effects were likely to be permanent.

The idea of parental determinism seemed to be supported by a wide variety of evidence from the psychiatric clinic as well as the experimental laboratory. It has been enormously influential among parents. Twentieth-century parents have confronted worries unknown to earlier generations; they have sought to choose the proper methods to raise their children from the often contradictory advice of the experts and blamed themselves when anything went wrong with their child's development. The belief in parental determinism is still widely held by many psychologists, and especially by psychiatrists. Here, for example, is a well-known psychiatrist writing about the significance of the first fifteen months:

> These are the months when the foundations are laid, not only for future emotional stability, but also for basic though global personality traits and for intellectual development. No part of the life experience will be as solidly incorporated into the individual, become so irrevocably part of a person, as infancy. (Lidz, 1976, p. 124)

The idea of early determinism is now at the center of a great debate within developmental psychology. Recent findings from a number of different kinds of research have challenged the idea of infancy as the predictor of the rest of a person's life. These new findings suggest that development is much more plastic, and that the past is much less of a prologue to the future, than had been assumed. No one denies that infants are sensitive beings who suffer when abused or maltreated. But recent evidence suggests that psychological damage or deprivation can be overcome (Clarke & Clarke, 1976). Further, studies of adult development across the life span suggest that while infant experience is an important first chapter in a person's life, it is not the whole story (Brim & Kagan, 1980).

Suppose it turns out that the critics of infant determinism are correct, and infant experience does not predict later development as strongly as formerly believed. Is this a scientific disaster for students of infancy? Would it mean that infant development is no longer an interesting or useful topic for study? Such a conclusion rests on two assumptions: that stability is more interesting than change; and that studying individuals at a particular age is justified only in terms of what they will become, not what they are now—which would clearly rule out research on older adults.

Instead of assuming that continuity from early to later life is the only useful issue, the scientific task becomes one of explaining how and why particular early experiences, for some children, continue to influence later development, and other experiences for other children do not. In any event, the basic story of infant development, the transformation of the helpless, speechless newborn into the active, sociable toddler is a fascinating story worthy of scientific study for its own sake.

Brain Development in Infancy

The ability to remember, to speak a language, to have a sense of self and a personal identity in relationship to society are the major achievements of the first two years of life. As we have seen, psychologists have debated about how to explain this remarkable transformation of a biological organism into a person; some emphasize the maturation of the brain, others emphasize experience. Today, while researchers still argue about how large a role the environment plays in mental development, they all agree that babies come into the world with brains biologically programmed to achieve the basic human competencies, given the natural human habitat of people and objects.

Psychological processes cannot be reduced to brain events; they represent a different level of reality, just as computer software programs differ from the hardware of the computer's machinery. But the structures and activities of the brain do influence psychological functioning. In particular, changes in the brain across the life span can be linked to developmental changes in thought and behavior. Currently, knowledge about the brain is increasing at a rapid rate. In the last twenty-five years, brain researchers—neuroscientists, psychobiologists, and others—have produced thousands of articles and have won twelve Nobel prizes. They are now able to map more accurately than ever before the brain processes involved in specific mental functions, such as silent reading, doing arithmetic, and voluntary and involuntary movements.

The human brain, as one researcher puts it, "is the most complicated living structure known on earth today. It represents the pinnacle of evolutionary progress, the ultimate achievement of nature" (Suomi, 1982, p. 53). Elephants and whales have larger brains than we do, but no other nervous system has the complexity of ours. It has been estimated that the number of pieces of information the brain can acquire and store is greater than the number of atoms in the universe (Piel et al., 1979). Although the basic architecture of the human brain is the same in every normal person, the specific "wiring" of each brain, the pattern of neuronal interconnection, is unique to each individual, even in identical twins. (See the discussion on Developmental Noise in Chapter 4.)

The part of the human brain that sets it apart from even our closest primate cousins, the advanced apes, is the cerebral cortex—the gray matter. The most primitive part of the brain is the base, where it joins the spinal cord. This part of the brain is sometimes called "reptilian." Over the course of vertebrate evolution, the brain grew forward, away from the spine. The middle portion of the brain contains structures we share with other mammals. As humans evolved, the cerebral hemispheres, the two walnut-like halves of the brain, came to occupy 85 percent of the total mass of the human brain. The cerebral cortex is the active working part of the brain. As the cortex continued to grow in the last million years of human evolution, because of the limited size of the skull, the brain came to be folded back on itself, giving it its familiar convolutions.

The cerebrum is the part of the brain most closely associated with mental activity and con-

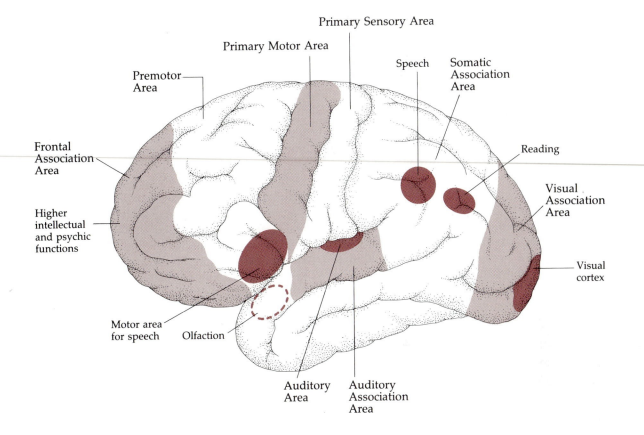

FIGURE 5.2
General Functional Areas of the Cerebral Cortex
Our sensory, motor, and intellectual functions all derive from specific areas of the cerebral cortex.

Source: *Human anatomy and physiology,* by A. P. Spence & E. B. Mason, 1983, Menlo Park, Calif.: Benjamin/Cummings.

scious experience. It is responsible for perception, memory, thought, language, and other intellectual functions. Some functions, such as speech, movement, vision, touch, smell, and hearing, are located in specific areas of the cerebrum (Figure 5.2). Thinking and memory in general, however, seem to depend on interaction between several parts of the brain.

The right and left halves of the brain also differ in function. Each half is responsible for sensation and movement in the opposite side of the body. The left hemisphere in most people is involved with speech and other analytic forms, while the right hemisphere is involved in such "holistic" processes as spatial relations, the perception of form, the appreciation of music, and insightful problem solving. Broad claims about "right brain-left brain" differences, however, are not supported by current research. Most mental activity depends on both sides of the brain working together (Springer & Deutch, 1981).

The development of human infants today reflects the evolutionary development of the human brain. Unlike the brain of any other animal, that of the human infant triples in size in the first year. While the brain was evolving to be ever larger and more complex, the size of the skull was limited by the size of the human birth canal. The accommodation between brain and pelvis came about through "premature" birth and a long period of development after birth. In comparison with other primates, human infants are born about six months "early" (Washburn & Devore, 1961).

The striking changes in a baby's psychological functioning over the first two years are closely tied to changes in the brain. At birth, the psychologically significant cortical areas of the brain are not fully developed. Nor do they all mature at the same rate. In newborns, only the sensory and motor regions are functioning, and thus the newborn's behavior is largely limited to reflexes. The premotor regions of the cortex, which provide information to the motor regions, develop at about the time infants learn to control their skeletal muscles. The association areas of the brain, which have extensive connections to most other areas and are viewed as "thought centers," are the last to develop. By the age of two, all cortical areas are functioning at a mature level and the average child

begins to talk (Figure 5.3). However, the connections between cortical areas remain incomplete. These connections, and the "thought centers" of the brain, continue to grow until the early teens. (This development is discussed in greater detail in Chapter 10.)

In general, recent research has shown that the mental capacities of newborns differ in both quantity and quality from older infants and children (Woodruff, 1978). Newborns do not live in a buzzing, blooming confusion, as early researchers had assumed. But the impressive sensory abilities of newborns to see and hear and taste are lodged in the more primitive, subcortical parts of the brain, not the cortex. At around three or four months, the cortex "turns on" and becomes functional.

This change can be seen clearly in records of the electrical activity of the brain. The EEG (electroencephalogram) is a device that records the levels of electricity given off by the brain. It

FIGURE 5.3
Behavioral and Cortical Development in Infants up to Two Years of Age

Age	Cortical Areas Functioning	Characteristic Behaviors
Birth to 1 month	Initial functioning of motor and primary sensory areas	Generalized actions; no reflex inhibition; no goal direction; little or no flexibility of action patterns
1 to 4 months	Initial functioning of motor, premotor, and other areas	Reflex inhibition; more visual attention paid to compound stimuli than to isolated stimuli
4 to 8 months	Initial functioning of sensory association and frontal association areas	Beginning differentiation of motor patterns; perception of sequential relationships; accidental goal direction
8 to 12 months	Initial functioning of additional association areas	Goal direction; anticipation; imitation of facial movements; incomplete body orientation in space; inability to inhibit past sensations and responses
12 to 18 months	All cortical areas functioning, but functioning of association areas is primitive	Trial-and-error search for new information and problem solution; incomplete perception of body as separate object in space
18 to 24 months	All cortical areas functioning at mature level, but interconnections between cortical areas are incomplete	Internalized mental images of goals; spatial and sequential concepts; perception of own body as a separate object from rest of environment

Source: "Some basic aspects of brain growth and development" by S. S. Suomi, 1982, in C. P. Kopp & J. B. Krakow, eds., *The child*, Reading, Mass.: Addison-Wesley.

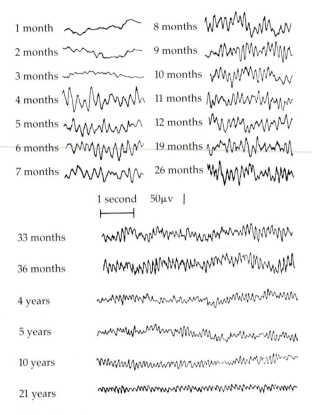

FIGURE 5.4
Development of the Occipital Alpha Rhythm
The alpha brain waves were recorded for the same person from infancy to adulthood. A persistent rhythm of 3 to 4 waves per second first appeared at about 4 months, which increased to 5 to 6 per second at about 1 year and from there to 10 per second by 10 years of age. This frequency persisted to adulthood.

Source: "Attention, consciousness, sleep and wakefulness" by D. B. Lindsley, 1960, in J. Field, ed., *Handbook of physiology*, vol. 2, *Neurophysiology*, Washington, D.C.: American Physiological Society.

is used to detect brain abnormalities as well as changes in mood, attention, and level of consciousness (Blakemore, 1977). The EEG has also been used to study the maturation and organization of the brain in infancy.

The electrical impulses given off by the brains of humans and animals may be considered a kind of noise produced by brain functioning. The rhythms in this "noise" indicate how well organized and integrated this activity is. Think of the sound of an orchestra tuning up versus the sound of the same orchestra playing a symphony. Before a baby is three or four months old, there are no organized rhythms in the sensory regions of the cortex. The onset of organized rhythms at around three months is believed to mark the time when the infant is progressing from a subcortical to a cortical level of functioning (Woodruff, 1978). (See Figure 5.4.)

But what specifically takes place in the brain during these early months? The growth of the brain involves a number of physical changes, the most basic of which are outlined here:

1. *Myelinization.* This is a process in which a fatty sheath develops around parts of many neurons (nerve cells), allowing them to conduct messages more quickly. Researchers believe that the myelinization of the motor areas at about one year of age accounts for the ability of the child to walk at that time and not earlier. Myelinization is thought to contribute to other developmental changes in childhood and early adolescence.

2. *The formation of branches (dendrites) and connections (synapses) among neurons.* Nerve cells branch out and connect with more and more surrounding cells. Although this process occurs most rapidly in the early years, it continues throughout the life span. The growth and survival of nerve cells depends on making connections with other cells. Researchers have recently discovered that the death of individual neurons is common during brain development, contrary to the popular belief that brain cells die only as part of aging or disease. In fact, the peak death of cells in any area occurs at the time that area is undergoing its most rapid development.

It turns out that during prenatal development, more neurons are formed than the brain will ever need. The growth of the brain after birth involves the elimination of these excess cells. It seems that the nerve cells "compete" with one another for survival, like animal species competing with one another for dominance. The survival of the "fittest" among nerve cells is determined by stimulation and use. Cells that are stimulated make connections with their neighbors and live. For example, using the right hand develops the neural connections that serve the right hand; those serving the left hand lose out, resulting in less skill and power.

3. *Glial cells.* In addition to neurons, there are other cells in the brain. Glial cells fill up the space between the neurons and it is believed that there are ten times as many of them as neurons. Little is known about their function, however. They grow most intensely after birth and continue to grow throughout life.

The fact that much of human brain development takes place after birth means that neuronal structure is susceptible to influence from the infant's environment; chief among these influences are nutrition and experience. Malnutrition during critical growth periods of the brain in humans can produce irreversible changes in the brain's structure (Winick, 1976). The greatest damage can occur during the period of most rapid brain development, which includes the final weeks of gestation and the first few months after birth (Dobbing, 1974). Early malnutrition seems to result in diminished mental capacity (Tizard, 1974), although similar malnutrition in older children and adults does not seem to have the same bad effects. The adverse effects of malnutrition on the mind may, to some extent, be reversed if adequate nutrition and behavioral stimulation are maintained into adolescence (Nguyen, Meyer, & Winick, 1977; Winick, Meyer, & Harris, 1975).

Experience also affects the growth and development of the nervous system. This is shown by experiments in which animals undergo sensory deprivation during critical early periods of their development. It seems that experience *induces* and *modulates* formation of synapses and may also maintain them. Vision researchers

Hubel and Wiesel received the Nobel Prize in 1981 for their work in this area (Hubel & Wiesel, 1965; Wiesel & Hubel, 1965). Additionally, varying types of prolonged experience, such as "enriched" experiences in which developing individuals (rats) are provided many social interactions and a good deal of living space, may have differing effects from "impoverished" experiences, such as small living space and absence of other individuals. Indeed, such varying effects have produced differences in behavior, in brain anatomy, and brain chemistry (Rosenzweig & Bennett, 1977, 1978).

Early Perceptual Development

The newborn is at the very beginning of its experience in the world. What does it bring to its first encounters with physical and social reality? How well, if at all, does the child see, hear, and smell? When a young infant looks at the world, does it see what we see—a three-dimensional world of objects in space? Can it recognize its mother? Are newborns capable of learning?

Although these questions have been asked for many years, it is only in the past decade or so that psychologists have been able to find answers to them. For a long time it appeared that very young infants were hopelessly inept as experimental subjects. Being nonverbal, they had to be approached with methods more appropriate to studying animals rather than older children or adults. Yet, unlike the rats or other animals psychologists were accustomed to working with, babies are uncoordinated in their responses—they cannot manipulate things or move around on their own. How then can they be studied?

In recent years, there has been a methodological revolution in studying perception and learning in young infants. Several ingenious experimenters figured out ways of using responses that infants can make, such as looking or sucking, or nonvoluntary responses such as heart rate, which indicate whether the child is paying attention to something.

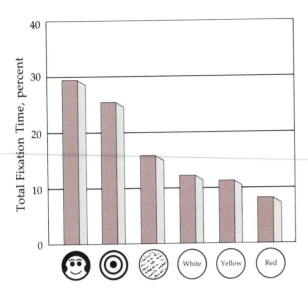

FIGURE 5.5
Visual Preferences of Newborns
Newborns as young as ten hours to five days old were shown these six disks. The face held their attention much longer than the bulls-eye, the newsprint, or the colored disks.

Source: "The origin of form perception" by R. L. Fantz, May 1961, *Scientific American, 204.*

For example, Robert Fantz (1961) was a pioneer in the use of looking as an indicator of early perceptual abilities. He presented infants with pairs of stimuli that differed in particular ways—a gray square and a square with thin stripes; a bull's-eye and a facelike circle; checkerboards with few and many squares. If the infant looked longer at one pattern than another, the experimenter could conclude two things: that infants could tell the difference between them, and that they preferred one pattern over another. Fantz (1961) discovered that newborns are not blind: they can discriminate even fine print from gray surfaces and they prefer to look at faces rather than several other complex patterns (Figure 5.5).

Capitalizing on infants' normal behavioral repertoire, researchers have also used sucking to study instrumental learning in very young infants. One experiment showed that infants as young as two days would increase the length of their sucking when music continued for as long as they sucked, but they would not do so when long sucks turned the music off (Butterfield & Siperstein, 1972). Earlier, Siqueland (1968) had shown that newborns could learn either to turn their heads or hold their heads still by rewarding them with a pacifier to suck on.

Another experiment using sucking provides even more striking evidence of the newborn's learning abilities. In this study, newborn babies learned to turn their heads to the right or left, depending on whether they heard a buzzer or a tone (Siqueland & Lipsett, 1966). In order to get to taste a sweet liquid, the baby had to turn to the right when the *tone* sounded. Similarly, when the *buzzer* sounded, the baby had to turn to the left to get the sweet drink. It took only a few trials for babies to perform perfectly—turning to the right when the tone sounded, and to the left when they heard the buzzer.

Heart rate has also been used to find out about infants' perceptual capacities and learning abilities. When a baby—or anyone, for that matter—is faced with a surprising or unexpected event, the heart rate slows down. There may be some truth in the old song—"I took one look at you, and then my heart stood still." Heart rate slowing, or deceleration, is part of the orienting reflex—the perceptive response system geared toward the processing and taking in of information (Sokolov, 1963). The orienting reflex is a set of systematic responses including pupillary changes to sharpen vision as well as changes in breathing, blood vessels, digestive processes, brain waves, and so forth. Psychologists in recent years have made increasing use of the mind's machinery—the psychophysiology of the brain and nervous system—as indicators of mental processes.

Heart rate, along with sucking, can be used as as indicator of **habituation**—becoming familiar with something. For example, the experimenter presents a certain picture over and over again. At first, the baby's heart rate slows down as he or she first notices the picture. Eventually, the heart rate rises again, showing that the picture is no longer interesting. When the experimenter changes the picture, the baby's heart rate goes down again, showing that the new picture is interesting. When it is no longer novel to the infant, the heart rate will rise again, and so on. The process of showing heightened attention to the new stimulus is called **dishabituation.** Newborns are able to show both habituation and dishabituation.

All of the techniques described above reveal what infants are able to perceive and what they prefer to pay attention to. Recent studies using such techniques have shown that very young infants are much more competent than was believed. They can see, hear, taste, smell, and even integrate data from different senses.

In the light of recent research, we know that William James was off the mark when he described the newborn infant's world as a "blooming, buzzing confusion." Currently, however, researchers are pulling back from an extreme emphasis on the skills of the newborn. The truth seems to lie somewhere in between the traditional "disorganized infant" and the more recent "competent infant." While newborns can attend to the world, their periods of alertness are brief and irregular, and their perceptual sensitivities are limited.

A great deal of development takes place in the first years; two months, eight months, and twelve months seem to mark major shifts in brain development, perceptual and motor skills, and sociability. By three months, babies are increasingly competent information processors. Between three and six months of age, they are ideal research subjects because they are highly curious about the world and have long periods of attentiveness, but their mobility is limited (Olson & Sherman, 1983). In the second half of the first year, the infant's sensory and perceptual skills become much more refined, and memory improves. The infant can recognize things seen and heard days and even weeks before (Fagan, 1973). In addition, recall memory improves. By eight months, the child can not only keep events in short-term memory for a longer time, but can retrieve memories from the past. The child's mental life is no longer restricted to what can be perceived in the here and now. Rather, the child uses mem-

ories of the past to evaluate the current situation (Mellar, 1974). Further, babies between 6 and 12 months begin to group and classify objects—a first step that will eventually lead to the use of abstract symbols. In the beginning, though, the infant's world is dominated by the sensations and perceptions of the immediate moment.

Vision

Vision is the most studied sense in infants. Researchers have charted their acuity, their scanning strategies, and their preferences. Though newborns actively explore the world with their eyes, their vision is much less sharp than that of older babies and adults. Their eyesight would be rated at about 20/800, or legally blind (Dobson & Teller, 1978). The physical structures involved in vision are not well developed at birth and, as shown above, the visual cortex of the brain is also immature, although it develops rapidly in the first few months (Banks & Salapatek, 1983; Cohen, DeLoache, & Strauss, 1979). Banks (1980) has shown that there is a dramatic improvement in the infant's ability to accommodate to visual stimuli between one and two months, and that maturation rather than experience is responsible for this change.

Despite the limitations of their visual equipment, young infants and even newborns scan the world in an organized way and can fix their eyes on sharply defined stimuli that catch their attention. Haith (1980) has described the newborn's scanning patterns in the form of a set of rules:

1. If I am awake and the light is not too bright, I open my eyes.
2. If I am in the dark, I maintain a controlled, detailed search.
3. If I am in the light and no forms can be seen, I search for the edges of things with broad, jerky sweeps of the visual field.
4. If I find an edge, I keep looking in that general vicinity. I try to look back and forth across the edge. If that edge is too far from the center of my vision, I look for another edge.

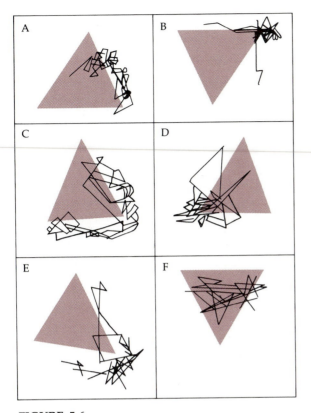

FIGURE 5.6
Newborn Scanning Patterns
The squiggly lines show the scanning
patterns of newborns as they observed the
triangles. The infants' concentration on the
corners indicates that they preferred
moderate stimulation. If they had preferred
constant stimulation, they would have
scanned all sides equally.

Source: "Visual scanning of triangles by the
human newborn" by P. Salapatek & W. Kessen,
1966, *Journal of Experimental Child Psychology, 3.*

5. While looking at an edge, I scan narrowly;
   I keep looking at areas that have the most
   edges.

Haith argues that these rules are biologically
adaptive, provided the experience keeps the
neurons in the visual cortex firing at a high
level. In addition to being attracted to edges
(Figure 5.6), newborns are also attracted to
moving objects (Kessen, Haith, & Salapatek,
1970).

Can infants see color? The evidence is clear
that by three months they perceive colors
much the way adults do and show the same
preferences as adults. Thus, they see the colors
red, blue, green, and yellow, and seem to prefer red and green (Bornstein, 1975). These findings have laid to rest an old debate about
whether people in different cultures see colors
differently.

Despite their limited visual skills, newborn
infants prefer to look at certain patterns over
others. As we saw in Figure 5.5, Fantz in his
pioneering studies presented infants with
grossly different patterns—disks with a face,
newsprint, a bullseye, and patternless red,
white, and yellow disks. Newborns and young
infants looked for the longest period of time at
the face, next longest at the bullseye and then
the newsprint. They looked much less at the
patternless disks.

When this finding was first reported, some
psychologists believed that infants like to look
at human faces. Later research showed that infants are attracted to faces not because they are
human, but because they have the kinds of
stimulus characteristics that babies find attractive: curved rather than straight lines, high
contrast, interesting "edges," movement, and
complexity. Faces also have a pattern that is especially interesting to infants: an outlined circle, that is, the face surrounded by hair, containing dots—the eyes (Caron et al., 1973). In
the first couple of months, babies shift the
areas of the face they prefer to look at: newborns look more at the outside of the face—the
hairline—but later, by the age of two months,
they focus their attention on the inside of the
face, including the eyes, mouth, and the nose
(Haith, Bergman, & Moore, 1977; Salapatek,
1975).

Another question researchers have asked in
recent years concerns depth perception: when
do infants begin to perceive the world in terms
of three-dimensional space? A number of studies have shown that infants in the earliest
months can tell the difference between two-
and three-dimensional stimuli. For example,
Fantz (1961) found that one-month-old infants
can differentiate between a circle and a sphere.

Another study placed two- and four-month-old infants on the deep side of a "visual cliff"—a glass sheet covering an apparent drop of several feet (Figure 5.7). Babies up to just over a year typically refuse to "go over the edge" even when beckoned by their mothers. Campos and his colleagues (Campos, Langer, & Krowitz, 1970) found that two-month-olds seemed to perceive the cliff, but rather than being frightened of it, they seemed to find it interesting, as shown by a decrease in their heart rate. More recent studies show that soon after they learn how to crawl, infants will cross the deep side of the visual cliff to reach their mothers (Campos et al., 1978). Some researchers are skeptical as to whether young infants really do have depth perception (Banks & Salapatek, 1983). The findings suggest that while two-month-old infants respond to cues indicating depth, they do not appreciate the meaning of depth in the way that older, crawling infants do.

FIGURE 5.7
The Visual Cliff
The visual cliff technique tests whether an infant can perceive depth.

Hearing and Other Senses

Although the auditory system is well developed a few weeks before birth, there is little conclusive evidence about whether or how much fetuses actually hear in the womb (Aslin, Pisoni, & Jusczyk, 1983). Newborns can hear very well at birth, in contrast to their blurry vision, although not as well as adults. They are startled by sudden noises and soothed by rhythmic or monotonous sounds, such as lullabies or washers and dryers.

One of the striking discoveries of recent years is the ability of very young infants to discriminate nearly all the phonetic contrasts found in human speech. For example, one-month-old infants can tell the difference between the sounds of "p" and "b." Peter Eimas and his colleagues (1971) found that infants would suck strongly on a pacifier connected to a recording mechanism to hear the sound "bah." Gradually they became habituated to that sound and sucked less. When the sound changed to "pah," they sucked harder again. Infants are able to note most of the contrasts used by the world's languages, even though

they may lose that capacity as adults. For example, Eimas (1975) found that babies can tell the difference between "r" and "l," although Japanese adults cannot. Similarly, there are contrasts in other languages that adult English speakers cannot hear but that young infants can. Thus, all infants come into the world prepared to learn any language they hear spoken around them.

When these findings first appeared, many researchers took them to mean that human infants possess specialized skills for processing information from speech. But recent studies in monkeys and other animals have shown that other species can make similar distinctions. Many researchers now speculate that the auditory capacities found in young infants are common to all mammals, and that human languages capitalized on these sound contrasts (Kuhl, 1978; Stevens, 1975).

In addition to being able to tell the difference between speech sounds, young infants are also able to recognize the voices of different speakers. Infants as young as four weeks (Mehler et al., 1978), and even three days (DeCasper & Fifer, 1980), have shown that they preferred listening to their own mother's voice over that of an unfamiliar woman.

There is also evidence that young infants have at least a rudimentary ability to integrate information from different senses. Thus, newborns will turn their eyes in the direction of a sound. If an object is placed within sight and reach, young babies will make swiping movements with their arms and hands. But there is no evidence that they expect to see anything when turning to the source of sound or to touch anything when they reach toward an object (Harris, 1983).

One study showed that one-month-old infants were upset by hearing their mother's voice come from a speaker placed some distance from where she was actually standing (Aronson & Rosenbloom, 1971). Studies by Spelke (1979; Spelke & Owsely, 1979) showed that four-month-old babies would look at whichever of two television screens were appropriate to the sound track they were hearing. One screen showed a bouncing toy kangaroo, the other a bouncing monkey. The filmed objects bounced at different rates while a central speaker broadcast the sound from one of the films.

Finally, newborns have a functioning sense of smell. They turn away from unpleasant odors such as vinegar and ammonia and can distinguish among a variety of other smells (Lipsitt, Engen, & Kaye, 1963). Breastfed newborns can recognize and prefer the odor of their own mother's milk to that of another woman (Russell, 1976). Newborns can also distinguish a variety of tastes and have a preference for sweetness even before they have tasted milk (Lipsitt, 1977).

All in all, this recent research has challenged traditional views of how infants learn about the world. Both Piaget and the learning theorists have agreed that the infant painstakingly and slowly builds up impressions of the world and learns to connect sight, sound, and touch. It now appears that infants come into the world with a head start in perceiving and recognizing

reality. Yet this is not to say that infants do not have a lot to learn. Rather, the new findings suggest that the infant comes into the world prepared to learn the events and categories that are important and "natural" to human life.

The Growth of Competence

By three and a half months, a baby can control its looking behavior as well as an adult. But its ability to use its hands is still limited. The development of grasping is one of the best charted areas of infant development (Halverson, 1931; White, Castle, & Held, 1964). Learning to use the hands as tools to pick things up is only one part of the task of learning to be a manipulator and controller of objects. The other part is getting the eyes and hands to work together.

Babies first try to reach for objects at about two months, but they can only make gross swipes in the direction of the object. They cannot yet oppose the thumb to the other fingers so that an object can be grasped, nor can they keep their hands in view. The eyes do not yet know how to lead the hand. The mouth is more in charge of grasping than the eyes. Anything in the hands will find its way to the mouth. The strong connection between grasping and sucking has to be broken before the child can begin to explore the objects it can reach.

Eventually, the eyes do take over from the mouth in guiding the hands. Hand watching—the baby's fascinated discovery of its hands as objects to look at—is the milestone that marks this important transition. By four months, the hand slowly approaches the object, touches it with spread fingers, closes the fingers, and brings the object to the mouth. By five and a half or six months, the eyes are in charge of the hand, the separate phases of grasping have smoothed out, and the child can efficiently pick up a one-inch cube. By a year, the infant can pick up a pencil and make a mark on paper, or hold a bead in a precise pincer grip. While maturation plays an important role in the growth of eye-hand coordination, experience plays a role also. Experiments have shown that babies given interesting objects to look at and grasp at will move through these phases at a faster rate than those in a bland, monotonous environment (White & Held, 1966).

Once the child has mastered grasping, he or she starts on a career of active exploration and play that will bring increasing contact with and knowledge of the world. Let us look once again at Gesell's description of the six- to seven-month-old baby to get some idea of what everyday behavior looks like in the middle of the first year. At this age babies can sit, but they still need some support to hold their bodies upright. The first thing the baby does on waking is to survey the scene, looking around for some object to hold, mouth, and bang. In Gesell's example, it is a clothespin that comes to hand. (Gesell was writing before washing machines and laundromats had obliterated clotheslines and clothespins from many families' backyards.) As we look in on the baby, he is sitting up in his high chair playing with the clothespin.

> His eagerness and intentness show that his play is serious business. He is discovering the size, shape, weight and texture of things. He is no longer content merely to finger his hands, as he did at 16 weeks. He wants to finger the clothespin, get the feel of it. He puts it to his mouth, pulls it out, looks at it, rotates it with a twist of the wrist, puts it back into his mouth, pulls it out, gives it another twist, brings up his free hand, transfers the clothespin from hand to hand, bangs it on the high chair tray, drops it, recovers it, retransfers it from hand to hand, drops it out of reach, leans over to retrieve it, fails, fusses a moment, and then bangs the tray with his empty hand, etc., throughout his busy day. *He is never idle because he is under such a compelling urge to use his hands for manipulation and exploitation.* (Gesell & Ilg, 1949, pp. 108–9, emphasis added)

Curiosity and Its Biological Significance

What is this "compelling urge" to explore, exploit, and manipulate? Why are infants as busy as they are? Some psychologists have tried to explain the child's curiosity as a kind of "instinct," a hunger for novelty, variety, and complexity. Some writers have stressed what Karl Groos in 1901 called the joy of being a cause. Children delight in making something happen: making noise, turning on light switches, splashing in a mud puddle, tearing paper. Robert White (1965) has used the term "effectance motivation" to describe the child's need to gain a feeling of mastery over the environment.

Nonhuman creatures also like to explore and play, and they learn in the absence of strong instinctive drives. For example, Konrad Lorenz described jackdaws playing high-speed games in strong winds. Gavin Maxwell describes his pet otter playing for hours with a rubber ball. Laboratory studies have shown that animals will learn and work simply to experience new sounds and sights. One study, for example, found that monkeys would spend up to ten continuous hours taking apart puzzles for no other reward than the privilege of doing so (Harlow, 1950). Berlyne (1960) found that rats will explore mazes that are unfamiliar to them. Other studies showed that rats and monkeys will "work" when the only reward is the opportunity to explore. For example, monkeys solved problems to get the chance to look out a window or listen to sounds from a tape recorder (Butler, 1958).

The studies mentioned above were carried out in the confining settings of standard laboratory devices, while, for several years, a zoologist named Kavenaugh (1967) studied the behavior of a wild species of mouse in a more complicated environment—cages with mazes, wheels, and switches that could be controlled by the animals themselves or the experimenter. Kavenaugh found that the mice would take advantage of almost any chance to change their environment. Also, they had a strong tendency to counteract changes that were unexpected or not under their control. For example, the mice would go in and out of their nests often during the course of the day. But if the experimenter picked them up and placed them in their nests, they would leave immediately, no matter how many times they were put back. Or, if the mice were running in a wheel and the experimenter turned a switch to make the wheel go around by motor, the mice would promptly turn the switch off. But if a mouse had turned on the motor and the experimenter turned it off, the mouse would promptly turn it back on again. In other words, something the mice usually initiated by themselves was avoided when it was imposed by force—they would respond by doing the opposite.

The mice also preferred complicated and challenging tasks to simple ones. For example, they preferred running in square wheels and wheels with hurdles to round ones. For no tangible reward, they would quickly learn to find their way through mazes with hundreds of blind alleys. As M. B. Smith (1968) observes, commenting on Kavenaugh's study, these mice seem very much like humans, especially children. Their curiosity, playfulness, and resistance to control suggest that these same traits in humans are part of our evolutionary heritage as mammals.

Why should mammals play and explore and learn things incidentally? For the higher animals such behavior is very adaptive in the evolutionary sense of aiding in survival. The lower forms of life have very simple repertoires of behavior. A jellyfish or a starfish can respond only to a few stimuli. The more advanced an animal is on the evolutionary scale, the more information its nervous system takes in, and the more varied are its responses. Despite the proverb saying that curiosity killed the cat, an incurious, immobile cat—or rat—that took no interest in its environment except when hungry or thirsty or fearful would be less likely to survive than an alert animal that noticed and remembered things even when it was not motivated by strong bodily needs. The curious animal would have noticed various paths through its terrain and could use this knowledge to escape predators. Hence, it would be more likely to survive and produce descendants. It makes good evolutionary sense, then, for the higher animals to be endowed with intrinsic motives for the processing of information from the environment. In the same way, negativism—or resistance to external control—would also be an evolutionary advantage. An animal that struggled to get away from a predator or a dangerous situation would be more likely to survive than one that simply gave up and surrendered helplessly to its "fate."

In humans, both the range of sensitivity and the response capabilities of the organism increase exponentially. For an infant to become a competent member of a social community, an enormous number and variety of things must be learned. Hence cognitive motivation—the inclination to learn and do things for the sheer pleasure of it—should be equal to the task. It makes sense also that a baby's cognitive system should be most sensitive to the kinds of information noted above: **contingency,** or knowledge of the kinds of events it can change and influence; and **discrepancy,** or new, surprising, puzzling events—happenings that are most likely to advance the organism toward greater knowledge.

Contingency and Discrepancy

In humans, as in animals, both contingency and discrepancy attract attention. They arouse the "orienting reflex," the tendency to turn to or explore a stimulus. Both also stimulate emotional responses: a sudden noise (discrepancy) or the awareness that "something out there is tracking my movements" (contingency) can signal danger. Discrepant and contingent events can also be pleasurable, interesting, or fun. John Watson (not John B. Watson, the founder of behaviorism) has studied contingency awareness in early infancy and finds that babies as young as eight to ten weeks can learn to play what he calls The Game and show great delight in doing so (1972, 1983).

The Game consists of an adult making some stimulus contingent on what a baby does—touching Johnny's nose when he wiggles his legs, or tickling his belly if he widens his eyes. Watson's experimental version of The Game used mobiles which moved when the baby pressed its head against a special pillow. After about four or five days of playing with this mobile for about ten minutes a day, babies began to smile and coo vigorously—earlier by a month than the usual appearance of this kind of emotional reaction.

The notion of discrepancy refers to the fact that, at any age, our attention is aroused by an event or stimulus that deviates in some way from our expectations. Thus, the loud ticking of a new alarm clock may be bothersome at first, but after a while we stop hearing it. If the ticking stops suddenly, we may notice the silence.

The studies of habituation mentioned earlier also illustrate the relation between discrepancy and attention. During the first days after birth, an infant's attention is attracted by changes in the ongoing level of stimulation—a sudden noise, a light going on, a moving object. Eventually, with more days and weeks of experience in the world, the infant appears to build up some kind of mental representations of familiar objects or events that enable it to recognize them. For example, after about a week's feeding experience, babies show an anticipatory reaction to the sight of the bottle. This behavior is one of the first signs of memory or expectancy in the infant and was given a name by German psychologists: the *Flaschenerkennugsreaction,* or bottle recognition reaction (Spitz, 1965).

At any age, there is tendency for people to pay most attention to events that are somewhat but not too deviant from expectations. One study showed that four-month-old infants look a long time at an image of a face in which the eyes were not in their normal position, but would not look very long at a face without eyes (Kagan, 1970). Many researchers now believe that it is the attractiveness of moderately discrepant events that leads cognitive development along. If the environment is monotonous, such as in an institution where infants lie on their backs staring at the ceiling, their development is apt to be retarded (although not necessarily permanently).

On the other hand, a child confronted with too much novelty and change may become detached and uninterested in the world. Infants seem to have a "biological fuse" (Papousek & Papousek, 1979) which regulates information coming in from the environment, leading them to turn away from confusing events. Infants work hard to solve difficult problems, but if the tasks are too hard to solve, they may become detached. Hunt (1965) refers to this as "the problem of the match": for development to proceed the baby must confront situations that are just hard enough to be interesting, but not so hard as to be unbearably frustrating. Fortunately, outside of extreme situations such as barren institutions or severely disturbed families, most babies find themselves in environments that feed their curiosity.

The Development of Intelligent Behavior in Infancy: Piaget's Six Sensorimotor Stages

The best account of how the infant uses its cognitive motivation to progress from helpless newborn to competent toddler is contained in the work of Jean Piaget (1952, 1954). The major landmarks of the infant's progress are described in Piaget's six-stage model of intellectual development during the time between birth and the onset of language. He calls this the sensorimotor period because the child is functioning at a practical, nonsymbolic level of intelligence—like an animal.

This model was originally based on close observations by Piaget and his wife of their three children—Jacqueline, Lucienne, and Laurent, born in 1925, 1927, and 1931. In these days when most research involves large numbers of subjects and complicated laboratory devices, it is remarkable that a monumental contribution to developmental psychology was based on the observations of three children growing up in their everyday home environment.

These were not, however, the casual observations of an ordinary parent. Piaget made hundreds of detailed observations of his children's behavior and the day-by-day changes that took place. He also devised many simple but ingenious experiments to test his theories of the babies' thought processes—hiding a toy just as the child is reaching for it, for example, to see if he or she would search for it when it was not in sight.

Since Piaget's pioneering work, his findings have been followed up by many investigators working with large numbers of infants. Recent research has modified some of his conclusions. For example, the new experimental techniques for studying sucking as well as looking and heart rate have revealed that young infants are more perceptually competent than Piaget could have known. (We will discuss some of these modifications and revisions later on.) Despite these revisions, Piaget's observations of infant cognitive development are among the most well-documented findings in psychology.

Although Piaget began his career in the 1920s, his ideas are at the forefront of contemporary research in infant development. As we saw in an earlier chapter, Piaget's views of infants, and of human nature itself, differed from those of the other leading developmental theories, behaviorism and psychoanalysis. Piaget saw infants as actively striving to learn about the world, while other theorists saw them as the passive objects of forces in the environment or of their own instincts. Further, Piaget was the first to see infancy as a time of intellectual growth, the necessary forerunner of later symbolic thought and language. He showed that the major concepts we use to understand our world—time, space, object, substance, number, cause—have their roots in the first two years of life. Babies grasp these concepts in an almost literal way through the actual manipulation of objects.

Piaget's ideas about infant mental development were more tied to actual observations than those of any other developmental theorist. Freud, as we saw, based his ideas about infancy mostly on the free associations of adult patients. Skinner and other behaviorists worked mainly with animals and hardly at all with children, though the same cannot be said of more recent behaviorists such as Bandura and Mischel. Further, although Piaget freely used mentalistic concepts such as intention, image, and insight, along with a host of more abstract theoretical terms, these were always tied to observable behavior.

Some knowledge of Piaget's work is essential to any student of child development. Unfortunately, Piaget is a difficult writer to understand. Although his theoretical notions are based on some observation or experimental demonstration, they are frequently couched in a set of terms that are unfamiliar even to many psychologists.

One concept central to Piaget's account of sensorimotor intellectual development, as we saw in Chapter 3, is that of *scheme,* a system of actions for dealing with the world. For example, a young baby has a sucking scheme: it will suck anything that comes into its mouth. The infant may also be said to have a looking scheme, a grasping scheme, a scheme for pushing an object with another object.

A behaviorist might use the term "response" to refer to what Piaget calls a scheme. But to Piaget, the term "response" suggests an automatic, robotlike connection between a stimulus and its resulting action. To him, a scheme is not only a response, a habit automatically triggered by stimulus, but also the *meaning* the child attributes to an object or event. A scheme is *not* just the observable behavior itself—the sucking, grasping, and so on—it is also the mental framework or cognitive structure that lies behind an action.

To Piaget, schemes are the raw material of intellectual development. Thinking is simply carrying out real actions in one's head. For example, just as the baby joins toys together and takes them apart, the adult puts together concepts, takes them apart, puts them in order. Thus, sensorimotor actions are transformed in the course of development, but they are not a totally different kind of behavior from adult logical thought. Sensorimotor schemes are transformed in three ways to more advanced, logical behavior: they come to be more adapted to reality, they can be combined with one another, and they come to be internalized—that is, carried out mentally, rather than in real overt behavior.

Two other essential Piagetian concepts are the twin processes of **assimilation** and **accommodation,** which we first encountered in Chapter 3. These are the basic mechanisms that move cognitive development forward at any age; they describe what happens when mind meets matter. For example, consider a seven-month-old baby given a lollipop for the first time. The baby will put the lollipop in its mouth, thus *assimilating* the lollipop to a sucking scheme or, to put it another way, defining the lollipop as "something to suck." But then the baby discovers that the lollipop is somewhat different than other things he or she has sucked before. It is not a soft, milk-giving nipple, or a hard, dry object like a rattle, but a hard thing that gives off a sweet taste and gets to be sticky after a while. As a result of these discoveries, the sucking scheme will change somewhat to *accommodate* the new knowledge. Thus, assimilation and accommodation explain how the child's mind gradually changes through constant daily encounters with the world and its objects.

A major theme in Piaget's account of infancy is the development of a very general scheme called the object concept or sense of **object permanence.** Piaget discovered that babies do not share the commonsense notions about objects that adults and older children take for granted. (See the discussion on Piaget's Stage 3 later in this chapter.) For example, we assume that people and things are solid objects which exist and can move through space. We assume our friends, family, and possessions continue to exist when we are not looking at them. We also recognize ourselves as objects like others which also exist and move in space. A magician's tricks play on our strong belief in the permanence of objects. If we did not have this belief we would not be surprised when a magician pulls a rabbit out of a hat, or makes something disappear. In fact, infants are not surprised at such tricks (Charlesworth, 1969).

Piaget (1970) argued that, to a baby in the first months of life, the world seems like a kaleidoscope or slide show. There are no permanent objects, but only "perceptual pictures" which appear, disappear, and sometimes reappear. An object out of sight is not only out of mind, but out of existence as far as the child is concerned.

The concept of object permanence is a good example of why emotional and social development are so closely bound up with intellectual development. The object concept is fundamental to all aspects of psychological functioning. Consider the emotional life of a person who did not believe that other people, things, and his or her own body were solid objects in space, but only fleeting, fragmentary images. Beyond early infancy, such a world is encountered only in nightmares, schizophrenia, or under the influence of strong drugs, extreme fatigue, stress, or hypnosis.

Before going on to describe the six stages of infant development, it will be useful to keep several things in mind. First, the ages given for the various stages are only a rough average. Different children pass through the sequence at different ages, and a child at a particular stage of development may still show behavior associated with earlier stages. Each stage is labeled for the highest level of behavior the child is capable of, but the child may not operate at his or her highest level all the time. Further, the rate of a child's progress may be influenced by environmental circumstances. For example, "hand watching"—the baby's looking at its hands—is a developmental milestone in early infancy. One of Piaget's children was three months slower than another in attaining this landmark. Piaget explained this "delay" on grounds that the slower baby had been born in the winter, and since she had been bundled up in blankets more than her brother, she had not had the opportunity to have her hands free.

While the precise age at which a child does something was not crucial to Piaget, the *sequence* of stages was. Thus, Piaget held that the sequence of stages is constant: no stage is ever skipped on the way to a later one and the order of the stages is never varied.

The following summary of Piaget's six sensorimotor stages of infant cognitive development presents the highlights of each period. Special attention will be paid to development of the object concept, and to the development of intentionality—the purposeful seeking of some goal. To Piaget, intentionality was the essence of intelligent behavior. In a remarkably short time, the infant progresses from being a creature of reflexes to one who carries out voluntary, purposeful acts. Piaget described the step-by-step changes that result in this transformation. (See Figure 5.8.)

There is space only to touch on some of the major changes at each stage. Piaget traced out several other aspects of development during infancy which are not dealt with here. For example, he followed the development of imitation and play, and concepts of space, time, and causality. Piaget's observations on infancy are presented in two books, *The Origins of Intelligence* (1952) and *The Construction of Reality in the Child* (1954). A good introduction to Piaget is by Ginsburg and Opper (1979). A more advanced work is by Flavell (1963).

Stage 1: Exercising Reflexes (Birth to 1½ months)
The baby comes into the world with a large number of innate reflexes or "wired-in responses." Some of these reflexes persist unchanged into adulthood, such as sneezing when our noses are tickled; others are specific to newborns. Piaget was interested only in a few reflexes which change with experience. Sucking, looking, vocalizing, grasping, and body movements are the behaviors that will develop through constant use and through repeated encounters with objects and events. Even during this very early period, these reflexes change as a result of experience; for example, the baby may suck at the breast differently from the way it sucks at a bottle or at nonnutritive things such as thumbs and blankets.

Like the behaviorists, Piaget saw reflexes as the source of psychological development. But there are profound differences between the two approaches. For traditional behaviorists, reflexes remain the basic units of behavior; the behavior of the child and the adult is a vastly complicated chain of reflexes that has been modified and linked together as a result of learning. Further, the behaviorists see the environment as the force that shapes behavior.

In contrast, Piaget was always concerned with the child's mind. Reflexes, even at the beginning of life, are not just a set of movements, but visible signs of mental processes. Reflexes become intentional actions, and later, mental structures. Especially in the early part of his career, Piaget (1927) was interested in consciousness, what the baby is experiencing, as well as in the baby's structures of thought. Even at the

FIGURE 5.8
Piaget's Six Stages of Sensorimotor Development

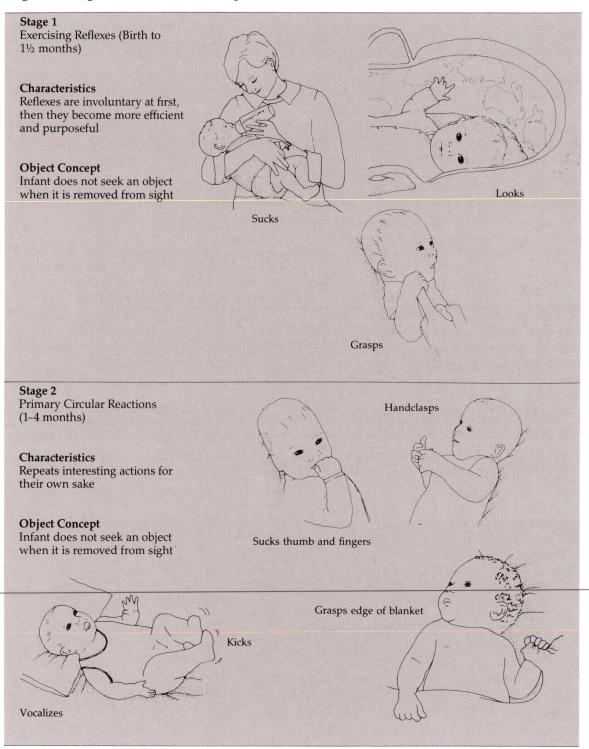

Stage 1
Exercising Reflexes (Birth to 1½ months)

Characteristics
Reflexes are involuntary at first, then they become more efficient and purposeful

Object Concept
Infant does not seek an object when it is removed from sight

Sucks

Looks

Grasps

Stage 2
Primary Circular Reactions (1–4 months)

Characteristics
Repeats interesting actions for their own sake

Object Concept
Infant does not seek an object when it is removed from sight

Handclasps

Sucks thumb and fingers

Grasps edge of blanket

Kicks

Vocalizes

Stage 3
Secondary Circular Reactions
(4–8 months)

Characteristics
Repeats an action to produce
or maintain an interesting effect

Object Concept
Infant will search for a partially
hidden object but will stop
looking if it disappears

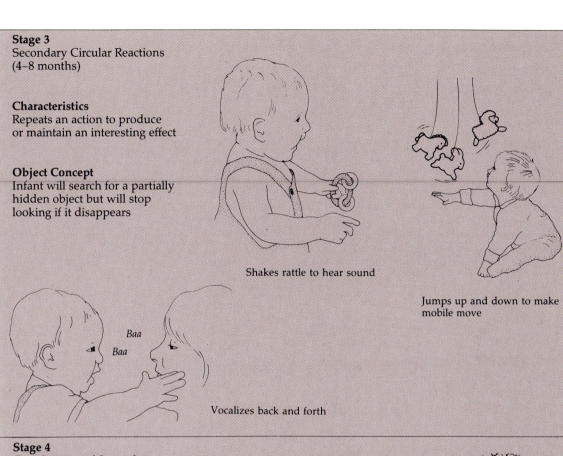

Shakes rattle to hear sound

Jumps up and down to make
mobile move

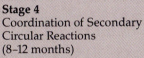

Baa
Baa

Vocalizes back and forth

Stage 4
Coordination of Secondary
Circular Reactions
(8–12 months)

Characteristics
Combines actions to obtain a
goal, applies actions to new
situations

Object Concept
Infant will search for a
completely hidden object, but
will search in the first place the
object was hidden even after
seeing it moved

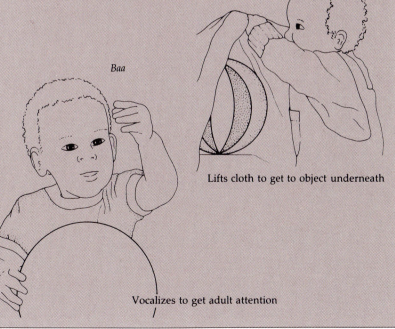

Baa

Lifts cloth to get to object underneath

Vocalizes to get adult attention

FIGURE 5.8 (continued)
Piaget's Six Stages of Sensorimotor Development (continued)

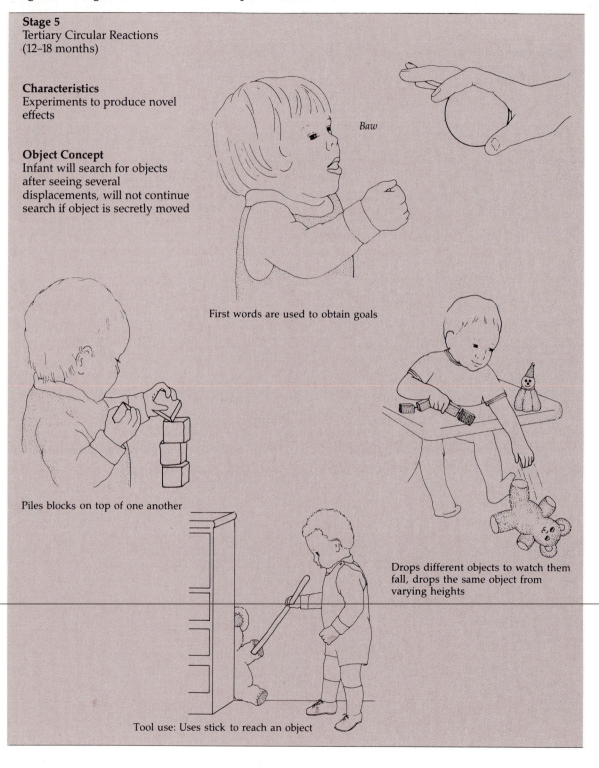

Stage 5
Tertiary Circular Reactions
(12–18 months)

Characteristics
Experiments to produce novel
effects

Object Concept
Infant will search for objects
after seeing several
displacements, will not continue
search if object is secretly moved

Baw

First words are used to obtain goals

Piles blocks on top of one another

Drops different objects to watch them
fall, drops the same object from
varying heights

Tool use: Uses stick to reach an object

Stage 6
Beginning of Representational
Thought (18–24 months)

Characteristics
Can think of absent objects and
past events, solves problems
mentally

Object Concept
Infant will search for object
secretly hidden, certain that it
must exist somewhere

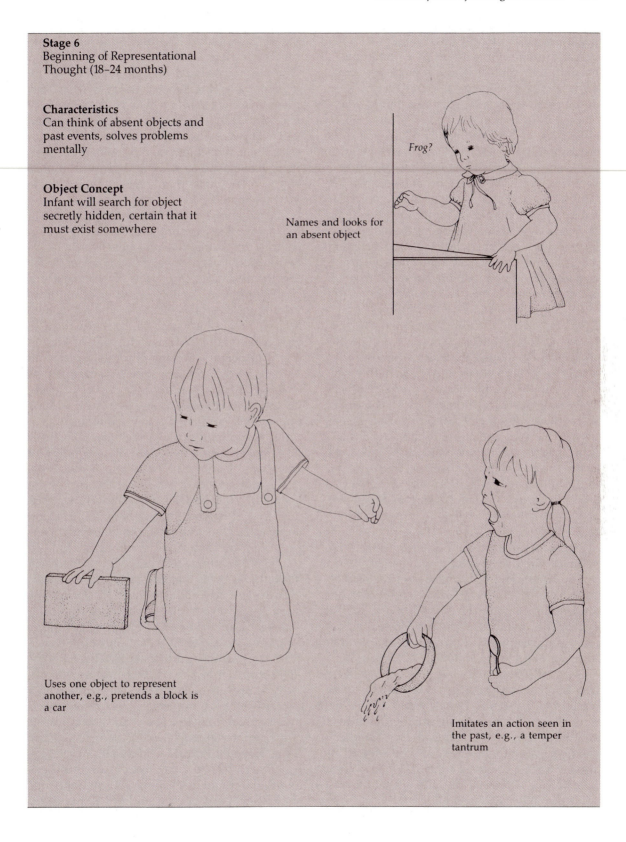

Names and looks for
an absent object

Uses one object to represent
another, e.g., pretends a block is
a car

Imitates an action seen in
the past, e.g., a temper
tantrum

beginning of life, Piaget saw the baby as "a particularly interested witness to a multitude of events: a picture passing through his visual field, a sound he hears, a sound that he hears at the same time as he sees something, and so on" (p. 208).

Further, as we saw earlier, Piaget saw the environment not as something that happens to the child, but rather, something the child is constantly striving to act on and master. The "interested witness" is not a passive spectator. Babies, when they are awake, are perpetually trying to assimilate everything they encounter by sucking, grabbing, looking, and listening. At the same time, accommodation or learning is going on—reality is constantly altering the baby's schemas.

Stage 2: Primary Circular Reactions—The First Habits (1 to 4 months) The first step of psychological development occurs when the baby is able to get some control over the reflexes. No longer simply an "interested witness" the baby can now make some things happen: he or she finds a way to repeat an interesting action, waving a hand, sucking a thumb, kicking the legs. Piaget saw in this kind of behavior the first sign of voluntary behavior: "The basic law of dawning psychological activity could be said to be the search for the maintenance or repetition of interesting states of consciousness" (1977, p. 202).

Piaget calls the typical behavior of this stage **primary circular reactions**. By "circular reactions" he simply meant behaviors that are repeated over and over. *Primary* circular reactions are actions centered on the body and carried out for their own sake. The baby looks in order to see, moves in order to move, sucks in order to suck.

Thumbsucking is an example of a primary circular reaction; another example was two-month-old Laurent's "scratching." Piaget described how Laurent scratched rhythmically at anything his hand touched—his mother's shoulder, his father's hand, his crib sheet. This scratching can go on for a quarter of an hour at a time, several times a day. It is a forerunner of what will later be grasping.

Stage 3: Secondary Circular Reactions—Making Interesting Sights Last (4 to 8 months) This stage is marked by the emergence of intentional grasping and **secondary circular reactions.** While *primary* circular reactions involve only the child's own body, *secondary* ones involve objects. The child discovers by chance that some movement makes something happen; for example, kicking makes a mobile bounce. The child then repeats the action to produce the effect.

Piaget considered this stage to be the first of the *intentional* sensorimotor adaptations, in contrast to the first two stages, which he labeled elementary sensorimotor adaptations. For the first time, the baby seems to have a goal in mind. An action is performed in order to produce a certain effect, not just for its own sake. Earlier, as we saw, the baby may kick its legs just for the function pleasure of kicking them. In Stage 3, kicking becomes a means to an end, a way to make something happen, to shake a doll hanging from the crib or carriage. Or the child repeatedly shakes a rattle to hear the sounds, not just to shake something.

But the intentionality of the Stage 3 infant is of a limited kind. It is only the beginning of deliberate, purposeful behavior, because the goal is not yet clearly set out at the start of the behavior. That is, the baby discovers by accident that a behavior such as kicking or shaking an object will make something interesting happen, and the baby will continue to kick or shake to make the effect last. But the effect will not have been the child's goal from the outset.

The object concept also advances during this stage. If an object falls to the floor, the baby will now lean out of crib or high chair to look for it. Earlier, the child would only have stared at the spot where it disappeared. There is a curious limitation in the child's behavior with objects, however, which illustrates why Piaget concluded the young infant lacks a concept of the permanent object. The child in hot pursuit of an object will stop dead if the object disappears behind a screen (Figure 5.9). For example, Piaget placed a toy duck close to seven-month-old Jacqueline's hand. As she was about to touch it, he slipped it under the crib sheet.

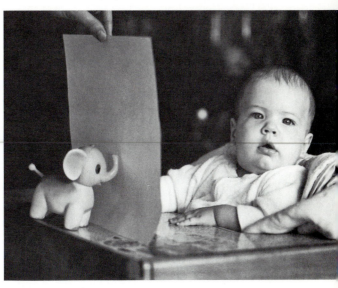

FIGURE 5.9
Object Permanence
An infant who does not yet understand the concept of object permanence will think that an object does not exist if it is removed from sight.

She immediately took her hand away, although she was perfectly able to move the sheet. Even when Piaget repeated the experiment and put her hand on the covered duck, she still did not raise the sheet.

Another curious aspect of behavior with hidden objects is this: the child will reach for a partly hidden object, but only if a certain amount shows. Six-month-old Laurent would reach for a pencil if he saw three or four centimeters of it sticking out from a screen, but not if he saw less than that.

As Piaget interpreted it, the child at this stage does not seem to believe that the rest of the object exists behind the screen. Rather, he or she seems to believe that the object is either made or unmade each time it emerges from or goes behind the cover. Thus, a baby will scream for his or her bottle if part of it is visible, but if it is then completely covered, the baby will act as if the bottle no longer exists.

Stage 4: Coordination of Secondary Circular Reactions (8 to 12 months) This stage is the first one in which what Piaget regarded as true intelligence appears. He defined intelligence as problem solving, the use of certain means to reach certain goals. The two major developments of Stage 4 are the appearance of clearly intentional, goal-directed behavior and the beginning of object permanence. Both of these new abilities can be seen in the baby's successful search for a hidden object. The intentionality of the Stage 4 infant is apparent in the determined way he or she will use one scheme as means and another as goal. For example, the child will push aside a pillow with one hand to pick up a toy with the other. Earlier, even if the toy was not hidden by the pillow or some other obstacle, the child might have lost interest in the toy and begun to play with the pillow. Now it is much easier to tell the difference between means and ends in the child's behavior.

Although the child can pull off a cover to find a hidden object, the object concept at this stage has a peculiar limitation. Piaget first noticed this peculiarity in the behavior of a visiting 13-month-old cousin. This boy, who knew how to walk, was playing with a ball when it rolled under an armchair. He reached under the chair and pulled it out. Then the ball rolled under a sofa at the other end of the room and disappeared behind the bottom fringes. The boy thought for a moment, crossed the room, and reached under the armchair again, carefully examining the place the ball had been before!

Later, Piaget carried out several experiments with his own children in which he hid an object first in one place, then another. Nine-month-old Laurent was seated between a coverlet (A) on his right and a wool garment (B) on his left. Piaget hid his watch under the coverlet, and Laurent retrieved it. When Piaget put the watch under the garment, Laurent looked attentively, but the moment the watch disappeared Laurent turned back to the coverlet and looked for the watch there. Piaget showed him the watch again, hid it under the garment, and again Laurent looked for it under the coverlet. This strange behavior, often called the "A, not B" phenomenon, has been corroborated by other researchers and has even been

found in dogs (Thompson & Melzack, 1956).

There is as yet no firm explanation of this behavior, but it seems clear that the Stage 4 child still does not think of objects in the same way we do. To an infant in this stage, the object seems somehow attached to its surroundings; it is still in the place it "belongs," even though it was seen moving. Piaget gave examples of similar behavior in older children. Thus, at three and a half Lucienne saw a visiting relative drive off in a car, and then went to the room where he was staying to see if he was still there. Even adults sometimes lapse into this kind of behavior, when we keep looking for a lost wallet in the place it is "supposed" to be, even though we have already looked there.

Stage 5: Tertiary Circular Reactions—Discovery of New Means through Active Experimentation (12 to 18 months)   During this stage ba-

bies become toddlers, able to move around on their legs with their hands free. Like scientists, children now experiment with objects to discover their properties and possibilities. A child may drop a ball from different heights to see how it falls, or the child may run a toy car down a board, varying the slant of the board each time. Piaget called these experimental manipulations **tertiary circular reactions**.

Another important landmark of this period is the child's discovery of the tool—for example, the discovery that a stick or string can be used to get hold of an object. This is a type of intelligent behavior that is believed to have been central in human evolution. Apes, especially chimpanzees, are also able to use simple tools such as sticks. But their intelligence remains permanently at the Stage 5 or 6 level (Chevalier-Skolnickoff, 1977).

In Stage 5, children reach a new level of object permanence: they no longer go back to A after seeing an object hidden at B. But they can find the object only if they can see it being hidden. For example, if you put a toy in a box, then put the box behind a screen and dump the toy out, the child will not look behind the screen when shown the empty box. In other words, the child can deal with *visible* displacements, but not *invisible* ones.

Stage 6: Beginning of Representational Thought—The Invention of New Means through Mental Combinations (18 to 24 months)   The major achievement at this time is the ability to use mental images to solve problems. This stage marks the transition from sensorimotor action to mental representation. Earlier, children can understand that something can stand for or mean something else. For example, when mother puts on a coat it means that she is going out. The Stage 5 child may use words as tools, to ask for things. But before Stage 6, the child cannot use symbols or images to solve problems. Stage 5 children solve problems by trial and error, manipulating objects in the real world. Stage 6 children can manipulate objects in their heads. For example, when Jacqueline was at Stage 5, Piaget put a stick outside her playpen. By turning the stick this way

and that, she was able to get the stick through the bars. With Lucienne and Laurent, Piaget waited until Stage 6 to present the stick problem. After sitting and staring briefly, each of them was able to get the stick through the bars without any overt manipulation. By this fateful step, the toddler enters a new world. The sensorimotor world of bodily actions, of the here and now, is transformed into a world of meaning.

The new capacity to represent events and objects is the great achievement of the sensorimotor period. But there is still a long way to go between the first sensorimotor symbols and the symbolic capacity of the adult. These early symbols are private and personal to the child, rather than the agreed-upon symbols of language. Thus, though they are immensely useful to the child in dealing with the world, the personal symbols are limited in their usefulness for communication between the child and others. Even when they begin to use words and phrases, children attach their own idiosyncratic meanings to them. Further, these early images are closely tied to sensorimotor experience. They are like a movie of real events that children play back in their heads. At this stage the child cannot yet think about imagined events and possibilities. The complete transition to symbols and the flowering of spoken language come with the next stage of development—the preoperational. We discuss the emergence of language in Chapter 8.

A related aspect of a child's new mental powers is the completion of object permanence. He or she can now follow objects through invisible displacements. For example, at the age of 19 months, Jacqueline watched her father as he put a coin in his hand, then put his hand under a blanket. He withdrew his closed hand; Jacqueline opened it and, finding no coin, searched under the blanket until she found it. Piaget repeated the test by hiding his hand in various other places before dropping the coin, but Jacqueline always found it. She now had a mental image of where the object was traveling.

No longer a prisoner of the present moment, the child can remember past events and anticipate future ones. His or her play also reflects this new capacity for mental representation. The child is now able to treat one object as another: a napkin can be treated as a blanket to cover a doll, a cup can be treated as a hat. Play becomes symbolic; it becomes the medium of emotional expression.

> It is primarily affective conflicts that appear in symbolic play. . . . If the child has been frightened by a big dog, in a symbolic game things will be arranged so that dogs will no longer be mean or else children will become brave. (Piaget & Inhelder, 1966, pp. 57–60)

Revising Piaget

How well have Piaget's observations of his own three children held up under the scrutiny of several decades of research? The answer is, remarkably well. Most of Piaget's basic description of how infants change in the first two years of life has been confirmed by many studies, as well as by ordinary observation. It is easy for anyone who is friendly with a baby to check out Piaget's observations, and countless students of developmental psychology have done so. More formal investigators also emerge with descriptions of the stages of infant development that correspond surprisingly closely to Piaget's. McCall (1979; McCall, Eichorn, & Hogarty, 1977) analyzed a number of infant intelligence tests, as well as other studies, and discovered a series of stages in infancy that correspond quite closely to those of Piaget.

On the other hand, some recent findings do not tally with Piaget's ideas. Piaget seems to have underestimated the competence of very young infants. He was not aware that newborns are as perceptually acute as they are in the ways indicated earlier in the chapter. As we have seen, these recent discoveries about infant competence have come about because of technical developments such as devices to track sucking and heart rates. Piaget's naturalistic, home observations could not have revealed such perceptual competencies.

Further, Piaget did not entertain the idea that babies' minds may be ahead of their motor capacities. But the recent work of John Watson (1983) and others shows that even though young babies cannot move through space, or manipulate objects with their hands, their minds can register contingencies—that is, they can recognize when their own behavior is making something happen in the world. Thus, Watson suggests that the first three months of life might be a "natural deprivation period": during this time, under normal circumstances, the child lacks an opportunity to exercise the intelligence it actually has.

Watson carried out a number of experiments in which he tried to supply babies with contingency experience during this natural deprivation period. He devised a mobile that could be attached to a crib and operated by a pressure-sensitive pillow placed under the baby's head. After a few days of play with these mobiles, two-month-old infants advanced to Piaget's stage of "secondary circular reactions," which, according to Piaget, usually begins around the fourth month. Further, the babies began to smile and coo at the mobile after a few days of playing with it, in advance of the normal time for this kind of emotional expression.

Watson's work, like other studies which show that children can reach a certain stage earlier than Piaget said they could, is not really a challenge to Piaget's theories: Piaget did not place great emphasis on age. However, several other lines of research do pose a more serious challenge to Piaget. For example, Bruner and Koslowski (1972) suggest that the development of eye-hand coordination in grasping may be a maturational phenomenon that is refined by experience. Such studies suggest there may be strong, innate components to behavior that Piaget thought must be learned through painstaking practice and experience.

Maturation and Infant Development

In general, there is growing evidence that the major turning points in infant development depend on maturational change. At around two to three months, a number of important transitions occur in emotional expression, as well as cognition and sleep (see box Can Newborn Babies Imitate Facial Expressions?). The most striking change for the parents is that the baby smiles at them, shows joy, and begins to seem like a real person. In rural Kenya, mothers begin to refer to their infants as "children" at this time, while earlier they call them "monkeys" (Super & Harkness, 1982). The fact that babies begin to smile at the same age in different cultures around the world and in very different conditions, even when blind (Freedman, 1964), suggests that there is an underlying maturational factor at work. This is further evidence of changes in brain structure between two and four months (Yakovlev & Lecours, 1967).

Another major turning point in emotional and cognitive behavior occurs at around eight months. Babies begin to be distressed at being left by their mothers and, in turn, to be wary of strangers. It is at this time that the child begins to find hidden objects and develops the sense of object permanence. Again, this set of changes occurs at remarkably similar ages in infants around the world. The timing and patterning of separation distress is very similar for children raised in urban America, in the barrios and Indian villages of Central America, as well as for children separated from their mothers each day in day care.

Generally, infants below the age of seven or eight months across these diverse settings do not cry when the mother leaves. After eight months, distress becomes more frequent and reaches a peak soon after the first birthday (Kagan, 1976). Jerome Kagan and his colleagues argue that it is unlikely that this behavior reflects a learned fear or the quality of the child's emotional relationship to the mother or primary caretaker (Kagan, 1976, 1984; Kagan, Kearsley, & Zelazo, 1978). Although these explanations are often offered, they make the implausible assumption that all children have

Can Newborn Babies Imitate Facial Expressions?

In 1977, two researchers startled the world by stating that infants in the first week of life can imitate the facial expressions of adults. Meltzoff and Moore (1977) claim to have demonstrated if

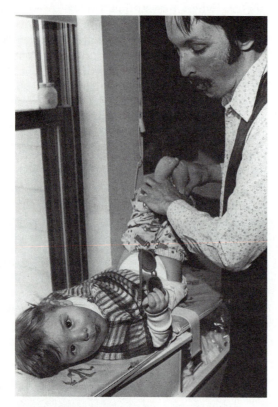

The difficulty many observers have is to determine who is imitating whom. Did the father or the baby initiate the facial expression here?

the mother or another adult sticks out her tongue, flutters her lashes, or opens her mouth very wide, the baby is likely to imitate these movements and will enjoy the game as well. Other researchers were startled because imitating facial expressions has been regarded

as a complex skill involving some kind of mental representation. Piaget (1962) had found that this kind of imitation does not emerge until late in the first year. Since Meltzoff and Moore presented their findings, the question of facial imitation in newborns has resulted in a lively controversy.

Details of the debate and the methodological issues involved are reviewed in Olson and Sherman (1983, pp. 1021–25). Briefly, the controversy centers around the problem of recognizing behavior that looks like imitation but really is not. For example, infants may stick out their tongues simply in response to being excited. An experimenter standing in front of an infant and sticking out his or her tongue might get the infant to stick out its tongue because of excitement, not imitation, or it might be that the infant sticks out its tongue to any slender object moving toward its mouth (Jacobson & Kagan, 1979). This would not be imitation, but rather an innately released response, like the sight of a pebble releasing a pecking response in a bird, or a red spot on a herring gull's beak releasing food-begging behavior in herring gull chicks.

All in all, it has been very difficult in practice to distinguish imitation from these various forms of pseudo-imitation. Further, other researchers have had difficulty replicating the original findings of Meltzoff and Moore. One investigator found that she could reproduce their results only when the experimenter believed that infant imitation of facial expressions is possible (Waters, 1979, reported in Olson & Sherman, 1983). An experimenter who did not believe in the possibility, or who did not know the purpose of the experiment, could not reproduce the results. These and other problems of replication suggest that a subtle process of social interaction and influence is going on in these experiments. Imitation is such a basic tool of learning that it is important to know more about it. But as of now, the question of whether newborns can imitate facial expressions remains unanswered.

similar experiences with fear and similar relations with their mothers. Rather, Kagan argues, the universal appearance of separation distress and fear of strangers reflects the growth of memory in the second half of the first year. The child gains the ability to remember past events, to compare past and present, and to anticipate what might happen in the future. This makes it possible for the child to detect and sometimes to fear unusual and unpredictable events. The twin fears of strangers and separation decline in the second year when the child has greater understanding that the mother will return and that strangers are not usually threatening. In sum, these fears reflect a general maturational change in psychological functioning; between 8 and 12 months the child becomes more thoughtful, and flexible. (Kagan, 1984). In fact, many researchers now agree that the development of memory is the key to understanding cognitive development in infancy and beyond (Siegler, 1978; Pascual-Leone, 1970).

The remarkably ordered shifts in cognitive and emotional functioning that occur in infancy pose a significant challenge to Piaget's theory. They suggest that the maturation of the central nervous system, not a long series of overt manipulations of objects, is the driving force in psychological development. Piaget himself believed that development follows a universal sequence, but he assumed that this was so because all children have similar experiences. Perhaps the strongest evidence against this view is the fact that handicapped children are not as impaired in their development as Piaget's theory of motor learning would suggest. For example, thalidomide babies, many of whom have no arms, seem to develop a normal object concept (Gouin-Decarie, 1969).

The Gibsons and Direct Perception

Still another challenge to Piaget has arisen in recent years. J. J. Gibson (1966, 1979) and Eleanor J. Gibson (1969; also Gibson & Spelke,

1983) have argued that children do not "construct" reality, but perceive it directly. For example, Piaget argued that the young infant sees the world as a flat patchwork of colors, and only gradually learns to see in three dimensions. The Gibsons, by contrast, argue that the perceptual world is rich in information, that the human newborn is well equipped in ways to explore it—and motivated to do so. Babies do not come into the world with innate knowledge, but they can detect valid information from birth. The difference between a newborn and an older child, according to the Gibsons, is that the latter is able to pick up more information from the environment, just as a wine expert can taste more than a novice in a sip of wine, or a musician can hear more of the details and structure of a symphony than someone who knows little about music.

The Gibsons have reminded developmental psychologists that perception has a purpose. Eyesight, hearing, touch, and the other senses evolved to convey knowledge about the environment. Every species has evolved in a particular habitat, and its perceptual systems are geared to extract the kind of information it needs to survive in that habitat. In particular, these systems extract information about the "affordances" of things. **Affordances** is a term introduced by J. J. Gibson (1979) to refer to the potential uses or meanings of objects. For example, a floor "affords" support for walking; a cave "affords" shelter from the rain; a cliff "affords" danger; an object "affords" grasping to a creature with hands. These affordances are specified by the actual nature and position of objects in the world, by the flow of visual information as an animal moves.

Another important term in the Gibsons' work is **invariant.** An invariant is a relationship that remains constant over change. For example, the size and shape of a ball remains constant, though it looks smaller as it rolls away. Even young infants appear to be sensitive to invariants and become more efficient in perceiving them as they develop.

Much of the recent experimental evidence on perceptual development in infancy supports the Gibsons' theory. Infants actively explore the environment from birth. They look in the direction of sound, follow objects with their eyes, swipe at things they see. In addition, they prefer novel objects to familiar ones, moving objects to stationary ones, and noisy objects to quiet ones, all of which serve to increase the amount of information available. On the other hand, some researchers have pointed to certain weaknesses in the Gibsons' approach. Their theory has little to say about what the perceiver brings to perception—what kinds of cognitive structures are necessary in the perceiver's head if perception is to take place. Also, they do not explain how other cognitive processes such as memory, imagery, and thought relate to perception. Nevertheless, some developmental researchers see in the Gibsons' approach a persuasive alternative to Piaget's views of perceptual and cognitive development. And there is widespread agreement that Piaget underestimated the infant's ability to perceive valid information about the world.

Concept Development in Infants

Recently, a new line of research has challenged both the Gibsons and Piaget. These studies focus on the infant's recognition of categories. The ability to classify events and objects into categories such as people, animals, food, furniture, and so on is the basis of language and symbolic thought. Recent studies suggest that infants between 6 and 12 months begin to be able to categorize everyday objects in much the way adults do, and they may have this capacity even earlier. (See review by Harris, 1983.) Because these findings suggest that infants go beyond the information given by the eyes, they challenge the Gibsons' insistence that memory and cognitive structures are not necessary to account for the infant's understanding of the world. These findings also challenge Piaget's belief that sensitivity to the abstract properties of objects develops much later than the second

half of the first year. In addition, they challenge his emphasis on motor activity as the key to cognitive development; the eye and the brain apparently can construct reality without the hand.

In categorization studies, infants are presented with a set of stimuli belonging to a set such as furniture or animals. After the infant has become familiar with the set, new examples are presented. For instance, after a series of male faces, infants are presented with a different male face or a female face. If the infant looks less at the item from the old category and more at the item from the new one, the researcher infers that the child has constructed a generalization about the old set that allows him or her to distinguish differences. When Fagan (1979) presented seven-month-old infants with a series of male faces, they seemed to construct a category of "male faces in general." They showed habituation—a lack of interest—in a new male face, but paid more attention to a female face.

Ross (1980) used a similar technique with a much more varied set of objects. Infants of 12 to 24 months were shown a variety of examples from categories of toys. Some sets contained very similar items: red, wooden, O-shaped letters, for example. Others contained very dissimilar items—furniture varying in material and size. Nevertheless, infants showed that they recognized the groups from which new items had been drawn; they turned away from a new instance of the old category, no matter how dissimilar it was to the earlier items, and they spent more time looking at the item from the new category. Still other studies have shown that infants as young as four to six months can discriminate on the basis of number; they can tell the difference between sets of things, such as toy dogs, that vary only in number—that is, they consist of two or three, three or four, or four or five items (Strauss & Curtis, 1981).

How do infants form categories? The Gibsons would argue that the child simply picks up information that is actually there in the world, without any mental processing. An alternative view is that the child forms a schema

Everyday play with animals, houses, and other common objects teaches classification skills.

or prototype—an image of a typical face, person, or animal that does not correspond to any particular example seen (Kagan, 1971).

Research with adults has shown that adults form categories using prototypes based on notions of "typicalness" (Rosch, 1975; Rosch et al., 1976). Strauss (1979) has demonstrated that the same kind of intellectual abstraction seems to account for categorization in infants. In Strauss's studies, 10-month-old infants were presented with faces that varied in different ways, such as the length of the nose, the distance between the eyes, and so forth. The faces in the first part of the experiment were selected to show extreme values, for example, very

wide or very narrow noses. When infants were later shown an average face they had never seen before, they treated it as more familiar than the faces they had actually seen. Thus, the infants seemed to have formed an abstract prototype of a face; faces that fit the prototype, even though they were novel, were not as "interesting" as ones with extreme features, even if they were not new faces.

All in all, the new research described above shows that, as Piaget had theorized, the conceptual foundations of the human mind are laid down in infancy. In contrast to Piaget, the new data suggest that these foundations do not consist mainly of internalized actions. Infants are more sensitive and accurate perceivers of objects and events than Piaget thought they were. Further, they are capable of a greater degree of abstraction than Piaget thought possible. The new data, as one research review put it, show "that the human infant, like his adult counterpart, ignores the isolated details of experience in favor of the more abstract information that organizes these details" (Caron & Caron, 1982, p. 139).

Despite all the criticisms, Piaget's theory and observations still dominate the study of mental development in infancy. The problems he chose to work on have kept psychologists busy for many years, and are likely to do so for years to come. Moreover, Piaget's writings have changed the way psychologists think about babies. Unlike the other leading theorists of infancy, such as Freud and Skinner, who hardly studied children directly at all, Piaget's theorizing is based on an enormous amount of observation. Because of Piaget's work, it no longer seems as plausible as it once did to think of infants as untrained animals, waiting to be conditioned by parents and the environment, or as helpless pawns in the grip of raging instincts. Above all, Piaget's image of infants as scientific explorers, continually discovering what the world is like, and continually revising their interpretations of it, has only been confirmed by the new research.

SUMMARY

1. Infancy lasts for the first year and a half or two, or until the onset of language. It is a period of dramatic physical, mental, and emotional change. During the past two decades, research on infancy has expanded enormously, challenging many earlier assumptions.

2. Conceptions of infants have varied greatly, both historically and in different psychological theories. For example, the behaviorists have traditionally viewed the infant as a blank slate, to be written upon by the environment. Freudians view the infant as a seething cauldron of aggression and sexual instincts. Until recently, most pediatricians and psychologists assumed that very young infants are virtually blind and deaf, and unaware of their surroundings. Recent research has revealed that infants are much more competent than formerly believed.

3. Traditionally, most psychologists have assumed that the experiences of infancy determine later emotional stability, personality, and intellectual development. Most also assumed that the behavior of the parents in infancy determined the quality of early experience. Today there is a great debate within developmental psychology about both infantile and parental determinism. Recent evidence suggests that development is much more plastic than originally assumed. Infancy is an extremely important part of life, but it is doubtful that, for most people, this stage significantly shapes the rest of their lives.

4. Studies of the perceptual capacities of newborns and young infants have made dramatic advances in recent years, thanks to new experimental techniques. It used to be thought that infants slowly and painstakingly had to build up knowledge about the world. Now it appears that infants come into the world with a head start, prepared to perceive reality in the ways that adults do. They have a lot of learning to do, but they do not seem to start from scratch.

5. Learning to control the eyes and the hands is a major part of the growth of competence. Controlling the eyes comes first, at about three and a half months. Controlling the hands, and coordinating eyes and hands, takes several months longer.

6. Infants are constantly active; playing, exploring, and manipulating objects. Some psychologists have theorized that there is a system of motivation inherent in information processes. Curiosity is a characteristic humans share with the higher animals. It seems likely that curiosity, playfulness, and resistance to imposed conditions evolved in the course of evolution because they increased the survival chances of the animals that possessed them.

7. In both animals and infants, events that are discrepant or contingent arouse attention. Discrepant events or stimuli depart in some way from expectations, such as a face with distorted features or an unexpected sound. Moderately discrepant events, rather than monotony or extreme novelty, appear to promote cognitive development. Contingency occurs when the behavior of an organism causes something to happen—or appears to. Infants are sensitive to contingency by 8 or 10 weeks and take great delight in playing games in which they can produce some effect in an object or another person.

8. Jean Piaget is the major theorist of infant intellectual development. His six stages of sensorimotor development begin with the reflexes of the newborn and end with the child's ability to represent events mentally. The central conceptual advance of the sensorimotor period is the achievement of object permanence. Thus, the child learns to recognize that objects are three dimensional, that they exist in space, and that they continue to exist when out of sight.

9. Although Piaget's observations and explanations of infant development have been revised somewhat by recent research, he remains the dominating influence in the study of infant mental development. His basic description of the child's cognitive development and interaction with the environment in infancy has been confirmed by later researchers.

Key Terms

accommodation   172
affordances   185
assimilation   172
contingency   170
discrepancy   170
dishabituation   164
habituation   163
invariant   185
object permanence   172
primary circular reaction   178
secondary circular reaction   178
tertiary circular reaction   181

CHAPTER 6

Of Human Bonds
Social Development in Infancy

The beast and bird their common charge attend
The mothers nurse it, and the sires defend;
The young dismissed, to wander earth or air,
There stops the instinct, and there the care.
A longer care man's helpless kind demands,
That longer care contracts more lasting bands.

—Alexander Pope,
Essay on Man

The last chapter presented an image of infants as scientific explorers, eagerly finding out about the world and the things in it. This image of the child is incomplete. It suggests that the infant is a kind of Robinson Crusoe, making a life for himself on a desert island. It leaves out the fact that from the moment of birth, babies are social and emotional beings as well as processors of information.

The Course of Social Development

Although babies differ in the rate at which they pass the many developmental milestones, their social development follows a regular course. Also, despite cultural variation in the handling of infants, researchers in different parts of the world have noted similar patterns of social development. The sequence of events may be outlined as follows. We will look at the details later.

1. The first stage of social development, from birth to about two months, has been labeled the period of the "behavior interaction system" (Bell, 1977). During this time, caretaking, triggered by the baby's crying, is the main interaction between infant and adult. This early period has also been called a time of "primary attraction to social objects." Babies come into the world "prewired" to attend to the kinds of stimulation provided by people, especially faces, but also the human voice. In addition, they are equipped with, or they develop in the first days and weeks, a set of actions that attracts the attention of adults, such as crying, vocalizing, smiling, clinging. Yet the evidence suggests that babies are not responding to people as such. During the early weeks there is no evidence that they can tell the difference between people and inanimate objects, much less one person from another. Rather, they seem to be responding to particular patterns of stimulation.

2. At about 4 to 6 weeks, the baby's gaze changes in a subtle way that has a dramatic effect on other people. In looking at someone's face, the baby searches out the eyes and focuses on them, its own eyes widening and brightening (Wolff, 1963). The other person gets the feeling that the baby is actually looking at him or her, as one human being to another. Parents are likely to feel that the baby sees them for the first time, and that they are engaged in a real relationship (Stern, 1977).

3. At about 8 to 12 weeks, another milestone in social behavior occurs: the social smile. Although newborn babies smile, before the baby is about three months old these early smiles are not true social smiles—they occur in response to inner states, such as being full. Now, at two to three months, the baby beams at people; the parents can "introduce" the baby to friends—not just present a doll-like object (Emde, Gaensbauer, & Harmon, 1976). Richard Bell (1977) labels the three- to six-month period as that of "the social interaction system."

4. At about the same time that the social smile appears, babies begin to babble. At first, this babbling is not social; we know it is not in response to the parent's voice because the babies of deaf mute parents begin to babble at the same time as those of hearing parents. Also, this early babbling seems to be done for its own sake, as a "primary circular reaction" to use Piaget's term; babies may babble less when with the mother than when alone.

5. During the first six months, babies learn to play the game of social interaction, to learn the rhythms of social exchange: I do this, then the other person does that, then I do this, and so on. The technical term for this kind of pattern is "reciprocity" or "synchrony." Newborns seem to be able to move their arms and legs in synchrony with adult speech; later in infancy they play The Game (Watson, 1972). As described in Chapter 5, each move of one person in The Game is contingent on the previous move of the other: baby babbles and the parent talks back; or baby closes eyes, opens them, and parent says "Peekaboo." This temporal patterning is the usual way of social interaction, and is done throughout the rest of life in the form of dialogue, conversation, turn taking, and so forth. Babies also learn during the first six months how to break off or avoid inter-

action, as well as how to begin and maintain it (Stern, 1974).

6. The first six months of a baby's social life may be described as a period of joining the human race—as Konrad Lorenz once put it—in which the baby learns how to be a person in interaction with other persons. The second half of the first year is generally recognized as the period of attachment. Babies fall in love for the first time. When they first become social, babies do not seem to differentiate very much between their parents and other people although they may be able to tell the difference between the mother and other women at three months or even earlier. They do not seem to have strong preferences, however, until about five or six months. By then, their preferences are clear. The creeping baby or toddler will approach and follow the mother, check back to look at her when playing and exploring, and cry if separated from her.

7. Although the bond between the infant and its mother has received the most attention, babies also become attached to fathers and other people they regularly interact with. At about seven or eight months, though, babies become wary and shy with strangers, and some may be markedly upset if approached by a stranger.

8. While the infant is becoming attached to the mother, an opposing process of separating from her and becoming a self-aware individual is beginning. This separation-individuation phase of development reaches a peak in the second year of life.

9. After 6 months, babies "share" objects with others, giving as well as receiving toys, food, and so on. At around 9 to 10 months they begin to point at interesting objects and people, and between a year and a year and a half they learn to look in the direction at which someone else is pointing. Pointing is one of the earliest forms of intentional communication. It is a gestural signal that the sender knows beforehand will be responded to in a particular way. This gestural communication about objects is probably the basis of later language development—using words as symbols to communicate about the world.

The sections that follow discuss the gradual socialization of infants as they become attached to and learn to interact with others. The box on Wild Children and the Problem of Human Nature illustrates what happens to infants who grow up without the benefit of human contact.

Attachment

We have seen that in the middle of their first year, babies develop strong emotional bonds to the people who care for them. "Attachment," on the one hand, is simply a descriptive word to describe the bonds that we can see in everyday life in both adults and children. We observe evidence of **attachment** in a toddler running to mother and hiding in her lap as a stranger approaches, or crying as mother goes out of the house. We can see it in adults also. At any airport, scenes of sad goodbyes and happy greetings reveal the existence of attachment. Attachment has been defined as a deep and enduring affectional tie that binds a person to another individual (Ainsworth, 1963; Bowlby, 1969).

On the other hand, "attachment" as a theory has been the subject of considerable theoretical debate and a massive amount of research. It is important in the following discussion to keep in mind the distinction between attachment as a *phenomenon*—including thoughts and feelings as well as observable behavior—and the theoretical notions that have developed to explain it.

Attachment in Animals

Attachment is found not only in infants in all cultures, but also in many animals, especially mammals. Dogs show their attachment to their masters in obvious ways; they wag their tails in greeting, follow at the master's heels, howl in protest when left behind. Primates, especially monkeys, have been a favorite subject for research in animal attachment. People who have raised monkeys or apes agree that these

Wild Children and the Problem of Human Nature

In the 1983 film about Tarzan, we learn how he came to be raised by apes and how he grew up to be "king of the jungle." Tarzan's parents, Lord and Lady Greystoke, are shipwrecked off the coast of Africa and survive long enough to produce a son. The baby is adopted by a chimpanzee mother who has lost her own infant. He becomes deeply attached to her. Yet, as a boy, he discovers he is different from the apes. Tarzan grows up to be a sturdy young man, whose human cleverness enables him to become the leader of his troop. Eventually he is discovered by an explorer who takes him back to England, restoring him to his family and his ancestral estate. Although he learns to speak well enough, he never completely fits into English society. Disillusioned with civilization, he returns to the jungle.

The perennially popular Tarzan story is just one example of the widespread fascination with wild or "feral" children, real and fictional—children raised apart from families and human culture. Other examples include the legend that Rome was founded by two children raised by wolves, Romulus and Remus. Kipling's *Jungle Book* contains the story of Mowgli, also raised by wolves. Every so often there are reports of wolf-children emerging from the forest.

The most famous and best-documented case of a real-life wild child is that of the boy who became known as the Wild Boy of Aveyron. The public part of the story began on a January morning in 1800. Around dawn that day, a strange-looking boy of about 11 or 12 emerged from the woods near a village in southern France. He was naked except for the tattered remains of a shirt, and was dirty and covered with cuts and bruises. Unable to speak except in grunts and shrieks, unhousebroken, and without any modesty, he seemed more animal than human. He had been seen on and off over several years, running wild in the forest. He had even been captured a couple of times, but had escaped.

This time, the boy was caught by the local tanner and did not escape. Word of the event spread rapidly. The first official report on the boy, containing eyewitness accounts of his behavior, was written three weeks later by a local public official. Several months after the first report, the boy became the talk of Paris, and soon the rest of Europe. To this day, the Wild Boy of Aveyron continues to inspire scientific analysis and popular retelling. In 1970, François Truffaut's *The Wild Child* (*L'Enfant sauvage*) portrayed the dramatic

A scene from the *Tarzan* movie series.

A scene from François Truffaut's *L'enfant sauvage.*

story of the relationship between the wild boy and the young doctor, Jean Itard, who devoted five years of his life to trying to restore the boy to his civilized heritage. In addition, two fairly recent books have carefully examined the case and Itard's methods in the light of modern psychological and educational knowledge (Lane, 1976; Shattuck, 1980).

Why was there such interest in the boy? As Roger Shattuck (1980) comments, people have always been intrigued by the "forbidden experiment"—raising a child apart from other people to discover what human nature is "really" like underneath the veneer of society and civilization. The forbidden experiment may actually have been carried out. In the seventh century B.C., according to the historian Herodotus, an Egyptian pharaoh wanted to find out which languages humans speak "naturally." He isolated two infants in a hut, to be cared for by a servant forbidden to speak to them. The infants' first word was said to be the Phrygian word for "bread." The Holy Roman Emperor Frederick II and King James IV of Scotland reportedly tried similar experiments. Frederick's two subjects died before speaking; King James's children were said to speak Hebrew.

At the time the wild boy emerged from the woods, the question of human nature had become an intensely debated political and philosophical issue. The American and particularly the French Revolution had raised questions about what kind of government human beings were suited for. Jean-Jacques Rousseau argued that in a hypothetical "state of nature" human beings are "noble savages," peaceful and cooperative. The selfishness and cruelty we see all around us, he claimed, are caused by the corruption of basic human nature by an unjust society. The opposing view, articulated most clearly by Thomas Hobbes, proclaimed that human beings in a "state of nature" are nasty, selfish brutes, constantly embroiled in a war of "all against all." Such a human nature requires strong constraints, continued Hobbes, and freedom and democracy are dangerous delusions that can lead to the breakdown of all social order. Echoes of this debate persist today.

The wild boy excited so much interest because he seemed to be a living example of a human being in a state of nature. People wondered whether he would turn out to be Rousseau's noble savage or Hobbes's nasty brute. However, these original hopes were soon disappointed. The child was taken to Paris, to the Institute for Deaf Mutes, to be observed by a panel of distinguished scientists, including the famous psychiatrist, Pinel. Neither a noble savage nor a brute, he appeared to be simply a deeply apathetic boy who spent his days rocking back and forth, oblivious to everything but food. The panel concluded that the boy was an incurable idiot and had probably been abandoned by his parents for that reason.

To this day, practically nothing is known of the boy's early life. He seemed physically normal in every way, except for his many scars. The most striking scar was a healed-over slit across his throat, suggesting that someone had tried to kill him and had left him for dead. He had apparently been in the woods for five, and possibly six years; in other words, from the time he was about five years old. Survival in the harsh conditions of those woods would call for considerable resourcefulness.

The wild boy would not have become a famous case had the panel's conclusion of hopeless idiocy not been challenged by Dr. Itard. Defying Pinel and his other superiors, Itard set out to prove that rather than being abandoned because he was an idiot, the boy was an idiot because he had been abandoned (Lane, 1976). Itard may have seen signs of responsiveness and intelligence underneath the vast indifference the boy displayed. The doctor also believed in Locke's doctrine of the *tabula rasa*, the mind as a blank slate. If lack of the right experiences had made the boy an idiot, then providing the right experiences could bring him back to normality. For five years Itard worked patiently with the boy, whom he named Victor, and in the course of his tutoring became almost a father to him. Itard was aided by a warm and patient woman, Madame Guerin, who became a mother to Victor and devoted herself to him until his death at the age of 40.

Dr. Itard's first step was to gain the boy's confidence by letting him do whatever he wanted—to eat, sleep, and run around outside. His next step was to break down Victor's most prominent and disturbing trait, his indifference to almost all sights, sounds, and sensations, including extremes of heat and cold. Itard started giving him hot baths, which the boy adored. Victor became very particular about the temperature of the bath, which then generalized to other things. For example, he stopped wetting the bed because he disliked cold sheets.

Itard's next step was to train Victor's other senses. He taught him how to distinguish shapes, letters, colors, objects, textures, sounds, tastes, temperatures, and weights. Itard's methods are the precursors of Maria Montessori's methods of early childhood education and are similar to behavior modification techniques.

During the first nine months, the boy made remarkable progress. By the end of this period, he was alert to his surroundings, wore clothes, and was orderly in his habits. He developed strong attachments to both Dr. Itard and Mme. Guerin, especially the latter. From a boy who never cried, he became one who shed many tears, such as when he was reunited with his "parents" after he had run away, or when pushed too hard in his lessons. Though he could not speak, he had learned a simple form of communication through writing. He gave evidence of a sense of justice and had enough imagination to make a small invention—a chalk holder out of a meat larder. The boy seemed on the way to becoming fully human.

But after reaching this point, Victor's progress slowed. Itard worked with him for over four more years but eventually gave up without achieving his goal of restoring the boy to normalcy. He particularly wanted Victor to learn to speak, but the boy could never understand the speech of others or learn to speak properly. Ironically, it may have been Itard's insistence on normal speech that hampered Victor's development. Although all this time Victor had been living at the school for the deaf, Itard never tried to teach him sign language.

The other stumbling block in Victor's education was his sexual development. Itard had been hoping that puberty would somehow bring about a major improvement in Victor, perhaps through his falling in love. But Itard was astonished to discover that the capacity for romantic love is not instinctive after all. Victor seemed to show only a slight preference for women over men; his approaches to women were bizarre and embarrassing. Itard was shocked by Victor's sexuality and was at a loss to deal with it.

Puberty, plus Victor's failure to speak, led Itard to end his program of instruction. After Itard's tutoring, Victor lived for twenty-two years with Mme. Guerin, supported by a state pension. An observer who saw him at around 30 described him as "fearful, half wild, incapable of learning to speak despite all attempts to teach him" (Shattuck, 1980, p. 177). His death did not stir any public notice.

Over the last century and a half, psychologists, psychiatrists, educators, and other scholars have continued to debate the issues in Victor's case. Why did Victor never learn how to speak? Was he abandoned after all because he was retarded? Was he autistic? Did he become psychotic from mistreatment and isolation? Could Victor have been restored to normality if Itard had known what we do today about child development and techniques of behavior modification?

Although much will remain unknown about Victor and his relationship with Itard, there is enough evidence to suggest answers to these questions. First, it seems unlikely that Victor was either retarded or autistic. His survival in the woods for several years under extremely harsh conditions, and the cleverness of much of his behavior from his earliest days in captivity onward, are incompatible with either of those diagnoses.

Could Victor's years of living in the wild, totally without human companionship, account for his condition? Lane (1976) argues that they could have, and he summarizes a variety of evidence on adults and children who had endured prolonged isolation. While many of the cases are poorly documented, there is a striking consistency in the accumulated reports. Living totally alone for long periods seems to result in mutism, sexual and social inhibition, and sensory anomalies such as indifference to extremes of heat and cold. Children who have been isolated for long periods rarely recover completely from their mutism.

It seems hard to believe that even previously normal people can lose the ability to speak simply through disuse, but Lane cites three cases that suggest they can. The most documented case is that of the Scottish sailor, Alexander Selkirk, who become the model for

Defoe's *Robinson Crusoe*. Marooned for over four years on an uninhabited island before he was rescued in 1708, he almost forgot how to make intelligible sounds. If he had not had a Bible and other books with him, and had he been isolated longer, his ability to speak might have deteriorated even more.

A recent case that is often compared to Victor is that of Genie (Curtiss, 1977). Genie is a California girl who, between the ages of 20 months and 13 years, was kept isolated in a small closed room, strapped to a potty chair. Her only human contact occurred when a family member entered the room just long enough to feed her baby food. Her father growled at her and beat her if she made any noise. When Genie was found, she could not stand erect, walk, talk, eat solid food, or control her bodily functions. After eight months in a rehabilitation center, she learned how to use the toilet, eat more normally, and walk. Genie next lived for three years as a foster child in the home of one of her doctors. After much training, she did learn to speak in a simple way and to understand a good deal more. But her language ability remained fixed at about the level of a four- or five-year-old child. Her voice continued to sound like that of a deaf person. All in all, she made greater progress than Victor, but still did not reach ordinary "normality."

Genie's case suggests that Victor's progress might have been limited even if Itard had had the benefit of modern knowledge. But in many ways he was less damaged than she was when found. Victor was physically strong and had adapted to his life alone in the woods. Although he made great strides under Itard's guidance, it is clear that Itard made several mistakes in dealing with Victor—mistakes that he could not be expected to realize were such at the time. First, he deprived Victor of any semblance of a normal social life with other children. Today, we know that play with other children contributes enormously to children's cognitive as well as socioemotional development. Also, Itard conceived of learning solely in terms of formal instruction. He did not try to find teaching opportunities in everyday household life or in play.

Ironically, Itard's most glaring mistakes concerned language—the thing he most wanted Victor to learn. As we have seen, he did not instruct Victor in sign language. Victor was actually quite adept at nonverbal communication and might have mastered that form more easily. Itard's methods of teaching oral speech were also flawed in the light of modern behavior modification techniques. Among other errors, he did not reinforce the sounds that Victor did make in order to increase and shape the boy's verbal behavior. There is no way of knowing what course Victor's life would have taken had he been able to benefit from current knowledge. Nevertheless, despite the effects of his long isolation in the woods, Victor did make enormous progress under Itard's patient care.

In the end, the story of Victor reveals that the notion of "natural man"—of a human nature apart from human culture and society—is fundamentally wrong. A human in prolonged and total isolation from others is a most unnatural human. Victor's story underscores the paradox of the human condition: we are both separate and social. Inside our skin, each of us lives out our life in a private psychological world that is unlike any other, and which cannot fully be known by anyone else. Yet, without other humans around us in our earliest years, we would not only not survive, we would not know ourselves. As the anthropologist Clifford Geertz (1973) points out, the human mind is a cultural as well as a biological product. The human brain and nervous system evolved along with human culture, which supplies us with language and other sets of symbols. We are born "unfinished animals" who need culture to complete us. Almost two hundred years ago, Itard himself made the same point:

> Cast upon this globe without physical strength or innate ideas, incapable by himself of following the fundamental laws of his nature which call him to the first rank of the animal kingdom, it is only in the heart of society that man can attain the preeminent position that nature has reserved for him. . . . (Quoted in Lane, 1977, p. 29)

animals insist on body contact and protest intensely when separated. Cathy Hayes, who adopted an infant chimpanzee she named Viki, recounts how Viki would cling to her from the moment she left her crib in the morning until she went to sleep at night:

> She sat on my lap while I ate or studied. She straddled my hip as I cooked. If she were on the floor and I started to get away, she screamed and clung to my leg until I picked her up. If some rare lack of vigilance on her part let a room's length separate us, she came charging across the abyss, screaming at the height of her considerable ability. (Hayes, 1951, cited in Bowlby, 1973, p. 58)

Observation of chimpanzees in the wild has also shown the intensity of their distress at separation. Monkeys and apes spend all of their infancies in close contact with their mothers. As the babies grow out of infancy, the mothers begin to lose interest in them and may push them away. For their part, young monkeys and apes are drawn away from their mothers when they become interested in examining objects, exploring places, and playing with other young primates.

It is obvious how clinging and separation protest help the infant survive. For all primates who live on the ground, among other wild animals, there is safety in numbers and danger in being alone. The isolated monkey or ape is more likely to suffer from cold or hunger, or to be eaten by a leopard or other predator. However, attachment patterns are not uniform among all primates. Even in the same species, groups with different patterns of social organization may show disparate attachment patterns.

Some monkey species quickly adopt abandoned infants. Infant bonnet monkeys, if separated from or abandoned by their mothers, are accepted quickly by others and do not show profound reactions to separation. Rhesus monkeys and pigtail macaques, on the other hand, remain alone if abandoned by their mothers. After frantically searching for their missing parent, the isolated infants seem depressed. They huddle and rock themselves (much the way Victor, the Wild Child, did), sometimes moaning softly (Rosenblum, 1971; Rosenblum & Kaufman, 1968).

Human Infancy in Evolutionary Perspective

John Bowlby (1969) argues that human attachment patterns evolved in similar ways and for similar reasons in diverse cultures over millions of years. Security lay in keeping close to the mother, and anxiety over actual or threatened separation was adaptive. Thus, he argues, human babies came into the world equipped with smiles and cries in order to increase the likelihood of receiving protective and comforting responses from the mother. Bowlby concludes from his reading of the primate evidence that babies are preadapted to mothers who are warm and responsive and who intervene promptly when the baby cries.

More recent biological research has shown, however, that primate attachment is more complicated than Bowlby assumed, and that attachment patterns for primates may not be directly relevant for human beings. Primate researchers have found striking individual differences in mothering and other forms of social behavior.

For example, one researcher contrasted "restricted" with "laissez-faire" baboon mothers. Restrictive mothers keep their infants close to them at all times, while laissez-faire mothers let their infants wander. The infants of the more restrictive mothers survived better in the early months, but the laissez-faire infants were better able to survive if orphaned. Further, infants of mothers who held high status in their baboon group were less likely to have mishaps occur to them (presumably because other baboons took more notice of them). Thus, the laissez-faire style of mothering could be considered the better style for high-status mothers. In general, as Hinde observes, "there is no best mothering style, for different styles are better in different circumstances, and natural selection would act to favor individuals with a range of potential styles from which they select appropriately. . . . *Natural selection must surely have operated to produce conditional maternal responses, not stereotypy"* (1982, pp. 70–71, emphasis in original).

A Nurturance Gap

Natural selection does not necessarily imply that mothers and children are adapted to an idyllic relationship in which the needs of one partner mesh perfectly with the needs of the other. Rather, the need of the infant for mothering is not matched by the need of a mother to mother. Studies of rhesus monkeys (Hinde, 1983) and other species have shown that mothers force independent behavior on their offspring before they would prefer it. Evolutionary theorists argue, in fact, that conflict between infants and parents is built into natural selection (Trivers, 1974). Hinde explains that "in practice, mothers of probably all species actively promote their infants' independence before the infants are ready for it" (1969), and continues: "Infants are presumably adapted to cope with mothers who reject them" (1983, p. 62).

Indeed, human evolution seems to have created a nurturance gap in early infancy. While the human brain and head grew enormously over the course of evolution, the human pelvis was not able to grow in the same proportion. How could a large-skulled baby be born through a narrow pelvis opening? One way the problem was solved was by means of separated skull bones (Konner, 1977). Babies are born with soft spots on their heads where the bones do not meet. Thus, the baby's skull can be molded as it passes through the birth canal.

Another "solution" was premature birth. Over the last million years, human infants came to be born "prematurely"—that is, at an earlier point in their development than other primate infants. The psychological consequences of this change were enormous. The result has been a newborn that is more helpless and therefore more burdensome to the mother, as well as less attractive; the social smile, for example, does not appear until the second

month of the baby's life. At the same time, because of the large human brain—in particular the cortex, as we saw in Chapter 4—the mother's behavior is less determined by reflexes and "instinct" and more by learning, culture, and custom. While a baby baboon is well developed enough to help determine its own relationship to its mother, explain Washburn and Devore, "the human infant is exposed to maternal whim, custom, or vagary in a way that is true of no other primate" (1961, p. 42).

In short, evolution does not always act to increase the survival chances of the new infant, as Bowlby and others had assumed. Sometimes qualities that are necessary for survival at one stage of the life cycle may result in disadvantages at a later or earlier stage (Konner, 1977). The human way of life, based on language, culture, and a great capacity for learning, depends on large brains and walking on two feet, leaving the hands free to use tools and carry things. The survival advantages of this way of life clearly outweigh the disadvantages of separated skull bones and a nurturance gap in early infancy.

Harlow and Love in Infant Monkeys

The late Harry Harlow shares credit with John Bowlby for making attachment a central concern in developmental psychology. For much of his career, Harlow had studied learning in primates. When he began to lose many of his monkeys to disease, he separated infant monkeys from their mothers at birth in order to raise them in germ-free isolation. He noticed that although these monkeys grew up to be more healthy, they did not know how to get along with other monkeys. They were either too aggressive or too withdrawn and submissive.

Eventually Harlow began a series of systematic studies to determine what the isolated monkeys lacked. He first tested the traditional idea that mother-infant bonds were based on feeding. Both Freudians and learning theorists held to this oral view of attachment—or what Bowlby once called "the cupboard theory of

FIGURE 6.1
Harlow's Experiments with Attachment
Harlow's cloth and wire "mothers."

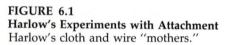

love." Harlow provided convincing evidence that this explanation of attachment was not valid.

In a series of now-classic studies, Harlow and his associates raised infant monkeys with substitute "mothers"; one a wire mesh cylinder, the other a similar cylinder covered with terry cloth (see Figure 6.1). Either cylinder could be set up with a bottle. The result was that the infant monkeys spent most of their time clinging to the cloth mother, even when only the wire mother provided them with milk. Harlow concluded that "contact comfort"— being able to cling to a soft, warm surface—is more important for attachment than food.

There was other evidence that the baby monkeys became attached to the cloth mother. It was used as a security base when a frightening "bear monster" was put next to them. Like toddlers burying their faces in their mothers' laps, they ran to the cloth mother, then ventured

away from it to explore the new object. The infants raised with the wire mother did not cling to it, but clutched themselves and rocked back and forth, like children who grow up in institutions. The attachment to the cloth mother was also lasting. After being separated from it for varying lengths of time, cloth-mother-reared monkeys still showed signs of attachment when reunited (Harlow & Zimmerman, 1959).

Harlow's early studies suggested that contact comfort, rather than feeding, was the key to the development of social attachment. But later research challenged this conclusion in two ways. First, a number of studies showed that some young animals form strong bonds without any physical contact. Sight and sound can also form the basis for attachment. For example, one study showed that a young lamb could become attached to an adult ewe even when the two were separated by a wire fence (Cairns & Johnson, 1965).

The second discovery was that contact comfort is not enough to guarantee normal social development. When the surrogate-reared monkeys returned to the company of other monkeys, they were socially incompetent. Like the totally isolated monkeys, they were either too aggressive or too withdrawn. They were sexually incompetent as well: surrogate-reared males seemed unable to have normal sexual relations; and while a few of the females managed to be impregnated, they were totally incompetent mothers. They ignored, abused, and even attacked their infants.

In his later work, Harlow and his associates tried to find out exactly what it was that the surrogate-reared monkeys lacked. Was it the lack of a mother, or the lack of social contact and interaction? Could the missing ingredient be supplied by peers? Could the isolated monkeys be rehabilitated later? Harlow began a series of studies in which he varied the length and conditions of isolation. Some infant monkeys were raised in total isolation, with no surrogate mothers. Others were raised without mothers but in the company of other young monkeys.

Monkeys raised in complete isolation at first showed bizarre symptoms when released: they were physically clumsy, injured themselves and other monkeys, and hugged and rocked themselves for long periods of time. But those who had been reared with peers and then isolated for three months were able to recover when returned to their age-mates. Longer isolation resulted in more long-lasting impairment, but interaction with peers enabled the young monkeys to recover. The most dramatic findings in this line of research concerned monkeys isolated for their first year, a treatment usually resulting in "social vegetables"—profoundly debilitated animals. Novak and Harlow (1975) showed that these monkeys could be rehabilitated by interaction with monkeys younger than themselves.

In addition, monkeys raised with peers but without real or surrogate mothers seemed surprisingly normal, almost indistinguishable from mother-reared monkeys. Harlow concluded that his earlier ideas about the absolute necessity of the mother were wrong. Social interaction, rather than a particular person per se, seemed enough to encourage seemingly normal social development.

As Harlow himself recognized, these studies may not be completely applicable to human development—and rehabilitated monkeys may have had impairments that were not detected in his studies. But the studies point to the important role that age-mates play in the development of social behavior. The box on the Nazi "Forbidden Experiment" helps to illustrate this point.

Attachment in Human Infants

According to Bowlby (1969), attachment in human infants develops through a series of phases:

1. In the **preattachment phase,** newborns respond to people in a nondiscriminating way. They will look at any face and can be comforted by anyone. Crying, smiling, and rooting are forms of attachment seen in all human babies; these behaviors provoke caretakers to approach and contact the baby. This phase ends at about two or three months, when the infant begins to show signs of knowing the difference between its mother and other people.

2. In the **attachment-in-the-making** phase, which lasts until six or seven months, infants can discriminate between familiar people and strangers. They smile, vocalize, and reach out more often to people they know. They may cry when familiar people leave the room. Toward the end of this period, the infant actively seeks to be close to one particular person and begins to be wary of strangers.

3. The **clear-cut attachment** phase begins at about six or seven months and continues into the second year. The infant clearly prefers one or more specific people. At this time, babies are learning how to crawl and walk and thus can actively seek physical contact with the objects of their affection. Usually, the prime attachment figure is the mother, but the father or a grandparent can also hold that role. In fact, infants commonly are attached to more than one person. During this phase, infants will try to follow or protest when an attachment figure leaves their sight—which is known as **separation anxiety** (Figure 6.2)—and will warmly

A Nazi "Forbidden Experiment": Children Reared Together without Parents

In the spring of 1945, six three-year-old orphans, along with thousands of other children and adults, were liberated from a German concentration camp called Tereszin. These were German-Jewish children, three boys and three girls, whose parents had been killed in Hitler's gas chambers. They had arrived at Tereszin when they were a few months old and had remained there for three years. It is impossible to imagine an environment more deprived or terrifying. Tereszin was a transit camp, a place people passed through, staying only days, weeks or months on the way to the extermination camps in Poland. Day and night there were arrivals, departures, disappearances, deaths. The children's contact with adults was minimal. No single person looked after them for more than a few weeks at a time: none of the children had any experience of parental love or family life.

In August 1945, the children arrived at a residential nursery in an English country house, where they stayed for a year. Recognizing that the six orphans had been subjected to a unique if unplanned experiment in childrearing, Anna Freud and Sophie Dann (1951) observed and described their adjustment to life during their year at the nursery. At first, the children were uncontrollable. Wild, restless, and noisy, they destroyed all the toys available to them and damaged much of the furniture. Toward adults, they alternated between cold indifference and intense hostility. Even more striking than their rejection of the adults, however, was their intense attachment to one another:

French Jewish mothers and their babies, in detention in France. Eventually, all were sent to a concentration camp where all were killed. The six German children described in this box were remarkably lucky to have survived.

The liberation of Auschwitz on January 27, 1945. Only 300 children were left alive. Tereszin was liberated in the spring of the same year.

> It was evident that they cared greatly for one another and not at all for anybody or anything else. They had no other wish than to be together and became upset when they were separated from each other, even for short moments. No child would consent to remain upstairs when the other was downstairs, or vice versa. . . . If anything of the kind happened, the single child would constantly ask for the other children while the group would fret for the missing child. (Freud & Dann, 1951, pp. 130–31)

The children's devotion to one another was also revealed in their remarkable sensitivity to one another's feelings. Although they quarreled a great deal among themselves, they showed none of the usual rivalry and competitiveness of brothers and sisters or groups of normally reared children. They gladly shared their possessions, looked out for each other's safety in traffic, picked up one another's toys, admired each other's play constructions, handed food to the others before eating themselves. A child given a present would demand the same for all the others, even the absent ones. Freud and Dann describe many incidents of behavior which would be considered admirably altruistic in adults; for example, one cold day Paul lost his gloves during a walk. John gave him his own gloves and never complained that his own hands were cold. Such incidents were routine.

Eventually, the children made friends with the nursery staff. They began to treat the adults the way they treated one another, becoming concerned about their feelings and comfort, trying to help them with their work. After a while, the children formed more personal relationships with adults, but these attachments lacked the intensity of ordinary children's emotional bonds to their parents. They never equaled the strength of the children's ties to one another.

Summing up their impressions of the children's psychological functioning, Freud and Dann observed that despite the extreme deprivation they had experienced, the children did not suffer from any gross impairment. "They were neither deficient, delinquent, nor psychotic. . . . That they were able to acquire a new language in the midst of their upheavals bears witness to a basically unharmed contact with their environment" (1951, p. 168).

Freud and Dann describe only the first year of the children's life after their liberation. But their judgment that the children were psychologically intact was apparently confirmed by their subjects' later development. Thirty-five years after the events described in the article, Sophie Dann reported that the six are leading effective lives as adults (cited in Hartup, 1983).

The story of the six children is remarkable in many ways. First of all, as Freud and Dann point out, it is a challenge to firmly held assumptions about child development. Neither common sense nor any developmental theory would have predicted that infants raised in such terrible conditions would survive as functioning human beings, much less the sensitive and altruistic young children described in the article. They were obviously not unscarred by their experiences, but they were without the major defects that might have been expected. They had survived several factors usually considered disastrous in childrearing: they had had no chance to form an attachment to a mother or mother substitute, no stability in their relationships or surroundings, and no families to socialize them and transmit the rules of language, culture, and morality. Evidently the six children were able to raise themselves, becoming at once parents and children for one another.

There is a striking parallel between these findings and some of Harry Harlow's research. Harlow found that monkeys raised with peers but without mothers became intensely attached to one another and did not show any major developmental disturbances. In contrast, monkeys raised by their mothers, but not allowed any peer contact, were markedly inadequate in their peer behavior (Alexander & Harlow, 1965; Harlow, Harlow, & Suomi, 1971). Taken together, these studies reveal the importance of the peer affectional system in the development of the individual children. Above all, however, the story of the six children is a moving demonstration of human resilience in the face of extreme deprivation and brutality.

FIGURE 6.2
Separation Anxiety
Toward eight to nine months of age, infants become very upset when separated from their mothers or other attachment figures.

greet him or her when the person returns. Meanwhile the infant begins to treat strangers with increasing wariness and usually with alarm. This type of behavior is commonly referred to as **stranger anxiety.**

The development of clear-cut attachment is related to cognitive development. This is the period during which the infant is able to think of absent objects (8–14 months). Thus, the child is able to remember mother even when she is out of sight and can realize she is gone.

Bowlby and other attachment theorists argue that attachment is not simply a set of overt behaviors. Smiling, following, clinging, and the like are indicators of the emotional bond between child and parent but in themselves they do not constitute that bond. Nor does the absence of overt attachment behavior mean that the bond is gone. Bowlby conceives of attachment as a behavioral system organized around a "set goal," which operates like a thermostat. Just as a thermostat can be set at, say, sixty-five degrees, a child's set goal would be a certain degree of proximity to the parent. When the temperature is at or about sixty-five, the furnace is turned off. If it drops below that level, the furnace turns on. Similarly, a child who is confident that the parent is available, say in the next room, can play happily without staying physically next to the mother. If, however, the mother gets ready to go out, this may turn on the attachment system and the child will seek nearness. Being sick or tired or frightened will also lead children—and adults—to come closer to their attachment figures. For both the child and the furnace, activity is triggered by a discrepancy between a goal and ongoing events.

Bowlby's theory has been modified somewhat by more recent attachment researchers, who feel that his concept of a set goal underestimates the child's desire to explore the environment. Everett Waters observes that if attachment evolved solely around the advantages of staying close to adults, "the goal could be more effectively accomplished by a tendency to cling unremittingly" (1980, p. 36). Revising Bowlby's model of the attachment system, Mary Ainsworth (1973) proposes a second set goal: the exploration of the environment. The aim of the system is to maintain a comfortable balance between the two goals. Ainsworth also described the *secure base phenomenon:* the tendency for a child to use the mother or other attachment figure as a base from which to explore. For example, when babies learn to crawl, they do not always remain close to the mother. Rather, they make little excursions away from her. Every so often they return to her for a bit of affection, to show her some-

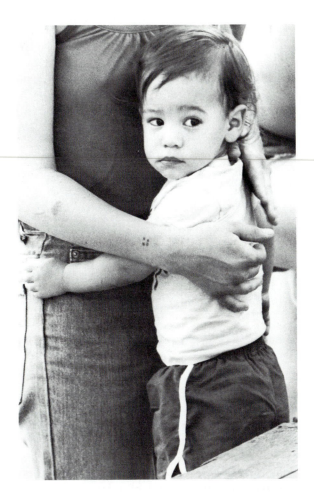

children who go to the playground with their mothers. One child spends most of the time clinging to the mother, afraid of the situation and the people in it. The other goes off to play in the sandbox or on the swings. Ainsworth argues that it would be wrong to consider the first child more attached to the mother. Rather, the first child's clinginess reflects insecurity, while the security of the second child's attachment is the basis for his or her freedom to explore.

Attachment after Infancy

Bowlby has described a fourth phase of attachment, following the clear-cut attachment phase, which he calls **goal-corrected partnership.** During clear-cut attachment, the mother is extremely important to the child but she remains an "object" in the environment. The child does not understand that she has goals and motives of her own. After the age of two or so, children become more sophisticated. They anticipate how the parents will react to events and can begin to influence and manipulate their behavior. For example, children often tease their parents by pretending to be hurt, or pretending to do something "bad."

Attachment does not end at infancy. Children continue to be attached to their parents through childhood, and most people maintain some degree of attachment to their parents throughout their lives. But most adults find their primary attachment in marriage or love. Robert Weiss has found that intimate adult relationships meet Bowlby's criteria for attachment:

> In all these instances, individuals display need for ready access to the attachment figure, desire for proximity to the attachment figure in situations of stress, heightened comfort and diminished anxiety when in the company of the attachment figure, and a marked increase in discomfort and anxiety on discovering the attachment figure to be inexplicably inaccessible. (1982, p. 173)

In other words, your attachment figure is the

thing, or just to check that she is still there. The child's explorations stop abruptly if the mother moves away or if the child is frightened or hurt.

Ainsworth and other recent attachment theorists have emphasized the emotional aspects of attachment. She suggests that the child's set goal is not simply to maintain a particular degree of physical closeness to the parent, but rather to maintain a feeling of security. Anything that makes the child uncertain or insecure—such as being hurt—will bring the child closer. As illustrated later in Figure 6.3, feeling secure enables the child to play and explore freely. Paradoxically, in some situations the *absence* of strong signs of attachment may indicate a more secure attachment. Consider two person you would call for first if you were suddenly sick or hurt, and also the person you would worry about the most if he or she did not show up on time and could not be reached.

Of course, attachment in adults also differs from that of infants. Weiss points out that adults are attached to peers, not caretakers; adults can attend to other business and relationships even when attachment bonds are threatened, and they can tolerate separation better. Finally, adult attachments are usually directed toward someone who is also a sexual partner (see box on the Prototype Hypothesis).

Becoming Attached

Although the child comes into the world equipped to form attachments, there is great individual variation in the patterning of attachment. Bowlby has argued that babies tend to attach themselves especially to one figure, usually the mother, a characteristic he calls "monotropy." Other researchers argue that the child's main attachment is not always to the mother. For instance, Schaffer and Emerson (1964) found that only half of the 18-month-olds in their studies were attached solely to the mother, and in a third of their cases the main attachment was to the father. Usually, children had one very strong attachment and multiple lesser ones.

Why do children become attached to one person rather than another? Traditionally, as we have seen, psychologists thought that food was the crucial reinforcer, and that babies become attached to the person who feeds them and takes care of other bodily needs. It seems clear, however, that simply feeding and taking care of a child is not enough to produce an attachment. For example, the Israeli kibbutz is a collective farm where children spend most of their time in communal nurseries; they see their parents for an hour or two each day, and all day on the Sabbath. Children are fed and cared for mostly by nurses. Yet all observers of kibbutz children agree that they become deeply attached to their parents, not the nurses. Mel-

ford Spiro (1954) notes that even though they do not provide physical care, or day-to-day socialization, the parents play a crucial role in the child's psychological development. They provide the child with a kind of love he does not get from anyone else. Another observer, who has done psychotherapy with people who grew up in kibbutzim, agrees that kibbutz children become attached to their parents rather than their caretakers: Pelled (1964) claims that none of her clients had a strong and lasting tie to a nurse.

The emotional quality of the interaction between a child and an adult, not the amount of time it lasts or the content, seems to be crucial for attachment. More specifically, the key feature seems to be responsiveness to the child.

Becoming Attached **207**

The Prototype Hypothesis

While attachment persists beyond infancy, we do not yet know how much or whether a person's attachment experiences in infancy influence his or her later attachments in adulthood. Freud, Bowlby, and more recent attachment theorists have argued that the infant's first attachment becomes the "prototype" for all future relationships. Similarly, Erikson's notion of basic trust emphasizes that the task of infancy is to establish a sense of trust in other people.

Bowlby argues that this sense of trust, or lack of it, comes from "working models" of the world and self that the child builds in the course of early experience with attachment figures. If a child has been lucky enough to have loving parents, he or she will develop a model of the world as a good place with helpful people in it. Such a child will also develop a working model of the self as a lovable person. A child unlucky enough to have uncaring parents is likely to feel not only unwanted by Mom and Dad, but incapable of being wanted, loved, or cared for by anyone. Thus, Bowlby assumes that the models of self and others that the child builds are fairly accurate reflections of actual experiences the child has had and that whatever expectations

develop during the early years "tend to persist relatively unchanged throughout the rest of life" (1973, p. 208).

There is as yet very little evidence testing this "prototype" hypothesis, and some research findings contradict it. On theoretical and clinical grounds, there is reason to doubt that the child's inner representations are photographic copies of actual events. Although Freud proposed the "prototype" hypothesis, in his later work he emphasized the power of the child's fantasy to modify reality rather than simply reflect it. Thus, Freud was in a sense a forerunner of Piaget, who documented how the child constructs reality out of the raw material of experience.

No analyst says that what actually happens to a child does not matter, but many analysts argue that whatever the parents do or fail to do, they simply provide raw material for the child's inner elaborations of experience. As Edmund Bergler puts it, "Given an unfavorable home situation, one child might grow into adulthood correcting the frustrating influences. Another, starting with an ideal home situation, could magnify small incidents into 'injustices,' and later, as a neurotic adult, continue to feel that he has been wronged" (1964, p. 9).

Schaffer and Emerson (1964) found that parents who responded quickly to the child's crying, or who were more sociable with their children, were likely to arouse stronger attachment as measured by the child's protests at his or her departure. In some families, infants were more attached to their fathers, who were home little, than to their mothers, who were home all day. In these families, the mothers were not very responsive to or sociable with their infants, whereas the fathers played with the children and were very attentive when they were home.

Emotional intensity also seems to play a role in the development of attachment. If caretakers are bland, neutral, apathetic, and unstimulat-

ing, the child's attachment may be inhibited. The other extreme can also cause difficulty for the child: children can become strongly attached to emotionally intense parents, even abusive ones (Main, 1981). In general, families are more emotional in both positive and negative ways than other groups. A study that compared mothers to nurses in an institution for young children found that mothers were not only more affectionate than the nurses, but also more often cross and angry (Tizard & Tizard, 1974). Children, too, are more emotional with their parents than others. Families are places where, as one family therapist put it, "you're dealing with life and death voltages" (Whitaker, quoted in Framo, 1972, p. 3).

Problems of Attachment

Bowlby's work on attachment in human infants grew out of earlier work on **maternal deprivation**—the term refers literally to the loss of the mother, but it has come to mean the loss or lack of any main caretaker. The most extreme form of maternal deprivation would be experienced by orphaned infants raised in hospitals. The classic study that introduced the concept of maternal deprivation was carried out by René Spitz in 1945. He compared the unwanted infants in a South American foundling home with infants in another institution who were being raised by their juvenile delinquent mothers. The foundling home infants received good food and medical care, lived in clean surroundings, and were cared for by a succession of nurses. By the end of their first year, however, they scored in the mentally retarded range on developmental tests. Emotionally, these children were apathetic; they rarely talked, smiled, or even cried. Also, despite good hygiene, they were extremely susceptible to disease. During a measles epidemic, all of the children under 30 months contracted the disease, and about a quarter of them died, a rate far in excess of home-reared infants with measles. In contrast, the infants who were being raised by their own mothers in the institution for delinquents developed normally. Spitz concluded that the lack of "mothering" was responsible for the plight of the foundling infants.

From the work of Spitz and others—and his own research on children who had been separated or had lost their mothers—Bowlby (1951) concluded that, in order to have normal social development, a child must have a loving relationship with one person—who is almost always the mother—which is unbroken and which occurs in the child's own family. Summing it up, he equates mother love in infancy and childhood for good mental health with vitamins and proteins for good physical health.

Within developmental psychology, the assumptions surrounding the maternal deprivation concept have been controversial. For example, the early investigators who observed the apathetic, sickly, retarded children in orphanages concluded that they were suffering from a lack of mother love. Other researchers have argued that there is nothing magical about mother love; what children need is personal attention and stimulation. The children in the earlier studies had not been getting these. In the institutions, they had been confined to their cribs, lying on their backs almost all the time, without toys, playmates, attention, social interaction, or even varied sights and sounds. Luckily, children may be more resilient than had been thought originally. Deficits brought about by early deprivation may not be irreversible if deprived children are placed in good environments.

During the 1950s, Wayne Dennis (1960, 1973) studied an orphan home in Iran that was comparable to the one Spitz had studied. When the children reached the age of 6, the girls in the home had been transferred to another very bad institution, while the boys had been transferred to a much better one where they were given some education and more varied experiences. At age 2, IQ scores of both boys and girls were about 50; but by age 16, the boys' IQs averaged around 81, still lower than normal, while the girls' IQs remained at around 50. Dennis argued that the difference between the boys and girls could be attributed to the environmental change after age 6. He argued further that lack of stimulation—or "experiential deprivation"—rather than the absence of maternal care in itself had also caused the poor development of the orphans.

In both Spitz's and Dennis's orphanages, the children were deprived of both mothering and stimulation. What would happen if infants were raised without mothering but in a good institutional environment? The question is answered in a study by Tizard and Rees (1974). These authors followed the development of children who had spent their first two years in British residential nurseries. There was a high ratio of staff to children in the nurseries, and the babies were provided with toys, books, outings, and other stimulating experiences. At the same time, they were cared for by a constantly changing staff. The children had about fifty to eighty different caretakers during the preschool period, which tended to impede the development of personal bonds; in addition, the agencies that ran the nurseries disapproved of close personal relationships between members of the staff and the children. Here, then, was a "natural experiment" in which it was possible to assess the effects of an environment that was rich in stimulation but denied children a close and continuous relationship with a mother figure.

Between the ages of two and four and a half, some of these children were adopted, some returned home to their biological parents, and some remained in the institution. To make valid comparisons in this study, it was important to ensure that the children's personal characteristics did not influence these outcomes. Tizard and Rees were confident that external factors, such as a parent finding employment, determined whether the child would go to a home or remain in the institution.

At the age of two, when they were still institutionalized, these children's intellectual growth was essentially normal, although they were a bit slow in language development. At age four and a half, all the children's IQs were at least average; the adopted children's scores were above average (115), the still-institutionalized children were slightly above average (105), and the children who had been returned to their families had the lowest scores, although still average (100). Thus, the slow language development seen at two was a delay, rather than a permanent deficit. The reason the children who had returned to their own parents scored lowest, according to Tizard and Rees, was that they had lost some environmental advantages; they had few books or toys and were read to less often. At eight and a half, all the children were still average or above, although the children who had remained in the institution declined slightly. A small group of children who had been adopted after four and a half had lower scores than those who had been adopted earlier. Tizard and Rees do not believe, though, that the older adoptees had passed a critical period in their development;

rather, they suggest that the lower scores resulted from the lesser interaction between these children and their adoptive parents: children adopted above the age of four and a half are likely to be in school all day.

This and other studies have shown that children who spend their infancies in institutions need not be intellectually impaired. Intellectually, at least, there is little support for the belief of many social workers who are inspired, mistakenly, by Bowlby's conclusion that any bad home is better than a good institution. But what about emotional development? Bowlby (1969) has stated that if children do not form an attachment to a mother figure in infancy, their capacity for social relationships will be forever impaired. Such children will be apathetic and affectionless or they will be indiscriminately friendly to many without the capacity to have a deep relationship with anyone.

The data on this issue is much sparser than that on intellectual development. The best evidence comes from the same British residential nurseries discussed above. Tizard and Hodges (1978) found that at the age of two, when the children were still in the institution, they were both more clingy and more diffuse in their relationships than home-reared children. By the age of four the institutionalized children were still clingy. Most had not formed deep attachments with anyone, but some were closely attached to their housemothers. They had also become very friendly with strangers and clamored for attention. By age eight the still-institutionalized children were attention seeking, restless, disobedient, and unpopular with other children.

What about the children who had been adopted *after* infancy? Even the children adopted after four usually developed deep relationships with their adoptive parents. Thus, it seems that it is possible for children who were not attached to anyone in infancy to develop their first bonds as late as four or six.

In contrast to their ability to develop parent-child bonds, however, the late-adopted children at the age of eight had problems in school similar to those of the children who had remained in the institution. It is not clear whether the lack of early attachment was responsible for these problems, or whether the children had learned patterns of interaction in the institution which worked there but not in the outside world. It is also uncertain whether these children continued to have difficulties in social relationships in adolescence and adulthood.

Separation

As we have seen, Bowlby has stated that an unbroken attachment relationship is necessary for normal development. Relationships can be "broken" by daily separations such as day care, transient separations such as a child or parent going to the hospital, long-term separations, or, finally, permanent loss. The effects of separation can be divided into short-term effects—the child's immediate reactions—and long-term effects, which are not seen until several years later (Rutter, 1981). The short-term effects of separation are well documented. The impact of separation on a child's psychological development is, however, highly controversial.

Researchers have studied the immediate reactions of young children to separation primarily by observing those who are admitted to hospitals or residential nurseries. Most, but not all, young children go through a set of processes that resembles adult grief in some ways (Robertson & Robertson, 1971). Children above the age of six months cry and scream and reject all efforts to comfort them—the period of "protest." If the mother appears during this time, they may be ambivalent to her. After a few days, children become miserable, apathetic, and hopeless. This is the period of "despair." Finally, there may be a stage when the child seems to be content and to have lost interest in the missing parent. If the mother visits, the child may ignore her, avoid her, or cry. This is the stage of "detachment" (Robertson & Bowlby, 1952). The detachment is more apparent than real, however. After the child returns home and resumes normal life, he or she may become excessively clingy to the mother and not let her out of sight. If children remain in the institutional setting, they are likely to suffer developmental retardation.

The full-blown distress syndrome described above does not appear to be a reaction to the separation from the mother in itself. Separation is particularly upsetting when combined with being in a hospital, a strange and frightening place for the child. Children who are cared for by familiar people, in a family setting, or who receive personal care from a substitute mother, show much less distress. The least disturbing situation would be where a child is cared for at home by a grandmother or other family member or friend. However, Bowlby and others have argued that even though children may not show extreme distress, any separation can still be "dangerous" (Bowlby, 1973, p. 22). The danger arises, according to Bowlby, from a distortion in the child's attachment to the mother. He claims that children are likely to be angry at their mothers for leaving them. Because being angry and hostile toward a loved one is so painful and anxiety-arousing, the whole pattern of feelings and responses toward the attachment figure can become tangled and distorted. Further, Bowlby argues, since models of attachment figures are built up in childhood and are likely to remain unchanged, separation experiences in early childhood may impair a person's close relationships in adulthood.

As we have seen, these views are extremely controversial. It is true that the tangle of love, hostility, and anxiety Bowlby describes can be found in adult neurotics. But, even if adult neurotics did have separations and insecure attachments to their parents in early childhood, such a finding would prove nothing about whether such conditions in childhood must *necessarily* lead to impairment in adulthood.

Indeed, there is some evidence suggesting that separation is not necessarily bad. For one thing, there is a very high rate of separation in normal individuals; one large-scale study showed that by the age of four and a half, a third of the children had been separated from their mothers for at least a week (Douglas, Ross, & Simpson, 1968). Another study showed that certain "happy" separations may actually protect children from the stresses of later, more difficult ones (Stacey et al., 1970). It seems clear that the circumstances of the separation, not the separation itself, determine whether the effects will be beneficial or harmful.

Patterns of Attachment

The largest and most systematic body of research on attachment is based on the work of Mary Ainsworth and associates (1978). At first, they used naturalistic observation to document the growth of attachment, observing parents and children in the United States and in Uganda. This work, along with other research, confirmed that attachment generally follows the same course in very different cultural settings.

In her Uganda study, and in a longitudinal one in Maryland, Ainsworth noticed some striking individual differences in attachment patterns. Most children seemed to have secure, confident relationships with their mothers, but there remained some children who seemed to be insecurely attached. They clung strongly to their mothers when upset and were highly distressed when separated from them. Yet they seemed tense with their mothers and were difficult to soothe when upset.

Because longitudinal research is expensive and time consuming, Ainsworth decided to devise a brief laboratory procedure that would give a reasonably accurate picture of the relationship between an infant and his or her mother. Thus, Ainsworth designed the **strange situation,** a technique which stimulated a large body of research.

The strange situation is a drama that unfolds in eight scenes over a 30-minute period. As shown in Figure 6.3, the cast of characters is a baby, usually 12 or 18 months old, the mother, and a stranger. Each succeeding scene exposes the child to increasing levels of stress in order to evoke high-intensity attachment behavior. Lest the procedure sound too cruel, it should be pointed out that the episodes are interrupted and the infant calmed if he or she becomes very distressed.

When the exercise begins, the mother and

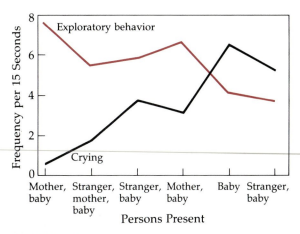

FIGURE 6.3
An Infant's Reaction: The Strange Situation
When a stranger enters the room, a baby will cry more and explore less than if it were alone with its mother. This chart illustrates a one-year-old's reaction to the strange situation over the period of a half hour.

Source: "Attachment, exploration, and separation: Illustrated by the behavior of one-year-olds in a strange situation" by M.D.S. Ainsworth & S. M. Bell, 1970, *Child Development, 41.*

infant are introduced to the laboratory playroom, and the child is put down on the floor to play with an attractive array of toys. Next, a female stranger enters the room, talks to the mother, and tries to play with the baby. The mother then slips out of the room, leaving the baby with the stranger. After three minutes the mother returns to the room and is reunited with the baby, then both the mother and the stranger leave the room, leaving the baby alone. The stranger returns first and tries to play with and soothe the baby. Finally, the mother returns for the second and final reunion.

From children's reactions to this exercise, especially their behavior during the reunion episodes, Ainsworth identified three different patterns of attachment: Type A or avoidant children ignore the mother when she returns, or they may approach her tentatively, turning or looking away. These infants pay little attention to the mother when she is in the room and do not seem distressed when she goes out. If distressed, they are as easily comforted by the stranger as the mother. About 20–25 percent of the middle-class American children who have been studied fit this pattern.

Type B, securely attached children, were the largest group—about 65 percent of the American middle-class sample. When their mothers return, these children go to them immediately, calm down after being held or hugged, and resume their play with the toys. Securely attached infants in the preseparation episodes use the mother as a secure base, but are friendly to strangers.

Type C infants are described as "resistant." They seem to be ambivalent toward the mother. When reunited, they both seek and resist physical contact; for example, a resistant baby typically runs to the mother when she reenters the room but, when picked up, squirms angrily to get down. Resistant babies are likely to be fussy and wary throughout the episodes of the strange situation. About 12 percent of Ainsworth's sample fit this pattern.

Ainsworth believes that both Type A and C babies are insecure and conflicted about their relationship with the mother. In home observations, she notes, A and C babies were more fussy than B babies. Both gave signs of being in conflict about being close to the mother. The A babies seemed to dislike physical contact, while the C babies seemed to want more from their mothers than the mothers were willing to give.

Ainsworth's methods have been widely used by other researchers. Some studies have found that children remain highly stable in their classifications between 12 and 18 months (Waters, 1978); others have found considerably less stability (Thompson, Lamb, & Estes, 1982; Vaughn, Gove, & Egeland, 1980). Part of the difference may be explained by social class: classifications were more stable in middle-class families where the environments were secure and relatively constant; in poor families that experienced considerable stress and instability,

classifications were less stable over time. These findings suggest that early attachment patterns are not necessarily permanent: if the family situation changes, children's relationships can change also.

Relations with Others

Most research on attachment has focused on the mother, but the father is being recognized more and more as an important attachment figure for infants (Lamb, 1981). A study by Mary Main and Donna Weston (1982), for instance, showed that a one-year-old who has an insecure relationship with the mother could have a secure relationship with the father. Researchers are also beginning to look at attachment in the context of all the child's relationships, not just the mother and father. Children obviously grow up in families in which there may be brothers and sisters, grandparents, aunts, uncles, and cousins (Lewis, 1982). One study found that the more social support the mother had from other people, the more likely was her infant to be securely attached. Additional results suggest that other people in the social network can compensate for a poor relationship with the mother (Parke & Asher, 1983).

Some research seems to show that levels of security and insecurity, as demonstrated in the strange situation in infancy, are related to how a child behaves with other children during the preschool period. For example, several studies have shown that toddlers who were rated as securely attached to their mothers were more sociable with other children, more likely to be leaders, and more curious and engaged with their surroundings than infants who had been anxiously attached (Lieberman, 1977; Matas, Arend, & Sroufe, 1978; Waters, Wipman, & Sroufe, 1979). Teachers described these children as more forceful, self-directed, and eager to learn. Children who had been insecurely attached as toddlers tended to remain on the sidelines and withdraw when other children tried to play with them.

These studies have been taken as evidence that the early relationship between mother and

child determines children's later peer experiences, as well as their problem-solving competence. But there are problems with this interpretation of the data. First of all, there are methodological flaws in some of the studies (Campos et al., 1983). Further, the good adjustment of a nursery school child may reflect the *current* secure state of the parent-child relationship, rather than a delayed effect of the attachment relationship at 18 months. Moreover, children with poor relationships with their mothers do not necessarily have poor peer relationships. Lewis and Schaeffer (1981) studied a group of abused and neglected infants who had insecure relationships with their mothers. These children, who ranged in age from 6 to 33 months, were placed in a day-care nursery for eight hours a day with other children who came from similar backgrounds but had normal relationships with their mothers. After four months in the nursery, there were almost no discernible differences between the two groups of children. The connections between early attachment and later social relationships remain an open question.

Second Thoughts about the Strange Situation

Recently, a number of serious questions have been raised about whether the strange situation really does reveal the quality of the mother-child relationship (Campos et al., 1983; Connell & Goldsmith, 1982; Lamb et al., 1984). Jerome Kagan points out that the classification of the child as "secure" or "insecure" is based largely on the two three-minute episodes during which the mother leaves and returns. "Is it reasonable," he asks, "that a history of interaction comprising over a half a million minutes would be revealed in six minutes in an unfamiliar room?" (1984, pp. 62–63).

Apart from the argument based on reasonableness, Kagan and other researchers have suggested that the child's behavior in the strange situation may reflect characteristics of the child, rather than the quality of the mother-child relationship. One study found that the

degree to which the child is upset by the strange situation is the best predictor of the child's response to the mother when she returns (Gaensbauer, Connell, & Schultz, 1983): infants who were distressed during the separation episode showed more attachment behavior to the mother; those who were not distressed, but played happily with the toys, were likely to go on playing when she returned. Such infants would be classified as avoidant and therefore insecure. But a child could be close to his or her mother and still not appear to be very anxious in the strange situation. The amount of distress a child displayed could be due to a host of factors apart from the underlying emotional bonds to the mother. Such factors could be children's temperamental vulnerability to anxiety in unfamiliar settings, illness or fatigue, events just before going into the laboratory, whether or not the child is used to being left with babysitters, the behavior of the stranger, and so on. (We will discuss the temperament issue later in this chapter.)

Childrearing practices may also affect the child's responses to the strange situation. Two mothers who are equally loving may encourage different degrees of independence and "toughness" in their children. Cross-national data supports this suggestion. While three-fourths of American children are usually classified as securely attached, in northern Germany only one-third of the children are so labeled, and one-half are regarded as "avoidant" (Grossman et al., 1981). The researchers who conducted this study did not conclude that all these children were less securely attached to their mothers; rather, they believe that the children's behavior reflects the strong cultural value placed by people in that part of Germany on emotional reserve and independence. In contrast to the German findings, studies of Japanese (Miyake, Chen, & Campos, 1985) and Israeli (Sagi et al., 1982) infants find large numbers of Type C infants. Again, these results are in line with the prevailing cultural values and practices.

Given these and other problems of method and interpretation, many researchers are coming to doubt whether strange situation classifications truly reflect the security or insecurity of

a child's attachment. One detailed review of the literature concluded that claims regarding the validity and reliability of this procedure are not well founded (Lamb et al., 1984). The recent evidence suggests that attachment is a complicated phenomenon; as Ainsworth and her colleagues have pointed out, it is strongly related to the child's emotional experiences. But we cannot assume that the specific behaviors observed in the laboratory reflect, in a simple and direct way, the complex emotional bonds between children and their mothers.

The Effects of Infants on Their Caretakers

During the 1930s, 1940s, and 1950s, many psychologists believed that the key to psychological development was parents' handling of the baby's biological drives. A great deal of research time and energy was given to the study of infant care techniques, such as breast or bottle feeding, weaning, and toilet training. These studies had been derived from Freud's writings, although some people believe they misunderstood what Freud was saying. Despite all this research, however, there is no evidence that specific infant care practices have any effect on adult personality (Caldwell, 1964). Or, as one writer put it, "If the child is father of the man it is for reasons other than missing out on the breast, and a too early acquaintance with the potty" (Schaffer, 1977, p. 10).

Why did these studies fail? First, they did not take into account the active role of the child in the socialization process; they assumed that particular practices would affect all children in the same way. Second, they looked at single events, such as weaning, rather than the overall relationship between the parents and children. Third, they overemphasized early experience, ignoring the possibility that later events could also influence the child. Finally, they assumed that child outcomes can be predicted directly from parental behavior—that the parent is the "cause," and the child, "the effect" (Danziger, 1971).

This is not to say that parents have no effect on the child. Rather, developmental researchers are now looking at parent-child interaction as a two-way process. For example, a study by Moss and Robson (1968) clearly showed how great a role babies play in interacting with parents. In six-hour home visits with fifty-four one-month-old infants, the researchers recorded the frequency with which the baby or the mother initiated contact. The infant was the initiator in about four out of five instances. In the first few weeks of life, the baby's fussing or crying usually starts a round of interaction.

The baby's personality also helps to maintain or disrupt the flow of caretaking. Some babies, for instance, exceed the tolerance limits of their parents. If a child does not calm down in response to the mother's efforts, she may respond less often. After three months, most babies cry and fuss less and need somewhat less physical caretaking. Robson and Moss (1970) found that mothers of three-month-old infants reported feeling less attached to them if their fussiness had not diminished.

Richard Bell (1974) describes how a vicious cycle can get started when infants exceed the parents' tolerance limits. He reanalyzed data from a study by Sylvia Bell and Mary Ainsworth (1972), who had looked at the relationship between infant crying and maternal indifference toward crying episodes in the four quarters of the first year. He found that, especially toward the last half of the year, the more the infant cried during any given three-month period, the more the mother ignored the cry in the following quarter. Thus, the cycle seemed to have developed: when the baby could not be consoled by the mother's efforts, the mother withdrew, which caused the baby to cry still more, and mother withdrew still more.

Babies That Are "Different"

Most babies have an enormous influence on parents simply because of their "babyishness." A cute baby can cause parents, grandparents, unrelated adults, and even children to make funny faces and noises and indulge in a whole

FIGURE 6.4
Cuteness as an Adult Releaser
According to some ethologists, "cute"
features of babies trigger a nurturant,
caring response in adults.

repertoire of other antics. As we saw in Chapter 2, some ethologists speculate that babyish "cuteness" evolved in many species to trigger a nurturant response in adults (Lorenz, 1943). Not just baby humans, but also kittens, puppies, monkeys, and birds have fat cheeks, big eyes, prominent foreheads, big heads, and small bodies (Figure 6.4).

Unfortunately, not all babies are born cute. We see the effects of infants on their caretakers most sharply when the child clearly deviates from expectations about what a normal baby should be like. Premature babies, for example, are often scrawny. Because their reflexes are immature, they are less responsive than full-term babies—less likely to gaze at the parent's face, for example, or turn to a sound. To com-

FIGURE 6.4
Cuteness as an Adult Releaser
According to some ethologists, "cute" features of babies trigger a nurturant, caring response in adults.

pound the problem, the cry of a premature baby is more disturbing to adults than that of a full-term infant.

In a study by Frodi and his associates (1978), parents were shown videotapes of either a normal, full-term newborn, or a premature one. The sound tracks were dubbed so that half of the normal infants seemed to emit a premature cry and half of the prematures a normal cry. Parents found the premature baby's cry more

annoying than the normal cry. Further, it elicited more physiological arousal—a sign of stress. The most negative reaction occurred when the premature cry was paired with the image of a premature infant. It is not surprising that premature babies may be at greater risk for child abuse (Lamb, 1979).

Studies of blind babies also reveal how the appearance and responsiveness of infants affect the way adults respond to them. Mothers of blind babies often have difficulty forming attachments to their children. Selma Fraiberg and her associates (1974) discovered that because eye contact is an essential ingredient in social interaction, its absence in blind children is profoundly disturbing to parents. She observes that normal babies, from their first days, "woo" their mothers with their eyes: "The engagement of the eyes is part of the universal code of the human fraternity, which is read as a greeting and an acknowledgement of 'the other' long before it can have meaning for the infant" (1974, p. 220).

Even after years of research, she notes, the observers and clinicians in the 1974 study could not help feeling that some vital element was missing in social exchanges with blind children. Fraiberg also saw contrasts in the way professional visitors respond to films of sighted and blind babies. With sighted children, the observers respond to the babies' moods. They smile when the baby smiles, frown when the baby frowns, laugh when the baby looks indignant in response to the experimenter's taking a toy away. With blind babies, observers' faces remain solemn, not only in response to the blindness itself, but mirroring the lack of expression on the child's face.

Fraiberg and her colleagues found ways to help parents to understand their baby's alien experience. For example, they discovered that in the absence of an "eye language," blind babies develop "hand language," "smile language," and "voice language"—subtle cues that parents can use to gauge the babies' reactions and intentions. When parents do find a way to "read" their blind child, the development of the child's attachment to the parents parallels that of sighted children.

Temperamental Differences between Infants

Obviously, marked differences in infants such as prematurity, blindness, or some other handicap will affect how their caretakers treat them. But more subtle differences also affect interaction. A dramatic rise of interest in infant temperament is one of the most significant developments in the study of human infancy (Campos et al., 1983).

Thus, many researchers in a variety of fields from psychosomatic medicine to education are now paying attention to what parents and pediatric nurses have always known—that there are marked individual differences even in very young infants. One baby cries a lot of the time, one baby cries very little. One baby stops crying right away when the parent tries to soothe its fretfulness, another keeps crying no matter what the parent does. One baby notices every sound, another is oblivious to loud noises. One baby lies still most of the time, another kicks and thrashes. These individual differences help determine what kinds of demands will be made on the parents in the earliest weeks and months of life.

For example, consider the simple trait of "cuddliness." A study by Annaliese Korner (1973) found that normal infants differ to an "amazing" degree in how cuddly they are. One baby molds to the parent's body when cuddled, another stiffens and squirms. Schaffer and Emerson (1964) followed thirty-seven infants and their mothers over their first eighteen months. Nine of the children were classified as "noncuddlers," nineteen "cuddlers," and the rest as "intermediate." Throughout the eighteen months, the noncuddlers resisted being held, even when they were tired, frightened, or ill. The cuddlers consistently enjoyed all kinds of physical contact.

Cuddliness was associated with other differences among babies. The noncuddlers tended to be more active, restless, and intolerant of physical restraint. They were also less likely to enjoy security blankets, cuddly toys, or their own thumbs. In addition, the noncuddlers were more advanced in their motor develop-

ment than the cuddlers. The latter were more placid, needed more sleep, and formed attachments earlier and with greater intensity.

In the past, most psychological theories would have pointed to the mother as the cause of the baby's resistance to cuddling. But Schaffer and Emerson could find no evidence that the mothers of cuddlers and noncuddlers handled their babies differently. The authors conclude that a baby's like or dislike of close physical contact is a general expression of the infant's personality—not a reaction to the parents. They see cuddliness as an aspect of a more general temperamental characteristic, the child's activity level. Schaffer and Emerson conclude that cuddly babies may need more hugging and physical contact than their noncuddly counterparts, and feel deprived if they do not get it.

Looking at the issue from the parent's side, Korner (1973) observes that the child's degree of cuddliness must affect the mother; imagine the feelings of a mother who wants physical closeness and whose child resists it—or a mother who is not fond of physical contact paired with a child who is always seeking it. What matters for the parent-child relationship is not so much the characteristics of the child, or the parent, but how well their personalities fit together.

There are other ways the personalities of parents and children can clash. For example, babies also differ in sensory sensitivity; how much stimulation they need and how much they can take (Korner, 1973). A highly sensitive baby may be overwhelmed by ordinary household stimulation unless shielded from loud noises, bright lights, sudden changes. Conversely, infants who are insensitive or have high sensory thresholds may need a great deal of stimulation for optimal development. These babies may show the effects of inattention and neglect more than those who are highly sensitive to environmental stimuli.

Much of the recent research on temperament is focused on the kinds of differences in infants that may lead to difficulties in early parent-child relationships and later problems. But recently researchers have become interested in *invulnerability*—how infants and children are able to develop normally and even thrive in the face of extreme deprivation and stress. (See the box in Chapter 11 on Resilient or "Invulnerable" Children.) Many factors probably explain why some children are resilient in the face of stress, but temperamental differences probably play an important role in a child's degree of vulnerability (Rutter, 1981).

What Is Temperament?

Temperament, like love, is one of those terms that everyone understands but has a hard time defining. Most researchers agree that temperament is an aspect of personality—an individual's characteristic way of behaving and approaching the world. But *personality* usually refers to the more complex and subtle kinds of individuality seen in adults and older children—a person's unique hopes, fears and fantasies, moral character, basic attitudes and values, styles of thinking, and especially his or her concepts of self and others.

Temperament, by contrast, concerns emotional reactions that can be identified in infants and young children, as well as adults (Figure 6.5). These reactions seem to be rooted in psychophysiology, especially the emotional arousal system. Thus, Allport defines temperament as the "characteristic phenomena of an individual's emotional nature, including his susceptibility to emotional stimulation, his customary strength and speed of response, the quality of his prevailing mood, and all peculiarities of fluctuation and intensity in mood" (1937, p. 54).

Over the years, the interpretation of temperament has accumulated a number of associated notions, many of which are no longer valid. For example, psychologists used to believe that different temperaments were associated with particular body types. Other outmoded notions about temperament held that temperament is unchanging, that it is uninfluenced by the environment, that a person's temperament is constant in all situations (Goldsmith & Campos, 1982.) Many current temperament researchers

FIGURE 6.5
Temperamental Differences between Newborns
Although temperament is not fixed at birth, temperamental differences are apparent between newborns.

fluence; rather, they assume that temperament and life experience interact with one another (Buss & Plomin, 1975; Thomas & Chess, 1977). Nor do they assume that temperament reveals itself in everything a person does. Temperament is a *predisposition* to react in particular ways to particular situations, not a constant feature of behavior. A child with a difficult temperament could have a "good" relationship with one parent, and a "poor" one with the other.

As babies grow into children, their emotions and moods are not expressed as directly. For instance, young children learn not to be "cry babies"; a child who temperamentally may be inclined to get very upset will learn not to show his or her true feelings. In addition, the older child's emotional reactions to events are guided by cognitions: expectations, assumptions, models of self and others. Temperament influences experience, and experience influences cognitions, but temperament does not influence cognitions directly (Buss & Plomin, 1975; Shaver & Rubinstein, 1980).

Finally, there is the issue of the origins of temperament. Most researchers believe that temperament is determined to some extent by genes, but they differ as to the degree. Also, as we saw in Chapter 4, there is a great deal of controversy about the measurement of heritability, as well as about the methodology of twin studies. Figure 6.6 from a study by Buss, Plomin, and Willerman, shows correlations between identical and nonidentical twins on four temperaments: emotionality, activity, sociability, and impulsivity.

Although these findings support the hypothesis that the four temperaments have a genetic component, the authors do not deny that environment plays a major role also. For example, in this same study, the correlations for all except the emotionality items decreased sharply from early to later childhood. As Buss and Plomin have stated elsewhere,

> It is not that parental inputs, peer influences, and the experiences of everyday life are unimportant in influencing personality, but that these

believe, by contrast, that temperament and other psychological traits can change with development (see Derryberry & Rothbart, 1984; Lerner & Lerner, 1983). Thus, a child may be a cheerful, calm, easy-going infant, and then become a difficult, cranky, tantrum-throwing preschooler.

Researchers do not necessarily assume that temperament is immune to environmental in-

determinants are not the only ones. . . . The initial inherited potential is modified by life experiences. . . . Although the *origin* of the temperament is inheritance, its final *outcome* depends on modification by the environment. (1975, p. 236)

Most temperament researchers would probably agree with that statement, although some would go further and argue that temperamental characteristics themselves vary in heritability; some may be completely determined by the genes, and others not at all (Goldsmith &

Gottesman, 1981). In any event, heritability is no longer part of the *definition* of temperament (Plomin, 1982).

Whichever way temperament is defined, and however large or small the contribution genetics makes, it is clear that infants and children differ from birth. The debates among researchers concern the ways children differ and the source of these differences—not whether they differ. And regardless of how much early temperament persists into childhood and later life, the individuality of babies affects how parents and infants interact with one another.

FIGURE 6.6
Items and Correlations on the Temperament Scales

A Priori Scale Assignment	Correlations			
	Males MZ*	Males DZ*	Females MZ*	Females DZ*
Emotionality				
Child cries easily.	.56	.10	.47	.23
Child has a quick temper.	.34	.10	.40	.70
Child gets upset quickly.	.64	.10	.66	.00
Child is easily frightened.	.58	.11	.70	.00
Child is easygoing or happy-go-lucky.	.46	.00	.38	.00
Activity				
Child is off and running as soon as he wakes up in the morning.	.88	.41	.86	.00
Child is always on the go.	.48	.02	.72	.01
Child cannot sit still long.	.76	.25	.65	.27
Child prefers quiet games such as coloring or block play to more active games.	.77	.00	.21	.03
Child fidgets at meals and similar occasions.	.67	.38	.68	.31
Sociability				
Child makes friends easily.	.74	.26	.47	.00
Child likes to be with others.	.61	.27	.29	.05
Child tends to be shy.	.57	.10	.51	.00
Child is independent.	.58	.25	.44	.24
Child prefers to play by himself rather than with others.	.55	.10	.73	.46
Impulsivity				
Learning self-control is difficult for the child.	.75	.55	.83	.69
Child tends to be impulsive.	.81	.00	.68	.39
Child gets bored easily.	.83	.13	.49	.59
Child learns to resist temptation easily.	.72	.35	.70	.52
Child goes from toy to toy quickly.	.82	.44	.83	.62

*MZ = monozygotic
 DZ = dizygotic

Source: "The inheritance of temperaments" by A. H. Buss, R. Plomin, & L. Willerman, 1973, *Journal of Personality, 41.* Copyright © 1973, Duke University Press (Durham, N.C.).

The New York Longitudinal Study

The major body of research on infant temperament and its later development is the New York Longitudinal Study (NYLS). Alexander Thomas and Stella Chess began the study in 1956 with 141 middle-class children born in that year. Later, 95 children of Puerto Rican working-class parents were added, and still later other special groups became part of the study.

At the time they began the project Thomas and Chess were out of step with most other developmental researchers. The prevailing view, as we have seen, was that the environment, especially the family—and in particular the mother—determined the kind of personality a child would have. Thomas and Chess, along with their collaborator, Herbert Birch, felt that too much credit was being given to the environment—to "nurture" rather than to "nature." They believed that the dominant learning and psychoanalytic theories of development were underestimating the importance of constitutional differences in children. In addition to their theoretical interests, these researchers were concerned about the impact of the prevailing theories on people's lives; they felt that parents were being unjustly blamed for any psychological problems their children developed.

Thomas and Chess used parental interviews as the main source of data. The questions to parents focused on detailed descriptions of children's reactions to everyday events. How did the child react, for instance, to wet diapers, to the first taste of cereal, to baths and bedtime, to new people and objects, to changes in routine? The interviewers insisted on step-by-step descriptions, rather than on general interpretations. For example, if a mother said that her child cried when he was put to bed at night, she would be asked, "What did you do when he cried?" Then, " How did he react to what you did?" Then, "What did you do then?" The questioning went on until the interviewer was satisfied that the episode had been described from beginning to end (Thomas & Chess, 1977). The parents were interviewed every three months during the baby's first year, then every six months. When analyzing the written records of the parental interviews, the researchers found that individual infants differed in nine distinct components of temperament, such as activity level, quality of mood, intensity of response. Figure 6.7 illustrates the typical behaviors in each of these nine elements.

Looking at the behavior profiles of all the children in the nine categories, the researchers found that the sample fell into three general types: "easy," "difficult," and "slow to warm up." The "easy children" got hungry and sleepy, and soiled their diapers at regular, predictable times. Yet they were not upset by novelty and change. They were cheerful much of the time, liked new food, reached for new toys, and smiled at new faces. At the other extreme, "difficult children" were irritable, fearful, and irregular in their bodily functions. They tended to have intense and negative reactions; they cried a lot, threw tantrums at slight frustrations, and were generally unhappy and unfriendly. Children who fit the "slow to warm up" pattern were in-between the easy and difficult groups. Initially, they did not take to most new things—the first bath, new foods. But slowly they did adapt. These children were also mild rather than intense in their reactions, and were relatively inactive.

Not every child in the study could be classified into one of the three groups. Forty percent were "easy," 10 percent were "difficult," and 15 percent were "slow to warm up." The remaining 35 percent did not fit into any of the three categories. The temperamental patterns did not seem to reflect the parents' methods of childrearing or parental personality. Boys and girls did not differ in temperamental traits, nor did the middle-class and working-class samples.

Although temperament and other aspects of individuality are clear in infancy, babies are not locked into their early temperament patterns for life. Perhaps the most surprising finding of the NYLS was that children who started out with similar temperaments could end up quite differently, while children with different tem-

peraments could end up very much the same. Retrospectively, these developmental outcomes could be understood and explained, but they could not have been predicted beforehand.

Thomas and Chess found that environmental factors played a crucial role in the child's emerging behavioral style. They use the term **goodness of fit** to suggest the degree of harmony or discord between a child's characteristics and the behavior and expectations of the parents. A baby with a difficult temperament whose parents are calm and patient, and whose environment is unchanging, may become smoothly adapted to everyday life. In contrast, an "easy" baby may encounter trouble later on. For example, in his earliest years David had been one of the most cheerful, friendly, active children in the study. When seen as a teenager, however, he was obese, inactive, and apathetic. All during his childhood his parents had been in constant conflict with one another and the outside world. At the same time, they constantly told David what a superior child he was and blamed his school problems on his teachers (Thomas & Chess, 1977).

Other Temperament Research

Other researchers have also emphasized the importance of the infant's traits meshing with the needs and expectations of the parents. Korner, as we noted earlier, pointed to the possibilities of mismatches between infant's and mother's needs for cuddling and stimulation. In another longitudinal study of 128 infants, Sibylle Escalona (1963) also found that children's development could not be predicted from their earlier characteristics. Some quiet, passive infants developed into active, resourceful preschoolers; some unusually lively infants became shy and unhappy. There were many examples where mothers behaved in a similar manner yet the outcomes of their children were very different. Conversely, opposite kinds of maternal behavior could lead to similar outcomes in the children.

Looking back over the records, Escalona concluded that to understand a child's development it was necessary to look at both child temperament and parental behavior, as well as the opportunities and constraints in the environment. Altogether, these factors made up what Escalona termed each child's **experience pattern.**

Compatibility between parents and child may change as the child grows older. A good or a bad fit in infancy may not predict the same kind of relationship later on. In the NYLS, marked and even dramatic change occurred in a number of families as new abilities or shortcomings appeared in the child, or the environment offered new opportunities or demands. For instance, Dorothy had been a typical "difficult" child. When she was an infant, her father rejected her while her mother was confused and ambivalent. In early childhood Dorothy had severe behavior problems, but during her elementary school years she suddenly turned out to have musical and dramatic talents. Teachers and others praised her to her parents, and in their eyes their daughter was transformed from a "rotten kid" to a highly talented person with an "artistic temperament." Her symptoms disappeared. When last interviewed at the age of 22, Dorothy still had some stormy moments, but she was successful both academically and socially, and she seemed to be well launched into adult life (Thomas & Chess, 1980, pp. 118–19). A contrasting example is another girl who had been an "easy" baby and who had developed well until she entered adolescence. At that point, she became sexually "promiscuous," dropped out of a series of schools, and eventually became alienated from family and friends.

In general, the Thomas and Chess findings about change, continuity, and predictability are comparable to the findings of other longitudinal studies that began in infancy. The Fels longitudinal study, for example, also followed a group of children from infancy to early adulthood. The findings of this study were first reported in a book published in 1962, *Birth to Maturity,* by Jerome Kagan and Howard Moss. In the preface to the second edition (1983), Kagan reviewed the major conclusions of the original

FIGURE 6.7
Behavior Illustrations for Ratings of the Various Temperamental Attributes at Various Ages

Temperamental Quality	Rating	2 Months	6 Months
Activity level	High	Moves often in sleep. Wriggles when diaper is changed	Tries to stand in tub. Bounces in crib. Crawls after dog
	Low	Does not move when being dressed or during sleep	Passive in bath. Plays quietly in crib and falls asleep
Rhythmicity	Regular	Has been on 4-hour feeding schedule since birth. Regular bowel movement	Is asleep at 6:30 every night. Awakes at 7 A.M. Constant food intake
	Irregular	Awakes at a different time each morning. Size of feeding varies	Variable length of nap. Variable food intake
Distractibility	Distractible	Will stop crying for food if rocked. Stops fussing if given pacifier when diaper is being changed	Stops crying when mother sings. Will remain still while clothing is changed if given a toy
	Not Distractible	Will not stop crying when diaper is changed. Fusses after eating even if rocked	Stops crying only after dressing is finished. Cries until given bottle
Approach-withdrawal	Positive	Smiles and licks washcloth. Has always liked bottle	Likes new foods. Enjoyed first bath in a large tub. Smiles and gurgles
	Negative	Rejected cereal the first time. Cries when strangers appear	Cries at strangers. Delays playing with new toys
Adaptability	Adaptive	Was passive during first bath; now enjoys bathing. Smiles at nurse	Used to dislike new foods; now accepts them well
	Not Adaptive	Still startled by sudden, sharp noise. Resists diapering	Does not cooperate with dressing. Fusses and cries when left with sitter

1 Year	2 Years	5 Years	10 Years
Walks rapidly. Eats eagerly. Climbs into everything	Climbs furniture. Explores. Gets in and out of bed while being put to sleep	Leaves table often during meals. Always runs	Plays ball and engages in other sports. Cannot sit still long enough to do homework
Finishes bottle slowly. Goes to sleep easily. Allows nail cutting without fussing	Enjoys quiet play with puzzles. Can listen to records for hours	Takes a long time to dress. Sits quietly on long automobile rides	Likes chess and reading. Eats very slowly
Naps after lunch each day. Always drinks bottle before bed	Eats a big lunch each day. Always has a snack before bedtime	Falls asleep when put to bed. Bowel movement regular	Eats only at mealtimes. Sleeps the same amount of time each night
Will not fall asleep for an hour or more. Moves bowels at a different time each day	Nap time changes from day to day. Toilet training difficult because of unpredictable bowel movement	Variable food intake. Variable time of bowel movement	Variable food intake. Falls asleep at a different time each night
Cries when face is washed unless it is made into a game	Will stop tantrum if another activity is suggested	Can be coaxed out of forbidden activity by being led into something else	Needs absolute silence for homework. Has a hard time choosing a shirt in a store because they all appeal to him or her
Cries when toy is taken away and rejects substitute	Screams if refused some desired object. Ignores mother's calling	Seems not to hear if involved in favorite activity. Cries for a long time when hurt	Can read a book while television set is at high volume. Does chores on schedule
Approaches strangers readily. Sleeps well in new surroundings	Slept well the first time he or she stayed overnight at grandparents' house	Entered school building unhesitatingly. Tries new foods	Went to camp happily. Loved to ski the first time
Stiffened when placed on sled. Will not sleep in strange bed	Avoids strange children in the playground. Whimpers first time at beach. Will not go into water	Hid behind mother when entering school	Severely homesick at camp during first days. Does not like new activities
Was afraid of toy animals at first; now plays with them happily	Obeys quickly. Stayed contentedly with grandparents for a week	Hesitated to go to nursery school at first; now goes eagerly. Slept well on camping trip	Likes camp, although homesick during first days. Learns enthusiastically
Continues to reject new foods each time they are offered	Cries and screams each time hair is cut. Disobeys persistently	Has to be hand led into classroom each day. Bounces on bed in spite of spankings	Does not adjust well to new school or new teacher; comes home late for dinner even when punished

Figure 6.7 continues on pp. 224 and 225.

Temperamental Quality	Rating	2 Months	6 Months
Attention span and persistence	Long	If soiled, continues to cry until changed. Repeatedly rejects water if wanting milk	Watches toy mobile over crib intently. "Coos" frequently
	Short	Cries when awakened but stops almost immediately. Objects only mildly if cereal precedes bottle	Sucks pacifier for only a few minutes and spits it out
Intensity of reaction	Intense	Cries when diaper is wet. Rejects food vigorously when satisfied	Cries loudly at the sound of thunder. Makes sucking movement when vitamins are administered
	Mild	Does not cry when diaper is wet. Whimpers instead of crying when hungry	Does not kick often in tub. Does not smile. Screams and kicks when temperature is taken
Threshold of responsiveness	Low	Stops sucking on bottle when approached	Refuses fruit he or she likes when vitamins are added. Hides head from bright light
	High	Is not startled by loud noises. Takes bottle and breast equally well	Eats everything. Does not object to diaper being wet or soiled
Quality of mood	Positive	Smacks lips when first tasting new food. Smiles at parents	Plays and splashes in bath. Smiles at everyone
	Negative	Fusses after nursing. Cries when carriage is rocked	Cries when taken from tub. Cries when given food she or he does not like

studies in the light of research that had been done since 1962. In general, they held up well. Two of the major findings of the study concerned the continuity issue. The most publicized generalization of the book had been that after the age of five or six years, a moderate degree of consistency develops over time in such qualities as aggressiveness toward peers, dependency on friends, lack of shyness with strangers, and academic performance. But the other major conclusion received much less attention: with one exception, the qualities of the infant failed to predict what he or she would be like in the future. Psychologists at the time

1 Year	2 Years	5 Years	10 Years
Plays by self in playpen for more than an hour. Listens to singing for long periods	Works on a puzzle until completed. Watches when shown how to do something	Practiced riding a two-wheeled bicycle for hours until he or she mastered it. Spent over an hour reading a book	Reads for two hours before sleeping. Does homework carefully
Loses interest in a toy after a few minutes. Gives up easily if she or he falls while attempting to walk	Gives up easily if a toy is hard to use. Asks for help immediately if undressing becomes difficult	Still cannot tie his or her shoes because of giving up when not successful. Fidgets when parents read to him or her	Gets up frequently from homework for a snack. Never finishes a book
Laughs hard when father plays roughly. Screamed and kicked when temperature was taken	Yells if feeling excitement or delight. Cries loudly if a toy is taken away	Rushes to greet father. Gets hiccups from laughing hard	Tears up an entire page of homework if one mistake is made. Slams door of room when teased by younger sibling
Does not fuss much when clothing is pulled on over head	Looks surprised and does not hit back when another child hits her or him	Drops eyes and remains silent when given a firm parental "no"	When a mistake is made on a model airplane, corrects it quietly. Does not comment when reprimanded
Spits out food he or she does not like. Giggles when tickled	Runs to door when father comes home. Must always be tucked tightly into bed	Always notices when mother puts new dress on for first time. Refuses milk if it is not ice-cold	Rejects fatty foods. Adjusts shower until water is at exactly the right temperature
Eats foods he or she likes even if mixed with disliked food. Can be left easily with strangers	Can be left with anyone. Falls asleep easily on either back or stomach	Does not hear loud, sudden noises when reading. Does not object to injections	Never complains when sick. Eats all foods
Likes bottle; reaches for it and smiles. Laughs loudly when playing peekaboo	Plays with sibling; laughs and giggles. Smiles when he or she succeeds in putting shoes on	Laughs loudly while watching television cartoons. Smiles at everyone	Enjoys new accomplishments. Laughs when reading a funny passage aloud
Cries when given injections. Cries when left alone	Cries and squirms when given haircut. Cries when mother leaves	Objects to putting boots on. Cries when frustrated	Cries when unable to solve a homework problem. Very "weepy" if not getting enough sleep

welcomed the news of continuity, but were not yet prepared to be skeptical about infant determinism.

The single quality that did carry over from infancy to later years was the tendency of some children to be fearful and inhibited when confronted with unfamiliar but nonthreatening events. A later study by Garcia-Coll, Kagan, and Resnick (1984) pursued this theme of behavioral inhibition. Out of 100 21-month-old children, the researchers selected the 28 most inhibited and the 30 least inhibited. At 31 months, the inhibited children were still shy and fearful. When they were 4 years of age, the majority still maintained their characteristic style—they were restrained, quiet, and gentle. Kagan suggests that this quality, which has the rare distinction of persisting past infancy, may do so because it is partially rooted in biology: a tendency toward emotional arousal in response to unexpected, unfamiliar events. In general then, results show that children with extreme scores on inhibition remain extreme; children with less extreme scores do not necessarily maintain their same rankings over time (See the box on "Difficult" Children for a discussion of the "difficult" temperament.)

The Transactional Model of Development

Arnold Sameroff (1975; Sameroff & Chandler, 1975) has spelled out in detail the implications of a *transactional* model of development. He contrasts such a model with a *main effects* model and an *interactional* model. A **main effects** model predicts later development directly from a child's early status. Such a model might forecast that a difficult baby would become a child with behavior problems because constitutional weaknesses predisposed the child to emotional difficulties, regardless of what the parents did in raising the child. This type of model could also predict that being raised in a bad home would produce a maladjusted adult regardless of the child's emotional makeup.

Retrospective studies, which look at the lives of adults or children backward through time, often find some constitutional or environmental handicap early in life, such as birth complications or an unstable family situation. But prospective studies, in which infants are followed into later childhood or adulthood, do not support the main effects model. Of course, certain extreme constitutional defects, such as severe brain damage, will result in deviant development in any environment. Similarly, there are extreme environmental conditions that would probably result in deviant development in any child. The case of Genie, who as we saw earlier was kept isolated and confined to a potty chair,

would be one example. But these extreme situations do not account for the vast majority of children who develop psychological disorders. Hence, main effects models do not fit the evidence concerning either constitutional or environmental influences on development.

An **interactional model** does take both constitution and environment into account. It would predict that difficult children raised in a stressful, unsupportive environment would have poor outcomes. Children without constitutional problems raised in a good environment would have the best outcomes. Finally, children with poor constitutions and good environments, or children without problems raised in a poor environment, would be in-between.

This model would lead to better predictions than the main effects model, but it has a major inadequacy. It assumes that child and the environment remain constant. In fact, parents and children are constantly changing, in response to their influence on one another and due to the developmental changes that are transforming the infant. The interactional model is too static; to overcome its limitations, Sameroff proposes a transactional model.

The **transactional model** views development as a step-by-step process of reciprocal interactions between the child and the environment. It emphasizes the possibility of change in the child's environment and the child's active participation in his or her own growth. A good illustration of how a transactional model works is the case of Dorothy, described earlier. Here was a difficult child whose parents treated her harshly until she developed a strong talent in music and drama. Her father's attitude changed from anger and rejection to pride and acceptance, and her development in adolescence and early adulthood seemed excellent. Both the main effect and the interactional model would have predicted a very poor outcome for Dorothy. But she changed, her environment changed, and so did her parents. It is these changes in the course of development that the transactional model emphasizes.

The transactional model can be applied to continuity as well as change. It assumes that if

"Difficult" Children

In the years since Thomas and Chess began their pioneering study of individual differences, many researchers have become interested in infant temperament. The concept of difficult temperament has received special attention because of evidence that "difficult" babies may be at risk for later behavioral difficulties and psychopathology.

Thomas, Chess, and Korn (1982), for example, have recently found that having a difficult temperament in the first few years correlated significantly with adjustment problems in childhood and early adulthood. Another study noted that "difficult" babies were more likely than other children in the first two years of life to have injuries requiring stitches (Carey, 1970). Still another found that children rated as difficult had a harder time later on in adjusting to a new baby in the family (Dunn, Kendrick, & MacNamee, 1981).

Recently, much of the work on temperament, especially the concept of difficult temperament, has been challenged by John Bates (1980). Bates argues that difficult temperament is a parent's perception rather than a characteristic of the child. He suggests that parental reports about a child's irritability, irregularity, fearfulness, and other major components of the difficult child concept have little correlation with objectively gathered information on the same qualities.

At first glance, Bates's arguments seem convincing. Most studies on temperament do rely on parent reports. How can we expect parents, who are obviously so emotionally involved with their children, to be accurate observers? His argument seems to bring up several separate questions: Do infants have any qualities that could reasonably be called temperamental traits? Can parents give reasonably valid reports about their children's temperament? How should we interpret any discrepancies between a parent's description of his or her child and those of an outside observer?

All of these questions plunge us deep into the heart of a complex issue in psychology: the problem of validity. Validity concerns the degree to which a measure actually assesses what it intends to assess. Most of the time, psychologists try to measure ambiguous, unobservable concepts such as intelligence or temperament. There is often no consensus about what the criteria for validation should be. In the debates over temperament Bates and others believe that "objective" observations and laboratory measures give the most valid picture of children's temperaments. But other researchers feel that parents' reports are the most valid sources of information about a child's temperament. Thomas, Chess, and Korn (1982) argue that to rate a child's temperament you need information on the child's behavior in many aspects of daily life; only an observer living in the house for days could duplicate what the parents know. They argue further that the behavior of a parent and child being observed in the laboratory, or in the home, may not resemble their typical behavior. Rather than choosing a single method, other researchers suggest that study on temperament could benefit from using both methods together. Using multiple measures of traits is already prominent in personality research (Campbell & Fiske, 1959).

Parental reports, like any other psychological measure, have their strengths and weaknesses. Parents are likely to be most accurate when they are describing specific behavior close to the time when it occurred. Pediatricians, for example, regularly assume that parents can report on children's colds and symptoms of other illnesses, temperature, appetite, sleeplessness, and so on. If parents are asked about the child's motives and inner psychological states, though, they are likely to be less accurate, but not by great margin. Most studies of parental accuracy report modest but significant agreement between mothers and fathers about their child's temperament, and between parents and objective raters. A carefully done study by Judy Dunn and her associates reported much higher agreement between parent and researcher observations. Dunn and Kendrick (1980) compared temperament ratings based on mothers' interviews *and* direct observations of forty mostly working-class families with children ranging from 18 to 43 months. The mothers were asked for detailed descriptions of their children's behavior and then the researcher simply observed activity in the home for an hour on at least two separate days. Agreement between parents and rater was quite high.

The evidence concerning temperamental differences does not all come from parental reports. As we have seen, many researchers have observed individual differences in young infants that can influence how their parents react to and care for them. Such infant qualities as fussiness, cuddliness, activity level, and responsiveness have emerged from objective observations.

Recently, several studies have looked at individual differences in newborns and also at the impact of these differences on interaction with caretakers. One study rated visual attentiveness, activity, and fussiness in twenty-eight healthy newborns (Breitmayer & Ricciuti, 1983). The researchers found that nurses were influenced by these characteristics as early as the second day of life. Babies who were more attentive—that is, those who were bright-eyed rather than sleepy or closed-eyed—received the most contact and were talked to more. Babies who were highly active when being washed or diapered were contacted the least. Irritable infants received the fewest affectionate comments and gestures.

Other researchers have related newborn differences to difficulties in later mother-child interaction. Judy Dunn (1975) found that babies who were irritable during the first ten days received relatively little affectionate contact by the mother at ten months. A study in Japan found that irritable newborns were more likely at age one to be fearful and insecure in their relationships with their mothers (Miyake, Chen, & Campos, 1983). These findings do not mean that the newborn's characteristics determine later development. While infants begin to influence their social worlds very early, they need not necessarily continue to elicit the same kind of interaction later on.

Laboratory studies provide another important source of data about temperament. In the laboratory, babies can be presented with controlled sets of stimuli—pictures, sounds, unfamiliar people—and their reactions can be recorded on videotape and physiological tracking devices (Rothbart & Derryberry, 1981). Using these records, researchers have looked at how long it takes different babies to react to new stimuli, how intensely they respond, and how long it takes them to return to "normal."

In general, this data suggests that infants do differ objectively in ways that can reasonably be called temperamental. Several of the temperamental traits that have emerged from observational and laboratory studies, such as inhibition and fear of the unfamiliar, are components of the "difficult child" construct.

There is evidence that having a "difficult" baby is more stressful in some cultures than in others (Lerner & Lerner, 1983). In a British working-class sample, one study found difficult temperament to be a high risk factor for the development of later problem behavior (Graham, Rutter, & George, 1973). Another study compared temperament and child care practices in a middle-class Boston community and in a farming and herding community in Kenya. The researchers found that difficult temperament was more stressful for the Boston parents. For instance, the Boston parents were much more bothered by their infants waking up in the middle of the night than the Kenyans. Thomas and Chess (1982) found similar contrasts between their middle-class sample and their Puerto Rican working-class parents. Middle-class parents expect that their babies will quickly become regular in their sleep and feeding schedules, adapt readily to new situations and people, and learn to feed and dress themselves. These expectations may be especially hard for children with difficult temperaments. It is important to note that, in each community, what parents expect of their children is shaped by the demands and pressures in their own lives, as well as by their ideals of proper childrearing.

In sum, then, the concept of the difficult child is not just a parental invention. Whether a difficult baby will later develop behavior problems depends on the parents' responses to the child, the cultural context and resources of the family, the child's particular experiences with other adults and children in school and the neighborhood, as well as the child's evolving perceptions of self and others.

a child continues to show the effects of some inborn or early defect, there must be a continuing difficulty in the ongoing transactions between the child and the environment. As we noted earlier, most infants who suffer birth problems such as prematurity, lack of oxygen (anoxia), or birth injuries develop normally. If such a child is born into a family at the upper end of the socioeconomic scale, the effects of the birth complications will disappear. By contrast, poor socioenvironmental conditions tend to amplify the effects of early complications.

Developmental Research and Public Policy

Theories and research in child development have often had a profound impact on child care practices, public opinion, and government policies. The work of Spitz and Bowlby, for instance, revolutionized the treatment of infants and children who cannot be cared for by their own families; such children are no longer placed in large institutions for months and years on end. Instead, they are placed in adoptive homes as soon as possible or in foster homes until permanent arrangements can be made.

Hospitals too have changed their practices in caring for sick children. In the past, they often regarded parents as intruders whose presence upset the children as well as hospital routines. One English psychiatrist recalled the long lines of parents outside hospitals, waiting for the half hour's visit they were permitted with their children *each week* (Hinde, 1982). Now, most hospitals in England and America allow and even encourage parents to be with their children as much as possible, and sometimes to stay with them overnight. As a result of these changes, hospitalization is now much less frightening and lonely for children than it used to be.

Not all applications of developmental research to practice and policy are so justified and beneficial, however. Sometimes, the mass media gives widespread publicity to findings that later fail to hold up in the light of further research. Often the dissemination of research findings, valid or not, can have unintended harmful consequences. The recently popular notion of mother-infant **bonding** in the first hours of life is a prime example of both problems and is illustrated in the box on The Rise and Fall of "Bonding." The original findings were supported only weakly, if at all, but many parents who for one reason or another had missed out on the experience of early "bonding" felt that an essential ingredient was missing in their relationship to their child.

Problems can also arise when research findings are exaggerated either by researchers themselves or others. Such overextensions are especially likely to occur when the topic is the object of public controversy, such as day care.

Day Care

As we have seen, babies develop deep and persisting emotional bonds to one or more of their caretakers as they approach their first birthday. The term "attachment" is a useful way to refer to these emotional ties. It is necessary, however, to separate the *facts* of attachment from practical policy matters concerning child care. For many influential writers, findings about attachment seemed to provide scientific backing for traditional beliefs about mother-child relationships: a woman's place is in the home; working mothers are placing their children at risk for serious personality disorders in later life. Some child care "experts" have considered working mothers and day care as equivalent in kind, if not in degree, to the more severe forms of "maternal deprivation." (Recall that "maternal deprivation" is itself a questionable way to describe the effects of being raised in institutions lacking in stimulation and individualized care.)

John Bowlby's work deserves much of the credit—and blame—for this extreme emphasis on the importance of the mother and the dangers of separation. In fact, in England, this set of ideas has been labeled "Bowlbyism" by its critics (Riley, 1983). Bowlby, however, is not

The Rise and Fall of "Bonding": Developmental Research, the Media, and Social Policy

"There is a sensitive period in the first few minutes of life during which it is necessary that the mother and father have close contact with their neonate for later development to be optimal" (Klaus & Kennell, 1976, p. 14). This statement by two pediatricians helped to revolutionize hospital childbirth practices in the late 1970s. Early and prolonged contact in the hours and days after birth, Drs. Klaus and Kennell argued, can have an important influence on the parent-child relationship and the child's future development; without such contact, the mother may become less emotionally attached to her infant and the child's future development could be impaired.

The idea of "bonding," and the image of some special kind of emotional epoxy glue secreted almost as part of the birth process, captured the attention of the mass media and the public. The movement convinced the medical establishment to make major reforms in the way hospitals deal with childbirth. It also led other researchers to study bonding. After further research had been done, however, serious flaws became clear in the original studies: the results could not be replicated. Some researchers found that early contact enhances a mother's behavior toward her infant, others did not. The effects found were short lived, disappearing after a few months. Usually, only a few measures out of the many used in each study showed differences between experimental and control groups. Such differences therefore could have been due to chance, not cause and effect. Often the observed differences had little relevance to how much a mother is attached to her baby. For example, one study found that mothers in the early contact group were more likely to lean on one elbow or sit up than other mothers.

According to a major review of bonding research (Lamb & Huang, 1982), the most charitable conclusion about early contact is that it has limited, short-lived effects on certain types of mothers under certain circumstances. A more critical reading of the literature leads to the conclusion that early contact has no significant impact on the mother-child relationship. Even Klaus and Kennell, in the 1982 edition of their book, acknowledge that there are many routes to attachment, and that almost all parents become attached to their babies regardless of hospital practices.

The rise and fall of the bonding concept contains important lessons about the public impact of psychological research:

1. The mass media can have an important influence on public attitudes through the dissemination of research findings. Yet the media tend to be uncritical in their coverage and publicize some kinds of findings prematurely, before they have been confirmed by other researchers. Later research which modifies or rejects dramatic claims is not likely to receive as much publicity.

2. There is great public interest in some kinds of behavioral research and a willingness to accept research findings, particularly when they agree with existing beliefs and attitudes. For a variety of reasons, the bonding concept was readily accepted by the public and the medical establishment. It fit in with prevailing notions about the importance of mother love and very early experience in relation to a child's future development.

3. Another reason the bonding notion may have won such ready acceptance is its biological emphasis. Klaus and Kennell's claims about a sensitive period were based on parallels with other nonhuman mammals as well as a belief that the physiological changes of pregnancy and birth promote maternal behavior in human mothers. Currently, the public, the media, and many social scientists are receptive to sociobiological explanations of human behavior. The research literature, however, does not support the biological assumptions underlying the bonding notion (Lamb & Huang, 1982). Despite the massive physiological changes that occur in pregnancy, birth, and lactation, hormones do not appear to play a major role in the onset of maternal behavior in primates or humans. Nor is there

support for the idea of a specific "sensitive period" during which humans and other animals become attached to their young; such periods occur only in the ungulates—goats and sheep.

4. The bonding idea may also have won public acceptance because it seemed to promise a "quick fix" for some major social problems. As explained in Chapter 2, the mothers in the original bonding studies were poor, black, young, and unmarried. Such mothers are at high risk for child neglect and abuse and other parenting failures. The bonding proponents claimed that early contact could remedy many of the problems in the mother-child relationship in such families. As Lamb and Huang point out, it is much cheaper and more convenient to allow skin-to-skin contact between mother and newborn on the delivery table than to provide other social services and supports.

5. Whatever the flaws in their methodology, Klaus and Kennell helped to bring about major reforms in contemporary obstetric practices. Before these changes, hospitals tended to treat childbirth purely as a surgical process. Fathers were kept out of the delivery room, and the baby was whisked away to the nursery right after birth. Reformers had argued in the early 1970s that the birth of a child is a major emotional event in a family and should be treated as such. The new family, for example, should be left alone as soon as possible after birth to share their feelings in privacy. But the medical establishment remained skeptical until Klaus and Kennell's work gave scientific backing to the reformers' arguments. The new

birth practices have been extremely popular with parents, without any apparent cost in medical standards. Unfortunately, without the exaggerated claims about the effects of bonding, these humane changes might not have happened.

6. Publicity given to overstated research claims can have harmful consequences. While many people enjoyed happier births as a result of the bonding movement, countless others who did not experience early contact were needlessly alarmed. Such parents included those who had had their babies before the mid-1970s, those whose babies had been born sick or immature, those who adopted children, and those who for one reason or another simply did not have the opportunity to be with their babies immediately after birth. Publicity about the importance of early contact led many parents to believe that they were lacking an essential ingredient in their relations with their children. One father said of his two-year-old daughter, born by cesarean section, "We're all getting along just fine, considering we didn't have the chance to get bonded" (Brody, 1983, p. 25).

Despite the fact that strong claims about the effects of early contact were not supported by the research evidence, it was a "good" hypothesis. It was "good" precisely because it could be easily tested and rejected. All in all, the rise and fall of bonding illustrates the need for public skepticism about scientific claims promoted by the mass media, especially those that promise quick fixes for psychological and social problems.

the only one responsible for these views: he insists he never said a mother had to be with her child twenty-four hours a day or could not go to work. But even while allowing for some leeway in the mother-child relationship, Bowlby emphasizes that separation is always risky for a child.

Some child care "experts" still believe that infants need their mothers with them all the time. For example, Selma Fraiberg (1977) has argued that good and constant maternal care is

"every child's birthright"; instead of providing day care, our society ought to encourage mothers to stay home with their children—and ought to encourage inadequate mothers to do better. Such messages have created enormous guilt in working mothers. These arguments have also contributed to declining levels of public funding for day care and preschool education.

The traditional assumption has been that children of working mothers are likely to become delinquent or have behavior disorders. More recently, there has been concern that children in day care would develop insecure attachments to their own parents, or become attached to the day care staff rather than their own parents. In addition, it was feared they might develop cognitive and social deficits. Evidence to dispute these assumptions, however, is plentiful (see Clarke-Stewart, 1982; Kagan, Kearsley, & Zelazo, 1978; Rutter, 1981; Scarr, 1984). Children from stable homes do not suffer from good day care, and even day care for very young children does not usually result in emotional disturbance, provided the care is good.

One careful study compared children who were in day care five days a week from the age of three months with babies of similar backgrounds who stayed home with their mothers (Kagan, Kearsley, & Zelazo, 1978). The day care arrangements were exceptionally good: there was a high staff-to-child ratio, and the children received a good deal of individual attention and stimulation. The researchers found no significant differences between day care and home care children in emotional, social, or cognitive development. When tested in the strange situation, children from both groups were equally attached to their mothers.

These recent findings from American day care centers compare with those from other countries. We have already mentioned studies showing that communally raised children in Israel develop normal attachments to their parents. Children in China, the Soviet Union, and many other European countries experience group care from early infancy without apparent ill effects (Clarke-Stewart, 1982; Scarr, 1984).

In general, what counts is the quality of the care given by parents or child care workers. There is nothing magical about parental care in itself—as we know from statistics on child abuse and neglect. Good day care is not necessarily worse than home care; certainly, reasonably good day care is better than the worst homes as the place for children to spend time during the day. One study found that even normal homes may be somewhat less pleasurable places to be than good day care centers.

Mothers caring for toddlers at home gave them more orders, directions, and reprimands. In the day care centers, the staff talked to the children less, but smiled at and touched them more. The children cried more at home (Rubenstein & Hawes, 1979).

Research on day care has implications that go far beyond scientific questions. It touches on deeply emotional public and private conflicts. Out-of-home child care has always been controversial, and support for it grudgingly given, because it goes against some strongly held assumptions about the family. One assumption has been that the well-functioning family should not want or need help in rearing its children (Grubb & Lazerson, 1982). Another, as we have seen, is that mothers should stay home and devote themselves to the care of their children. In support of this idea, it has also been assumed that women with children do not really have to work, and do so only to earn "pin money" or to "fulfill" themselves. As a result of these assumptions, child care in America has remained an underfunded patchwork system, far less adequate than in the European countries closest to us in cultural values.

Ironically, these beliefs are at odds with social reality. Most mothers work out of economic necessity. Most father's jobs today do not pay enough to support traditional notions of an adequate standard of family living, such as buying one's own home or putting the children through college. Further, in a time of high divorce rates, many mothers are the major economic providers for their children.

No one doubts that a strong and caring relationship with parents is central to a young child's well-being and development. But such a relationship is compatible with a wide range of caretaking environments. Indeed, historically and cross-culturally, childrearing patterns vary greatly. The traditional pattern of childrearing, by mothers at home, is rare. As Robert Hinde (1982) puts it, if we are going to make biological arguments about child care, then we must state that as far as evolution is concerned, there is no "one best way" to raise young children. Natural selection is likely to have produced infants who can adapt to a variety of conditions.

SUMMARY

1. Babies come into the world predisposed to social behavior. At first, children are attracted to the kinds of stimulation provided by other people—for example, faces and human speech sounds.

2. A major milestone of the first year of life is forming an attachment to a parent. Usually the mother is the main attachment figure, but sometimes it is the father. Infants form deep attachments to those who are sympathetic and emotionally responsive to them. They do not become strongly attached to people who simply care for their physical needs in a nonresponsive, nonemotional way. A secure attachment enables the baby to use the parent as a secure base from which to explore and learn about the environment.

3. From the first days of life, the influence between babies and their parents flows in two directions. Some of the infant qualities that determine the demands that will be made on parents are prematurity, handicap, cuddliness, amount of crying, soothability, and sensory thresholds.

4. A great deal of research is now concentrating on the temperaments of babies and young children. Temperament is the aspect of personality involving emotional arousal. Although temperamental characteristics such as irritability or fearfulness can be found at all ages from infancy through adulthood, they do not necessarily show continuity across the life span. A child's temperament during a particular period can have a profound impact on parent-child relations.

5. A transactional model of development is now widely favored among developmental psychologists. Transactional models assume that both the child and the environment are constantly changing and influencing one another. A child's development is a step-by-step process in which both change and continuity can occur. Transactional models also assume that self-righting tendencies are built into early development.

6. For optimal social-emotional development, children need strong, caring, continuing relationships with their parents. Children raised in institutions without much social interaction and environmental stimulation are likely to be severely impaired in both cognitive and emotional development. Good institutions do not produce such devastating effects although children raised in them may have difficulties in their social relationships. There is no single family environment that is best for children, and they can thrive under a wide variety of conditions.

Key Terms

attachment **193**
attachment-in-the-making **201**
bonding **229**
clear-cut attachment **201**
experience pattern **221**
goal-corrected partnership **205**
goodness of fit. **221**
interactional model **226**

main effects model **226**
maternal deprivation **208**
preattachment **201**
separation anxiety **201**
strange situation **211**
stranger anxiety **204**
temperament **217**
transactional model **226**

PART III

Giant Step
The Transition to Childhood

*A*lthough people in other times and places may not have divided up the human life cycle in the same way we do now, one boundary line does remain constant: the line separating infancy from the rest of the life span. The most obvious distinction between infants and noninfants is language: as noted earlier, infancy means "being without speech." The change from communicating just basic, primal needs as an infant to being a talking child does not occur all at once. But the mastery of language has profound implications for the developing person as well as for society.

The child leaves the practical here and now world of sensation and action, pleasure and pain, that infants share with other intelligent animals and is cast into a strange new world of memories, images, symbols, and concepts. With language come new knowledge and new powers, but also new demands, expectations, taboos, and judgments. In learning language, we learn about society's major categories of experience. We learn of male and female, good and bad, right and wrong, beautiful and ugly, polite and rude, past and future, life and death.

The next chapters cover major aspects of the passage from infancy to childhood: the development of a sense of self and the mastery of language. Many scholars used to believe that thinking and knowledge of the world did not begin until the child learned a language. We now know that babies can think and engage in intelligent action long before they can speak. The young child learning a language is learning a code to express what he or she already knows about the world.

The order of the chapters here reflects this newer understanding. Chapter 7 discusses the origins and later development of identity: it seems clear that before there can be a self-concept, there has to be a self. Chapter 8 deals with the child's mastery of language itself. Chapter 9 covers more generally the preschool years, that magical and often trying period between the arrival of speech and the age of reason at six or seven. Having entered the realm of symbols, the child must now rework the practical knowledge of infancy—to represent in words and images what he or she knows about the world on the level of action. Yet cracking the language code is only the first step in becoming a competent communicator. Children must recognize that other people have their own points of view, as well as their own needs and feelings. They must learn about gender and other social categories and roles. Between the arrival of speech and the beginning of school, children have enormous tasks to accomplish.

CHAPTER 7

The Origins of Identity

One great splitting of the whole universe into two halves is made by each of us; and for each of us almost all of the interest attaches to one of the halves; but we all draw the line of division between them in a different place. When I say that we call the two halves by the same names, and that those names are *"me"* and *"not-me"* respectively, it will at once be seen what I mean.

—William James,
Principles of Psychology

The most exciting idea in contemporary psychology is that it may at last be possible to construct an experimental mentalism: a psychology which does justice to the richness and complexity of the mental processes that cause behavior but is nevertheless empirically disciplined in the ways a science ought to be.

—Jerry Fodor, Thomas Bever, & Merrill Garrett,
The Psychology of Language

The problem of the self is with us again. . . .

—Ernest Hilgard,
Annual Review of Psychology, 1980

237

How does it happen that by the age of two or so, the newborn infant has been transformed into a person—someone with a mind, a social identity, and a sense of self? Until recently, only psychoanalysts and philosophers were bold enough to speculate how a baby's inner sense of self might develop. Now, however, we are beginning to have answers based on experiments and observation.

A widespread interest in the sense of self is one of the most surprising developments in psychological theory today. Psychologists in almost every branch of the field, working on different problems, now find that some concept of the self, however defined, is necessary to explain human behavior. Psychologists who study the brain, information processing, or memory, as well as personality and clinical psychologists, have been using concepts of consciousness, awareness, purpose, and other terms inextricably tied to the self, as well as the construct of self. In developmental psychology, there is a growing recognition that the sense of self is the center of the developmental process—the core of what it is that develops across the life span.

In this chapter, we examine how self-awareness emerges in an infant's first year of life and then outline the development of self in childhood and beyond. To begin with, it will be useful to spell out some of the themes and assumptions that will guide the discussion here:

1. The capacity for self-awareness is the most fundamental difference between humans and all other animals. But despite the large gap that separates us from other species, this capacity is not some unique and miraculous gift. Rather, it is a further step in the evolution of the mammalian brain. Consciousness, the ability to pay attention and be aware of one's surroundings, began with the mammals. It was, as one writer put it, as much a biological adaptation as a hand or an eye (Jerison, 1982).

Animals even have a rudimentary form of self-awareness; any animal that moves through the world must be aware of its own position and movement through the environment (Neisser, 1976). But only humans have *reflective* self-consciousness. They not only *think*, but they are *aware* that they are thinking; and they are aware of an "I" behind their thoughts and actions. The trait of reflective self-awareness seems to be the result of a quantum leap in the evolution of the human nervous system, the increase in the size and complexity of the human brain that accompanied the emergence of human speech and culture.

2. The term **self** simply means the person *as seen from his or her own point of view*. In other words, John's self is simply John, not some mysterious entity "inside" John or separate from him. My self is the person who is writing these words. Your self is the person who is reading them. All this may seem too obvious to mention, but discussions of the term "self" have been bedeviled by a great deal of conceptual confusion. Some writers have viewed the self as a little man—a homunculus—inside the person. Others have confused the self with the self-concept—the person's ideas or images of him- or herself. Recently, many philosophers and psychologists have agreed that the simplest and most useful definition of self is the one given here—the self as the person, the human being, whose behavior and thoughts are being studied (see Mischel, 1977).

3. Self-perception is not fundamentally different from any other form of perception. During our waking hours we are continuously perceiving the external world. Similarly, self-awareness has been described as "a kind of continuous apprehension of an inner reality, the reality of one's mental states and activities" (Churchland, 1984, p. 73). Moreover, part of our ongoing perception of ourselves is as physical objects in the external world. Our bodily selves are a constant part of the visual field (J. J. Gibson, 1979).

4. Information about the self is available to the infant from birth. We do not know for certain whether newborns use this information, but it is unlikely that infants go through a period in which they cannot tell the difference between themselves and the world, or themselves and other people. This statement is directly contrary to traditional views of infants. Practically every writer on infancy, including

Piaget, has assumed that infants have no sense of self. Recent evidence, however, suggests that infants are born ready, perceptually and cognitively, to differentiate themselves from the external world and from other people (Harris, 1983; Stern, 1983). The infant develops not from a state of nondifferentiation but from less to more information about the self and the world.

5. There is no particular magic moment at which the sense of self emerges. Self-awareness develops gradually. It begins with the first crude differentiations of the young infant and continues to grow, with cognitive development and sophistication, across the life span. Adults also differ in the amount of attention they pay to their mental states and the kinds of discriminations they make:

> A novelist or psychologist may have a running awareness of her emotional states that is far more penetrating than the rest of us enjoy; a logician may have a more detailed consciousness of the continuing evolution of his beliefs; . . . a painter may have a keener recognition of the structure of his visual sensations; and so forth. Self-consciousness, evidently, has a very large *learned* component. (Churchland, 1984, p. 73)

The Rediscovery of the Self

The concept of self has had a curious history in psychology. Around the turn of the century, psychology was declared to be "the science of selves" by two early presidents of the American Psychological Association (Broughton & Riegel, 1976). Then, with the behaviorist revolution, the term "self" became virtually taboo. There was no place in an experimental science for such an unobservable mentalistic concept.

For almost fifty years, the self was considered, with some justification, to be beyond the reach of study. You could not point to something and say, "There, that is a self, that is con-

sciousness, that is intention." Further, mainstream experimental psychologists assumed that all behavior could be explained in terms of stimulus and response. Belief in the self seemed naive, romantic, and unscientific. It made as much sense to suggest that humans had selves as to suggest that a watch has spirits that make it go. In fact, the concept of self was dismissed as "the ghost in the machine."

Why do we now see an interest in the self emerging in developmental psychology after almost a century of neglect? One reason is that, like Mount Everest, it is there. All languages have some version of "I" and "You" in their structures, and without the underlying concepts, the two-year-old child would never be able to learn to use these terms. Legal institutions also recognize that people have selves, that they are active agents who most of the time carry out intentions. Elaborate legal procedures—hearings and trials—exist to determine individual responsibility and intentions.

Beyond this, the problem of consciousness and the self could not be disposed of. As Julian Jaynes (1976) has pointed out, even the behaviorists who argued that consciousness does not exist did not believe that they themselves were not conscious. Behaviorists simply refused to *talk* about consciousness. As a method, he continues, behaviorism "gave psychology a thorough housecleaning. And now the closets have been swept out and the cupboards washed and aired, and we are ready to examine the problem again" (p. 16).

But why are psychologists now willing to entertain commonsensical notions they rejected earlier? One important reason is that the self is turning out to be a useful explanatory construct. As we have seen, there has been a cognitive revolution in psychology. There has been a revival of interest in such mental processes as language, dreaming, and emotion. Advances in brain physiology have also renewed interest in the ancient problem of the relation between the brain and consciousness and the self (Popper & Eccles, 1977). Cognitive psychology presupposes an active organism, rather than the passive one of stimulus-response, or S-R, theory. An active

organism has goals, can selectively attend to the environment, and can modify or reject environmental influences. Ironically, research done in the S-R tradition itself undermined its original assumptions of a passive organism. Researchers kept discovering odd effects that could not be explained in S-R terms—effects due to such inner states as expectancy, or mental set (S. White, 1976).

From the belief in an active organism, it is only a short step to the concept of the self, or active agent. Michael Lewis and Jeanne Brooks-Gunn observe that

> If one holds to a model of active cognition, one must logically hold to a belief in the self. It does not appear logical to believe in plans, intentions, and hypotheses testing without a belief in the organism's possession of some notion of self. How can an organism make a plan or test a hypothesis without also having an agency of the plan, or a tester of the hypothesis? (1979, p. 248)

Finally, in addition to all the theoretical reasons for the rediscovery of the self, a methodological breakthrough was made. What had once seemed a hopelessly vague phenomenon suddenly became available to experimental research. Such breakthroughs had occurred before: the discovery of rapid eye movement (REM) during sleep made it possible to make routine the study of dreams. New techniques had also made it possible to study perception and attention in very young infants, as we saw in Chapter 5.

As explained later in this chapter, the breakthrough in the study of the self occurred when Gordon Gallup, Jr., used mirrors to study self-recognition in chimpanzees (1970). Just as rapid eye movements indicate an inner process of dreaming, so does self-recognition in a mirror indicate an inner identity. As Gallup observes, if you did not have an identity, you would not be able to figure out the source and meaning of your mirror image. If apes could demonstrate self-awareness, it could no longer be considered "unscientific" to speak of the self in humans.

Issues in the Study of the Self

With the rediscovery of the self, traditional issues have become newly relevant. Two themes are particularly important: the first concerns a distinction between two major aspects of the self, the "I" and the "Me." The second theme concerns the relationship between knowing about one's self and knowing about other people. Both of these issues are important to understanding how the experience and concept of self develops from infancy onward across the life span. Each of these themes is dealt with, either implicitly or explicitly, by all who write about the self.

The "I" and the "Me" The idea that the self is double was first proposed by William James (1842–1910), one of the founding fathers of

William James

Different Beginnings

Every human society faces the task of caring for dependent infants. Many different solutions to the problem have been tried; none is more "natural" than any other.

In the upper classes of many societies, a nanny or nurse lives with the family to care for the infant. This used to be a common pattern in Western societies until fairly recent times.

Carrying the child in a pouch or sling is a common practice. Mothers often carry children this way; so do fathers and siblings. Older children are important child care providers in many cultures.

Hoti Indians, Venezuela

Nigeria

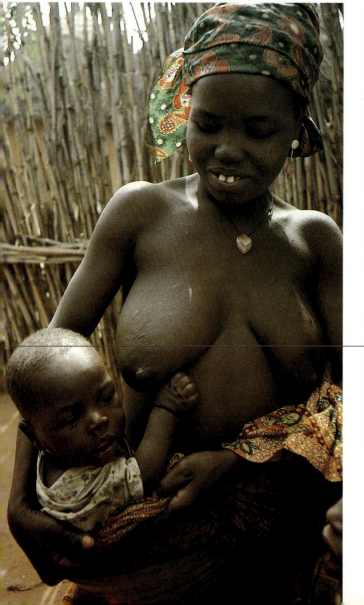

Chihuahua, Mexico

Navaho child on cradle board. In cultures using this device, the infant can be "parked" inside the tent or on a convenient tree while the mother works at her tasks.

Guatemala

Child and nurse in Israeli kibbutz nursery. On the kibbutz, infants and children live in groups apart from their families, but family contact is frequent and close ties develop among parents and their children.

Child's room in American home. American infants spend more time alone than those in other cultures.

modern psychology. James pointed out that the self is both subject and object, I and Me, at the same time:

> Whatever I may be thinking of, I am always at the same time more or less aware of *myself*, of my *personal* existence. At the same time, it is I who am aware; so that the total self of me, being as it were duplex, partly known and knower, partly object and partly subject, must have two aspects discriminated in it, of which for shortness we may call one the *Me* and the other the *I*. (1890/1981, p. 53)

James insisted that the terms "I" and "Me" did not signify anything "mysterious"; he was not postulating two entities within the mind. The core of the "I" experience is the sense of bodily existence. We feel "the whole cubic mass of our body" all the time, which gives us "an unceasing sense of personal existence." Even our thoughts and feelings are accompanied by bodily sensations, such as a quickened heartbeat or suppressed breath. A second source of the "I" experience is the sense of agency—the awareness that we are thinking our thoughts and causing our actions.

The "I" aspect of self also involves a sense of continuity, the feeling that "I am the same self that I was yesterday." This sense of continuity persists throughout life. While the "Me" changes as a person develops from baby to child to adult to old man or woman, the "I" shifts much more slowly and always retains a sense of sameness. Memory contributes to this sense of continuity. "However different the man may be from the youth, both look back on the same childhood and call it their own" (1890/1981, p. 352).

Although James regarded the "I" as the central nucleus of the self—the "self of selves," the "pure principle of personality identity"—he believed the "Me" is much less elusive and easier to study. Indeed, he referred to the "Me" as "the empirical self" and assumed it to be based on actual, observable qualities. Until recently, most research on the self has in fact focused on the "Me" aspect as the object of knowledge. Hence, there have been many studies on the

self concept, especially self-esteem. Very little attention has been paid to the "I" aspect of the self, or to the task of mapping out the various senses of the self as they develop across the life span. However, with the recent revival of interest in the self, researchers have recognized that both the "I" and the "Me," and the relations between them, are essential for understanding how the sense of self develops across the life span (Damon & Hart, 1982; Harter, 1983).

Thus, it makes sense to think that infants are "I" before they are "Me." James himself was describing adults when he wrote about the "I" and the "Me," but contemporary researchers have found the distinction useful for understanding infant development. Lewis and Brooks-Gunn (1979) contrast the "existential self" of infancy with the "categorical self" which develops around the time the child learns to use language. In early infancy, before children know anything *about* themselves, they know that they exist; they are aware of their bodily selves. This early "I" aspect of self is based on sensorimotor knowledge.

For example, babies learn that when they cry, open and close their eyes, suck their fingers, kick their legs, and so forth, something happens: they hear their own cries, the world goes dark, their fingers experience sucking, the legs wave in the air and bump against things. In the earliest months of life, these sensations cluster together to define the baby's bodily self.

The Self after James

William James died in 1910, three years before John B. Watson launched behaviorism. As a result, James's work became lost in the wake of this new movement and was essentially forgotten by the mainstream of academic psychology. It turned out, however, that his ideas were not dead, but only in a state of "hibernation" (Schlenker, 1985). With the emergence of cognitive psychology in 1965, James was rediscovered. Many psychologists today regard his *Principles of Psychology* (1890/1981) as the most important book ever published in the field and highly relevant to current issues, especially the problem of the self (Scheibe, 1985).

While the concept of the self was latent in mainstream psychology, it was awake and lively in clinical psychology. Karen Horney, Harry Stack Sullivan, and Carl Rogers felt that the self was the most important concept in understanding normal and abnormal behavior. Erik Erikson's work focused on the self under the heading of "identity" and made the term "identity crisis" a household word.

The concept of self also remained alive and well in two other disciplines, sociology and psychiatry. In sociology, the self has remained the central concept in one of the dominant theories of the field—*symbolic interactionism*—stemming from the writings of George Herbert Mead (1934), James Mark Baldwin (1906), and Charles Horton Cooley (1902). (See Chapter 3.) These writers argued that the self arises out of social interaction. Cooley's central idea was the *looking-glass self:* we can know ourselves only by the reactions of other people to us. To him, society acts as a mirror which reveals us to ourselves. Without society, we would have no selves. Mead elaborated on Cooley's ideas. His central concept is "role-taking": if children are told they are nice, or smart, or beautiful or bad, dumb or ugly, that is the way they will think of themselves. From the ability to see ourselves from the point of view of others, we are able to "take the role of the other" through the use of shared symbols, such as language. Mead saw the emergence of this kind of self-awareness as the crucial development of early childhood.

The other field for which the concept of self remained extremely important was psychiatry. Here the concept was put to practical use. While philosophers and psychologists could debate about whether the self was real or an illusion, psychiatrists were using it to make important decisions about real people that would greatly affect their lives: is this person crazy or not? Clinicians assumed then, and still do, that a sense of self is part of the basic equipment of a functioning human being.

The concept of self often reveals more about itself by its failures than by its normal functioning. By the term "failure" I don't mean the every-

day, garden variety identity problem such as "Who am I" and "What am I really like?" Many essentially "normal" people spend a lifetime trying to figure out the answers to those questions and never do succeed. (We will discuss why it is harder to know ourselves than others in later chapters.) Psychiatrists see patients with many kinds of identity problems, but the issue here is a more basic aspect of self.

Take, for example, the patient who thinks he is Napoleon; or the autistic child who struggles to understand how to use "I" and "You" but cannot grasp the difference; or the man who feels he is a robot controlled by mysterious powers; or the one who believes he is turning into someone else; or the woman who feels "there is someone else living in my body and looking out of my eyes." All of these people appear to be having problems with their "existential selves"—the "I" as opposed to the "Me." Specifically, a secure existential identity involves

1. A sense of being separate and distinct from other people and the outside world.
2. A sense of embodiment, of living in a body that feels solid and real and located in space.
3. A sense of agency—of being the doer of the things one does, and the thinker of one's thoughts.
4. A sense of continuity—"I am the same person I was, and I always will be even though I will change in many ways."
5. A sense of singularity or unity—"In spite of my many moods, social roles, states of health, I am one person."

This very basic sense of permanent identity seems related to the concept of permanent objects which the infant acquires in the first year. As the concept of object permanence grows, so does the infant's sense of its bodily self as a permanent object. It experiences itself as solid and substantial, and located in space and time. The early self is almost completely a body-self because the infant is only capable of sensorimotor experience at this period. However, the body-self remains with us throughout life and is our orientation to reality (Schor, 1959). (Self-psychology and object relations theory are discussed in greater detail later in this chapter.)

Self-recognition in Primates

Gordon Gallup, Jr., began his work with chimpanzees with a general interest in mirror images as a kind of stimulus. In an early experiment, he placed mirrors outside the cages of two male and two female wild-born chimpanzees. At first, the chimps treated their images as if they were seeing other chimps, making friendly or threatening gestures and sounds. After about three days, however, their behavior changed. The chimps began to act as if they recognized their reflections as themselves: for example, they would use the mirror to clean their teeth or groom parts of their bodies they could not ordinarily see.

Gordon Gallup, Jr.

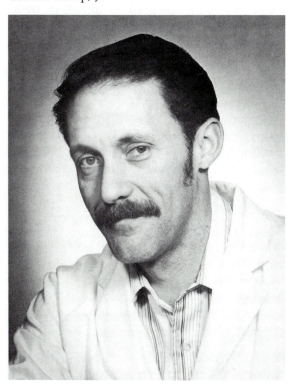

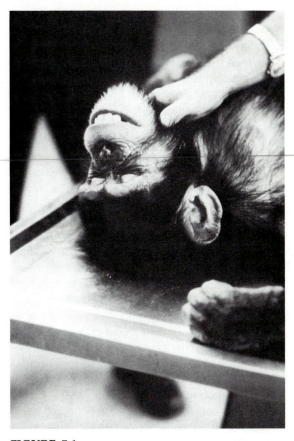

FIGURE 7.1
Experiments with Self-recognition in Primates
A rouge mark applied to a chimp's face is a method by which experimenters can gauge the chimp's self-recognition.

To provide a more rigorous test of self-recognition, Gallup devised an ingenious technique. Placing the chimps under anesthesia, he painted bright red dye on their foreheads. Since the dye was odorless and nonirritating, and had been placed on the chimps' foreheads without their knowledge, the mirrors would provide the only evidence to the chimps that the marks were there. When they woke up and saw themselves, there was a dramatic increase in the amount of touching of the dyed area on their heads as well as in mirror watching. Also, the chimps smelled and stared at their fingertips after touching the red dye. This provided strong evidence that they knew they were looking at themselves, not other chimps, or they would have had no reason to examine their own fingers. (See Figure 7.1.)

As a control experiment, Gallup followed the same procedure with chimpanzees who had no previous experience with mirrors. These animals did not touch the red marks on their heads, nor did they give any indication that they recognized themselves.

Gallup also discovered that social experience is necessary for self-recognition. Chimpanzees raised in social isolation were unable to recognize their mirror images as reflections of themselves (Gallup et al., 1971). This finding supported earlier evidence that when isolated chimps are given social experience, they show signs of self-recognition (Hill et al., 1970). Gallup's findings provide striking experimental confirmation of Mead's hypothesis that social interaction is necessary for the emergence of self-awareness—that there is an intimate relationship between knowledge of others and knowledge of the self. But his results contradict Mead's notion that language is the key to the emergence of self. The opposite, in fact, may be true: a concept of self may be a necessary precursor of language development (Terrace & Bever, 1976).

It is not clear exactly how social interaction encourages the development of self-awareness. We know from the work of Harlow and others (see Chapter 6) that isolation leads to profound cognitive and social impairment. The inability of isolated chimps to recognize themselves in a mirror may be due to this general retardation of development. Also a chimp—or a person—who never saw another creature like itself would lack an image of its whole body, and would never have seen a face before. Hence, a chimp raised in total isolation, looking into a mirror for the first time, would not only have difficulty recognizing the face reflected there as its own, but would also have no face schema, no previous knowledge of the kind of pattern or object a face is. It is interesting that although normal chimps stopped gazing into mirrors after thoroughly exploring themselves, isolated chimps stared obsessively at their mirror images, without giving any indication of recognizing the image as themselves. Oddly enough, self-recognition can occur in apes raised in the homes of humans (Gallup, 1979). Home-reared chimps can recognize themselves in mirrors, but many show active avoidance or dislike for members of their own species!

Self-recognition in Other Primates

Gallup's findings of self-recognition in chimpanzees have been replicated by other investigators. Orangutans have shown self-recognition; and Koko, Penny Patterson's gorilla, is reported to make faces at herself and to powder her face in order to stare at her ghostly image (1978). But the great apes seem to be the only primates to have this ability. The existence of profound gaps between humans and great apes on one side, and all other animals on the other, is one of Gallup's most striking discoveries. He did not expect to find such a gap. In fact, at the outset, he assumed that with enough experience, any animal should be able to recognize itself. "I was more surprised by the inability of monkeys to recognize themselves than in the chimpanzee's success," he commented (quoted in Desmond, 1979, p. 173).

Since negative evidence is inconclusive, there is a possibility that some future study may reveal self-recognition in monkeys. But the present lack of evidence is not for want of trying. Gallup followed up his original work with numerous attempts to find self-recognition in monkeys (1977). For example, one monkey received 2,400 hours of mirror exposure to no avail. Other monkeys showed no recognition after as much as seven years of exposure.

Why did the monkeys fail to recognize themselves? One reason is that recognizing oneself in a mirror is a much more complicated task than it seems at first. It is more complicated than simply identifying an object in a mirror. Monkeys do perceive that reflections of food or other objects are only reflections, and so they will turn away from the mirror to reach them.

The French psychologist Henri Wallon (1949, cited in Merleau-Ponty, 1964) has described the nature of the task the child faces in learning to recognize itself in the mirror. Children learn to recognize other people first. It seems easier to relate two visual images—the father here and the image of father in the mirror—to each other. But the child does not have a complete visual experience of his or her own body. The task is to understand that the mirror image is not one's actual body, but what one's body looks like at the very place where it is felt to be. The child must understand that the visual and tactile images of the body—the mirror image over there, and the felt body over here—are one and the same.

Thus, mirror self-recognition appears to require a particular cognitive capacity, the ability to integrate information coming from different senses. This ability, in turn, appears dependent on having a particular kind of nervous system, one with a capacity for **cross-model association**. Information coming from the various senses can be associated in the brain. Information coming from one sense—the sound of a bell, or the touch of an orange—can give rise to a mental representation of a whole object. Human language is based on this ability to form associations between two different sets of environmental stimuli: the sound of a word, and the sensory image of the thing the word represents.

Until recently, scientists believed that only humans were capable of cross-model association, and that only humans have the necessary brain structures. However, in 1970 two scientists demonstrated that chimps and orangutans are able to integrate different senses; they could pick out by feel an object that matched the image they were being shown (Davenport & Rogers, 1970). Also, recent work in neuroanatomy has suggested that the parts of the brain responsible for cross-model association and language in humans are minimally developed in apes, but are greater than those for monkeys (Geschwind, 1979).

Even in humans, identifying one's image as oneself requires experience. Babies, as we shall see in more detail later, respond socially to mirrors at first, just as apes do. Monkeys never progress beyond the social response stage. People born blind who gain their sight later re-

spond to their first glimpse of a mirror as if they are facing another person, and they respond to mirror space as if it were real (Von Senden, 1960).

Mentally impaired humans also have difficulties recognizing themselves in mirrors. Some retarded adults and children totally lack this capacity. Studies that used the Gallup dye procedure (the dye was applied while the subjects were sleeping) failed to find evidence of self-recognition in children afflicted with Down's syndrome, as well as in people with other forms of retardation (Harris, 1977).

Further, schizophrenics have difficulties with their images in the mirror. They often spend long periods of time gazing into mirrors; and, in fact, prolonged mirror gazing has been associated with the onset of schizophrenia. Some schizophrenics lose the ability to recognize themselves, so they react to their mirror images as if they were confronting another person. One group of researchers devised a mirror that looked like the kind of distorting mirror one might see in an amusement park, but which could be adjusted to give a normal image (Orbach, Traub, & Olson, 1966; Traub & Orbach, 1964). In contrast to normals, schizophrenic patients had great trouble achieving an undistorted image of themselves. Each of these failures of recognition can be explained in terms of a lack of, or disturbance in, an underlying sense of identity.

Mirror Responses in Humans

Gallup's research provided the first clear test of self-recognition, but others before him had written about the significance of mirrors in charting human development. Some investigators used a baby's interest in the mirror as a sign of self-recognition. Another early researcher used the child's recognition of the mother in the mirror as a sign of self-recognition (Preyer, 1883). Darwin (1877) thought his own son could recognize himself when the boy would turn to the mirror and say 'ah' when called by name. But none of these behaviors are clear indicators of self-recognition. Babies and animals respond to their mirror images as if they were other organisms; monkeys can recognize objects other than themselves in mirrors, and children can be taught to label their reflections with a name without necessarily being aware of the origins of the image (Gallup, 1975).

We referred earlier to Henri Wallon's analysis of mirror recognition as a cognitive task (1949). He also elaborates on the significance of the mirror image for psychological development. In addition, the French psychoanalyst Jacques Lacan (1936/1977) emphasizes the importance of the visual image of the body as the infant's first experience of its body as a unit. Between 6 and 18 months, Lacan postulates a mirror-stage of development which transforms the infant's mental life. The infant identifies with its reflection in the mirror, and this "specular" or mirror image of itself then becomes a permanent part of its identity. The specular image later becomes the basis of the infant's identification with other people, acquisition of language, and, in general, entrance into the social order, the world of rules. Lacan's views concerning the looking-glass self are in accord with those of earlier writers, but unlike them, he regards the infant's identification with its mirror image as an alienating experience.

The first systematic study of mirror recognition in children was carried out by Dixon (1957) who simply observed children of different ages in front of mirrors. From these observations he derived four stages of mirror behavior. In the first stage, at 4 or 5 months, the infant looked more at the mother's reflection than at its own; in the second stage, at around 5–6 months, the infant played with its reflection as if it were another baby, smiling, vocalizing. From 6 to 12 months, a stage Dixon labeled "Who do dat when I do dat?," the infant seemed to pay attention to the *contingency* of the mirror image—the fact that every move one makes is also made by the person in the mirror. Between 12 and 18 months, infants acted coy, self-conscious, or fearful in front of the mirror, suggesting to Dixon that the infants were beginning to recognize themselves.

In 1972, in one of those odd coincidences that occur every so often in science, Beulah Amsterdam devised a procedure very much like Gallup's without knowing of his work. She applied a spot of rouge to the noses of infants of different ages, and then noted whether they touched their noses when shown a mirror. She found stages somewhat similar to Dixon's.

More recently, Lewis and Brooks-Gunn (1979) carried out a series of mirror studies using larger numbers of infants and toddlers and more carefully controlled marking and testing procedures than the earlier studies. Rather than simply applying rouge to the children's noses, for example, they told the mothers to wipe the children's faces "because they were dirty," and apply the rouge without mentioning or calling attention to it. The children's behavior in front of the mirror was videotaped both with and without rouge on their noses. Two observers watched the videotapes and coded many different behaviors: (1) facial expressions, (2) vocalizations, (3) attention (number and length of looks), (4) mirror-directed behaviors (pointing to the mirror, touching it, and so on), (5) imitation (bounding, clapping, making faces, acting silly or coy), (6) self-directed behavior (touching face or body, touching nose, pointing to self).

Lewis and Brooks-Gunn found a much more complex picture of infants' responses to mirrors than did earlier researchers. First of all, they did not find the clear-cut stages noted by Dixon and Amsterdam. Few behaviors occurred at only one age. Babies were delighted by the mirror, whether or not they knew they were looking at themselves. Few infants in these studies showed any kind of negative feeling in front of the mirror. In general, mirror-directed behaviors were constant and high at all ages, but self-directed behaviors (touching the mark or one's body) increased with age.

What about self-recognition? Lewis and Brooks-Gunn raise the question about what is a good measure of this ability. Clearly, touching a mark on one's face soon after looking in the mirror shows that the child realizes the image in the mirror is not another person, but a "picture" of the bodily self. But mark touching

is a stringent criterion and indicates that self-recognition does not occur in most children until they are close to 2—around 21 to 24 months. It was never seen before 15 months. If any kind of body touching in front of the mirror is taken to be the measure of self-recognition, then children of 9 to 12 months have this capacity. If acting silly or coy and pointing to one's image is the measure, then self-recognition is common by 15 to 18 months. These studies confirm the notion that recognizing oneself in a mirror is a complex cognitive act that occurs when the child is able to manipulate symbols. It occurs after the child has established a primary, sensorimotor identity, and before the child learns to use "I" and "you" correctly.

Lewis and Brooks-Gunn also looked at infant's responses to videotapes of themselves and others. These studies were used to assess how three kinds of information contribute to visual knowledge of the self: **contingency** (the fact that the mirror duplicates every move we make in front of it), social categories such as age and sex, and the specific features of one's own face. Thus, children's attention to "live" TV images of themselves and to **noncontingent** or previously filmed tapes could be compared. The researchers could in this way tell the difference between children's preferences for seeing "moving pictures" of themselves, as opposed to a mirrorlike "who do dat when I do dat" contingency presentation. By comparing noncontingent tapes of the self with tapes of another child of the same sex and age, the child's ability to recognize his or her features could be assessed. Children as young as 4 months perceived that the live TV images were contingent. However, the ability to recognize the self did not begin to occur until 15–18 months, and was established in most children at 21 to 24 months.

Still another series of experiments used photographs. Babies from 6 to 24 months were shown slides of themselves, their mothers, a man and woman, a 5-year-old girl and boy, and boy and girl babies the same age as the subjects. The researchers noted how long the baby looked at each slide and how much he or she smiled at each. They found that at around

15 to 18 months, children began to differentiate between unfamiliar people of different ages, between the self and other babies of the same age, and between boy and girl peers.

These and other studies show that age is an important social category for babies. Lewis and Brooks-Gunn found that babies were less frightened when approached by children than by adults. To find out whether they were responding to size or facial features, midgets were recruited to approach babies of about 6 months of age. If infants showed fear, it would indicate that facial features were the cue. If they showed happiness, or no fear, this would suggest that they were responding to height cues. To the amazement of the researchers, the babies showed surprise at the sight of the midgets: an adult face on a child-sized body violated their expectations.

There is also evidence that infants can discriminate between the sexes. Kagan and Lewis (1965) found that 6-month-olds could discriminate between photographs of males and females. Lewis and Brooks-Gunn (1979) found that by 18 months children are 90 percent accurate in applying verbal levels of "mommy" or "lady" to pictures of women and "daddy" or "man" to pictures of men. Thus, from an early age, children use the dimensions of age and gender, as well as familiarity, to construct knowledge of themselves and other people. They also begin to prefer others who are like the self in age and gender.

Early Origins of Self

Gallup's work leaves us with a tantalizing question. What is the origin of the identity that child or chimp recognizes in the mirror? Looking in a mirror will not provide you with an identity if you do not already have one. Rather, the mirror provides an image of what one already knows. If you do not know who you are, there is no way to know who or what your mirror image is. As Gallup and his associates put it, "without an identity or sense of self, the source and significance of the reflection would,

as is apparently the case for monkeys, forever remain unknown" (Gallup, Wallnan, & Suarez, 1978, p. 7).

Physical Bases of Self-awareness

As we have seen, a basic distinction has been drawn between two aspects of the self: the "I" and the "Me," the self versus the self-concept, the self as subject versus the self as object, the "existential self" and the "categorical self" (Lewis & Brooks-Gunn, 1979). Infants are "I" long before they are "Me." That is, the "I" may be thought of as a sense of *primary identity* that develops in early infancy and which the child will later refer to as "I." Margaret Mahler and associates explain: "We use the term *identity* to refer to the earliest awareness of a sense of being . . . it is not a sense of *who* I am, but *that* I am, and as such, this is the earliest step in the process of the unfolding of individuality" (Mahler, Pine, & Bergman, 1975, p. 8).

A person who is experiencing an "identity crisis" usually is not confused about his or her primary identity. Identity crises usually are about the kind of life we should lead and the kind of person we are or should be. Primary identity, by contrast, deals with what R. D. Laing (1970) calls "ontological" security and insecurity—concerns about one's very existence in the world as a physical and mental being.

Knowledge of the body is the most basic knowledge about the self, and an intact body image or schema is essential to normal functioning. The idea of a disembodied person is hard to grasp; we tend to think that even ghosts have a human form. Our knowledge of the world depends on our bodies—eyes to see with, ears to hear with, hands to touch with, sensations produced by movement.

Throughout life, the bodily self continues to be the most constant, inescapable experience we have. Brain researchers and physicians recognize that an image of our bodies, or "body schema" as Henry Head termed it, is essential for controlling the movement of our limbs and carrying out the simplest activities. Feedback from muscles, joints, and tendons collaborates

to form "proprioceptive sensation" which tells us what our bodies are doing from moment to moment and whether our movements are doing what we intend them to do. Oddly enough, one of the limitations of computers is that they have "minds" but no bodies. As Hubert Dreyfus puts it, "what distinguishes persons from machines, no matter how cleverly constructed, is not a detached, universal immaterial soul, but an involved, situated, material body" (1979, p. 236).

Knowledge of the body as physical object and as an agent of action develops long before language. Babies seem to be able to tell the difference between themselves and other people very early, in the first few months. The traditional assumption has been that babies learn to make the distinction between themselves and others through a long, slow process. For example, Piaget believed that babies do not distinguish between themselves and others until

8–12 months. This is the stage when babies acquire object permanence—the capacity to represent absent objects and people. However, recent research on infants suggests that they may never experience a truly undifferentiated world. The distinctions between self and others are learned very early, at least by the second or third month, on the basis of early inborn perceptual and cognitive abilities (Samuels, 1984; Stern, 1983; Watson, 1983). (Recall the evidence of John Watson and others in Chapter 5 that babies are aware of contingency—of the effects of their actions—during the earliest weeks and months of life.)

Recently, Daniel Stern (1983) has presented an impressive array of evidence showing that from birth, infants have the ability to form distinct schemas of self and others. Much of this evidence comes from the recent infant studies which show that infants are prepared to perceive and recognize the "natural categories" of the world, such as human faces, speech sounds, colors, and objects (Chapter 5). In contrast to what Piaget and most other writers on infancy had postulated, this new research suggests that infants do not have to piece together their knowledge of the world from scratch. Stern shows how these abilities enable the infant to establish a rudimentary sense of self very early in life, and to distinguish between self and world, and self and other people.

Further, as P. L. Harris (1983) points out, information about the bodily self is as directly available and specific as anything else. It is not indirect or inferential. When we move, the world flows by in a way that tells us precisely where we are and where we are going. J. J. Gibson (1966) uses the term "visual proprioception" to refer to the information about the self we pick up from this optical flow. Although some psychologists have suggested that babies cannot tell the difference between themselves and other people, this confusion must exist only at the very beginning of life, if ever. As Ulric Neisser points out, "No other object can possibly be confused with the self, and no other event offers the same information as a self-initiated one" (1976, p. 192). (See box on Informational Bases for the Development of Self-awareness in Infancy.)

Emotional Bases of Self-awareness

The experience of distinct emotional states is probably another source of self-awareness in early infancy. After years of neglect, there has recently been a tremendous upsurge of interest in and research on human emotion. Emotion is one of the most crucial issues in research on cognition (Norman, 1980). Human information processing cannot be understood without taking it into account, nor can we understand it without some concept of self. Emotions are *about* the self, although the self changes dramatically with development. As Campos and associates put it, "Emotions draw attention to the physical and social boundaries of the self" (1983, p. 816).

Emotional expression patterns appear to be biologically based and prewired in infants, and related to survival. For example, a newborn will make an expression of "disgust" if a bad-tasting liquid is put into its mouth. A 10-week-old will express fear if an object looms quickly toward its face. While very young infants experience basic emotions concerning their physical survival, adult emotions concentrate more on maintaining the concept of self. Complex emotions such as shame, guilt, jealousy, and depression depend on complex self-concepts. Guilt, for instance, results from our failure to live up to our own moral standards.

Recent research has established that emotions are similar among all peoples of the world (Ekman, 1982; Izard, 1977). Different things make people in different cultures happy, sad, or angry, and there are different rules for displaying emotions. Some cultures, like the English, value a "stiff upper lip", or not showing strong emotions. In contrast, others such as Italian, Greek, and Jewish cultures, approve of displaying strong feelings. Nevertheless, happiness, sadness, anger, and other basic emotions are expressed by the same facial patterns in different cultures. All people smile when they are happy, frown and clench their teeth when angry, wrinkle their noses in disgust, and so forth. Currently, emotion researchers believe there are several of these primary, basic emotions: interest, surprise, fear, distress, anger, disgust, as well as happiness and sadness (Figure 7.2). It was Darwin (1872) who first suggested that emotions are similarly expressed in different cultures; he believed that the facial movements involved in emotional expression were biologically adaptive in various ways, such as signals to others about internal states and external events.

These facial expressions are remarkably similar across the life span. Despite the many ways in which emotions change as a person grows, there is a core of emotional experience that remains constant; happiness is happiness and fear is fear, whether the cause is the sight of a nursing bottle, a looming object, or passing or failing a crucial exam.

These distinct emotional states not only contribute to early self-awareness, but they also

Informational Bases for the Development of Self-awareness in Infancy

Recent research has shown that very young infants are much more competent than previously suspected. Many of their perceptual abilities suggest that they probably have some sense of themselves as persons. This is not to say that they have fully formed conceptions of themselves at birth. Rather, they are born with perceptual sensitivities which enable them to discover the distinction between themselves and the world. As the infant grows, it then specifies its own existence by assimilating a good deal of information from the world. Curt Samuels (in press) has summarized this information:

1. Body boundary: An individual can see or feel where his or her physical body ends, where the skin (or hair) stops, and where the background begins.
2. Double touches: When we touch our body, we experience an active touching (say on our fingertip) and a passive feeling (say on our belly); this is a double sensation of touch as opposed to a single sensation of touch which we feel when touching or touched by another person or object.
3. Intersensory coordination: We perceive double stimulation across our sense modalities when we move, i.e., we see an arm reach out and simultaneously feel the kinesthetic feedback from our movements.
4. Name identification: There is a consistent set of names that others use to refer to a given individual and this would assist in their individuation.
5. Place specification: When a person is addressed, there is a regularity in the spatial location of the visual fixation of the other(s), namely at the body (usually to the face) of the person being addressed.
6. Perspective as locus of awareness: Our sensory input is determined by the location in space of our body and our orientation. A perspective is individualized, available only to self.
7. Perceptual invariants: Our sensory mechanisms (perceptual systems) pick up information in the world, including the invariant relations of higher-order variables of stimulus energy.
   a. Nose and brow in visual field: Our visual field will always include certain parts of our physical body, namely the tip of our nose and our brow, thereby perceptually specifying an invariant and inescapable self.
   b. Motion flow pattern: When we move through space and time, our visual field undergoes a radial expansion, a flow pattern specifying self-movement.
   c. Mirror contingency: When we look at ourselves in a mirror, there is a one-to-one correspondence of each of our body movements with the movements of the mirror reflection.
8. Efficacy of personal will on self-action: When we will to turn our head to the side, we immediately do it; this degree of efficaciousness can only apply to self-behavior, not another's.
9. Emotional isolation: The affective internal fluctuations are state changes of which the self may be aware—and which are felt as one's own—and are not discernible on the emotional display(s) of the social other(s).
10. Social contingency: Interactions with others in the world are characterized by interdependent relationships of mutual causality, leading to perceptions of efficacy.
11. Stream of consciousness: Our internal cognitive flow is ceaseless (or nearly so) but is private; others are not directly aware of our thoughts.

Source: "Bases for the development of self in infancy" by C. Samuels, *Human development*, in press.

Surprise Brows rise, eyes widen, mouth forms oval shape.

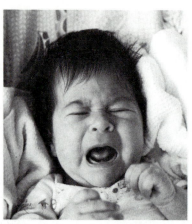

Distress Eyes close tightly, mouth is squared and angular.

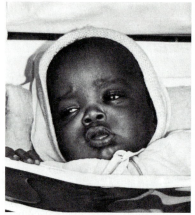

Sadness Inner corners of brows rise, lower lip is drawn out and down.

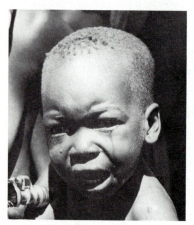

Fear Brows draw inward and upward, eyelids lift, mouth retracts.

Joy Eyes twinkle, mouth smiles, cheeks lift.

Anger Brows draw together and downward, eyes are fixed, mouth is squared.

Interest Brows rise or are knit, mouth is softly rounded, lips purse.

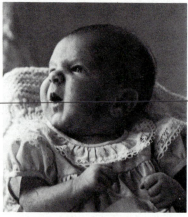

Disgust Nose wrinkles, upper lip rises, tongue pushes outward.

FIGURE 7.2
Facial Patterns Characterize Basic Emotions

give continuity to our personal identity. Thus, Robert Emde has proposed that there is an emotional or "affective core" of the self that *"guarantees our continuity of experience across development in spite of the many ways we change; it also guarantees that we can understand others who are human"* (1983, p. 165, emphasis in original).

Self-psychology and Object Relations Theory

While laboratory research has been making discoveries about the emergence of self-awareness in infants, clinical psychology has also been focusing on the development of the self. "Object relations theory," a variant of psychoanalytic theory, has come to be widely influential. While traditional Freudians believe that mental problems reflect conflicts among instinctual wishes—between id, ego, and superego—these theorists believe that problems of the self and its relations to other people are the main source of psychopathology (Eagle, 1984; Greenberg & Mitchell, 1983).

Margaret Mahler (1968) and Heinz Kohut (1971, 1977) are among the most prominent writers in this school of thought. These theorists all place the self at the center of personality development. They all assume that the major developmental process is the shift from total dependence and lack of a sense of self to an increasing awareness of one's separate physical and psychological identity. For example, Mahler, Bergman, and Pine (1975) suppose that the infant moves from a state of "symbiosis," a merging of self with mother, to a process of separation and individuation. Kohut posits that the infant first relates to others as "selfobjects," or parts of the self, and later comes to develop a cohesive sense of self.

For the most part, the discussions of early development by these theorists are speculations based on clinical work with adult patients, rather than experimental studies or longitudinal evidence (Klein, 1981; Peterfreund, 1978). As we saw earlier, recent research makes it seem highly unlikely that infants are ever

Margaret S. Mahler

without at least a rudimentary sense of self. Nevertheless, because of the wide influence of object relations theorists, particularly Mahler, it will be useful to discuss them here.

Mahler's work can be considered the "second major theory" of development in the psychoanalytic tradition (Galenson, 1979, p. 153). Although her name is far from being a household word, her ideas have been extremely influential in current psychoanalytic thought, as well as among other scholars and popular writers.

Mahler's theory traces the development of selfhood from birth through the age of three. She sees the newborn as being in a normal "autistic state," with little awareness of the outside world. The autistic period is followed by a "symbiotic" period during which the infant comes to be dimly aware that it is being cared for by someone, but believes that the mother and self are one.

The psychological birth of the child, according to Mahler, takes place in four phases, occurring after the period of "normal symbiosis."

At about four to six months, the child first begins to differentiate the self from the mother. Mahler describes this as the "hatching" process, comparing the baby to a chick emerging from a shell. She believes that sitting up and the onset of visually directed reaching are the landmarks that usher in this period of active exploration.

The second subphase from around a year to a year and a half is called the "practicing" period. First by crawling, then by walking, the baby is able to move away from the mother and becomes increasingly aware of its own separateness. Mahler suggests that learning to walk upright and free is a momentous experience in the child's life, the peak of body mastery and the beginning of a "love affair with the world." Toddlers at this age are intoxicated with their own abilities. Although the mother is still extremely important, the child seems less emotionally dependent on her than before.

During the last half of the second year, the love affair with the world ends, and the child enters a crisis period. There are temper tantrums, mood swings, and a struggle of wills between parent and child. "No" becomes the child's battle cry. Mahler calls this third period the "rapprochement crisis." The child's increased cognitive abilities make the child aware of its own separateness, as well as the fact that the parents too are separate beings with their own interests. The child not only battles with the parents, but also struggles with his or her own conflicting desires over independence and autonomy. The toddler realizes that he or she is a separate being, small, alone, and vulnerable, dependent on the love and care of the parents.

During the fourth and final phase, the child

learns to cope with aloneness. The child's internal image of mother, unstable during the rapprochement crisis, now becomes more a secure source of emotional constancy. At the same time, the child achieves a definite sense of his or her own individuality.

Mahler, like Bowlby, believes that the quality of mother-child interaction in infancy has a profound impact on later development. Difficulties during a particular phase, according to her, are likely to place the child at risk for particular kinds of psychopathology. Thus, an infant who fails to negotiate the "autistic" phase of early infancy may develop into an autistic child—one who is totally withdrawn and unable to establish a relationship with anyone. Problems during the "symbiotic" phase of development may lead to a symbiotic psychosis, marked by an inability to tolerate any separation from the mother. Problems during the various phases of separation-individuation may result in a variety of personality disorders and difficulties in relationships. In her later writing, Mahler suggests that the early experience of separation-individuation is a critical determinant of later personality, both pathological and normal. Moreover, she has come to believe that all humans are caught in an eternal struggle between the wish for "oneness" with a loved person and the wish to be a free, autonomous individual.

Evaluation of Mahler

Mahler's behavioral descriptions capture much of the emotional quality of parent-child interaction during the first two years. Observers—and parents—of young children have long pointed to a crisis in human relations during the second and third year of life, variously called "the terrible two's" or a crisis of willfulness and obstinacy. In previous centuries, parents believed it was their duty to "break the will" of the child at this period, which was achieved by whipping or other punishment (Hunt, 1970). Freud thought that conflicts over bowel training were the main battleground between parents and children at this time. Eric Erikson describes this period as a crisis in autonomy.

However, there are serious weaknesses in Mahler's theory. Her speculations about early infancy are at odds with what we now know about the perceptual capabilities of babies. As we saw earlier, in the first two to three months they can make complex perceptual discriminations and can perceive distinctions between self and others (Watson, 1983). There is a large body of experimental work on early infant capacities which suggests that infants never experience an undifferentiated world—an autistic or symbiotic phase. Separation and individuation appear to begin at birth (Klein, 1981; Stern, 1983).

Further, Mahler overlooks the child's contribution to mother-child interaction, and portrays the infant as living in an essentially two-person world, with the mother the only significant other. Thus, many of her assumptions are at odds with current thinking about infant temperament, the importance of the father and other members of the social network, and transactional models of development (see Chapter 6). Finally, there is no evidence to support Mahler's idea that specific forms of mental illness result from faulty mothering at specific phases in infancy.

Despite these weaknesses, however, Mahler provides some compelling descriptions of struggles that recur throughout life—the wish to be a separate, autonomous human being versus the fear of being alone and vulnerable; the longing for "oneness" with another person versus the fear of being smothered by intimacy. In her vivid descriptions of the emotional conflicts of selfhood, she has made an important contribution to our understanding of human development.

The Acquisition of Standards and the Beginnings of Self-evaluation

It is part of the human condition to wonder not only who or what we are, but what we should or should not be. Earlier, we contrasted the two aspects of self described by William

James—the "I" and the "Me." As we saw, the I, or sense of self as subject, develops first. Later on, infants develop a sense of themselves as objects, with recognizable features and characteristics such as size, gender, and age (Lewis & Brooks-Gunn, 1979). Soon, the child begins to apply not just social categories to the self, but rules and standards.

Some standards have to do with morality, such as not hurting other people or not taking things that belong to someone else. Other standards have to do with achievement, with meeting some goal of excellence, such as balancing a tower of blocks or completing a jigsaw puzzle. Other rules have to do with correctness, such as the rules of language—learning the correct word to use for an object, or later learning to say "he went," rather than "he goed." Still other norms and standards have to do with appropriateness, such as the norm that after you say "hello" to someone when you first see them, you don't say it again in that same encounter. Other norms have to do with politeness.

Socialization is largely a matter of learning these various sets of norms. In the beginning, of course, babies have no knowledge of norms and must be taught by adults. Being told "no" or "don't touch" when reaching for a dangerous or breakable object is probably the baby's first encounter with rules. As children begin to be able to think of themselves in relation to other people, they begin to apply standards to themselves and evaluate themselves in terms of those standards. As a result of these inner and outer evaluations, the child may feel pride and satisfaction, or guilt and shame. And children may begin to develop some general conceptions of themselves as good or bad, smart or dumb, helpless or effective.

The tendency to apply standards to oneself is part of the same ability to stand outside of and observe ourselves, which enables us to recognize ourselves in mirrors and to "see" ourselves through the eyes of another person. These evaluative aspects of the self-concept have been studied and discussed mostly in connection with older children. It is difficult to study conscience and self-esteem, or feelings or control or helplessness, in children who do not speak very well. More important, most theorists have assumed these aspects of the self do not develop during infancy, but appear at around five or six years.

There is evidence, however, that even young infants are sensitive to norms, and that in the second half of the second year, with the growth of self-awareness and self-recognition, they begin to apply standards to themselves across a wide array of behaviors. For example, parents have reported that their 7- or 8-month old babies hesitate when approaching "taboo" objects such as electric wires (Church, 1968). Many of the behaviors that Gesell reports as typical of 18-month-olds have to do with norms in the form of rituals or completions of acts—saying "thank you" and "bye-bye," closing doors, handing over a dish when finished eating, mopping a spill.

Jerome Kagan (1981) and his associates have carried out a series of studies which provide more systematic evidence about the growth of self-awareness and sensitivity to standards in the second year of life. These studies aimed at both describing the major psychological changes that occur in the months before and after the child's second birthday and explaining what the central mechanism underlying these changes might be. The studies began by presenting a wide variety of tasks to two groups of children who were studied over a ten-month period; a younger group was studied from age 13 to 20 months, and an older group from 20 to 24 months. The tasks were intended to quantify the major observable psychological changes that occur during the second year:

1. The appearance of intelligible language: one- or two-word utterances usually occur by the end of the second year.
2. Concern with parental prohibitions and standards, and a preoccupation with things that are broken, dirty, out of place.
3. Mastery behavior: the desire to do well on certain tasks, to seek challenges and avoid tasks that are too difficult, and to exercise control and autonomy.
4. Social interaction: the growth of the ability

to engage in conversations and reciprocal play.

5. Symbolic play: the ability to tell the difference between reality and make-believe.

The general kinds of behavior the researchers looked at included spoken language, symbolic play, imitation, recall memory, social play with a peer, and performance of a number of other cognitive tasks. The first phase of the research suggested that the various surface changes in behavior between 15 and 20 months derive from a more basic change in functioning, the growth of self-awareness.

During this period, children seemed to become more aware of their actions and psychological states, as well as of their ability to meet various kinds of goals and standards. It is interesting to note that unlike the mirror research described earlier, these studies did not originally set out to investigate self-awareness. Rather, self-awareness emerged as a construct that explained a great deal of the empirical data. There is a striking degree of agreement between the mirror studies of self-awareness and these findings.

The second phase of the research examined more closely the emergence of the behaviors observed earlier which seemed to be the best indicators of the child's growing self-awareness. This phase of the research included intensive naturalistic observation of six children over a period of ten months, from age 17 to 27 months. For example, one of the behaviors examined in this part of the study was showing distress at being unable to imitate a model. While seated on the floor playing with an array of toys, the child was joined by a woman researcher who said she was also going to play. The woman would proceed to carry out a number of acts—put a toy telephone to a doll's ear,

make three animals "walk in the rain" by fluttering her fingers to indicate rain. After carrying out these acts, she would get up and say, "Now it's your turn to play."

The tendency to show distress—fretting, crying, clinging to the mother—reached a peak at 20 months and declined thereafter. Kagan concluded that the children became upset because they felt obliged to imitate the model, yet could not do so. They did not become upset when they were simply interrupted in their play, or when the woman performed acts that were easy to imitate, or when their mother performed the acts. The distress seemed to result from a combination of the difficulty of the task, plus the uncertainty of the relationship with the strange woman.

This behavior suggests two significant things about infants during this period. First, they are beginning to impose obligations on themselves to perform tasks they see adults doing (the woman did not *ask* the children to imitate her); second, they appear to have some idea of what they can and cannot do—in other words, some notion of their own competence.

Another indicator of concern with standards was more positive: children would smile as they accomplished some goal, such as building a tower of six blocks or putting in the last piece of a jigsaw puzzle. Smiling suggests a capacity to set a goal for oneself, as well as the ability to know when it has been reached. Still another behavior which seemed to indicate growing self-awareness in the second half of the second year was directing adults—not only by asking for help, but also by telling adults to engage in particular play activities such as eating a toy banana, or talking on a toy telephone, and in general getting adults to do childish things. Such directions seemed to reflect not only the child's desire to turn the tables on the adults by giving them orders, but also the child's recognition of childish or silly behavior.

The most direct evidence of self-awareness, however, is self-description. Children's earliest words are not about themselves; rather, children refer to objects around them—they name a ball or ask for it. The earliest words are often an extension of the act of pointing to some-

thing (Bates, 1976). In Kagan's studies, self-description begins at about 19 months, peaks at around two years, and then declines. The earliest form of self-description is simply describing what one is doing, such as saying "up" when climbing on a sofa. Later, around 22 months, children use "I" plus a verb ("I go") or their name plus an action verb. Later still, children began to produce sentences in which "I" is followed by a predicate describing a psychological state; sleepy, tired, want, can't. The increase of self-talk seems to indicate children's increasing preoccupation with themselves and their activities around the age of 2. The activities of objects and other people become less salient. About one-third of the 2-year-old's instances pertain to the self.

The fact that these variables arise in several samples of children, including Fijian and Vietnamese, at a similar age and in roughly the same order suggests to Kagan that they reflect maturational changes in the central nervous system. The cognitive abilities that develop one after another in the first two years seem to be milestones on the way to higher levels of consciousness. First there is recognition memory. Then there is recall memory, the ability to retrieve the past and compare it with the present. Object permanence, the ability to search for a hidden object, depends on inferences made on the basis of recall memory. Finally, there is self-awareness—and the realization that the self is an entity, a combination of body and mind which is both unique and similar to others.

It seems likely that the growth of self-awareness and other cognitive capacities depends on the maturation of the central nervous system. As we saw earlier in Chapter 5, certain periods in infancy are marked by rapid changes in the development of the brain. These growth spurts seem to be related to the emergence of new motor skills and cognitive abilities. Thus, changes around 3 months are associated with the onset of social smiling and the shift from reflexes to more voluntary contol over action. Brain changes at around 8 months have been linked to the onset of object permanence. The months around the second birthday are also times of marked brain maturation (Rabinowicz, 1979). By the age of 2, the brain has reached 75 percent of its adult size (Tanner, 1978). Also, the branching of nerve fibers comes to resemble the adult pattern, the sensory areas of the cortex reach a similar level of maturation, and EEG patterns reveal that the brain has reached a higher level of organization. All of these changes seem to provide the basic "hardware" for the new abilities that emerge around 18 months to 2 years, from toilet training to the use of symbols and the emergence of self-awareness.

The Self after Infancy

After infancy, the "I" as observer and active agent and the "Me" or observed self change as cognitive, emotional, physical, and social development go forward. The onset of conscious self-awareness around the age of two does not mean that the development of the self is complete. In fact, the development of the "categorical self"—the awareness of the self having certain attributes—is the point at which most previous theorists thought the self began. Thus, G. H. Mead believed that self-awareness was made possible only through the acquisition of language.

Gallup's work with chimpanzees shows that self-awareness can occur without language or any other kind of symbol use. Yet Mead was correct that human selfhood does not fully develop without language (M. B. Smith, 1978). Language makes it possible to take part in human society the same time it gives us tools for private thought. With language, the development of the self becomes "historicized" (Luckmann, 1979); that is, the child's identity is shaped by being born into and living in a particular family at a particular moment in history.

In this section, we review some of the major trends in the sense of self over time. More detailed descriptions of the self in childhood, adolescence, and adulthood will be presented in later chapters. Many theories of the self (Ep-

stein, 1973; Kelly, 1955; Sarbin, 1968) consider it as a structure of knowledge. That is, they view the self as a set of schemas that have a powerful role in organizing an individual's experiences. Hazel Markus (1980) has elaborated and performed research on what she terms *self-schemata*. Epstein argues that the self-concept is a theory that individuals construct about themselves across the life span. Orville Brim (1976), suggests that it is possible to look at people's notions about themselves the way we look at other theories—in terms of how valid and consistent they are and how open to change.

The notion of the self as a theory does not require that components of the self-theory be conscious. Brim points out that scientific theories also contain hidden assumptions and unrecognized premises. Similarly, each of us has a variety of beliefs about ourselves; some we are fully aware of, others we are only dimly conscious of, some we are not aware of because we take them for granted—as the fish does not notice the water—and still others are deeply repressed or "disowned" beliefs about the self.

"Good Me," "Bad Me," "Not Me"

The psychiatrist Harry Stack Sullivan (1953) has written about the hidden aspects of the self. On the basis of his clinical work, he proposes that anyone's self-system contains conflicting views of the self. The self is divided into three parts or "personifications"—the "good me," the "bad me," and the "not me"—bound together by a growing conception of "my body." Sullivan believes that this triple division of the self is inevitable, since every society teaches children that there are right and wrong forms of behavior.

The "good me," according to Sullivan, reflects the child's experiences of parental approval. The "bad me" reflects impulses, wishes, and actions that have met with parental disapproval and caused some degree of anxiety. The "not me" contains impulses and actions that have met with such extreme disapproval and produced so much anxiety that they cannot be claimed as part of the self. These disowned aspects of the self can be found in the nightmares of normal people, as well as in the delusions and hallucinations of schizophrenics, and cases of multiple personality like the fictional Dr. Jekyll and Mr. Hyde. They are also revealed in the "uncanny emotions" most children feel—feelings of horror and dread about one's own impulses.

Sullivan believes that a child's self-system reflects actual experiences he or she has had with the parents. In contrast, Freud and many of his followers believe that children's unconscious tendencies to blame themselves reflect their own inner tendencies as much as their parents' actions. Sometimes children have extremely severe superegos, and hence feel extremely guilty, in families where the parents are mild and fairly nonjudgmental. As we have seen in the discussion of temperament (Chapter 6), some children are more prone to anxiety and emotional arousal than others.

Clinical speculations like Sullivan's are hard to test. Yet research on the self-concept which includes only aspects of the self that are easy to talk about may be severely limited. Sullivan's work points out that any person's self is highly complicated, not always fully conscious, and entangled in powerful emotions.

Research on the Self after Infancy

The most difficult task confronting current self researchers is how to investigate the "I" component of the self. Even those who acknowledge the importance of self as knower find it easier to study a person's knowledge and understanding of the self. Thus, much of the work on children's conceptions of themselves consists of self-descriptions. The "I" aspect of the self, as well as out-of-awareness aspects of a person's self theory, are likely to be overlooked. Nevertheless, there is some knowledge of how such aspects of the "I" as continuity and distinctness change over time.

Damon and Hart point to four trends in the development of the self from early childhood through adolescence:

1. Self descriptions shift from physical to behavioral to social to psychological aspects of the self.
2. Self descriptions come to focus on stable social and personality characteristics.
3. Reflective self-awareness grows, along with a conception of the self as an active processor and manipulator of internal experience.
4. Diverse aspects of the self are integrated into a unified self-system.

Figure 7.3 presents a model created by Damon and Hart to illustrate the development of self-understanding from infancy through adolescence. It is based on a variety of studies, most of which used verbal methods. The front face of the model represents the "Me" or categorical self; the side face, the "I" or existential self.

Development of the "Me" On the "Me" face of the model, the vertical axis describes four levels of understanding, from infancy and early childhood to late adolescence. The horizontal axis presents four aspects of the self—the physical, active, social, and psychological. Several studies of self-concept development focus on this progression from the physical to the psychological (Broughton, 1978; Selman, 1980). Thus, infants recognize their own faces in mirrors and photographs. In early childhood, children use physical characteristics to describe themselves ("I have red hair," "I have a bike"). But they also use activities as descriptions (I play," "I can ride a bike"). In late childhood, they use family and group membership characteristics ("I am Catholic," "I am a boy scout") to describe themselves. Children at this age also categorize themselves in comparison to others ("I'm no good at math," "I can't play baseball," "I can draw better than most kids").

Adolescents view themselves primarily in mental terms; when asked to describe themselves, they use personality and interpersonal traits ("I am shy") as well as moral characteristics and personal belief systems ("I am honest," "I lack will power," "I believe in nonviolence").

The outlined boxes across the diagonal in the model describe this developmental shift from

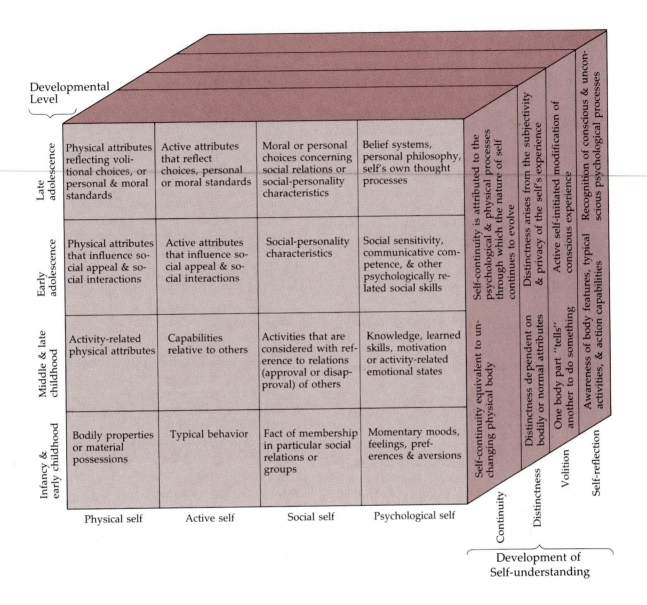

	Physical self	Active self	Social self	Psychological self	Continuity	Distinctness	Volition	Self-reflection
Late adolescence	Physical attributes reflecting volitional choices, or personal & moral standards	Active attributes that reflect choices, personal or moral standards	Moral or personal choices concerning social relations or social-personality characteristics	Belief systems, personal philosophy, self's own thought processes	Self-continuity is attributed to the psychological & physical processes through which the nature of self continues to evolve	Distinctness arises from the subjectivity & privacy of the self's experience	Active self-initiated modification of conscious experience	Recognition of conscious & unconscious psychological processes
Early adolescence	Physical attributes that influence social appeal & social interactions	Active attributes that influence social appeal & social interactions	Social-personality characteristics	Social sensitivity, communicative competence, & other psychologically related social skills				
Middle & late childhood	Activity-related physical attributes	Capabilities relative to others	Activities that are considered with reference to relations (approval or disapproval) of others	Knowledge, learned skills, motivation or activity-related emotional states	Self-continuity equivalent to unchanging physical body	Distinctness dependent on bodily or normal attributes	One body part "tells" another to do something	Awareness of body features, typical activities, & action capabilities
Infancy & early childhood	Bodily properties or material possessions	Typical behavior	Fact of membership in particular social relations or groups	Momentary moods, feelings, preferences & aversions				

Developmental Level

Development of Self-understanding

the physical to the psychological in the dominant conception of the self. But Damon and Hart point out that at each age all four aspects of the self remain important. Thus, even young children have some notion about their psychological selves—they know, for example, about their own likes and dislikes. And adolescents are highly concerned with their physical selves even though they conceive of themselves mainly in terms of inner psychological characteristics such as emotions and thoughts.

FIGURE 7.3
The Development of Self-understanding
The "Me" (physical, active, social, and psychological) and the "I" (continuity, distinctness, volition, and self-reflection) concepts of self have been charted for the four developmental levels of childhood and adolescence.

Source: "The development of self-understanding from infancy through adolescence" by W. Damon & D. Hart, 1982, *Child Development, 53.*

Development of the "I"   The angled, depth face of the model shows how the "I" or existential self develops from infancy onward. This aspect of self, as we have seen earlier, is based on experiences of continuity, distinctness from others, volition, and self-reflection. Development shifts from one pole to the other along these dimensions. Thus, in infancy and early childhood, continuity is based on the visual image of the face and the sense of one's body as a permanent object; the "I" knows what the "Me" looks like, and that it is located in a particular body (Lewis & Brooks-Gunn, 1978). Around the age of six or seven, children often cite their unchanging name as a basis for continuity. Between six and nine, children develop a sense that certain basic aspects of their identity are unchangeable: their humanity, their gender, their uniqueness and individuality (Guardo & Bohan, 1971). In adolescence, the past and future senses of the self become increasingly salient (Secord & Peevers, 1974). Adolescents begin to develop a sense of their own autobiographies; they become the heroes and heroines of life stories that begin in early childhood and extend, however uncertainly, into the distant future.

The sense of separateness also has its rudimentary beginnings in infancy. From birth, as we have seen, infants are sensitive to contingency—they can tell the difference between events that they make happen and those where they have no control. By the age of three, children develop a rudimentary sense that their own thoughts and perceptions are private and cannot be perceived by others (Flavell, Shipstead, & Croft, 1978).

Later, the sense of being a separate and distinct self develops further. Between 8 and 12, children come to be aware of the distinction between an inner and outer self. They realize that we can feel one way and act in ways that will conceal our true feelings from others. One study examined adult's recollections of how they developed a feeling of being a separate individual in childhood (Bannister & Agnew, 1977).

One man recalled that when he was three, he was riding inside a barrel on a wheelbarrow, being pushed along by his brother. At some point in the journey, the brother stopped to talk to someone:

> I was crouched down in the barrel and suddenly realized with great clarity that I could hear this man speaking, but he didn't know I was there, he didn't know I could hear him, and that I was able to know about him without him knowing about me. In some way this sticks in my mind as one of the times I realized I was an individual, that I was a self. . . . It was to do with being secret and in myself. (P. 121)

One woman recalled discovering a "separate me" the day she deliberately tripped her little brother and then pretended to her parents that he fell accidentally:

> My deceit was discovered and this seemed to be the first appreciation that I wasn't just the "good little girl" which seemed to be an imposed character; she had a nasty side too. Though it wasn't pleasant to have this nasty bit known, there was a positive side and that was that this was definitely "me" and not what others saw me as. (P. 119)

The sense of volition develops from the infant's awareness of making things happen to the adolescent's conception of the self as an active processor and manipulator of experience (Selman, 1980). Still later, the older adolescent realizes that the self controls only conscious experience, while unconscious experience can also affect behavior.

The fourth aspect of the "I" is self-reflection, the ability to observe ourselves. This is the capacity that George Herbert Mead referred to as the ability to "take the role of the other." As we have seen, at about 18 months of age, the infant "I" becomes aware of what the "Me" looks like and begins to apply such categories as gender, age, goodness and badness, and competence to the self. Eventually, with the approach of adolescence, children come to be aware of their own awareness. As Susan Harter (1983) puts it, it is as if a new part of the self is formed, a sort of "super I" which can observe both the "I" and the "Me."

There is a good deal of agreement among researchers who have studied the development of self-understanding about the trends we have just described. But these trends, especially at the later ages, are probably not universal. They describe the development of the self in modern Western societies, not in other places and times.

Some fundamental aspects of the self are indeed universal. Anthropologists point out that people everywhere have a sense of their physical and mental individuality: every language has the personal pronouns "I" "you," and "he". Moreover, as Irving Hallowell (1971) points out, no society can function without self-awareness. Individuals need to be self-aware in order to carry out the many different social roles they are assigned. But the *concept* of the self has been elaborated more in Western societies than in others, and more in recent times than in the past. Many cultures identify the self with the social roles the person occupies—son or daughter, hunter or farmer, member of this clan or the other, the embodiment of an ancestor's soul (Mauss, 1950/1979). Only Western societies have identified the person with the self—and endowed individual selves with religious and moral status and legal rights (see box on Cross-cultural and Historical Perspectives on the Self).

The Social versus the Solitary Self

Most writers on the social development of the child stress the social origins of the self. The "looking-glass self" expresses this view of the self as social product. Many writers in this tradition assume that our awareness of ourselves is inseparable from our awareness of others. Thus, G. H. Mead wrote, "No hard and fast line can be drawn between our own selves and the selves of others, since our own selves exist only insofar as the selves of others exist" (1934, p. 164). Another tradition portrays the self as a solitary mind, locked into a separate biological brain and body. Descartes provided this view in his famous statement: "I think, therefore I am."

Cross-cultural and Historical Perspectives on the Self

Do people everywhere have selves? Is there a society in which concepts such as "self," "person," and "individual" do not exist? Strange as it may seem, some anthropologists claim that many cultures fit that description. Clifford Geertz (1965) argues that our ideas about the individual would be regarded as peculiar by many of the world's cultures. He explains that in Bali, people make no distinction between the person and the social roles he or she occupies. No attention is paid to anything psychological or physical that distinguishes one individual from another. Only the roles, not the actors, are real: "Physically, men [and women] come and go— mere incidents in a happenstance history of no genuine importance, even to themselves. But the masks they wear, the stage they occupy, the parts they play, . . . constitute not the façade but the substance of things, not least the self" (p. 50).

Other anthropologists do not go quite so far in denying the reality of the individual self. They recognize that while cultures differ in how much they elaborate the concept of the self, people everywhere carry on internal dialogues, distinguish between themselves and others, and have some notion of personal identity over time (Fogelson, 1982; Schweder & Levine, 1984). Yet we cannot simply apply our own familiar conceptions of selfhood to other cultures. Despite the universal core of similarity, the differences remain profound.

For example, anthropologists often distinguish between "shame cultures" and "guilt cultures" (Rosaldo, 1984). In the first, people are punished for wrongdoing by being publicly ostracized or humiliated. In guilt cultures, people may be deeply distressed by misdeeds known only to themselves. The historian Lynn White points out that the all-seeing God in the Judeo-Christian tradition has made Western society a guilt culture. He notes that no other culture has a practice comparable to the Catholic practice of confession, in which individuals of every social level examine their consciences and whisper their misdeeds to a priest: "And since knowing ourselves is the cornerstone of individualism, no other society has so motivated the development of self-conscious individuals at every social level" (1978, p. 55).

Within Western society, conceptions of the self as well as the experience of selfhood have changed historically (M. B. Smith, 1978). In his book *Sincerity and Authenticity* (1972), Lionel Trilling traces changes in the concept of the self over several centuries of European history. Historians generally agree, he notes, that something like a "mutation in human nature" (p. 19) took place during the sixteenth and seventeenth centuries. People became more aware of their individuality, especially their internal psychological life. This new self-awareness was different from the kind of examination of conscience that Christianity had always encouraged. Now people came to emphasize and to value their unique individuality. It was a time when large, bright mirrors were manufactured and used widely, portraits and self-portraits began to be painted, privacy within the home increased, benches were replaced by chairs, and people began to keep diaries and write their autobiographies. Unlike their ancestors and people in other cultures, they came to see their inner selves as separate from any roles they might play in society.

Sincerity came to be an important social value. The ideal received its classic statement in Polonius's advice to his son Laertes in Shakespeare's *Hamlet*:

This above all: to thine own self be true,

And it must follow, as the night the day,
Thou canst not then be false to any man.

Trilling points out that neither the word or the concept of sincerity existed before the sixteenth century. People of that era became preoccupied with pretense and false identity—individuals claiming to be someone other than who they really were. It was a time of dramatic increases in social mobility; it became more and more possible to leave the social class and place into which one had been born. Thus, people worried about being deceived by imposters, and it became a virtue for a person's words and actions to correspond to his or her inner feelings and beliefs.

In more recent times, Trilling observes, the ideal of sincerity lost its value. Even before Freud, people were aware that the true self might be hard to find, that the feelings we have at any moment might not be our true feelings. Thus, in the middle of the nineteenth century, the poet Matthew Arnold wrote:

Below the surface-stream, shallow and light
Of what we *say* we feel—below the stream,
As light, of what we *think* we feel—there flows
With noiseless current strong, obscure and deep,
The central stream of what we feel indeed.

(Quoted in Trilling, 1972, p. 5)

"Authenticity" is the name of the new ideal of self; it is not enough to be "sincere" in playing the roles society demands of us. The new ideal insists that the true self is completely separate from, and even opposed to, society and its roles. Trilling and others have argued that the search for the "true self" has been carried to a pathological extreme; people have come to identify unconscious impulses and even insanity as the only "authentic" versions of self. A recent study of American society has concluded that the current preoccupation with the self may have become socially destructive and self-defeating, undermining the quality of public life as well as our intimate commitments to one another (Bellah et al., 1985).

Many contemporary psychologists view the emergence of self-awareness as a product of biological maturation. Kagan (1981) is a recent proponent of this view. Piaget's work often suggests an image of the child as a solitary thinker, reinventing knowledge of the world. Still others, such as R. W. White (1963) and M. B. Smith (1968), suggest that while a social environment is necessary for normal development, the self is not completely a social product. These writers argue that the social product view of the self is an "oversocialized conception" (Wrong, 1961) of human beings. It portrays people as little more than reflections of their environment. Pointing to Piaget's work on sensorimotor development, White argues that the child's own actions provide important information about the nature and capacities of the self. Smith points to Kavanaugh's studies of wild mice (see Chapter 5) as evidence that human strivings for autonomy are rooted in our biological heritage as mammals.

There are, as noted earlier, parallels between the development of the self and the development of language. For a long time, it was thought that language is a social product—acquired by the child through parental instruction, imitation, and the gradual shaping of the child's behavior. The psycholinguistic revolution started by Noam Chomsky argued the exact opposite. (We shall look at these issues in more detail in the next chapter.) Chomsky argued that children come into the world with an innate Language Acquisition Device (LAD) built into their brains. A baby has to be exposed to a sample of language for the LAD to operate, but basically the LAD theory assumes that children come into the world "knowing" all about language from birth.

Currently, there seems to be a consensus that neither extreme position is correct. The capacity for language is biologically programmed in the human species, just as walking on two feet is. Neither of these activities has to be taught. Only an extreme degree of social isolation can keep a normal child from learning language. Even a deaf, mute, and blind child such as Helen Keller could acquire language quickly and enthusiastically.

But experience in the social and physical world counts for more than the early LAD notion assumed. For example, words and sentences refer to things in the world. To use them correctly the child must have some knowledge of how the world works, and also some notion of what communication is about. Thus the child must have some notion of objects, and must have some nonverbal experience of sharing attention to those objects with another person (Bruner, 1978). In sum, children do teach themselves to talk, but they do not do it alone. They do need social interaction, but language is not simply a *product* of social interaction.

It seems reasonable to think about the self in the same way. We have a primary, or sensorimotor kind of self which we share with animals. The evidence from Gallup's work with chimps and Kagan's work with two-year-olds suggests that self-awareness is also genetically programmed. Thus, our biological inheritance gives rise to our existence as both "Me's" and "I's," social selves and individual, nonsocial primary selves. Yet if we were raised in total isolation, neither of these would develop.

We are also dependent on others for knowledge of who and what we are. We learn that we are persons because we live among persons and are treated from infancy on as one of them. We are strongly influenced by the views other people have of us—more precisely, what we *think* other people think of us (again, more on these matters later). Yet we are more than our social selves. As Neisser (1976) has pointed out, all of us have unique possibilities for perceiving and acting because no one occupies any one else's exact position in the world or has had exactly the same history. Ultimately, of course, we are all biologically separate beings. No matter how difficult Mead and Baldwin find it to distinguish between self and others, if one of them stepped on a tack, neither would have any doubts about whose foot it was! Not only pain, but death comes to us as individuals: part of the price we pay for our symbolic capacities and our self-awareness, the awareness of our own mortality.

Even in the most intimate relationships, some sense of separateness remains. Many clinicians and marriage counselors feel that only a firm sense of being a separate, unique individual permits us to enter into genuinely close relationships with others. A child or adult who lacks this kind of self-constancy may feel threatened by closeness to others and may withdraw from relationships in order to protect the secret self. An extreme form of this process occurs in schizophrenia. Laing (1969) has given vivid descriptions of the schizophrenic's vacillation between feeling completely alone and isolated, and feeling engulfed, almost drowning. Such a person is likely to have a greater fear of being loved than being hated.

In sum, then, as the British child analyst Donald Winnicott (1965) suggests, there is a core of personality, "a still, silent center" (p. 190), that remains, in healthy people, forever apart from the world and other persons: "Although healthy persons communicate and enjoy communicating, the other fact is equally true, that *each individual is an isolate, permanently non-communicating, permanently unknown, in fact, unfound*" (p. 187, emphasis in original).

SUMMARY

1. In recent years there has been a great revival of interest in the self. Once a central topic in psychology, it was considered an unnecessary and even unscientific concept for several decades. Now psychologists in developmental psychology and other fields find it useful to invoke some notion of self to explain behavior.

2. William James proposed that the self has two distinct aspects—the "I" and the "Me." The "I" is the self as observer and actor, the "Me" is the self as observed. This distinction has proved extremely useful to contemporary developmental psychology. The "I" or existential self develops first in infancy; the "Me" or categorical self develops in the second year, along with the capacity to use symbols.

3. One widely used method of studying self involves mirrors. Gordon Gallup, Jr., carried out extensive studies of mirror responses in animals. He discovered that only chimpanzees and presumably other higher primates realize that their image in a mirror is a reflection of their own bodies. Such recognition implies that apes already have some rudimentary concept of self. Apes raised in isolation, however, are not able to recognize themselves.

4. In human infants, recognizing oneself in the mirror is a gradual process. Babies of 9 to 10 months love to play with mirrors and touch parts of their bodies while looking into mirrors. But the clearest evidence of self-recognition—touching a mark on one's face soon after looking into a mirror—does not occur in most children until the last quarter of the second year. Babies of all ages respond to the contingency of mirrors—the figure in the mirror moves when they do—but they do not recognize their own faces until 15 to 18 months.

5. In the second year, the development of the categorical self begins. Children begin to apply the categories of age and gender to themselves and others and to prefer those who are like themselves. Also at this age children begin to evaluate themselves. They become concerned with parental prohibitions and standards and begin to apply standards of competent task performance to themselves.

6. After infancy, both the "I" and the "Me" change as cognitive social and emotional development proceeds, and the child accumulates experience. Research on the self after infancy relies for the most part on verbal procedures, such as self-descriptions. Between early childhood and adolescence, children describe themselves in increasingly psychological terms. Reflective self-awareness grows also; the "I" becomes the observer of its own inner and outer experiences. The "I" aspect of the self also changes in the following ways between early childhood and adolescence: the sense of continuity includes both past and future selves; awareness of the private inner self increases; awareness of both conscious and unconscious mental processes increases, along with a sense of control over conscious thoughts.

7. Some writers have viewed the self as a social product and claimed that self-awareness is inseparable from our knowledge of others. Other writers emphasize that the self is basically solitary. There is good reason to believe that both views are true: both are different aspects of the self experience.

Key Terms

contingent **247**
cross-model association **245**
noncontingent **247**
self **238**

CHAPTER 8

The Development of Communication and Language

In the beginning was Alpha and the end is Omega, but somewhere in between occurred Delta, which is nothing less than the arrival of man himself and his breakthrough into the daylight of language and consciousness and knowing, of happiness and sadness, of being with and being alone, of being right and being wrong, of being himself and being not himself, of being at home and being a stranger. . . .

—Walker Percy,
The Message in the Bottle

A human language is a system of remarkable complexity. To come to know a human language would be an extraordinary intellectual achievement for a creature not specifically designed to accomplish this task. A normal child acquires this knowledge on relatively slight exposure and without specific training. . . . For the conscious mind, not specially designed for the purpose, it remains a distant goal to reconstruct and comprehend what the child has done intuitively and with minimal effort. Thus language is a mirror of mind in a deep and significant sense. It is a product of human intelligence, created anew in each individual by operations that lie far beyond the reach of will or consciousness.

—Noam Chomsky,
Reflections on Language

What happens when a child hears someone saying a word and understands that the sound coming from the other person's mouth is not just a noise, but the name of something? Actually, there is no magic moment when the child crosses the border into language; as we shall see in more detail later, the first words arise gradually from nonverbal communication about objects. There is, however, one important source of information about what it means to discover language. This information comes from reports about the language learning of deaf and blind children such as Laura Bridgeman and Helen Keller. Helen Keller's autobiographical account of her own breakthrough into language is, on one level, a dramatic, moving document about courage and achievement—not only Helen's but also that of her teacher, Annie Sullivan—in the face of overwhelming odds.

In one day, Helen became totally transformed both intellectually and emotionally. From a wild, seemingly unteachable creature,

Helen Keller reading, around 1888.

she became a thoughtful, sensitive and curious human being. But the description of seven-year-old Helen's breakthrough into language is also a valuable scientific document. It contains clues concerning the nature of human language—what it means to enter into a world of socially shared symbols. It reveals clues as to the differences and similarities between human language and the communication systems of nonhuman primates such as chimpanzees.

Helen's Breakthrough

The turning point in Helen Keller's life occurred on a spring day in 1887. Several weeks before, her parents had hired a teacher, Annie Sullivan, to live with them and try to teach sign language to their daughter. At first, the teaching seemed to be fairly successful. Miss Sullivan had brought a new doll for Helen, and while Helen played with it, she slowly spelled the letters d-o-l-l into the girl's hand. Helen was fascinated by this finger game. She imitated her teacher and was delighted to make the letters correctly. In the next few days, she learned to spell out the letters for such words as "pin," "hat," "cup," and "sit," "stand," and "walk." When she wanted a piece of cake, she spelled out the word in her teacher's hand, and Miss Sullivan got her a piece.

But Helen still did not realize that she was dealing with words. She was simply associating the finger movements with particular objects. She did not know that the movements of her fingers were spelling out the *names* of things. As she wrote later, "I was simply making my fingers go in monkey-like imitation."

After a while, the teaching reached an impasse. Miss Sullivan could not get Helen to understand, and Helen grew bored and angry with her teacher's efforts. But eventually, understanding came. The following is Helen Keller's account, slightly abridged, of her discovery of language:

> One day, while I was playing with my new doll, Miss Sullivan put my big rag doll into my lap also, spelled "d-o-l-l" and

tried to make me understand that "d-o-l-l" applied to both. Earlier in the day we had had a tussle over the words "m-u-g" and "w-a-t-e-r." Miss Sullivan had tried to impress upon me that "m-u-g" is *mug* and "w-a-t-e-r" is *water*, but I persisted in confounding the two. In despair she had dropped the subject for the time, only to renew it at the first opportunity. I became impatient with her repeated attempts and, seizing the new doll, I dashed it upon the floor. I was keenly delighted when I felt the fragments of broken doll at my feet. Neither sorrow nor regret followed my passionate outburst. I had not loved the doll. In the still, dark world in which I lived there was no strong sentiment or tenderness. . . . She brought me my hat, and I knew I was going out into the warm sunshine. This thought, if a wordless

This scene from the 1962 film *The Miracle Worker* depicts the climactic moment when Helen realizes that "everything has a name." Anne Bancroft portrays Miss Sullivan, and Patty Duke is Helen.

sensation may be called thought, made me hop and skip with pleasure.

We walked down the path to the well-house, attracted by the fragrance of the honeysuckle with which it was covered. Someone was drawing water and my teacher placed my hand under the spout. As the cool stream gushed over one hand, she spelled into the other the word *water*, first slowly, then rapidly. I stood still, my whole attention focussed upon the motions of her fingers. *Suddenly I felt a misty consciousness as of something*

Helen Keller and Anne Sullivan, around 1890.

forgotten—a thrill of returning thought; and somehow the mystery of language was revealed to me. I knew then that "w-a-t-e-r" meant the wonderful cool something that was flowing over my hand. That living word awakened my soul, gave it light, hope, joy, set it free! There were barriers still, it is true, but barriers that could in time be swept away.

I left the well-house eager to learn. Everything had a name, and each name gave birth to a new thought. As we returned to the house every object I touched seemed to quiver with life. That was because I saw everything with the strange new sight which had come to me. On entering the door I remembered the doll I had broken. I felt my way to the hearth and picked up the pieces. I tried vainly to put them together. Then my eyes filled with tears for I had

remembered what I had done and for the first time I felt repentance and sorrow.

I learned a great many new words that day. I do not remember what they all were; but I do know that *mother, father, teacher*, were among them—words that were to make the world blossom for me, "like Aaron's rod with flowers." It would have been difficult to find a happier child than I was as I lay in my crib at the close of that eventful day and lived over the joys it had brought me, and for the first time longed for a new day to come. (Keller, 1917, emphasis added)

Clearly, Helen realized the meaning of language at the well. But what was it exactly that she "got," and what did she know afterward that she did not know when she was signing d-o-l-l for doll and w-a-t-e-r for water? If we could understand what happened to Helen, we would understand a great deal about what language is. (See box on Signs and Symbols.)

The Speaking Creature

For centuries, language has been considered the unique possession of human beings. When Linnaeus classified the entire animal kingdom over 200 years ago, he applied the label *homo sapiens*—man the wise—to our species because of this talent for language. Not only do we have this talent, but we use it constantly. A Martian who landed among us probably would find that the most noticeable thing about humans is the fact that they talk all the time—and for all kinds of purposes—to gossip, to joke, to argue, to buy and sell, to work together.

The next thing the Martian might notice is that different groups of humans speak in ways that sound very different and are incomprehensible to one another. Although it is obvious that specific languages such as English, Chinese, or Russian are very different from one another on the surface, at a deeper level they are all very similar. Thus, linguists speak of "language" or "human language" without referring to any particular one. All languages are equally

Signs and Symbols

What happened when Helen Keller realized that the word w-a-t-e-r *meant* the cool wet substance flowing over her hand? What was the nature of her breakthrough? According to Walker Percy (1975), what Helen discovered was the difference between a *sign* and a *symbol*. Signs direct our attention to something other than themselves: dark clouds and thunder lead us to expect rain; to a dog in Pavlov's experiment, the bell indicates that food is about to appear; to a year-old baby, the sight of mother putting on her coat indicates that she is going out.

In contrast to signs, symbols do not direct our attention to something else. As Percy notes,

> A symbol . . . does not direct at all. It "means" something else. It somehow comes to contain within itself the thing it means. The word *ball* is a sign to my dog and a symbol to you. If I say *ball* to my dog, he will . . . look under the sofa and fetch it. But if I say *ball* to you, you will simply look at me and, if you are patient, finally say, "What about it?" The dog responds to the word by looking for the thing; you conceive the ball through the word *ball*. (1975, p. 153)

Piaget made a similar distinction. Describing normal development, he traced the child's gradual shift from signs to symbols. For Piaget, a symbol is not a label for a specific object, but rather, something that stands for a mental image or a concept—a class of objects and events. One hallmark of true symbol use is using words to evoke absent objects (see Mandler, 1983).

Helen Keller's experience at the well was thus a realization of what the toddler discovers gradually. But the discovery that w-a-t-e-r- *is* water was only part of her breakthrough. Symbols also establish a shared world among symbol users. Helen realized that words could free her from the isolation of her own mind, and put her in touch with other people's thoughts. Percy compares Helen's experience to the earlier breakthrough of the human species. He imagines a group of cavedwellers sitting around the fire, thinking about the day's hunt:

> One of them tries to recapture it, to savor it, and so repeats the crude hunting cry meaning *Bison here*; another, hearing it, knows somehow that the one doesn't mean *get up and hunt now* or do this or do anything, but means something else, means *Remember him, remember the bison*, and as the other waits and sees it, sees the bison, savors the seeing it, something happens, a spark jumps. . . . (1975, p. 38)

complex and detailed; there is no such thing as a primitive or advanced language. In every language, it is possible to make statements, ask questions, give orders, make requests, and so forth. Further, anything that can be said in one language can be said in another. Some languages may have words that do not correspond to terms in others—for example, Eskimos are said to have many different words for "snow"—but it is always possible to express a particular meaning or concept in any language.

The Martian might also discover that other species communicate with one another. Bees dance to direct other bees to a source of nectar, birds sing, cats spit, and primates have call systems, to describe just a few examples of animal communication. So what, if anything, is unique about human language? Human language does share many features with animal communication systems, but none of them has all of the human characteristics. The linguist Charles Hockett (1960) has identified at least thirteen "design features" that are shared by every single one of the world's languages.

As shown in Figure 8.1, some of these features are: *interchangeability*, the speaker can

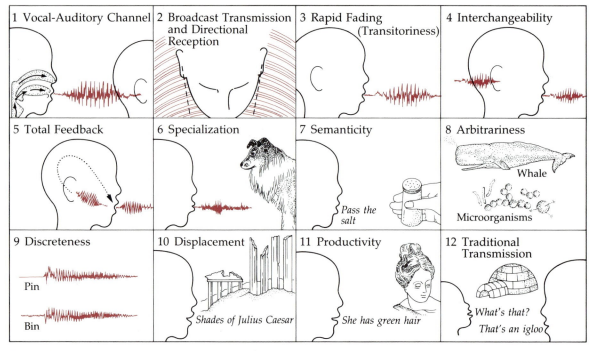

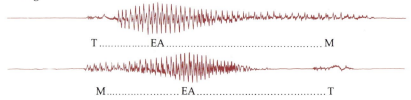

usually repeat any message he or she has heard; *total feedback,* the speaker hears everything he or she says; *specialization,* the communication system does not serve any other function, such as breathing; *arbitrariness,* there is no relation between the word and the thing it stands for ("salt" is not salty, and "dog" is *hund* in German, *chien* in French, *perro* in Spanish); *discreteness,* the communication system can be broken down into sounds, words, and sentences, and small distinctions, such as the difference between "p" and "b" can make a difference in meaning; *duality of patterning,* the communication system consists of two levels—a sound system and a system of meanings. Different combinations of the same sound may have different meanings. For example, *m, ea,* and *t* can be arranged as *meat* or *team.*

FIGURE 8.1
Hockett's "Design Features"
Hockett has identified 13 "design features" that are shared by each one of the world's languages.

Source: "The origin of speech" by C. F. Hockett, 1982, in S.-Y. Wang, ed., *Human communication,* San Francisco: W. H. Freeman.

The most important features of human language, however, are **semanticity, displacement,** and **productivity.** Semanticity means that the signals in the communication system refer to features of the world. Displacement means that it is possible to refer to things that are remote in space and time. Productivity, also referred to as *creativity* or openness, means that it is possible to say things that have never been said before.

Noam Chomsky (1966), a noted linguist, points out that the creativity of human language itself has several characteristics. First of all, human language is unbounded. There is no limit to the number of thoughts that can be put into words. In the next few minutes you or I or anyone else can start a list of sentences that no one has ever uttered before:

> While thinking about erupting volcanoes, my Aunt Evangeline was embraced by a lisping lobster.

You can take somebody else's sentence and make a novel one out of it. You can take a line from a poem,

> I have known the inexorable sadness of pencils

and change it to

> I have known the inexorable sadness of pencils and pens

(with apologies to Theodore Roethke, 1957, p. 55). Or you can make up a sentence like

> This is the fire that burned the stick, that beat the dog, that chased the cat, that killed the rat, that ate the cheese. . . .

Not only are you and I able to make up an unlimited number of sentences never heard before, but we can *understand* each other—we can interpret one another's sentences. We can do so because our productivity, though unbounded, is constrained within tight limits: the meaning of our words is *structure dependent*— that is, governed by the rules of grammar. The linguistic meaning of "grammar" is not the set of seemingly trivial rules we struggled with in elementary school. Rather, the grammar of a language is the complex system of rules that enables the speaker to decode strings of sound and thus understand their meaning. Our knowledge of grammar reveals itself in the kind of intuition that tells us *Ball the me throw* is not a proper English sentence, but that *Colorless green ideas sleep furiously*, while nonsensical, *is* a grammatical sentence.

Another aspect of creativity in human language is that what people say is not tied in fixed ways either to external stimuli or to emotional states. Not only can we make up whatever sentences we want to, but we can also speak them when we want to. You can say "Hello" when you pass someone on the street, but nothing compels you to. In contrast, animal communication usually involves fixed relationships between signals and situations. The response to these signals commonly is fixed also. When a baboon barks, the sound that means danger, all baboons scatter. Even when this sound is played repeatedly on a tape recorder, they continue to scatter each time (Bronowski, 1978).

While animals have only one way to say any one thing, people can express the same meaning in a variety of ways. For example, if you want someone to close a window, you can ask directly, "Would you please close the window?" or you can ask indirectly, "It's cold in here," or "There's a draft on my neck," or "Could you close the window?"

Another defining characteristic of human language is that it can be used to describe new situations. In contrast, primates in the wild can communicate very little about the environment. A chimp who has found a fruit tree can give a series of hoots which indicate pleasant excitement, but he has no way to describe what he has found—where it is, how much there is, or what the other chimps should do about it. Similarly, a chimp who sees a lion approach can give a danger call, but he cannot say whether the danger is a hunter, a lion, or how many of each, where they are coming from, or what the other chimps should do. It is obvious that even a simple system of names would be a great advantage to a species trying to survive under dangerous conditions.

The Development of Language in Children

Over 300 years ago, Descartes observed that "there are no men, not even the insane, so dull and stupid that they cannot put words together in a manner to convey their thoughts." All normal children learn to speak. Whether their parents are professors of linguistics or residents of the poorest slums, or even if they have been orphaned or abandoned like the street children of some Third World cities, children learn to speak at pretty much the same rate and in the same sequence of stages.

Recent research has confirmed Descartes' observation. Even severely mentally retarded children learn to speak, although at a slower rate than normal children. Eric Lenneberg, a specialist in the biological basis of human language, has studied some retarded dwarfs with brains no larger than those of chimpanzees. These "bird-headed dwarfs," despite their handicaps, have "perfect language," and some even learned to speak several foreign languages in addition to their native one (1973, p. 51).

Knowing language is not even dependent on being able to speak. One of the most surprising of the findings reported by Lenneberg is that children who have never been able to speak may still develop the capacity for language. He studied children who were incapable of making speech sounds—some had minor brain damage that prevented them from coordinating their speech movements, others were born with cleft palates or without tongues. Lenneberg tested these children by giving them a variety of commands, such as "Pick up the pencil and put it in the big box," or asking them to answer questions by nodding "yes" or "no."

These findings suggest that all children need in order to speak a language is to grow up in an environment where they hear people talking to one another and, above all, where they are spoken to. Even blind children, who cannot see the objects that language refers to, nevertheless learn language at the same rate as seeing children. Children who hear no language, because of isolation or deafness, will not learn how to speak; but deaf children can learn to communicate fairly easily through sign language or lip reading.

In addition, there is evidence that the urge to communicate, and to do so in systematic ways,

emerges in children who are radically deprived of linguistic input. A study of isolated deaf children of hearing parents revealed that these children invented their own sign languages, consisting of words and sentences (Feldman, Goldin-Meadow, & Gleitman, 1978; Goldin-Meadow, 1982; Goldin-Meadow & Mylander, 1984).

Cracking the Code

What is the nature of the task confronting the infant who is learning language? It consists of several parts, each corresponding to a major aspect of language. First, the child must analyze the sounds of adult talk and learn how to produce them. This aspect of language is called **phonology.** Part of the task is breaking the sound stream into discrete units; another part is perceiving the variations that matter and distinguishing them from variations in sound that do not signal a difference in meaning. **Phonemes,** for example, are the smallest units of sound that make a difference in meaning. The phonemes of the world's languages are constructed from the same set of contrasting sounds, and individual languages select certain of these contrasts to signal meaning and ignore the others. For example, "l" and "r" are phonemes in English, but not in Japanese.

The second major task confronting the child is figuring out what the sounds mean, how they are related to the things and events of the world. This aspect of language is called **semantics.** Sometimes, it is assumed that language learning is easy to explain because the child can figure out from the scene or situation what the adult is talking about. But the task of decoding the meaning of words and sentences is much more complicated than it might seem at first glance. For example, suppose a child is looking at a canary in a cage, and the parent says "bird." The child might make the correct inference that the sound "bird" means the creature with wings and feathers in the cage. But he or she might also assume the word means the beak, or the wings, or the feet of the bird, or the bird-on-a-perch or the bird-on-a-perch in

a cage, or the color "yellow." Complicating things still further, the parent might say, while the child is looking at the bird, "Time to go to Grandma's!"

Another difficult semantic issue is the fact that the meaning of some words depends on who is speaking them. For example, parents say "you" when talking to the child, but children must learn to use "I" when speaking of themselves. Similarly, a cup near the child is "this cup" for the child, but "that cup" to the person across the table.

Another major task for the child is learning how to put words together to make sentences. **Syntax** consists of the rules by which words may be combined and ordered to form larger units, such as clauses and sentences. Syntax also includes rules governing the use of suffixes such as -s, -ed, -ing.

Finally, the child must learn how to put all this linguistic knowledge to use in social situations. **Pragmatics** describes the rules for taking part in a conversation and how to do things with language, such as give orders, ask for things, be sarcastic. Much pragmatic knowledge involves indirect and nonliteral ways of saying things. For example, when someone asks another person, "Do you know what time it is?" the answer "Yes" is usually not enough.

Noam Chomsky

How Do They Do It? Theories of Language Acquisition

Obviously, children who hear no speech will not learn to talk. But what exactly do children require from adults in order to master the rules of language? How necessary are parental "lessons"? Most ordinary people, and until recently most psychologists, have assumed that children learn language by imitating what they hear around them, especially at home, and being reinforced for well-formed utterances. Psychologists believed that language was just another form of learned behavior that could be explained in terms of stimulus, response, and reward. B. F. Skinner's book, *Verbal Behavior* (1957), was the most detailed statement of the behaviorist explanation of language learning.

According to Skinner, the child acquired language from the older generation piece by piece, as a collection of words, phrases, and sentence patterns. Thus, a child at the breakfast table might imitate a parent asking for toast by saying "Toast." The child would be rewarded for saying the proper words in the particular situation and for putting words together. Sentences were simply strings of individual words, and no complicated—or even simple—mental processes needed to be invoked to explain language.

In the same year that Skinner published his *magnum opus* on verbal behavior, a linguist named Noam Chomsky published a book, *Syntactic Structures*, which presented views diametrically opposed to those of Skinner. This

book, and Chomsky's 1959 scathing review of *Verbal Behavior*, helped to set off a revolution in both linguistics and psychology. Essentially, Chomsky argued that when Skinner used the terms "stimulus," "response," and "reinforcement" outside the laboratory and applied them to language and other human affairs, they lost all their technical meaning and were simply vague metaphors, with no particular claims to being scientific. Chomsky's work was a major influence in the shift away from behaviorism and toward cognitive psychology.

Chomsky argued that Skinner and other behaviorists fundamentally misunderstood the nature of human language, and the process of language acquisition. At the core of his revolutionary view of language was the insight that language is both creative and governed by a set of complex, abstract rules. Creativity, as we saw earlier, refers to the ability to express new thoughts and to understand sentences we have never heard before, all within a framework of grammatical rules. In other words, all of us are constantly creating wholly new sentences which are not even similar in pattern to sentences we have heard in the past. Chomsky felt that this innovativeness was the chief feature of language that any theory of linguistics had to explain. Thus, he insisted, it is wrong to think of a language as a collection of words and sentences that a person has learned how to speak. Rather, language has to be a set of *rules* for making up new sentences and for understanding those of others.

Chomsky pointed out that the essence of language was not *performance*, the act of speaking, but rather the underlying *competence* that makes it possible for us to speak and understand each other—and also to tell the difference between the normal use of language and ungrammatical speech, the ravings of maniacs, or the random output of a computer.

Part of the mystery of language as revealed by Chomsky is the fact that we know complicated sets of rules that we are not aware we know. For example, all of us, even five-year-old children, know how to form tag questions, such as "They shoot horses, don't they?" Try filling in the following blanks:

I made a mistake, _____?
You and I are going to the movies tonight, _____?
John isn't coming with us, _____?
Ellen can't play the piano, _____?
You don't know how to do it, _____?

Undoubtedly, you could complete the sentences without conscious thought, and almost instantly. Yet if you tried to explain to someone the steps you actually went through, it would probably take you a while. Tag questions are grammatically very complex (Brown & Hanlon, 1970). We can explain what has to be done to derive a proper tag for a sentence, but we do not know how speakers actually do it. This is the kind of implicit knowledge that Chomsky defined as the essence of language, and what the acquisition of language is all about.

Through examples such as these, Chomsky (1959, 1968, 1975) demonstrated that knowledge of language could not be learned by S-R principles; it would be impossible to learn all the rules in several lifetimes. Further, Chomsky proved that language is not just a matter of learning to string together words and phrases. Language exists at two levels; it has a **surface structure**—the actual words in a sentence—and a **deep structure,** or meaning. Thus, two different surface structures can have the same meaning:

The dog bit the elephant.
The elephant was bitten by the dog.

And the same string of words can have two different meanings, as in the following sentences.

Flying planes can be dangerous.
The shooting of the hunters was terrible.

In sum, then, what the child acquires in learning language is not a collection of words and sentence patterns, but a system of rules for mapping meanings and intentions into sequences of sounds. Probably the most startling aspect of Chomsky's nativist approach was his explanation of language learning: the capacity for language, he argues, is a genetically determined mental faculty. The human brain comes equipped with the ability to abstract the prin-

ciples of language, just as the heart has the capacity to pump blood (Chomsky, 1980). Children learn language because the human mind is programmed like a computer to understand how language works. In support of his position, Chomsky pointed to the similarity of all languages, the same stages that all children go through in learning language, as well as the fact that all children except for a few with particular handicaps master their native language, in spite of variations in intelligence, motivation, and personality. Chomsky also claimed that the speech children hear around them is too fragmentary to provide them with a suitable basis for figuring out the rules of grammar if they did not already have some idea about how language works. Everyday, normal adult speech consists of false starts, disconnected phrases, and so forth.

Chomsky's notion of an innate **Language Acquisition Device,** or LAD, stirred up an enormous controversy when he introduced it in 1957, and the issue remains unresolved (Wanner & Gleitman, 1982). Yet there is actually a great deal of agreement that Chomsky's view of the nature of language and of language acquisition is substantially correct. Few researchers today accept the behaviorist version of language learning. Both Chomsky and his critics agree that the child brings a good deal of cognitive organization and activity to the process of language acquisition. Further, they agree that from an early age children seem to assume that language is rule governed, and that in the course of language acquisition a child will make a succession of hypotheses about these rules.

For example, Jerome Bruner (1978) rejects as "impossible" the S-R theory that assumes we learn language by association, as well as Chomsky's "magical" theory which assumes we know all about sentences before we start. Nevertheless, he concludes that

> Chomsky has taught us something . . .
> profoundly important. It is that the child
> is equipped with some means for
> generating hypotheses about language
> that could not simply be the result of

learning by association and reinforcement what words go with what in the presence of what things. There is indeed something pre-programmed about our language acquiring capacity. . . . There appears to be some readiness . . . quickly to grasp certain rules for forming sentences, once we know what the world is about to which the sentences refer. (1978, pp. 64–65)

The debate in psycholinguistics today is not so much between Chomskians and behaviorists, as it is between Chomsky's *innatism* and the *constructivism* of Piaget and Bruner. The argument concerns how many of the rules of human language are preprogrammed in the brain, whether language should be viewed as a specific skill or part of cognitive development, and how important a role the environment and parental teaching play in language development.

Further, many child language researchers disagree with Chomsky's emphasis on the formal rules of grammar and criticize his lack of attention to the study of meaning (semantics) and the use of language (pragmatics). During the 1970s, the study of meaning and the social rules of language came to dominate the study of child language. Charles Fillmore (1968) and others argued that semantic structures are a fundamental part of language, along with the kind of formal rules Chomsky has emphasized. These researchers claimed that a child's early speech reflects semantic roles such as agent and action rather than grammatical categories. For example, when a child says "Doggie run" or "Daddy eat," he or she is expressing a relationship between an action and the agent or source of that action. In contrast, Chomsky and his followers argue that the child is expressing the grammatical categories of subject and predicate, or noun and verb.

While the debate between these two views of language rages on (Gleitman & Wanner, 1984), many important new findings about early child language have been made. Researchers continue to be surprised at how much young children know about word meanings and the rules of communication.

Before the First Word

Most children produce their first word some time around their first birthday. The first word will be something like ma-ma, da-da, ga, or ba. Between 18 months and 2 years, the child begins to put two words together, to say things like "Allgone milk," "More juice," or "Mommy book." Some months later, the child is capable of saying things like, "I have a cup. And you have a cup. Just like Daddy has, and Johnny has, and Mary has."

Before babies produce their first words they have a great deal of preparation to do. We saw earlier that learning a language consists of several tasks: mastering the sound system, figuring out what the sounds mean, knowing how to use speech to communicate with and influence others. Work on all of these tasks begins early in infancy.

From birth, babies are active soundmakers. During the first few weeks they are fairly quiet when they are not crying. Sounds of pleasure—cooing and gurgling—begin at around three months. Vocalizing is one of the principal forms of primary circular reaction (see Chapter 5).

Babies also seem to come into the world prepared to pay special attention to speech sounds. One study found that newborns move in synchrony with human speech (Condon, 1975). Another found that within the first month of life babies will stop crying if they hear a human voice, but not a bell or other sound (Menyuk, 1971). Eimas and his colleagues found that infants as young as one month can hear the difference between closely related consonants such as "p" and "b" (1971). Thus, babies are able to make the perceptual discriminations necessary for speech long before they begin to use them in speaking. As we saw in Chapter 5, a study by Spelke (1979) demonstrated that given two video monitors showing talking heads the infant will look at the one that is synchronized with the soundtrack. When the soundtrack changes, so does the visual fixation.

More recently, in addition to issues of sound and sentence structure, issues of *semantics*—or meaning—and *pragmatics*—how people use language—have come to the fore of current research. What is the meaning of early language? How does it describe the world? And how does the child use language to communicate with other people and get them to behave in certain ways? These issues raise questions about the cognitive and social precursors and prerequisites of language use. What knowledge about the world, and what kind of social interaction skills, must a child have in order to learn to use language? In what ways do parents and child communicate before the child's first word?

Social Precursors of Language Use

In recent years researchers in language development have come to realize that the child learning language is not a solitary Robinson Crusoe reinventing the rules of syntax and talking to himself. Dialogue, not monologue, is the basic form of speech. When babies produce their first words, they are trying to convey messages (Bates, 1976).

People of all ages use language to communicate for all kinds of reasons, from the most mundane to the most profound. They use it to get other people to hand them things, to buy and sell things, to express anger and love, to joke, or to discuss religion, politics, the structure of the universe, or the latest gossip. Thus, conversation is a form of social interaction. Adult conversation is an intricate form of social interaction that has been compared to a dance. Even casual conversation proceeds according to a complex set of rules governing verbal and nonverbal behavior. Usually, the speakers are unaware of the rules they are following, but they will be uncomfortable if those rules are violated. People with severe mental problems, such as schizophrenics, frequently seem "peculiar" to us because their interaction often violates these rules.

How To Carry On a Conversation

The most basic and universal rule of human dialogue is that the speakers take turns. This

turn-taking has been the subject of a great deal of research (Duncan, 1975; Sacks, Schegloff, & Jefferson, 1974). Although most of the time we communicate smoothly, turn-taking involves a precise sense of timing. There are subtle cues which regulate the exchange of speaker and listener roles. Just as smooth dancers avoid bumping into each other and stepping on each other's feet, conversational partners avoid overlapping with one another—speaking at the same time. The person who is listening will usually not start to speak until the speaker has given signs indicating that his or her turn is up. This is done through a variety of subtle verbal and nonverbal cues—dropping one's voice, stopping one's gestures, relaxing one's body, looking away.

In addition to turn-taking, conversations usually involve the speakers' being oriented to one another, and to a topic of conversation. The first problem in carrying on a conversation is for the would-be speaker to get the attention of the listener. Later, the two partners must pay attention to one another. Thus, the speakers usually face one another and look at each other in patterned ways. Here again, the rules are both precise and subtle: glances must be exchanged in the right rhythm, and each partner must look at the other just long enough—not so little as to seem shifty or inattentive, not so long as to stare. In fact, as Daniel Stern points out, "Two people do not gaze into each other's eyes for over ten or so seconds unless they are going to fight or make love or already are" (1977, p. 18). Listeners look at speakers longer than speakers look at listeners; in adult conversations, the speaker usually looks at the listener at the beginning and end of utterances, but not as much in the middle. It seems to be hard to concentrate on speaking when looking directly at the other person (Kendon, 1967).

The other feature of a conversation is that it is *about* something. It has a theme. It refers to things, people, and events in the world. The speaker must get the listener to understand what the speaker is talking about—they must both have the same subject in mind for the conversation to proceed. If you want somebody to hand you something, or if you want to make a comment about a thing or person, you first must get the listener to know what or who it is you are talking about. As the conversation proceeds, each speaker builds on what has already been said and anticipates the information that will be needed by the other person. In general, speakers and listeners follow what Paul Grice calls "the cooperative principle" (1975).

Protoconversation

In recent years, researchers have been looking for precursors of conversation in infancy. These studies make it clear that children take part in conversation-like behavior—or **proto-conversation** (Bullowa, 1979)—practically from the moment of birth.

At the beginning of life, of course, babies are not able to communicate intentionally. But adults, particularly the mother or caretaking adult, treat even newborn babies *as if* they were in fact communicating and able to take turns in conversations. For example, Macfarlane (1974) studied how mothers greet their newborns. He found that a mother will assume the infant's acts to be purposeful. In the first months of life, whatever the infant does—burp, yawn, blink—can count as a turn in conversation (Snow, 1977). Even if the infant does nothing, the mother often engages in a monologue punctuated by a pause, which turns it into a one-sided dialogue. This can be seen in the following one-sided "conversation" between a mother and her baby:

> "Aren't you my cutie?"
> (Pause)
> "Yes." (Mother speaking imagined response from infant.)
> "You sure are." (Stern, 1977)

Later, mothers are more demanding; by eight months or so, only vocalizing by the baby will "count" as a turn. There is some debate about whether these early interactions should be considered as the actual forerunners of later conversations in which two people exchange roles, or whether they are simply forms of maternal behavior (Schaffer, 1979). Also, as Stern points out, the way mothers and babies gaze at one another is very different from the way adults gaze at one another in a conversation. Usually adults exchange glances that last a few seconds, whereas mothers and babies can look into each other's eyes for thirty seconds or so. In any case, the baby is receiving valuable lessons in the rhythms of conversational exchange.

Toward the end of the first year, protoconversations become more like adult conversation in that they are more reciprocal and intentional on the part of the child (Schaffer, 1979). From early on, the child has been an active participant in social interaction. For example, Stern (1977) found that babies of three and four months use gazes toward and away from the mother's face to regulate the degree of social contact. But near the end of the first year, babies are more likely to keep up their end of the "conversation" by using their "turn" to vocalize, and they are also more likely to initiate a protoconversation. While adults begin conversations with words, babies begin their careers as intentional communicators by sharing objects with adults—either by giving, showing, or pointing.

Thus, unlike protoconversation in early infancy, exchanges between adults and older babies tend to be *about* something. The attention of both partners to the conversation tends to be focused on the same thing. This joint attention, or "intersubjective sharing" (Bruner, 1978), is the basis of genuine as opposed to proto communication.

Joint Attention and Pointing

Jerome Bruner (1983) notes that joint attention is prominent among primates: a chimpanzee, for example, habitually follows the line of sight of another animal to see what he or she is looking at. A study by Butterworth (1981) showed that infants as young as 6 months will also follow their mother's gaze to see what she is looking at. By one year, babies look out along the mother's line of regard and search for an ob-

ject. If there is none, they return to the adult's eyes and look out again. They seem to expect that the adult was looking at something.

At 9 to 10 months, infants begin to point to things; at first, they point to get the attention of the adult and show him or her what they are interested in. Pointing is one of the first clear indications of a communicative act—of the child's making a gesture to communicate something intentionally. How do we know the pointing child is trying to get the other person to focus on a particular object or event? Observation of children around age one shows that when they point to something, they check to see whether the adult is paying attention (Bates, 1976). Also, one-year-olds know that the adult's pointing is a communicative gesture. They look in the direction the adult is pointing in, not at the pointing hand or the face of the adult (Lempers, Flavell, & Flavell, 1977).

It is interesting to note that pointing does not seem to be derived from reaching for an object (Bates, 1976; Werner & Kaplan, 1963). When children reach for things they want, they make effortful movements of the arms and body. They lean toward the object and hold their arms out, with hands opening and closing. The movements of reaching, as Bruner (1978, p. 70) points out, are "reeking" with the intention to possess the object.

When babies first begin to reach for objects, they are not intentionally communicating with adults. Later, however, around nine months, reaching becomes a ritualized gesture: instead of straining desperately toward an object, the child will reach toward it, opening and closing the hand, while looking at the adult and not, as before, at the object. The response called for in the adult is to hand over the object, and the child will not be satisfied until the adult does so or distracts the child's attention with something else.

By contrast, the pointing gesture—pointing with an index finger outstretched—does not seem to be aimed at getting the adult to hand over an object, but rather to look at something. The object of a pointing gesture seems to be "Look at that" or "Tell me about that." The aim seems to be to get the attention of the adult and begin an interaction. The child is satisfied if the adult names the object or says something about it.

Before the child points in order to communicate with another person, there is a period of noncommunicative pointing, or pointing for self (Bates, 1976). The child will point to objects up close or to interesting events at a distance, such as a dog barking. During such episodes, children do not make eye contact with the adult or otherwise try to get the adult's attention. To researchers who have studied it, this pointing seems to help the child single out the object to attend to it better.

Both pointing and reaching seem to be the direct predecessors of the child's early use of language: asking for and commenting on things. In other words, just before the time when the first words appear, children are using gestures as a form of intentional communication which functions in ways similar to language.

The recent research on pointing provides additional evidence against Piaget's charge that young children are egocentric—that is, unable to take another person's view. As Leung and Rheingold have shown, by the time babies reach their first birthday, pointing is a well-established behavior which resembles the adult gesture in both form and function. They conclude that

> The infants have learned not only to look where others point, but also that others will look where they point and will find what they see worthy of comment. We propose that at a very early age infants have acquired the ability not only to take the visual perspective of others but also to share with them their own view of the world. (1981, p. 220)

From Actions to Symbols

The relation between language and thought is one of those tangled issues that has been endlessly debated by linguists, philosophers, and psychologists. Piaget believed that language is a product of cognitive development; Vygotsky theorized that language is a separate system of knowledge. (We will discuss the debate about the relation between thought and language in a later section.) Despite the disagreements, most researchers believe that language starts out as an expression of what one-year-olds already know about the world.

Piaget's six stages of sensorimotor development (Chapter 3) trace the child's increasing understanding of objects, space, time, and causality. Children have a great deal of specific information about the objects around them. They know that some objects such as people, animals, and cars seem to move on their own; others, such as toys, can be moved. They know that objects can be acted on, moved from place to place, and handed back and forth. Some objects, such as sticks, can be used to get hold of and do things with still other objects.

Before a child begins to speak a language, he or she must not only have a practical understanding of objects and actions, but must also be able to *represent* them mentally. The child must be able to form and remember inner images of sights and sounds. Piaget (1951) has described how symbolic representation rises out of imitation and play. For example, he reports how a year-old infant imitated Piaget's opening and closing of a match box by opening and closing his own hands and mouth and trying to reproduce the sound of the box. Delayed imitation is a more advanced skill. An often-quoted example of delayed imitation involves Piaget's 16-month-old daughter Jacqueline imitating a little boy who threw a spectacular temper tantrum by screaming, pushing the playpen backward, and stamping his feet. Jacqueline did not imitate this behavior until the next day and again two weeks later after a visit from the same boy. The delay between the event and the imitation suggested to Piaget that Jacqueline could hold the event in memory. Around this same time, symbolic play emerges. The child pushes a box, pretending it is a car, or pretends to fall asleep, or rubs hands together saying "soap" and pretending to wash.

Tools and Words

Another cognitive prerequisite for language is understanding how to use tools (Bates, 1976). Although using a stick to reach an object seems, at first glance, a very different form of behavior from using a communicative gesture or sound, in fact the two kinds of behavior have an underlying similarity. In both instances, the child must keep a goal in mind while paying attention to something else. Wanting a toy on a high shelf, for example, the child can look for a tool such as a stick to knock it down or a chair to stand on. Or the child can get an adult to reach the toy.

Intentional communication involves a more psychological kind of causality than nonsocial tool use; the child knows that the adult can be activated by messages (Bretherton & Bates, 1979). Later, during Piaget's Stage 6 (the invention of new means through mental combinations, see p. 181), the child can think ahead several steps and predict the effects of a given cause. Thus, Piaget describes his daughter Jacqueline's first "lie" at the age of 16 months. Taken away from a game and put into her playpen, she called to her parents to no avail. Then she expressed "a certain need," although she had just taken care of that need ten minutes before. Taken from her playpen, she immediately tried to resume the game. Thus, knowing that asking would not free her from the playpen, she thought up—or imagined—a more effective method (Piaget, 1954, p. 301).

In sum, then, language emerges out of a complex web of cognitive and communicative skills. But the acquisition of language is something more than the direct expression of sensorimotor knowledge or social interaction. However well prepared the child may be for the task by these other skills, language is a complex body of knowledge which must be mastered on its own terms (Shatz, 1982; Slobin, 1982). Further, it seems likely that, once the child learns to speak, concepts and words develop together. Children may learn their first words to express what they already know, but then words can be "invitations," as Roger Brown (1958) once put it, to form concepts.

Perhaps language even contributes to the shift out of the sensorimotor mode of thought, rather than being simply a result of that shift (Gopnik & Meltzoff, 1984).

The One-Word Stage

When do the child's first words appear? Although everyone agrees that the first stage of child language is one in which the child uses a single word at a time, there is a debate about when this actually occurs. Some writers suggest that the first words appear around nine months, others that the one-word stage begins at around a year and a half. While it is true that children differ a great deal in the rates at which they begin to speak, another explanation for the differences in opinion seems more likely: there is, in fact, no single magic moment at which the first word springs out of nowhere. Rather, the child gradually shifts from simply babbling to vocalizing as a form of communication, to using a word idiosyncratically as a form of communication, to using a word as an adult would with the right meaning. The debate about when language begins seems to reflect differences about the point in this process at which different observers are willing to credit the child with having language. Consider the following notes by a mother on her child's first words:

> Jacqueline actually started by making noises [such as] "P," "AH-AH," "Mm" very definite and then attempted to make words like Mummum, Dad-dad (9 months). At 11 months was using some words but not understanding. Bow-wow always for a dog but for other objects too. "Bird," "Mumum," "Dadad"—knew all these and would use them at appropriate time, but also for others. . . . At 14 months was saying her first words. Mum, Daddad, Gone. "There-it-is." (All in one word.) (Grieve & Hoogenrand, 1979, p. 94)

Most studies of the one-word stage begin in the late end of the continuum, when the child is using recognizable words in adultlike ways. In recent years, however, there has been rising interest in the period between babbling and the first "true" words. Michael Halliday (1975) calls the phenomenon "protolanguage." He studied his own son Nigel between the ages of 8 and 16 months, noting the sounds he was making and the situations in which he was making them. For example, "Mnning" seemed to mean "Give me that"; "A-da," "Look at this picture"; "Uh uh," "Let's not do that"; and "Ah," "Yes, I want what you offered." Other researchers have collected similar instances.

Despite the recent upsurge in interest in protolanguage, it is still a relatively uncharted area. The sounds are hard to transcribe accurately, and both sound and meaning shift. It is often hard to tell whether the meaning of an utterance is in the child's head or the observer's. One fascinating question is whether the sounds of protolanguage derive from, and evolve into, adult words, as one researcher suggests. For example, in a study of a one-year-old, David, the boy was saying "Mmmm" while reaching for objects. Later, he began to say "More" and "Mine" in the same situation.

Also, at around one year, David would make "l" or "d" sounds while showing or pointing at an object. These utterances turned into "look", "that," or "there" when showing or pointing (Carter, 1979).

Sooner or later, children produce words that the adults around them recognize as true language. Usually these words include the most familiar important and interesting objects and events in their world (Nelson, 1973). Children's first words commonly refer to *people*—Mama, Dada, Baby—and *food*—juice, milk, cookie, as well as things connected with food, such as bottle or cup. They also learn the names for toys, familiar household objects, clothing, vehicles, animals, as well as those for body parts and for events, such as baths, pee-pees, and poo-poos, and words to get parents to do or stop doing something: up, down, open, more, no. Each child learns a somewhat different array of these items as first words.

Early Word Meaning

An important part of early language learning is figuring out exactly what words refer to. For example, a parent holds up a big red beach ball and says, "Ball." The child repeats, "Ball." They are playing what Roger Brown (1958) has called the Original Word Game. The two players are the teacher and the learner. The teacher names things, the player tries to figure what exactly the name refers to. The learner forms hypotheses about the meaning of the word and tests these hypotheses by trying to name things correctly. The teacher corrects the learner. Adults play the game whenever they encounter a word whose meaning they do not know.

For beginners at the Original Word Game, it is difficult to figure out what aspect of an object or event is being encoded in the word. For example, when the father holds a red ball and says, "Ball," the child may not be sure whether the word refers to the ball, the color, the shape of the ball, or the act of holding it. A child who learns to call a dog a "doggie" will typically overextend the word to refer to all four-legged animals. In a detailed study of such overextensions, Eve Clark (1973) found that size, shape, gesture, movement, sound, and other properties could be the basis for such generalizations. Thus, a child who said "mooi" to refer to the moon used the same word to refer to cakes, round postmarks, the letter O, and other things. Another child generalized the word "fly" to all small insects, specks of dirt, crumbs, and his own toes.

In these examples, the child uses one property of the object to extend the word. Sometimes children use several properties for overextension. A one-year-old child whose parents are researchers on child language learned to call the family dog by her name, Nunu (de Villiers & de Villiers, 1979). He then extended the name to all dogs, then to animals and birds, and also to furry objects such as slippers and coats. One day he puzzled his parents by pointing to some pitted black olives and saying, "Nunu." Suddenly they realized that the two shiny black olives looked like the dog's shiny black nose. Some of this child's overextensions seemed to his parents to be early metaphors; the child seemed to be saying not that the olives *were* Nunu, but they were *like* Nunu. Conversely, a child may also underextend the meaning of a word. He or she may think that the word "cat" applies only to the family cat, not cats in general (Anglin, 1977).

Children do not use their first words only to label things. When children say "ball," they are trying to communicate something to someone *and* might be saying something *about* the ball. The meaning of a child's saying "ball" could be simply to name the ball, but it could also mean, "Look at the ball," "Give me the ball," "The ball is rolling." Usually, parents are able to figure out remarkably well what their baby is trying to say because the context, along with the child's intonation, visual attention, and nonverbal behavior, supply clues. For example, if the baby says "ball" while pointing to a picture of a ball in a book, that would most likely be an act of naming. If the child strains and reaches for a ball that had rolled under a sofa, the word is most likely a demand or request for the ball. If the child has given the ball

a push and is watching it roll, the word may mean "The ball is rolling."

In recent years, researchers have been using context to make the kind of "rich interpretations" parents do about children's utterances in the one-word stage. They have been looking at the child's words not as vocabulary items or names, but as **holophrases**—or one-word sentences. Greenfield and Smith (1976) intensively studied the development of two boys from age 7 to 22 months and concluded that children's one-word utterances describe the relations between objects and actions, not just the objects themselves. The single words are describing the *roles* objects play in events. For example, if children say "Dada" when father opens a door or throws a ball, they are describing the father as the agent of an action. If they say "door" or "ball," they are indicating the object of actions. There is some disagreement among researchers as to whether early words should be consid-

ered holophrases. Lois Bloom (1973) argues that the term "holophrases" suggests that the child in the one-word stage already has knowledge of syntax—that is, knows what a sentence is. However, the consensus among researchers now seems to be not that the child's first words are sentences, but that they involve certain concepts and relations between things.

Language Comprehension during the One-Word Stage

If you have tried to speak a foreign language, you know that it is usually much easier to understand what someone is saying to you in that language than it is to express yourself fluently. Similarly, when a child is learning his or her primary language, comprehension also usually comes before production.

Until fairly recently, there was little systematic knowledge of language comprehension during the one-word stage. Researchers have been looking into this topic, and their findings support the notion that babies at this stage understand much more than they can say. Jane-Ellen Huttenlocher (1974) studied four babies who were between the ages of 10 and 13 months at the start of the study. She found that these children could locate objects before they could name them, and later they showed a remarkable knowledge of word combinations. One little boy, at a year and a half, and with only two words in his speaking vocabulary, was able to distinguish between "your bottle" and "baby's bottle" (he had a baby sister) and between such commands as "Give mommy the baby's bottle" and "Show mommy your bottle," "Give me your diaper" and "Show me the baby's diaper."

Thus, at the end of the one-word stage, children are already able to express—through words, intonations, gestures, and actions—meanings that will later be expressed by combining words into sentences. And they already have the cognitive skills to decipher sentences spoken to them.

The Two-Word Stage

Somewhere around the second birthday, the child begins to put two words together to form sentences. How do we know these are genuine sentences, and not just random pairs of words? To answer such questions about early language, researchers usually record a large sample of a child's speech—about 500 sentences. Such studies have shown that children in fact do not put two words together randomly. They are more likely to say "Throw ball" or "Mommy throw" than "Ball throw." Children seem to select the word orders that express the basic concepts coded into all languages, such as *agent* plus action, *action* plus object. Nelson (1973) found that children's first words and sentences dealt mostly with agents of action—people, animals, cars, and movables—or objects of actions—toys, food, clothing.

Of course, being in the two-word stage does

not mean that all children ever say is two words. They continue to use single words and begin to utter complex sentences that are not of their own creation, but rote imitations of what other people have said. Adults sometimes do the same thing. If, say, a man who does not know Italian memorizes some lines from an Italian opera, he can mimic the sound, but he cannot break the sentences down into parts and express the same idea another way, which is what we do all the time with our native language. Autistic children often use sentences this way, too. In effect, such sentences are like long words.

Children usually begin to combine words within a few months of beginning to say one word at a time. Some researchers have pointed out an intermediate, transitional period when the child says single words in succession which

could be parts of two-word utterances (Bloom, 1973; Scollen, 1974). For example, a child might say:

Baby.
Chair.

Or,

Car.
Go.

And later say:

Baby chair.
Car go.

Scollen terms these one-word-at-a-time sequences "vertical sentences." Another form is what Patricia Greenfield and Joshua Smith (1976) call a "two-person" sentence, in which the adult might point to a stove and say "stove" and the child may say "hot."

The arrival of two-word utterances is a significant advance in language development. For the first time, the child's utterances have a structure that is independent of the individual words. The child does not string words together in a random fashion, but rather is sensitive to the word orders that adults use. For example, they say "My teddy" and "Mommy hat" to indicate possession, not "Teddy my" or "Hat Mommy."

Further, for the first time, the child is using words in ways that are not patterned directly on adult speech. Adults do not say things like "All gone milk." These babyish constructions illustrate the basic nature of language and of language learning: language is not a collection of sayings, but a set of rules and strategies—a set of recipes, in effect—for mapping ideas into words and sentences. The process of language learning involves trying to figure out what the rules are, testing your hypotheses, and then modifying them if you are wrong. The same process can be observed when toddlers make mistakes they never heard anyone else make: saying "mouses" for "mice," or "he goed" for "he went." Such mistakes illustrate, however, that children have learned the rules of English not badly, but too well, and are applying them to instances where English is irregular.

By contrast, the two-year-olds' combinations, although they use English words, reflect the two-year-olds' thoughts, activities, and social world. Children of this age from cultures around the world have been found to encode the same kinds of meanings in the same kinds of ways. (See Figure 8.2.) In short, children in the two-word stage speak a kind of "two-year-old-ese." Only later do children learn the rules of their own particular language.

Children at the two-word stage talk about the same things they talked about at the one-word stage, but they can talk about more than one aspect of a situation. Instead of saying just "Doggie" on hearing a dog bark, the child can say "Doggie bark." The child who in the one-word stage might pick up Daddy's shoe and say "Daddy" can now say "Daddy shoe." The relationship of possession is extremely interesting to children at this stage. In addition to describing actions and events, and what belongs to whom, they are also interested in *recurrence* ("More milk"), *nonexistence* ("All gone milk"), and *location* ("Car outside"), as well as *naming* and *labeling* ("Baby chair"). As acts of communication, children mainly use two-word utterances the way they used one-word utterances, and earlier, reaching and pointing: to request things, and assert things—to get the other person to attend to some thing or event.

FIGURE 8.2
Functions of Two-Word Sentences in Child Speech, with Examples from Several Languages[1]

Function of Utterance	Language			
	English	German	Russian	Finnish
Locate, Name	there book that car see doggie	buch da [book there] gukuk wauwau [see doggie]	Tosya tam [Tosya there]	tuossa Rina [there Rina] vettä siinä [water there]
Demand, Desire	more milk give candy want gum	mehr milch [more milk] bitte apfel [please apple]	yeschë moloko [more milk] day chasy [give watch]	anna Rina [give Rina]
Negate[2]	no wet no wash not hungry allgone milk	nicht blasen [not blow] kaffee nein [coffee no]	vody net [water no] gus' tyu-tyu [goose gone]	ei susi [not wolf] enää pipi [anymore sore]
Describe Event or Situation[3]	Bambi go mail come hit ball block fall baby high-chair	puppe kommt [doll comes] tiktak hängt [clock hangs] sofa sitzen [sofa sit] messer schneiden [cut knife]	mama prua [mama walk] papa bay-bay [papa sleep] korka upala [crust fell] nashla yaichko [found egg] baba kreslo [grandma armchair]	Seppo putoo [Seppo fall] talli 'bm-bm' [garage 'car']
Indicate Possession	my shoe mama dress	mein ball [my ball] mamas hut [mama's hat]	mami chashka [mama's cup] pup moya [navel my]	täti auto [aunt car]
Modify, Qualify	pretty dress big boat	milch heiss [milk hot] armer wauwau [poor dog]	mama khoroshaya [mama good] papa bol'shoy [papa big]	rikki auto [broken car] torni iso [tower big]
Question[4]	where ball	wo ball [where ball]	gde papa [where papa]	missä pallo [where ball]

[1]The examples come from a variety of studies, published and unpublished. Data from the three non-Indo-European languages are drawn from the doctoral dissertations of Melissa Bowerman (Harvard, 1973: Finnish), Ben Blount (Berkeley, 1969: Luo), and Keith Kernan (Berkeley, 1969: Samoan). (Luo is spoken in Kenya.) The examples given here are representative of many more utterances of the same type in each language. The order of the two words in the utterance is generally fixed in all of the languages except Finnish, where both orders can be used freely for some utterance types by some children.
[2]Bloom (1970) has noted three different sorts of negation (1) nonexistence (e.g., *no wet*, meaning 'dry'), (2) rejection (e.g., *no wash*, meaning 'don't wash me'), and (3) denial (e.g., *no girl*, denying a preceding assertion that a boy was a girl).
[3]Descriptions are of several types: (1) agent + action (e.g., *Bambi go*), (2) action + object (e.g., *hit ball*), (3) agent + object (e.g., *mama bread*, meaning 'mama is cutting bread'), (4) locative (e.g., *baby high chair*, meaning 'baby is in the high chair'), (5) instrumental (e.g., *cut knife*), (6) dative (e.g., *throw daddy*, meaning 'throw it to daddy'). (The use of terminology of grammatical case is suggestive here; cf. Fillmore's (1968) discussion of deep cases as underlying linguistic universals.)
[4]In addition to wh-questions, yes-no questions can be made by pronouncing any two-word sentence with rising intonation, with the exception of Finnish. (Melissa Bowerman reports that the emergence of yes-no questions is, accordingly, exceptionally late in Finnish child language.)

Source: *Psycholinguistics*, 2nd ed., by D. I. Slobin, 1979, Glenview, Ill.: Scott, Foresman.

Luo	Samoan

en saa
  [it clock]
	Keith lea
	  [Keith there]

ma wendo [this visitor]	

miya tamtam
  [give-me candy]
	mai pepe
	  [give doll]

adway cham
  [I-want food]
	fia moe
	  [want sleep]

beda onge
  [my-slasher absent]
	le 'ai
	  [not eat]
	uma mea
	  [allgone thing]

chungu biro
  [European comes]
	pa'u pepe
	  [fall doll]

odhi skul
  [he-went school]
	tapale 'oe
	  [hit you]

omoyo oduma
  [she-dries maize]
	tu'u lalo
	  [put down]

kom baba
  [chair father]
	lole a'u
	  [candy my]
	polo 'oe
	  [ball your]
	paluni mama
	  [balloon mama]

piypiy kech
  [pepper hot]
	fa'ali'i pepe
	  [headstrong baby]

gwen madichol [chicken black]	
	fea Punafu [where Punafu]

Individual Differences

Most studies of language learning focus on changes that all children go through, such as the one-word stage, the two-word stage, and so on. Recently, some researchers have described striking individual differences in early language use. For example, when Katherine Nelson (1973, 1981) examined the first fifty words acquired by the eighteen children she was studying, she found two patterns of lan-

guage use. Children were either "referrers" or "expressers." Referrers, the majority of the children, had a large proportion of nouns—words referring to objects—in their vocabularies. They also had some verbs, proper names, and adjectives, and were likely to use words to refer to objects and events—"The truck is red." The "expressers" had more diverse vocabularies. They tended to use language to express needs and feelings or to have an effect on other people; their vocabularies contained a large number of social routines, such as "Stop it," and "I want it."

Other researchers have found individual differences in the strategies children use to acquire various aspects of language. Some studies have noted differences comparable to the referential-expressive distinction discussed by Nelson. Others have revealed additional contrasts. For example, Lois Bloom and her colleagues (Bloom, Lightbown, & Hood, 1975)

found that some children tend to use a lot of nouns while others emphasize pronouns. Thus, some children prefer to use "it" to refer to almost any object, while others prefer to use specific object labels, such as "dog," "cat," "truck," and "car."

Another individual difference has been labeled "analytic" versus "gestalt." Several investigators discovered to their surprise that one-year-old children, presumably in the one-word stage, sometimes come out with complete sentences, such as "I don't know where it is" (Branigan, 1977) or "I like read *Good Night Moon*" (Peter, 1977). Branigan, in the same study, found that of the three children he observed, one produced one word at a time, another used whole but "compressed" sentences, while the third used a mixture of both patterns. These "compressed" sentences are not like adult sentences: they are said very fast, with no pauses, and with the "words" running into one another (like Jacqueline's "There-it-is," expressed earlier). One researcher calls them "gestalts" to emphasize their wholistic character.

Katherine Nelson (1981) has suggested that the three characteristics go together. That is, there seem to be two strategies that can be used to master the complexities of early language: an analytic approach emphasizing the referential function of speech, and a gestalt style emphasizing the social and expressive uses of language. Nelson stresses that she is not talking about two types of children; all children use both approaches, but some emphasize one strategy over another. Both routes lead to language competence.

As yet, very little is known about the reasons for the differences in strategy. Some researchers have suggested the differences may be due to caretaker speech, the number of children in the family, or the educational level of the parents. Others suggest the reasons may be inherent in the child. Another unanswered question is the persistence of the stylistic difference and its possible influence on later language development. Research on individual differences in early language has only recently begun; eventually we may know more about the causes and consequences.

Beyond Two Words

After the age of two and a half or so, children's utterances get to be more complicated in two distinct ways—they use more complicated forms, and they express more complicated thoughts. Figure 8.3 provides an 18-month-old's sentences and some from the same child nine months later. As de Villiers and de Villiers point out, the changes are found not only "in the addition of grammatical morphemes, but [also] in the elaboration of different parts of the sentence and the appearance of well-formed questions and negatives" (1979, p. 55).

The child's early language has been aptly described as "telegraphic." When adults send telegrams or write classified ads, they eliminate all words but those necessary to get the information across: "Lost wallet. Rush funds." "Mother ill. Come home now." "3 Br. River

FIGURE 8.3
Early Sentences

Eve at 18 Months	Eve at 27 Months
More grapejuice.	This not better.
Door.	See, this one better but this not better.
Right down.	There some cream.
Mommy soup.	Put in you coffee.
Eating.	I go get a pencil 'n' write.
Mommy celery?	Put my pencil in there.
No celery.	Don't stand on my ice-cubes!
Oh drop a celery.	They was in the refrigerator, cooking.
Open toy box.	I put them in the refrigerator to freeze.
Oh horsie stuck.	An I want to take off my hat.
Mommy read.	That why Jacky comed.
No Mommy read.	We're going to make a blue house.
Write a paper.	You come help us.
Write a pencil.	You make a blue one for me.
My pencil.	How 'bout another eggnog instead of cheese sandwich?
Mommy.	I have a fingernail.
Mommy head?	And you have a fingernail.
Look at dollie.	Just like Mommy has, and David has, and Sara has.
Head.	What is that on the table?
What doing, Mommy?	
Drink juice.	

Source: *Early language* by P. A. de Villiers & J. G. de Villiers, 1979, Cambridge, Mass.: Harvard University Press.

view. Must sell." What is left out of both early language and telegrams are all the little "function words" that modulate the meaning of the content words—articles such as *the* and *a*, prepositions such as *in* and *on* or *to* and *from*, as well as word endings such as *-s* to indicate plural or possession and verb endings such as *-ing* and *-ed*.

After the two-word stage, children enter a phase during which they add these **morphemes** to their speech. (Morphemes are the smallest units of meaning. A word is a morpheme, but so are such suffixes as -ing and -ed.) Roger Brown (1973) calls it the "modulation of meaning" phase. Brown, who with his associates has carried on major studies of early language development, considers both the one-word and two-word stages as one stage of language development in which basic semantic and grammatical roles are being learned (Figure 8.4). During Brown's second stage, the modulation of meaning, he has determined that children master the fourteen most common morphemes in a consistent order. This order of morpheme acquisition has been confirmed by other researchers. The first morpheme to be mastered is usually the progressive tense -ing, as in "I eat*ing*." Other early morphemes are the plural -s, the prepositions *in* and *on*, and the articles *a* and *the*. Only much later do children learn how to use the forms of the verb *to be*—*is*, *are*, and so on.

The regularity of the order in which English-speaking children learn the fourteen morphemes is striking. What accounts for it? Frequency in adult speech has little relation to the order of morpheme acquisition. Rather, the answer seems to be informativeness and complexity, both in form and meaning. Forms that supply important information are likely to be learned sooner than those that do not. Also, the easier a concept is to grasp, and the easier it is to figure out how a morpheme is used, the earlier it will appear. Thus, -ing, one of the first forms to be learned, shows little variation. It is pronounced only one way; it describes something going on in the here and now. The past tense is more complicated both conceptually and formally. The regular past tense, -ed,

is pronounced differently depending on the verb it is attached to. For example, at the end of "talked" it is a "t" sound, at the end of "listened" a "d," and at the end of "waited," "ed." Also, many verbs have irregular past tense forms—it broke, he went, she ate. The future tense is still more abstract than the past tense, and is acquired later. The various forms of the verb "to be" are complicated and are among the last function words to be acquired. Also, they often do not supply much information: "I am walking" may be the correct form, but it is not more informative than "I walking."

Besides using morphemes to fill in their utterances, children past the two-word stage increase the complexity of their sentences in other ways. They learn to ask questions (who, what, why, where, when), express negation (no and not), and combine two or more ideas or propositions in a single sentence: "I have a book and Mommy have a book"; "I show you how to do it." During the first period of language development, children are learning to

FIGURE 8.4
Stages of Early Language Development

Stage*	Focus†	Examples
I	Basic semantic and grammatical roles	
	Nominations	That ball
	Nonexistence	Allgone ball
	Recurrence	More ball
	Attribution	My ball, Adam ball
	Possession	Adam hit.
	Agent-action	Adam hit ball.
	Agent-action-object	
II	The modulation of meaning	
	Progressive aspect	I walking.
	In, on	*In* basket, *on* floor
	Plural	Two ball*s*
	Past irregular	It broke.
	Possessive inflection	Adam*'s* ball
	Uncontractible copula	There it *is*.
	Articles, *a, the*	That *a* book. That *the* dog.
	Past regular	Adam walk*ed*.
	Third person regular	He walk*s*. She run*s*.
	Third person irregular	He *does*. She *has*.
	Uncontractible progressive auxiliary	This *is* going.
	Contractible copula	That*'s* book.
	Contractible progressive auxiliary	I*'m* walking.
III	Modalities of the simple sentence	
	Yes-no questions	{ Will Adam go? { Does Eve like it?
	Wh Questions	{ Where did Sarah hide? { What did Eve see?
	Negatives	Adam can't go.
	Ellipsis of the predicate	Yes he can.
	Emphasis	He *does* want to go.
IV	Embedding one simple sentence within another	
	Relative clauses	{ What is that playing the xylophone? { You got a pencil in your bag.
	Various kinds of subordinate clause	{ I see what you made. { I went where your office was. { I want her to do it. { You think I can do it.
V	Conjunction of one simple sentence with another	
	With no parts deleted	{ We can hear her and we can touch her. { I did this and I did that too.
	With various redundant constituents deleted once	
	Subject deleted	He's flying and swinging.
	Predicate deleted	No, you and I had some.
	Predicate nominal deleted	John and Jay are Boy Scouts.

*Only Stages I and II have received exhaustive analysis; the later stages have been closely analyzed but are not complete.
†The focus on a stage describes the new frontier that is being explored for the first time in that stage.

Source: Adapted from *Psychology* by R. Brown and R. J. Herrnstein, 1975, Boston: Little, Brown & Co.

encode more and more of what they already know. Thus, although the child in the one-word stage can only express the proposition, "Daddy, throw the ball" or "Mommy give cookie" one word at a time, it is unreasonable to suppose that the child does not know who is to do what with what object (Antinucci & Parisi, 1973). Between the ages of two and four, children come to be increasingly able to fill in the missing parts of the sentence.

They also express more complex ideas in their utterances. Earlier, the child learned how to combine words; now the child learns how to combine phrases and propositions. For example, both questions and negatives may be viewed as a proposition with an extra proposition added. Consider the following three sentences:

> The baby is sleeping.
> The baby is not sleeping.
> Is the baby sleeping?

Both questions and negative sentences may be viewed as sentences with an extra thought or proposition in them. In negative sentences such as the one above, the 'not' expresses the extra proposition, "It is not the case that. . . ." Questions contain the extra, unexpressed proposition, "Tell me" (Clark & Clark, 1977, p. 347).

Children know how to ask questions and say no in the one-word stage, but they do not express these concepts in grammatical form before they are around two and a half. The earliest questions are simply a rising intonation on a word: "Doggie?" Children also learn to express the concept *no* very early through head shaking. Babies often repeat the word "No" when approaching forbidden objects.

The stages children go through in learning both negatives and questions are quite similar. They begin by putting a negative word or question word at the beginning of a sentence. "No sit there." Later they put these elements inside sentences and begin to use auxiliaries. The process of mastering the adult system in both negatives and questions is very gradual.

Brown argues that "wh-" questions—questions that begin with who, whose, what, where, when, why, and even how—involve "one of the most elegant and powerful sets of rules in all languages" (1973, p. 14). Of course, not all languages have "wh-" questions, but all of them have some way of expressing the same meaning. "Wh-" questions may be viewed as declarative sentences with one element unknown: *Who* is reading the book? *What* is John reading? These questions say in effect, "I know all about this sentence except for one point, and on this point I should like specific information." The missing point always refers to some major part of a sentence—subject, verb, object.

By the age of 5, children have mastered most of what there is to know about their native language. But at least in English, some of the finer points of syntax remain a problem. For example, children will misunderstand the sentence "Mary promised John to walk the dog," assuming that it means "Mary told John to walk the dog." Carol Chomsky (1969) found that children often assume that words such as "ask" and "promise" mean "tell," and they have trouble identifying the subject of a sentence like "The doll is easy to see." By the age of 9 or 10, these difficulties usually have disappeared. However, mastering the English language is a task that can occupy a lifetime. There are always new words to learn, new thoughts to express, and better ways to make words fit meaning.

Current Controversies

Since the late 1950s, when B. F. Skinner and Noam Chomsky first published their theories, there has been an explosion of knowledge about language and language learning. We have discovered a great deal about the various stages of language development and the kind of knowledge the child has acquired at each stage. Yet we still do not know exactly what language is or how children learn it. There is no single, universally accepted explanation of language acquisition. Three issues illuminate some of the controversies currently being debated by psychologists and psycholinguists:

the relation between language and thought, the role of the social environment in language learning, and the question of whether chimpanzees and gorillas, the "higher apes," can be taught some form of language.

Language and Thought

As we have seen, there have been several shifts in how psychologists and psycholinguists have viewed language acquisition. Before Chomsky, it seemed to many researchers that language was simply a form of behavior learned bit by bit through imitation and reinforcement. Then Chomsky revolutionized thinking about language by arguing that children have an innate capacity, programmed into the brain at birth, to learn grammar quickly and spontaneously.

Much of the research in linguistic development has been a reaction against Chomsky's insistence that language is a unique form of knowledge, unrelated to any other form of intelligence. Many researchers also objected to Chomsky's emphasis on formal grammar—the notion that the young child is learning about subjects and predicates and types of sentences. To them, the evidence is clear that young children use language to convey meaning. It is also clear that the meanings they express reflect their sensorimotor understanding of the real world of objects and events. In other words, *language reflects thought.* The relation between language and thought is at the center of a continuing debate.

The view most diametrically opposed to Chomsky's is what has been called "the strong cognition hypothesis" (Rice, Huston, & Wright, 1982, p. 258). It is associated with the work of Piaget and others, such as Furth (1966) and Macnamara (1972). To these researchers, language is like a map of thought, a direct reflection of what the child knows about the world. Just as the real contours and features of the land determine what goes into a map, they

feel, so does the knowledge of objects and events determine language. The task of the child learning a language is to figure out which sounds express what he or she already knows.

The earliest stages of language learning do seem to fit the strong cognitive model. Children's first words and sentences do seem to map their sensorimotor understandings. To give a very simple example, a child knows how to give a dog a biscuit before he knows how to say the word "dog." Eventually, he will be able to say "Doggie eat" or "Johnny feed Doggie," thereby expressing the semantic roles of agent, action, and object. Later, according to this view, the child will map these semantic roles into the grammatical categories of subject, verb, and object. Proponents of the strong cognitive hypothesis also point to studies of older children which seem to show that concepts come before language and are independent of it. For instance Hans Furth (1966) showed that the cognitive development of deaf children who lack language is similar to that of hearing children. Piaget (1980) cited studies of his colleagues which showed that teaching children the meaning of words does not advance their conceptual understanding of what the words mean. One such study (Sinclair-de-Zwart, 1967) taught four- to six-year-old children the meanings of "more" and "less," but this linguistic knowledge did not improve their understanding of quantity.

Although the strong cognitive hypothesis seems very plausible, many researchers have pointed to serious flaws in it. They agree that there are a number of cognitive prerequisites for language use, such as being able to form mental representations of objects and events. But they believe it is wrong to suppose that language reflects nonverbal thought in any simple and direct way.

For example, very young children learn certain aspects of language which have no relation to the real world or semantic meaning. German children, in the earliest stages of language acquisition, learn how to use a gender system containing masculine, feminine, and neuter categories (Gleitman & Wanner, 1984). Yet gender systems have only a slight connection to the categories of the real world: German children learn that "stone" is masculine, while French children learn that it is feminine.

Another discrepancy in the relation between thought and language is the observation that children come to use increasingly complex forms to refer to the same concepts: children first refer to themselves by means of their names, then they use "me," and then "I" (Cromer, 1974).

In general, then, many researchers argue that language is a complex body of knowledge in itself and cannot be completely explained in terms of nonlinguistic thought. As Dan Slobin puts it, "A sentence is not a verbal snapshot or movie of an event" (1982, p. 131). Children know much more about events than will appear in language. They must figure out which particular aspects of a situation are important in the language they are learning and ignore the rest. Slobin gives the example of a child who wishes to report that Daddy, not someone else, has just thrown a particular ball. The child learning English would say *"Daddy* threw the ball." This sentence includes one word for each of the semantic elements (agent, action, object) plus stress on the agent, and an extra word, "the," showing that the object is definite, rather than indefinite (a).

At first glance, the sentence looks like a simple mapping of the child's knowledge of the situation into the appropriate words. But, as Slobin points out, there is more to the task than meets the eye, especially if we take other languages into account:

> Why indicate that the object, and only the object, is definite? And why indicate definiteness by a little word that precedes the object name? And why *not* indicate other facts, which are also obvious—the sex of the agent, for example, or that the action just took place, or that the balls are round? These are facts that receive obligatory grammatical coding in some languages. (1982, pp. 132–33)

In German, for example, the child would say *"Vater* varf den Ball." The German equivalent of "the ball," "den Ball," says that the ball is

not only a definite object, but is singular and considered to be masculine. In Hebrew, gender is also coded, but it is the gender of the agent and appears in the verb.

Word order also varies across languages. In English, German, and Hebrew, the word order tells who did what to whom, and the usual order is subject-verb-object: "The dog bit the cat" has a different meaning from "The cat bit the dog." In some of the world's languages, however, word order does not convey meaning. In Turkish, for example, word order is used to communicate emphasis. Semantic relations are indicated by adding on suffixes and other such inflections (changes in word form). Thus, "top," the word for ball, becomes "topu" when it is the object of an action. As speakers of English, it seems more natural to us to use word order to express meaning, but young children acquire Turkish as easily as any other language.

Summing up, it seems clear that learning to use language involves both cognitive and linguistic skills. Language is a complex form of knowledge that builds on, but does not simply reflect the child's understanding of the world. Slobin (1982) suggests the metaphor of a waiting room to describe the connection between thought and language in early development. The child enters the room when he or she has a particular concept or event to be put into words. Inside the waiting room, the child has both a semantic task and a grammatical task. That is, the child must figure out what particular aspects of the situation are coded in the language and exactly how they are encoded. The child leaves the waiting room when these problems have been solved. Slobin emphasizes that the main point of the waiting room metaphor is the two doors: the young child enters through a cognitive door and leaves through a linguistic door.

If we extend Slobin's metaphor to later stages of development, it seems reasonable to suppose that the child can enter and leave through both doors. That is, eventually, and especially when the child goes to school, he or she will begin to learn concepts from language. Indeed, as Vygotsky (1962) and Bruner (1983)

have pointed out, human societies are based on symbols, concepts, and information that are available only in language—cousin, democracy, exploitation, God, heaven, and hell.

The Role of Social Experience

As we saw earlier, Skinner and Chomsky take diametrically opposing views about the role of the social environment in language learning. Skinner believes that language is completely shaped by parents and other speakers; Chomsky holds that a child only has to hear language being spoken to activate the Language Acquisition Device. Each child, in effect, reinvents language in order to learn it. Without going back to Skinner's model of language as no more than a set of responses, many researchers have been investigating the possibility that parental input does play a major role in language learning.

In recent years, researchers have been carrying out studies of parental speech to small children (Snow & Ferguson, 1977). They have found that much of the time parents talk to children in slow, short, simple sentences and repeat themselves often. Parents frequently use baby talk and exaggerated intonations to gain the child's attention and make their meaning clear. This way of talking to small children is called "Motherese."

Studies of parental speech were inspired by Chomsky's assertion that the language children hear is too fragmentary and ungrammatical to provide a basis for learning grammar. Some researchers felt that this description of adult speech to children was wrong, and further, that parental speech must be important in language acquisition. They are right that Chomsky was wrong: the language young children hear is *not* fragmented and ungrammatical. Yet there is no evidence that any of these parental speech patterns play an important role in the development of grammatical competence.

For one thing, children growing up without much parental attention, and even without parents, learn to speak. In some cultures, parents typically speak very little to children. Fur-

ther, one study (Newport, Gleitman, & Gleitman, 1977) found that parental speech, or Motherese, is not simplified in ways that correspond to the child's acquisition of the fundamental properties of language. These authors conclude that some aspects of language learning are sensitive to the environment, but others are not. The child's growth in the universal aspects of language, such as sentence length, is not influenced by parental input. But using certain language forms peculiar to English does seem to reflect parental styles. As they put it, "the mother has little latitude to teach her child about the nature of language; but she can at least improve his English" (1977, p. 147).

Even if what parents say to young children is perfectly regular and understandable, the basic problem remains. The child still has to figure out the implicit rules of language and how to put what he or she wants to say into words and sentences: "The child must make use of parental input to discover the UNDERLYING, UNSPOKEN regularities of his language. . . . A perfectly tailored input, like a perfectly tailored reinforcement schedule, does not account for the child's ability to fashion a grammar based on that input" (Slobin, 1979, p. 105, capitals in original).

There is something fundamentally wrong with the notion that language is mastered by learning how to map particular situations into particular sentences, or by learning how to insert new words into familiar sentence patterns. The whole business of understanding what other people are saying, and finding words to express what you want to say, is much more complicated than that. In real life, people, including parents, express the same idea many different ways. For example, in a half-hour observation of a mother trying to get her two-year-old daughter to sit still and have her hair combed, the mother used nineteen different ways of expressing the same idea, including the following:

Cmon and let me set your hair.
Why don't you lemme fix your hair?
Lemme get the snarls out of your hair.
(Quoted in Slobin, 1979)

Simplified lessons in sentence construction are unlikely to enable the child to deal with this complexity. Roger Brown (1973) gives an interesting example from his own adult experience. To help himself better understand the process of language acquisition, Brown enrolled in a Berlitz "total immersion" course in Japanese, a language of which he had no prior knowledge. Like a preschool child learning his native language, Brown spent most of his waking hours in conversation with his teacher. No English was spoken, and no written words were used. The teacher programmed lessons in an almost Skinnerian way, carefully adding new elements one at a time. On the last day of the course, a Japanese friend met Brown at the door of the school. The friend asked him in Japanese what seemed like a simple question: "Where is your car?" Despite his "total immersion" in the new language, Brown was completely unable to understand or answer this sentence or any other in Japanese. Understanding a well-drilled sentence is very different from understanding one that comes to you from the infinite number of sentences in a language. Fluent speakers of a language are not tied to particular sentence patterns in either their understanding or their speech.

Even more "natural" ways of influencing children's language growth do not seem to work very well. Courtney Cazden (1965) systematically presented expanded versions of children's utterances back to them. When a child said "Doggie eating," the adult might say, "Yes, the doggie is eating his food." These "expansions" were presented over several months, yet the children who heard them showed no learning advantage over a control group.

Actually, parents seem to pay very little attention to their children's syntax. If they do try to correct the child, their lessons are likely to be ineffective. Children will process parental speech in line with their own current linguistic capacity. They are unlikely to learn new structures. When children at the two-word stage try to imitate longer sentences, they still produce only two-word utterances (from Ervin Tripp, 1964, p. 334):

Adult: I'll make a cup for her to drink.
Child: Cup drink.

Or consider the following example of a mother trying to teach her child a correct construction (from McNeill, 1966, p. 69).

Child: Nobody don't like me.
Mother: No, say "Nobody likes me."
Child: Nobody don't like me. (Eight repetitions of this dialogue)
Mother: No, no, listen carefully; say, "nobody likes me."
Child: Oh. Nobody don't LIKES me.

Since correcting children's syntax is so hard, perhaps it is not surprising that, as Roger Brown found (Brown & Hanlon, 1970), parents do not seem to do much of it. In fact, most of the time parents are not even aware of their children's syntax. They are concerned more with whether what the child says is true, not whether it is well formed. For example, if a child asks, "Why the dog won't eat?" the mistake never seems to register. But if the child says, using correct syntax, "Why won't the dog eat?" and the dog is in fact eating, or has just eaten, the parent will correct the child. It is paradoxical that this pattern of reinforcing children for truth but not correct grammar usually ends up producing "an adult whose speech is highly grammatical but not notably truthful" (Brown, Cazden, & Bellugi, 1969, p. 70).

Linguistic Apes?

Recently, several researchers claim to have taught the rudiments of human language to apes. Beatrice and Allen Gardner (1969, 1980) appeared to have taught Washoe, a chimpanzee, to communicate in sign language. Francine ("Penny") Patterson made similar claims for a gorilla, Koko. Other researchers taught chimpanzees to communicate with colored plastic chips and a computer language. Currently a great debate is raging about whether apes and chimps actually can use human language or not. Serious methodological and conceptual

problems have been pointed out in the linguistic ape research. Some critics argue that these apes are just performing tricks, like circus animals or well-trained dogs (Sebeok & Umiker-Sebeok, 1980). Others suggest that while apes can be taught to master a very simple form of language, their achievements are quite different from those of human children in the early stages of language learning.

Even if we grant that apes can be taught some version of a human language, this would not really challenge the claim that language is unique to homo sapiens. Using language is not a natural form of ape behavior in the natural environment, but a product of human manipulation in a human environment. There is no evidence that apes use anything remotely like human language in the wild. Apes, like other animals, do have complex systems of communication, but these systems have little in common with human language. There is hardly any possibility that some day someone will come upon a group of chimps in the jungle discussing the nature of communication, or anything else.

Animal communication systems are not geared to carry on discussions of any kind. Rather, they are essentially sets of signals—something like the flags code that ships at sea use to communicate with each other. There is a limited set of messages you can signal, and only one way to signal each particular message. Monkeys and apes have highly complex communication systems, which use a rich set of postures, gestures, facial expressions, and vocal signals. Each species has its own set of signals. For example, vervet monkeys have about thirty-six sounds evoked by twenty-one different situations and carrying about twenty-two different messages (Struhsaker, 1967). There is an "airborne predator call," uttered when monkey-eating eagles fly overhead, a "snake chutter," uttered when snakes are sighted, and an "anticopulatory squeal scream" used when a vervet is not in the mood.

Apart from predator calls, primates communicate emotional states, not objects or events. Even predator calls probably express an emotional message of extreme danger, rather than

a specific reference to something in the world. The vervet monkey's system seems to be a special case, not a typical example of primate communication, nor a step on the way to human language. Even in the example above, the call is more like a scream of terror than a warning such as "Look out! There's a snake!" In contrast, humans are unique in their ability to communicate detailed information about the environment, calmly, as well as to communicate emotion. Our emotional message system uses gestures, expressions, and tones of voice—we laugh, cry, scream, frown, smile— and we have much in common with the communication systems of other primates. Emotional expression in both humans and apes is tied to the "older," more primitive parts of the brain—specifically the limbic system. We can, of course, express emotion in words, but the ability to use language depends on parts of the human brain that have no counterparts in the apes. Their brains are symmetrical, but ours is

Ape in the wild attending to a potential danger.

lopsided because areas controlling language have developed in the left hemisphere. (See Figure 8.5.) This asymmetry can be found in the human fetus, which shows that it is not caused by language learning in childhood (Geschwind, 1979).

The development of these brain areas gives humans an almost unlimited ability to associate words with objects in the environment as well as other words. An ability to make references to the environment would have been a great selective advantage for our human ancestors who were beginning to use tools, share food, hunt and gather, and set up home bases. Even a small set of names for pebbles, plants, and animals would have greatly facilitated their way of life (Lancaster, 1975).

The experiments with apes show that with intensive training they can be taught to name things. Washoe learned the sign language names for many objects and actions and could intelligently generalize them. For example, she used *dog* for all dogs, including those in a picture book. Having learned to sign *open* in relation to a closet door, she would ask for the opening of closed containers, a refrigerator, and even a bottle of soda. This is a highly significant finding, since many authorities had assumed that even the rudiments of symbolic language were far beyond the capacities of any ape.

Though apes can take the first steps toward language, however, their ability to go further seems severely limited. Apes differ in a number of ways from human infants learning language. For one thing, although apes can be taught to learn a rudimentary form of language, human children are predisposed to learn it. They learn it easily without having to be taught or coaxed into learning through rewards. There are also enormous differences in the sheer number of words and combinations of words that chimps and children produce. Beyond this are even more profound differences.

The next big step in language development is combining names into sentences. In all human languages, as we have seen, the meaning is not just in the separate words but in the

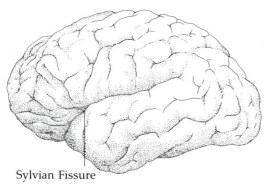

Sylvian Fissure

Left Hemisphere

Right Hemisphere

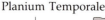

Planium Temporale

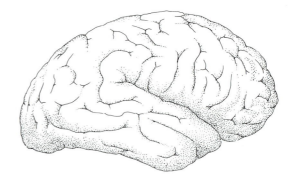

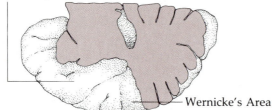

Wernicke's Area

FIGURE 8.5
Our Cortical Asymmetry
The asymmetry of the human cortex is apparent in two places shown here. Notice that the sylvian fissure is angled more steeply in the right hemisphere than in the left. The fissure defines the upper margin of the temporal lobe. If one looks at the planum temporale, which is the upper surface of the temporal lobe, one can see that it is much larger on the left side than on the right. The enlarged section is part of Wernicke's area, which is responsible for language.

Source: "Specializations of the human brain" by N. Geschwind, 1979, in *The brain*, Scientific American, San Francisco: W. H. Freeman.

ordering as well. Thus, in English, "John tickled Mary" has a different meaning than "Mary tickled John," and other combinations, such as "Mary tickled" or "Tickle Mary, John." This **structure dependence** is one of the major defining characteristics of human language.

There is little evidence of structure depen-

dence in apes. Washoe did combine signs, but in no particular order. Thus, when she wanted to be tickled, she would say "me tickle," "tickle me," "you tickle," or "tickle you." Washoe's combinations have been described as a kind of complex naming rather than sentences. Further, even though chimps do have an impressive ability to learn names, they still do not use this ability in the way even young children do. The first and most frequent question children ask is "What is this?" Recall Helen Keller's excitement at discovering that "everything has a name" and her eagerness to learn as many as she could. Laura Bridgemen was another deaf-blind child who was taught sign language. Her reaction to the discovery of names was similar to Helen's:

The truth began to flash on her, here was a way by which she could herself make up a sign of anything that was in her own mind, and show it to another mind. . . . She had thus got the "open sesame" to the whole treasury of the English language. She seemed aware of the importance of the process; and worked at it incessantly, taking up various articles, and inquiring by gestures and looks what signs upon her fingers were to be put together in order to express their names. (Howe, 1837, in Dennis, 1972, p. 67)

Apes do not seem to know or care that "everything has a name." Although Washoe was asked "What's this?" thousands of times, the Gardners give no evidence that *she* ever asked for the name of a new object. Researchers who have worked with other linguistic apes have noted a similar lack of intellectual curiosity. Chimps are very clever animals, but they use their intelligence to solve practical problems, such as getting food that is hard to reach. They use their people-given "language" skills mostly in the same way—to get goods and services from their caretakers. The trainers of Dana, a computer-using chimp, report that

The chimp is signing I want to hold (top) the cat (bottom left).

Dana's persistence in conversation has been strictly pragmatic—once the desired incentive has been achieved, the conversation ENDS! . . . Dana has never initiated conversations to "broaden her

Clever Horses and Linguistic Apes

Clever Hans was a German horse who became famous around the turn of the century. He could apparently solve complicated arithmetic problems shown to him on a blackboard by tapping out the answers with his hoof. Owned and trained by a man named Von Osten, he could also solve problems presented to him by total strangers.

Hans was studied by numerous scientists over a period of years. Unable to uncover fraud or trickery, many were willing to credit Hans with a genuine ability to do arithmetic. Finally, in 1911, the mystery was solved. Professor Otto Pfungst discovered that instead of solving arithmetic problems, Hans was responding to the behavior of humans. Those who tested him gave subtle, unintentional cues. They would raise their eyebrows, nod, or stop nodding at the right "answer" and Hans would stop tapping. Pfungst proved his explanation by showing that if Von Osten or another questioner could not see the blackboard, Hans could not solve the problem.

Clever Hans and his trainer have gone down in the history of science as an example of unintentional fraud. But as Lewis Thomas (1983) observes, the horse deserves more credit than he gets. Even though he could not do arithmetic, he was an extraordinary observer of human beings.

In recent years, the Clever Hans story has been retold as a rebuke to those who claim that apes can be taught to use human language (Sebeok & Rosenthal, 1981). Like Clever Hans, the apes were said to be responding to subtle cues given by their trainers. And the trainers, like Herr Von Osten, were said to be attributing human capabilities to their animal friends. But the debate over human language has obscured the actual accomplishments of apes. They are much more intelligent, and have a much more complex social life, than previously thought.

Further, they are capable of using symbols. However, the transition from sign to symbol (see box on p. 273) is much more difficult for the ape than for the human child (Savage-Rumbaugh, 1979; Terrace, 1985). Initially, apes learn to show signs when they want to eat or play. But like Helen Keller before the incident at the well, they are using "words" without realizing what they represent. Thus, Austin and Sherman, the apes trained by Duane and Sarah Rumbaugh (1978), could punch the word "key" in order to unlock a box with food in it. But they could not *name* the key—they did not realize the word "key" referred to an object that could be held up and pointed to. Nor did they realize that the word "key" could be used to communicate about an absent object.

Eventually, through a complex training process, the Rumbaughs were able to teach Austin and Sherman how to use symbols and to communicate with them. First, they had to build complex cognitive schemata around each word. For example, the apes were taught to recognize that the word "key" could refer to different kinds of keys, that keys could open different kinds of things, and could be used by different individuals. The chimps were also taught that words could be used for communication and exchange between themselves. Ultimately, the Rumbaughs' efforts were rewarded, as the following incident shows:

> On one trial Sherman requested *key* erroneously when he needed a wrench. He then watched carefully as Austin searched the tool kit. When Austin started to pick up the key, Sherman looked over his shoulder toward the keyboard, and when he noticed the word "key," which he had left displayed on the projectors, he rushed back to the keyboard, depressed "wrench," and tapped the projectors to draw Austin's attention to the new symbol he had just transmitted. Austin looked up, dropped the key, picked up the wrench, and handed it to Sherman. (Savage-Rumbaugh, Rumbaugh, & Boysen, 1978)

All in all, the ape research has revealed that the cognitive capacities of nonhuman primates are much greater than had been believed. But it has also opened the way to a deeper appreciation of the fundamental differences between apes and humans.

horizons," if you will. She has never asked for the names of things unless they held some food or drink she apparently wanted; she has never "discussed" spontaneously the attributes of things in her world. . . . (D. Rumbaugh & Gill, 1976, p. 574)

Recently, other researchers have become even more skeptical about claims concerning ape linguistic competence. Some scholars have claimed that the original researchers were taken in by the "Clever Hans" effect—the tendency of animals to respond to subtle nonverbal cues unconsciously supplied by the experimenters themselves. (See box on Clever Horses and Linguistic Apes.) Other researchers, after examining the records of chimpanzee "conversations," have found that most chimpanzee "utterances" were direct imitations of the researchers who were conversing with them. Nevertheless, although apes have not been proved capable of humanlike language, they are clever animals who seem capable of at least a simple form of symbol use.

In a sense, the discovery of the symbolic capacities of apes is like finding a "missing link" in the evolution of human language, the forerunner of something that was to undergo massive development over aeons of time as humankind evolved from its primate ancestry. It remains a mystery why apes have the kinds of abilities shown in the recent studies when they never use anything like symbols to communicate with each other in the wild. Why should they be so smart if they don't talk? No one really knows. But it seems that the connection between ape intelligence and a system of symbols was the spark that set off the further evolution of both human intelligence and human language. We do not know how the capacity for human language originated, but it became part of human biology. As birds have wings to fly and fish have gills and fins to swim, hu-

mans have tongues, lips, and breathing passages tailored to the task of producing articulate speech and a neurological apparatus geared to the demands of producing and analyzing speech sounds.

These anatomical adaptations probably did not emerge all at once. Human language as we know it today may be a relatively recent development. Phillip Lieberman (1975) has advanced the surprising hypothesis that Neanderthals—the large-brained hominids who lived in the Stone Age—could not have produced the speech sounds that are the basis of all known human languages. He came to this conclusion after he had reconstructed the vocal tracts of Neanderthal fossils. Despite their large skulls, their necks and throats were more like those of apes and newborn babies than of modern adult humans. If his reconstructions are correct, then the Neanderthals may have represented an intermediate stage in the physiological evolution of language. Their tools and level of culture—recall the burial site at Shanidar mentioned in Chapter 1—were much more sophisticated than those of our earlier ancestors, but they may have possessed a more primitive form of language than anything known on earth today.

The complexity of the languages that young children learn so easily still defies the best minds that have tried to fathom it. No one has managed to program a computer to simulate the language ability of a five-year-old child. Computers can solve complicated mathematical problems, play chess, and even to a limited degree translate written into "spoken" words. Cleverly designed computer programs can even seem to do a kind of psychotherapy. But no computer can carry on a simple conversation, ranging from one topic to another, the way ordinary humans do every day.

SUMMARY

1. Language has long been considered the definitive characteristic of human beings. All normal children learn to speak in the first few years of life without any formal instruction. Recently, some researchers have claimed that apes can be taught to use language. Although this research has shown that apes have more ability to associate symbols and objects than anyone had thought, there is strong doubt whether they have learned more than the rudiments of language.

2. Two of the most important features of human language are *structure dependence* and *productivity*. Structure dependence means that words must be arranged in specific ways to convey meaning. Productivity refers to the fact that human language is unbounded; people are always making up sentences that they have never heard before, and there is no limit to the number of ideas that can be expressed.

3. Until recently, most psychologists believed that children learned language piece by piece, as a collection of words, phrases, and sentence patterns: adults would simply teach children to associate words with objects, and then they would teach them how to put words together. This was the behaviorist interpretation championed by B. F. Skinner. The linguist Noam Chomsky demolished this view of language and language acquisition. He showed that it would be impossible to learn language in this way. Chomsky demonstrated that any language is fundamentally a set of *rules* for understanding and making up sentences. He argued that children must come into the world with a predisposition to learn the rules of the language they hear around them.

4. Although babies do not begin to speak until their second year, their preparation for language begins at birth. Babies are born with a predisposition to attend to and discriminate the sounds of speech. They are also active soundmakers. In addition, during their first year, babies take part in protoconversations: they take turns exchanging looks and glances with their caretakers.

5. Learning a language is also dependent on having reached the upper levels of sensorimotor cognitive development. Early language reflects the infant's sensorimotor understanding of objects and actions. It also requires the ability to form internal representations of objects and actions.

6. At some point around the first birthday, babies say their first word and enter the one-word stage of language. Before they begin to use recognizable words, most babies make up their own idiosyncratic sounds for things. The first words include the most familiar important and interesting people and objects in their worlds. One of the problems facing the child at this time is figuring out exactly what it is a word refers to. Overextensions are typical at this stage; the child will use one or more properties of a word or concept and overextend its meaning; for example, a young child may call all four-legged animals "dog" until corrected. Some researchers believe that one-word utterances are usually *holophrases*—not just names of things, but precursors of sentences which include some notion of action.

7. Around the second birthday, children begin to put two words together. During this stage, children in all cultures use two-word utterances to express several kinds of meaning. Among the functions of two-word sentences are naming and locating things ("See doggie"), asking for things ("More milk"), refusing something ("No nap"), indicating possession ("Mama cup").

8. Between age two and five, a child's language becomes more complex in terms of both words and sentences. Children master the fourteen most common morphemes in a regular order. That is, they learn to use such function words as *a* and *the*, prepositions such as *in* and *on*, as well as word endings such as *-s*, *-ing*, and *-ed*. During this time children's sentences also grow longer and more complex.

9. Currently, there is no single explanation of language acquisition that all researchers agree upon. Most researchers agree with Chomsky that babies are born with an innate biological predisposition to learn language. Some scholars, however, believe that the process of learning language is helped a great deal by special, simple ways of talking to children—a form of talk called "Motherese." Other scholars doubt whether such environmental supports make any significant contribution to basic linguistic competence.

Key Terms

deep structure **278**
displacement **274**
holophrase **287**
Language Acquisition Device (LAD) **279**
morpheme **293**
phoneme **276**
phonology **276**
pragmatics **277**
productivity **274**
protoconversation **281**
semanticity **274**
semantics **276**
structure dependence **302**
surface structure **278**
syntax **277**

CHAPTER 9

Early Childhood
The Preschool Years

The End

When I was One,
I had just begun.

When I was Two,
I was nearly new.

When I was Three,
I was hardly Me.

When I was Four,
I was not much more.

When I was Five,
I was just alive.

But now I am Six, I'm as clever as clever.
So I think I'll be six now for ever and ever.

> —A. A. Milne,
> *Now We Are Six*

No one can remember being an infant. It is hard even to imagine what the wordless world of infancy could be like. Early childhood, however—the years between two and six—is a more familiar psychological landscape, though not because we have very many clear memories from those years. At most, we carry around a few blurry mental snapshots of events that often do not have any clear significance. The world of early childhood is easier to imagine than to remember.

Much of the time preschool children live in the same everyday world we do. But this world can shift into another world which is also familiar to us because we return there periodically, in dreams and especially in fairy tales. In fairy tales, everyday, practical reality coexists with a magical reality of shifting appearances and spooky places. It is a world populated by ordinary people as well as by giants, fairy godmothers, evil witches, and devouring wolves. It is a place in which inanimate things, such as trees and rocks, can talk; ugly beasts can be transformed into handsome princes, and wishes can make things happen.

Early childhood is also the age of amusing sayings "out of the mouths of babes." For example, there is the story of the four-year-old girl at a wedding. As the groom slipped the ring onto the bride's finger, she whispered loudly, "Is he sprinking the pollen on her now?" Proverbs and conventional expressions conjure up literal images in the young child's mind. Hearing her mother say that "Daddy is tied up at the office," a three-year-old is likely to imagine father bound up with ropes.

During the years between two and six, children are transformed from being the practical, intelligent animals they were as infants into symbol users, conceptual thinkers, and functioning members of society. Children also become aware of the social identities they have inherited: gender, race, nationality, religion, family, social class. Autobiographical memory begins as well as the stream of consciousness, that inner, private movie of images, perceptions, memories, and daydreams that will run constantly until the end of life.

Children also begin to develop more distinct

personalities; preschool children come to vary enormously in such traits as shyness, boldness, aggressiveness, cheerfulness, and kindness. Some are noisy, rambunctious, rebellious; others are quiet, reserved, thoughtful. Individual talents may appear: for leadership, for speaking well, for music or art. At the same time as they are becoming individual persons, they are also learning the typical ways of acting and thinking, which comprise the roles, rules, and rituals of their cultural group.

Conceptions of Early Childhood

There are three general ways of conceptualizing young children. There is a *commonsensical* view, predating the field of psychology, which sees young children as simply small and ignorant versions of older children and adults. Traditionally, the age of seven or so has been recognized as the age of reason, but generally, people assumed that younger children perceived and understood the world in much the same way as adults did, given their lack of knowledge. This moderate view contrasts with that of Freud, who argued that children under the age of five live in a very different psychological world. He saw young children as *"emotional* aliens" (Elkind, 1974, p. 107, emphasis added), their minds and bodies a battleground between raging instincts and the terrors of punishment and loss.

The third view is Piaget's, which emphasized the *cognitive* handicaps of the preschool child. Despite Freud's insistence on young children's emotional and sexual perversity, Freud credited them with adultlike cognitive abilities; he believed even young infants could have mental images of absent objects. Piaget, on the other hand, assumed that children's thinking is radically different from adults'. He demonstrated that some of the most basic concepts about the world are cognitive achievements rather than simple perceptions of reality. He pointed to previously unsuspected contradictions and flaws in the thought processes of young children. For example, if you show two clay balls of equal size to a child and then roll one into a sausage shape, he or she is likely to believe the sausage is larger, or has more clay in it, than the ball because it is longer. Similarly, if you line up two rows of pennies, each row containing the same number, and then move the pennies in one row farther apart, the preschool child will say that there are more pennies in the longer row (see the Tests of Conservation figure in Chapter 10, p. 359).

Recently, evidence has been growing that preschool children are not as cognitively inept as previously thought. For example, they can and do count (Gelman, 1979). Many theorists seem to be returning to the older view that young children are not massively and qualitatively different from adults after all. Researchers are not arguing that preschoolers are miniature adults in their thinking abilities. Rather, they are pointing to the precursors of later skills—the concepts and capacities out of which more advanced abilities will grow.

Let us look at some examples of young children's thought. Kornei Chukovski (1966) is a Russian children's writer who collected and wrote about young children's questions and comments. Like Piaget and Freud, he examined young children's speech as a way of understanding their thought processes. Here is a selection of these sayings:

- "Mother, who was born first, you or I?"
- "Daddy, when you were little, were you a boy or a girl?"
- "Why do they put a pit in every cherry? We have to throw the pit away anyway?"
- (A little girl feeding cabbage leaves to chickens, and being told by her mother that chickens don't eat cabbage) "I'm giving it to them so that they may save it for after they become rabbits."
- "Daddy, please cut down this pine tree, it makes the wind."
- "Lie down on my pillow, mommy, and we'll look at my dream together."
- "Isn't it wonderful? I drink coffee, water, tea, cocoa but out of me pours only tea."
- "Do women give birth to girls and men to boys?"
- (On being told a pregnant woman had a baby in her belly) "She ate up a baby?"
- "The rooster, could he completely, completely, completely, forget that he is a rooster and lay an egg?"
- (A four-year-old, who became so upset after his mother said "Yes" when he asked if all people die [that] she said she was only joking) "Of course you were joking, I knew it. At first we'll all become little oldsters, and then we'll become youngsters."
- A five-year-old girl had been upset by the sight of a pig who had been killed by a train. Later she saw a healthy, lively pig. "The pig glued herself up" she exclaimed happily.

These examples lend support to all three views of children mentioned above. Freud would find evidence of preoccupation with sex, bodily functions, family relations, and death. Piaget would find examples of the cognitive deficiencies he has analyzed. Yet it is also clear that the preschool child is a novice and simply ignorant of basic facts about life, death, and the world.

Despite their differences, there is an underlying similarity in all these views. They each agree that early childhood marks an encounter between the ways of adult society and a mind that is in some sense "primitive." Or, to put it another way, early childhood represents a passage from the ignorance of infancy, through confused knowledge, and on to a more or less accurate understanding of basic natural and social realities. Paradoxically, the child's earliest encounters with language and adult society, en route to more ordered forms of thought, produce results that are often unique and sometimes bizarre.

Symbols and Socialization

While infants have practical or sensorimotor intelligence, the central feature of the preschool years is the beginning of symbolic thought. Language is the most striking evidence of this new ability, which Piaget called the "semiotic function" (semiotic means "pertaining to signs and symbols"). Children of this age are able to use a wide variety of **symbols**—private ones of their own invention, plus socially agreed upon systems such as words, numbers, music. It can be argued that this is the single most important transition in human cognitive development (Piaget, 1951; Piaget & Inhelder, 1969).

Piaget pointed out that the child's first words emerge as part of a general flowering of symbolic behavior. Deferred imitation and pretend play also reflect the ability to use symbols to evoke people, objects, and events in their absence. As an example of deferred imitation, recall how one of Piaget's daughters at 16 months saw a playmate having a tantrum. An hour or two later, she laughingly pretended to scream and stamp her foot as the other child had done (Piaget & Inhelder, 1969). The games of make-believe typical of preschoolers are additional evidence of symbolic thinking. This kind of play emerges quite early; Piaget cited the example of his daughter at 15 months pretending the corner of a tablecloth was her pillow, resting her head on it, closing her eyes, and sucking her thumb, smiling all the while.

Pretend play represents an important intellectual achievement because it reveals a clear distinction between a symbol or signifier—the cloth and the thing signified, a pillow. Piaget also recognized that symbolic play serves an important function in the child's emotional life. Children use play to deal with conflicts, fears, and disappointments. For instance, Piaget described how Jacqueline, at two and a half, responded when told she could not carry her new baby sister, Nonette. She folded her arms, pretending to rock and talk to an imaginary baby. She said, "Nonette's in there. There are two Nonettes." Later, she pretended she was Nonette (Piaget, 1951/1962). Young children may also invent an imaginary playmate whom they take very seriously, asking for example, that a place be set at the table for him or her. (We discuss symbolic play in more detail in a later section.) Throughout life, symbols continue to function in two ways—as expressions of private thoughts and feelings, and as vehicles of communication and problem solving.

Public and Private Symbols

While Piaget recognized that symbols can take a great many different forms—imitations, concrete objects, mental images, drawings, and words—he made a major distinction between two broad classes of signifiers: personal symbols and conventional ones.* In the child's personal symbols, the signifier often resembles the significate; thus, the tablecloth looked like the pillow the child was pretending it to be. Further, the meaning of the symbol to the child is private and idiosyncratic; a tablecloth is not a socially agreed-on symbol for a pillow.

In contrast, words and other conventional symbols are arbitrary. They have no resemblance to the things they stand for; the word "rose" does not resemble a rose, the word "automobile" does not resemble the machine we drive. Words, mathematical symbols, musical notes are simply symbols that society has agreed represent certain things.

Personal symbols can be real objects, as in the tablecloth example or a block used to signify a car. They can also be imitations, or mental images. Thus, it is likely that the child who imitated the tantrum, or pretended that the cloth was a pillow, had at the time a mental image of the real objects and events. A personal symbol can be a true symbol in that (1) it is something that stands for something else, and (2) it is used to evoke that other thing in the latter's absence. But it differs in an impor-

tant way from conventional symbols such as words. The latter can easily be used for communication; while it is often possible to figure out the meaning of a child's personal symbol, conventional symbols are used expressly to communicate a specific meaning from one person to another.

As we saw in the last chapter, the invention of a way of referring to objects and events marked a great step for humankind. Similarly, the acquisition of language is also a great step for the child, because the child can now become socialized. Infants lack not only language but also are ignorant of the most elementary social categories and standards of morality, politeness, and competence. And though infants have a sense of self, they have not yet developed their central core of identity: knowledge of their own gender. The process of acquiring all this knowledge is what is meant by the term **socialization.** The two processes are related; symbols, especially the shared symbols of language, make it possible to communicate with other people and to learn from them.

The term "socialization," as we have seen, has had a controversial history. It has often been seen as a process of social molding, in which a particular culture reproduces itself in succeeding generations, like a rubber stamp or a cookie cutter. This model assumes that socialization means conformity; it leads to what sociologist Dennis Wrong (1961) has called an "oversocialized" conception of human nature. It assumes a passive model of the child and ignores the role of the child in his or her own socialization. This interpretation also ignores the possibility of tension between the society and the individual.

Socialization is most usefully defined as simply the process of becoming human, of acquiring the basic human skills of language, social interaction, and body management. A person can learn the basic rules of his or her culture without necessarily being a conformist. As Roger Brown (1965) has pointed out, revolutionaries, poets, and reformers have learned the rules of their culture very well, but may bend or change the rules in the interests of a higher norm.

---

*Piaget's terminology differs from that of most other scholars, although his concepts are similar. He uses the term "symbol" to refer to private, personal symbols, and "sign" to refer to conventional symbols.

Cognitive Limitations in the Preschool Period

Although Piaget regarded the use of symbols as the major achievement of early childhood, he usually referred to that stage of development as the preoperational period. As we saw in Chapter 3, **operations,** in Piaget's theory, are mental representations and actions—or, to use everyday language, thoughts. But they are thoughts that can be transformed in various ways. For instance, they are reversible: the school-aged child can undo a mental action; he or she can add three to, say, nine and then subtract it. Piaget believed that preschool children are in a transitional period between the sensorimotor schemes of infancy and the use of operations.

In recent years, however, alternative explanations of cognitive development have been advanced. Information processing theorists generally reject the notion of massive, stagelike transformations of thought. Rather, they see development as a process of gradual change in several distinct information processing capacities. Children become increasingly able to regulate their attention and perception, their memory skills improve, and they can think up more ways to solve problems. Further, the older the children get, the more they build up a store of knowledge about the world.

Despite the recent criticisms, Piaget's work provides the most detailed and systematic account of the preschool child's thinking. The recent research, as one investigator put it, is not as much anti-Piagetian as "neo-Piagetian" (Gelman, quoted in Hunt, 1982). Piaget's ideas and the problems he chose to work on remain the starting place for most of the current work on cognitive development in early childhood.

Piaget believed that the most pervasive characteristic of the young child's thinking is centeredness, the tendency to focus attention on one detail or part of an event. Young children can deal mentally with objects and events, but have difficulty grasping the *relations* among those objects and events. **Centering** means the flexibility of thought is limited, as is the child's ability to process information from all aspects of the situation. Thus, the child looking at the ball of clay rolled out into a sausage may focus on its length, ignoring its height and the possibility that the sausage could be rolled back into a ball.

One of the most prominent forms of centration described by Piaget is *egocentrism.* When he says the young child is egocentric, Piaget is not using the term in an emotional or moral sense. That is, he is not saying that children are selfish or inconsiderate, or that they do not care about other people. Rather, he is using egocentrism in an epistemological sense; that young children consider their own point of view the only possible one, and do not realize that other people may have a different point of view. He is fond of using as an analogy the pre-Copernican belief that the sun and stars revolve around the earth. Many preschool children actually believe that the sun and moon follow them as they walk. The child's belief that Mommy could see his dream is another example of egocentrism: "If I see it, it's obviously there and another person can see it too." In general, then, Piaget argues, young children cannot imagine that the world could look different from another person's point of view.

Yet, as we saw in an earlier chapter, recent studies have shown that preschool children are not completely unaware that other people may have a different point of view. We will discuss these studies later, after first reviewing in a bit more detail Piaget's work on early childhood.

Forms of Egocentrism

Piaget regarded the entire course of cognitive development as a series of cognitive revolutions. At each of the major stages, children must reconstruct their understanding of the world. Each stage has its own form of egocentrism which gradually gives way to a "decentered" view of the world. Piaget believed that infants start life in a kaleidoscope of sensations, unable to tell where their own bodies end and the world begins. By the end of infancy, this fluctuating, unstable reality evolves into the three-dimensional world of permanent objects. Children become aware of themselves as objects in a world of physical objects.

The last stages of sensorimotor development contain the seed of the next stage of development. The concept of the permanent object implies that the child is able to represent an object mentally when it is out of sight. But the coming of what Piaget called the symbolic or semiotic function plunges children into a new kind of egocentrism that will take several years to overcome.

Although Piaget recognized the onset of symbolic thought as a great advance, it seems almost as if he viewed the preschool child as having taken one step forward and three steps back. Having acquired the use of symbols, two-year-old children must go back and start all over again, translating what they knew as infants into mental representations.

Between the ages of two and four, according to Piaget, the once solid world of the older infant becomes unstable and shifting once again, only this time on the level of concepts and mental images. For example, older babies reverse their own actions to bring about an original state; they can turn a bottle over to get at the nipple, they can find their way around at home and in the backyard. But all of this is on the practical level of action. They cannot represent these actions mentally. When children are in the preoperational stage, they have mental representations of objects and events but they cannot do mental manipulations with them in the way that the baby can do physical manipulations with actual objects.

When children do achieve this flexibility of thought, they have advanced to the next stage of Piaget's developmental scheme, the stage of concrete operations. As discussed in an earlier chapter, operations are the mental versions and direct descendants of the baby's manipulations of objects—joining, separating, ordering and reordering, acting and reversing the action. And, as we have seen, not all psychologists agree with Piaget's way of conceptualizing mental processes. But most of them view cognitive development as essentially a matter of getting to be more and more adept at manipulating one's thought process. The chief difference between other cognitive psychologists and Piaget is how each characterizes thought processes.

Constancy of Identity

While the young infant has to master the notion that objects continue to exist when they are no longer in sight, newly symbolic children must master the concept of constancy or invariance. They must discover that the identity of individuals and objects remains the same through time and in different contexts, and that matter can change form and still remain the same in quantity. Piaget's notion of quantitative invariance or **conservation** is exemplified in the understanding that a cup of water poured into containers of differing sizes and shapes will not change the amount of water, despite the obvious variation in water level. Piaget regarded the capacity to understand conservation as the essence of mature intelligence and as a necessary condition for all rational thought.

At first, identity is plastic: the same individual is a different person at different times or in different costumes. For instance, at two and a half, Piaget's daughter Jacqueline did not believe that her younger sister Lucienne was really her sister when the baby wore a bathing suit and cap. She kept asking, "But what's the baby's name?" When Lucienne again put a dress on, Jacqueline exclaimed "It's Lucienne again." Similarly, Jacqueline seemed to believe that her mirror image and her picture in photographs were different people. Lucienne had similar concepts of identity. She referred to a picture of her sister Jacqueline at a younger age as "Jacqueline when she was Lucienne." She believed that all little girls are Luciennes and then become Jacquelines when they get older.

More recent studies have confirmed Piaget's finding that young children believe changes in appearance constitute changes in identity. Rheta De Vries (1969) trained a friendly black cat named Maynard to wear masks representing either a ferocious dog or a rabbit. Sixty-four boys, aged three to six, were interviewed individually in one of three situations. One group saw the cat turned into a "dog," another saw the cat turned into a "rabbit," while the third group first saw the "dog" change into a cat and then back to the "dog." After petting it and identifying the original animal, the child was told, "Now this animal is going to look different. You keep an eye on his tail end, and in a minute I'll show you." While screening the front of the animal from the child, the experimenter would put on or take off the mask and then show the transformed animal to the child, saying "Look, now he has a face like a dog. What is this animal now?"

The children were asked a number of questions about the nature and causes of the changed appearance. The petting procedure was repeated, and then the child was asked to identify the animal after watching the mask being removed and put on again. Finally, the child was asked, "Is there *any* way a real cat could be a real dog?"

The study revealed marked increases in the constancy of identity with age. The youngest children believed the masked Maynard was an entirely different animal. Even though they were told to "watch the tail," they believed that the cat had run away or disappeared, and that the changed animal *was* a real dog (or rabbit). They believed it could bark, eat dog food, and had a dog's "insides." Moreover, they were afraid of the "dog" and refused to pet it. At a second stage, the children expressed surprise and puzzlement about the change, revealing that they had some expectation of constancy, but they nevertheless still believed in the transformation. Later, children denied the reality of the identity change, but accepted the possibility that a person's identity could be changed by magic. Finally, the oldest children completely rejected the possibility of identity change.

De Vries also investigated children's beliefs in the constancy of gender identity—whether a girl could become a boy if she played with guns and wore boys' clothes. The age trends were similar to those in the studies involving Maynard and the mask. De Vries concludes that the belief in the constancy of identity is a necessary step on the way to later belief in quantitative constancy, such as the constancy of the amount of clay when it is changed from a ball to a snake.

How would the results of De Vries's studies relate to the psychoanalytic interpretation of early childhood thinking? Freud and his followers believed that the magical thinking of young children is a distortion of normal thought processes caused by strong *emotions*. A Piagetian would argue the reverse, that young children's ordinary experience of reality is different from adults' because of their limited *logical* abilities. Piaget believed that rather than being two independent processes, intellect and emotion are "two sides of the same coin." In other words, while the Freudians would say that children's fears and other strong emotions cause their thinking to deteriorate, the Piagetians would argue that the unstable cognitive structures of the preschool child lead to fear and anxiety: the world is an unpredictable place, and nice people and animals can be transformed into bad ones. De Vries's studies provide a test of these two interpretations, and her results support the cognitive or Piagetian explanation.

De Vries was able to separate the belief in inconstancy from fearfulness. Inconstancy of identity did not seem to be the product of thought processes distorted by fear, nor did it lead to fear if the transformed identity was not a fearful one. It was only when children believed that friendly Maynard had turned into a snarling dog that they were afraid of him.

Classes and Relations

The child learning to use language and concepts must deal not only with single entities such as an object, an animal, or a person, but also with complex sets of abstract relationships. To understand the word "dog," it is not enough to know that the term refers to the family pet. The child must also learn that the word is a concept—it indicates a class of animals with several characteristics in common. Different kinds of dogs such as beagles and collies are still dogs; all dogs are animals, but so are cats, cows, horses, birds, and even insects. Animals, in turn, are part of a still wider class of living things. Classes form nested hierarchies, like a set of Russian dolls that fit inside one another. It takes some time for children to master the notions of classes. Piaget refers to the child's earliest concepts as "preconcepts," and the years between two and four as "preconceptual." The years between four and seven or eight are called the "intuitive" substage.

At first, the relation between the individual object and the class is uncertain. The little Russian girl who thought the mangled pig had "glued herself up again," is an example of the difficulty children have with the concept of class. For her, all pigs were one pig, rather than members of a class. Piaget cited a similar example (Piaget, 1962, p. 225). When his daughter Jacqueline was two and a half, they would take daily walks on a road where there were many slugs. When she saw the first slug of the day, she would say "There's the slug." When she came to another one farther down the road, she would say, "There's the slug

again." This type of reasoning can explain why children may not be bothered by seeing Santa Claus in several department stores and on the street, or by the difficulties of Santa coming to every child's home on Christmas morning. It is characteristic of young children to be able to tolerate what would be glaring contradictions to older children or adults. It is when children begin to think about contradictions, such as the impossibility of Santa being in many places at once, or the sun and moon following everyone the way they seem to follow oneself, that they begin to overcome the tendency to assume that the way things look at any given moment is the way things really are.

Another aspect of learning to use concepts involves the relationship between a class of objects and its subclasses. For example, a bunch of flowers could include red flowers and white flowers, a group of toy animals could include cows and horses. To adults, it is clear that the number of objects in a general class has to be greater than the number in the subclass: there are more flowers in general than there are red (or white) flowers; there are more animals than there are cows (or horses).

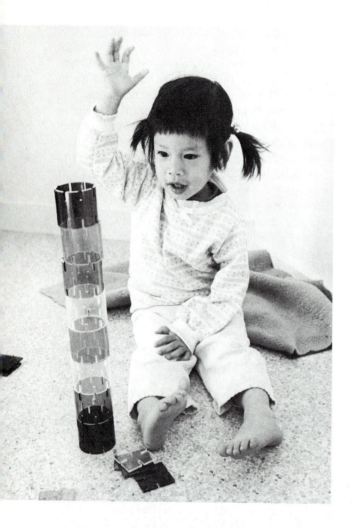

Piaget claimed that children below the age of seven or so cannot solve such class-inclusion problems. In a typical experiment, a child is shown a number of objects that divide into subclasses in some obvious way. Usually the two subclasses are unequal—there would be, say, four black beads and two white ones. The question that is put to the child is this: "Are there more black beads or more beads?" Until the age of seven children cannot seem to solve this problem. They are likely to say there are more red flowers than flowers, more black beads than beads. Piaget argued that young children are unable to compare one of the parts with the whole; if they "center" their attention on one of the subclasses, they cannot think of

the whole class of which it is a part. Thus, Piaget saw the child's difficulties with the class inclusion problem as one aspect of the general egocentrism and inflexibility of preoperational thought.

Recent studies have questioned Piaget's explanation. It seems that at least some of the child's trouble with the class inclusion task resulted from communication problems which made it hard for the child to understand what the experimenter was really asking. When problems are put in a different way, many six-year-old children can solve them. For example, James McGarrigle (in Donaldson, 1978) used four toy cows, three of them black, one white. He placed all the cows on their sides and explained they were sleeping. Then he asked the crucial question in two different ways: the standard Piagetian way and the restated way, such as "Are there more black cows or more sleeping cows?" The standard (Piagetian) form of the question was answered correctly by 25 percent of the children, the second form by 48 percent. Evidently the emphasis on the whole category—the sleeping cows—made it easier for the children to compare the class with the subclass. Yet note that even with the changed wording, a majority of the children still failed to solve a problem that is self-evident to adults. Further, these children were not young preschoolers, but six-year-olds.

Young children also have difficulty with the concept of class in certain other tasks. If asked to sort objects into groups that are alike, adults will form groups based on common attributes or conceptual similarities, such as furniture, eating utensils, animals. Young children, however, form "complexes" in which objects may be included for a variety of reasons. Inhelder and Piaget (1964) found that children of two or three, when asked to group together certain blocks, typically built something with the blocks, such as a house or a train. Older children, four- or five-year-olds, are able to sort blocks by one category, for example into red ones and blue ones; but when asked to do the task another way, they are usually unable to sort by size or shape. They are unable to shift to the other property.

Here again, however, the nature of the task seems to have a strong influence on the child's ability to deal with classifications. Studies by Eleanor Rosch and her associates (1976) have shown that even young children are able to classify objects into correct categories when an oddity task was used. The child would be shown three pictures at a time; say two different dogs and a car, or a car, a train, and a cat. The task was to "put together the things that are alike." On one kind of task, a "basic level sort" involving two different dogs and vehicles, the performance of the youngest children in the study, who were three years old, was virtually perfect. The other task involved a higher level of abstraction: two different kinds of animals, vehicles, or clothing would be contrasted with another type of object—for example, a dog and cat versus a guitar. This type of task was harder for the younger children, but 96 percent of the four-year-olds got it right. The results show that even very small children can classify objects in the same manner as adults.

Another kind of difficulty that Piaget claimed young children have is with relations, including size, time, and family membership. Here again, knowledge that seems self-evident to adults is shown not to be so for children. Piaget described a boy who, when asked if he had a brother, said "yes." But when asked if his brother had a brother, the boy said "no." Piaget argued that the boy's failure to understand the reciprocal nature of the brother relationship is part of a more general difficulty with relationships among things.

Transitivity

Much of Piaget's study of relational concepts concerned the problem of **transitivity.** For example, if you are taller than your friend John, and John introduces you to his friend Mary, and you see that John is taller than Mary, it is self-evident that you are taller than Mary. You know this without standing next to Mary and comparing yourself to her. It simply "has" to

be so. Piaget argued that this obvious truth is not apparent to children, and that they have trouble making the inference that if A > B, and B > C, then A has to be greater than C.

In a typical Piagetian experiment, the child is shown two sticks, one larger than the other (A > B). The smaller of the two sticks is hidden, and the larger stick is presented with a still larger one. Then, the child is asked how A, the hidden stick, and C, the largest, compare. Typically, preschool children answer that they do not know.

Recently, as with the class inclusion problem, there have been questions raised about Piaget's way of presenting the task. Some psychologists argue that part of the difficulty is remembering all the items and their characteristics. By the time item C comes along, the child has forgotten about A and its relation to B. Further, they believe that instead of solving the problem through logic, both adults and children may construct mental images of the items, lined up in the proper order, and just "read off" the answers (Flavell, 1977).

In one study, Paul Harris and his colleagues (see Donaldson, 1978) showed two strips of paper to four-year-old children. The strips were placed about three feet apart and were very similar in length—one was only about a quarter of an inch longer than the other. When the children were asked which was longer, the number of correct answers was the chance level—the differences were imperceptible. Then the child was shown a third strip of paper, equal to one of the other two. It was briefly placed next to each of the first two strips. Most of the children were now able to answer the question correctly, which shows that they were capable of making transitive inferences.

A series of studies by Peter Bryant (1974) has also shown that children's failures at the standard transitivity tasks are likely due to the child's failure to understand the task, or the shortness of young children's memory spans. Bryant argues that the child may have psychological abilities necessary to make inferences, but may have trouble putting them together well enough to succeed at a particular task. In some of these studies, Bryant trained young children to compare five sticks, two at a time. Thus, they learned that A > B, B > C, C > D, D > E. Only after the children could remember the comparisons did he ask for comparisons of separated items, such as B and D. When tested in this way, 79 percent of the four-year-olds could make the correct inference, a result that is markedly in contrast with Piaget's belief that children cannot deal with transitivity until they are seven.

Studies along the same line by Trabasso (1975) suggest further that there is more than one way to solve the transitivity problem. He hypothesized that if logical inference was the only way to do it, then questions about the relative length of differing pairs should be harder than questions about adjacent pairs, which have been seen together: A and B, C and D, and so on. On the other hand, if people were using mental images of the items lined up in a row, the wider comparisons ought to be easier. The results showed that for children of various ages, even young ones, the farther apart the items to be compared, the shorter the solution time. If there is more than one way to skin a cat, perhaps it is not surprising that there should be more than one way to solve an intellectual problem.

Looking at the World through Another Person's Eyes

As we saw earlier, Piaget believed that all the young child's cognitive limitations stem from one central failing—egocentrism, or to use Piaget's later term—the *centeredness* of the child's thought. This centeredness has two main aspects: first, the child focuses on one striking perceptual feature of an object or event; second, the child fails to realize that his or her own point of view is not necessarily what another person would see or experience.

In everyday conversation, when we say "I see," we can use the term "see" in either a literal or metaphoric way. We can see something, literally, with our eyes, or we can "see" or understand what another person is thinking or feeling or intending to say or do. For Piaget and many other researchers, this equation of visual seeing and taking the view of another person was not just a metaphor. Piaget believed that the ability to figure out what other people are seeing with their eyes reveals their general ability to understand another person's point of view, or to "take the role of the other." Role taking has been regarded by many theorists—G. H. Mead, Wallon, Flavell, Kohlberg—as the key social skill and the major step in the socialization of the child. In recent years, role taking in children has become an active area of research.

The Three Mountains Task

For many years Piaget's Three Mountains Task has been regarded almost as an operational definition of role taking. In this task, children of various ages are shown a papier-mâché model of three mountains (see Figure 9.1) and are asked to select photographs showing how the mountains look from different locations. Thus, the experimenter places a doll in various positions around the mountains, and asks the child what the doll can see. Another version of the task requires the child to move some model mountains around to reflect what a person in a different position might see. Still other variations of the same testing procedures have been carried out (Flavell et al., 1968; Laurendeau & Pinard, 1970).

In general, the task is challenging for children up to the age of 9 or 10. The younger the child, the more pronounced is the inability to describe the appearance of the mountain from a position other than his own. Thus, all 4- and 5-year-old children responded by giving their own perspectives (Piaget & Inhelder, 1956). Between 6½ and 7, some children showed awareness of the doll's point of view by making some attempts to pick a view other than their own. But they were still unsuccessful in identifying the doll's point of view.

Other research on egocentrism deals with young children's communication. Generally,

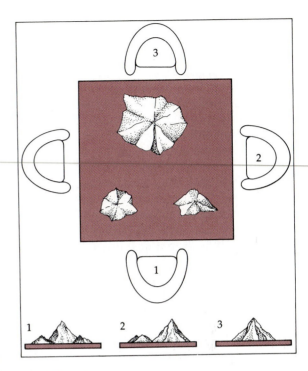

FIGURE 9.1
Piaget's Three Mountains Task
Piaget designed the Three Mountains Task to measure a child's egocentricity, or centeredism. The child would be placed at position 1 and then would be asked to describe the views from positions 2 and 3.

such studies show that young children fail to take their listener's perceptions into account. A typical experiment (Glucksberg, Kraus, & Higgins, 1975) places two preschool children out of sight of one another, such as across a desk with a screen in between them, and asks them to communicate about objects they both can see. Each child might have a set of objects to look at, and the task would be to pick out one object and get the other child to identify what it is. A typical response of a young child would be to point to an object and ask, "Is this it?"—disregarding, of course, the fact that the other child could not see what the first one is pointing to. These and other tasks seem to confirm the idea that young children are locked into their own point of view, unaware that another person might see things differently.

New Views on Egocentrism

As mentioned earlier, there was very little research until recently that challenged the idea that young children are pervasively and hopelessly egocentric. Since the mid-1970s, however, a number of studies by different researchers have undermined this view. Rather than being pervasively egocentric, the research showed, preschool children are aware that other people may have different points of view, but this ability will be revealed only if the tasks are simplified. It turns out that the Three Mountains Task, like many other Piagetian tasks, is a difficult one and insensitive to the basic ability it was intended to assess (Flavell, 1977).

Helen Borke (1975) developed a variation of the Three Mountains Task using materials that would have more appeal to young children. Three- and four-year-old children were shown a large red fire engine on a table. Then each child was introduced to Grover, a muppet from "Sesame Street." Grover was placed in a car, and he then "drove" to various points around the fire engine. Whenever Grover parked to look out at the fire engine, the child was asked how it looked to Grover. He or she could answer by turning a duplicate fire engine on a turntable until it matched Grover's view. Children who gave the wrong response were taken over to where Grover was parked. Then they were asked to go back and move the turntable so the engine was the way Grover saw it. If the child still gave the wrong answer, the experimenter moved the engine to the right position and explained that this was the way it looked to Grover.

After practicing with the fire engine, each child was shown three different displays, one at a time. One display was a replica of Piaget's three mountains. The others consisted of arrays of familiar objects, such as a toy boat on a lake, horses, cows, houses. The procedure was the same as for the fire engine task, but the children were not given a chance to look at the scene from Grover's point of view (Figure 9.2).

All of the children correctly predicted Grover's view over 80 percent of the time on the

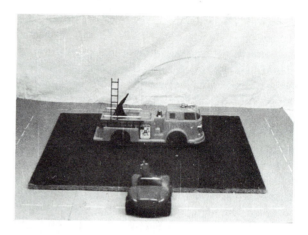

FIGURE 9.2
Simplifying the Egocentricity Test
Helen Borke's introduction to the perspectives task (above) and her variation of the Three Mountains Task (below) simplified Piaget's egocentricity test so children as young as three could demonstrate that they can understand another person's perspective.

two displays containing familiar objects. The Three Mountains Task was correctly answered only 42 percent of the time by three-year-olds, and 67 percent of the time by four-year-olds. Clearly, the familiar objects were easier for the children to deal with than Piaget's mountains. The mountains may have been less interesting or simply harder to differentiate, or both. Nevertheless, the majority of four-year-olds were able to succeed on the mountains task when they could rotate an exact replica of the scene.

A study by Martin Hughes (1975) also used a novel kind of perspective task. Here, children between three and five were shown a model of two walls intersecting to form a cross and two dolls—a boy and a policeman. The task was to hide the boy so the policeman could not see him. As in the Borke study, there was a practice period before the test proper. Children made very few mistakes during the training. The actual experimental task was to hide the boy from *two* policemen who were standing at the adjacent ends of the cross. Thus, the child had to consider the points of view of two other people. Nevertheless, even the youngest children had a success rate of 88 percent.

How can such results be reconciled with the findings of Piaget and others that even 9- and 10-year-olds have trouble figuring out the view of another person on the Three Mountains Task? John Flavell (1977) has suggested that there are two levels in the development of knowledge about another person's point of view. At the first level, children understand that other people may not see things the same way they themselves do, but they may not be able to figure out exactly how objects and scenes look to another person. At the second level, children can figure out what different visual experiences the other person is having. The Three Mountains Task, according to this interpretation, calls for second-level knowledge—an understanding of how to calculate changes in spatial imagery.

It seems clear now that Piaget underestimated the ability of young children and even infants to put themselves in another's place. For example, some studies show that infants in the first year are sensitive to another person's gaze. That is, if a four-month-old baby sees a person looking in a certain direction, the baby is also likely to look in that direction (Lempers, 1976; Scaife & Bruner, 1975). By nine months, babies understand what pointing means, provided that the adult's finger is on or near the object. By about a year, most children can both point to something and understand what an adult is pointing to, even if it is far away. This "joint visual attention" may be one of the foundations of later language development (Bruner,

1978). In any event, since joint attention or mutual orientation suggests some degree of knowledge about another person's point of view, even babies in their first year seem to be less than totally egocentric.

Children of two and three can understand that when a card with a different picture on each side is placed between the child and the experimenter, each one sees something different (Masangkay et al., 1974). The study by Lempers, Flavell, & Flavell (1977) revealed that by age three, children know that people see with their eyes, that they cannot see if their eyes are covered or if something is in between the person and an object, and that what another person sees is independent of what the self sees.

In addition to studies of visual perception, research on other kinds of role taking also reveals that young children are less egocentric than had been assumed. For example, four-year-olds were found to adapt their communications to the needs and capacities of their listeners. When speaking to much younger children, they made their speech more simple and attention getting than when they spoke to peers or adults (Shatz & Gelman, 1973). Four-year-olds were also able to choose appropriate gifts for their mothers, rather than picking toys they themselves liked (Marvin, 1984). Further, children of this age were also able to change how they spoke about an incident depending on whether the listener knew about it or not (Flavell, 1968). Another study found that children as young as two have a rudimentary ability to carry on conversations with one another, thus contradicting Piaget's notion that the egocentricity of children under five makes it impossible for them to carry on more than a "collective monologue" (Ervin-Tripp, 1976). As a result of all these studies, a consensus seems to be developing among developmental psychologists that preschool children are much less egocentric and more competent in social understanding than Piaget had thought them to be.

Helen Borke (1975) points out that Piaget himself was inconsistent on the subject of egocentrism. In some of his writings, he recognized that children as young as a year and a half, in transition to symbolic thought, are able to take the view of the other. Piaget also observed children reacting sympathetically to others. While he did not give much theoretical weight to this behavior, other writers, such as George Herbert Mead (1934) viewed sympathy to other people as an indicator of a simple form of role-taking ability.

Yet if little children seem to have more adult-like cognitive capabilities than earlier believed, adults are no longer viewed as paragons of perfect rationality. As adults, we are capable of logical, rational thought, but the older, more egocentric, intuitive kind of thought still remains. Adults are capable of more complex mental operations than children, but we do not always operate at the highest level. We may beg traffic lights to change when we are in a hurry and curse at and kick machines that refuse to work. Like little children, adults often at some gut level do not believe in chance. The gambler believes he can influence the dice or the roulette wheel; people who find they have a serious disease wonder, in anger and guilt, "Why me?" As mature rational adults, we scoff at superstition and magic, but we may walk around ladders, "knock on wood," and feel uncomfortable if we break a mirror. Baseball pitchers and other athletes are notorious for using good luck charms and special gestures to help them win games. Even Piaget himself admitted that he functioned at his highest or "operatory" level only part of the day, when he was devoted to his work. "The rest of the time I am dealing with empirical trial and error on a very low level," he explained. "Every moment I am enjoying pre-operatory intuition. At other times I go even lower and almost give way to magical behavior" (quoted in Tanner & Inhelder, 1956, p. 126).

Apart from believing in magic and superstition, we are always in danger of failing to differentiate our own point of view from another person's. If I do not like a certain movie, or if I feel very cold in a room, I am likely to feel that the movie simply *is* a bad movie, and that the room *is* cold. If you come along and tell me you like the movie, and feel too warm, I may have trouble understanding how you can possibly misperceive reality that way. And you are likely to feel the same about my reactions.

Sometimes it is a lack of knowledge or experience that makes us egocentric. It is hard for a white middle-class person to know what it is like to grow up poor or black, or for men to know what it is like to be a woman, and vice versa. It is hard for adults in the prime of life to remember what the world looks like through the eyes of a child, or to imagine what it looks like to an 80-year-old. It is possible to overcome the barriers of class, race, nationality, gender, age—good fiction helps us do this—but we never truly escape from the prison of our own experience. At the end of life, egocentrism is total: as someone once observed, the death of any single person ends a whole world.

Young Children as Novices

We mentioned earlier that one of the traditional ways of looking at young children was simply as ignorant adults. That is, in looking at the contrasts between 3- and 4-year-old children and those of 9, 10, or 11, people of former times were likely to assume that what younger children mainly lacked, and they gained as they grew older, was knowledge. In recent years, there has been a revival of this idea in developmental psychology.

Some psychologists are coming around to the view that at least some of the difference in the thinking of children and adults is due to the fact that children are absolute beginners in solving all kinds of problems. Consider, for example, the development of memory. There seems to be little doubt that the capacity to store items in memory increases with age—that is, adults have longer memory spans than children. A 4-year-old can repeat a list of about three or four random numbers, a 12-year-old about six or seven. Beyond this, however, how well a child or anyone remembers things depends not only on basic memory capacity, but also on how well we use whatever capacity we have—our strategies for remembering things. Some common, everyday memory strategies adults use include tying a string on one's finger, repeating a phone number after looking it up, taking notes in class, and making lists of things to do. Our memory performance also depends on how familiar we are with what we are trying to remember. Being "universal novices" (Brown & Deloache, 1978) means that children lack both basic knowledge about the world and knowledge about how to use their knowledge. This latter skill has been called **metacognition,** and it is this that develops through childhood and adolescence.

A study carried out in the Soviet Union illustrates the development of metacognitive skills (Isotoma, 1975). Three- to five-year-old children were asked to remember a list of five items to be bought at a realistic-looking play store set up at their nursery school. As a control condition, children were asked to remember five words of comparable difficulty. All the children remembered more items in the game than in the control situation. A key difference between younger and older children was in setting the task of remembering as a conscious goal. For example, three-year-olds would rush off to the store almost before the list was finished and come back with items not necessarily on the list. Four-year-olds listened attentively and tried to carry out the task as quickly as possible before they forgot the items, but they did not seem to have strategies for improving their memories. Between four and five, the children's approach to the task changed. They actively rehearsed the lists, checked their memories, and asked the experimenter for the names of forgotten items. The oldest children, six to seven years old, devised even more sophisticated strategies such as rearranging the items on the list to form logical connections among them.

Strategies for remembering do not account for all of the differences between adults and children. Micheline Chi (1978) has tested the hypothesis that adults' greater store of knowledge contributes to their superior performance. She tried to separate the effects of knowledge and age by comparing children who were experts in a certain area with adults who were not. Chi solicited children from a local chess tournament and had them compete against graduate students who knew how to play the game, but were not experts. She found that the children's ability to remember chess positions on a board was far superior to the adults', even though their memory capacity—as tested by memory for digits—was lower. The children in this experiment were about 10 years of age, but the general point seems applicable to preschoolers: at least some of the differences between young children and their elders are due to ignorance and inexperience. To some extent, a person can be a novice at any age when faced with a new kind of problem to solve; adults who never had any experience with computers might be confused and inefficient when first trying to learn how to work with them.

Emotional Development in Early Childhood

In contrast to the vast number of studies that have been carried out on young children's thinking, very little has been discovered about their emotional development. Emotions, however, have become a lively topic in developmental research (Campos et al., 1983; Izard, Kagan, & Zajonc, 1984). Many investigators now believe, as we saw in Chapter 6, that there is a core set of emotional responses that emerges in the first year. These responses are the precursors of the basic emotions—happiness, surprise, anger, fear, unhappiness. As the child grows, the experience of emotions becomes more complex, and the child's response to emotional arousal becomes more differentiated. Further, children come to understand the causes and consequences of emotional states: children as young as three can recognize the kinds of situations that are likely to determine basic emotions. During the preschool years, children come to be increasingly accurate in inferring the emotions of others from facial expression and verbal cues, as well as knowledge of the situation. Several studies show that happiness is the easiest emotion for young children to recognize, while sadness and anger are often confused.

One particular emotion that has been the focus of research attention for some time is fear. While babies are afraid of specific things and situations—loud noises, looming objects, strangers—preschool children become vulnerable to a new set of fears. A study carried out during the 1930s found that certain fears increased over the preschool period—fears of animals and imaginary creatures, of the dark, of being left alone, and of bodily injury (Jersild & Holmes, 1935). A more recent study (Bauer, 1976) found that 47 percent of four- to six-year-olds were afraid of animals, 74 percent were afraid of frightening dreams, and 74 percent were afraid of ghosts and monsters.

Freud believed that the fears of this period reflect the intense emotions aroused by the Oedipal conflict. A major statement about the conflict can be found in one of Freud's most famous case histories—the case of Little Hans (1909/1955). Recall that Hans was a five-year-old boy who developed a severe phobia: he was afraid to leave the house for fear that he would be bitten by a horse. After a long series of discussions with his father, guided by Freud, Hans's phobia gradually declined. Freud's hypothesis was that the feared horse symbolized Hans's father, and that the biting symbolized castration. The case history presents many details in support of this interpretation.

Both Freud's account of phobias and the theoretical assumptions on which it is based remain highly controversial (see Wolpe & Rachman, 1960). Nevertheless, Freud's analysis of emotional development in the years from three to six remains highly influential. As mentioned earlier, Freud felt that the most significant events in the socialization process were weaning, toilet training, and the renunciation of aggressive and sexual wishes toward one's parents. He believed that these oral, anal, aggressive, and sexual drives were powerful forces that were always at war with the civilized veneer of the presumably socialized individual.

Freud regarded early childhood as the period with the most profound impact on later life. The Oedipal crisis and its resolution represented to him the climax of psychological development. By identifying with the parent of the same sex, he argued, the child acquires a sexual identity as well as ideals and a conscience or superego.

Although relatively few developmental psychologists accept all of Freud's theoretical assumptions, they recognize that Freud did ask the important questions about early childhood: How do children develop a sense of their own sexual identity? How do children acquire a conscience—that is, how do they come to accept the values of their culture and learn to renounce their own desires and control their own impulses?

Let us look in a bit more detail at Freud's account of the **Oedipal conflict.** Freud's theory, as he himself admitted, is clearest when applied to boys. Oedipus was of course a male—a mythical Greek prince who unknowingly killed his father and married his mother. Freud believed that every little boy of around the age of four or five would like to do what Oedipus did. Developing an intense sexual interest in the mother, he becomes jealous of his father's relationship to her. The child feels hostile to the father and would like to get rid of him. These thoughts and feelings conflict with the little boy's love for his father, and also lead him to fear his father's revenge. Specifically, Freud thought that the child fears his father will castrate him. Terrified by this prospect, the little boy renounces his desire for his mother and identifies with his father. This identification results in the boy developing a sexual identity, as well as a conscience and a set of ideals for the self. (See the box on The Concept of Identification.)

Although for girls several details of the story change, Freud believed that girls also become jealous of and hostile to their mothers and want to be the exclusive objects of their fathers' affection. He called the girl's version of the family triangle the Electra complex.

Just as a description, Freud's account does fit the behavior of many children around four and five. Little boys and girls often do talk about marrying the parent of the opposite sex. A woman psychologist who had always thought

The Concept of Identification

Identification is a core concept in psychoanalytic theory and is also widely used in developmental psychology. It is generally defined as a psychological process in which a person assimilates aspects of another person to the self. In other words, a person comes to believe that he or she is like the other person. To psychoanalysts, identification transforms the person in major ways; personality is formed through a series of identifications.

In everyday usage, the term overlaps with a number of other concepts—imitation, sympathy, empathy. But identification involves more than acting like another person, or understanding another's emotions. It is a feeling of deep psychological similarity, almost as if one were the other person.

While the best-known example of identification occurs in the Oedipus complex, Freud believed that it also occurs when we must give up a love object, as when a beloved person dies. We console ourselves by becoming like the lost loved one.

Some psychologists have pointed out that one can identify with a role as well as a person. Thus, Kohlberg (1966) has argued that boys identify with their fathers because they are both males, and similarly, girls identify with their mothers on the basis of gender identity. A study of thirty-seven children whose parents had undergone sex change operations supports this view: the children identified with traditional sex roles and regarded their parents as deviant (Green, 1978). This study shows that children are not completely dependent on their parents for knowledge about cultural norms; they can learn from the culture itself.

A transsexual family

Freud's theories "complete nonsense" reports the following conversations with her daughters when each of them was four:

Rachel: When I get married, I'm going to marry daddy.
Mother: Daddy's already married to me.
Rachel: Then we can have a double wedding.

Bethany: When I grow up, I'm going to marry daddy.
Mother: But daddy's already married to me.
Bethany: That's all right. When I grow up, you'll probably be dead. (Berger, 1980, p. 340)

Despite the fact that children often do talk this way, there are some serious problems with Freud's theorizing about the Oedipus conflict. One major problem is that Freud does not really explain why the little boy identifies with his father, and how this identification solves the Oedipus problem. The girl's identification with her mother is also not clearly explained. A careful reader of Freud's work, Robert White comes to the conclusion that it would be more correct to say that the boy *renounces* his identification with his father at the resolution of the Oedipus complex, since he gives up his wish to take his place in the mother's bed (1963, p. 101).

A related and even more serious problem is that Freud uses identification to establish such important outcomes as sexual identity as well as conscience and ideals. Freud links all of these variables together and makes them depend on a complex series of emotional experiences unfolding in precisely the same way for children in all times and places. Yet we know that family structure varies dramatically in different cultures. In many cultures, children do not grow up in the kind of nuclear family households familiar to Western societies, especially that of the middle class. It seems likely that where family arrangements differ, the emotional dynamics of parent-child relationships also vary. Cross-cultural research shows that boys do not always have jealous or hostile relations with their fathers. In some cultures, for instance, the maternal uncle, not the father,

is responsible for disciplining the little boy. The boy thus becomes hostile to his uncle rather than his father, who is his mother's sexual partner (Malinowski, 1929).

Further, we know from everyday life that sexual identity and superego do not necessarily go together. A person can have a biologically appropriate sexual identity and no conscience, or have a variant sexual identity—such as homosexuality—and a strong conscience and ideals. The developments of gender identity and conscience seem to require separate explanations. And the Oedipal drama that takes place in many families also requires explanation.

Alternative Theories of Gender Identity

Since Freud, developmental researchers have continued to ask questions about how children acquire gender identity and social standards. But they have been dissatisfied with the complexities and gaps in Freud's Oedipal theory. Two major alternatives to the psychoanalytic account have been advanced, one based on social learning theory and the other on the cognitive-developmental theory.

The Social Learning Model

According to *social learning* theorists, the child learns sex-typed behavior the same way he or she learns any other type of behavior, through a combination of reward, punishment, and observation of what other people are doing. Proponents of this view include Dollard and Miller (1950) and Bandura and Walters (1963). In essence, they argue that it is unnecessary to invoke innate biological drives to account for sexual behavior, particularly sex role behavior, since learning can and does account for whatever behavioral differences are found between the sexes. Bandura, for example, describes sex role learning as a process of indoctrination that begins at birth:

Sex-role differentiation usually commences immediately after birth, when the baby is named and both the infant and the nursery are given the blue or pink treatment depending upon the sex of the child. Thereafter, indoctrination into masculinity and femininity is diligently promulgated by adorning children with distinctive clothes and hair styles, selecting sex-appropriate play materials and recreational activities, promoting associations with same-sex playmates, and through nonpermissive parental reactions to deviant sex-role behavior. (1969, p. 215)

Besides direct indoctrination, social learning theorists include modeling as a way of learning: the boy will be rewarded for imitating his father and discouraged from using his mother as a model for his own behavior; the girl will be rewarded for the reverse. Eventually the child will find imitating the appropriate models rewarding in itself.

The Cognitive-Development Model

The *cognitive-development* model of gender identity derives from the work of Lawrence Kohlberg (1966), whose approach is largely an elaboration of the theories of Piaget, but applied to the area of sexual development. Like the social learning theorists, Kohlberg argues against the notion that gender identity is instinctually patterned. Nevertheless, he does not believe that sexuality and sex role learning are based on conformity to cultural patterns. Rather, he argues, children's concepts of sexuality arise in the same way as all their other concepts about the world and the things in it. Sexual ideas and sex role concepts result from children's *active structuring of their own experience*, rather than from something directly taught by other people.

The key cognitive event is the categorization of one's self as male or female. Once this recognition of self is acquired, between the ages of one and a half to three, it organizes the way the child perceives and categorizes the rest of the world and his or her place in it. Other people are defined as belonging to one category or the other, male or female, so the child places himself or herself in one of these categories and begins the process of "cognitive rehearsal"—the lifelong accumulation of memories and fantasies in which he or she acts out the appropriate sex role. The little boy will imagine himself as a daddy with a wife and children. A little girl's fantasies of family life will feature her in the role of mother. The learning is gradual and changes with the child's stage of thinking—that is, young children may think that one's sexual identity is something that can change, like one's age.

Kohlberg's research also shows that, contrary to Freud, genital anatomy plays a surprisingly small part in young children's thinking about sex differences. Clothing styles and social role differences, such as the fact that males are more likely than females to be firefighters, are more impressive to childish minds. In general, then, the cognitive-developmental model implies that the development of gender identity is not a unique process determined by sexual drives and identification. Rather, it is part of the basic process of conceptual growth.

Evaluating the Theories

The learning theorists are surely right when they point out that parents and other people exert a great deal of social pressure directly and indirectly to encourage children not only to identify themselves correctly as male and female, but to become sex typed—that is, to adopt the behaviors that our society labels "masculine" or "feminine." From birth on, parents perceive boys and girls differently. One study found that newborn boys (or girls labeled as boys) are seen as strong, alert, and robust, while newborn girls are seen as delicate, pretty, and soft (Rubin, Provenzano, & Luria,

1974). In fact, there are no measurable differences in these attributes.

As boys and girls grow older, parents encourage them to be different in almost every way. Consider, for example, how parents furnish rooms for their sons and daughters, as Rheingold and Cook did (1975). Little girls' rooms contain dolls, dollhouses, doll carriages, housekeeping toys, as well as lace, ruffles, and floral designs. Boys' rooms contain sports equipment, model cars, trucks, and soldiers, and nonfussy decorations. Not all parents encourage children to live up to sex stereotypes, but the traditional ways remain firmly entrenched.

Yet social pressures and reinforcements cannot be the whole explanation of gender identity and sex typing. Much of young children's social behavior occurs without any obvious reinforcement. As we saw in the last chapter, imitation and reinforcement cannot in themselves explain how children acquire language; there is

little evidence that they account for young children's social behavior. Even Bandura recognizes that there is a large cognitive component in the socialization of children.

Since Kohlberg advanced his theory, major aspects of it have been supported by other researchers. Thus, as discussed in an earlier chapter, toddlers and even infants are able to differentiate between males and females, and gender is one of the first categories applied to the categorical self or the "Me" (Lewis & Brooks-Gunn, 1979). Other researchers have shown that nursery school children are more likely to imitate someone when the model's behavior has been labeled as appropriate for their sex (Masters et al., 1979). In other words, children do not blindly imitate behavior produced by models of the same sex.

Neither social learning nor cognitive-developmental theory relies on the most common-sensical explanation of sex role learning—biological inclination. There is some evidence that boys on the whole are more likely to be aggressive, to engage in rough-and-tumble play, and to be concerned with dominance (Maccoby, 1980). But it is hard to separate social experience from biological "presetting," since parents also treat boys and girls differently. Further, there is a great deal of variation *within* each sex, and the two sexes overlap considerably.

The Transsexual Phenomenon

Both the biological and psychological aspects of sex differences are more complicated than is generally recognized. The existence of **transsexuals** is a challenge to both social learning theories of sex identity as well as simple biological explanations. Transsexuals are individuals who are born as normal males and females and who are raised and treated as such. Yet somehow they grow up convinced that their real selves belong to the opposite sex. Feeling like prisoners inside their mismatched bodies, transsexuals often turn to surgery to make their anatomy correspond to their identity. In recent years several such cases have made headlines: a male tennis player who underwent a sex-

change operation stirred up a controversy when "she" tried to enter a women's tennis tournament. Most sex-change operations are done confidentially, however.

Transsexuals should not be confused with transvestites or homosexuals. *Transvestites* merely like to dress in the clothing of the opposite sex (recall Klinger in M*A*S*H, who dressed up as a woman to try to get a discharge from the army on "psychological" grounds). *Homosexuals* do not want to change their gender or dress like the opposite sex; rather they are attracted to members of their own sex. Transsexuals, however, have a core gender identity which is opposed to their biological sex. All of these kinds of "deviant" behaviors conflict with the social learning theories; such behaviors are obviously out of line with, and also highly resistant to, social reinforcement and modeling.

The Case of Jan Morris Although we do not know why transsexuals reject the gender identity assigned to them at birth, we do have some insight into what it is like to grow up believing that one was born into the wrong body. James Morris was a distinguished British newspaperman and writer of nonfiction books before he had a sex change operation at the age of 46 (Figure 9.3). The most prominent person ever to have had such an operation, he seemed a highly unlikely candidate for one. He had climbed Mount Everest, served four years in the army, and had married and become the father of five children. Yet since the age of 3, he had felt that he really was a girl.

Jan Morris told the story of her transformation from James in an extraordinary book, *Conundrum*. It begins with the moment she "knew" she was a girl trapped in a boy's body:

> I was three or perhaps four years old when I realized that I had been born into the wrong body, and should really be a girl. I remember the moment well, and it is the earliest memory of my life.
>
> I was sitting beneath my mother's piano, and her music was falling around me like cataracts, enclosing me as in a cave. . . .

FIGURE 9.3
Transsexuals
James Morris (left) transformed himself into Jan Morris (right) when he was 46 years old because "The machine was wrong."

> What triggered so bizarre a thought I have long forgotten, but the conviction was unfaltering from the start. (1974, p. 1)

For more than forty years after that, Morris lived what was outwardly a man's life, all the while tormented by "the tragic and irrational ambition . . . to escape from maleness into womanhood" (1974, p. 8).

James Morris and other transsexuals illustrate the problematic nature of sexual identity. Maleness and femaleness do not spring automatically from anatomy or hormones: possessing a penis or a vagina does not necessarily make us a man or a woman; nor does being given a sexual label and encouraged to live up to the role. Jan Morris's female identity was clearly her own creation. The rest of us also construct sexual selves through experience and over time, but if the final outcome is in accord with our anatomical equipment, the temptation is to attribute our destiny to biology.

Cognitive theory does not explain why some children do not accept the physical evidence of their own gender. But the existence of transsexuals does support one of Kohlberg's core claims: the importance of self-categorization as a boy or girl as a critical and basic organizer of psychological experience.

Biology and Gender

In recent years, it has become clear that both biological and psychological aspects of sex differences are more complex than had been realized. Most contemporary sex researchers agree that it is important to distinguish between the biological aspects of sexuality and the psychological aspects. "Male" and "female" are the terms used to refer to biological aspects of sex, but "masculinity" and "femininity" are psychological and behavioral characteristics. Figure 9.4 presents these physiological and psychological sex differences.

Masculinity and femininity are not to be confused with **gender identity.** Thus a tomboy is a girl with the traditionally boyish interests in, say, sports, tree climbing, and playing with soldiers, but there is no doubt about what gender she belongs to. A boy may have an interest in the things the culture places in the feminine world but he is still a boy. People may worry about their femininity and masculinity but,

with rare exceptions such as Jan Morris, they have no doubts about their gender identity. Furthermore, there appears to be very little relationship between being worried about one's masculinity or femininity and the actual degree of discrepancy between one's behavior and the cultural standards. Thus a male who seems very "masculine" to other people may have doubts about his masculinity during adolescence, whereas an "effeminate" male may go through life without any such worries at all.

Gender identity and masculinity-femininity are also to be distinguished from the third aspect of psychological sexuality, sex-object preference. Whichever sex a person is aroused by

---

FIGURE 9.4
Male and Female Characteristics

Characteristic	Male	Female	Explanation
Physiological			
Chromosomal composition	XY	XX	At the moment of conception, the sex is determined by whether the father's sperm cell contains an X or a Y chromosome; if it is a Y chromosome, the child will be a boy. But the chromosome pattern is only a "recipe"; the making of a "normal" male or female body is a complex process that sometimes goes awry.
Gonads Hormonal composition	Testicles Androgen, etc.	Ovaries Estrogen, progesterone, etc.	These hormones operate before birth to differentiate male and female fetuses and again at adolescence to produce secondary sex characteristics: deep voices, beards, and body hair in men; breasts and menstruation in women. If too much or too little of these hormones is produced, "female" fetuses can be born with masculine-looking genitals and vice versa for males.
Internal accessory organs	Seminal vesicles, prostate gland	Vagina, uterus, fallopian tubes	
External genitalia	Penis, testicles	Vulva	
Psychological			
Gender identity	I am a male	I am a female	This is the basic sense of one's social identity as male or female.
Sex typing	I am a masculine or effeminate male	I am a feminine or mannish woman	Typing refers to a person's conformity to the sex role standards of the particular culture; it involves certain interests, attitudes, fantasies, ways of moving and speaking. These vary from one culture to another.
Sex object preference			Preference is demonstrated by whether one is sexually aroused by members of one's own sex or the opposite sex.

is independent of gender identity and masculinity-femininity. Homosexuals are not confused about their gender identity. Nor do homosexual men and women necessarily differ from their "straight" counterparts in masculinity and femininity. Some homosexual men view themselves as masculine and take the masculine role in sexual encounters. Others view themselves as feminine and take the feminine role; whereas still others see their masculinity as independent of homosexual roles (Hooker, 1965).

Body, Mind, and Gender

Some of the most dramatic evidence for the ambiguity of sexuality has emerged from studies of "sex errors of the body": people born with physical characteristics of both sexes. Studies of such people, generally referred to as *hermaphrodites* or intersexed individuals, have provided new insights into the development and patterning of sexuality. Certain tests now make it possible to tell whether the child is "really" male or female—that is, whether the chromosomes are male or female in pattern. Previously, the doctor simply had to guess. Sometimes it was later discovered that children had been assigned to the wrong sex. In such cases the child might be reassigned to the appropriate gender.

John Money (1961) undertook a series of studies of children and adults who had sexual abnormalities of one kind or another. The most striking discovery of this research was the finding that children with the same anatomical structures could be assigned to either sex and grow up to be a psychologically "normal" member of that sex. These researchers argued that the biological aspects of sexuality are independent of the psychological aspects—that is, the sex category to which one is assigned at birth and reared in, one's own sense of gender identity, and one's preference in sex objects. Thus, not only can intersexed or hermaphroditic children be raised successfully as a member of either sex, but children relegated to the

wrong category can grow up to be psychologically normal members of the sex to which they were erroneously assigned.

Money originally concluded that every child is "psychosexually neutral" at birth. In his more recent research, however, he has moved away from the concept of complete psychosexual neutrality. One study (Money & Ehrhardt, 1972) examined a group of genetic females who had been born with enlarged male-appearing genitalia because their mothers had taken male hormones to avert miscarriage. After corrective surgery they were raised as girls. When interviewed during childhood and adolescence, these girls considered themselves female, but they were "tomboyish" girls—preferring activities like sports and games to more "feminine" pursuits such as playing with dolls. Money and Ehrhardt speculated that this "tomboyism" might be due to the masculinizing effects of prenatal hormones.

But there are many methodological problems with this study. For example, the parents knew that these girls had been masculinized in the womb and born with genital abnormalities. This knowledge might have affected how the girls had been raised. Although Money and Ehrhardt acknowledge that prenatal hormone levels may influence behavior to some degree, they do not believe that sex role differences are determined in a simple and direct way by biological forces. They argue that while sex typed traits such as tomboyism may be influenced by sex hormones, gender identity arises mainly from social experience (1975).

They describe a particularly dramatic case that shows how the gender label a child is given can override even normal anatomy and hormones. The story begins with the birth of identical twin boys. At the age of seven months, during a routine circumcision by electrocautery, one of the boys had his penis burned off. After some months of agonizing, the parents agreed to transform the little boy surgically into a little girl and raise her accordingly. By the age of four and a half, the little girl was a model of traditional femininity, in dress, interests, and activities.

Because such mistakes of nature—or, in this

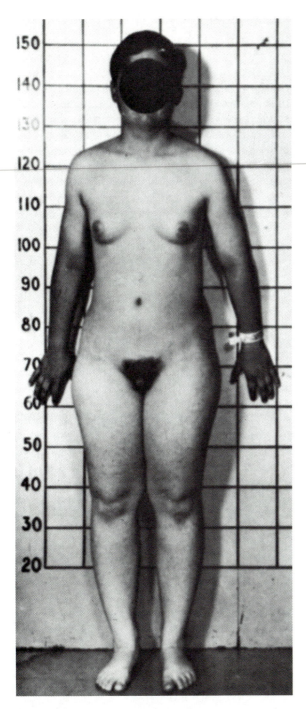

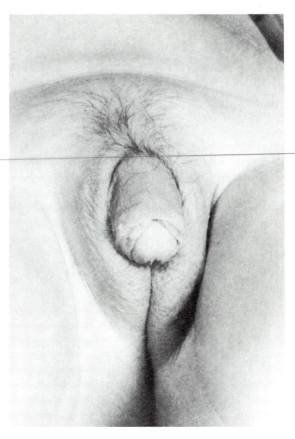

The ambiguity of hermaphroditism. The girl, *left*, underwent surgical feminization of her genitals after this picture was taken. The photo, *right*, shows how difficult it is to tell the sex of the child strictly upon visual examination.

case, medicine—are so rare, we assume that gender identity is a natural unfolding of innate biological inclinations. But the psychosexual neutrality concept argues that we assign children to one sex or the other on the basis of their anatomy and then believe that the psychological aspects of sexuality are caused by anatomy and physiology.

The child does not, however, remain psychosexually neutral for long; once the child has established a gender identity (during the period of language mastery from one and a half to three), it seems to be irreversible. Before that age a child can be reassigned to the other sex; after that age it becomes much more difficult. Thus, Money's work also provides strong support for Kohlberg's view of gender identity as a basic organizer of experience. Money compares the process to "imprinting" in birds. Recall from Chapter 2 that in certain species of birds there is a critical period during which a young bird will follow any moving object it sees, and later will try to mate only with something that resembles the "imprinted" object. Usually the baby bird sees its mother during the critical period. Experiments carried out by Lorenz and others, however, show that the baby birds can become imprinted on humans or vacuum cleaners or any moving object. Money suggests that sexual imprinting is something like that in humans. Kohlberg warns, however, that the notion of imprinting is only a metaphor in human sexuality. He argues that early sexual identities are difficult to reverse later because they are basic to other learning. They constitute the cognitive categories around which experience and memory have been organized, and any such categories learned early in life are hard to reverse.

The Oedipus Complex Revisited

Although the social learning and cognitive theorists have offered alternatives to Freud's account of gender identity, they have not dealt with the emotional conflicts Freud described in his account of the Oedipus complex. Recently, Kurt Fisher and Malcolm Watson (1981) have offered a cognitive interpretation of the Oedipus complex. They argue that these conflicts emerge and are then resolved as a result of the child's developing understanding of social roles in the nuclear family. These changes in understanding are not based on cool, analytic thinking but rather are intimately tied to strong emotions and interaction in the family.

The framework of this explanation is provided by Fisher's (1980) theory that cognitive development is the growth of hierarchies of mental skills. The skill learned in the Oedipus complex is the ability to understand and form mental representations of social roles (Watson, 1981). At age two or three, children's understanding of social roles is limited. They know their own gender, and they can assign people to the categories of girl, boy, Mommy, Daddy, and sometimes man and woman. But they have difficulty *relating* social roles and categories to one another; girls and boys of two or three do not yet understand they will be women and men when they grow up. Also at this age children do not grasp the meaning of the terms *husband* and *wife*. The child's awareness of single aspects of social roles sets the stage for the eventual emergence of the Oedipal conflict.

When children learn to relate one social role to another, they come to understand that boys will be men, girls will be women, husbands are married to wives and wives to husbands, and that men are the opposite sex of women. In general, children become aware that each social role is defined by its relationship to the complementary or opposite role. But children's grasp of social roles and categories at this age is still limited and confused, and it is these confusions, according to Fisher and Malcolm, that lead to the Oedipal conflict. The roles of parents and children in family involve both age and gender. In the Oedipus complex, the child focuses on gender but ignores the dimension of age. Thus, the child places him- or herself in the same category as the parent of the opposite sex. With age left out, the boy can substitute for Daddy, the girl for Mommy; children at this stage do not yet understand age change. They know that children grow up, but they do not realize that adults grow older at the same time. Confusion about age is illustrated in the following dialogue between a mother and her five-year-old son:

Billy: Mommy, I'm gonna marry you.
Mother: But, Billy, you can't marry me. You're not old enough.
Billy: Then I'll wait till I grow up, like Daddy.
Mother: But when you're grown up, I'll be as old as Grandma.
Billy: Really?
Mother: Yes, you'll be a young man and I'll be an old woman.
Billy: Well, I'll just wait till I'm old as Grandpa. Then I'll marry you. (Fisher & Watson, 1981)

The Oedipus conflict is resolved when the child reaches the next level of understanding

A Day in the Lives of Four Young Children

Nitsan Four-and-a-half-year-old Nitsan lives on a kibbutz outside Jerusalem. Following the traditional kibbutz childrearing pattern, she sleeps, eats, and goes to school with a group of other children, but sees her own family every day. She has four brothers and is the next to youngest child.

Nitsan's bedroom, which she shares with two other children.

Nitsan washing up in the morning. Each of the towels belongs to one of the other children she lives with.

Waiting for her parents to pick her up at the end of the school day.

Eating breakfast.

At home with the family. She spends a few hours at home every day, then returns to the dormitory to sleep.

Petra Petra is a five-year-old from Austin, Texas. She lives in a motel room with her brother, sister, and mother, who is divorced, on welfare, and employed as a housecleaner. Petra attends a Head Start school.

Portrait of Petra

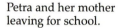

Petra and her mother leaving for school.

Petra and sister waiting to go to school.

Eating breakfast at school.

A make-believe tea party.

be more concerned about the masculinity of their sons and the femininity of their daughters. This encouragement does not just take the form of reinforcing appropriate behavior. Fathers of little girls seem to enjoy flirting with them and viewing them as coy and sexy (Chodorow, 1978). A review of this literature concluded that:

> Fathers appear to want their daughters to fit the image of a sexually attractive female person, within the limits of what is appropriate for a child, and they play the masculine role vis-à-vis their daughters as well as their wives. This may or may not generate rivalry between mother and daughter, but there can be little doubt that it is a potent force in the girl's development of whatever behavior is defined as "feminine" by her father. (Maccoby & Jacklin, 1974, p. 379)

The Development of Conscience and Ideals

As we saw earlier, Freud explained the development of moral standards and ideals as part of the resolution of the Oedipus complex. The child identifies with the parent of the same sex and "internalizes" a copy of that parent's moral standards and ideals. Developmental research, however, has not supported Freud's idea that adult standards are swallowed in one big gulp at the age of six or so. Researchers in both the learning theory and cognitive-developmental tradition view the child's acquisition of morals and ideals as a gradual process. Children grow up among adults who organize their lives around systems of social rules, as well as language, logic, and aesthetics. Adults may not always follow the rules they honor, and indeed may not even be able to state them explicitly. But from a very early age children spend a great deal of time observing adults and trying to figure out the rules implicit in their behavior. The end result is usually not simply a carbon copy of the parents' rules and standards. As Roger Brown points out,

> This process is not a simple "passing over" of the systems from one generation to another. What each child extracts at a given age is a function of his idiosyncratic experience and his present intellectual capacities. The systems governing the child change as he grows older and they need not in the end simply reproduce the rules that prevail in his society. The outcome can be unique and is sometimes revolutionary. (1965, p. 195)

In essence, Freud's concept of the superego refers to the capacity to think about one's own behavior and judge it according to community standards. It is literally an "over-I," a part of the self that observes the self. This capacity for self-awareness and self-criticism also develops much earlier than Freud had assumed. Jerome Kagan's research (1981), as cited in Chapter 7, showed that as early as the second year children come to be concerned with standards involving both a goodness-badness dimension and a success-failure dimension. Thus, toddlers are alert to "discrepant" events that have met with adult approval or displeasure. Such events have to do with dirt, the destruction of property, and harming others. All children experience parental disapproval over such things as rubbing dirty hands on a wall, spilling a glass of milk, breaking a dish, hitting, or taking a toy away from another child. Such experiences seem to create a sensitivity to all events that violate adult norms. Eventually children learn to apply the words "good" and "bad" to such events.

Also during the second year children come to be concerned about their own success and failure at achieving certain goals. Children smile when they accomplish some play task such as putting a final piece in a jigsaw puzzle, or putting the top block on a tower. They also may cry if they are unable to complete some task they have set for themselves. Mastery standards are different from normative ones because they are not as tied to the parents' expressions of disapproval. Yet children feel they should attain such goals. As Kagan points out, his research seems to have rediscovered and is able to consider several aspects of social roles at the same time. The confusions then disappear. For example, children come to understand that, as they grow older, the parents also age. Being able now to deal with both age and sex at the same time, children realize that they are not in the same social category as the parent of the same sex: little girls are female children, Mommies are female parents; little boys are male children, Daddies are male parents.

Children at this level of understanding are also more realistic about the social implications of Oedipal ideas. They realize the impossibility of replacing the parent of the opposite sex and the emotional losses that would follow if they could. They also recognize that people do not choose marriage partners from their own immediate families, and that they usually choose partners around their own age. In general, then, children come to understand the system of social relationships in the family.

Evaluation

This interpretation of the Oedipus conflict has much to recommend it. It explains the conflict as a part of a general process of psychological development rather than a unique series of psychological happenings triggered by sexual instincts. Also, unlike Freud's account, it explains girls' Oedipal conflicts as well as boys'.

The Fisher-Watson interpretation can also handle variations in social development much better than Freud's version. It does not assume that the Oedipus conflict is universal. Rather, Fisher and Watson argue, it occurs mainly in cultures that raise children in nuclear families. They do suggest that some sort of emotion-laden confusion exists about social roles in family and social systems. Every child who grows up will first be ignorant about social roles and relationships, then will understand them in confused ways, and finally will develop a clear grasp of them. During the period of misunderstanding, the child's confusions are likely to have an important impact on his or her emotional life.

The theory also allows for variations between families in the same culture. Children in different kinds of families are likely to experience different forms of cognitive confusion and emotional turmoil. In some families, the parent of the opposite sex encourages the child to develop a close, almost romantic relationship; in others the child is particularly close to the parent of the same sex, while in still other families the child may have strong emotional relationships with sisters, brothers, aunts, uncles, or other family members besides the parents.

Neither Freud nor the cognitive explanation of the Oedipal conflict assigns the parents themselves a central role in the process. For Freud, the Oedipal conflict is triggered by the child's sexual urges. The cognitive theory assigns a central role to the child's developing understanding of social roles. Both of these explanations may underestimate the parents' impact in encouraging their children toward sex-typing and heterosexuality. A number of studies have found that fathers are very active in sex-typing their children. Mothers may view their sons as "little men," but in general they focus less on the gender of their children than the father does (Johnson, 1963). Fathers tend to

Megan Megan is a three-and-a-half-year-old child with cerebral palsy. She lives with her parents and nine-year-old sister in the suburbs of New York. Until recently, she was immobilized by her disability. Now she is learning how to use crutches. Megan attends a school for handicapped children which provides physical therapy as part of the curriculum.

Megan being carried onto the school bus. Before she got her crutches, she had to be carried everywhere.

Megan's mother helps her dress.

Megan receiving physical therapy at school.

Megan having lunch at school.

Being greeted by her mother and sister after returning from school.

A joyful Megan on crutches, which have liberated her from immobility.

Spencer Five-and-a-half-year-old Spencer lives in an affluent middle-class suburb with his parents and two brothers. He is the middle child.

Waking up

Walking to school with his mother.

At school

Having dinner at home.

that violate social conventions, such as school rules and table manners. For example, preschool children, when questioned about moral transgressions such as hitting someone or taking someone's possessions, said such acts would be wrong even if there were no rules against them. But when asked about violations of conventional rules such as being noisy, the children said such behavior would be all right if there were no rule against it.

Far from being the savage little beast of Freudian theory, the child emerging from infancy soon develops an intuitive understanding of morality and other social standards. Of course children are "naturally" aggressive and sexual. But morality is "natural" also. Children at this age often do display a noticeable interest in sexual matters—it is the age of "playing doctor," of "show me," the discovery of sexual arousal and masturbation. It is easy to see how this dawning sexual interest can collide with strong parental disapproval and even disgust to produce guilt and anxiety in the child and sexual inhibitions in later life. But it is unlikely that the whole of a child's emotional and moral development depends on sexual matters.

Freud considered the psychological events of the Oedipal period as a result of biological maturation—the emergence of genital sexuality. He said nothing about another form of biological maturation—the development of the brain. Yet it is increasingly evident that brain changes in the first two years are associated with the emergence of complex ways of responding (see Chapter 5). The period between 15 and 24 months, when self-awareness and sensitivity to standards emerge, coincides with a major period of critical maturation (Rabinowicz, 1979).

The young child's sensitivity to norms and standards may well have arisen in the course of evolution, as Kagan (1981) suggests, as a curb on aggressive inclinations. Whatever the origin of these early intimations of morality, it seems as if the basic conflict Freud saw between instinct and civilization is really a conflict between two sides of human nature itself. Current research in young children's social understanding is oddly reminiscent of certain turn-of-the-century writers who suggested that

the two components of Freud's superego: concern with community norms and with values that define the ego ideal. "We did not have that distinction in mind as we studied the children's behaviors," he writes, "but the data invited the distinction" (1981, p. 127).

In general, then, it seems clear that children begin to acquire what Freud called the superego long before the time he postulated as the Oedipal period. By the time children reach that age, they already have begun to make complex judgments about morality and social convention. Elliot Turiel (1983) found that children as young as three can differentiate between events that violate moral standards and those children have an innate disposition to be moral. Two writers of that time argued:

> Moral ideas do not require to be created or implanted in the minds of children by their elders. Nothing is more certain than the child is born potentially a moral being, possessing a moral nature which requires only to be evoked and developed by environmental conditions. . . . If no amount of training can make a moral being out of a dog, it is because he possesses no moral nature to begin with. (Tracy & Stimpfl, 1909, cited in Kagan, 1981, p. 125)

Young Children and the "Facts of Life"

In addition to discovering the moral and other standards of the community, young children also confront for the first time other complicated and disturbing aspects of life. Both Freud and Piaget agreed that little children are often concerned with certain emotionally arousing themes that appear in play and dreams. These themes may relate to the body (eating, sucking, defecation and urination, and bodily damage), may be elementary family feelings (love, anger, jealousy), or may be questions and concerns about birth (where babies come from, how birth takes place). Sooner or later the question of beginnings leads to the question of endings—of death.

It seems likely that at least some of this preoccupation occurs because the young child emerges from babyhood knowing nothing about the facts of life and death, and must come to grips with mysterious and often frightening realities. Consider for a moment what it would be like to learn about death for the first time, that everyone you know, everyone in the whole world, including yourself, will some day be dead—buried in the ground, to remain there forever. It is little wonder that it takes a long time for children to absorb this reality. When my older son was 4 he was fascinated by cemeteries. He knew that everyone dies, but he believed that after people were buried they turned into little seeds that eventually grow into babies. My younger son later came to a similar conclusion at the same age. Only after the age of 9 do most children accept the fact that death is universal, but the concept that death is irreversible is still uncertain for 10-year-olds (Childers & Wimmer, 1971).

Thus, no sooner are they past babyhood than children confront the dilemmas of human existence that have perplexed philosophers and theologians for centuries. As Ernest Becker once wondered, why is it that most people do not go insane in the face of the contradiction between being, on the one hand, a self and mind that can speculate about atoms and infinity, and on the other hand, a body that "aches and bleeds and will decay and die"? (1973, p. 26).

There are other lessons to be learned about the body in early childhood. Toilet training, for example, involves not only a battle of wills, of learning to conform to rules that must seem at first arbitrary and artificial. It also means discovering that the natural substances one's body produces every day are disgusting to other people, and learning to feel this disgust oneself.

Where Do Babies Come From?

Of all the facts of life and death the young child must come to grips with, the most complicated is the origin of babies. The problem is that, as Selma Fraiberg (1959) points out, the truth is more fantastic than the child's own theories. It seems preposterous that a human being could start out as a tiny egg or seed no bigger than a pencil dot, that a whole live baby could be contained in a woman's belly, or once inside could find a way out. The father's role in all of this and the nature of sexual intercourse are additional mysteries. A study by Bernstein and Cowan (1975) compared children's understanding of where babies come from with several Piaget-type tasks. These authors found that while children's concepts of the origin of babies followed a developmental sequence, it was the most difficult of the four tasks presented to the children.

The facts are so strange and complicated that accurate information is often misinterpreted. For example, books about reproduction may, in the process of trying to explain things to children, lead them into erroneous ideas. Bernstein and Cowan give the example of a little girl who thought babies came from ducks. Her mother had given her a book which started out by describing how various animals mate and give birth, and then worked up to people. The little girl concluded that the ducks pictured earlier in the book turned into the babies portrayed later.

Fraiberg (1959) gives a similar example. A little boy of six believed that the doctor has to operate on the father to "get the seed out" and plant it in the mother. He believed that the operation was necessary because the seed was big, about the size of a marble. It turned out that he had seen an enlarged photograph of a sperm under high-powered magnification. A sperm the size of a marble seemed more plausible to him than one that was so tiny as to be invisible.

The issue of identity figures in all of this as children come to grips not only with their own origins, but their own future role in the process of making babies. The discovery that there are two sexes means that feelings, interests, and identity must be channeled in one direction to fit the roles as the child perceives them. The realization that children cannot grow up to marry their Mommy or Daddy means that young children, at the height of awareness of their own dependence and vulnerability, must face the realization that someday they must leave home. In view of all this hard knowledge, it is perhaps not surprising that most peoples have believed in a myth of a lost paradise, a time of innocence with no knowledge of shame, sex, or death.

Child's Play

Another reason early childhood may seem to adults to be a sunny and uncomplicated time of life is that young children spend so much time at play. Play is one of those everyday terms that seems to defy efforts to define it clearly. One five-year-old girl defined play as "fun stuff that kids do 'cause they like to do it" (Rubin, 1980, p. viii), and her definition will stand comparison with those of the experts. There are so many different kinds of play, and so many different definitions, it seems clear that the concept includes several aspects that may or may not be present in any particular episode of play: enjoyment, voluntariness, no practical aim, a make-believe alteration of reality (Sutton-Smith, 1980).

Within the general category of play, most scholars recognize several varieties: sensorimotor or exercise play, such as a child banging a rattle; play with body movements, such as jumping up and down or rough-and-tumble; play with language, such as making up nonsense rhymes; dramatic play, where children are assigned make-believe roles and identities; games with rules, such as marbles or baseball (Garvey, 1977). The origins and functions of play have been explained in various ways (Rubin, Fein, & Vandenberg, 1983). Earlier scholars viewed play in evolutionary or biological terms. Karl Groos (1901) believed that the play of children and the frolicking and mock fighting of young animals are an instinctively based preparation for adult life. Herbert Spencer (1873) argued for a "surplus energy" explanation of play: he believed that energy builds up in the body to fuel survival efforts, such as hunting and fighting. If survival demands are not made, this energy is released in play. G. Stanley Hall proposed that children's play "recapitulates" the history of the human race. Thus, infancy corresponds to the animal stage of the human species when it was still using four legs. Early childhood recapitulates the prehistoric era of hunting and fishing. Between 8 and 12, the child reenacts the "humdrum life of savagery" before the higher human traits emerged. Finally, adolescence is a turbulent transitional stage when the higher levels of civilization were reached. In fact, as noted earlier, Hall's ideas influenced the founding of the Boy Scouts. Scouting was thought to satisfy the various prehistoric instincts of young boys. Hall's ideas sound silly to us today, yet they seemed reasonable to his contemporaries and may be no more farfetched than current speculations about the origins of human behavior.

Although the playfulness of children seems to be a universal trait, found in all times and places, there has been great variation in the patterning of children's play. In twentieth-century America, play is defined as what children do, and work as what adults do. This sharp segregation of child and adult roles is found only in advanced industrial societies. In most times and places, children past infancy become participants in adult work. When work goes on in the family, and when families make rather than buy most of the necessities of life, there is plenty of work for even young hands to do. Children start off with simple tasks, such as gathering wood or feeding farm animals. As they grow older, their responsibilities gradually increase. In these circumstances children still play in between tasks, or sometimes the work itself becomes a form of play, as in the case of children in hunting societies.

If there was no separate world of childhood in preindustrial society, however, neither was there a separate serious adult world. For example, in Western society in past centuries, adults and children shared in the same games and stories. Hide and seek, blind man's bluff, and fairy tales were entertainments for all ages, not just children (Plumb, 1972).

In short, compared to people in other eras and cultures, contemporary American middle-class parents are unusual in expecting little from their children in the way of help with adult work. On the other hand, they make other demands on their children—to be independent, to be interested in achievement, and also to amuse themselves. Anthropologists who have studied childrearing in other cultures have been struck by the way young American children are *obliged* to play, to have fun (Goodman, 1970).

Even closely related cultures may vary widely in how they conceive of young children and their play. For example, some European countries have a more "serious" view of childhood than America. Martha Wolfenstein (1955) has pointed to some striking contrasts between French and American attitudes toward childhood. The French see the enjoyment of life as the right of adults, while childhood is a time of hard preparation. Everything children do must serve a useful purpose and not just be amusing. Further, French children are expected to be much more restrained in their behavior than their American counterparts. When preschool children go to the park with their parents, they are expected to sit quietly on the bench, or to squat at their parents' feet; they are not to run around, play with other children, or get dirty.

Becoming Social

Whichever way we choose to define play, one of its main functions in the lives of young children is to bring them together, to interact with one another. During the preschool years, children begin a lifelong career of dealing with peers in a wide range of social situations. Many of the skills older children and adults need to manage social interactions and relationships come into play at this early stage: communicating clearly, engaging others in conversation and activity, gaining entry into groups, making friends, managing conflicts, learning how to be tactful and supportive but also assertive when the need arises. Early play relationships give children a chance to learn and practice these skills. At the same time, young children also reveal marked differences in the level of their social skills.

In a study of children's friendships, Zick Rubin (1980) observed two bright, alert three-year-olds who attended the same nursery school every morning. Ricky entered the class

several weeks late, but quickly made friends and went on to become the most popular boy in the class. Danny was there from the beginning but never got the hang of how to get other children to play with him, or even pay attention to him. Nothing that Rubin could find about the boys seemed to explain why they differed so much in their social skills.

In general, however, researchers have learned a great deal about patterns of social interaction among children. For several decades children's friendships were a neglected topic, probably because the child's relationship with parents, particularly the mother, was seen as the most important influence in the child's life. Now the development of peer relationships from infancy on is being observed and analyzed, aided by the technology of videotaping.

Several researchers have examined the very beginnings of peer interaction in toddlers from ages one to two (Mueller & Lucas, 1975). These studies have shown that when toddlers come together, even if they have not met before, they are likely to make social overtures to one another. They are more likely to smile, exchange toys, imitate one another, and coordinate their play than to fight, cry, or take toys from one another. Among toddlers, objects play an important role in launching social interaction. Adults who want to meet new people are sometimes advised to walk around with an interesting object. Toys bring toddlers into contact by focusing their attention and requiring them to coordinate their behavior, allowing them to show, give, and take. However, toys are not essential for toddler interaction. Children do manage to touch, smile, and imitate one another without them, and toys can sometimes distract toddlers from interacting with one another.

By preschool age, from two to five, patterns of play become more complicated. The classic study of preschool play was carried out by Mildred Parten in the 1920s (Parten, 1932). She identified five ways young children play in the company of other children:

1. *Solitary play*—The child plays alone, paying no attention to other children.
2. *Onlooker play*—The child remains on the sidelines, watching other children play.
3. *Parallel play*—Children play next to one another, but don't interact.
4. *Associative play*—The child plays with another child; each one has his or her own goal.
5. *Cooperative play*—Children play together, sharing a common goal. They help each other and take turns.

Solitary and onlooker play are common at age two; as children reach four and five, associative and cooperative play become more frequent. Parten's classifications have held up reasonably well in later studies (Rubin, Maioni, & Hornung, 1976). However, recent research has shown that the proportion of different types of play varies with children's experience. Today children are more likely to have had group experience at an earlier age than those in past generations. By the time many children are three, they are already involved in a good deal of associative and even cooperative play.

Symbolic Play and Its Functions

Whether children play alone or with others, symbolic or make-believe play is the characteristic form of play in the preschool years. Its onset marks the transition between infancy and early childhood, and its decline marks the child's entrance into the next stage of life. In between, it is an activity that most young children engage in much of the time.

In the course of the preschool years, fantasy play becomes increasingly detached from the actual stimulus situation, as well as more complex and social. Thus, the earliest form of symbolic play appears at about one year; the child uses actual objects in a make-believe way: pretending to drink out of an empty cup, or pretending to go to sleep on a pillow. Later, symbolic play comes to include imaginary others; the child pretends to feed a doll, put it to bed. Also, objects are used in a nonliteral fashion. A stick can be a horse, a box, a car. Between three and five, play becomes sociodramatic, involving other children, complicated systems of roles, and extended plots sometimes lasting as long as a half-hour or forty-five minutes. Then, when children are at the height of their talents for pretend play, it gradually declines, to be replaced by games with rules (Rubin, Fein, & Vandenberg, 1983).

Within the field of psychology, ideas about the functions and value of symbolic play have varied. Piaget thought that while manipulating objects and playing games with rules contribute to cognitive development, symbolic play is an egocentric activity. He regarded symbolic play as "pure" assimilation, an activity that shapes reality to the child's wishes rather than an adaptation to reality. Such play reflects the young child's ability to make and use symbols; it may consolidate the child's cognitive skills, but it does not advance the development of logical thinking. However, Piaget believed that symbolic play does have a vital function in the child's emotional life. He is in striking agreement with psychiatrists and clinical psychologists who feel that in their make-believe play, children express their worries and fears and try to deal with them.

In recent years, several researchers have argued that symbolic play is not just expressive, but also contributes to intellectual development (Rubin, Fein, & Vandenberg, 1983). These researchers argue that symbolic play helps the child in the tasks of role playing, decentering, and reversibility. In make-believe play, the child transforms the identity of objects and the self, while at the same time keeping track of the original identity and function. Thus, a child can play at being Batman or Superman, and know he is still himself and he cannot really fly (although some children do get carried away in their pretend play). Similarly, the child does not believe that making cookies out of clay transforms the clay into something sweet and edible. The ability to switch back and forth between make-believe and reality is a kind of reversibility of thought—the very skill which Piaget emphasized as a key to further intellectual development. A study by Golomb and Cornelius (1977) found support for the hypothesis that practice in pretend play advances cognitive development, specifically children's performance on the conservation task involving liquids (see Chapter 10, pp. 358–59). Other studies have also found evidence that symbolic play has a cognitive function (Singer, 1973; Smilansky, 1968).

Education and Play

Disagreements about the value of play are not just abstract, theoretical issues; they have important implications for how preschools should be run. Traditionally, nursery schools have been play schools—they have encouraged free play, fantasy activities. At the same time, there have always been some who considered the "fun and games" approach of the traditional nursery school a waste of time. In past centuries, some parents and even some school systems began formal instruction in reading, writing, arithmetic, foreign language, and music during early childhood. For example, some nineteenth-century Massachusetts schools started instruction at age three (Kaestle & Vinovskis, 1978).

In a review of evidence on the effects of instruction, William Fowler (1962) has argued that very young children are capable of absorbing such instruction without any harmful side effects. He disputes the notion that young children are egocentric, fragile, and at the mercy of their emotional life. Maria Montessori (1973), an influential theorist of early childhood education who lived at the turn of the century, advanced a similar view. She disapproved of the free play approach of the traditional nursery school and believed that young children could learn reading, writing, and arithmetic very early. But she argued that this should not be done through formal instruction. Instead, she promoted the use of special educational toys and games that would be intrinsically appealing to children. Objects such as sandpaper alphabet letters or sets of colored rods representing numbers would teach the child basic concepts through sensory exercises and practical experience.

During the 1960s, there was a great revival of interest in Montessori's approach as well as other methods of skill training in early childhood. There was great public concern with speeding up the process of education. Making American kids smarter sooner was a way of competing with the Russians after they moved ahead of us in their space program. Also, at that time, preschools became a weapon in the war against poverty. Psychologists such as Benjamin Bloom (1964) and J. McV. Hunt (1961), argued that most of a child's intellectual development takes place in the preschool years, and that IQ is modifiable early in life, but becomes hard to change later.

Since that time, there has been great skepticism about the possibility of doing away with a whole system of inequality by adding a couple of years of preschool education. There has also been a growing skepticism as to whether raising IQ should be a major goal of early education, if indeed it ever was. We will discuss IQ tests in more detail in a later chapter.

In any event, disillusionment with skill-oriented approaches has led to a revival of interest in play. Further, the interest in children's play is part of a wider concern with the study

of symbolic processes in general. There is a growing recognition that symbols play a central role in emotional, cognitive, and social functioning. The results of a growing number of empirical studies (see Rubin, 1980) suggest that play, including the fantasy play of the preschool child, serves many functions: it reflects and advances children's understanding of role-taking and other cognitive skills, as well as expressing emotions and private experience. Further, the play of young children is more social and rule governed than Piaget had assumed (Garvey, 1974).

The Stream of Consciousness

Although symbolic play drops out of children's observable behavior after a certain age, it does not disappear completely. Rather, it goes underground to become part of the stream of daydreams and fantasies that flow through our minds when we are not concentrating on solving mental problems. Or as Piaget put it, all imaginative thoughts are "interiorized play." The characters and scenes that the young child acts out become the daydreams of the older child and the adult. In recent years, researchers have documented the fact that most people daydream every day. Daydreams vary from simple wishful images of beaches in Hawaii, heroic feats, or erotic encounters with movie stars to the more elaborate fantasies that made up "the secret life of Walter Mitty" in a story of that name by James Thurber. Some daydreams may be the forerunners of plans for actual behavior; some people turn their daydreams into stories, novels, and poems.

Although it is only in recent years that researchers have been studying fantasy and daydreams, the insight that there are two kinds of thinking goes back to Freud. Freud labeled as *secondary process* the kind of thought that is orderly, logical, realistic, and aimed at solving problems and making decisions. He labeled as *primary process* thought that is dreamlike, illogical, and based on emotionally arousing images whose meanings are unconscious. He believed

that there is a developmental progression from primary to secondary process thinking—that primary process thought is characteristic of infancy, as well as of dreams and mental illness in adults.

Piaget revised Freud's notions about primary process thought in the light of his own theories and empirical observations, and his interpretations are now widely accepted by contemporary psychoanalytic theorists (Gill, 1967; Holt, 1977). As we saw earlier, Piaget argued that when symbolic thought arises at the end of infancy, it makes possible two kinds of symbols, individual and social. The social type of symbol is typified in language. It consists of a set of arbitrary sounds with a socially agreed-upon meaning. For example, the word "dog" has no resemblance to a dog, but because it has a standardized meaning, people can use the word to communicate about dogs. By contrast, the individual symbol has a private meaning to the child. An individual symbol usually resembles the object in some way, even if only to the person whose symbol it is.

At first, when children begin to use symbols, all symbols are individual. Before children learn to use words the way adults do, as symbols referring to particular things, actions, and concepts, they use them in an idiosyncratic way—much like Humpty Dumpty in *Alice in Wonderland* who said his words could mean anything he wanted them to mean. Even after the child has become a speaker, there is a need for the more personal, emotional kind of symbolism: Piaget argued there are two basic reasons why the collective sign system of language needs to be complemented by a system of private images and symbols long after early childhood (Piaget & Inhelder, 1969). For one thing, language is not able to capture all aspects of experience—even the best writers cannot completely recreate in words any particular event or experience. In contrast to the idea some psychologists have advanced that thought is simply inner speech, Piaget argued that we experience, remember, and think in the form of images; we think in words only some of the time, particularly when we want to communicate with others.

Recent research into the stream of consciousness confirms this notion that we are constantly having private thoughts and fantasies even when we are engaged in ordinary activities or trying to solve cognitive tasks (Singer, 1978). Even abstract, strictly defined symbols, such as mathematical concepts, are accompanied by personal images. Such fantasies help us cope with unfinished emotional business, plan our behavior, and think through alternatives before acting on them. In short, though in the course of development our thinking becomes ever more directed by abstraction and logic, ever more shaped by the rules of social life, an underground stream of personal symbols based on our own unique experience persists.

Imagery and fantasy mean we are never completely socialized: whatever the external situation, in our minds we can be elsewhere, in a private world. I would like to conclude this chapter with a quotation from A. A. Milne, author of *Winnie the Pooh*, which is a marvelous recreation of some of the modes of thought of preschool children. In the following excerpt taken from his autobiography, he describes how he and his brother created their own private symbol which enabled them to escape, at least mentally, the stuffy, formal adult world in which they found themselves.

When they were four and five, Milne and his brother Ken caught a toad and killed it. They were not ashamed of this act, but regarded it as a significant and bloody ritual that somehow united them into a secret society of two. They devised a secret code so they could talk about it. Starting from the initials R. T., standing for Raw Toad, they ran through English, Latin, and Greek (classical education started early for children in that class and time) to reach the final code, FN:

> Thumbs on the same hymn book in Dr. Gibson's church, we would whisper "FN" to each other and know that life was not all Sunday; side by side in drawing room, hair newly brushed for visitors and in those damnable starched sailor suits, we would look FN at each other and be comforted. And though, within six months sharing some entirely different secret, yet forty years later, the magic letters had power to raise sudden memories in two middle-aged men, smoking their pipes, and wondering what to do with their sons. (1939, p. 65)

SUMMARY

1. Early childhood, the years between two and six, is the time during which the child learns to use symbols and begins to understand society. Thus, children learn the concepts, categories, and standards important to the adults around them.

2. Until recently, many developmental researchers believed that the thought processes of preschool children were qualitatively different from older children—in other words, that early childhood was a distinct stage of development with its own form of logic. More recent research suggests that while young children have certain limitations, their thought processes are not as different as previously believed.

3. Among the major developmental milestones of early childhood is the acquisition of gender identity, a conscience, and a set of ideals for the self. Several different theories have been advanced to explain these changes. Freudian theory argues that the resolution of the Oedipus complex leads the child to identify with the parent of the same sex. Social learning theory claims that children learn about sex roles and other social standards through imitation and reinforcement. Cognitive-development theorists argue that children first learn what gender they belong to, then imitate the parent of the same sex and

other role models. In general, the evidence indicates that gender identity is the organizer of sex role learning, but that children also learn through reinforcement. However, the existence of sexual deviants such as transsexuals suggests that sexual development is complicated and sometimes resistant to social pressure.

4. Piaget viewed young children as prelogical and egocentric. Egocentrism to Piaget is not selfishness, but the inability to understand a point of view other than one's own. Later, Piaget described young children's thought as "centered" rather than egocentric. Children, he believed, tend to focus on one aspect of a situation and are unable to shift their point of view or consider other aspects. Thus, young children are unable to understand the logic of classes and relations.

5. More recent research has challenged Piaget's view that young children operate according to a different logic and that their thought processes undergo a massive qualitative change. Some studies have modified Piagetian tasks to eliminate extraneous obstacles to the child's understanding of the principle involved. Young children do much better on such modified tasks. Other researchers argue that young children's problem-solving difficulties grow out of the fact that they are "novices"—they lack basic knowledge about the world as well as ways of using what knowledge they do have. "Metacognition" is the term which describes this kind of knowledge management skill. Preschool children are also novices about the basic facts of life and death. The process of learning about the origins of babies and permanence of death is gradual and often beset by misunderstanding.

6. Play is the characteristic activity of preschool children. Although children often play alone, more often it brings them together with one another. The skills necessary to win friends and influence people in the early years are similar to those needed in adulthood. Symbolic or make-believe play is characteristic at this age, regardless of whether children play alone or with others. Psychologists and preschool educators have differed about the meaning and importance of play.

Key Terms

centering   **314**
conservation   **315**
gender identity   **333**
identification   **327**
metacognition   **325**
Oedipal conflict   **326**
operations   **314**
socialization   **313**
symbols   **312**
transitivity   **319**
transsexuals   **331**

PART IV

Middle Childhood

The School Years

Middle childhood is a long period bounded on either side by major life transitions. Upon entering this stage, the child must make the sometimes wrenching passage from home to school. The small, familiar world of home is now a place that by law the child must leave for part of each day to enter the wider world of classmates, teachers, and other strangers. At the other end of the period, the child stands on the brink of adolescence. Sexuality blossoms, and serious choices about school, work, and the future must be made.

Many people look back on the years from 5 to 12 as an idyllic time. Bodies are strong, and minds are quick and logical. The burdens of adulthood seem infinitely remote. Even adolescence, with its worries about sex, appearance, morality, and identity, seems a long way off. The present, rather than the future, is the center of attention at this age. Each school year seems to go on forever, and summers last almost as long.

In reality, for children living through them, these years are not always idyllic. The world of the school and the playground can be a competitive, unaffectionate, even cruel society. Some children of this age may be haunted by fear of failure at school. Success in school and on the playground can build lasting self-esteem; failure can leave a lasting sense of inadequacy. For most children, however, the school years are a time of challenge. In the next two chapters, we look at the intellectual and social worlds of middle childhood.

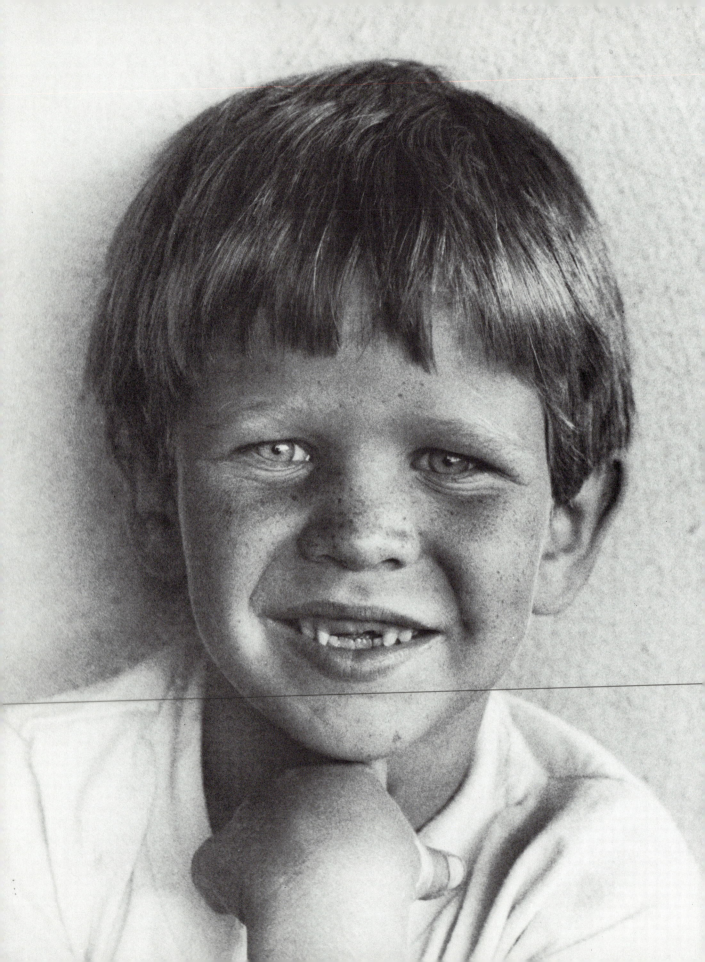

CHAPTER 10

The Age of Reason
Intellectual Development in Middle Childhood

And then the whining schoolboy, with
*   his satchel*
And smiling morning face, creeping
*   like snail,*
Unwillingly to school.

—Shakespeare

The world rests on the breath of the children in the schoolhouses.

—The Talmud

ou know your children are growing up, a writer once observed, when they start asking questions that have answers (Plomp, quoted in Peter, 1977, p. 103). It is no accident that formal education around the world usually begins for children between the ages of five and seven. Children can be taught to read and write when they are younger, but teaching and learning are much easier at the usual age for starting school. Societies that do not have schools also recognize the shift in children's psychological functioning between five and seven. Children in such societies are generally assumed to have acquired common sense; they are given responsibility for the care of younger children, for tending animals, and for helping the family in its daily tasks (Rogoff et al., 1976).

The historian Philippe Ariès (1962) has observed that, in medieval and early modern Europe, children entered directly into the stream of adult life once they reached the ages of five to seven. The quasi-adult status of the child over seven was codified into both civil and church law. English common law traditionally considered children over the age of seven to be legally responsible—that is, able to know right from wrong, to stand trial and be declared guilty (Rogoff et al., 1976). Judges were not required to treat all children as legally responsible, but they had the discretion to do so in particular cases. Similarly, the Catholic church places first communion at the age of seven, when children are held to know right from wrong and therefore be capable of sin and confession.

The major theorists of child development, despite their differences, also agree that there is an important shift in mental functioning around this time. For Piaget, this age marks a major turning point in cognitive development: the shift from intuitive to operational thought. For the Russian developmental theorists Vygotsky and Luria, this age is characterized by a critical shift in mental processes: the internalization of language. Russian researchers, following Pavlov, emphasize language as the basis for higher human thought. Between the ages of five and seven the more primitive *first signal system*—direct responses to stimuli—is replaced by the *second signal system;* language becomes the vehicle of thought and the regulator of behavior.

For Freud, this is the time when infantile sexual impulses are suppressed, and parental prohibitions are internalized to become the inner voice of conscience, or the superego. He believed that once the upheavals of the Oedipal crisis are resolved, sexual urges die down and remain "latent" until they reawaken at puberty. Hence, he labeled middle childhood as the *latency period.*

Despite all the evidence that children's minds are transformed in major ways between early and later childhood, some researchers have recently come to question whether the changes are as global and stagelike as had previously been thought. No one denies that young children often act as if they are much less competent than older children. The question is how to interpret the observed differences. Piaget, for example, assumed that there are fundamental changes in the structure of children's minds at early and middle childhood. Yet more recent research has pointed to a large number of factors that can make tasks hard for younger children, without implying any basic difference in cognitive competence.

In this chapter, we review various approaches to understanding the cognitive changes of middle childhood. First, we look at the evidence for a fundamental shift in mental functioning between five and seven and the possibility that changes in the brain may account for this shift. Next, we turn to Piaget's account of middle childhood. We will also sketch out the ways in which more recent research has revised and challenged Piaget's views. Finally, the chapter examines the impact of schooling on children's thinking and the use of IQ tests as measures of mental ability.

The Five to Seven Shift

About two decades ago, Sheldon White (1965) called attention to the **five to seven shift** as a

Sheldon White

major watershed in psychological development. He had observed that in many different experiments on children's learning, researchers found a dramatic shift in performance between the ages of five to seven. Younger children tended to respond directly to the physical properties of stimuli—color, size, and so on—while older children were more apt to categorize and apply verbal labels to them. "Before this age," he wrote, "the pattern of findings resembles those obtained when animals are used in like procedures. After this age, the pattern of findings approximates that found for human adults. The transition is from animal-like to human-like learning" (1965, p. 195).

Intrigued by these findings, White looked for further evidence of change in children between five and seven. He found many different kinds of behavior changes in the literature (1965, 1970). IQ scores, for example, come to be as predictive of adult IQ as they are at later ages.

Also, children younger than seven have difficulty locating themselves in space, so that they may get lost if they wander away from home; children older than seven seem to have more accurate mental maps. The ability to tell left from right emerges during this period. On classification tasks, preschool children are likely to group objects on the basis of color rather than form; after six, children tend to use form rather than color.

Some of the changes White documented are neurological or semineurological, such as the ability to copy complex geometric figures. (These tasks are used to assess brain damage in adults.) Another neuropsychological change occurs in the "phantom limb" phenomenon. If a child over eight loses an arm or a leg, he or she always reports feeling as if it were still there. Children four and younger never feel a "phantom limb."

A decade later, White reevaluated the evidence concerning the five to seven period in light of later research. Some of the behaviors he had documented were found in younger children, some abilities seemed to appear later, but the neurological findings held up over the years (Sheldon White, 1975).

Brain Development from Five to Seven

White has speculated that it may be the maturation of the brain that accounts for the changes in psychological functioning at around five to seven. For example, he points out that sheathing or myelinization of the brain is completed around this time. This might enable mental processing to go faster and improve memory.

There are also other kinds of brain change in this period. The maturation of the crossmodal areas is not completed until five (Geschwind, 1964; Tanner, 1970). These zones enable the child to integrate different sources of information, and probably support symbolic activity. Still another brain function that changes in middle childhood is the dominance of the left hemisphere—the side of the brain responsible for language. Such a change might account for the five-to-seven improvements in children's communication abilities, and in their ability to regulate their behavior by means of language (Kinsbourne & Hiscock, 1983).

Additional evidence that the five to seven shift may be influenced by changes in brain organization is the fact that the age of eight looms as a critical point in recovery from brain damage. In general, the younger the child, the less disastrous a particular injury is compared with a similar injury at a later age. One dramatic case was reported by A. Smith and Sugar in 1975. An infant had to have the entire cortex of the left hemisphere removed; although it was years before he could speak normally, by the age of 26, he had almost completed college, his IQ was above normal, and he had superior language abilities. This capacity to recover from *aphasia*—language deficits due to brain damage—declines markedly after the age of eight. A study of the records of a large number of brain-injured children revealed that all who became aphasic before eight, no matter how great the impairment, eventually regained their speech (Woods & Teuber, 1978). Many of those who became aphasic after eight failed to recover completely. In sum, it appears that the benefits of having a more developed brain come at the cost of a greater vulnerability to the effects of injury.

Despite such intriguing cues, neurology is probably not the whole explanation for the great shift from five to seven. As we have seen, some children can read at the age of two. Further, current psychological research has turned up evidence that preschool children are more intellectually competent—and older children more mature and uneven in their performance—than they had been thought to be.

Perspectives on the Five to Seven Shift

When children in modern, Westernized societies start school between the ages of five and seven, they are embarking on a long period of preparation for adulthood. Children between

the ages of five and seven in traditional societies enter into a status closer to adulthood; they are considered small adults. There are two points to be made here: first, the fact that virtually all normal children in America and Europe are in school once they reach this age poses a major theoretical challenge to psychological theorists (Cole et al., 1971). Is the mental growth we see at this time the result of universal psychological processes, or is it a kind of mental socialization? The modes of thought we think of as developing naturally at a particular age may in fact be dependent on the experience of school. The second point is, even though schooling—and simply living in a technological, bureaucratic society—may stimulate mental development in particular ways, there does seem to be a core of developmental change that leads both traditional and Western societies to alter the way they treat children after the ages of five to seven.

The invention of schools as institutions for the young, and the very idea of childhood as a separate stage of life, are relatively recent historical innovations. In their definition of these children as small adults, Western societies in past eras were closer to today's traditional so-

cieties than to contemporary Western practices. Anthropologists report that where people are free from Western influence, children's educations are part of adult life. For example, Meyer Fortes (1970) notes that among the Tallensi and other African peoples children and adults do not move in different "social spheres" as they do in the West. Everyone is involved in the same activities, but in varying degrees according to physical and mental development. The interests and motives of children and adults are the same, and—interestingly—there is no stormy transition period corresponding to Western adolescence. However, children are not passive in the hands of their parents. Fortes noted striking temperamental differences among Tallensi children, as well as incidents of disobedience, tantrums, and destructiveness. Misfits and incompetents could be found at all ages. But everyone is involved in the same social world.

Along with reports of the small-adult concept of childhood in non-Western cultures, the anthropological literature contains many reports of changes in the *treatment* of children at around the ages of five to seven. A study by Barbara Rogoff and associates (1976) surveyed the cross-cultural literature to find out how extensively the age difference is recognized. They discovered that, in one way or another, practically all of the societies studied shifted in the way they viewed and treated children over the age of seven. Generally, children from five to seven are thought to become sensible, rational, teachable, and ready to be integrated into adult society. They are expected to know the difference between right and wrong and to be able to take on responsibilities of various kinds, ranging from the care of younger children to the tending of animals and the beginning of serious participation in adult occupations. Children are expected to stop being childish, and to follow adult rules of manners and politeness. Further, these societies believe that children's personalities are fixed at this age; the traits and characteristics are set for life.

Children also assume new sexual roles once they reach this period. Peer groups are divided by sex, and there is greater sexual differentiation in chores and social behavior. In many societies, children are expected to become more independent from their parents; they may sleep apart from their parents or be sent to live with relatives. All in all, these new roles assigned to the children suggest that broad changes in psychological processes occur at this age which are recognized and acted upon by most societies.

Piaget and Concrete Operations

Jean Piaget offered the most comprehensive and unified account of the cognitive changes of middle childhood. In recent years, researchers have challenged some of his theoretical assumptions. But his work continues to be the starting point for much current research, and investigators are continuing to ask the questions he raised.

Piaget believed that at around seven or eight children undergo a mental revolution that affects all aspects of psychological functioning—not only intellectual processes, but emotional life, morality, and social relationships. Children are liberated from the egocentric magic universe of early childhood. The world becomes a more solid place as the child understands that various physical aspects of objects—their quantity, weight, and number—remain the same even though their appearance may alter. Social relations change as the child becomes able to see the world through other people's eyes. Fantasy play gives way to games with rules, and the child comes to understand morality as a matter of intentions rather than something to be judged only by consequences such as damage or punishment. In short, children become more adultlike in their thinking.

Piaget's belief that an immature system of mental processes gives way to a more mature system at the beginning of middle childhood is shared by other theorists, as we have seen. But Piaget had a particular theoretical model of these changes. Middle childhood is, in his terms, the concrete operational stage or period.

The concept of **operational thought** is central in Piaget's theory; it is the goal toward which he sees mental development proceeding. To have operational thought means that you can manipulate mental images of things. According to Piaget, preoperational children's thought is static. They are stuck with a picture of reality at a particular time, and cannot reverse the mental movie. Looking at a glass of water that has been poured into a tall, thin beaker, the four-year-old believes there is more now because the water is higher, or less because it is thinner. The eight-year-old can mentally reverse the action of pouring, imagining the water going back into the original glass and coming out the same as before.

An **operation,** then, is a mental manipulation. But operations have a very specific meaning in Piaget's theory. They are not just any mental manipulation; they are the mental versions of such acts as combining, separating, recombining, and ordering objects: think of a child stacking a set of blocks, separating them, and then ordering them from smallest to largest. An operation does not exist on its own, but as part of a system of operations—a structured whole. One of the most important features of a group of operations is reversibility, in which one operation can cancel out the effects of the other—as subtracting can cancel out the effects of adding, or moving through space from one place to another can be canceled out by returning to one's starting point.

Piaget called this the stage of **concrete operations** because it is less abstract than the next stage postulated by the theory—the stage of **formal operations.** The new mental manipulations the seven- or eight-year-old can perform are still tied to actual objects. Instead of having actually to *manipulate* liquids, blocks, or pieces of clay, the child can *think* about doing so. At this stage, however, children cannot yet manipulate mental objects such as ideas, hypotheses, and mathematical symbols.

Piaget regarded the onset of concrete operational thought as the most decisive turning point in the course of cognitive development. This is the age to which he devoted most of his attention—and many other researchers have replicated or varied his work. The task most often used to indicate whether or not a child has attained operational thought is the conservation of quantity experiment in which water is poured from one glass to another, or a ball of clay is rolled out into a snake. These are also the most famous experiments in developmental psychology. The editor of one of the leading journals on child development reports that more papers are submitted on conservation experiments than any other topic (Brainerd, 1978, p. 134). In short, conservation is to middle childhood what object permanence is to infancy. Both are concepts with profound implications for mental development, yet both can be easily demonstrated by anyone with access to an infant or young child.

Conservation Experiments

While conservation studies using substances such as liquid or clay are the most well known, other physical properties are also conserved in middle childhood (Figure 10.1). Conservation of length is tested by using two sticks lined up next to each other like tracks. After the child agrees they are equal in length, one is moved so that it is ahead of the other. The child is asked if the sticks are still the same length. Conservation of number is tested by presenting the child with two sets of objects—blue and yellow blocks, or bears and chairs, in one to one correspondence. Then, the experimenter bunches up one set of objects, or stretches them out, and asks the child if they are still the same. Whatever the answer, the child is asked to explain it. To demonstrate that he understands conservation, the child must point out that nothing has been added or taken away, or that the decrease in one dimension is compensated for by an increase in the other. Conservation of weight, volume, and area are also included among Piaget's tasks.

The empirical results of conservation studies are not as clear-cut as the theory would lead one to expect. All children do not become conservers in everything as soon as they have passed their eighth birthday. There is a good

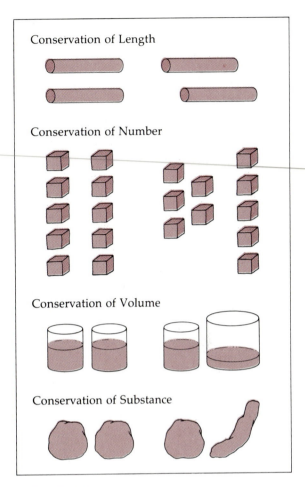

FIGURE 10.1
Tests of Conservation
The concept of conservation is to middle childhood what object permanence is to infancy. A child will be shown two identical objects or groups of objects and then the researcher will alter the position, shape, or container of one of the objects or groups. The child understands conservation if he or she recognizes that the altered object or group is still basically the same.

deal of individual variation. One researcher who reviewed a number of studies found that the percentage of conservers at each age varied from one investigation to the next (Fogelman, 1970). In many studies, the oldest and youngest children differed by about six years, yet a few of the youngest were able to master concepts still not understood by 10 percent of the oldest.

Moreover, some forms of conservation typically occur later than others. Conservation of substance occurs first, then conservation of weight, then conservation of volume. Piaget referred to this kind of uneven performance as *décalage*. Some of his critics regard the existence of these lags as a serious flaw in Piaget's theory, which he tried to explain away with the notion of décalage. If the theory postulates a set of mental structures the child either has or does not have, why should different kinds of conservation occur at different ages? Piaget and his followers argue that while children around seven or eight do begin to use more advanced mental structures, these do not appear all at once and transform the child's mind overnight. Some tasks, although they appear to be of equal difficulty, may in reality be harder to deal with than others. Thus, volume may simply be a harder concept than weight, which may be harder still than the amount of a substance.

Reworking Conservation

Researchers have tried to go beyond Piaget's work on conservation in a number of ways. They have addressed such questions as: Can evidence of conservation be found in children at younger ages than Piaget believed? Can children be *taught* to understand conservation? What actually takes place in children's minds as they shift from nonconserving kinds of responses to conservation?

A number of researchers, using different methods, have succeeded in producing conservation responses in younger children. Jerome Bruner (1966) developed his own theory of cognitive growth which centers on shifts in how children represent or encode the world at different ages. At first, he contends, children represent objects and actions *enactively*—through action, as a person might explain a spiral staircase by making spiral hand movements. Next comes *ikonic* representation: children's thought processes are dominated by the look of things.

Hence, the preschool child is struck by the height of the water in a tall thin container. Bruner postulates as his next stage the era of *symbolic representation,* in which the child interprets the world in terms of language or some other symbolic system.

Bruner contends that children understand conservation earlier than Piaget claims they do, but that this symbolic representation of reality is in conflict with the ikonic mode. The height of water in a tall, thin beaker is so striking to young children that they ignore what they actually know.

Briefly, Bruner tested his ideas by varying the standard conservation of liquid task: he poured the water behind a screen, with only the tops of the beakers visible. Then, with the liquid still hidden, the children were asked if there was still the same amount of water. Typically, they would say it was the same because

Jerome Bruner

"It's only the same water" or "You only poured it." Next, the children were asked to predict the level the water would reach after being poured, and then they were shown the actual level after pouring. Practically all of them agreed that the water would be the same after pouring when they could not actually see the uneven heights in the beakers. After the screen was removed, the youngest children, four years old, reverted to nonconservation—they could not resist the appearance of the water: "There is more because it is higher." But the increase in conservation responses among five- to seven-year-olds was dramatic. By getting children to think through the problem before seeing the results of pouring, Bruner apparently produced the realization that while the water looked different, it was really still the same in quantity. He also demonstrated the power of appearance: how things look dominates the thinking of young children.

Piaget and his followers challenged Bruner's theory, methods, and conclusions, contending that children who had been trained to conserve by Bruner and others did not really have as deep or "operational" an understanding as those who came by it naturally. An earlier study by Smedslund (1961) has often been cited by these critics. Smedslund trained a group of nonconserving children in conservation of weight by showing them that two equal balls of clay still weighed the same on a scale after one had been flattened or rolled out. Then he tricked the children by secretly removing a piece of the shaped clay. Very few of the trained children were surprised that the shaped clay now weighed less, indicating that they did not have a deep understanding of constancy. In contrast, children who were "natural" conservers were more likely to realize that some of the clay had been taken away or lost; half of the natural conservers continued to conserve.

Piaget and his followers have traditionally believed that conservation must develop "naturally." They insist that training in conservation tasks does not lead to changes in mental structure. Recently, however, other researchers have questioned these assumptions. Pointing to studies showing improved performance on many of Piaget's tasks after a little training, Rochel Gelman and Renée Baillargeon (1983) argue that if young children can benefit from training enough to improve their performance, then they may not differ as much in cognitive structure as Piaget had thought.

Further, questions have been raised about the concept of conservation as the hallmark of intelligent thought. Conservation may not be quite as universal in all cultures as Piaget assumed, as we shall see in more detail in the next section. In addition, it may not be as central and unshakable a part of childhood and adult intelligence as Piaget claimed. For example, some studies have shown that tricks like Smedslund's—removing clay or altering scales—can shake the beliefs in conservation of many adults (V. C. Hall & Kingsley, 1968). Finally, conservation does not apply to everything. The area inside a circle or other geometric figure does not remain the same if the shape is flattened; a clay pot will change in size and weight when it is fired.

Nevertheless, the concept of conservation or invariance captures something essential in human thought. As William James once observed, the sense of sameness or constancy is "the very keel and backbone of our thinking. . . . We do not care whether there be any *real* sameness in *things* or not . . . our principle only lays it down that the mind makes continual use of the *notion* of sameness, and if deprived of it, would have a different structure from what it has" (1890, vol. 1, pp. 459–60).

Seriation and Classification

Conservation is just one of several tasks that young children have trouble with and older children come to do easily. The **seriation** problem asks children to put a number of objects in a series according to one quantifiable dimension. Typically, the child is given a number of sticks of differing lengths and told to arrange them from the shortest to the longest. A preoperational child might take two sticks and put the shorter one on the left. Then he or she

might take another stick from the pile and compare it with only one of the first sticks, ignoring the other. Or the child might form several groups of sticks and arrange the sticks in each group according to size, but not put all of the sticks into one series. Piaget explained that children can focus on only one aspect of the problem at a time; in other words, they can focus on a comparison between two sticks, but not the total array.

By the age of six or seven, children approach the task in a systematic manner. First they scan the pile to find the shortest or the longest stick, then they scan the pile again to find the next shortest or longest, and so on. Each time the child considers the entire problem and orders the sticks without error. Once again, Piaget showed that a task that looks almost mindlessly simple to an older child or adult is actually a complex cognitive achievement.

The ability to classify objects is another achievement Piaget attributed to the concrete operational period. **Classification** consists of sorting objects into groups according to their similarities. Suppose a child is shown a collection of toy men and women, trucks and cars, chairs and beds. A concrete operational child would sort these objects into three groups: people, vehicles, and furniture. A multiple-classification problem, the next cognitive step in this period, sorts out objects according to two or more dimensions. For example, children can be presented with an array of cards varying in size and shape, such as circles and squares in red and blue. Those with a firm understanding of class properties sort the cards by shape or color, or by both dimensions together.

Piaget believed that children cannot master the logic of classes until the concrete operational stage; only then does the child master the two crucial properties of class: *intension* and *extension*. Intension is the definition of the class—the "roundness" of a circle, the "blueness" of blue. Extension is the list or sum of all the objects that fit the category. Both intension and extension must be coordinated. Thus, if the category is "furniture," all the chairs, tables, beds, and sofas set in an area should be grouped together, and a toy car should not be grouped with the furniture. Preoperational children are not yet capable of such coordination; they often include "extraneous" objects, and change the definition of the category as they go along.

Nevertheless, children are sensitive to categories from an early age. Recent studies show that children as young as one and a half to three may be capable of consistently classifying objects into categories (Gelman & Baillargeon, 1983; Sugarman, 1979). The class inclusion problem mentioned in Chapter 9 is another classification skill that is not completely absent in the preoperational period, but which is mastered around the age of seven or eight.

Beyond Piaget

When cognitive researchers began reinterpreting and revising Piaget's ideas, there seemed to be a fundamental incompatibility between his theories and the newer information processing approaches to cognitive development. Recently, though, there has been much less polarization and more overlap between the two approaches. Many researchers see themselves as "neo-Piagetians," extending his insights, rather than "anti-Piagetians" (Gelman, quoted in Hunt, 1982).

The two approaches share many assumptions. Both Piagetian and information processing researchers assume that children are active participants in their own learning and development. Instead of a passive child responding directly to environmental stimulation, both approaches assume that the most important determinants of children's responses are what goes on inside their heads—what they pay attention to, what they do with the information after they perceive it.

Information processing researchers depart most sharply from Piaget over the matter of stages. As we have seen, Piaget believes the child's mind goes through a series of complete reorganizations in the course of development. Each stage is marked by a different mental structure, which is based on a different logical model. Thus, in the concrete operational stage, the child's mind becomes capable of reversing mental operations. This central change accounts for the range of specific achievements such as conservation, transitivity, class inclusion, and so forth. Information processing researchers, by contrast, see intellectual development as a more complex, diverse process. Where Piaget saw one major transformation at each stage, these researchers believe that intelligent behavior consists of a set of separate skills—attention, perception, memory—which are applied step-by-step to solve particular problems. They may follow the problem solver's thoughts in minute detail, second by second; often they use flow charts to describe the process. Failure to solve a task, they believe, can result from difficulties in any one of these steps. Thus, a preschool child's failure to solve a problem might be due not to global cognitive incapacity, as Piaget had thought, but to a problem with one of the steps in the process.

A key assumption of the new approach is that the human mind at any age has only a limited capacity to process information. Our immediate, sensory register can hold impressions for less than a second. Short-term memory at any age can hold no more than about seven items of information—the number of digits in a telephone number, for example. If we rehearse the number, we can keep it in short-term memory long enough to make the call. If we rehearse still more, and call the number often enough, it may enter into long-term memory.

Chunking, or organizing information, is another way of remembering. If we notice that the last four digits of a telephone number are 1776, 1914, 1984, or some other well-known date, we can reduce the four individual bits of information to one—"Declaration of Independence," "start of World War I in Europe," or "Orwell." A sentence or a word can count as one chunk in short-term memory. This ability to use chunking and other encoding strategies begins to appear in middle childhood.

Memory is now a topic of great interest to both cognitive and cognitive-developmental researchers. As the above example shows, current research emphasizes the active role played by the individual in memory tasks. Most researchers believe that memory is an important factor in the observed differences between younger and older children on various tasks. One line of research follows the development of memory *strategies* such as chunking and rehearsal, as well as *metamemory*—the understanding of memory and how and when to use strategies. Children in middle childhood use strategies more often and more efficiently than preschoolers and have greater knowlege of memory and their own capabilities.

Some researchers have made ambitious attempts to translate Piaget's concepts into memory and information processing terms. The work of Juan Pascual-Leone (1970) and Robbie Case (1978) argues that changes in memory or basic processing capacity play a major role in cognitive development. Pascual-Leone has proposed an elaborate, mathematical model which attributes Piaget's stages to changes in "M-space" or working memory. He believes that the absolute capacity of the child's mind to deal with information increases with age; evidence for this view may be found in the fact that while a 3-year-old can repeat only three digits, a 10-year-old can repeat an average of six.

Case agrees with Pascual-Leone that increases in the capacity of working memory play a major role in cognitive development. But, instead of memory becoming larger in *attentional* capacity, he believes that children's minds become *more efficient* as their brains mature. Thus, when older children display the ability to count

faster, or take in more details of a scene in a given amount of time, they not only can absorb more information, but can process it more automatically, without giving full attention to every step in problem solving.

Still other researchers have argued that the way children *encode* and *represent* information may account for developmental change. Yet despite the differences among information processing researchers, they analyze Piagetian tasks in similar ways. For example, in solving the conservation task involving water in different containers, they would agree that the young child attends to one piece of information—the height of the water—not two—the height and the width. The older child is able to notice both height and width and relate the two to make a judgment about quantity.

Information processing research has not yet come up with a definitive explanation of the cognitive changes of middle childhood. Many unresolved issues remain. As Deanna Kuhn (1984) points out, it is difficult to disconfirm or disprove the various accounts of specific cognitive tasks. Information processing models, she continues, do not explain what Piaget saw as the core of operational thought—the feeling of logical necessity. To Piagetians, judgments in conservation and other tasks are not just problems to be solved. The heart of the matter, they argue, is the child's sense of logical necessity—the understanding that water poured from one container to another *must* remain the same in quantity, and that if A is less than B, and B is less than C, then A *has* to be less than C. As D. Kuhn explains, it is difficult to assess the distinction, but if researchers ignore it, they may miss what could be the most important aspect of cognitive development.

Despite the limitations of current knowledge, we now have a much more sophisticated understanding of the cognitive differences between younger and older children than we did a few years ago. It is clear that the notion of a unified mental structure emerging between the ages of six and eight is not tenable in light of current evidence. Preschool children are not as incompetent as had been previously thought, nor are older children and adults uniformly

What Makes Children Laugh?

One index of the cognitive sophistication of school-aged children is the kind of humor they enjoy. Preschool children have very little idea of what a joke is. For a 3-year-old, a joke may consist of going up to another child or adult and saying "do do" or "pee pee" or some other taboo word. At about the age of 6, children begin to feel a need for what Freud called a "joke façade" to disguise the sexual or aggressive nature of their jokes. The humor becomes less direct and more dissociated from the teller of the joke. Martha Wolfenstein (1954, 1978) traced how the joke façade becomes increasingly complicated in middle childhood. A 7-year-old girl told the following story:

> Once there was a little boy and he had to go to the bathroom. And he went over to the teacher and said, "I have to go to the bathroom." And the teacher said, "Raise your hand and say your ABC's. So the boy said, "A B C D E F G H I J K L M N O Q R S T U V W X Y Z." And the teacher said, "Where's your P?" And the boy said, "It ran down my pants." (Wolfenstein, 1978, p. 164)

The complications here involve a play on words and a shifting of blame for the taboo act from the child to an unreasonable adult who delays the boy's trip to the bathroom.

By the age of 11 or 12, children appreciate jokes where the taboo content is so indirect that it is never mentioned at all. Wolfenstein gives this example from an 11-year-old boy:

> There's this man who has beer with his meal all the time. One day he opens the beer and tastes it, and it tastes a little off. He sends it to the scientists to analyze. Four or five days later, he gets a reply: "Your horse has diabetes." (Wolfenstein, 1978, p. 166)

Sex and aggression are not the only sources of humor. Many jokes and riddles depend on ambiguity, the fact that words and statements have two meanings. Riddles are the elementary school child's favorite form of humor. Here are some examples of humor based on various kinds of incongruity:

> Why did the farmer name his pig Ink? (Because he kept running out of the pen.)

> Order! Order in the court! (Ham and cheese on rye, your honor.)

> If frozen water is iced water, what is frozen ink? (Iced ink—get it?)

The ability to appreciate ambiguity reflects the underlying cognitive skills of the elementary school child. To get the point, the child has to go back and forth between different ideas and meanings. The ability to shift mental gears this way is what Piaget termed "reversibility" and considered one of the hallmarks of operational thought. An information processing approach would see the ability to deal with ambiguity as evidence of older children's greater mental flexibility—their ability to encode two aspects of a situation at the same time.

Whatever the explanation, the amount of intellectual challenge in a joke determines how funny it is. At any age, jokes that are too easy or too hard to figure out seem less funny than jokes that present a moderate amount of challenge. The school-aged child does not find the preschoolers' crude attempts at humor very funny; adults are not greatly amused by the puns and riddles that delight 8-year-olds.

---

competent across all domains. Most researchers agree that what develops is a diverse set of cognitive skills, rather than a single, unified structure. There is also agreement that cognitive functioning is influenced by the nature of the specific task and by the social context in which it takes place (see box What Makes Children Laugh?). In sum, children's developing skills are related to their experiences, motives, and goals in everyday life.

Cognitive Growth, Culture, and Schooling

In recent years, developmental psychologists have become increasingly interested in the effects of formal education on intellectual growth. The reasons for this interest are both practical and theoretical. The practical issue concerns schools as social investments. Developing countries, which are just now creating school systems, are faced with decisions about their purpose and organization: Does education help to advance economic development? How much schooling should a country provide for its citizens? In Western countries, such as England and America, the issue is the role of education in advancing equality of opportunity: Do schools foster the intellectual growth of all children, thereby giving children from poor and minority backgrounds a chance to compete on more equal terms with their middle-class peers? Or do schools simply reflect and reinforce the class and cultural differences children bear when they enter school?

The theoretical issue concerns the basic direction and causes of human cognitive development. Traditionally, developmental theorists such as Piaget, Werner, Freud, Kohlberg, and others have assumed that there is an inherent tendency of the human mind to evolve in a particular way toward a specific end point. That end point is usually the Western-educated adult. In Piaget's theory, as several psychologists have observed, the end point of development resembles an experimental scientist.

When the Europeans first encountered so-called primitive peoples in the South Pacific, Latin America, Africa, and elsewhere, they found what seemed to be striking differences between "Western" thought and the modes of thought among native peoples. They discovered not only strange beliefs and practices, such as witchcraft, but seeming inabilities to think abstractly, logically, and mathematically. For example, the Lo Doga people of Northern Ghana have no concept of counting as a general procedure. When an anthropologist first asked someone to count for him, the reply was, "Count what?" (Goody, 1977). There were different procedures for counting different objects; cows were counted one way, cowry shells (used as money) another. Among the Kpelle, a Liberian people, there are few general terms for geometric shapes such as line, circle, triangle. The closest term for "straight line" is *pere*, which means path, but it can apply equally well to a curving or jagged line. Similarly, the closest term for circle is *kere-kere*, which refers to any roundish object, even if irregular or oval (Gay & Cole, 1967).

In the 1930s the Soviet psychologist Alexander Luria studied some of the preliterate peasant peoples who live on the steppes of central Asia (1976). His task was to assess the impact of the Russian Revolution on their lives, as well as the introduction of schooling and new technologies on their mental processes. He thus presented the peasants with logical problems in the form of **syllogisms,** which are a set of general premises and a conclusion based on those premises. The first sentence, or "major premise" of a syllogism, is always a general statement such as "All men are mortal." The second sentence, or minor premise, deals with a particular instance, "Socrates is a man." The conclusion is deduced from the first two sentences: "Therefore Socrates is a mortal." The conclusion is not based on personal experience, but on the logic of the premises. Syllogisms can be expressed abstractly, without any content:

All A are B.
C is A.
Therefore, C is B.

In Luria's day psychologists regarded the syllogism as a basic, natural form of human reasoning. Luria did not think the ability to solve syllogisms was natural, but he did see it as an indicator of the ability to engage in abstract thought. He found that illiterate peasants refused to make inferences from syllogisms. Thus, if they were presented with the following problem:

Cotton grows well where it is hot and dry.
England is cold and damp.
Can cotton grow in England or not?

they would say that they had never been to England, and therefore did not know if cotton could grow there. Nevertheless they were familiar with the content of the problem since they themselves grew cotton. When they were given a problem with unfamiliar content, their inferences had to be purely theoretical:

> In the far north, where there is snow, all
>   bears are white.
> Novaya Zemlya is in the far north.
> What color are bears there?

As in the first example, they would reply that they had no way of knowing what color the bears were in the far north since they had never been there. In general, they refused to draw conclusions about matters they had not experienced personally. However, Luria found that adults who had some education or who worked in modernized settings differed sharply from their more traditional peers. They would say something like, "The bear must be white because your words said all the bears are white in the far north."

Classification is another type of problem explored by Luria and other students of cross-cultural thinking. Luria showed subjects drawings of a bird, a rifle, a dagger, and a bullet and asked them which things belonged together and which did not fit. The most advanced cognitive response to a classification test is to group items into a general or superordinate category: the rifle, dagger, and bullet could all be labeled weapons. The least advanced response is a thematic grouping in which the items are linked by a story or theme.

Studies of nonindustrial societies typically find adults performing like Western children. Luria's peasants usually used thematic groupings. A peasant shown pictures of the bird, rifle, dagger, and bullet said "The rifle is loaded with the bullet and kills the swallow. Then you have to cut the bird up with the dagger, since there's no other way to do it" (1976, p. 56).

The Myth of "Primitive" Mentality

What are we to make of such findings? The traditional interpretation is that "primitive adults" are incapable of logical or abstract thought. As noted earlier, Europeans who visited preliterate societies were often impressed by what seemed to them bizarre beliefs and religious practices. After Darwin, scholars who had not themselves visited such societies used the observations of others as the basis of a concept of "primitive mentality" (e.g. Levy-Bruhl, 1923). The thought processes of individuals in preliterate societies were thought to represent earlier stages in human evolution. Some of the major theorists of developmental psychology—G. S. Hall, Freud, Werner, and Piaget accepted the notion of a "primitive mentality" in tribal peoples and in Western children.

While recent research on various preliterate societies has undermined the notion of "primitive mentality," studies of people in *modern* societies have shown that "illogical" thought also occurs under certain circumstances (Kahneman, Slovic, & Tversky, 1982). Thus, the difference is not as much between ordinary everyday thinking in preliterate and complex societies as between ordinary thought processes and those used by scientists in their work (Child, 1984).

Further, Western cognitive tasks are often inappropriate for non-Western peoples. Language differences, unfamiliarity with materials, and lack of motivation may make it hard to draw inferences about underlying *competence* from people's *performance* on the tests. The experimental situation itself is a product of Western culture; in some societies, an interview between a child and an adult may be unheard of. Almost everything happens in groups, and adults do not ask for the opinions of children (Greenfield, 1966). Moreover, tests where scoring depends on speed of problem solving may be inappropriate in societies where nobody ever has to hurry.

Nevertheless, certain conditions do produce dramatic changes in performance *within* particular non-Western cultures. These are urbanization, exposure to Western influence, and, above all, schooling. A large number of studies in recent years have shown that schooling improves performance on a wide variety of cognitive developmental tasks. Greenfield (1966) carried out a classic study among the Wolof of Senegal, using Piaget's water pouring task. Although about a quarter of the unschooled children did realize that the amount of water remained the same after pouring, about half the sample failed to conserve by the ages of 11 to 13, the oldest age tested. On the basis of her own and other research, Greenfield concluded that the unschooled children were not simply moving toward conservation at a slower rate, but that they would never reach it. While Wolof school children showed the typical Western pattern at younger ages of relying on how the water looked, and then moving on to conservation responses later, the tendency to rely on appearance increased among the unschooled. Greenfield concluded that her findings cast doubt on any simple maturational concept of development. Wolof children who had been to school differed more from those who had not than they did from European and American children. These findings also cast doubt on any biological or genetic explanation of differences between Africans and Europeans.

Since Greenfield's original study, many others have been carried out in countries around the world and have reached similar conclusions about the effects of schooling on conservation. There is increasing evidence that in many cultures adults apparently may not reach the level of concrete operations (Dasen, 1972). On the other hand, these studies also reveal great individual differences among unschooled peoples.

School, however, is not the only experience that affects cognitive performance on Piagetian and other tasks. One study compared Mexican children from pottery-making families with comparable children whose families did other work (Price-Williams, Gordon, & Ramirez, 1969). The researchers found that children experienced in pottery making reached an understanding of conservation of substance earlier than the others.

In contrast, another study (Steinberg & Dunn, 1976) found that in a different Mexican village children of pottery-making mothers were no better at conservation than other children. This study points to which specific kinds of experience may influence conservation. In the first village the children took part in all stages of the pottery-making process from rolling the clay to firing the pots. In this second village, however, the children participated only in the firing stage, in which the size and weight of the pots were actually transformed. These latter children, therefore, did not have the opportunity to see that the product was the same clay that had been rolled and shaped.

The experience of schooling seems to have the most wide-ranging effects on cognitive performance. One large-scale study on the effects of education presented a variety of tasks to over 800 5- and 6-year-old Peruvian children living in different social and cultural settings (Stevenson et al., 1978). The authors found that attendance at school improved performance on most tasks, regardless of social class, culture, or urban or rural environment. A similar major study was carried out in Yucatán with subjects ranging in age from 10 to 56 (Sharp, Cole, & Lave, 1979). This study also found that education had major effects, even when age and many other factors were controlled.

What is there about schooling that has such a marked impact on the way people perform cognitive tasks? Jerome Bruner (1966) has pointed to two features of schools which may account for these results: first, students in school are physically as well as psychologically detached from everyday, practical life; and second, schools employ techniques that amplify cognitive processes. That is, just as mechanical inventions such as eyeglasses and telescopes amplify human sight, inventions such as written language, mathematics, maps, and diagrams amplify human thought processes. Thus, according to Bruner, cognitive growth is pushed by outside elements in a particular direction as these symbol systems are internalized.

It is not that children in traditional cultures are not educated; rather, the kind of education they receive differs in many ways from going to school. In all societies, children are "educated" in the skills and knowledge they need for adulthood. Sylvia Scribner and Michael

Cole (1973) have analyzed many of the differences between the "informal" education that goes on in nontechnological societies, and the formal learning of the school. Traditional or informal education takes place in the midst of everyday life; children learn from watching and taking part in adult activities. While, in school, teachers use language as the major means of instruction—telling, explaining, dictating—informal instruction is based on demonstration or observation. The adult cooks, weaves, hunts, farms, or fishes, while the child watches and imitates. Adults in such situations rarely describe what they are doing in words. The schoolteacher communicates information, outside of any practical context, while the informal teacher teaches know-how. In school, learning becomes an act in itself, and words become an invitation to form concepts.

While individuals who are unschooled often approach each problem as a new one, those who have been to school treat problems as an instance of a general class. Schooled populations seemed to have "learned how to learn." Scribner and Cole (1978) presented Kpelle children with a series of problems involving geometric forms on cards that differed in color, shape, and number. The task was to guess the "right" cards—for example, all cards with red forms, or all cards with blue figures. Unschooled children and adults showed little improvement from one task to the next, while school children solved later problems much faster than earlier ones. They had figured out the general rule. Also, educated people are more likely to transform the materials in some way—to group items on a list of words to be remembered, or classify objects into broader categories.

In general, the detachment of school from everyday life also fosters a more abstract attitude. Schools are places where people verbalize about thought processes, something that is rarely found in traditional cultures. Patricia Greenfield (1966) had an interesting problem in this regard while doing her research among the Wolof. In the typical Piaget conservation procedure, the children are asked to justify their answers: "Why do you think this glass has more (or less, or the same) water?" The unschooled Wolof children had trouble answering; they did not distinguish between their own thoughts or statements and outer reality. The idea of explaining a *statement* had no meaning to them; it was the *event* in the real world that had to be explained. In short, they lacked the self-consciousness about thought processes that is found in Western and schooled populations.

Literacy

Some researchers view literacy itself as the chief factor in both cultural differences and individual development. The invention of a relatively easy way of putting spoken words into written form occurred only once, when the alphabet was invented in Greece in about the eighth century B.C. All existing phonetic alphabets are based on the Greek original. The crucial feature of the Greek alphabet was that it could represent all the sounds of speech. Previous forms of writing were based on pictures, syllables, or simply consonants, and were hard to learn and understand. (See table below.) Alphabetic writing made it easy to capture the spoken word or the private thought in a form that was both permanent and easily understandable. According to many scholars, the invention of writing changed the whole Western cultural tradition and led to the development of recorded history, logic, mathematics, and science (Goody & Watt, 1963; Olson, 1977).

Some Greek Letters

| Greek Form | | | Trans- | Approximate |
Capital	Small	Name	literation	Pronunciation
A	α	alpha	a	drama
B	β	bēta	b	bible
Γ	γ	gamma	g	good
Δ	δ	delta	d	dog
E	ε	epsīlon	e	era

In a similar way, many developmental psychologists believe that learning how to read and write has a great impact on the individual child's mental processes (Luria, 1976; Olson, 1977). Written language is a very different psychological phenomenon from oral speech. Ordinary speech, especially that of children, is embedded in the here and now of everyday events and situations. Speakers in face-to-face conversation rely on tone of voice, gestures, and eye contact to make their meaning clear. Often the meaning of an utterance is dependent on the situation and can therefore be highly abbreviated. If a surgeon says "scalpel" during an operation, the meaning is clear. By contrast, in written language, the meaning is in the text—the words on the page (Olson, 1977). Because there can be no help from gestures or tones of voice, written language must be more precise and elaborated than speech.

The psychological effects of learning how to write have been studied by a number of Russian researchers (Luria, 1976). Their work suggests that literacy has a significant impact on verbalized thoughts, or inner speech. Instead of immediately putting our thoughts into words, as in a conversation, writing slows us down, making us choose our words and think of different ways to express our meaning. Further, when we write, our words are out there in front of us, to see, to think about, to change. The inner preparation for writing makes us more aware of our own idiosyncratic thought processes, as well as the various possibilities contained in language itself. Once a person becomes literate, spoken language is also affected and becomes more elaborated, more attuned to individual meanings (Bernstein, 1975).

The Limits of School Learning

The results of schooling and literacy should not be idealized, however, and the intellectual ca-

pacities of the unschooled should not be overlooked (see Laboratory of Human Cognition, 1983). As many scholars have pointed out, all people have the ability to reason logically, to classify, to abstract. Preliterate cultures have complicated systems of law, myth, religion, kinship, and technology. Rather than viewing the differences between such cultures and literate societies as deficits, we should think of them simply as differences in the way abilities are combined and used in dealing with particular problems. There is no reason to believe that the newly educated Wolof, Yucatecan, or Soviet Asian peasant is suddenly acquiring a capacity for abstraction and logical thought. We cannot expect a person who has never been to school to realize that a syllogism is a logical puzzle, a kind of game, the first rule of which is, "Ignore what is really true and pay attention only to the words in the first two sentences of the three I tell you."

Syllogisms are often mind boggling even to highly educated people. For example, Mary Henle (1962) once presented a syllogism something like the following to a group of graduate students:

> A group of women were discussing their household problems. One woman said:
>
> It's so important to talk about what's on our minds.
> We spend so much time in the kitchen that household problems are on our minds.
> So it's important to talk about them.

Is the conclusion justified? Just as Luria's peasants did, many of the graduate students refused to accept the logical task. They argued against the premises, saying such things as, "Just because a woman spends time in the kitchen doesn't mean she can only think about household problems."

People in all societies seem to do best at solving problems in real-life situations, using familiar materials and modes of thought. Westerners can be inept at tasks that peoples in other cultures are skilled in. For example, Yale students were less accurate than Liberian rice farmers at estimating the number of cups of rice in a large pile or container (Cole et al., 1971). In contrast, the Kpelle farmers were less skillful at estimating length and distance, a task unfamiliar to them. Some Pacific peoples have skills at navigating on the open seas that amaze Western sailors. In short, the particular ways of thinking that educated Westerners take for granted are far from "natural."

Class and Culture in American Schools

A study of the demands of formal schooling and of cultural differences in problem solving can help explain why so many poor and minority children in America have trouble in school. It should not be too surprising that such children often find school an alien and alienating experience. Starting off with a reasonably good

preparation for school, some children will experience the pleasure of success and develop the skills and self-esteem that make further success possible. Other children find the school and its language and culture foreign and difficult. Their initial failures make them hesitant to keep trying; and they become aware of being labeled as deficient and unlikely to succeed. To salvage their self-esteem they may resist and reject the school and its methods, either silently or through open disobedience and disruption. Meanwhile, day by day, year by year, they fall further and further behind in knowledge, skills, and test performance. Getting used to the language games played in school is especially difficult for children who may have had little previous experience with books or with verbalizing their thoughts, or whose home language is not the standard English of the school. Traditionally, it has been all too easy to assume that minority children suffer from "incapacities" and "deficiencies."

Black English

One such deficiency belief that has recently been exploded is the idea that the language of black slum-dwelling children is impoverished. During the 1960s, many of the psychologists and educators who designed the Head Start program for disadvantaged preschoolers assumed that poor black children suffered from poor communication skills and ungrammatical language. Research into black language and its use in the black community, however, has demolished such notions. Linguists have discovered that Black English is not simply an error-filled version of "good" English, but a completely different dialect with a complex grammatical structure and its own rules of pronunciation (Labov, 1972). Thus, when ghetto children come to school, they are in effect learning standard English as a second language. Some educators have suggested that teachers of ghetto children should indeed teach standard English as a second language, using methods that have proved successful with other children faced with a language barrier.

The idea that black children do not communicate well has also been laid to rest. In fact, speaking ability is highly valued in the black community, and black children may even have an advantage over white. From an early age, ghetto children play complex games of verbal insult, variously called sounding, signifying, or "the dozens" (Kochman, 1972). In these games, children hurl insults back and forth, trying to be quick, clever, and outrageous, and to get the opponent to lose his "cool." The insults, often obscene, are aimed at the opponent personally, or at his family. (The players are usually male.)

New Questions about Schooling

In recent years, doubts have been raised about whether schooling actually does induce general mental growth. For example, although the Yucatán study described earlier did find marked differences between schooled and unschooled groups, the authors conclude by raising serious doubts about whether the skills learned in school are anything more than a complex skill like carpentry or tailoring. Further, they wonder if it is ever possible to tell whether schooling has a general effect on cognitive growth; the tests that are used to measure cognitive growth are variants of the very tasks that are correlated with school performance, such as IQ tests, syllogisms, Piagetian tasks, and so forth.

Other writers have pointed to negative consequences of schooling, and still others have raised questions about whether it has any effects at all, positive or negative (Jencks, 1972). School learning may be narrow, limited, and unusable for application outside of school even for similar problems. Wertheimer (1945) pointed out that students often solve geometry problems in a completely blind and uninsightful way that could not even be applied to other geometry problems. One result of schooling is often fear and dislike of what has been studied: math anxiety is widespread, and many students dislike science, serious literature, and anything intellectual.

Nevertheless, even the most severe critics of

current schools recognize that literacy and education are necessary in a technological, bureaucratic world. Further, they recognize that a good education does more than teach useful skills—it can help individuals fulfill their intellectual and emotional potentials. Finally, literacy and education still play their historic roles in advancing human freedom. As one psychologist put it,

> Everything that a person learns makes him less susceptible to control. People with knowledge are necessarily harder to manipulate than those who lack it, for the same reason that skilled chess players are harder to beat than duffers. Truth does make us free. Real education is not primarily a technique for manipulating students, as some have suggested, but just the opposite. This isn't because schooling makes people rebellious, but because it enables them to see more possibilities for action. (Neisser, 1976, p. 185)

Schooling and the Classification of Children

The start of elementary school is in many ways the beginning of the child's adult career. Attitudes toward learning are taking shape, self-concepts are being formed, and prophecies are being made. From the first grade on, children are being judged, labeled, ranked, categorized, compared, and contrasted by teachers, classmates, and most significantly, by themselves.

Smart, dumb, teacher's pet, athletic, pretty, good sport, popular, bully, fast learner, slow learner, gifted, learning disabled—these are some of the labels and roles that are being assigned. Research on the social organization of elementary school classrooms (Sexton, 1967) reveals that, within several weeks, children acquire a social position among their classmates based on several criteria: how much they are liked by other children, how competent they appear to be at school work, and how much power or influence they have over others. Most children know what their status is, and these social positions may persist for many years.

Teachers' assessments of children's ability also begin very early and may have great influence on the kind and quality of education the children will receive. In kindergarten and the first grade, teachers begin to judge which children seem to have the characteristics necessary for success in school and in the wider society. Often such assignments are based on economic class or minority group status (Rist, 1973); and on the basis of these assessments and expectations of future performance, children may be grouped and treated differently by the school. These assessments often generate self-fulfilling prophecies—beliefs that help to bring about their own fulfillment (Rosenthal & Rubin, 1980).

Of all the classifications that are made, the most familiar and those with the greatest impact on people's lives are IQ tests. Any reader of this book is likely at some time to have taken an intelligence test in one form or another. The results of these tests are used to make decisions about which children should be placed in

© 1984 United Feature Syndicate, Inc.

programs for the gifted and which in programs for the mentally retarded. More generally, they help determine the kinds of hopes and expectations to be set up for each child's future, in school and in the world.

The IQ Controversy

Currently, there is no consensus among psychologists about the scientific worth of IQ tests. Some believe that they are definitive measures of intellectual ability, the most valid and reliable measures psychology has produced. Others feel that the concept of intelligence has never been clearly defined, that the content and scoring of IQ tests are arbitrary, and that what an IQ score tells about a person's intellect is unclear. In addition, many psychologists believe that IQ tests are biased toward the kinds of skills and information that middle-class white families encourage.

Aside from their impact on individual lives, IQ tests in America have been embroiled in social policy questions and political debates. Thus, they have been used to justify claims that certain racial and class groups are inferior to other groups. In the early decades of the twentieth century, some mental testers reported that a majority of such European "races" as Italians, Poles, and Jews were feeble minded; recently arrived immigrants had been given IQ tests, and since they were unfamiliar with both the English language and the content of the items—for example, names of baseball teams—they received low scores. Despite these obvious limitations, such findings had a significant impact on restrictive immigration laws passed in the 1920s (Kamin, 1974; S. Gould, 1981).

At the moment, a number of lawsuits are in progress which aim at banning the use of IQ tests for placing children in special classes for the mentally retarded. The opponents of testing, who include many psychologists, argue that labeling children as mentally retarded does more harm than whatever good the children may get out of special classes into which they

are placed as the result of such testing. Testing opponents claim these classes are used as dumping grounds for difficult children. Further, they argue that the tests discriminate against blacks and other minority groups. In contrast, however, many other psychologists and school administrators argue that mental testing is a fair and reasonable way of assessing children's educational needs.

Defining and Measuring IQ

Part of the reason for the controversy is that intelligence has proved difficult to define and measure. Think for a moment about what you would consider a good definition of intelligence. Would you say it is the amount of knowledge a person has? Is it the speed with which someone can solve problems? Is it creativity—the ability to think up new uses for a common object such as a brick? Is the ability to draw well, or play the piano well, or diagnose and repair an engine a kind of intelligence?

A prominent dictionary defines intelligence as "the ability to learn or understand or to deal with new or trying situations" and "the ability to apply knowledge to manipulate one's environment or to think abstractly" (*Webster's Ninth New Collegiate Dictionary*, 1984). This definition states that intelligence is a capacity or aptitude for knowledge and reasoning, not how much one knows. The description suggests that it is possible for a person to be highly intelligent, yet ignorant or even illiterate. It is this notion of intelligence as some underlying capacity that makes it so hard to measure. Most intelligence tests ask people to define words, to read, to solve arithmetic problems. They may also ask people to picture things in space, memorize, put block designs together (see Figure 10.3). Tests ask people questions about general information—capitals of states, writers of famous works, names of presidents. Clearly many of these items test for knowledge, not the underlying capacity for knowledge.

Roger Brown and Richard Herrnstein (1975) have pointed out that around the turn of the century IQ tests were called "mental" rather than "intelligence" tests. They suggest that the change was unfortunate, because people are more likely to be able to agree about what a mental test is than about what intelligence is. To call them intelligence tests also leads to what Stephen Jay Gould calls the fallacy of *reification*—the tendency to convert an abstract concept into a material object or thing (from the Latin word *res,* meaning thing), having an independent existence of its own. An example of reification is the assumption that IQ tests measure intelligence the same way that scales measure weight and thermometers measure temperature. Trying to find a way out of the problem, a psychologist once suggested that "intelligence is neither more nor less than that which intelligence tests test."

Alfred Binet and the Birth of Mental Testing

Alfred Binet produced the first mental test in 1905 at the request of Paris school authorities. They asked him to provide an objective way of selecting, before the start of school, those children who did not have the ability to learn in the standard school program. Although he had been interested in theories of intelligence and in studying intelligence in the laboratory before he was called upon to develop a test, he had to put aside whatever theoretical notions he had in order to do the job. His task was clear and practical. He had to devise a test that predicted learning difficulties, whatever else it did or did not do.

Binet's test is the parent of IQ tests used today. Its American version, the Stanford-Binet was developed by Lewis Terman and first published in 1916. The Stanford-Binet is an individual rather than a group test so it is not routinely used by school systems. But it is the criterion against which other IQ tests are validated. To be judged acceptable, a new IQ test must correlate highly with the Stanford-Binet.

Ironically, the "father" of intelligence testing disagreed with many of the assumptions of the more recent IQ testers. Binet insisted on three principles for the use of his tests, all of which

Alfred Binet

were discarded by later testers (S. Gould, 1981). First, he saw his tests as practical devices designed for a limited purpose, rather than indicators of an innate and permanent characteristic of a child. Second, he believed his tests should be used to identify children with learning problems, rather than a way of ranking normal children. Third, he believed that the tests should be used to diagnose the kind of help a child might need, rather than to label children as inferior and incapable.

The Meaning of IQ Scores

Binet assumed that intelligence in children has something to do with the relationship between a child's age and the kinds of problems he or she could solve. He assumed that a bright child would perform like an older child, a dull child like a younger one.

On Binet's test, children were assigned a mental age. However, building upon the suggestion by William Stern, it was Terman who developed the concept of an intelligence quotient, which is mental age divided by chronological age, then multiplied by 100. If the child's mental age and chronological age are the same, his or her IQ will be 100. A child with a mental age of 10 and a chronological age of 8 would have an IQ of 125 (10/8 × 100). A 12-year-old child with a mental age of 10 would have an IQ of 83.

Today, IQ scores are based on a normal curve. The mean of the population is set at 100; two-thirds of the population's scores fall between 84 and 116. Figure 10.2 illustrates this intelligence curve and provides the common labels for the various ranges of scores.

The items included in the Stanford-Binet are short, easily scored tasks. At two, for instance, children are asked to point to parts of the body. At four, they are asked to supply opposites, as in "Brother is a boy; sister is a _____."

Children are also asked at this age, "Why do we have houses?" "Why do we have books?" An eight-year-old is read a story and asked questions about it.

IQ tests are supposed to measure a person's basic "smartness," not previous learning. But typically, non-middle-class and minority children do less well on IQ tests than their middle-class counterparts. Serious attempts have been

FIGURE 10.2
The Intelligence Curve
The intelligence curve shows the normal distribution of standardized IQ scores according to the Stanford-Binet intelligence scale.

Source: Adapted from *Stanford-Binet Intelligence Scale: Manual for the third revision of Form L-M* by L. M. Terman & M. A. Merrill, 1973, Boston: Houghton Mifflin. Copyright © 1973 by Houghton Mifflin Company, reproduced by permission of the publisher, The Riverside Publishing Company.

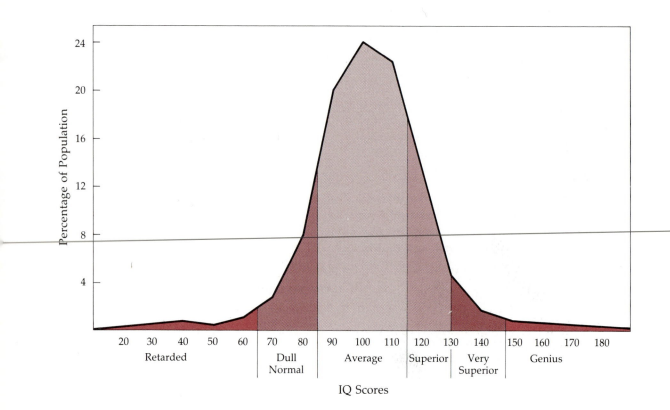

IQ Scores

made to construct tests that would be fair to all cultural groups; yet it has proved difficult to find test items that would be equally familiar or unfamiliar to all groups.

It is crucial to realize that intelligence tests are essentially measuring the child's ability to do well at school. By and large, when children are motivated, comfortable, and have some familiarity with the content of the test items, current IQ tests do give a fairly good indication of how children will master the skills taught in school. But IQ tests cannot measure some independent essence, some mysterious X in the child's mind which predicts school performance.

Different Mental Abilities

Is intelligence one general talent, or are there different sorts of abilities? While psychologists differ about whether there is a general "smartness" factor, and how much it accounts for, they agree that people differ in how they perform on various tasks: some people are better at verbal than numerical problems; others do best figuring out spatial puzzles. The Wechsler Intelligence Scale is an IQ test that uses items similar to the Stanford-Binet's, but groups

them into different kinds of tasks (Figure 10.3). There is the Verbal Scale of tests using verbal problems (including arithmetic problems) and a Performance Scale consisting of various picture

---

FIGURE 10.3
The Wechsler Adult Intelligence Test

Test	Description
Verbal Scale	
Information	Questions tap a general range of information; for example, "How many nickels make a dime?"
Comprehension	Tests practical information and ability to evaluate past experience; for example, "What is the advantage of keeping money in a bank?"
Arithmetic	Verbal problems testing arithmetic reasoning.
Similarities	Asks in what way certain objects or concepts (for example, *egg* and *seed*) are similar; measures abstract thinking.
Digit span	A series of digits presented auditorily (for example, 7-5-6-3-8) is repeated in a forward or backward direction; tests attention and rote memory.
Vocabulary	Tests word knowledge.
Performance Scale	
Digit symbol	A timed coding task in which numbers must be associated with marks of various shapes; tests speed of learning and writing.
Picture completion	The missing part of an incompletely drawn picture must be discovered and named; tests visual alertness and visual memory.
Block design	Pictured designs must be copied with blocks; tests ability to perceive and analyze patterns.
Picture arrangement	A series of comic-strip pictures must be arranged in the right sequence to tell a story; tests understanding of social situations.
Object assembly	Puzzle pieces must be assembled to form a complete object; tests ability to deal with part-whole relationships.

Source: Wechsler Adult Intelligence Scale and Wechsler Adult Intelligence Scale–Revised. Copyright © 1955, 1981 by The Psychological Corporation. All rights reserved.

and manipulation problems. Wechsler believed that general intelligence contributes to performance on all the scales.

Louis Thurstone (1938) objected to the emphasis on general intelligence. He found evidence for 7 different kinds of mental ability that were relatively independent of one another: these are verbal comprehension, word fluency—the ability to think of words rapidly—number ability, memory, spatial ability, reasoning, and the ability to grasp visual details quickly. Another researcher, J. P. Guilford (1967), came to the conclusion that intelligence is made up of 120 different kinds of ability.

He is responsible for emphasizing and developing measures of creativity—the ability to solve problems in new and original ways. According to Guilford, intellectual activity can be divided into two different kinds of thinking. **Convergent thinking** requires people to choose the one right answer out of several alternatives. It makes people "narrow" their thoughts. Intelligence tests and multiple choice tests call for convergent thinking. **Divergent thinking,** on the other hand, calls for thinking in many different directions and devising novel solutions to problems. Divergent thinking, or creativity, is important not only to artists and writers, but also to scientists, engineers, and those trying to solve social problems.

Guilford's work has been incorporated into a number of different tests of creativity. A test item may ask, "How many uses can you think up for a toothpick, a brick, a paper clip?" or "Imagine the consequences if all laws were suddenly abolished." Some doubts have been raised about whether performance on creativity tests is truly independent of intelligence, and whether such tests actually predict creative accomplishments in real life. One significant finding from this research, however, is that disadvantaged children often do as well or even better on creativity tests than middle-class children. One study concluded that while advantaged children did better on standard intelligence and achievement tests, they also seemed to "pay a price" for their skills. They lacked spontaneity and were so fearful of making a mistake that they produced very few responses to creativity items. In contrast, the disadvantaged children lacked self-confidence on academic tasks but were able to be spontaneous and flexible in dealing with creativity problems (Yando, Seitz, & Ziegler, 1979).

Whatever the number and relationship of the various mental abilities, it seems clear that a single IQ score does not give a clear picture of a child's abilities. Three children with the same overall IQ in the average range could be very different in the patterning of their abilities: one child might be talented verbally but below average in numerical skills, one child could be a whiz with numbers and poor verbally, while the third might be average in everything.

Heredity, Environment, and IQ Change

It has been widely assumed that IQ tests measure some fixed, innate capacity in children. Yet the founder of intelligence testing, Binet, did not believe that a person's intelligence was unchangeable. In fact, he devised a set of mental exercises to improve the functioning of those who scored low on his tests.

The chief difference between strict hereditarians and their opponents, as Stephen Gould (1981), points out, does not lie in the belief that intelligence is either all inborn or all a matter of the environment. Few people deny that IQ, like most human traits, is to some degree heritable. Rather, Gould claims, the differences have to do with social policy and educational practices: "Hereditarians view their measures of intelligence as markers of permanent, inborn limits. Children, so labeled, should be sorted, trained according to their inheritance, and channeled into professions appropriate for their biology. Mental testing becomes a theory of limits. Antihereditarians, like Binet, test in order to identify and help" (pp. 152–53).

Psychologists can be found on all points of the heredity-environment continuum. The most well-known hereditarian today is Arthur Jensen (1969, 1980), who declares that the research evidence shows that 80 percent of the IQ differences among individuals are due to heredity. Further, he contends that the average fifteen-point difference between the IQ scores of blacks and whites is also due to genetic differences.

At the opposite pole from Jensen is Leon Kamin of Princeton. Kamin (1974) argues that there is little evidence that IQ tests measure anything more than a person's opportunity and willingness to learn how to answer the kinds of questions that appear on the tests. He contends that studies purporting to show hereditary influences on IQ are so methodologically flawed that no conclusions can be drawn from them. Such studies either compare the IQs of adopted children with their biological and adoptive parents, or the IQs of separated identical twins.

As discussed earlier, the results of these studies appear to show that separated twins closely resemble each other in IQ, and that adopted children's IQs are more strongly correlated with their biological than with their adoptive parents. The problem Kamin points to in twin studies is that they do not control for the similarity of environments in which the twins are placed. The assumption of such studies is that twins reared apart are living in very different circumstances while in fact they are likely to be placed in families offering similar advantages. Hence, the resemblance in their IQs could result from the similarity of their environments.

The problem with adoption studies also concerns the similarity of adoptive parents. While almost anyone can have a biological child, adoptive parents are a highly selected group. Adoption agencies try to place children in "good" homes, so that there is less variation in education, income, and IQ among adoptive parents than among natural parents. The similarity of adoptive parents results in a lowering of the correlation between their IQs and those of their adopted children. It is a well-known statistical fact that when there is little variation in one variable there will appear to be little correlation with another variable.

Kamin also contends that there has been systematic bias in favor of hereditarian views in the research reports and summaries of the literature, as well as in textbooks. One of his

claims of bias was corroborated in a dramatic way. In 1974, Kamin pointed to certain inconsistencies in the papers of C. W. Burt, an English psychologist whose twin studies strongly supported the hereditarian interpretation of IQ. Evidence later emerged that Burt was guilty of massive scientific fraud, making up much of his data and even inventing nonexistent coauthors for his papers (Hearnshaw, 1979). Contemporary hereditarians such as Jensen argue that the discrediting of Burt's work has little effect on the evidence and that other studies support their position. To Kamin and others, however, Burt is only the most flagrant example of how IQ tests have been misused to promote certain ideologies and social policies.

Most psychologists fall somewhere in between Jensen's hereditarianism and Kamin's argument that the heritability of IQ is zero. Generally, most psychologists believe that both genetics and environment play a role in intelligence, but that it is impossible to come up with precise percentages. As we saw in Chapter 4, the techniques that genetic researchers use to study heritability in plants and laboratory animals are difficult to apply to humans.

In addition to being criticized for his claim that 80 percent of the variation in IQ scores can be explained by heredity, Jensen has also been taken to task for applying that estimate to group differences. Even if variation within a particular population is strongly influenced by genetics, it does not follow that differences *between* groups are genetically caused. Group differences and individual differences are not comparable (Hirsch, 1970; Mackenzie, 1984). The contribution of heredity to any trait varies with the population being studied and the environmental conditions under which it develops. For instance, the height of people in a well-nourished, healthy population is probably determined largely by heredity. But in a poorer and less healthy group, genetic differences may have less chance to express themselves. And the height of the less well-nourished population will be shorter. For example, as noted in an earlier chapter, recent generations of Japanese have grown taller than their parents and grandparents. Thus, it would be inappropriate to apply heritability estimates derived from one population to another.

There is a further complication in comparing racial groups. Genes function not only as determiners of certain traits, but as significant social markers. Black skin is not only an inherited physical characteristic, but also a trait that exposes its bearer to prejudice and often to life in a poor and stressful environment.

As the height example shows, a trait can be influenced by heredity and still show strong environmental effects. The evidence on IQ also shows such environmental effects. In fact, a study by DeFries and his colleagues (DeFries et al., 1982) shows generational differences in IQ that parallel the generational height differences among Japanese. These researchers examined IQ test data from parents and offspring in three ethnic groups—Chinese, Japanese, and Caucasian (white). Offspring of the two Asian groups scored substantially higher than their parents. Interestingly, in contrast, the children in the Caucasian sample scored lower than their parents. The differences across generations seemed to be related to education and occupation—a finding that argues for important environmental influences on mental test performance.

Research on adopted children usually cited for hereditarian findings also demonstrates that the mean IQs of adopted children are much higher than those of their biological mothers (Skodak & Skeels, 1949). A study of black children raised in middle-class, white families showed that their IQs were higher than those of black children in general and higher than the national average of white children as well (Scarr & Weinberg, 1976). Other research compared children of white mothers and black fathers with children of black mothers and white fathers. The mulatto children who had white mothers had somewhat higher IQs, even though their racial heredity was similar to those who had black mothers (Willerman, Broman, & Fiedler, 1970).

In another study along these lines, a German researcher compared the IQ scores of children fathered by black and white American soldiers occupying Germany after World War II

(Eyferth, 1961). Although racial prejudice was widespread in Germany, separate black and white communities did not exist. The results of this study showed that there were no significant differences between the two groups of offspring. This and other studies of racially mixed children support an environmental rather than a genetic explanation of race differences in IQ (Mackenzie, 1984).

Thus, how well one does on a test of vocabulary or information—"Who wrote the *Iliad*?" "What does plagiarize mean?"—clearly depends on having the opportunity to learn about such things (see Figure 10.4). Cultural bias is also revealed in other kinds of questions. The Wechsler scale for children asks, "What is the thing to do if a child much smaller than you starts to fight with you?" The "correct" answer is to try to avoid the fight, and this is how middle-class children typically respond. Black children, however, often state that they would fight back. One black child, when asked why, said, "My mother says if someone mess with you, you mess em back" (Kagan, 1978, p. 183). Such differences reflect different values and conditions of life, not different degrees of intellectual competence.

In the passion of the debate over race differences in IQ, the basic message of the data is often overlooked: differences between the races are trivial when compared to individual differences within each race. Thus, knowledge of a person's race is of no practical use in predicting his or her IQ.

Changes in Individual IQ Scores

If being raised in different environments contributes to IQ differences between individuals, do changes in environment and life circumstances lead to changes in a single individual's IQ scores over time? The answer is yes. As a result of various longitudinal studies, we now know that an individual's IQ can vary a great deal. Thus, Binet was correct when he rejected the idea that a child's IQ was fixed for life.

Repeated testing from infancy through adulthood reveals that infant intelligence tests are

FIGURE 10.4
The Chitling Intelligence Test
Many intelligence tests reflect a cultural bias toward the white middle class. The "Chitling Test," published by *Newsweek* in 1968, illustrated this point by turning the tables. Some samples of the multiple-choice questions are provided here.

1. A "gas head" is a person who has a:
   (a) fast-moving car
   (b) stable of "lace"
   (c) "process"
   (d) habit of stealing cars
   (e) long jail record for arson

2. "Bo Diddley" is a:
   (a) game for children
   (b) down-home cheap wine
   (c) down-home singer
   (d) new dance
   (e) Moejoe call

3. Which word is most out of place here?
   (a) splib
   (b) blood
   (c) gray
   (d) spook
   (e) black

4. If a pimp is uptight with a woman who gets state aid, what does he mean when he talks about "Mother's day"?
   (a) second Sunday in May
   (b) third Sunday in June
   (c) first of every month
   (d) none of these
   (e) first and fifteenth of every month

5. A "handkerchief head" is:
   (a) a cool cat
   (b) a porter
   (c) an Uncle Tom
   (d) a hoddi
   (e) a preacher

6. If a man is called a "blood," then he is a:
   (a) fighter
   (b) Mexican-American
   (c) Negro
   (d) hungry hemophile
   (e) red man, or Indian

7. Cheap chitlings (not the kind you purchase at a frozen-food counter) will taste rubbery unless they are cooked long enough. How soon can you quit cooking them to eat and enjoy them?
   (a) 45 minutes
   (b) 2 hours
   (c) 24 hours
   (d) 1 week (on a low flame)
   (e) 1 hour

Answers   1. c   2. c   3. c   4. e   5. c   6. c   7. c

Source: "Taking the Chitling Test" by Adrian Dove, *Newsweek*, July 15, 1968. Copyright © 1968 by Newsweek, Inc. All rights reserved. Reprinted by permission.

not predictive of later IQ, except in cases where a child is seriously impaired. By the age of 7 or so, IQ scores do predict adult IQ fairly well, but there are still wide individual fluctuations (see box on Change in Individual IQ Scores). In one longitudinal study, carried out at the Fels Institute, the average range of IQ change between the ages of 2½ and 17 was 28.5 points (McCall, Appelbaum, & Hogarty, 1973). A third of the children changed by more than 30 points, and one in seven changed by more than 40. Longitudinal studies at the Institute of Human Development in Berkeley also revealed IQ change. Between ages 6 and 18 the IQs of almost 60 percent of the 252 children studied changed 15 or more points (Honzik, Macfarlane, & Allen, 1948).

Changes in IQ are influenced by motivation, such as intellectual interests and ambitiousness, as well as by the ups and downs of life experience. Illness, emotional troubles, or a crisis in the family are often associated with lowered IQ scores; and thus improvement in a child's life situation can lead to a rise in his or her IQ. In adulthood, IQ can also rise or decline, and it is not true that IQ necessarily declines with age. Intellectual challenge, or being married to a spouse with a higher IQ, can raise an individual's IQ (Eichorn, Hunt, & Honzik, 1981).

Change in Individual IQ Scores

Longitudinal studies have shown that an individual's IQ scores can vary widely over time. One such study, carried out at the Institute of Human Development in Berkeley, showed that a child's life circumstances at the time of testing had a great impact on test performance. In 1948, Marjorie Honzik, Jean Macfarlane, and Lucille Allen described changes in children's IQ scores between the ages of 2 and 18 as well as some of the apparent reasons for those changes. The following describes some of the individuals discussed in their article.

Case 423 was a girl who was always above average, but whose scores sagged during adolescence. In her high school years, she deliberately turned away from intellectual success. She became much more interested in good dates than good grades, which she regarded as "unfeminine." Her rejection of school was also a way of rebelling against her parents, who placed a high value on academic achievement.

Case 764 was an example of a child whose IQ gradually decreased, from 133 to 77. An only child, she had a difficult relationship with her mother, who both overindulged her and complained about her. The girl was also quite obese throughout her childhood, which created problems in her relations with peers.

Case 553 was a boy whose mental test scores increased markedly. Small and thin, he was plagued by a variety of illnesses throughout childhood. He had three operations as well as three serious illnesses. Nevertheless, he was successful both intellectually and socially.

Case 715 was a girl with extremely variable scores. She had intermittent but severe bouts of both eczema and asthma throughout the years of the study. Her family also suffered from severe stress and emotional tension. To make matters worse, she was obese and had difficulty getting along with other children. Her highest scores came when she was taking adrenalin to control the asthma.

The article concludes with a warning about

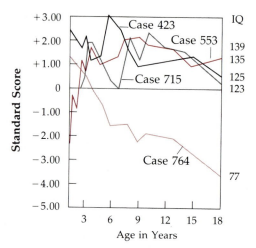

IQ Changes in Individual Cases

Source: Table (below) and chart are adapted from "The stability of mental test performance between two and eighteen years" by M. Honzik, J. Macfarlane, & L. Allen, 1948, *Journal of Experimental Education, 17.*

using IQ tests for practical purposes. The fluctuations observed in scores of the children studied show that single test scores, or even two such scores, may give a misleading picture of a child's abilities. The table below illustrates the distribution of the range of changes in IQ during the twelve-year period when all of the children in the study were 6 to 18 years old.

Amount of Change	Guidance Group Percent (N = 114)	Control Group Percent (N = 108)	Total Percent (N = 222)
50 or more IQ pts.	1	—	0.5
30 or more IQ pts.	9	10	9
20 or more IQ pts.	32	42	37
15 or more IQ pts.	58	60	59
10 or more IQ pts.	87	83	85
9 or fewer IQ pts.	13	17	15

In sum, then, an IQ score is not an absolute measure of a child's innate intellectual capacity. The concept of intelligence, and the relationship of IQ scores to such a concept, remains as vague as it was in Binet's day. IQ tests are reasonable predictors of school performance, which is their intended purpose. But they are of limited usefulness for children outside the white middle class. There are important intellectual qualities they do not measure, such as the ability to find new solutions to old problems, or to ask new questions. People who have actually been creative and innovative in their adult lives do not necessarily have higher IQs than their less creative peers. Nor is IQ or school performance as predictive of adult success as is generally supposed (Jencks, 1972). IQ scores and claims about their implications for individuals and groups should be regarded with a healthy skepticism.

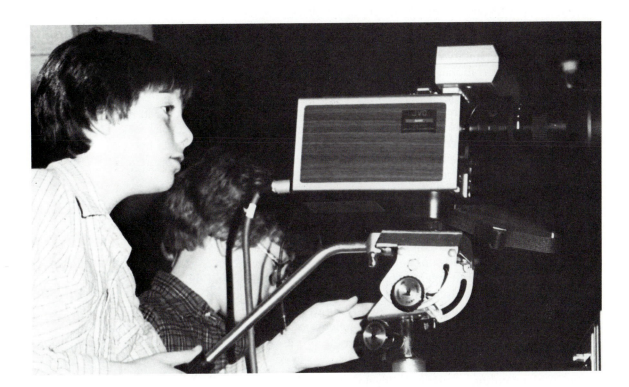

SUMMARY

1. Around the ages of five to seven, children undergo numerous physical, cognitive, emotional, and social changes. Researchers often refer to this period as the five to seven shift. This age is also recognized in many societies as a time when children come to be reasonable, educable, and capable of controlling their own behavior. In traditional societies, children enter into adult roles as apprentices. In societies where children go to school, this is the age at which formal education begins. One of the most significant changes at this time is the child's increased skill in language. Children can now communicate with others more effectively and can use language and thought to control their own behavior.

2. Psychologists have tried to describe and explain the changes at five to seven and the psychological attributes of middle childhood from a variety of perspectives. For Freud, this age marks the resolution of the Oedipus complex and the start of the latency period. For Erikson, this is the time when the child develops either a sense of industry and competence, or a sense of inferiority and inadequacy. For the Soviet school of psychologists, it is the time when language is internalized. Sheldon White compiled an inventory of the changes in the five to seven period that are reported in the research literature. He suggests that the maturation of the brain may account for at least part of the changes at this time.

3. The most influential conception of the cognitive changes of middle childhood is Piaget's. For Piaget, this is the first time the child becomes capable of operational thought. Children can now reason systematically by performing mental actions in their heads and can imagine what the reverse of such actions would be. Reversibility is one of the crucial hallmarks of operational thought. The concrete operational child can solve problems in conservation, seriation, and classification.

4. In recent years, researchers have discovered that the changes that appear at five to seven are more gradual than had previously been thought. Many of the tasks Piaget used as evidence of the stage of concrete operations can be solved by younger children if experimental methods are modified. Though development is more complex and piecemeal than it once seemed to be, the five to seven period still marks a time when important cognitive skills are consolidated and mastered.

5. Information processing researchers have offered alternative explanations of Piaget's account of the cognitive changes of middle childhood. These researchers reject the idea of a massive, unified change in cognitive structure. Instead, they view intelligent behavior as the outcome of several different processes, including attention and memory. Further, they regard problem solving as a step-by-step process. According to this view, younger children do not suffer from general cognitive incompetence; rather, they have difficulties with some of the components or steps in the process of solving intellectual tasks.

6. Our understanding of cognitive development in middle childhood is complicated by the fact that children in modern societies begin to attend school at this time. Schooling cultivates mental skills that would not develop "naturally" in a society without schools or literacy. Both schooling and literacy foster abstraction, an ability and willingness to solve nonpractical problems, and the ability to be more reflective about language and thought. Nevertheless, people in nonliterate cultures can reason logically and think abstractly. In general, people in any culture do best at solving familiar problems in familiar situations.

7. IQ tests are widely used and are highly controversial. They were originally developed to identify children who might have learning difficulties in school and thus be in need of special instruction. More recently, intelligence and aptitude tests have been used to rank normal children. Controversy has centered around the following issues: the extent to which IQ is innately fixed, whether the tests are fair to minority and disadvantaged children, whether racial differences in IQ scores have a genetic basis, whether the tests are used to help children with learning problems or to stigmatize them.

Key Terms

classification   362
concrete operations   358
convergent thinking   378
divergent thinking   378
five to seven shift   354
formal operations   358
operation   358
operational thought   358
seriation   361
syllogism   366

CHAPTER 11

The Social and Personal Worlds of Middle Childhood

Children know nothing about childhood, and have little to say about it. They are too busy becoming something they have not quite grasped yet, something which keeps changing. . . . Nor will they realize what is happening to them until they are too far beyond it to remember how it felt.

—Alistair Reed,
The World of Children

fter the age of five to seven, children take a giant step toward adulthood, socially as well as intellectually. John and Elizabeth Newson (1976) are British anthropologists who studied 700 four-year-olds from all socioeconomic classes. Observing the same children three years later, they saw a remarkable transformation. At four the children seemed still to be "prisoners of their own egocentricity," although we know from psychological research that preschool children are not in fact as globally egocentric as they had been thought to be. Nevertheless, the Newsons were struck by the subtle and sensitive capacities for social understanding that had emerged in three years. One of the ways this sensitivity revealed itself was in the older children's ability to restrain their impulses. Before expressing emotions, they would anticipate the reaction of others and modify what they did or said. Thus, when upset, they often managed not to cry, or at least to save their tears for home or the privacy of their own rooms. Even positive emotions were constrained. Where four-year-olds would literally jump for joy with delight, the seven-year-olds often assumed a cool nonchalance.

Another aspect of this social understanding is an appreciation of the differences in social distance and degrees of formality. While the mothers of four-year-olds often worried that their children would misbehave and thereby "show them up" or "let them down" in public, the same women three years later assumed they could count on their children not to do so. The seven-year-olds recognized a code of social conduct which taught that different situations demand different kinds of behavior. They could read social cues and modify their behavior accordingly. Thus, the parents in the Newson study were willing to put up with a great deal of disruptive and defiant behavior in the privacy of their homes, but they expected their children to be discreet outside the home. A mother who engaged in shouting matches with her son at home could control his behavior at the doctor's or principal's office with a lift of her eyebrow.

In recent years, developmental psychologists have been trying to understand the processes underlying such changes in social knowledge. **Social cognition** is the term used to describe the development of children's social skills and understandings, and it includes several more specific aspects of social relations: **role taking,** the ability to see things from another person's point of view; **personality perception,** or the child's conceptions of other people; **moral judgment,** the understanding of rules and conventions, as well as norms of justice and fairness.

Role Taking

Role taking, or social perspective taking, is seen by many authors as the master social skill. It is necessary not only for communication with other people, but eventually leads to a broader, societal point of view. By taking the role of what George Herbert Mead called "the generalized other," children come to understand moral rules, laws, and social conventions (see Damon, 1977).

Since thinking about other people is intimately related to thinking about ourselves, children's self-awareness and conceptions of self are included in studies of social cognition, as are their conceptions of friendship and social institutions such as government and money. In general, then, social cognition includes thinking about what goes on inside people's heads, what goes on between people, as well as thinking about social groups, institutions, and what society is all about.

Just as little children are not as egocentric as previously thought, older children and adults are not immune from all forms of egocentrism. John Flavell (1974, 1977) suggests that social understanding, or "people reading," may be thought of as a complicated game. Young children know that the game exists and have some sense of what it is about; with age and experience they come to be increasingly skilled players. The child's earliest tasks are to become aware that people have perceptions, thoughts, intentions, memories—and that these exist both in the self and others. A later task is to realize that other people's inner experiences may not be the same as one's own.

As we saw in Chapter 9, an elementary form of interpersonal awareness develops around age two or three. During the elementary school years, however, there is a marked increase in children's ability to make inferences about what other people are experiencing. They are, for example, increasingly able to solve such complicated inference problems as Piaget's Three Mountains Task—to figure out what view a person would have from different places around a set of model mountains.

When children reach middle childhood, they also become increasingly skilled at *metacognitive* aspects of social cognition. As explained in Chapter 10, metacognition is the ability to think about thinking. It can also be applied in social situations, such as the ability to think about what another person is thinking, and anticipate his or her behavior. An illustration of this kind of role taking is shown in the Peanuts cartoon in Figure 11.1. Charlie Brown plans a course of behavior based on what he thinks is Lucy's plan to trick him; she, however, manages to stay one step ahead of him—by realizing what he thinks she is going to do, and doing the opposite.

Researchers have studied the growth of this ability by playing a simple game in which the child is asked to hide a coin in one hand (De Vries, 1970) or under one of two cups. A child who has first hidden the coin in his or her right hand has to decide which hand to hide it in next. A very young child does not think about the other person's thoughts in making the choice. An older child might think the other person would choose the right hand again and therefore hide the coin in his or her left one. A still older or more sophisticated child would realize that the other person would expect the hider to switch hands and therefore try to fool him by hiding the coin in his right hand the second time. Around the age of 8 to 10, the child is likely to realize that the other person can also follow this same line of reasoning, and may be expected to choose the right hand, and so hides the coin in his or her left hand.

FIGURE 11.1
© 1962 United Feature Syndicate, Inc.

Another kind of task used to assess role taking is asking children to tell the same story from the point of view of different characters (Feffer & Gourevitch, 1960; Kurdek, 1977). Before age 6, children simply repeat the same story. By 6, children can tell a story from different points of view, but the perspectives do not mesh. Around 7 or 8, the events of the different stories go together better, and by the age of 9, Feffer found that "simultaneous coordination occurs"; children integrate each character's emotional reactions into the stories.

The most detailed attempt to work out a model of the development of role-taking abilities has been conducted by Robert Selman (1976, 1980; Selman & Byrne, 1974). His model extends from the preschool period to maturity, but we will concentrate on middle childhood here. Between 6 and 8, labeled as Level 1, *subjective* role taking occurs. The child understands that different people may have different thoughts and attitudes about things. The Level 1 child can distinguish between accidental and intentional actions and realizes that other people can also.

At Level 2, around 9 or 10, *self-reflective* role taking occurs. The important gain here is the child's realization that his or her own thoughts and feelings can be the object of another person's thinking. Children can step out of their own shoes and see themselves as if being observed by others. In Level 3, which occurs between ages 10 and 15, role taking is *mutual*. The child can look on the interaction between the self and another person in an impartial way, as if he or she was a spectator. The young person becomes aware of the recursive, back and forth mirroring of perspectives, as in the Peanuts cartoon in Figure 11.1 (She thinks that I think that she thinks . . .).

At Level 4, which arises in adolescence and adulthood, perspective taking grows more complex in a number of ways. The person realizes that perspectives among individuals form a system, and that the society as a whole has viewpoints—that there are legal and moral perspectives that lie outside of particular individuals. Also at this level, the person realizes that an individual may have more than one perspective—that people may have conflicting and even unconscious motives.

Personality Perception: Self and Others

In addition to the striking advances in social understanding that children make in middle childhood, there are changes in the way they describe and presumably perceive themselves and other people. It is possible for anyone to describe a person of any age in two different ways. We can describe individuals in terms of how they look, what they own, what they do, and the social categories they belong to—age,

sex, race, religion, class—or we can describe them in terms of their psychological interiors—their motives, values, thoughts, and feelings. The trend in middle childhood is for children to focus less on behavior and external aspects of themselves and others, and more on inner characteristics. As one researcher puts it, "with increasing age the child becomes less of a Skinnerian, more of a Freudian" (Rosenberg, 1979, p. 202).

A study by Livesly and Bromley (1973) asked 320 English boys and girls between 7 and 15 to write descriptions of themselves and other people they knew well. They were instructed to describe what sort of person the individual was, and not to use physical characteristics. In spite of the instructions, the younger children were likely to describe people's appearance, possessions, family: "She is pretty; he has a new brother." Almost half of the 7-year-olds failed to mention a single psychological quality. The number and proportion of psychological descriptions increased significantly with age, with the greatest change between the ages of 7 and 8. In fact, differences between 7- and 8-year-olds were often greater than those between 8- and 15-year-olds. Livesly and Bromley suggest that the eighth year is a critical period in the development of social perception, a finding that is consistent with other research.

Children's descriptions also become less egocentric. Peevers and Secord (1973) classified descriptions according to whether they were egocentric ("He scares me," "He gives me things"), mutual ("We both like sports"), or other-oriented ("She's quiet and shy," "He's unathletic and likes to read"). While younger children were able to use other-oriented descriptions, this type of description increased dramatically with age.

Understanding Other People's Feelings

Between the ages of 6 and 12, children become increasingly able to recognize other people's feelings and motivations. One study examined children's perceptions of social interaction as

A scene from the 1945 movie *Our Vines Have Tender Grapes.*

portrayed in a complex and realistic movie (Flapan, 1968). Children in this age span were shown excerpts from the film *Our Vines Have Tender Grapes.* A major episode portrays a father who punishes his young daughter rather severely for not sharing her roller skates with a neighbor's son. He takes the skates away from her, gives them to the boy, and sends her to bed without dinner. Later, the father regrets his actions and tries to make up for them by taking the girl to a circus.

Children were first asked to tell the story of the movie as if to someone who had not seen it, then they were asked for the reasons why the characters behaved as they did. The children's spontaneous responses were coded according to whether they simply reported actions or situations—"It was summer," "The girl was skating"—or dealt with motives or explanations of behavior—"She was crying because her father punished her."

A third category contained statements in which the child mentioned thoughts, feelings, and intentions that were not outwardly expressed or labeled in the film. The youngest children generally gave accurate accounts of the film but at a concrete descriptive level: "The boy wanted those skates. And the boy said she was a dirty pig. And then the boy told the lady about it. And then the girl pushed him down." The older children's descriptions were more psychological and more integrated; they explained the actions in terms of thoughts and intentions: "The father was reading the newspaper, but he was thinking about something else. He couldn't really read it. He wanted to go up to her and say it wasn't so bad. But he decided he better not."

The most striking developmental changes occurred between 6 and 9, confirming once again the ages of 7 and 8 as an important transitional phase. Another striking difference between the 6- and the 9- and 12-year-olds was the older children's greater awareness of the feelings, thoughts, and communications of the girl's parents. They could easily pick up on indirect communications. For example, the film shows the mother trying to get out of spanking her daughter by telling the father she is busy making supper. Later, the mother sees the father looking upset after he had punished the girl, and she tells him a circus is passing through town.

Six-year-olds typically took such statements at face value. When asked why the mother said she had to make dinner or mentioned the circus, they would say: "It was getting time to eat," "The mother thought the father would like to go to the circus." The older children recognized that the mother was trying to avoid spanking her daughter, and that the mother mentioned the circus as a way for the father to make up to the girl for what happened earlier. While to older children and adults the father's discomfort about punishing the girl is a central element in the story, none of the 6-year-olds appeared to even perceive that the father felt sorry, confused, or conflicted.

Self-concepts

The development of children's conceptions of themselves parallels the development of the ways they conceive of other people. Younger children describe themselves in terms of overt, behavioral characteristics—what they look like, where they live, what they own, what they like to do. As they grow older, the self is increasingly described as a private, unique world of thought and experience. The course of development we have just sketched is not universal. In more traditional cultures, both children and adults are more likely to describe themselves in terms of their family and role relationships. Here is a 9-year-old American boy's answer to the question, "Who am I?"

> My name is Bruce C. I have brown eyes. I have brown hair. I have brown eyebrows. I'm nine years old. I LOVE! sports. I have seven people in my family. I have great! eyesight. I have lots! of friends. I live on 1923 Pinecrest Drive. I'm going on 10 in September. I'm a boy. I have an uncle that is almost seven feet tall. My school is Pinecrest. My teacher is Mrs. V. I play hockey. I am almost the smartest boy in the class. I LOVE! food. I love fresh air. I LOVE school. (Monetmeyor & Eisen, 1977, p. 317)

By 11 and 12, children's self-descriptions have a more psychological flavor. The following example from the same study is by an 11½-year-old-girl:

> My name is A. I'm a human being. I'm a girl. I'm a truthful person. I'm not pretty. I do so-so in my studies. I'm a very good cellist. I'm a very good pianist. I'm a little bit tall for my age. I like several boys. I like several girls. I play tennis. I am a *very* good swimmer. I try to be helpful. I'm always ready to be friends with anybody. Mostly I'm good, but I lose my temper. I'm not well-liked by some girls and boys. I don't know if I'm liked by boys or not. (P. 317)

To see where this trend is heading, read the response of a 17-year-old girl in the same study:

> I am a human being. I am a girl. I am an individual. I don't know who I am. I am a Pisces. I am a moody person. I am an indecisive person. I am a very curious person. I am not an individual. I am a loner. I am an American (God help me). I am a Democrat. I am a liberal person. I am a radical. I am a conservative. I am a

pseudoliberal. I am an atheist. I am not a classifiable person (i.e., I don't want to be). (P. 317)

The tendency to move from exterior to interior conceptions of the self does not simply reflect age differences. One study (Rosenberg, 1979) interviewed children from 8 to 16 about their self-conceptions, asking them such questions as, "What does the person who knows you best know that other people do not?" "What things are really best about you?" "What are your weak points?" "What are some things that are not so good about you?" "How are you different from other people?" "How are you like other people?" The younger children had no difficulty answering the questions, but the developmental trend from exterior to interior ways of conceiving the self emerged quite strikingly. For example, when asked what the person who knows them best knows about them, younger children typically referred to some form of behavior—"That I cross the street when I shouldn't," "That I sometimes play hooky from school." Older children usually referred to inner thoughts or wishes.

The finding that the development of self-conceptions moves from outer to inner characteristics does not mean that older children and adolescents no longer see themselves as physical beings with observable characteristics. Nor does it mean that younger children have no inner world of thought and feeling. As children grow older and more inward looking in their conceptions of self, such aspects of self as appearance, possessions, behavioral characteristics remain as part of the self-concept. But for most individuals, they are not the central, defining characteristics of the self, unless they are invested with psychological meaning.

Similarly, younger children do not lack psychological interiors—they experience thoughts, feelings, images, memories. And as we saw earlier, by age seven children have a high degree of self-awareness and social sensitivity in actual face-to-face interactions. What is at issue here is the distinction between practical activity and the ability to think about and describe that activity. Self-conceptions seem to follow the

same transformation as cognitive development in general. As we saw in the last chapter, the limitation of what Piaget terms concrete operational mode of thought is the ability to engage in a more abstract, second-order level of thought: thinking about thinking.

Whether the increasing ability to think about thinking is due to maturational processes or environmental influences such as schooling, it reveals itself in several ways as the child advances toward and through adolescence. First, children become increasingly introspective; as Piaget (1928) put it, they "get into the habit" of watching themselves think. By adolescence, introspection may take the form of an obsessive brooding about the inner world of the self and its relation to others. In contrast, during middle childhood it is simply an increasing alertness to one's own thought process. Second, children's descriptions of themselves as well as others become more inferential, more based on assumptions about underlying motives and personality styles. A young child might say, "I like to play the piano and the guitar," whereas the older child might say "I like music," while the adolescent might say, "I am a musical person," or "I am a musician." Piaget (Piaget & Inhelder, 1958) points out that adolescents use facts to form inferences about an unseen, underlying reality. The new ability to probe beneath the surface of things results in an altered conception of self.

The tendency to look at ourselves and others in terms of deep underlying dispositions is a mixed blessing. We may exaggerate the consistency of people's personalities, leap to conclusions about people's character on the basis of little evidence, and form stereotypes that are highly resistant to change. Walter Mischel puts it this way:

> There is a great deal of evidence that our cognitive constructions about ourselves and the world . . . often are extremely stable and highly resistant to change. Studies of the self-concept, or impression formation in person perception and clinical judgment, . . . all of these phenomena and many more document

the consistency and tenacious continuity of many human construction systems. Often these construction systems are built quickly, and on the basis of little information. But once established, these theories, whether generated by our subjects or ourselves, become exceedingly difficult to disconfirm. (1968, p. 1012)

Moral Development

As we saw in Chapter 10, even very young children come to be aware of the existence of rules, conventions, social standards, and norms. In middle childhood, children's understanding of moral and social standards increases, along with the ability to articulate such principles. Piaget (1932) was the first to investigate the development of moral reasoning. He presented short story problems to children, assessing not so much their conclusions but how they reasoned about the problem. For example, a child might be asked who was naughtier, a boy who accidentally breaks fifteen cups, or a boy who breaks one cup trying to reach the jam jar while his mother is out. Piaget presented a number of such stories, varying the amount of damage done as well as the characters' intentions. He found that younger children tend to attribute blame according to the amount of damage done, regardless of intentions. Older children take motives or intentions into account. A person with good intentions, even if he or she does great damage, is not considered morally blameworthy, but rather, unlucky or clumsy.

On the basis of this research, Piaget suggested there are two broad stages of moral growth. In the first stage, sometimes called *objective morality* or *moral realism*, an act is judged bad if it causes damage, departs from the established rules, or is punished by authority figures. The more advanced stage, called *subjective* or *autonomous morality*, develops in the middle years. During this stage children have a less rigid and absolute view. They recognize that the rules are not sacred and untouchable but

are based on social agreement and can be changed if human needs and circumstances change. They also realize that moral judgments are made in terms of people's intentions, as well as standards of fairness and justice. Piaget believed that this second type of moral reasoning was not usually achieved before the ages of 12 or 13.

Recent research has modified and elaborated Piaget's views, but it has supported his essential insight about the nature of changes in moral thinking during childhood (Karniol, 1978). Some researchers have pointed to flaws in Piaget's stories, such as the demands they make on children's memories and the fact that the difference in accidental and intended damage is very great. When these flaws are corrected, young children can show more advanced reasoning than Piaget had thought them capable of demonstrating (Surber, 1977).

Kohlberg

Building upon Piaget's work, Lawrence Kohlberg carried the study of moral development into adolescence and adulthood. Although Kohlberg confirmed many of Piaget's essential ideas, such as the shift from a morality of consequences to a morality of intentions, he advanced a more complicated model of development. Kohlberg proposes that moral development progresses past the point at which Piaget left it. Piaget's second stage of morality corresponds only to the middle of Kohlberg's scheme of development. Kohlberg's model contains three major levels of moral development, with two substages in each level (see Figure 11.2).

Like Piaget, Kohlberg presents moral dilemmas in story form. Unlike him, however, Kohlberg's stories contain genuine dilemmas in which one moral principle is pitted against another. There is no obvious right or wrong answer, even to adults. Here is Kohlberg's best-known story dilemma:

In Europe, a woman was near death from a special kind of cancer. There was one drug the doctors thought might save her. It was a form of radium that a druggist in the same town had recently discovered. The drug was expensive to make, but the druggist was charging ten times what the drug cost him to make. . . . The sick woman's husband, Heinz, went to everyone he knew to borrow the money, but he could only get together about $1000, which is half of what it cost. He told the druggist that his wife was dying, and asked him to sell it cheaper or let him pay later. But the druggist said, "No, I discovered the drug and I'm going to make money from it." Heinz got desperate and broke into the man's store to steal the drug for his wife. Should the husband have done that? (1963, pp. 18–19)

In looking at the responses of children and adults to these stories, Kohlberg is concerned not with whether the person would recommend stealing the drug or not, but the reasons behind the choice. Scoring is based on three levels and six substages of morality. The interviews themselves and the rating scheme are quite complicated, so there is room here only for the briefest sketch of Kohlberg's system.

The first level is called **preconventional,** which emphasizes avoidance of punishment and the satisfaction of desires. A person at the preconventional level would argue for or against stealing the drug depending on which course of action would lead to the least trouble. "Steal the drug because you'll get in trouble if your wife dies"; "Don't steal the drug because you'll be caught and go to jail." At the **conventional level,** the reasons are based on maintaining social approval. Unlike the preconventional person, the individual at the conventional level has internalized the moral rules and would feel guilty about breaking them. Examples of conventional level responses to the dilemma would be: "If you don't steal the drug and save your wife, people will think you're inhuman"; "If you steal the drug, you'll always feel guilty about breaking the law."

The **postconventional** or principled level is based on principles of right and wrong that go beyond conventional morality. For example, at Stage 5, the person recognizes that rules and laws are based on some notion of a social contract. While recognizing that the law may sometimes be unjust and arbitrary, the Stage 5 person gives great weight to the will and welfare of the majority. Stage 5 answers to the dilemma might be: "Stealing is wrong, but it would be reasonable for anyone in these circumstances to steal the drug"; "Heinz wouldn't be completely wrong to steal the drug, but it wouldn't be right. The end doesn't justify the means."

At Stage 6, the highest level, reasoning is based on universal ethical principles that may sometimes conflict with conventional morality, the law, and the will of the majority. Real-life examples of Stage 6 morality would be the civil disobedience of Thoreau, Gandhi, and Martin Luther King, or the refusal of one soldier to obey orders at the Mylai massacre. Stage 6 responses to the Heinz dilemma would be: "The preservation of a human life is a higher value than blind obedience to law. It is morally right to steal the drug"; "Heinz should not steal the drug because that is not a fair way of deciding which of the many people who have cancer should get the scarce medicine."

Kohlberg's research (1963, 1983) revealed that among children aged 7 to 16 the stages appeared in the predicted order. Between 7 and 10, preconventional responses are dominant. From age 10 on, conventional responses become dominant and remain so. In fact, most adults stay at the conventional level. About 20 percent of all 16-year-olds reach Stage 5 and a majority of adults never attain Stage 6. This last stage has rarely been found in other cultures where studies have been carried out, such as Taiwan, Turkey, Mexico, and Kenya (Gibbs, 1978; Snarey, 1985); among middle-class urban subjects in those same countries, however, the age trends for the earlier stages are similar to what Kohlberg found in the United States.

Kohlberg's work raises questions about development and cultural differences such as those discussed in the last chapter (Gibbs, 1978; Simpson, 1974; Snarey, 1985). Does

FIGURE 11.2
Kohlberg's Six Moral Stages

Level and Stage	Content of Stage	Social Perspective of Stage	How People Answer the Heinz Dilemma	
			Pro	*Con*
Level 1: Preconventional Stage 1—Punishment-Obedience Orientation	*What is Right* *Reasons for Doing Right* To avoid breaking rules backed by punishment, obedience for its own sake, and avoiding physical damage to persons and property. Avoidance of punishment, and the superior power of authorities.	*Egocentric point of view.* Doesn't consider the interests of others or recognize that they differ from the actor's; doesn't relate two points of view. Actions are considered physically rather than in terms of psychological interests of others. Confusion of authority's perspective with one's own.	He should steal the drug. It is not really bad to take it. It is not like he did not ask to pay for it first. The drug he would take is only worth $200; he is not really taking a $2000 drug.	Heinz shouldn't steal; he should buy the drug. If he steals the drug, he might get put in jail and have to put the drug back anyway.
Stage 2—Individualism, Instrumental-Exchange Orientation	Following rules only when it is to someone's immediate interest; acting to meet one's own interests and needs and letting others do the same. Right is also what's fair, what's an equal exchange, a deal, an agreement.	*Concrete individualistic perspective.* Aware that everybody has his own interest to pursue and these conflict, so that right is relative (in the concrete individualistic sense). To serve one's own needs or interests in a world where you have to recognize that other people have their interests, too.	Heinz should steal the drug to save his wife's life. He might get sent to jail, but he'd still have his wife.	He should not steal it. The druggist is not wrong or bad; he just wants to make a profit. That is what you are in business for, to make money.
Level II: Conventional Stage 3—Mutual Interpersonal Expectations, Relationships, and Interpersonal Conformity; "Good boy," "Good girl" Orientation	Living up to what is expected by people close to you or what people generally expect of people in your role as son, brother, friend, etc. "Being good" is important and means having good motives, showing concern about others. It also means keeping mutual relationships, such as trust, loyalty, respect and gratitude.	The need to be a good person in your own eyes and those of others. Your caring for others. Belief in the Golden Rule. Desire to maintain rules and authority which support stereotypical good behavior. *Perspective of the individual in relationships with other individuals.* Aware of shared feelings, agreements, and expectations which take primacy over individual interests. Relates points of view through the concrete Golden Rule, putting yourself in the other guy's shoes. Does not yet consider generalized system perspective.	If I were Heinz, I would have stolen the drug for my wife. You can't put a price on love, no amount of gifts make love. You can't put a price on life either.	He should not steal. If his wife dies, he cannot be blamed. It is not because he is heartless or that he does not love her enough to do everything that he legally can. The druggist is the selfish or heartless one.

Stage	What Is Right	Reasons for Doing Right	Social Perspective of Stage		
Stage 4— Social System and Conscience Orientation	Fulfilling the actual duties to which you have agreed. Laws are to be upheld except in extreme cases where they conflict with other fixed social duties. Right is also contributing to society, the group, or institution.	To keep the institution going as a whole, to avoid the breakdown in the system "if everyone did it," or the imperative of conscience to meet one's defined obligations.	*Differentiates societal point of view from interpersonal agreement or motives.* Takes the point of view of the system that defines roles and rules. Considers individual relations in terms of place in the system.	When you get married, you take a vow to love and cherish your wife. Marriage is not only love, it's an obligation. Like a legal contract.	It is a natural thing for Heinz to want to save his wife, but it is still always wrong to steal. He still knows he is stealing and taking a valuable drug from the man who made it.
Level III: Postconventional, or Principled Stage 5— Social Contract or Utility and Individual Rights Orientation	Being aware that people hold a variety of values and opinions, that most values and rules are relative to your group. These relative rules should usually be upheld, however, in the interest of impartiality and because they are the social contract. Some values and rights like *life* and *liberty*, however, must be upheld in any society and regardless of majority opinion.	A sense of obligation to law because of one's social contract to make and abide by laws for the welfare of all and for the protection of all people's rights. A feeling of contractual commitment, freely entered upon, to family, friendship, trust, and work obligations. Concern that laws and duties be based on rational calculation of overall utility, "the greatest good for the greatest number."	*Prior-to-society perspective.* Perspective of a rational individual aware of values and rights prior to social attachments and contracts. Integrates perspectives by formal mechanisms of agreement, contract, objective impartiality, and due process. Considers moral and legal points of view; recognizes that they sometimes conflict and finds it difficult to integrate them.	The law was not set up for these circumstances. Taking the drug in this situation is not really right, but it is justified to do it.	You cannot completely blame someone for stealing, but extreme circumstances do not really justify taking the law in your own hands. You cannot have everyone stealing whenever they get desperate. The end may be good, but the ends do not justify the means.
Stage 6— Universal Ethical Principles Orientation	Following self-chosen ethical principles. Particular laws or social agreements are usually valid because they rest on such principles. When laws violate these principles, one acts in accordance with the principle. Principles are universal principles of justice: the equality of human rights and respect for the dignity of human beings as individual persons.	The belief as a rational person in the validity of universal moral principles, and a sense of personal commitment to them.	*Perspective of a moral point of view from which social arrangements derive.* Perspective is that of any rational individual recognizing the nature of morality or the fact that persons are ends in themselves and must be treated as such.	This is a situation that forces him to choose between stealing and letting his wife die. In a situation where the choice must be made, it is morally right to steal. He has to act in terms of the principle of preserving and respecting life.	Heinz is faced with the decision of whether to consider the other people who need the drug just as badly as his wife. Heinz ought to act not according to his particular feelings toward his wife but considering the value of all the lives involved.

Source: Adapted from "Moral stages and moralization: The cognitive-developmental approach" by L. Kohlberg, 1976, in T. Lickona, ed., *Moral development and behavior,* New York: Holt, Rinehart & Winston; and "Stage and sequence: The cognitive-developmental approach to socialization" by L. Kohlberg, 1969, in D. A. Goslin, ed., *Handbook of socialization theory and research,* Chicago: Rand McNally.

moral development follow an invariant, universal set of stages? Does the failure of most adults in this country and elsewhere to reach the highest stages mean that they are morally immature? Many social scientists believe that Kohlberg's scheme is culturally biased in favor of educated, modernized, middle-class individuals, at least in its descriptions of postconventional reasoning. Recently, however, Kohlberg (1984) has revised his thinking about Stages 5 and 6. Stage 5 now includes the notion that human life is more important than property. Stage 6 is recognized as a mode of thought found only in rare individuals, not the expectable outcome of ordinary human development.

Kohlberg has also been criticized for his complicated scoring system, which is highly subjective and demands special training (Cortese, 1984; Kurtines & Greif, 1974). Thus, the moral dilemma is usually not obvious, and not something that can be determined by an untrained observer. Even with training, raters disagree with one another about a quarter of the time. The fact that Kohlberg and his colleagues have revised both the scoring system and their theoretical assumptions shows that gauging moral development is far from precise.

Despite the criticisms, Kohlberg's work is a major contribution to developmental psychology. He showed that there is indeed a regular progression in the development of moral reasoning. Moreover, Kohlberg rescued the topic of moral reasoning from the oblivion into which it had fallen after the early decades of the twentieth century. During the heyday of behaviorism and psychoanalytic theory, the topic of morality seemed quaint and unscientific. Piaget himself, in his later work, turned away from his early interest in moral reasoning. Kohlberg's efforts have made this very important aspect of human social life a central concern for psychology.

Women and Moral Reasoning

Recently, a new charge of bias has been made against Kohlberg's theory. Carol Gilligan, in her book *In a Different Voice* (1982), claims that

Kohlberg, along with most developmental psychologists, devalues women's distinctive psychological perspectives. She argues that women and men differ in their basic orientation to life. Women, she writes, from infancy onward, emphasize attachment and connectedness to others; men and boys typically emphasize individuation and separateness. Thus, in dealing with hypothetical moral issues, women stress care and sensitivity to the needs of everyone involved in the dilemma, while men see moral issues as matters of individual rights and the application of abstract rules.

To illustrate the difference, Gilligan presents the responses of two 11-year-olds, Amy and Jake, to the Heinz dilemma. Jake sees the dilemma as a conflict between the value of property and that of a human life. Since he believes that, logically, life is the higher value, it is obvious to him that Heinz must steal the drug. It's "sort of a math problem with humans."

Amy, by contrast, sees the problem as one of relationships. If Heinz steals the drug, he might go to jail, and would not be able to help his wife if she got sick again. They should "just talk it out and find some other way to get the money," Amy feels, or they should talk to the druggist and get him to realize that he should give the drug to the woman and let the couple pay for it later. Thus, Jake is convinced that logic requires Heinz to steal the drug, while Amy is convinced that if Heinz and the druggist talked the problem over, stealing would not be necessary. Gilligan argues that girls and women typically reason the way Amy does, and that Kohlberg's scoring system penalizes this kind of morality of care.

Gilligan's book has found a large audience among the general public as well as in the field of psychology. It has been widely hailed as a vindication of women's special view of what is important in life. Further, Gilligan's claim that Kohlberg's scoring system devalues concern with relationships is correct. Kolhlberg's original scoring system did rate concern with relationships as Stage 3, "conventional," but his new scoring system has separated the content of a person's responses from the quality of reasoning. Thus, it is possible for caring responses to be scored at any level from 1 to 6 (Colby & Damon, 1983; Colby et al., 1983).

Despite the appeal of her arguments, however, Gilligan's claims have been challenged by other researchers. Some recent studies have failed to find evidence that males and females actually do differ in moral judgment scores (Pratt, Golding, & Hunter, 1984; Rest, 1983; Walker, 1984). These researchers argue that where such distinctions have been found, they are due to educational and occupational differences; when these factors are equated, the sex differences disappear. Still more recently, the claim that there are no sex differences in moral reasoning has been challenged (Baumrind, in press). The issue remains highly controversial, like many other aspects of moral development research.

Whatever the outcome of the controversy, Gilligan's work has made an important contribution to the psychology of morality. She has focused attention on a special, typically female point of view about what is important in life—a point of view that has traditionally been ignored, misunderstood, and devalued. Gilligan reveals the limitations of theories of moral development based on the male perspective and the moral strength in what have traditionally been regarded as women's weaknesses. Nevertheless, it seems incorrect to say that this way of looking at moral issues is seen in all women all the time, and never in men.

The Sense of Justice

William Damon (1977) has argued that Kohlberg's stories are inappropriate for children, since they deal with adult issues such as the value of human life and the institution of marriage. Damon found that where he obtained a "worm's eye view" of the child's social world in his own studies, presenting children with dilemmas drawn from familiar experiences such as how to divide eight pieces of pizza among seven children, they showed remarkable sophistication in moral and other forms of social understanding in middle childhood.

Damon presented children with several illustrated stories concerning children who have to divide money or candy earned from a joint project such as making bracelets or objects for a fair. In each story, the children are said to differ in some way—one is bigger, one is poorer; one makes better bracelets quickly, another is younger and works more slowly. The children were asked to describe the fairest way of dividing the candy or the money.

Damon found a clear progression between the ages of four to nine in children's thinking about fairness. He identified three stages in this progression. The youngest children did not distinguish between justice and each individual's own desires. At a later phase of this early stage, children would allocate the candy or the money on the basis of some observable characteristic: "She should get it because she's the prettiest." At the second level, which emerges at around five or six, children advocate simple equality: Everyone should get the same treatment under all circumstances. This is less a commitment to the abstract ideal of equality than a seemingly easy way to avoid fights. Following this desire for equality, the idea of equity emerges: some children are more deserving than others, because of talent or effort. At this stage, children recognize only one kind of claim.

During the third stage, which emerges between seven and nine, children recognize that several different valid claims can exist. The child thus attempts to reward everyone who has a special claim. Finally, at a later point, children take on the more difficult task of deciding which of the competing claims is most justified in the given situations. Certain claims will be considered irrelevant.

Moral Behavior

So far, we have been discussing moral reasoning, or "story-problem morality" (Brown & Herrnstein, 1975). What is the relation between a person's statements about moral issues and his or her actual behavior? The question is a complicated one. For one thing, Kohlberg's theory does not assume any necessary relation between moral level and behavior, since in the dilemmas it presents, either course of action can be justified at any moral level. The theory looks for the reasons people give for their actions, not the actions themselves. On the other hand, the theory "prefers" certain values, such as human life, over other values such as law and order. There is some evidence that in situations of actual moral choice, people at Stage 6 are more likely than those at other stages to disobey authority when it conflicts with what they view as higher principles (Haan, Smith, & Block, 1968). One review of the literature indicated that out of seventy-five studies relating moral judgment to behavior, fifty-seven, or 76 percent, found some evidence of a relationship. On the other hand, many studies did not find such correlations; and even when they were found, the correlations were not strong ones.

In general, the evidence for consistency between moral standards and moral conduct is less than overwhelming. Many psychological experiments have shown that people of all ages will behave in ways that they and others consider immoral. A classic study by Hartshorne and May (1928) laid to rest the notion that there is some general trait of conscience or morality that predicts moral conduct in all situations, as well as the notion that people can be clearly categorized as moral or immoral. Hartshorne and May tested children for many types of immoral behavior, such as cheating, lying, or stealing, and in various situations and settings. They also examined children's moral judgments. In general, they found little consistency between statements of morality made in different situations—for instance school versus playground—or between statements about morality and actual behavior. Thus, cheating in one situation did not necessarily predict lying or cheating in another situation. Practically all children engaged in some form of immoral behavior some of the time. More recent research has not challenged Hartshorne and May's essential conclusion about the weakness of the links between moral reasoning and moral conduct.

Damon (1977) followed up his hypothetical story study with one in which he examined children's real-life judgments. He asked groups

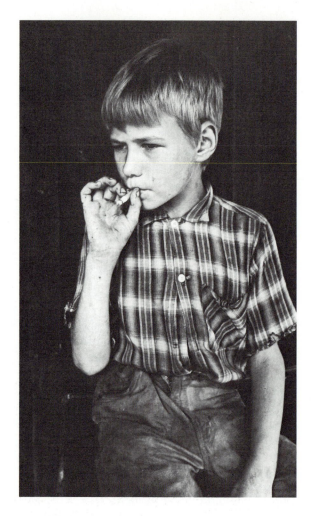

consisting of three children of the same age and one younger child actually to make bracelets. Then he asked the three older children, in the absence of the younger one, to divide a reward of ten candy bars among the four children. Damon's initial hypothesis was that children's responses in the real-life situation would be similar to their interview responses. He found that half of the 144 children did, in fact, reason the same way in both situations. Nineteen of the children had more advanced scores in real life than in the hypothetical situation, while 52 subjects scored lower. In other words, the model response was to use the same kind of moral reasoning hypothetically and in real life, but for most children where there was a discrepancy between words and deed, self-interest won out over principle.

Often in real-life situations, moral issues are not as clear as they are in story problems. We live in a complex culture which presents us with mixed messages and goals that may sometimes be incompatible—to be honest, successful, well liked, helpful, and competitive. In pursuing one worthy value, we may be tempted to sacrifice others. In a study carried out in an Italian city, Leonard Pearlin (1971) discovered that sometimes parents' messages can have unintended effects. Working-class parents who wanted their children to have an occupation of a higher social level than their own frequently urged their children to work hard and succeed in school. The children, however, were likely to respond to these pressures not by working hard, but by cheating.

Jules Henry (1963), an anthropologist who studied American high schools, found a contradiction between the norm that cheating is wrong, and what amounted to almost a counternorm in favor of cheating. The children he studied were under a great deal of pressure to cheat from the grading system, parental pressures, peers, and even from teachers who seemed indifferent to the cheating going on under their noses. Henry observed that a child who refused to share test answers with a classmate would be regarded as the deviant, blameworthy person. Other writers have pointed to other contradictions in American life: parents and other moral authorities preach nonviolence to children, yet they use and threaten violence in conflicts with friends and neighbors (Goode, 1971); most people subscribe to the norm of marital fidelity, yet extramarital affairs are common. Susan Isaacs (1966), an English psychologist, pointed out some time ago the confused and conflicting messages adults present to children regarding the treatment of animals. Children are told to be kind to animals, and their acts of cruelty are condemned. Some pets are treated almost as members of the family. But most adults eat dead animals, wear clothing made from dead animals, and kill animals that are dangerous or a nuisance. Some adults even kill animals for sport.

American society is not necessarily more inconsistent than other societies. There is little evidence anywhere of a society whose norms and ideals are indicators of what people actually do (Harris, 1968). The idea of socialization as simply the transmission of moral rules from one generation to the next is off the mark. If every society manifests contradictions between what adults preach and what they actually do, then growing children are faced with a much more complex task than simply learning a consistent set of moral values.

Parental Influence in Middle Childhood

Although children in middle childhood are moving out into the world, and parents must share their influence with the child's friends, the school, and the mass media, the family retains an important place in their lives. Home and family frequently provide a refuge from the pressures and demands of life, a "haven in a heartless world" (Lasch, 1977). At the same time, the outside world can serve as a refuge from the emotionally charged atmosphere at home. By the age of four, the Newsons (1977) found, children were beginning to reserve their worst, most uncontrolled, and angriest behavior for the family—who are willing to tolerate in the privacy of the home behavior that would not be tolerated elsewhere. Indeed, the family remains the place where people experience their most intense joys, sorrows, and rages. It is, as one family therapist put it, "the place where you're dealing with life and death voltages" (Whitaker, quoted in Framo, 1972, p. 3).

As children move out into the wider world, they come to see their parents in a new light. Harry Stack Sullivan has written about the transformation of children's relations to parents in the juvenile years. He explains, "the juvenile gradually has the opportunity to pare the parents down from godlike figures to people" (1953, p. 31).

Children also learn during the school years about their parents' social position in the

world. They learn about the prevailing systems of class and caste—which occupations, levels of income, styles of dress and speech, and so forth are valued by the larger society, and which are not. In a society in which money buys not only the necessities of life, but also identity and status, children learn early about access to economic resources and the possibilities for self-realization they provide. The consumption of goods and services locates a person in the stratification system. Lee Rainwater (1977) has studied the social meaning of income and found that there is a "standard package of goods and services" families are expected to have. Those unable to buy the standard package not only feel deprived, but something less than "whole and usual" persons. Thus, children who fall below the standard may judge their parents and themselves as counting for little in the larger society.

By contrast, children who grow up rich and affluent come to have what psychiatrist Robert Coles (1967) calls a sense of "entitlement." Coles has studied children from all walks of life in his several-volume study, *Children of Crisis,*

and finds that privileged children, despite differences among themselves, develop a special kind of identity that they always possess, whether they grow up to be stockbrokers or dropouts. They have the sense that they and their families count for something in the world, that their needs will be met, that life is full of choices, and that within the limits of their abilities almost any kind of future is open to them. This is not to say that affluent children are necessarily happier than children lower down in the social strata; rather, the quality of children's joys and sorrows reflects to some degree the place they and their families occupy in the stratification system.

It is obvious that children's behavior, attitudes, and views of themselves are derived from the circumstances in which they grow up. But how can we translate this observation into psychological theory? Are children simply products of the way they have been brought up? Until fairly recently, most social scientists assumed what might be called a social determinist point of view. The assumption was that social influences, specifically the parents, de-

most infinite number of ways, many researchers have identified two major dimensions: authority and affection. The first dimension concerns the degree to which parents try to control their children's behavior, the kind of discipline they use, and the consistency of their efforts along these lines. The second dimension concerns the amount of love the parents feel toward the child, and how much the parents express that love. All parents have some ambivalence about their children; but in the more loving parents, positive feelings outweigh the hostile ones.

These two dimensions of parental behavior have been researched both separately and together. Different studies have defined the two dimensions in different ways. Nevertheless, there is general agreement that a moderate amount of control, consistently enforced, has a positive effect on children. Children with moderately controlling parents—not too strict and not too lax—have been found to be better able to control their impulses (Block & Haan, 1971; G. Patterson, 1976), have higher self-esteem (Coopersmith, 1967), and are more competent, happy, and self-reliant.

Studies of parental warmth have concluded that children whose parents are loving and accepting are more likely to be securely attached in infancy (Ainsworth et al., 1978) and more open to exploration and learning in early childhood (Matas, Arend, & Sroufe, 1978). Also, children of more affectionate parents have been found to be more compliant (Patterson, 1976), higher in self-esteem (Coopersmith, 1967), and more considerate and altruistic (Hoffman & Saltzstein, 1967; Zahn-Waxler, Radke-Yarrow, & King, 1979).

A classic series of studies by Diana Baumrind (1971, 1973) examined both dimensions of parental behavior. She and her research team, using in-home observations and other techniques, identified three patterns of parenting:

1. *Authoritarian* parents were high on the control dimension and low on the warmth dimension. They valued obedience and order and discouraged verbal give-and-take with other children.

termine the kind of person a child grows up to be. Children's personalities are determined by the way their parents have treated them: a child who has been rejected will suffer from low self-esteem; a child who has been treated with kindness and reasonable discipline will grow up to be self-confident; a boy brought up in a fatherless home will have trouble with his masculinity; a child who has experienced trauma or ill treatment in early childhood will bear the mental scars for life. The assumption that parents and home life are responsible for crime, juvenile delinquency, school failure, and mental illness is not only a major theme in psychological theory, but a widespread popular belief as well. Each year dozens, if not hundreds, of books and articles promise parents that if they follow the prescribed methods their children will turn out to be happy and successful.

Dimensions of Parental Behavior

There is a considerable body of research on the influence of childrearing practices on children's development. Although parents vary in an al-

2. *Authoritative* parents were high in both control and warmth. They encouraged discussions about rules and expected their children to be both compliant and independent.
3. *Permissive* parents tended to be high in warmth and low in control. They made few demands on the children and let children do what they wanted as much as possible.

Baumrind found that children of authoritative parents were highest in competence; they were independent and socially responsible. Children of authoritarian parents tended to be passive and dependent, while children of permissive parents lacked social responsibility and were not particularly independent.

Limits of Parental Influence

In recent years, as we have seen in earlier chapters, researchers and theorists in developmental psychology have been questioning the assumptions underlying the studies cited above—that the direction of influence flows in one way, from parents to children; and that a particular kind of parental behavior leads directly to a particular outcome in the child. Although there is no doubt that parental practices and attitudes have a profound influence on child development, everyday experience shows that there is another side to the picture. Many of the most successful adults in American life have childhood histories that current theorists would regard as unfavorable, if not disastrous. Sociologist Alice Rossi has observed that "There is often a predominance of tension in childhood family relations and traumatic loss rather than loving support, intense channeling of energy in one area of interest rather than an all-around profile of diverse interests, and social withdrawal . . . rather than gregarious sociability" (1968, p. 235).

In the folklore of every family and community are stories of a promising youth from an ideal family who became a drug addict, the school failure who became a leading surgeon, and the orphan who became a respected judge.

(See the box on Resilient or "Invulnerable" Children.) Further, in everyday life and naturalistic studies such as the Newsons', parents repeatedly comment on temperamental differences between their children which seem to resist the most strenuous efforts to change—one child has a sunny, easy disposition and seems to cooperate naturally. Another child is headstrong and wild; and still another is negativistic, "opposing all parental demands on principle, and then considering the matter" (Newson & Newson, 1976, p. 375). As we saw in Chapter 6, children differ in temperament and these differences have an important impact on parent-child relations. Parents find themselves frequently striking one of their children, while another child has never been touched in anger. A longitudinal study by Buss (1981) also confirms these anecdotal reports. Buss found that on the basis of the observed activity level of preschool children, it was possible to predict parent-child interaction several years later. Parents of children who had extremely high activity levels were more likely to get into hostile power struggles with them. As Buss put it, "It may be dangerous to be the parent of a highly active child."

In recent years, researchers have been recognizing the complexity of parent-child relations and the difficulties of untangling cause and effect. They have been questioning the parental determinism model of development, as well as the assumption that a child's personality and behavior will continue to be the same in adulthood (Brim & Kagan, 1980). Further, there is a growing realization that parent-child relationships are embedded in wider family systems. The marital relationship of the parents—especially the amount of conflict—has an impact on children's development, as does the family's social network of friends and relatives (Lerner, Spanier, & Belsky, 1982). Despite the considerable amount of energy that has gone into studies of childrearing practices, the parental determinism model of development has not been strongly supported. By 1976, there had been eight major reviews of research in this field. In a study of these reviews, Richard Bell (1976) concluded that there has been a

Resilient or "Invulnerable" Children

Eleanor grew up in difficult circumstances. Although she came from a wealthy and socially prominent family, her childhood was highly stressful. Her first misfortune was being born homely and awkward to a glamorous, "belle of the ball" mother. Eleanor's mother could not stand to be touched by her little girl and ridiculed her in front of guests. Her father was a charming alcoholic playboy Eleanor adored but saw rarely.

By the time she was 10, both parents and a younger brother had died. Eleanor was raised by her strict maternal grandmother in cold and splendid isolation. Painfully shy, she did poorly in school, lied, stole, and suffered from numerous fears. Eventually, however, she grew up to be one of the most admired public figures of the twentieth century—Eleanor Roosevelt. She is remembered not just for her activities as First Lady, but for her moral leadership and public service after her husband's death.

Eleanor Roosevelt is only one of many eminent people who experienced a difficult childhood (Goertzel & Goertzel, 1962). Another is Daniel Patrick Moynihan, currently U.S. senator from New York, and formerly the U.S. ambassador to the United Nations. Moynihan grew up in the slums of East Harlem; when his father abandoned the family, Daniel had to spend his adolescence shining shoes and tending bar in his mother's saloon.

In recent years, a number of researchers have become interested in children who survive and even thrive under hardships that often devastate others. Norman Garmezy (1976, 1983), one of the pioneers in this line of research, coined the term "invulnerables" to describe these children. Garmezy's interest in invulnerability grew out of his research on the children of schizophrenic parents. He found that the majority of such children did not become schizophrenic or disturbed themselves. And he found some children like Michael, a 10-year-old boy with a schizophrenic mother, a father in prison, and a sister in a home for the retarded. Since Michael's birth he had known nothing but poverty and chaos. Yet his teachers described him as charming, bright, popular, a good student, and a natural leader.

Eleanor Roosevelt at work.

Since his discovery of such children, Garmezy has been trying to understand resilience in the face of stress. He found that those who cope well with hardship seemed to share several characteristics. The central quality they had in common was a strong sense of self. These children had both self-esteem and a sense of personal power—what has been termed an internal locus of control (Lefcourt, 1973). Despite the bleakness of their circumstances, resilient children believe they can exercise some degree of control over their lives. They perceive some degree of choice in situations where others might see none at all. Instead of giving up or showing what Martin Seligman (1975) has called "learned helplessness," such children keep plugging away at problems, making do with very little. For example, one young girl had no food in the house to take for lunch except some stale bread. She cheerfully made herself "a bread sandwich." In general, these children seem to face challenges rather than flee from them.

Resilient children also seem to have at least one adult in their lives who provides emotional support and encouragement. If not a parent, this supportive adult can be a grandparent or a teacher. Here, too, such children often seem to be able to make do with little. Eleanor Roosevelt, for example, had had little contact with her father before his death, yet memories of his affection for her sustained her through difficult times.

The term "invulnerable" may be somewhat misleading. There may be limits to how much stress even an "invulnerable" child can bear. And childhood hardship may leave scars on the adult that are subtle and hard to see. Further, "invulnerability" suggests an imperviousness to pain; yet the ability to cope does not mean a lack of suffering. A woman I know who overcame a childhood marked by rejection by both her mother and stepmother, and the death of her abusive but sometimes affectionate father, put it this way: "We suffer, but we don't let it destroy us."

failure to reach stable findings and little agreement between studies carried out.

The research literature even documents the idea that certain parental actions may produce opposing effects. Wesley Becker (1964) reviewed a number of studies on the effect of parental discipline which were based on interviews and questionnaires rather than home observations. He found that, in boys, strict discipline on the part of parents may result either in sons who are extremely nonagressive or extremely aggressive. Becker also pointed out that all the different approaches may result in the very kind of behavior the parent is aiming at. Strictness may foster well-controlled, obedient behavior, but it may also result in children being fearful, dependent, and submissive; further, it may dull their intellectual striving and inhibit their ability to deal with aggression in themselves and others. Conversely, "permissiveness" may result in children who are outgoing, sociable, assertive, and intellectually striving; but it may also lead to less persistence and more aggressiveness.

Even when correlations are found between parental practices and child behavior, they are generally low. As mentioned earlier, it is possible for correlations to be statistically significant and yet be low in their ability to predict individual differences. (Recall that a "significant" finding, statistically speaking, is one that is unlikely to have occurred through chance alone.) Further, even strong correlations in themselves provide no information about cause and effect. For example, one finding in the literature is a correlation between aggressive behavior in boys and severe physical punishment or parental hostility. This finding is usually taken to mean that parental severity produces an aggressive child. Richard Bell (1968) however, has pointed out that correlations between parents' behavior and the child's personality characteristics can often be explained as children's effects on parents as well as parents' effects on children.

Thus, the association between children's aggression and punishment can be explained as resulting from the influence of the child's aggressiveness on the parents' disciplinary practices. Bell and others have suggested that, temperamentally, children differ in aggressiveness and docility. Parents, for their part, have a number of ways of trying to control their children. They may begin with soft words and go on to use physical punishment only when other means have failed. Bell offers similar explanations for correlations between parental behavior and such child behaviors as achievement, assertiveness, independence, and guilt. Further, correlations do not reveal the process by which they came about. As R. Bell and Harper observe, "the love-oriented permissive parent and the sweet little child who is doing chores may have done some real shouting and hair-pulling before you appeared on the scene to observe their currently peaceful truce" (1977, p. 213).

Those who argue that children influence their parents do not deny that parents influence their children. Rather, they argue that the one-way model that has prevailed in the past results in an oversimplified view of the socialization process. They suggest that parent-child relations occur in a reciprocal social system in which each party influences and accommodates the other. Parents are more powerful and know more than their children, but their power is offset to some extent by differences in children's temperamental abilities and their ability to resist or modify their parents' attempts to control them.

The parental determinism model of socialization is also at odds with recent work on cognitive development. While studies of parent-child relations have traditionally used a passive model of the child, in which children reflect the social input they have received from their families, studies of children's cognitive development portray them as selecting and processing information from the environment. Today, most theorists, even social learning theorists such as Bandura (1969), recognize that cognition plays an important role in socialization and that children are not simply passive recipients of environmental influences.

If we take cognition seriously, then children's interpretations of their experience play a key role in the socialization process. In fact, numerous developmental psychologists have pointed to children's conceptualizations of events in their lives as the key to understanding their subsequent responses. Although it may be possible to predict the child's behavior from his or her interpretation of experience, it may be difficult or impossible to predict how a child will interpret the objective events.

The most general statement of the need to incorporate the child's point of view into research was made by Kagan (1967) in his article on the need for relativism in psychology. Traditionally, he notes, psychologists frame the relationship between parental behavior and child outcomes in absolute terms. They assume, for example, that there is a definable set of behaviors that can be labeled social rejection and that these rejecting acts lead to inevitable changes in the self-concept of the child. A lack of expression of affection or harsh physical punishment are the usual indicators of parental rejection. In many cultural settings, however, these behaviors do not necessarily imply rejection for either mother or child. Kagan concludes that "rejection is not a fixed, invariant quality of behavior *qua* behavior. Like pleasure, pain, or beauty, rejection is in the mind of the rejectee. It is a belief held by the child; not an action by a parent" (1967, p. 132).

Another reason why parental action should be viewed in relative rather than absolute terms is that a child's perceptions of a particular instance of parental behavior, such as a spanking or a display of affection, depend on internalized standards based on previous experience. Bronfenbrenner (1958) observes that the child who is used to a high level of parental support may be more sensitive to a lack of affection than the child who is not accustomed to much warmth. Danziger (1971) notes that a researcher's view of parental severity may have little to do with how the child experiences the parent's behavior. While the researcher uses statistical standards or the norms of the professional subculture as a basis for evaluating the parent, children have only their own experience to rely on, at least until they are exposed to discrepant norms outside the home.

The greatest theoretical emphasis on the importance of the child's perceptions is found in the psychoanalytic literature. Although psychoanalytic ideas served as important inspiration for the parent-as-cause model, Freud himself, as well as those who followed closely in his tradition, stressed that it is children's fantasies about their parents, rather than parental behavior itself, that are the determining influences in personality development. Edmund Bergler, in a rather extreme statement of this position, argues that parents are "truly helpless" against this decisive force in the child's development:

> The reality presented to the child is merely raw material. *What the child does with this raw material depends entirely upon his own unconscious decisions.*
>
> Given an unfavorable home situation, one child might grow into adulthood correcting the frustrating influences. Another, starting with an ideal home situation, could magnify small incidents into "injustices" and later, as a neurotic

adult, continue to feel that he has been wronged. (1964, p. 9, emphasis in original)

To emphasize the contribution children make to their own development is not to deny the obvious fact that parents do have a profound impact on their children. Certainly the type of parents we have, whether they are kind or cruel, strict or lax, responsible or neglectful, shapes the childhood we experience and the memories we will carry into adulthood. But the people we become as adults always involves an interplay between what happens to us and what we make of those happenings.

One quality of parents that does have a major influence on their children's later lives, however, is their social class. As noted earlier, the social class one is reared in has emerged as a major predictor of many kinds of behavior—performance in school and college, occupational aspirations and status, the likelihood of serious mental illness. The social class of a boy's father is a better predictor of his eventual education and occupation than his own IQ during childhood (McCall, 1977). In the Fels longitudinal study, family social class was correlated with autonomy and competitiveness in women, with a more positive attitude toward fathers in men, and with less traditional sex roles in both men and women (Kagan & Moss, 1962).

Social class is such a powerful variable because it comprises a host of influences: the quality of housing and neighborhood; the family's resources of time, money, and energy; the cultural level of the home; the amount and kind of stress in the family; as well as child-rearing methods and the kinds of beliefs the child is exposed to, the way children spend their time, and their sense of what kinds of lives they might have. Lillian Rubin, in a study of working- and middle-class families, has described the set of class-linked influences that impinge on the growing child:

> For the child, especially a boy, born into a professional middle-class home, the sky's the limit, his dreams are relatively unfettered by constraints. In his earliest

conscious moments he becomes aware of his future and of plans being made for it—plans that are not just wishful fantasies but plans that are backed up by the resources to make them come true. All around him as he grows, he sees men who do important work at prestigious jobs. At home, at school, in the neighborhood, he is encouraged to test the limits of his ability to reach for the stars.

For most working-class boys the experience is the reverse. Born into a family where survival is problematic, he sees only the frantic scramble to meet today's needs, pay tomorrow's rent. . . . Such boys face "a series of mounting disadvantages"—that is, poverty, lack of education and vocational guidance, no role models in prestige occupations, no personal contacts to help push a career along—that all come together to . . . form a vicious circle from which few ever escape. It is in this process that the class structure is preserved—as if in ice—from one generation to the next. (1976, p. 38)

Television and Children

The other major influence in the home, apart from the family, is television. Nearly all American children watch TV, and they spend more time at it than they do in school; more time, in fact, than in any other activity except sleeping (Liebert & Poulos, 1975). School-aged children watch more television than anyone. The amount of viewing increases from the age of 3, reaches a peak at 11 and 12, and declines somewhat in adolescence (see Huston & Wright, 1982). The average American child watches television three to four hours a day, every day of the year (Comstock et al., 1978).

Television achieved its dominant place in children's out-of-school lives in a relatively short period of time. Television sets came onto the market in the years after World War II and became practically universal in American homes by the mid-1950s. This massive change in the socialization of children has led to a great deal of public and private concern. American parents and social commentators are deeply ambivalent about television. On the one hand, television has been portrayed as a dangerous addiction, a "plug-in drug" (Winn,

Fred Rogers from "Mister Rogers' Neighborhood"

1978) that wastes children's time, impairs their imagination and intellectual functioning, interferes with family life, and encourages violence. In one survey, 80 percent of parents said they worried about their children's television viewing (Medrich et al., 1982).

On the other hand, parents and scholarly writers also recognize that television is a tireless source of information. It brings major events and far-off places into the home, as well as knowledge of different groups in American life. Through such programs as "Sesame Street" and "Mister Rogers' Neighborhood," television has shown its effectiveness as an educator. Every once in a while the power of television is revealed in some dramatic fashion: a program such as *The Day After* captures the public's attention and focuses it on the dangers of nuclear war. A broadcast of *The Deer Hunter* results in several people killing themselves by playing Russian roulette; in an episode of "Happy Days," Fonzie takes out a library card and over the next few days thousands of teenagers go to their local libraries and take out cards (Gitlin, 1983).

Why is television so popular? Grant Noble (1975) speculates that it serves important needs in modern industrial societies. Television enables people both to "escape" from society and at the same time to participate in it. In some ways, television provides a "community" akin to the village society of days gone by. By exposing isolated individuals to the same familiar content, it resembles the village pump from which people used to get the latest "news" and gossip. For children as well as adults, television shows a range of people, places, events, and social roles and occupations and reveals how others—individuals, communities, and societies—live. Television can act as eyes and ears in near and faraway places. Noble recognizes that television often presents distorted views of social reality, but he also sees its potential as a tool for social learning. He concludes that in "modern industrial societies where individuals necessarily lead fragmented and discontinuous lives we need information about our fellow [mankind] as much as we need water" (p. 242).

Two decades of studies have documented both the positive and negative effects of television. Studies of television violence have shown that violent programs may kindle violence in real life and that well-designed, educational, and prosocial programs can increase children's knowledge and improve behavior. But the findings are more complex than is generally assumed. (See box on Does Television Violence [Really] Cause Aggression?)

Television and Social Stereotypes

Apart from the effects of violent programs, parents and many other people worry about the impact of television on children's views of social reality. Every television program presents some version of reality, whether it is a news program or a situation comedy. The worry is that television offers distorted or exaggerated views.

In general, television presents highly stereotyped images of male and female roles, minorities, and old people. According to George

Does Television Violence (Really) Cause Aggression?

Most psychologists agree that viewing violence on television causes people to be more aggressive than they would otherwise be. Despite the apparent consensus on the issue, social psychologist Jonathan Freedman (1984) has recently reviewed the research and concluded that there is very little convincing evidence that, in natural settings, television violence actually does cause people to be more aggressive.

Freedman relied on research done outside the laboratory. Although much of the research on the effects of violent programs has been carried out in laboratory settings, he argues that such findings may tell us little about the effects of television in the real world. First, he believes that the typical laboratory measures of aggression, such as punching a Bobo doll, do not really correspond to real-life aggression, since there is no possibility of retaliation or punishment. Second, he feels that these experiments encourage or at least give permission to subjects to act aggressively. Thus, the subjects may assume that because the experimenters have chosen the films, they approve of the content. If the subjects are then given an opportunity to behave aggressively, they may think that the experimenter permits such behavior. Finally, showing one violent program in isolation may be quite different from the usual diet of television programs in which violent programs are often mixed with nonviolent ones.

After eliminating laboratory studies from consideration, Freedman was left with a relatively small number of studies dealing with the effects of television violence in natural settings. Some studies were field experiments: for example, students in a residential school are randomly assigned to view various types of television programs and then measured for aggressiveness. In general, the field experiments produced inconsistent results. Some studies supported the hypothesis that viewing television violence increases aggressiveness, but the effects were not strong. Other studies failed to find any evidence that television violence increases aggressiveness.

It is interesting also that the field studies found no consistent difference between aggressive and nonaggressive individuals in their responses to televised violence. Some researchers believe that individuals predisposed to be aggressive will be more affected by violence. This was confirmed by some of the studies. But others indicated that highly aggressive subjects were markedly *less* aggressive after viewing violent television.

Although field experiments provide the best way to test the effects of watching violent programs, they are difficult to carry out. Therefore, much of the research is correlational. That is, the researcher records the amount of violent television people watch and relates that to a measure of aggressiveness. Although the results of these correlational studies are not totally consistent, they do indeed confirm that children and adolescents who watch more violent programs than others tend to be more aggressive. However, while this is an important finding, the correlations are not very high. Further, since correlation does not necessarily imply causality, these findings do not establish that viewing violent programs causes aggressiveness. It may be that people who are aggressive in the first place choose to watch more violence or that some other factor is responsible for both the behavior and the program preference.

After reviewing several other kinds of studies, Freedman comes to the overall conclusion that the available evidence does not support the hypothesis that viewing television violence causes increased aggression in the real world. The hypothesis may not be wrong, and future research may support it, but the current evidence, he contends, does not.

Freedman himself asks how it can be that our intuitions and theoretical expectations about the effects of television violence are not borne out? After all, people learn about the world from television and children are especially likely to imitate what they see. Freedman points out, however, that social learning theory does not assume that children are indiscriminate mimics. Children imitate behavior that is successful and rewarded. Thus, he argues, if television typically showed violence being rewarded, we might expect an increase in aggression. But if instead it presented violence in many different circumstances—legal versus illegal, justified versus not justified, successful or not successful, punished or rewarded—it would be difficult to predict what messages people would come away with and how their behavior would be affected.

Freedman's conclusions may not be convincing to those who believe that there is too much violence on television, and that it is bound to have harmful effects, especially on children. But Freedman deals only with the hypothesis that violent programs cause aggression. It is possible that television violence could be innocent of producing increases in aggression, and yet still be harmful to children and adults. For one thing, there is evidence that television in general makes young people more fearful about the world and worried about growing up. George Gerbner and his associates (Gerbner et al., 1977; Gerbner et al., 1980) have found that viewers of all ages and all socioeconomic categories who watch television frequently were imbued with a "mean world syndrome." In contrast to light viewers, those who watched frequently were more worried about risks of crime and more suspicious of other people. The violent world of television can, according to Gerbner, both instill and magnify the fear that the world is a mean and dangerous place.

Apart from instilling fears of victimization, the pervasiveness of violence on television can desensitize our feelings: there is evidence that television violence can make children more tolerant of aggression. As an 11-year-old put it, "You see so much violence that it's meaningless. If I saw someone really get killed, it wouldn't be a big deal. I guess I'm turning into a hard rock" (quoted in Greenfield, 1984, p. 51).

Gerbner and his colleagues, in the social world portrayed on American television,

> Men outnumber women three to one, young people comprise one-third and old people one-fifth of their real numbers, professionals and law enforcers dominate the occupations and an average of five acts of violence for prime-time hour (and four times that number per weekend daytime hour) involve more than half of all leading characters. (Gerbner et al., 1980, pp. 10–11)

Sex role stereotyping is pervasive, although there are some notable exceptions, such as "Cagney and Lacey." Generally, women are portrayed as weak and passive and men as powerful and effective. Commercials are even more stereotyped than the programs. Minorities are usually portrayed as poor and powerless, which reinforces existing stereotypes. (Bill Cosby's hit show, which portrays an upper-middle-class black family, is a notable exception.) Old people are relatively rare in TV land—television has been compared to Shangri-la, the mythical country where no one ever grows old. And when old people are seen, they are often portrayed as silly but harmless fools.

The evidence indicates that television does influence children's perceptions of social reality (Noble, 1975). For very young children, television is reality; they think what is happening on the screen is real. As they grow older they recognize that fictional programs do not present reality, but they believe that what they see on realistic entertainment programs represents something that probably happens in real life (Greenfield, 1984). Children as well as adults are especially likely to be influenced by television portrayals when they have little firsthand experience with the reality in question. One woman told a researcher that "they're showing all the black people in one way on almost all the shows, so maybe this is true" (Graves, 1976, p. 1).

Television can also be used to break down stereotypes. A series produced for public television, which aimed at changing sex role attitudes in 9- to 12-year-old children, was effective, especially when the show was discussed in classrooms (Johnston & Ettema, 1982). An experimental study using a commercial program, an episode from "All in the Family," was also effective in decreasing sex role stereotypes (Corder-Bolz, 1980).

Neither children nor adults are completely vulnerable to television's messages, however. The beliefs a person already holds influence the way he or she will perceive a particular program and the impact it will have. For example, children with stereotyped and nontraditional sex role attitudes who watched the same program tended to remember it as being in agreement with their own views (Liben & Signorella, 1980). The impact of television on children can also be modified if parents and other adults encourage discussion and criticism of the programs children watch.

Why Children Watch

In general, television may be harmful for some of the children some of the time or beneficial for some of the children some of the time. For most children its effects are mixed; some good, some bad. Television cannot be understood as an isolated variable, apart from all the other circumstances and influences in a child's life. Television plays many roles in children's lives; they report that it would be the most deeply missed form of entertainment if it was not available (Medrich et al., 1982; Schramm, Lyle, & Parker, 1961). Children often use television as a kind of mild analgesic to cope with everyday stresses. One study asked children what they would prefer to do if they wanted to relax or be entertained, if their feelings were hurt, or if they felt angry or lonely. Television was chosen most often for relaxation and entertainment, and frequently to remedy hurt feelings and deal with anger and loneliness (Lyle & Hoffman, 1972). Children with social adjustment problems may turn to television as an "electronic friend." Heavy television watching may be a symptom, not a cause, of the shy,

distractible behavior frequently attributed to it (Parke, 1978).

Although children often turn to television when they are lonely, it also plays an important role in peer relationships. Children typically watch television alone, rather than with friends, but it is a prime topic of conversation among school-aged children. Sixth graders spend almost as much time talking about what they saw on TV as they do about school events (Lyle & Hoffman, 1972). A child who watched no television might feel left out of many conversations with peers.

Television also functions as a time filler, something to do in between more purposeful activities. Several studies show that most children's television watching is unplanned. Sometimes children do plan to watch a certain program, but mostly they just flip the dial until they find something interesting.

What do children find interesting on TV? Contrary to the widespread idea that violence is a prime attraction, it is humor that young viewers look for and enjoy. Young children like cartoons, but school-aged children prefer situation comedies; those relating to families are the overall favorite (Lyle & Hoffman, 1972). Children enjoy programs with characters close to their own age. Such programs may help children put their own everyday family problems in perspective, although the conflicts are presented in stereotyped ways and, unlike real family problems, are solved simplistically in half an hour.

Apart from the effects of violence, one of the chief worries about children and television concerns what has been called "the displacement problem." Television takes up a lot of time, so it must have displaced other activities. The most worrisome charge is that television has produced a generation of nonreaders and illiterates. Some popular writers look back nostalgically to a time when children spent long hours reading books, when families spent their evenings reading aloud or engaging in leisurely conversations with one another. There is no evidence, however, that this image of family life was ever typical for past generations.

Social science research on the displacement problem is mixed. Some studies find declines in reading as a result of the introduction of television (Himmelweit et al., 1958); others find that children can be heavy television viewers yet also read a lot and be active in extracurricular activities (Lyle & Hoffman, 1972). In general what television seems to replace is activities comparable to itself: audio and visual media such as radio, movies, comic books. None of the major studies has shown a marked decline in leisure reading with the advent of television (Huston & Wright, 1982).

Television and the Family Television is a complicated issue in families. Despite parents' worries over their children's viewing, most parents allow their children to watch a lot of television and have a hard time controlling what the children do watch (Medrich et al., 1982). Part of the reason for this ambivalence is that parents like to watch television themselves, and it also serves a child care function. When children watch TV, parents know that they are safe at home, out of trouble, and being entertained. Parents who live in crowded cities or dangerous neighborhoods are especially likely to see television as a better alternative than allowing the child to roam the streets. It also allows school-aged children to occupy the time of younger children they are babysitting for, in their own homes or someone else's.

Television use varies in families in different demographic circumstances. Blacks generally watch more television than whites, who in turn watch more television than Asian families (Medrich et al., 1982; Stein & Frederick, 1975). Mothers with more education exercise more control over their children's watching, but highly educated working mothers may experience a conflict: their values incline them to limit their children's access to television, but they rely on it to keep the children occupied when neither they nor other activities are at hand to provide alternatives.

Summing it all up, it seems clear that while television is a pervasive presence in children's lives and does have some demonstrable effects, it is not the major menace it is sometimes said to be. But this does not mean it is a good agent of socialization or a good use of children's time. Television is not so much a menace like heroin or toxic waste as it is like white bread— it is easy to take in, it fills you up, but it isn't very nourishing.

Peers in Middle Childhood

School-aged children live in at least three separate worlds, each with its own rules and styles of behavior: the family, the school, and the peer group. The society of children has been compared to an autonomous republic with its own culture and traditions (see the box on Nicknames). The existence of a large body of language and lore, such as games, jokes, taunts, jeers, rituals, and superstitions, has been documented by several writers, most notably Iona and Peter Opie (1959).

The lore and language of childhood are passed on from one generation of children to another without adult help and often against

Nicknames

A 1976 study by Rom Harre on the origins and functions of nicknames among English schoolchildren found that the nicknaming system is a powerful force in the social order that children create for themselves. Nicknames are used to mark certain children as outcasts, but they also are used by certain cliques who have the privilege of using each other's nicknames as a sign of their special relationship to one another. Finally, some names, such as "Fatty" or "Flea Bag," seem to repeat themselves generation after generation and assign their owner to a particular slot or "office" in the society of children. Being assigned to such a slot may bring a child a certain amount of teasing or scapegoating, but being without a nickname was a worse fate among the children Harre studied. It meant they were peripheral to the group and friendless.

the wishes of adults. Especially among boys, the peer culture is frequently subversive of adult standards and values; at home a boy can be a model of politeness and proper speech; among his peers, the same boy could be an expert on dirty jokes and daring, near-delinquent exploits. It is likely that living in two contradictory worlds and being two different selves, contributes both to cognitive development and to the identity problems that arise in adolescence. In any event, the movement away from parents in middle childhood is the first step toward the independent identity and separate sense of self that are required of adults in our culture.

Developmental psychologists, as well as parents and other adults, have had mixed feelings about peer groups. Psychologists recognize that peer interaction plays an important role in a child's development, and parents become concerned if their child has troubles getting along with peers or seems to be a loner. On the other hand, both parents and psychologists worry about the subversive influence of peer groups.

William Golding's novel *Lord of the Flies* paints a haunting picture of the society of children as evil; the novel is sometimes referred to by psychologists as an accurate reminder of the dangers of peer influence. (The book tells the story of a group of English choirboys who survive a plane crash on a tropical island. Freed from the restraints of adults and of "civilization," the boys become cruel and bloodthirsty.) Harry Stack Sullivan (1953) presents a less extreme but still unflattering picture of the society of children. Juveniles, he declared, are often viciously competitive and shockingly insensitive to each other's feelings of self-worth; social relations are often carried on with a degree of crudeness that is rarely matched in later life.

Yet, at the same time, he recognized that the education for life that comes from peer groups is immensely important. Sullivan, along with Piaget, recognized that peer relations involve a completely different social system from that of parents and children, and that important developmental tasks are carried out by both systems. The child-adult system is one of unilateral authority or constraint. However democratic they are in their interactions with children, parents do not relate to their children as true equals. Parents define reality and set the rules. Children typically regard parental authority as both legitimate and in their own self-interest (Damon, 1977). Finally, the norms and laws of the larger society define parents as the responsible authorities in relation to their children.

Peer relations have an entirely different egalitarian and reciprocal basis. In them children learn the arts of negotiation, debate, and compromise, as well as a sensitivity to what matters to another person's feelings and the ability to understand another person (Youniss, 1980). In recent years, researchers have confirmed the importance of the contributions that peers make to a person's development. As one author explains, "Experience with peers is not a superficial luxury to be enjoyed by some children and not by others, but is a necessity in childhood socialization" (Hartup, 1976, p. 303).

Sex and Aggression

In addition to learning the arts of social interaction and making friends, there is evidence that children learn from their peers how to cope with aggression and sex. Studies of primates (Harlow, 1962) suggest that rough-and-tumble play with age-mates, in which play escalates into aggression and returns to play again, contributes importantly to normal development. Primates deprived of peer contact are handicapped in dealing with aggression and the emotions it arouses; they tend to be either too aggressive or too timid. While primate behavior cannot always be generalized to humans, this seems to be one instance where the analogy holds true. For example, Gerald Patterson and his associates (G. Patterson, Littman, & Bricker, 1967) show how children's assertiveness and aggressiveness are shaped through interaction with peers.

Despite the myth of the "heart-to-heart" talk about sex between parent and child, it is children who are the main source of information about sex for one another. As one researcher puts it, if parents were given the sole responsibility for the socialization of sexuality, the human race would not survive (Hartup, 1976). Because of the incest taboo, parents and children are often uncomfortable discussing sex with one another; peer groups not only tell children what they want to know about sex and are afraid to ask their parents, but also provide practical experience and role models. Sex researchers from Kinsey (1948) to the present have confirmed that children's sexual learning comes mostly from other children. Sexual lore and misinformation are part of the culture of childhood that is passed on from one generation to the next. Such works as the Opies' *Lore and Language of School Children* (1959), and Martha Wolfenstein's 1954 study of children's humor document the pervasiveness and traditional nature of sexual interests in children.

Sex Roles in Middle Childhood

The society of children not only teaches its members about sex, but about sex roles as well. It is a society divided in two by sex, and it is more traditional and stereotyped than adult society. Parents may try hard to avoid sex typing their children, only to have their efforts sabotaged by the peer group—as well as television.

Segregation by sex, and the rigidity with which conventional sex roles are enforced, rises and falls over the course of middle childhood. Damon (1977) interviewed children concerning their views about a boy who played with dolls. He found that younger children, around four and five, were fairly libertarian on the issue; early elementary school children were much less tolerant; while by the end of elementary school children were increasingly libertarian once again.

In part, the segregation of the sexes in middle childhood arises out of the nature of children's activities in those years. The male peer group tends to run in large, loose packs because boys play team games such as baseball and are freer than girls to roam neighborhood streets. Girls tend to play in groups of two or three in or near the home (Lever, 1976, 1978).

In general, boys tend to be more intolerant of girls and of the idea of sexual equality. It is a truism that a tomboyish girl is socially acceptable, but an effeminate boy is disdained by his peers and is apt to be a source of worry to his parents, especially his father. Some writers have suggested that sex role development in girls involves learning how to be like an adult and not a child, while for a boy it involves learning how to be masculine, and not feminine (Emmerich, 1959). Thus, a certain amount of rejection of things female may be built into male development. Some psychoanalytic writers claim there is a traditional male fear of women, due to the fact that for all children during their earliest years the mother is the main authority as well as the principal nurturer. Girls can identify with this early authority figure but boys must break free of the primordial female influence (Chodorow, 1974, 1978). The involvement of fathers in the rearing of infants, if this theory is correct, should make male sex role development less problematic. Whatever the origins of sex role stereotyping in middle childhood, it is a profound influence on children's views of the world, themselves, and their future possibilities.

Friendship and Social Skills

The kinds of social relations children have with their peers are in some ways very similar to those that adults carry on with one another. Contemporary Western adults develop two types of social relations; sociability with friends, acquaintances, coworkers, and neighbors; and more intense, intimate kinds of relations with lovers, spouses, and close friends (Weiss, 1973). These two kinds of relations do not substitute for one another. People can be lonely if they have a close relationship but no network of friends. They can also be lonely if they have friends but no intimate relationship. Whether or not children's friendships have an enduring effect on later relationships, the skills and understanding involved in the two kinds of sociability are similar in childhood and adulthood.

To make and continue friendships involves a number of social skills. Michael Argyle (1972) has compared social behavior to driving a car. The skills involved in social interaction include knowing how to approach a person and enter into an activity or conversation, how to keep a conversation going, manage disagreements that may arise, and gauge how others are reacting—whether they are bored or appear hostile or confused—and how to react accordingly. Social skills also include knowing how to break off a conversation or social encounter.

While everyone has to learn how to drive a car, most people seem to come by their social skills naturally. Yet many people are uncertain about these skills. Shyness and problems in self-assertion are widespread among adults, and psychologists have devised a variety of ways to train people in such skills.

A study of third and fourth grade children (Gottman, Gonzo, & Rasmussen, 1975) assessed children's knowledge of social skills and their actual popularity with classmates. Among other tasks, each child was asked to pretend that a researcher was a new child in school with whom he or she wanted to make friends. Children tended to proceed in a fixed sequence: offering greetings (saying "hello" or "hi"), asking for information ("Where do you live?"), offering inclusion ("Wanna come over to my house some time?"), offering information ("My favorite sport is basketball"). Not all children completed the whole sequence, but the order of responses was as shown. Children received one to four points for each response, with those offering information scoring higher. The study found that children who scored highest were more likely to be popular among their classmates.

Young children use their social skills to enter into daily interaction with others. As several studies have recently shown, young children define a friend as somebody you play with and share things with (Hartup, 1983). If you play with somebody one day, the person is your friend. If you do not play with him or her on a given day, that person is not your friend. Young children may have ongoing friendships, but they still think of a friend in terms of doing and playing. As we saw earlier, younger children tend to perceive themselves and others externally, in terms of their physical attributes and activities rather than as psychological beings. As children grow toward adolescence, a new kind of relationship appears. Two individuals single each other out to become close friends. As various psychologists have pointed out, this kind of intimate friendship looks very much like love. Sullivan puts it this way:

> If you will look very closely at one of your children when he finally finds a chum— somewhere between eight and a half and ten—you will discover something very different in the relationship—namely that your child begins to develop a real sensitivity to what matters to another person. And this is not in the sense of "what should I do to get what I want" but instead, "what should I do to contribute to the happiness or to support the prestige and feeling of worthwhileness of my chum." (1953, p. 245)

Sullivan regarded the close relationships of later childhood as the beginning of the capacity for interpersonal intimacy. More recent systematic studies of children's views on friendship confirm his observations about the resemblance between the close friendship of later childhood and adult intimacy. Selman (1980) found that children progress from defining friendship as momentary physical interaction to enduring psychological attachments based on common interests, mutual understanding, and trust. A study by James Youniss (1980) also confirmed the developmental progression from the here and now interaction of young children to the psychological bonds of later childhood. Many of the children Youniss interviewed saw close friendships as exclusive, like adult couple relationships. When asked how a friendship might end, many children said that if one of the friends began a new relationship with a third person, that would end the friendship:

> "A new guy makes friends with one of them."

"If someone else gets in the friendship
and ruins it."

"They meet people they like better and
just drift apart."

"Mary might get another friend that she'd
like better than Sue and leave Sue out
in the cold."(1980, p. 203)

There is fairly strong evidence that peer relationships in childhood are related to later mental health. Sullivan observed that many of his adult patients had failed to form close friendships with other children when they were young. More systematic studies have tended to confirm Sullivan's clinical observation. Hartup (1983) points to studies that show a connection between a child's popularity and his or her emotional adjustment. Henry Moss (1968) examined the Berkeley longitudinal data and found that adults rated as "warm" or "aloof" at age 30 tended to have contrasting patterns of peer relations during preadolescence. The aloof adults were not necessarily socially isolated, but they had difficulty keeping friends. One study (Cowen et al., 1973) found that children who were disliked by their classmates were more likely to appear as psychiatric patients later in life. Another researcher concluded that unpopular children were more likely than others to receive bad-conduct discharges from the armed forces (Roff, 1961).

It is not clear how these findings should be interpreted. Did the unpopular children's poor social relations *cause* their later mental problems? Did their mental problems prevent them from developing social skills in the first place? Or is it possible that, as Michael Argyle (1972) has suggested, people are apt to label others as mentally ill simply because they lack social skills? Argyle and his colleagues have carried out a number of studies which show that many mental patients are not mentally ill at all, but are grossly unskilled in social interaction. Some people have never learned such skills; others become so anxious in social situations that they cannot use the skills they have.

The findings cited above do not mean that a child who has few friends or who likes to play alone is headed straight for the psychiatrist's couch or worse in later life. While the correlations may be statistically significant, they do not allow for individual predictions with a strong degree of confidence. While peer popularity and rejection show significant stability over time in a statistical sense, they also demonstrate that an individual child can change his or her position in the peer group. Further, as the biographies of outstanding artists and scientists suggest, some children who go on to accomplish great feats may not fit the current ideal of popularity, nor enjoy a wide circle of friends. More often they are social isolates. In addition, as Zick Rubin (1980) has pointed out in a study of children's friendships, there are considerable individual differences between children in their preferences for social interaction. Some children like to have many friends, some like to concentrate on one or two close relationships, others like to spend a lot of time by themselves.

The Social Ecology of Middle Childhood

Children's peer relations are influenced not only by their skills and tastes, but also by the

environment in which they live. Most studies of children's social behavior take place in a particular setting, say a classroom or recreation area, and use a particular kind of child—often middle-class American. The impact of the wider environment—cultural, social, and physical—is often ignored. In recent years, however, researchers have begun to pay greater attention to the *ecology* of human development (Bronfenbrenner, 1979), the way environmental influences shape individuals and social interaction. Although groups of children may be found in cultures around the world, the nature of these groups varies a great deal. In most of the world's cultures the age grading commonly found in America and other Western societies is unknown. In most places, children play in mixed age groups. In America, by contrast, children and adults are highly age conscious, and friendships and play groups tend to be organized by age, just as school classrooms are. Children, of course, do interact with children younger and older than themselves, but generally it is considered "appropriate" for children to spend most of their time with their age-mates. A child who seems to prefer the company of older or younger children is likely to be viewed by adults as having some psychological or social problem (Z. Rubin, 1980).

Part of the reason for the different patterns of children's friendships is that in many cultures children associate mostly with other children in their kin group, who also typically live near by. In many non-Western settings, even the schools are not as age graded as they are in our culture. Indeed, as noted in the first chapter, the degree of age grading we know today is a relatively recent phenomenon, historically speaking (Ariès, 1962). Not all contemporary Western societies share the typical American concern for peer popularity. For example, the upper-middle-class French child is not supposed to make friends with children who are not related to him or her (Pitts, 1968). The extended family is a "total society," and no one is supposed to have any relationships outside of it. The child is supposed to find friendship among his cousins or among children of adult "friends of the family" who have family-like sta-

tus. Nevertheless, the child eventually goes to school and participates with peer groups. Paradoxically, because the family does not recognize sociability among unrelated children, whenever peer groups do arise they possess a delinquent, antiadult quality.

Some researchers feel that the degree of age grading that prevails in American society today is excessive and deprives children of benefits they could derive from more interaction with older and younger peers. While friendship and aggression typify relations between children who are close in age, children are more likely to show nurturance and dominance when they interact with younger children and dependency in interaction with older children (Hartup, 1979). Such cross-age relationships can often be helpful to both children, as is shown in studies of tutoring programs where, for example, fifth graders tutor first and second graders (Allen, 1976). The older children gain from exercising competence in a responsible, adultlike role, and the younger children may find it easier to learn from and model themselves on slightly older children rather than the teacher.

Neighborhoods

Children's relations with their peers are also shaped by the neighborhoods in which they live. Children, like the elderly, are particularly involved in and dependent on the social and physical worlds around their homes. The neighborhood a child lives in often determines how that child will spend his or her free time, the time unorganized by family and school.

To a large extent, the character of a neighborhood is a product of larger social forces. The neighborhood a child lives in depends on his or her parents' social class, income, race, ethnic group, and marital status. But neighborhoods also vary a great deal in other ways that influence the lives of the children who live in them. A recent study carried out in Oakland, California, examined the impact of neighborhoods on 750 sixth grade children (Berg & Medrich, 1977, 1980; Medrich et al., 1982). One part of the research involved a field study of five different neighborhoods. Researchers explored the physical and social aspects of each area and hung out with the neighborhood children, observing their activities and talking with them. The contrasts cut across traditional class and economic lines.

One neighborhood, "Mountainside," is in a beautiful, wooded area high in the Oakland hills and is populated by affluent, mostly white families. The adults who live there consider it idyllic. It is safe, and its large single-family homes are only a few minutes from local shopping and a short drive to work in the city.

In contrast to the parents, however, many of the children find the neighborhood oppressive. Because it is hard for them to get around, they find themselves painfully isolated. The steep, winding streets lack sidewalks, and the long distances between places make it hard to walk or bike anywhere. There are few buses. The children are dependent on their parents for chauffeuring them, and the parents must spend considerable time organizing their children's activities. There are few places for children to congregate, and thus few opportunities for informal, spontaneous friendships. Not surprisingly, the children tend to have only one or two friends.

Another affluent neighborhood offers a completely different environment. In the "Rosewood" area, houses are close together and sidewalks wide. Because of the density of the population, there are many children of all ages on the street, skateboarding, bicycling, or just hanging out. Children can casually interact with neighbors of all ages, from babies to old people. The neighborhood also offers some rugged, undeveloped areas which children can safely explore. From an adult point of view, "Mountainside" and "Rosewood" are very similar—they offer safe, comfortable, middle-class settings for raising children. And yet the contrast in the daily lives of the children in the two neighborhoods is remarkable.

Another neighborhood that offers a lively, spontaneous social life for children differed in almost every other way from "Mountainside" and "Rosewood." The mostly black "Eastside" neighborhood is one of the poorest sections of the city and has one of the highest crime rates. Yet "Eastside" children are on very easy terms with the people, places, and happenings in the area. With their house keys around their necks so they can get in and out whenever they want, they wander in large groups to and from the school, stores, the recreation center, and one another's houses. "Eastside" children reported having four or five friends, but these often included adults such as shopkeepers and mail carriers. The study found that black children in general seemed to have a more inclusive orientation toward friendship than white children, who were more selective. Despite the poverty of the "Eastside" area, the researchers felt that the vitality and richness of neighborhood life there saved it from being a bad place for children to grow up in.

Unfortunately, "Eastside" is not the typical inner-city neighborhood. Two other neighborhoods were marked by the tension that pervades many urban areas. "Bancroft" is in the middle of the socioeconomic scale, but is in the process of shifting from being all white to racially mixed. Neighborhood tensions are reflected in the way children spend their free time. "Bancroft" children stay close to their homes, often using their backyards to build tunnels and forts. Their isolation is reminiscent of the children of the "Mountainside" neighborhood, but it is an isolation based on fear and hostility rather than geography. There is a schoolyard, a library, and a recreation center in the area but these stand vacant most of the time. Families and children turn inward, reflecting and reinforcing the lack of neighborhood sociability so prized in some of the other neighborhoods studied.

Tension was also found in the poorest neighborhood in the study. Children in the "Glenn" area spend a great deal of time inside their own houses, partly because many of them have adultlike responsibilities such as cooking, cleaning, and babysitting, but also out of fear. "Glenn" children fear both traffic and other people. As in other poor neighborhoods, younger children are often harassed by teenagers and adults. When they venture out to play, it is with groups of other children who are similar in ethnic background. This neighborhood contains street gangs based on ethnic ties, and the children talk a lot about fights. "Glenn" children hardly ever dare to play alone, and they worry more about violence and intimidation than those in other areas.

The five neighborhoods described here are only a sample of the great variety of environments in which children live. The study did not include any clearly suburban areas or rural settings. But the brief descriptions illustrate how many different factors contribute to the character of a neighborhood, and how profoundly the character of a neighborhood can influence the things children do, the kinds of social interaction they experience, and their sense of well-being. As the Oakland researchers concluded, "Two children growing up five miles apart may be as different and as uncomfortable with one another as two children raised in different countries" (Berg & Medrich, 1977, p. 12).

SUMMARY

1. During middle childhood, children's social understanding advances markedly. They are able to understand other people's intentions and feelings and become adept at inferring the thoughts, intentions, and feelings that lie behind overt behavior. Children's understanding of social rules also advances.

2. Children's conceptions of themselves and others shift during middle childhood. Younger children view themselves and others in terms of observable characteristics and activities. Older children's concepts stress inner psychological characteristics. This emphasis on inner experience may be peculiar to our own culture, rather than a universal feature of development.

3. Children's ability to reason about moral dilemmas advances during middle childhood. According to Piaget and Kohlberg, children move from an early, self-centered emphasis on the effects of behavior to an emphasis on moral principles. Damon's research has shown that in middle childhood children develop a sophisticated understanding of fairness and justice, recognizing a number of aspects of equity and merit. Gilligan has raised important questions about gender differences in moral concerns.

4. Moral behavior bears only a loose relationship to moral reasoning. For many children, their actual behavior is in line with their moral principles. Other children can reason at a higher level while their behavior in a real-life situation reflects self-interest rather than principle. For a small proportion of children, behavior is ahead of moral reasoning. In general, moral behavior, such as honesty, varies a great deal for each individual depending on the situation.

5. Parents remain a significant influence on children during middle childhood. Research on parent-child relations has emphasized authority and affection as the two major dimensions of parental behavior. Generally, researchers have found that children do better in terms of personality and achievement if their parents are high on warmth and moderate on control. However, despite many positive findings linking parental behavior and child outcomes, developmental researchers are coming to realize that it is hard to untangle cause and effect in parent-child relations. Further, in real life there are many people whose

development does not correspond to theoretical expectation. The social class a child is born into does have profound effects on later personality and achievement.

6. Television is a pervasive influence in the lives of children, particularly for school-aged children. Two decades of research have shown that television can have both positive and negative effects. Violent programs can encourage aggressive behavior in some children some of the time, and educational programs such as "Sesame Street" can make a difference in children's learning. But the results of research on television's effects are mixed, and it has proved difficult to arrive at clear-cut generalizations. We do know that television serves several functions in the lives of children and families—it is a coping device for dealing with mild stress, a time filler, a topic of conversation among peers, and a device used by parents to keep their children occupied.

7. Friendship is a central part of childhood experience and peer relations make important contributions to children's development. Unlike adult-child relationships, peers relate to one another on a reciprocal, egalitarian basis. This kind of interaction helps to lay the groundwork for adult relationships. Peers are also an important source of information about sex and aggression. Researchers have found that children who are liked by other children have certain skills that less-liked children seem to lack. For example, "popular" children know how to approach other children and be included in ongoing activities. Difficulties in peer relations in childhood and adolescence have been linked to emotional problems in adulthood, but it is by no means clear that a lack of friends in itself puts children at risk for later difficulties.

8. Neighborhoods can have a profound influence on the quality of a child's everyday life. Affluent neighborhoods are generally better than poorer ones, but there are qualities that cut across economic levels. The following are some neighborhood distinctions that make a difference for school-aged children: the relative ease of finding playmates and getting places, availability of play space, dangers from traffic, availability of other children, and presence of adults. Children in different neighborhoods of a single city can have totally different environments.

Key Terms

conventional level   **395**
moral judgment   **388**
personality perception   **388**
postconventional level   **395**
preconventional level   **395**
role taking   **388**
social cognition   **388**

PART V

The Transition to Adulthood

*A*dolescence is a time of great change in body, mind, and relations with others. It is a period when, paradoxically, the most "primitive" aspect of human life, our sexuality, awakens just as our minds become capable of the highest, most abstract levels of human thought.

In all times and places, young people have had to cope with the biological changes of puberty and with the transition from being a child to being an adult. But we know from cross-cultural and historical research that adolescence as a distinct psychological stage of life—a prolonged period between childhood and adulthood—is not universal. We think of adolescence as a time of emotional upheaval and the search for an identity. But this kind of adolescent experience seems to occur only in societies that are complex, changing, literate, and urban. It is less likely to be found when one generation gradually takes the place of the previous one. Adolescence as a distinct period of life occurs when young people have choices to make about what they will do with their lives and who they will be.

Even in our own society, not all young people undergo some typical "adolescent experience." Adolescents are no less unique as individuals than are babies, children, or adults. Young people from different social classes, ethnic groups, and regions of the country are no less different from each other than are their parents.

As we shall see in the next two chapters, adolescence is almost as perplexing a subject for psychologists to study as it can often be for young people to experience. Researchers and theorists have portrayed adolescence in contradictory ways. Yet it is a rich and exciting period to examine. And at this stage, unlike previous ones, it is possible to supplement the observations of researchers and theorists with first-person reports from the objects of study—the adolescents themselves.

CHAPTER 12

Adolescence
Basic Perspectives

Our society has passed from a period which was ignorant of adolescence to a period in which adolescence is the favorite age. We now want to come to it early and linger in it as long as possible.

—Philippe Ariès,
Centuries of Childhood

If we listen to boys and girls at the very moment when they seem most pimply, awkward and disagreeable, we can partly penetrate a mystery most of us once felt heavily within us, and have now forgotten. This mystery is the very process of creation of man and woman: . . . a change that amounts almost to rebirth and is the moment of greatest *instinctive* self-awareness in our lifetime, even if, while it is happening to us, we have not yet achieved our highest level of conscious understanding.

—Colin Macinnes,
The World of Children

The twentieth century has been called "the age of adolescence." It is a time of life that fascinates children long before they reach it and adults long after they leave it. **Adolescence** is more than a particular span of time between 12 and 20; it is also a label for a state of mind. The search for identity is a central theme in our culture, and it is in the teen years that this questioning arises for the first time.

Adolescence itself is an unavoidable part of the social landscape. For writers of all kinds, from novelists to Hollywood scriptwriters, the struggles of adolescence provide an endless source of comedy and drama. Fashions in clothes, music, entertainment, and even food are aimed at or reflect the large, vaguely defined territory of youth. Some of our major social problems are problems of adolescence—delinquency, teenage pregnancy, drug abuse, school dropouts, and unemployment.

The images of adolescence that surround us are contradictory. Teenagers, especially boys, are often portrayed as cruel young savages, preying on their elders. Or they are sensitive idealists who will redeem our corrupt society and lead the way to a better future. Adolescence is a time of painful emotional turmoil and conflict with others, or it is a time of carefree fun, of beach parties and football games. Adolescents are awkward, shy, and easily embarrassed; or they are sleek, sexy creatures who make adults feel inept in their presence. They are still children, incompetent, dependent, and in need of adult protection; they are adults who have been deprived of their rights and responsibilities.

Psychology also offers contradictory images of adolescence. Many theorists portray it as a time of emotional turbulence and rebellion that no young person can escape. Yet researchers have failed to find convincing evidence that crisis is an inevitable and universal part of adolescence. Still, even those who deny that adolescence fits the image of extreme stress and conflict admit that the image fits some adolescents some of the time, or even many adolescents much of the time. There does seem to be a general agreement that while adolescence may not always fit the image of storm and stress, changes that occur during the teen years, as well as the demands placed on young people, make this a period that can be trying both for the youths and their parents.

When does adolescence begin and when does it end? The traditional textbook answer states that adolescence refers to the teen years, between 12 and 20, or to the time between reaching sexual maturity and full adult status. Many writers observe that adolescence is spreading at both ends of the period. Younger children have become more like adolescents and adults have become more like youths. The bobby-soxers of the 1940s who mobbed performances by Frank Sinatra were between 15 and 18, but the teenyboppers of the 1960s were still younger. Record companies recognize the sub-teens, 9 to 13, as a distinct market, while people 14 and older are considered adults (Kett, 1977). Clothing styles have become less determined by age; the young set the trend for those both older and younger than themselves.

The end of adolescence is even harder to define than the beginning. **Puberty,** the onset of sexual maturation and changes in body size and shape, at least gives a clear signal that the child has entered a new phase of life. But what is the signal that adolescence is over and adulthood has arrived? Many laws and regulations set the boundary between childhood and adulthood, deciding at which age a person can, or must, "go to school, go to jail, marry, work, obey parents, speak freely, worship God, see a movie, inspect school records, receive parental support, provide support to parents, have counsel, testify, own a credit card, endure beatings, buy, sell, smoke, drink, drive" (Simon, 1975, p. 1). But these legal rights and responsibilities have no regular pattern and have different meanings for different individuals. For one young person, having a driver's license means he can have dates and cruise down Main Street on Friday nights. For another, it represents a way of getting to a job, or the possibility of working as a driver.

Traditionally, a person became an adult in our society by settling down to marriage and work and, generally, taking on an identity that would last for life. Many young people still follow this pattern. They marry at 17 or 18, he works a full-time job, and she starts to have babies. It does not seem appropriate to call such people adolescent, despite their chronological age. On the other hand, increasing numbers of young people continue to go to school through their twenties and even into their thirties, putting off final decisions about love and work. Kenneth Keniston (1971) argues that a new stage of life, a kind of second adolescence which he calls "youth" has emerged in recent years between adolescence and adulthood. Others have suggested that, in some ways, the issues of adolescence persist throughout life. Decisions about marriage and work are no longer made once and for all at one fateful turning point between adolescence and youth. At any age in the adult years, people divorce and seek new mates or decide to change careers. The cartoonist Jules Feiffer once commented in a radio interview, "If I'm moody and depressed, obsessed with sex, and don't know what to do with my life, and I'm 38, they call it a mid-life crisis. If I'm 18, it's called an adolescent crisis. But it's really the same thing."

The Discovery of Adolescence

Given the current concern with adolescence, it is surprising to realize that it was barely recognized before the end of the nineteenth century (Demos & Demos, 1969; Kett, 1977). A key element in our special version of adolescence is the opening of a "space" between childhood and adulthood. Thus, Erikson writes of adolescence as a "moratorium," a time of exploration and the discovery of one's identity.

Just as the idea of the unconscious had existed before Freud put forth a systematic theory based on it, various notions of "youth" and its problems have been expressed by earlier writers. Rousseau had actually used the term "adolescence" in *Emile,* describing it as "a second birth" and a time of rebelliousness and emotional upheaval. Still earlier, in the fourth century, St. Augustine in his *Confessions* had described something that sounds surprisingly like a modern adolescent experience. But adolescence as an experience or idea did not touch the lives of large numbers of young people until the dawn of the twentieth century.

The awareness that adolescence is a relatively recent social invention is itself relatively recent. For many years, psychologists considered adolescence as an inevitable, universal process, triggered by the biological changes of puberty. Yet anthropologists such as Margaret Mead argued that while the biological changes of puberty are universal, the cultural and psychological meanings of these physical changes are not. Some societies take hardly any notice of puberty, others have elaborate "puberty rites," which may not even coincide with the physical changes themselves (Goodman, 1970). In some cultures, the transition from childhood to adulthood is smooth and gradual; in others the change is abrupt and dramatic, with the person moving directly from childhood to adulthood by means of a complicated and sometimes bloody set of trials and ceremonies.

Keniston (1971) has argued that psychologists in the past tended to overestimate the uniformity of stages of the life cycle because they failed to distinguish between three separate processes: physical maturation, age grading, and psychological change. Physical maturation is obviously universal, although in modern, technological societies it occurs earlier. Age grading, or putting people into different social categories according to age, also occurs in every society although there is wide variation in how the life course is divided up. But though every society recognizes age differences, they do not necessarily assume that people of different ages have different kinds of experiences, emotional qualities, or modes of thought. In most preindustrial societies, as we saw earlier, people of all ages live in the same social world.

Adolescence as a Distinct Stage of Life

Recently, historians have been taking a detailed look at how adolescence emerged both as a social reality and a psychological concept around the beginning of the twentieth century. Tamara Hareven (1982) has described the complex process by which stages of life emerge and are "discovered." First, individuals become aware of a distinct phase in their lives, different from the way they had been thinking and feeling. The characteristics and problems of this stage are echoed by others in the same age group. Then this phase is recognized and described by psychologists and later by popular writers. Next, if there is a social problem connected to the particular stage, it may attract the attention of reformers and public agencies. The needs and problems of the age group may be dealt with by laws and institutions. Finally,

public recognition of the new life stage affects the experience of individuals.

The emergence of adolescence as a distinct stage follows the pattern described by Hareven. Evidence shows that in the second half of the nineteenth century, young people began to experience certain problems and tensions in their early teen years. Adults observed them congregating in groups and beginning to show "adolescent" styles of behavior. This emerging concept of adolescence was articulated by G. Stanley Hall in his encyclopedic work in 1904. Concern with youth gangs and other unruly groups of teenagers led to public recognition of the distinct needs of young people—and to institutions that made adolescence even more of a social reality than it had been.

As Hareven points out, the concept of childhood had emerged in a similar way. And in the twentieth century, the concept of middle age has gone through the same cycle of private experience to public recognition to private experience.

Adolescence seems to develop under a particular set of social and economic conditions. First, it emerges in societies that are complex, literate, changing, and urban, rather than in those in which the lives of the children simply repeat the lives of their parents and grandparents. In most times and places, young people have not had to search for an identity in their teens because they have been given one at birth.

Second, adolescence seems to have emerged with the founding of mass, compulsory education systems, particularly the large public high school. Compulsory education laws helped to define adolescence by setting a precise chronological age for it and providing an institutional setting in which large numbers of teenagers could be brought together to create their own society for a good part of their daily lives. At least for some of these young people, the extension of education is also a way of extending psychological development and mastering more complex levels of intellectual skill.

The complete set of conditions that are necessary for adolescence to develop did not exist until just three generations ago. Whether or not they worked with their own families, most Americans until the twentieth century went to work at the age of 10 or 12. A shortage of labor ensured that anyone willing to work could do so.

As in traditional and tribal societies, young people often began their adult work careers before the onset of sexual maturation. As Joseph Kett observes,

> The onset of male puberty failed to coincide with any fundamentally new life experience. . . . [T]he twentieth century has argued that no matter where the boy is, what he is doing, or what he has been through, with the onset of puberty he becomes an adolescent. In the 1830's, in contrast, popular definitions of youth took their cue more from social status than from physiology. If a sixteen-year-old boy were in district school, he was called a child, and for the most part treated like one. If in college, he was usually described as a youth. Strictly speaking, the same boy could be a child for part of the year, and a youth for the remainder.* (1971, pp. 294–95)

Kett (1977) uses the term "semidependence" to describe the status of youth aged 10 to 21 in the nineteenth century. In some ways, young people were much more independent of their parents than today's youth, because they often lived and worked outside the parental home. Young people could even be legally emancipated and freed of obligation from their parents (Marks, 1975).

By the end of the nineteenth century, however, there was no longer a need for vast armies of unskilled labor. Young men who would have been mature enough to be workers were now considered immature, useless, and even dangerous. Idle youths crowding the

---

*The focus on males in this quotation is typical of much of the research on adolescence. Adolescent girls have not been studied nearly as much as boys have. The reason for this neglect may be that adolescent boys are more troublesome, or that their future occupational success has been regarded as more important.

streets of American cities were seen as a threat to public order and a corrupting influence on other young people.

The youth crisis resulted in several major social and legal policies concerning children and youth. Compulsory education, child-labor laws, the juvenile court, and the child-guidance clinic were the major innovations of the time. In effect, as David Bakan (1971) has pointed out, these laws added adolescence onto childhood as a kind of second childhood to deal with the social changes that were taking place. Adolescence was now marked off from childhood by puberty and from adulthood by legal barriers that prevented the youth from working, leaving school, and living apart from parents. As one legal scholar observes, "By the early 20th century, the notion that a child upon reaching puberty could assume status independent of his parents had virtually disappeared. The state compelled the extension of childhood—enjoining longer supervision, more protracted education, and the postponed assumption of adult economic roles" (Marks, 1975, p. 88).

The industrial and economic changes at the end of the nineteenth century altered the conditions for success and placed new demands on middle-class families. By 1900, education beyond grade school was required for middle-class occupations. No longer a meandering road, the route to success now resembled a steep ladder. A missed step anywhere along the line could be disastrous. Adolescence became a more burdensome time for parents because teenaged children no longer contributed to the family income, but had to be supported economically and emotionally through a trying period. Too much independence and autonomy in the young came to be seen as a "prescription for failure." There was a new emphasis on obedience, purity, restraint—and for males, achievement. If a young man did what he was supposed to, he would be rewarded in adulthood with success and a place in society.

These changes in society and family transformed the experience of growing up; adolescence was not just a problematic age for the rest of society, it became an important part of

the individual's biography. Adolescence became a time of crucial decisions about work, love, and values. This delay between maturing physically and becoming an adult socially and legally led to the psychological experiences we have come to associate with adolescence—uncertainty and indecision, conflicts over independence and the family, the discovery of the private and unique world of the self, the search for an identity, and the questioning of adult values and assumptions.

Is Adolescence a Time of "Storm and Stress"?

"Adolescence" became a household word in Hall's time. His work seemed to provide the answers to many of the questions people were asking about the troublesome young. Underneath the vast collection of ideas and facts presented in his book were two central themes: first, adolescence is a time of severe psychological crisis—"storm and stress"—marked by violent impulses, great mood shifts, and vulnerability to external influences that could lead to either religious conversion or crime; second, he used a biological framework to interpret these psychological changes. Hall believed that individual development actually recapitulates the development of the human race; adolescents are reenacting a time when the human race was making great leaps toward civilization.

Hall's work was enormously influential. His ideas were taken up by psychologists, educators, child guidance workers, and social policy makers. His scientific credibility, however, was attacked by such prominent psychologists as Edward Thorndike, who pointed to absurdities in the doctrine of recapitulation. Hall's evolutionary theories still are not taken seriously today, but many later theorists share his views about the turbulence of adolescence. Recent psychoanalytic writings, as in the works of Anna Freud and Peter Blos, agree with Hall that adolescence is a distinct phase of development and that it is a time of storm and stress.

Anna Freud presents a description of adolescence that strikingly resembles Hall's. She por-

Rites of Passage

Every society uses rituals to mark stages of the life cycle or passage from one social status to another. Birth, puberty, marriage, and death are the times most likely to be celebrated in all cultures. In our own culture, graduation from high school or college is also an important passage. Various rituals marking important life transitions are illustrated here.

Catholic first communion, Peru

Mormon baptism, U.S.A.

Catholic baptism, Lesotho

Bar Mitzvah, Israel

Masai headdress for
puberty cermonies, Kenya

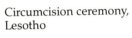

Circumcision ceremony,
Lesotho

These boys
are being
initiated
to manhood
by having
to live by
themselves.

Lovale circumcision
ceremony, Zimbabwe

Python Dance of betrothed, young women, Movehda tribe

Initiation of young women, Lesotho

College graduation

Jewish American wedding

Caraja Indian virgins in ceremonial dance, Bananal Island, central Brazil

The Changing Meaning of Age

Though every culture recognizes various stages of the life cycle, the conception of each age and stage is different from one culture to the next. In our own society, the meaning of age has changed dramatically in the past several decades. The cartoons illustrate the older version of how middle-aged or older adults were viewed, while Joan Collins and Ronald Reagan show that being in one's fifties or seventies no longer means what it once did.

Joan Collins

"I just want to say that I'm perfectly willing to serve as treasurer, provided every penny doesn't have to come out exactly even."

Ronald Reagan

"Goodness, Mr. Harrison, seventy-eight isn't old!"

trays it as a time of intense and contradictory emotions:

> Adolescents are excessively egoistic, regarding themselves as the center of the universe . . . , and yet at no time in later life are they capable of so much self-sacrifice and devotion. They form the most passionate love-relations, only to break them off as abruptly as they began them. . . . They oscillate between blind submission to some self-chosen leader and defiant rebellion against any and every authority. . . . Their moods veer between light-hearted optimism and the blackest pessimism. (1936, pp. 137–38)

While Hall suggested recapitulation as the cause of adolescent upheaval, Anna Freud attributes it to the upsurge of sexuality. She argues that when sex drives reawaken after the so-called latency period, the young person's entire personality is disrupted and must be reorganized. Adolescence is a "developmental disturbance," she observes (1969), which is something like the onset of psychosis, yet is part of normal development. "People cross and recross the border between mental health and illness many times during their lives," and adolescence is one of those times. Peter Blos comments that "no parent, no matter how devoted and well-intentioned, can spare the child this frenzied conflict" (1962).

In contrast to this widely held image of adolescence as a time of "frenzied conflict," many studies of large samples of adolescents give a very different view. These studies suggest that most adolescents grow toward adulthood in steady, bland, and nonturbulent ways. According to the researchers, adolescence is not that much different from any other period of life. As Gold and Douvan ask, "Where are the tensions, the crises, the muddles, the befuddled, struggling, exasperating personalities, lurching through the teen years?" (1969, p. 3). Another researcher concludes: "Taken as a whole, adolescents are *not* in turmoil, *not* deeply disturbed, *not* at the mercy of their impulses, *not* resistant to parental values, *not* politically active, *not* rebellious" (Adelson, 1979, emphasis

in original). How can we explain the contrast between these diametrically opposed views of adolescence? Is there any way to reconcile or integrate the two?

Those who view adolescent conflict as inevitable could respond in two ways to the researchers' findings. First, they might question how deeply the researchers had penetrated into the hearts and minds of the young people they studied. Second, they might look at the lack of storm and stress as a bad sign; thus, Anna Freud (1969) has argued that children who remain calm and easy to get along with during adolescence may be crippling themselves by resisting the maturational process, and may be more in need of therapy than the more outwardly disturbed.

The consensus of most researchers in the field, however, is that adolescence is not necessarily a time of extreme turmoil. The images of adolescence that appear in the media and the clinical writings may have been too strongly influenced by problems of young people from the top and bottom of the socioeconomic scale. The juvenile delinquents, teenage gangs, high school dropouts, and unemployed youth who appear in the media are likely to come from the poorest parts of the population. (Although, as we shall see in the next chapter, class differences in rates of delinquency have been greatly exaggerated.) During the days of student protest in the 1960s, it was largely upper-middle-class young people who made headlines because they had the luxury of being able to reflect on the state of the society and the world, and on their own inner goals. The clinical literature about emotional turbulence and identity crises in adolescence also reflects the experience of upper-middle-class young people. To engage in a search for self, to try to find a way of life that fits one's inner needs, *is* a kind of luxury. It is more likely to occur if your family does not need you to work as soon as you are old enough to get some kind of job, and also if they have encouraged you to be an independent, question-asking kind of person.

Most American teenagers, however, live in middle- or lower-middle-class families that value conformity to traditional values more than they do autonomy in their children. These children of those who work with their hands, or sell things, or do clerical work are more likely to relive the lives of their parents and live in the same towns and neighborhoods their parents do.

Probably the most reasonable conclusion to draw is that there is no single, typical adolescent experience that every young person goes through. Daniel Offer (Offer, 1969; Offer & Offer, 1975), carried out a longitudinal study of high school boys which did not support the notion of adolescent turmoil as a universal pattern. Nevertheless, he did find that storm and stress was one of the three patterns of psychological change during adolescence. About the same number of boys experienced a smooth, gradual, and continuous type of development. The third group experienced intermittent periods of turmoil.

However, Offer and other critics of the storm and stress concept of adolescence do not argue that it is a time with no emotional conflicts or problems. He found that parents of the boys studied reported the years between 12 and 14 to be the most difficult time they had had in raising their children. There was a great deal of "bickering" and "infighting" about seemingly small issues such as haircuts, dress, and so on.

It is significant that this much turbulence appeared in Offer's sample; the study has been criticized for using adolescents purposely selected for their apparent normality (Siegel, 1982). A study that used a large general population, the "Isle of Wight" study, found "some appreciable misery or depression" in nearly half the adolescents (Rutter, Tizard, & Whitmore, 1970). Thus, it does seem that we are justified in believing that adolescence is indeed a time of emotional unsteadiness, if not extreme alienation or turmoil. The chief problem with the "storm and stress" notion which has come down to us from Hall is its biological framework. The psychologists who followed Hall did not accept his Darwinian notions of "recapitulation." But they did share his assumption that the psychological changes of adolescence are inevitable and universal.

It is not necessary to accept those assump-

tions to recognize that, particularly in contemporary society, adolescence can be a troubled and troubling period of life. Erik Erikson's description of adolescence as a "normative crisis" (1959) is a term that many scholars of adolescence feel comfortable with. The term "crisis" does not imply chaos or a complete disruption of personality, but rather, the kinds of problems that could occur in any period of life in which major changes are taking place and important choices must be made.

Physical Development

The most conspicuous changes of adolescence are physical ones. As J. M. Tanner has pointed out,

> During the years from 12 to 16 young people experience the most dramatic changes in their growth and development they have known. It is true that physical development is even faster in infancy, but the subject himself was not the fascinated, charmed, or horrified spectator that watches the developments, or lack of developments, of adolescence. (1972, p. 1)

At puberty, which marks the end of childhood and the beginning of adolescence, growth not only speeds up, but the individual begins the road to sexual maturity (Figure 12.1). Within a few years, the young person will have reached adult size and weight. Girls begin to menstruate and develop breasts, hips, and pubic hair; boys show a great increase in

---

FIGURE 12.1
The Physical Effects of Sex Hormones
The secretion of sex hormones at puberty has a complex effect on physical growth and bodily function.

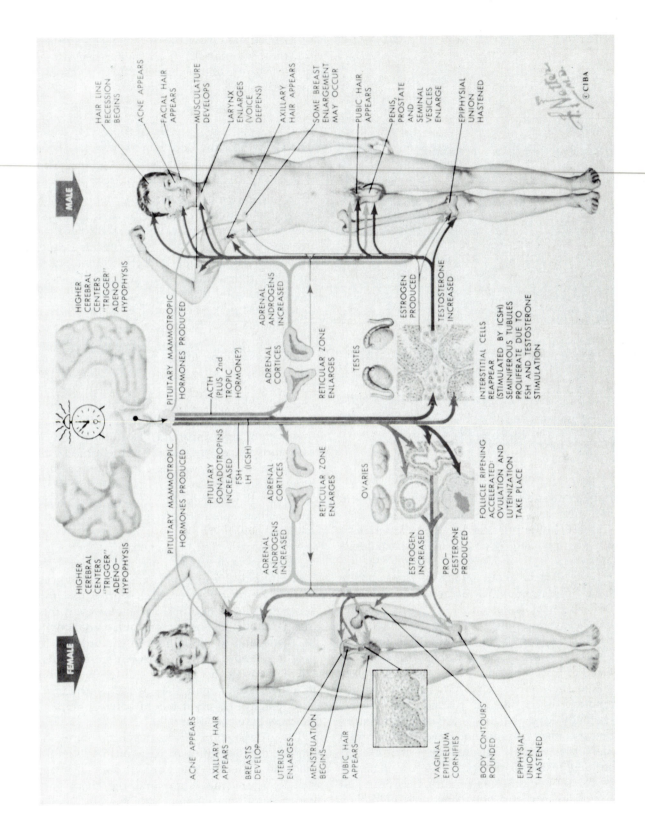

muscle size and strength, their voices deepen, and their sexual organs change. For both boys and girls, these physical developments are usually accompanied by an upsurge of sexual feelings.

Several facts about biological development have important implications for psychological aspects of adolescence. First, girls develop, on the average, about two years earlier than boys; second, individuals vary a great deal in terms of when puberty begins, how long it takes to complete the process, and how closely linked the various developments are. For example, it is possible for a healthy girl to have reached adult height and have adult-sized breasts, and yet still not have had her first menstrual period. Finally, there has been a striking historical change in the onset of puberty. In the nineteenth century, European and American girls did not menstruate until they

were about 17. Now the age of the first menstruation is about 12 or 13. Better health and nutrition are usually given as the explanations for this change.

The Growth of the Body

At the peak of the adolescent growth spurt, children may gain two to five inches in height in a single year. To the child experiencing it, growth may seem even faster. When I was 12, I left school at the end of the term shorter than my closest friends; when I returned to school in the fall, I was the tallest. In the United States and Britain, the girls' spurt usually comes at age 12, the boys' at 14.

The question of how tall one is going to be as an adult concerns both young people and their parents during this time. The socially "ideal" body type for a man is muscular and tall, but not too tall. The ideal woman, of course, is shorter than the man. Few people live up to the ideal in all its dimensions, but it is influential even in adulthood. Adolescents are even more concerned about their body's size and shape since it is in the process of changing and the final outcome is as yet unknown. The growth spurt may confuse matters. A girl who gets her growth spurt early and is taller than all the boys in the sixth grade will probably not be taller than all the boys in the tenth grade. The boy who seems very short at 13 or 14 may catch up in height later. The best guide to a young person's adult height is his or her height before the spurt starts; the correlation is .80 (Tanner, 1972). However, this means about 30 percent of adult variation in height is due to differences in the amount of height gained during the growth spurt. Thus, people can end up taller or shorter in relation to other adults than they were as children. Girls reach their adult height between 15 and 18, boys between 17 and 20.

The growth spurt affects the entire body, not just height. But different parts of the body develop at different rates and times. Legs get longer before the torso, and the torso gets wider before the shoulders. Thus, as Tanner

(1971) points out, a boy stops growing out of his trousers before he stops growing out of his jackets. The hands and feet grow to adult size earlier than the rest of the body, leading some boys and girls to feel their hands and feet are too large and awkward. Eventually, the rest of their bodies will catch up, and their hands and feet will be much more in proportion to the rest of them.

Along with the obvious external changes, muscles grow in size and strength, as do hearts and lungs. For boys, these changes in size and strength are greater but for a short while girls may have larger muscles than boys. One organ that changes very little during adolescence is the brain. While the average 10-year-old weighs about half what she or he will weigh as an adult, at the start of adolescence the brain weighs about 95 percent of what it will weigh in adulthood (Tanner, 1970).

Sexual Development

Sexual maturation also follows a typical sequence of events, although there is great individual variation (Figure 12.2). In girls, the arrival of the first period—an event called **menarche**—is both the public and private sign of puberty. But actually, menarche is one of the latest, rather than the earliest events in sexual maturation. The first event in the sequence is the budding, or the enlargement, of the breasts, which usually begins around the age of 10 and continues for about three years. Pubic hair usually grows next, although it can come earlier in the sequence. The inner and outer sexual organs then develop, followed by the first menstrual period. Finally, body hair grows, the hips widen, and fat deposits increase to make the body shape more womanly.

These events in girls can occur anywhere between age 9 and 17, with the average age of first menstruation being 12. The arrival of menstruation does not mean that a girl's reproductive system is functioning like that of an adult woman. The first period usually occurs without ovulation—that is, with no egg available to be fertilized.

In boys, the first sign of puberty is the enlargement of the testicles and scrotum, followed by growth of the pubic hair and then the penis. These changes usually begin around age 13 and take about two years to complete (Tanner, 1978). The first ejaculation of seminal fluid often occurs at around 13, although there is great variation in age—from as early as 11, to as late as 16. The event can occur spontaneously, as in a "wet dream," or through masturbation. Underarm and facial hair appear about two years after pubic hair does. The rest of the development of the body hair and the beard continues throughout puberty and beyond. The changing of the voice is a relatively late event in the sequence, and so does not signal the beginning of the process, as many people believe.

Over the past several generations, the age of puberty has declined in Western countries (Roche, 1979). Girls begin to menstruate about two years earlier than they did in the last century; puberty in boys also comes earlier, although still later than in girls. This **secular trend** also affects the growth spurt; it too occurs several years earlier than it did a century ago, and people grow to be taller and heavier.

The secular trend reveals the impact of environmental factors on biological processes. Apparently, it has been caused by improvements in the standard of living in Western and modernized countries over the past century. Poverty, illness, and malnutrition can delay physical development; good nutrition and health care can speed it up. Cross-cultural evidence confirms the importance of these factors; girls in technologically advanced societies menstruate earlier than girls in less advanced ones (Tanner, 1978). Recently, the secular trend has begun to level off, suggesting that there is a threshold for sexual development, an age below which puberty will not occur no matter how well nourished and healthy a population may be.

Because the secular trend has reduced the age of puberty for boys and girls, the physical and emotional changes of adolescence are happening at ages we still think of as part of childhood. Our culture's conceptions of adolescents

FIGURE 12.2
Tanner's Five Developmental Stages of Puberty

	Characteristic		
Stage	**Genital Development** **(Boys)**	**Pubic-Hair Development** **(Boys and Girls)**	**Breast Development** **(Girls)**
1	Testes, scrotum, and penis are about the same size and shape as in early childhood.	No pubic hair.	There is elevation of the papilla only.
2	Scrotum and testes are slightly enlarged. The skin of the scrotum is reddened and changed in texture. There is little or no enlargement of the penis at this stage.	There is sparse growth of long, slightly pigmented, tawny hair, straight or slightly curled, chiefly at the base of the penis or along the labia.	Breast bud stage. There is elevation of the breast and the papilla as a small mound. Areolar diameter is enlarged over that of Stage 1.
3	Penis is slightly enlarged, at first mainly in length. Testes and scrotum are further enlarged than in Stage 2.	The hair is considerably darker, coarser, and more curled. It spreads sparsely.	Breast and areola are both enlarged and elevated more than in Stage 2 but with no separation of their contours.
4	Penis further enlarged, with growth in breadth and development of glans. Testes and scrotum are further enlarged than in Stage 3; scrotum skin is darker than in earlier stages.	Hair is now adult in type, but the area covered is still considerably smaller than in the adult. There is no spread to the thighs.	The areola and papilla form a secondary mound projecting above the contour of the breast.
5	Genitalia are adult in size and shape.	The hair is adult in quantity and type with distribution of the horizontal (or classically "feminine") pattern. Spread is to the medial surface of the thighs but not elsewhere above the base of the inverse triangle.	Mature stage. The papilla only projects with the areola recessed to the general contour of the breast.

Source: *Fetus into man: Physical growth from conception to maturity* by J. H. Tanner, 1978, Cambridge, Mass.: Harvard University Press.

were formed when girls were beginning to menstruate at 14, 15, and even 17. Now girls of 9 or 10, and boys of 11 and 12 are experiencing the beginning stages of pubertal development and their psychological impact.

The Psychology of Early Adolescence

The idea of change can be disturbing to a person who is reasonably content with things as they are. Children want to be grown up, but the idea of all the unknown factors that are involved is frightening. One writer recalls that, "When I was a kid I wanted everything to stay the same. I wanted to live in the same house, go to the same school, keep the same friends . . . forever. When I was ten I used to tell my mother that I would grow up, get married, have children, but never leave home" (Goodman, 1979, p. ix).

In some cultures, the passage from childhood to adulthood almost fits that description. But early adolescence in our culture has been singled out as "a specific and stressful stage of the life cycle'' (Hamburg, 1974) because of the other changes that have been superimposed at the physical onset of puberty.

Metamorphosis   The idea of a marked change in a person's body is both fascinating and frightening, especially if it is one's own body that is doing the changing. The feeling that one's body is stable, dependable, and whole is basic to a feeling of security. A common theme of literature and folklore is the theme of metamorphosis or transformation—the ugly duckling becomes a beautiful swan, Alice in Wonderland shrinks and grows, a human being changes into an animal or an insect or a golden statue. Though our bodies are constantly changing, our images of them may take time to catch up with reality. Fat people who lose weight may still feel fat, aging people may picture themselves as younger in their mind's eye, and people who have suffered the amputation of some body part often experience the ''phantom limb'' phenomenon—the sensation that the missing arm or leg or breast is still there (Schilder, 1935).

In early adolescence, the young person must somehow come to terms with a radically altered body and the uncertainty about what its final size, shape, and attractiveness will be. Further, many of these bodily changes are a public event, which alters the way other people act toward an individual, and the demands they make. Phyllis Lafarge, a writer, recalls her own experience of bodily change in early adolescence:

> Self-consciousness about my body and appearance were overwhelming for several years. I did not put it into words, or even think it, but there was always the possibility that my body, like some not quite predictable tyrant, . . . would betray me, that something else would bulge or sweat or all at once sprout hair and so depart from the firm, predictable body of childhood. (1972, p. 281)

Aside from the possibility of embarrassment, puberty had another meaning to this writer; it was proof that her body, and the self that in-

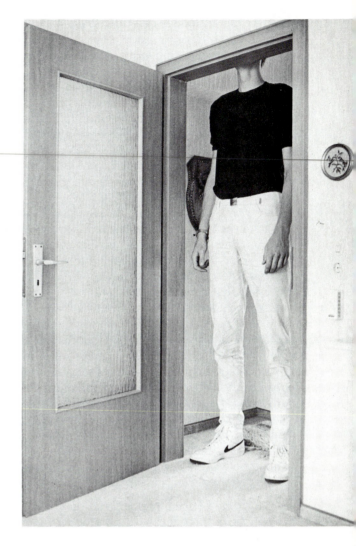

habited it, were fated to change, and this early change was the forerunner of later, and less welcome ones; after her mother's first-period talk, she wept, out of a feeling of ''extreme mortalness.''

The Onset of Puberty   Clearly, then, the physical changes of puberty have great psychological significance in their own right. For girls, the arrival of the first period is the social and individual symbol of puberty. The event may be greeted with celebration, shame, fear, or indifference. In many cultures, there are elaborate rites of passage on the occasion, and the girl may be introduced to menstrual taboos which she will have to practice the rest of her menstruating years. Individual families in our own society also vary in how they greet a daughter's first period. Some girls, as in the movie *Carrie,* are given no information beforehand, and may fear they are bleeding to death. One woman who had this experience reported that when she told her mother she was given a furious lecture about "what a bad, evil, immoral thing I was to start menstruating at the age of eleven" (Weideger, 1975, p. 169).

Only a small proportion of American girls today have their first periods without advanced warning. But in the first half of this century, girls in some immigrant cultures were not told about it. The custom was to explain menstruation and what to do about it after the event, not before. In some families, the subject was so taboo that parents never did discuss it or instruct girls in how to wear sanitary cloths (Able & Jaffe, 1950). Even today, families vary in how openly menstruation is discussed—for example, is the father informed of his daughter's menstrual experiences?

Girls themselves are likely to feel ambivalent about menstruation. Even those with negative attitudes feel pleased with it as a badge of womanhood. Ann Frank expressed this complex mixture of feelings in her diary:

> Each time I have a period—and that has only been three times—I have the feeling that in spite of all the pain, unpleasantness, and nastiness, I have a sweet secret, and that is why, although it is nothing but a nuisance to me in a way, I always long for the time when I shall feel that secret within me again. (1972, p. 117)

Menstruation, particularly if it is painful, can turn a girl's attention inward. A vivid fictional example of this shift in focus is given by Nadine Gordimer in her novel *Burger's Daughter.* The heroine gets her first period the night her mother has been taken to prison for political activities. (The novel takes place in South Africa.) The public events, however, are overshadowed by the inner drama. Outside the

prison where her mother is being held, surrounded by a crowd of political activists, she finds that her

> real awareness is all focused in the lower part of my pelvis, in the leaden, dragging, wringing pain in there. . . . The internal landscape of my mysterious body turns me inside out, so that in the public place, on the public occasion (all the arrests of the dawn swoop have been in the newspapers, . . .) I am within that monthly crisis of destruction, the purging, tearing, draining of my own structure. I am my womb, and a year ago I wasn't aware—physically—I had one. (1979, pp. 15–16)

The pain and physical disability involved in menstruation are the subject of a great deal of misunderstanding. There are two contrary myths. One states that women are debilitated by menstruation—that they are literally "unwell"—and must stop their normal activities. The other myth is that menstrual discomfort is "all in the head" and caused by a woman's unconscious rejection of her femininity or some other psychological process. Some of the booklets which prepare girls for menstruation take this line, suggesting that having a positive mental attitude and plunging into activities will remedy the condition.

The trouble with both myths is that they claim to speak for all women all of the time. Menstruation is not always debilitating. Women athletes have won Olympic competitions and other sporting events during their periods. A study of college women indicated that only one-third found their periods somewhat debilitating, and almost none who said they were severely so (Brooks-Gunn, Ruble, & Clarke, 1977). Some women, however, do have painful periods. Recently, menstrual cramps have been found to be associated with changes in the level of the hormone prostaglandin.

The onset of menstruation is also a signal to the girl and her family that childhood is ending and that it is time to put away childish things. One 15-year-old girl told a researcher: "It was like growing up over night. I felt that I was not

The Meaning of Puberty in Males For boys, sexual maturation is a very different process. The most obvious sign of it is ejaculation, which may occur either as a result of masturbation, or during sleep in the form of a nocturnal emission or "wet dream." Because it is so much more clearly sexual than menstruation, the first ejaculation is not usually celebrated in the same way as the first menstrual period. (In fact, making love may also be a taboo subject in discussing menstruation. A girl can be told all about periods and what to do without mention of sex.) Gordon Shipman found that only 6 percent of the boys in the sample he studied felt positive about their first ejaculation. He suggests an unlikely scenario: "Imagine an American boy coming to the breakfast table exclaiming, 'Mom, guess what? I had my first wet dream last night. Now I'm a man!' It is not without significance that such an imaginary episode is greeted in American culture with laughter" (1971, pp. 333–34).

For both boys and girls, adolescence brings an upsurge of sexual feelings that must be dealt with one way or another. As Robert Coles puts it, adolescents often "feel themselves in the presence of an enormous internal energy suddenly exerting itself—a gift, a threat, a mystery, a force to be reckoned with. Out of nowhere, it seems, the body is visited by this transforming presence" (1985, p. 2).

Despite the sexual revolution, the onset of sexual feeling is still fraught with uncertainty and the possibilities of shame, guilt, and embarrassment. Most teenagers still find it hard to talk to their parents about sex (Coles & Stokes, 1985). And although sex is a favorite topic of conversation among teens themselves, they still hesitate to confide to one another their deepest worries and concerns, lest they be thought "weird" or ignorant. Above all, today's adolescents still face the same developmental task that each generation has had to deal with—integrating sexuality with the nonsexual aspects of the self (Miller & Simon, 1980). The reflective, conscious, continuing "I" must be reconciled with the newly sexual "Me" which is revealed by the body as well as the reactions of others.

a little kid anymore. I couldn't ride my bicycle anymore . . ." (Kagan, 1972, p. 97). A study of body image changes in girls before and after menarche concluded that it is a pivotal psychological event (Koff & Silverstone, 1978). When asked to draw a picture of a person, postmenarchal girls were more likely to draw a female figure, and also to differentiate male and female figures. When asked about their satisfaction with various body parts, postmenarchal girls were more likely to be satisfied with the feminine parts of their bodies. (For a discussion of how some individuals' perceptions of their bodies can become distorted, see the box on Eating Disorders.)

Eating Disorders

The Duchess of Windsor once said that "You can't be too rich or too thin." Many adolescent girls carry the second part of that statement to a life-threatening extreme. **Anorexia nervosa** is sometimes called the "slimmer's disorder." Its main symptoms are a substantial loss of weight—25 percent or more—due to dieting and an intense fear of obesity. Anorexia results in death in about 15 to 21 percent of the cases (Halmi, 1978), one of the few psychological disorders with a fatal outcome.

Anorexics are obsessed with body size and have a distorted perception of their own appearance, fearing they are grossly obese when their weight is normal, and believing they look normal when they actually resemble concentration camp victims. One young woman wrote that, after she had lost fifty pounds over a few months, "I never felt lovelier or more confident about my appearance: physically liberated, streamlined, close to the bone" (Spitzer et al., 1983, p. 224).

The vast majority of anorexics are female; a small percentage are male. Anorexics are generally "good" girls who have previously

This woman weighed 120 lbs. at age 18 (below). Nineteen months later, suffering from anorexia nervosa, she had dropped down to 47 lbs. (right).

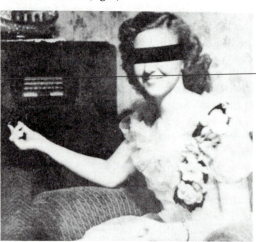

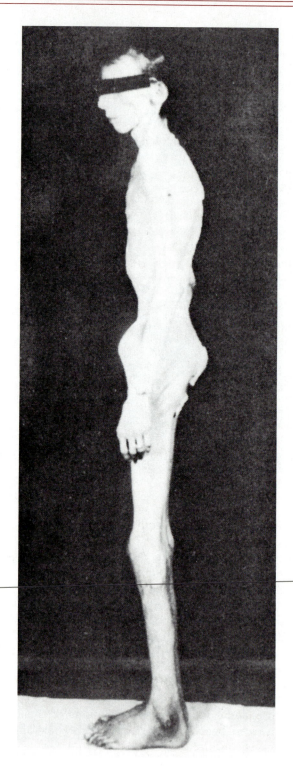

given their parents little cause for concern; they often do well in school and commonly are from the upper socioeconomic classes. Typically, anorexia begins with a diet, which then turns into a fierce determination to eat as little as possible. Anorexics remain obsessed by food, even while they avoid eating it. They count calories, collect recipes, cook for other people. Some may binge on occasion.

Several theories have been advanced to explain the condition, but none has been accepted as the definitive account of why people become anorexic. Psychoanalysts generally see anorexia as a flight from sexuality; anorexic girls fear and reject the signs of puberty. Anorexia not only causes breasts and hips to shrink, but also makes menstruation stop. Another explanation has been advanced by family therapist Salvador Minuchin and his associates (Minuchin, Rosman, & Barker, 1978). They see anorexia as the symptom of an intense power struggle in the family: a ''good'' girl, unable to express anger openly, uses her refusal to eat as a weapon against her parents. One of the treatments used at Minuchin's clinic is to serve a meal to the patient and tell her parents to make her eat it. Eventually, the girl either eats or the parents literally force her to. Once the power struggle is resolved, the family and the therapist can deal with the family's conflicts and communication problems. Behavior therapy and drugs have also been used to treat anorexia.

Some researchers feel that the disorder is so bizarre and powerful that there must be more than psychological or family conflicts at the root of it—that there must be some biological malfunction involved. Others deny that it is bizarre. They see it as an extreme form of the obsession with dieting and weight that afflicts practically all American women (Chernin, 1981). In fact, the condition is unknown outside of the developed countries where slimness is considered attractive.

Bulimia, or *bulimarexia,* is another increasingly common eating disorder. Like the anorexic, the bulimic is usually a young woman from the upper levels of the socioeconomic scale. She is also preoccupied with weight and body image. But while the anorexic is iron-willed in her avoidance of food, the bulimic alternates between dieting and wild binges. Bulimics stuff themselves with enormous amounts of food—boxes of donuts, quarts of ice cream, the contents of refrigerators. Once the binge begins, nothing stops it until exhaustion or extreme stomach pain sets in. Afterward, bulimics purge themselves by vomiting or taking laxatives. Their lives are dominated by fears of obesity and of losing control over their eating. Nevertheless, bulimics usually manage to maintain normal weight. Unlike anorexics, they are interested in dating and sex.

Both eating disorders represent the extreme forms of the struggle for slimness that most American women undergo. Bulimia is extremely widespread. Judith Rodin, who has done major research on obesity and eating behavior, estimates that about 35 to 60 percent of college women are binge eaters (quoted in E. Hall, 1984). Rodin, like many other writers, believes that eating disorders reflect a pathology in society, rather than a mental illness that afflicts only those clearly identified as anorexics or bulimics. She observes that women today feel too fat even if they are five pounds underweight.

> The current body ideal is ridiculously slim, and almost all women aspire to it. It's unfortunate because women are genetically programmed to be fatter than men, to lay down more fat cells, and store more fat. When you put that genetic program in the context of pressures on women to be thin, it's not surprising that there's so much erratic eating behavior among women today. (Interview with E. Hall, 1984, p. 42)

It's not surprising either that anorexia has taken on a kind of glamour. A study of the obsession with weight among normal women found that the anorexic girl is often regarded as a cultural heroine, a victor in the war against weight (Chernin, 1981). One anorexic became a celebrity at her high school; even the most popular girls came to consult her about the secrets of her ''success.'' Another writer calls anorexia the illness of our era; described and discussed in intellectual journals and the mass media, it has become ''a glamorous cross between two Victorian favorites, consumption and hysteria, but updated for a modern audience'' (Gilbert, 1979).

Although adolescence brings sexual feelings to both males and females, sexuality for adolescent boys is more focused on the genitals and more easily aroused. Masturbation is almost universal in boys, and is the most common cause of their first ejaculation. According to data collected by Kinsey between 1938 and 1948, 21 percent of 12-year-old boys, 82 percent of 15-year-olds, and 92 percent of 20-year-olds had masturbated to orgasm. The comparable figures for girls are 12 percent, 20 percent, and 33 percent (reported in Gagnon, 1974, p. 240).

Recent studies (Coles & Stokes, 1985; Sorenson, 1973) report similar but somewhat lower rates; Kinsey's figures, however, are still believed to be correct. His study was based on interviews especially designed to elicit honest answers. The later studies were based on surveys in which people were more likely to underreport questionable or deviant behavior. It is surprising that many of today's teenagers still regard masturbation as in some way shameful (Coles & Stokes, 1985).

It is a popular assumption that the differences in masturbation rates reflect differences in sex drive, but social mores may play a large role also. It is true that the adolescent boy is focused on his genitals in a way that the girl is not; she bleeds, but his penis becomes capable of erection and ejaculation. This physical contrast is reinforced by differences in socialization and peer group patterns. For example, explicit sex can be much more a part of boys' peer groups than it is of girls', even before adolescence. As Gagnon and Simon point out, "It is possible for young boys to be both playing games of tag and using *Playboy* to masturbate" (1973, p. 51). Most boys learn about masturbation from other boys, rather than discovering it on their own. Kinsey, Pomeroy, and Martin (1948) found that many boys observe each other masturbating and for some it is a group activity, or even a game. For example, the "circle jerk" is a contest to see who can ejaculate first or squirt sperm the farthest. In contrast, girls rarely even talk about masturbation with one another. Most of them discover it without knowing anyone else does it.

Despite the support boys get from their peers, masturbation is still surrounded by guilt and anxiety, which in turn increase the emotional power of sexuality. In the not too distant past, most people, including the medical profession, believed that masturbation caused insanity, as well as a host of physical ailments including pimples, poor posture, and weak eyes. Today, masturbation is recognized as a "normal," almost universal practice, whose effects are no different from any other sexual activity. But for many people, especially young adolescents, it remains a guilt-ridden, dirty secret.

These early adolescent differences in the way boys and girls come into their sexuality may make for difficulties between them later in life. Traditionally, while boys are learning to express their sexuality directly, girls have been encouraged not to seek sexual pleasure, but romance, love, and marriage. Sexuality can be a

dangerous activity for girls; even today, parents, female peers, and boys may express disapproval of a girl who admits an open interest in sex. In addition, sex involves troubles for girls which boys do not have to face. With adolescence, a girl becomes a sex object to males; this can bring the harmless attention of adolescent boys, the less welcome attention of older men, and the increased and ever-present danger of rape. Thus, there is a certain justification for parents to be more worried about their daughter's sexuality than their son's, but the warnings reinforce traditional sex roles and may interfere with girls' appreciation of their sexuality.

The other bodily changes of early adolescence also have a profound impact on the boy's sense of self and relations with others. Height, weight, muscular development, and coordination often determine whether a boy can participate in sports and be attractive to girls. Thus, a boy's physical development, like a girl's, can become an important basis for social ranking. Boys can be as concerned about their physical changes as girls are about breast development and periods. Women are often thought to be more obsessed with their looks than men, but there is evidence that both sexes learn very early about what the ideal female or male should look like, and both worry about whether they live up to the ideal. In one large study of young adolescents, one-half of the boys and four-fifths of the girls had concerns about their appearance (Frazier & Lisonbee, 1971). In another study of young people between the ages of 12 and 17, about half the boys wanted to be taller and almost as many of the girls wanted to be thinner (Scanlon, 1975). One man, now a psychologist, recalls his acute embarrassment at the age of 12 when his basketball team was asked to take off their shirts during gym class:

> Why was it so embarrassing, this exposure of skin and the display of our chests and backs? Some of us had acne, and that was humiliating, but I think more than anything, we simply were not up to the ideal stature, and the ideal

posture, size and strength. The ideal was evidently present in all our minds. . . . The only part of us which showed sufficient development at age twelve was the legs, and for those whose legs were thin, or whose ankles were excessively fat, or whose budding truly incongruous leg hair was already unsightly and growing uglier by the day, there was no escape if they couldn't procure long sweat pants. . . . (Cottle, 1972, p. 297)

The Impact of Physical Attractiveness

This concern with appearance is more than a silly adolescent preoccupation. There is a considerable body of evidence which shows that physical attractiveness matters (Adams, 1977; Langlois & Stephan, 1981; Sorell & Nowak, 1981). Though we give lip service to the idea that the ''inner'' qualities of a person are more important than physical appearance, there is a widely held stereotype which tells us that ''what is beautiful is good.'' Individuals who

are judged to be more attractive than others are also judged to have better psychological qualities. They are judged to be not only more likable, but also more intelligent and competent. As a result, these differential expectations cause attractive and unattractive people to be treated differently than others. In turn, attractive and unattractive people tend to internalize both the cultural stereotypes and other people's attitudes toward them. Thus, they may tend to behave in ways that confirm the stereotype.

In effect, from nursery school on, children who are thought to be physically attractive are better liked by peers and adults than those judged as unattractive (Dion & Berscheid, 1972). Further, a bad act committed by an attractive child is judged less severely than the same act committed by an unattractive one (Dion, 1972). Physical attractiveness has also influenced how intelligent adults judge even newborns to be (Corter et al., 1978). In general, peers, teachers, and adults are inclined to think well of the child blessed with physical attractiveness.

In later life, attractiveness has an overwhelming influence on impressions adults form of other adults in many situations, especially dating and marriage. College students, for example, *say* they look for intelligence and friendliness in dating partners, but the evi-

dence suggests that physical attractiveness determines whom they choose to date (Berscheid et al., 1971). Given the fact that, for the most part, good looks are a matter of good luck—being born with the right facial and body configuration—this bias in favor of beauty must be regarded as a painful and yet unnoticed source of inequality in our society.

Western culture has long valued physical attractiveness; the heroes of fairy tales are always the beautiful princess and the handsome prince. But the importance of appearance has grown as modern society has become what social commentators have called a "visual culture," thanks to photography, the movies, and television. Our looks have come to represent our identity in a way that was impossible before inexpensive photographic portraits became available and cameras and the family photo album became household necessities.

Further, the movies and then television provided ideal types of people to compare ourselves with. Adolescents are the most affected by these standards—more likely to model themselves on popular stars, to become distressed at the gap between themselves and the ideal. Recently, the role models have come from television—"Charlie's Angels," "Dynasty," and the "Dukes of Hazzard." One commentator has pointed out how old high school yearbooks mirror the prevailing beauty standards of the time:

> Class of 1944, Veronica Lake and Betty Grable; 1950, Jane Russell; 1955, Marilyn Monroe; 1960, Kim Novak; 1968, Faye Dunaway and Janis Joplin; 1978, Farrah Fawcett and Mick Jagger. (Appel, 1983, p. 97)

The Timing of Puberty

The two basic facts about the physical maturation process are its inevitability and its variability. Some adolescents look mature at 12, others look like children until they are 16 or 17. A casual visitor to a seventh grade classroom may have a hard time believing that all the children in it are close to the same age. These differences in the timing of maturation may have a significant psychological impact.

For boys, the evidence seems clear that early maturation is a great social asset. Researchers in the Berkeley longitudinal studies examined the self-concepts, behavior, and social standing of early and later maturing boys. They found the early maturers to be more popular and self-confident. The early maturers were taller, stronger, and more muscular and athletic—coming closer to the ideal masculine build. They were perceived by others as more good looking, more mature, and were more often chosen as leaders. The late-maturing boys were less poised or relaxed and were more talkative, bossy, and restless. They had less self-confidence and felt more inadequate. Some of these differences persisted into adulthood, even though the late maturers had grown to normal height or taller. The early maturers were more responsible, cooperative, sociable, and self-centered. They were also more likely to be supervisors and managers at work and to have more active and organized social lives (M. C. Jones, 1965).

But early maturation may not be as much of

a psychological asset as it is a social one. In addition to the qualities just mentioned, early-maturing boys were also more rigid, moralistic, humorless, and conforming. The late maturers as grown men were still more impulsive and assertive, but they were also more insightful, perceptive, playful, and able to cope with ambiguity. It seems that the early maturers' smooth identification with adult masculine roles was not without its psychological costs.

Harvey Peskin (1967) has suggested that the stressful adolescence of the late-maturing boys provides better psychological preparation for adulthood than the early maturers' seemingly comfortable adolescence. Looking at the timing of puberty in a different Berkeley longitudinal sample, Peskin found that the early-maturing boys were actually made anxious and upset by the onset of puberty. They fled from their distress about the fixed, conventional identity the world offered them. In contrast, the later-maturing boys had more time to prepare for the onset of puberty and so were less stressed by it. Since they were less frightened by their own thoughts and emotions, they were more intellectually curious than the early maturers, who tended to avoid problem solving or new situations:

> In terms of cognitive and problem solving strategies, the disparity between the internal and external states of the early maturer would lead him to seek and find rapid solutions after minimal exploration; the late maturer, expecting to find neither an easy niche nor an ersatz adult-styled role, creates new possibilities for his larger tolerance for the pubertal change. (Livson & Peskin, 1980, p. 73)

The above descriptions should be applied cautiously to particular individuals. Not all early-maturing boys are smashing social successes in adolescence or constricted, overly conventional personalities as adults. Even very high statistical correlations leave room for a great deal of individual variation. Further, times have changed enormously since the Berkeley longitudinal subjects were teenagers. There has been a sexual revolution and a sex role revolution. Standards for masculinity have relaxed somewhat, and there is greater tolerance for individual differences. The traditional "macho" male style is now only one of several versions of masculinity, making life a little easier for the later-maturing boy. On the other hand, the more open sexual atmosphere of the times may make the onset of puberty less shocking for the early-maturing boy.

Whether or not the early-maturing boy "pays" for his social success with his later development, it is clear that his physical status is an asset in adolescence. The evidence is less clear for girls. In the Berkeley studies, it was the early-maturing girl who was at a disadvantage (H. E. Jones, 1949). She was rated as less popular, less poised, less expressive, and more withdrawn and unassured than her classmates. Late-maturing girls were considered more attractive and were higher in sociability, leadership, and prestige. More recent studies suggest that early maturation still poses difficulties for girls.

It seems plausible that early maturation should put a girl at a disadvantage. Being taller than boys and other girls is a violation of the ideal body type for girls, which is petite. As one early-maturing girl told a researcher, "I felt clumsy, my feet were too big, my body too tall." However, this same researcher (Faust, 1960) found that early maturation was only a temporary disadvantage; eventually, the early-maturing girl is well liked and has high prestige, like her male counterparts. Perhaps her pioneering experience at being adolescent makes her a source of useful information to her classmates as they catch up to her. In addition, Peskin (1973) found that girls who had undergone the stress of early maturation turned out, in adulthood, to be more self-possessed and self-directed than their late-maturing peers.

The Transition to Junior High School

The physical changes of early adolescence are dramatic, but they are not the only changes in the child's life in this period. The arrival of puberty means that parents and other people define the young person in a new way, as an adolescent or teenager; the child may feel ready to join the new social category. But in addition to this new social role, there are institutional changes: early adolescence is the time of the shift from elementary school to junior high school. The junior high school was specifically designed to ease the transition from elementary school—where the children had stayed with a single teacher most of the day—to the larger and more complicated world of the high school, with its shifting classrooms and teachers. It was also designed to be a place where pubescent young people could be among their peers. Ironically, however, as junior high schools function in practice, they may simply make a difficult transition come earlier in a child's life.

Junior high school children must learn how to make their way in large, complex, highly bureaucratic institutions. They must learn how to relate to a changing set of teachers, rather than to just one—who may have seemed like a mother or father figure. Often it is also necessary to make new friends. Further, the entrance into junior high school is taken as a signal that the child has entered a new phase of life. Parents may begin to think of their sixth or seventh grader as an adolescent, although their image of adolescence may be based on stereotypes of older teenagers. Children themselves may feel called upon to think of themselves and act in ways that correspond to some notion of adolescence.

Both the parents and the school begin to escalate their academic demands at this time. Tracking—sorting students by level of academic performance—often begins in the seventh grade, giving each child hard evidence as to how the school and, by implication, the larger society regards his or her talents and potential. As Kagan (1972) observes, tracking may

frighten those who find themselves in the top track, making them wonder if they can live up to the demands that will be made of them. For those in the bottom track, the pain and anger of being publicly labeled as inferior may kill whatever interest they had in academic success, leading them to reject school and all its values. To defend their self-esteem, they may join the antischool culture of prankishness and rebellion. Since the tracking hierarchy corresponds in most cases to the socioeconomic stratification system, it becomes yet another instance of what has been called "the hidden injuries of class" (Sennett & Cobb, 1974).

Academic Performance and Self-esteem

The difficulties of the transition to junior high school are definitively reflected in a sharp drop in academic performance. A large number of the children who do well in elementary school perform at a fair or poor level in junior high (Finger & Silverman, 1966; Hanson & Johnson, 1985). Further, children whose performance drops may never improve their grades later. The problem seems to be mainly one of motivation; intelligence appears to have little relation to changes in performance in junior high school. As Kagan (1972) points out, the motivation to deal with problems of body image, role change, and relations to peers overrides motivation for academic achievement.

A study of sixth grade students in a middle-class suburban school found that all of them admitted some degree of worrying about the transition to junior high school (Hamburg, 1974). Among their worries were the following: fear of academic failure, fear of having to deal with a different teacher and a different group of students every hour, concern about being able to make and keep friends, concern about what would be expected of them now that they would be treated as adolescents, confusion about the size and complexity of the junior high school. Many students worried about getting lost and not being able to locate their classrooms. The children found it extremely reassuring to learn that their classmates had the same worries they did.

Given all their other concerns, it is not surprising that young people's images of themselves become unstable. Harter (1983) summarizes a number of studies which show that self-esteem drops with the transition to junior high school. Young people become self-conscious and uncertain about how to evaluate themselves. Their estimate of their competence declines, as does the correlation between their actual achievement and how well they think they are doing. These findings suggest, as Harter points out, that a person's self-esteem may not be an enduring attribute. Instead, our judgments of ourselves may undergo periods of instability as we enter new environments or take on new roles, not just in early adolescence, but across the life span.

SUMMARY

1. Adolescence is a time of life that looms large in American culture. Much of our popular literature and the mass media use the emotional conflicts of adolescence as a theme for comedy or tragedy. Adolescents set fashions in music and dress. Many of our major social problems—crime, drug use, teenage pregnancy, and unemployment—involve adolescents.

2. Before the twentieth century, adolescence was not recognized as a distinct time of life. Although other writers had described aspects of adolescent experience, G. Stanley Hall is credited with popularizing it, describing it as a time of high idealism as well as storm and stress. Hall thought that the psychological changes of adolescence were brought about by biological changes, recapitulating an earlier stage in human evolution. Anthropologists have pointed out,

however, that adolescence is not universally recognized as a major stage in the life cycle. Historians note that adolescence emerged when young people were no longer in the labor force but instead began to attend high school in large numbers.

3. Some of the major theorists of adolescence, particularly those in the psychoanalytic tradition, view it as an inevitable period of emotional turmoil. This view has not been confirmed by empirical researchers. Surveys of adolescence have found that while some young people fit the storm and stress model, most do not. Nevertheless, adolescence is one of those periods of the life cycle when troubles are more likely to arise.

4. Physical growth during adolescence is more dramatic than at any other period except infancy. Sexual maturation occurs, and the whole body enlarges. Sexual maturation is a gradual process, but the chief milestones are menarche in girls and nocturnal emission in boys. There is wide variation in the timing of physical maturation, and these variations have psychological consequences. Early-maturing boys have been found to be socially advantaged, while late-maturing boys seem to be less popular and confident. Other research suggests that these psychological differences are reversed in adulthood, with late-maturing boys doing better in life than those who had matured early. For girls, early maturation also seems to create more social problems than being a late maturer.

5. The psychological stresses of adolescence arise from the bodily changes that occur so dramatically, as well as from changes in demands and expectations that young people must face. Adolescents are often desperately concerned about their normality and their attractiveness, measuring themselves against their peers as well as idealized standards. In addition to physical maturation, young adolescents have to deal with the transition from elementary school to the larger and more confusing worlds of junior and senior high school. Also, parents and teachers and other adults begin to demand more of the young person in terms of general maturity as well as academic purpose and achievement.

Key Terms

adolescence **428**
anorexia nervosa **442**
bulimia **443**
menarche **437**
puberty **429**
secular trend **437**

CHAPTER 13

Thought and Identity in Adolescence

Youth seeks to be, know, get, feel all that is highest, greatest, and best in man's estate. . . . It is the glorious dawn of imagination, which supplements the individual limitations and expands the soul towards the dimensions of the race.

—G. Stanley Hall,
Adolescence

Every step of the upward way is strewn with wreckage of body, mind, and morals. There is not only arrest, but perversion, at every stage, and hoodlumism, juvenile crime, and secret vice seem not only increasing, but develop earlier in years in every civilized land.

—G. Stanley Hall,
Adolescence

Some years ago, a 13-year-old boy suddenly found himself preoccupied with thoughts about death. He was not frightened at the idea of his own death—at least that was not what was uppermost in his mind. Nor had anyone close to him died. Rather, what bothered him was the inevitability and universality of death.

> What seemed to me absolutely insupportable was simply that there was no getting around it. You could live to be a hundred and twenty. Doctors could invent all kinds of medicines and serums. You could be the King of England, or the President of the United States. Still, in the end, you would die. Everyone now alive would die. I felt it to be intolerable that we should be so completely overruled, that it should be made so brutally plain to us that our wishes, our will, our achievements and our individuality counted for nothing. (Jacobson, 1966, p. 229)

Although these words are the recollections of a gifted writer many years later, they illustrate how the general quality of adolescent thought differs from that of younger children. Before adolescence, the child tends to live in the present moment, in the here and now world of concrete reality. Adolescents, in contrast, have the capacity to manipulate ideas, to think forward and backward through long stretches of time, to deal with imagined possibilities and impossibilities. Thus, an 8- or 9-year-old child brooding about death would likely be concerned about its more factual horrors—the pain and suffering of dying, the separation from loved ones, being buried in the ground. But the 13-year-old described above, while not immune from such concrete fears about death, was concerned with its more theoretical implications—the fact that the most powerful individuals are powerless against death and the inconsistency of death with the values we prize most in life: our wishes, achievements, individuality.

Many of the changes and characteristics typical of adolescence owe as much, if not more, to these advances in cognitive development

than to sexual maturation and physical growth. Not until adolescence does the child have, as Flavell puts it, "the conceptual wherewithal to worry about the world situation, plan for the future, or experience romantic love" (1963, p. 42).

Before taking a more detailed look at the cognitive changes of adolescence, a word of caution is in order: we should not assume that specific kinds of cognitive changes we see in American and European adolescents are common to all humankind. Like puberty, the capacity for abstract forms of thought and self-awareness are universal. But as we mentioned in the last chapter, it is only in certain kinds of societies that adolescence is recognized as a stage of life, with a distinct set of psychological and social characteristics. Adolescence, like a concern with self, "is a luxury item that emerges in surplus economies" (Munroe & Munroe, 1975).

Piaget and Formal Operations

Jean Piaget put forth the first and most important theory of adolescent thought, and most of the research on the subject is based on his work (Inhelder & Piaget, 1958; Piaget, 1972). He wrote about adolescent thought in three different forms. First, he discussed how the sophisticated thought of adolescents differs from the thought processes of younger children as well as from those of adults. Piaget believed that, although the new mental powers put the adolescent at the same intellectual level as the adult, they also plunge him or her into a new kind of egocentricity.

Second, Piaget described a series of experimental tasks which showed how formal operational thought differs from earlier stages of cognitive development. Finally, he presented his theory of formal operations in a highly abstract way, drawing heavily on mathematical and logical symbolism. He believed that each stage of cognitive development can be expressed by a distinct logical-mathematical model.

Piaget and his associates theorized that adolescents reach a level of thought called **formal**

operations. Recall that the *concrete operational* child can deal realistically with objects and the relations between them. He or she can classify objects, count them, and tell the difference between *apparent* and *actual* changes, such as those involved in the concept of conservation. All of this marks a great advance over the preschool child's uncertain grasp of the distinction between illusion and reality. But the mind of the concrete operational child is limited by its realism. It does not yet possess the powers and attitudes of the competent adult mind, which begin to appear in early adolescence.

Once a child reaches the level of formal operations, several crucial characteristics distinguish his or her adolescent thought from earlier forms. The first is the *detachment* of thought from concrete reality. While the preoperational child can transform reality in fanciful, make-believe ways, the adolescent in the formal operational period can depart from reality logically and systematically. A rough way to illustrate the differences among levels of thought is to compare them to literary genres: the preoperational child's world is found in fairy tales; the concrete operational child's world is the realistic novel or the nonfiction book; the adolescent's formal operational world is found in the kind of science fiction that describes a hypothetical society or situation in convincing, consistent detail.

The ability to deal with the hypothetical and the possible is one manifestation of the adolescent mind's "detachment" from reality. Another is the ability to separate the *form* of thought from the *content*. The adolescent can deal with the Xs and Ys of algebra and the Ps and Qs of formal logic. He or she can also deal with the logic of a series of statements, without regard for their literal truth. Consider the following sentences:

All cows are purple.

There is a cow in my bathtub.

What color is it?

To a 9-year-old, the statements are likely to sound silly because cows are not purple, and it is unlikely that there is one in the bathtub. The

adolescent, by contrast, is likely to recognize that the statements form a chain of reasoning, and that logic requires the cow in the bathtub to be purple.

A second feature of formal operational thought is its *combinatorial property*. One of the tasks Piaget uses to study the transition to adolescent thought involves discovering why objects float. The child is handed a bucket of water and a collection of objects such as needles, paper, matches, pebbles, an aluminum pan lid and is asked which objects will float and why. The concrete operational child will typically try to solve the problem in terms of size or weight separately. The adolescent will realize that it is the combination of the two properties taken together that determine whether an object will float or sink.

Second-order thinking is another major feature of the formal operational period. The adolescent is able to manipulate representations of reality or, as Piaget put it, perform operations on operations. One function of this second-order thinking is the understanding of proportions. The concrete operational child can understand multiplication; that 4 times 3 is 12, or 5 times 3 is 15. But the adolescent can recognize that 4 is to 12 as 5 is to 15 because they have the same form or proportion, 1:3.

The ability to understand analogies is another example of this more abstract, second-order kind of thinking. Adolescents can solve the following kinds of problems, while younger children have difficulty doing so (Sternberg & Nigro, 1980):

WIN:LOSE is the same as which of the following?
   DISLIKE:HATE
   EAR:HEAR
   ENJOY:LIKE
   ABOVE:BELOW

Adolescents can understand relations and see connections among phenomena that seem at first glance to be dissimilar. The ability to relate statements to one another also means that the adolescent can detect inconsistency.

Finally, the adolescent's thought tends to be more *exhaustive* than that of the younger child, taking more of the information in a situation into account as well as more of the possibilities inherent in it. An adolescent will also show greater *flexibility* than a younger child. Piaget finds that younger children tend to approach problems with their minds set on a particular solution which they cling to even in the face of contradictory evidence. Older children are more willing to try a series of different ways of solving a problem if the first attempt fails. All of these general characteristics of adolescent thought reveal themselves in the experimental tasks Piaget devised to assess the development of formal operations.

Liquids and Pendulums

The major work on formal operations, *The Growth of Logical Thinking from Childhood to Adolescence* (Inhelder & Piaget, 1958), presents fifteen experimental tasks for demonstrating the differences between concrete and formal thought. I will discuss just two of these.

The Colored and Colorless Liquids Problem   The child or older person is shown four similar, numbered flasks, each containing a colorless liquid. A smaller flask, labeled "g," also contains a clear liquid. Two glasses with liquid in them are presented to the subject. While the subject watches, the experimenter puts several drops from "g" into each of the glasses; the water in one of them turns yellow. The experimenter then asks the subject to produce the yellow liquid, using any or all of the five flasks. The solution is to mix fluids from flasks 1 and 3 with a few drops from "g." Any other combination gives a colorless mixture, and certain of the fluids can eliminate the yellow color.

The Pendulum Problem   The subject is given a string that can be shortened or lengthened, a series of weights that can be hung from the string, and a rod from which to suspend the weights. The task is to figure out what determines how fast a pendulum swings. Other factors the person might take into account are the height of the release point and the strength of

the push he or she gives to get it started. Since the length of the string is the only factor that influences the rate of oscillation, the task for the subject is to eliminate all the others.

Problems such as these are extremely difficult for children to solve before the age of 12 or 13. Not all adolescents solve them either, but they typically tackle the problems in a different way than younger children. Children at the concrete operational level typically proceed in an unsystematic, trial-and-error fashion. They begin to manipulate the materials with little planning or consideration of all the possibilities. For example, the child might simply start mixing the colorless liquids randomly. Or, in the pendulum problem, the child might compare different weights on different length strings. A child at the concrete operational stage might be more systematic than this, but only up to a point. For example, he or she might systematically combine each of the four liquids with the contents of flask "g," but fail to go on to mix the liquids two at a time. Or the child might go on to combine two or more liquids at a time, but unsystematically and without keeping a record of what was combined and the results.

What do young people at the stage of formal operations do differently? Mainly, they start out with a plan, rather than randomly manipulating the materials. They consider all the possible solutions to a problem and figure out how to identify the correct one. Thus, in the liquids problem, the person would list all possible combinations and form a strategy of attack: "First I'll try mixing all the liquids one at a time with the liquid from flask 'g,' then, all pairs of liquids with 'g,' then all possible combinations of three liquids with 'g.'" In the pendulum problem, the task is to think of each factor that might explain the speed of oscillation and to plan a series of trials in which all but one of the possible factors is held constant. Through a process of exclusion, the causal factor can be identified. Thus, the subject might test the hypothesis that the weight is a crucial factor by varying the weight while keeping the other factors—length of string, strength of push—constant.

In sum, then, adolescents reason differently from children in that they subordinate reality to possibility; reality is only one part of a wider world of possibility. Adolescents imagine how things could be otherwise and realize that what actually occurs is but one of a number of things that *might* have occurred. Another characteristic of Piagetian adolescent thought is its *combinatorial* property. While younger children can consider each factor in a problem on its own, they have trouble combining them. Thus, they cannot consider all combinations of the liquids; and on the pendulum problem they are not able to focus on one variable while keeping in mind the others that must be held constant.

Emotional Implications

The shift to more abstract, "formal" levels of thought has profound implications for the adolescent's emotional life. As we saw earlier, most theorists have seen adolescence as a time of stress, conflict, and preoccupation with sexuality. Piaget argued that we cannot interpret this age only in terms of puberty and generational conflict.

Emotions do not exist in isolation from mental structures—that is, ideas and the capacity to manipulate them. The cognitive changes of adolescence affect all of experience; the youth may experience intense feelings in connection with sexual urges and bodily changes, yet these emotions are aroused and interpreted within a framework of thought. As Piaget points out, the adolescent's discovery of romantic love is deeply involved with the general tendency at this age to construct theories and ideologies. Children experience love, he explains, but "what distinguishes an adolescent in love from a child in love is that the former generally complicates his feelings by constructing a romance or by referring to social or even literary ideals of all sorts" (Inhelder & Piaget, 1958, p. 336). Adolescents in love are apt to view themselves and the loved one as characters in a romantic novel; they may be more in love with love and with romantic fantasy than with the flesh and blood person.

The shift to more abstract modes of thought also influences the way adolescents think about themselves. There are many similarities between Piaget's account of the cognitive changes of adolescence and Erikson's description of the process of identity construction. Erikson (1968) explains that identity is a sense of sameness and continuity despite growth and environmental change. An identity is an integration of previous self-images in the light of one's hopes and goals for the future. Piaget (1967) writes that adolescents' new perspective of time, their ability to think beyond the present, makes it possible to develop a "life plan"—a concept of the kind of adult they want to be—and a set of plans for reaching that goal.

Thus, the ability to think about thoughts, to notice and be concerned with inconsistency, and to deal with hypothetical possibilities is turned on the self in the process of constructing an identity. Adolescents can think about their own thoughts and apply abstract standards of competence, morality, beauty to themselves. They can construct an ideal model of the kind of person they would like to be and become dissatisfied with the kind of person they think they are. All of these concerns are central to Erikson's description of the process of identity construction.

Evaluation of Formal Operations

Piaget considered the stage of formal operations as the highest level of human intellectual ability and the chief accomplishment of the adolescent years. Adults are more sophisticated than adolescents because their thought processes are tamed by reality and experience, but they do not have more advanced cognitive structures, according to Piaget. A great deal of research has been based on Piaget's approach to adolescent thought; some of it has supported him, some has been critical of his ideas and methods. A review of many major works in support of Piaget's claims may be found in Neimark (1975); critical and contrasting approaches to adolescent thought are reviewed in Keating (1980).

The debate between Piaget and his critics centers around his explanation of the nature of adolescent thought. No one denies that during adolescence young people become increasingly able to deal with sophisticated cognitive problems, and many researchers agree that adolescents have a greater capacity to deal with abstract ideas than children. The issue is how to interpret these changes. The evidence of adolescent cognitive superiority to younger children can be found in IQ data. For example, a study of the performance of large samples of children and adolescents on the Stanford-Binet test (Garfinkel & Thorndike, 1976) reveals striking age changes. Thus, while 76 percent of 7- to 9-year-olds pass the age 8 items, 99 percent of 14- to 16-year-olds do. While 1 percent of the younger children can pass the average adult items, 55 percent of adolescents can.

Many other studies of thinking processes reveal similar age trends. Consider games such as Twenty Questions (Bruner, Olver, & Greenfield, 1966; Neimark & Lewis, 1967), the point of which is to use the fewest possible questions to figure out what object someone is thinking of. Younger children tend to solve the problem by asking a lot of specific questions directed at finding out exactly what the other person is thinking about: "Is it a cat?" "Is it the Empire State Building?" In contrast, adolescents and adults are likely to use an information processing strategy to figure out what category the object belongs to and progressively narrow the possibilities. Knowledge that the object is an animal rather than vegetable or mineral will prompt the older person to ask a series of questions such as, "Is it human rather than animal?" "Is it real as opposed to fictional?" "Living or dead?" This methodical, hypothetical, abstract approach to problem solving, which Piaget regarded as the essence of formal operational thought, reveals a liberation of thought from concrete reality, an ability to plan ahead and develop and test hypotheses.

Recent studies carried out by information processing researchers also support Piaget's claims about a shift in intellectual function at around age 12 (Sternberg & Powell, 1983). Piaget argued that, with the onset of formal op-

erational thought, children become able to construct "relations between relations." For example, a number of studies dealing with reasoning about analogies—A is to B as C is to D—find that the ability to solve such problems occurs around the transition from childhood to adolescence (Gallagher & Wright, 1979; Sternberg & Rifkin, 1979).

Generally, critics agree with Piaget's descriptions of major differences between the cognitive capacities of adolescents and children; this is even taken for granted in practical applications such as school curricula. More fault has been found, though, with Piaget's experimental tasks, and there are still more reservations about his complicated mathematical models of adolescent thought.

Piaget believed that the cognitive changes of adolescence are rooted in the same developmental processes that guide infants through the six stages of sensorimotor learning and the later stages of childhood. At each stage, the child's basic cognitive structures are reorganized. Piaget theorized that the shift to adolescent intelligence involves the acquisition of formal logic; that the logician's description of logical structures illustrates the psychological makeup of the adolescent mind. His use of logic is the most abstruse and controversial aspect of his work on adolescent cognitive development. It would take too much room to describe it here, and given the criticisms by logicians as well as other psychologists, it is unlikely to emerge as the best scientific model of adolescent thought (Flavell, 1977; Neimark, 1979; Parsons, 1960).

Aside from concentrating too much on abstract logic, Piaget has also been criticized for paying too little attention to the kinds of tasks used in assessing formal operations. The problem of telling the difference between *performance*—how well a person does on a particular task—and his or her underlying *competence* is a persistent one in psychology. The familiarity and difficulty of the tasks affect how well a person will do. For example, some problems are extremely simple to solve when they are described in practical, concrete terms, but become mind boggling even for professors of logic if described as abstract, logical problems in terms of A, B, then C.

Several researchers have tried to show that the generally poor levels attained by adolescents and adults on formal operations tasks are due to the vague and ambiguous instructions used by Piaget and Inhelder. One study (Danner & Day, 1977) tried to evoke formal operational behavior through explicit instructions, suggesting that paper and pencil would be useful. Then the researchers presented problems using the traditional instructions. Although the technique was much more successful for 17-year-olds, some 10-year-olds were able to solve the Piagetian problem. Findings of this and other studies suggest that the capacity for formal operations may occur at a younger age and is more widespread than Piaget believed.

Even taking task difficulties into account, the lack of universality of formal operations poses a problem for Piagetian theory. The theory implies that anyone who has mastered concrete operations in childhood should eventually, through further experience and maturation, internalize these operations and reason at a formal operational level. Formal operations is assumed to be the built-in, inherent direction of the human mind. Yet even among college students and adults, rates of successful performance are only about 40 to 60 percent (Niemark, 1975). Further, while formal thought is far from universal in our culture, it seems to be practically impossible to demonstrate in nonliterate cultures (Berry & Dasen, 1974).

Some researchers have raised questions about whether Piaget's conception of intelligence may represent not a basic human ability, but a habit of mind peculiar to certain segments of Western civilization. Indeed, most of the problems Piaget uses to study formal operations are problems in chemistry and physics; those who have taken science courses are more likely to succeed at them, while those unfamiliar with experimental procedures may be handicapped. Robert Hogan regards the capacity for formal operations as a cold-blooded, detached mode of thought: "Such a habit of mind requires a very special cultural context to support it, a culture characterized by leisure, by

distance from the immediate demands of physical survival, and a social system that supports and rewards this detached and rather narcissistic form of thought" (1980, p. 539).

Piaget acknowledged the validity of many of the criticisms of formal operations. Even in his earliest statements about adolescent thought, he recognized that this stage of development was more dependent than the earlier ones on particular social and educational environments. Piaget (1972) suggested that, unlike his earlier stages, formal operations may be a more specialized ability, dependent on a person's particular talents, training, and experience. While success at Piaget's original tasks may favor those with scientific training, other people may reason in an abstract, hypothetical-deductive way dealing with other problems. An auto mechanic might show such a high level of thought in trying to figure out what is wrong with a car, thinking of all the possible causes of the problem, isolating variables, testing various hypotheses; hunters in a nonliterate society might show such reasoning in tracking and capturing animals (Flavell, 1977; Tulkin & Konner, 1973).

The Information Processing Approach

Since the 1970s, Piaget's account of adolescent thought has also been challenged by researchers using an information processing approach to cognitive development. While they agree that children's problem solving changes around the age of 12, they disagree with his account of how and why the shift occurs. As we mentioned in an earlier chapter, researchers using this approach focus on the various processes that contribute to thinking and problem solving. Like Piaget, they are interested in underlying mental processes; unlike Piaget, however, they reject the idea that cognitive development consists of changes from one tightly knit, logical structure to another.

Rather, they believe that children acquire particular cognitive skills in addition to the increased capacity or rate of mental processing. Among the skills that may account for developmental change are greater knowledge of the physical and social world, strategies of memorizing, the ability to focus attention. After the age of 11 or 12, children performing a cognitive task can skillfully ignore distracting stimuli, such as irrelevant pictures, and process only pertinent information (Hagen & Hale, 1973). The growth of **metamemory** is another skill children acquire over time. Metamemory refers to a person's use of strategies for remembering: tying a string around one's finger or putting a package to be mailed next to the front door. Information processing researchers have studied the development of such mnemonic strategies repeating what is to be remembered or organizing information in some fashion such as making an outline (Kail, 1979).

Memory is also implicated in other cognitive processes: to solve a problem, it is necessary to remember what the problem is. Thus, information processing researchers have pointed to increases in memory capacity as a general mechanism of cognitive development. As we saw in Chapter 10, Juan Pascual-Leone (1970) has proposed that increases in children's processing capacity—the number of pieces of information they can keep in mind at the same time—correspond to movement from one of Piaget's stages to the next. Case (1978) makes a similar argument. There is also growing evidence that memory does indeed play an important role in Piaget's tasks (Trabasso, 1977). It seems fair to say that while Piaget's influence remains strong, many researchers are coming to favor an information processing approach over one of cognitive development—which is not as much anti-Piagetian as it is neo-Piagetian.

In sum, then, the scientific status of formal operational thought is not settled, and Piaget's claim that it is the culmination of human cognitive development seems dubious: some adults may never attain formal thought while some preadolescents may show evidence of it. Further, some researchers postulate a stage of cognitive development *beyond* formal operations (Broughton, 1983). Yet Piaget has called attention to the development of an important quality of human thought. Formal operations may not represent the level at which most adolescents and adults think most of the time.

Nor are the more sophisticated forms of thought necessarily impossible for children. But there are observable differences between the way children typically think and the way adolescents and adults typically do. Before adolescence, it is rare for anyone to become concerned about identity, justice, the purpose of life, or the nature of truth and beauty.

The Emergence of Identity

"What do you want to be when you grow up?" Children are often asked that question, but their answers are seldom taken seriously. At adolescence, finding the answer becomes a major life task. There is a popular stereotype of a person having an "identity crisis": a college student or older person becomes engaged in a prolonged and endlessly discussed "search for self." The search may involve leaving home or school, moving from place to place, seeking out some guru, or entering therapy. The stereotype portrays a middle- or upper-middle-class young person; Holden Caulfield, the hero of J. D. Salinger's novel *Catcher in the Rye*, fits the image perfectly. There are many real-life people who match Salinger's stereotype, which is based on literary examples as well as psychiatric case histories. Many novelists have had identity crises, and psychiatrists often see late adolescents and older people who are having trouble "finding themselves." But most people manage to find an identity calmly and without living up to the stereotype.

Nor is identity an issue only for the middle class. As mentioned in Chapter 12, middle-class adolescents have more options, and since they are more likely to go to college, they have more time to make up their minds. But few young people in this society are exempt from choosing an identity, no matter how little thought they give to it. Every young person must choose what particular direction to take in work, sexuality, politics. Identity formation does not always take the form of a self-conscious "search for self." Most of the time, it proceeds gradually and often without con-

scious awareness that identity construction is in process. As one researcher observes,

> Identity is the result of minute, seemingly inconsequential choices: whom one chooses for friends, what school one attends, what courses one takes, what one reads or does not read, whether one learns to play tennis or fly airplanes, whether one takes drugs or robs a store. Choice and action, however transient or impulsive, become part of one's life history and part of one's meaning for society. (Josselson, 1980, p. 202)

The terms **identity** and **identity crisis** have migrated from the original clinical writings in which Erikson first propounded them to become media clichés and a part of the "psychobabble" of everyday life. Erikson himself has been amused and appalled by the faddish use and misuse of the term. He had coined the term "identity crisis" to describe the confusions of some disturbed young men who had recently served in World War II. They had lost a sense of personal sameness, continuity, and control over their lives. Later he applied the term to delinquents and disturbed adolescents and then extended its meaning to include the normal developmental changes of adolescents. Erikson does not approve of the use of his term when referring to an "identity crisis" of a corporation, or a nation. More seriously, Erikson was surprised to find that a technical term he coined to describe mental patients has become part of the way people talk about themselves, "flamboyantly display[ing] a conflict which we once regarded as silent, inner, and unconscious" (1968, p. 19).

Despite the overextensions and misuses of "identity" and "identity crisis," the concepts remain a useful way of understanding psychological development during adolescence in cultures like ours. In contrast to other places and times, modernized industrial societies impose a prolonged period of transition between childhood and adulthood. During this transition, the individual is faced with new expectations and choices. In cultures where a person is regarded more as a member of a family or clan than as an individual, or where young people inherit the occupations and status of their parents, identity usually is decided at birth.

Identity as a Theory of Self

Identity, as we saw in Chapter 7, may be conceived of as a schema (Markus, 1977), an image or concept that a person implicitly holds about him- or herself. This view of the self-concept as a theory was first put forth by Epstein (1973) and was later elaborated by Brim (1976). It is consistent with the perspective known as **implicit** or naive **psychology**—the idea propounded by theorists such as Fritz Heider (1958) and George Kelly (1955) that people in their everyday lives behave like scientists, building theories about the social world. Individuals continually make, test, and revise hypotheses and organize their observations into broader theories. Like scientists, according to implicit psychology, people construct theories in order to understand, predict, and control their worlds. Without some theory of self and others, it would be impossible to make choices, respond to others, and in general behave effectively. Some of these beliefs about self and others are conscious; some are implicit but available to awareness, like knowledge of exactly what motions one makes in driving or walking; others may be deeply repressed. These varying levels of awareness are also typical of scientific theory. As Brim points out, "in scientific theory generally, digging out the hidden assumptions, the unrecognized axioms and premises, . . . is an integral part of the growth and development of science, as it is for the self theories of human beings" (1976, p. 244).

Defining identity as a kind of theory of the self is a useful way of organizing knowledge about identity in a broader framework. Erikson has defined identity as a *process* that goes on throughout the life span but becomes a critical developmental task at adolescence. A conception of identity as a theory of the self makes it clear why this should be so. At adolescence, young people in modernized societies must revise their theories of self in ways that more traditional, unchanging societies do not. As the anthropologist Ruth Benedict (1938) once pointed out, just in going from childhood to adulthood, young people must go from being asexual to sexual; from having no work responsibilities to choosing a career; from being sub-

ordinate to adults to taking on the rights and privileges of adulthood, to feeling and acting like and thinking about oneself as a grown-up. We may in fact think of traditional societies as ones in which most of a person's self theory is given from an early age by society, although even in these cultures individual differences are recognized.

The thought of identity as a kind of theory about the self suggests another reason why this concern arises at adolescence. When an adolescent gains the capacity for more abstract hypothetical modes of thought, he or she is also likely to be concerned with issues of self-consistency and continuity. For example, a younger child might act like a model of politeness and good behavior when in the presence of parents and teachers, and yet might be a swearing, smoking, near-delinquent adventurer among his peers. When he gets to be an adolescent, this boy may be bothered by what he may now see as inconsistency. He may wonder which is his real self—the rebel or the conformist—and try to integrate the two ways of behaving, or else choose between them.

Research Findings

So far, we have talked about the concept of identity but not research on the topic. How well have Erikson's descriptions stood up to empirical study? Actually, identity is a rather elusive topic for research. For one thing, Erikson (1968) has purposely kept his definition vague. He writes within the tradition of psychoanalytic clinical literature; much of the writing of others on identity is also within those parameters. Another problem is that identity is an abstract way of referring to a person's inner organization of needs, values, goals, and self-images, much of which is not fully conscious. Thus, asking people directly about their identity may not be the best way to find out about it.

Nevertheless, some research has provided useful information about the development of identity during adolescence. Some of the studies attempt to translate Erikson's terms directly

into research categories; others define identity more broadly in terms of self-concept. Still other research does not deal explicitly with identity or self, but with the process of identity formation during adolescence—sexual development, vocational choice, and problems of adolescence such as delinquency and mental illness.

According to a series of studies which examined the self-concepts of a large sample of young people from 8 to 18 (Rosenberg, 1979; Simmons et al., 1979), there is a generalized pattern of self-image disturbance in young adolescents, starting about the age of 12. Compared to younger children, early adolescents are highly self-conscious and have uncertain, shaky images of themselves. They have lower

overall self-esteem, and lesser opinions of themselves with regard to certain qualities they value. They believe that parents, teachers, and peers think less well of them and so are more likely than younger children to feel depressed. These findings lend support to Erikson's views about the importance of identity during adolescence, but the problems seem to occur at an earlier age than he assumed.

What happens as a person progresses through the teenage years? On the whole, except for the fact that self-esteem rises again, there are few differences between early and later adolescents; the striking contrasts are found between the 8- to 11-year-olds, and the 12- to 14-year-olds.

Although it would seem at first glance that sudden changes in self-concept around the age of 12 are likely to be due to the physical and sexual changes of puberty, the authors of these studies suggest a different answer. They do not deny that puberty affects young people's concepts profoundly, but they also found a very strong environmental effect. The data showed that the onset of self-concept disturbance was not related to age, but rather to entrance into junior high school. Like puberty itself, the transition to a new and challenging environment has an unsettling effect on young people's view of themselves. Both the physical and the environmental changes come at a time when adolescents are cognitively able to see themselves from the point of view of another. As a result, the young person becomes much more concerned with what other people think of him or her, less sure of what the self is really like, and uncertain as to how well the self lives up to one's own or other people's standards. Eventually, most individuals establish a more stable sense of self, but they can never return to the unreflective self of childhood.

The most direct attempt to measure and study Erikson's notions about identity has been carried out by James Marcia and his associates. Marcia (1966) developed an interview technique to place college students into one of four categories. The interview asks questions about occupational choice and religious and political beliefs and values. Students are classified ac-

cording to whether or not they have gone through an active decision-making period, or "crisis," and the degree to which they are now committed to an occupation and set of beliefs. By using these two criteria, Marcia classified students into the following four identity statuses:

- *Identity Achievement:* These individuals have gone through a decision-making period and seem to have developed firm commitments.

- *Foreclosure:* These are persons who are committed to an occupational goal and a set of beliefs, but seem to have passively accepted their parents' goals for them rather than going through a period of decision making on their own.
- *Moratorium:* These are individuals who are currently struggling with occupational or ideological issues, trying to make a choice among a set of alternatives. They are considered to be *in* an identity crisis.
- *Identity Diffusion:* These are young people who have no set occupational or ideological commitments and may or may not have experienced a decisional crisis.

The following answers to the question "Have you ever had any doubts about your religious beliefs?" gives the flavor of these distinctions:

- (Identity Achievement) "Yeah, I even started wondering whether or not there was a God. I've pretty much resolved that, though. The way it seems to me is. . . ."
- (Foreclosure) "No, not really. Our family is pretty much in agreement on these things."
- (Moratorium) "Yes, I guess I'm going through that right now. I just don't see how there can be a God and yet so much evil in the world. . . ."
- (Identity Diffusion) "Oh, I don't know. I guess so. Everyone goes through some sort of stage like that. But it really doesn't bother me much. I figure one's about as good as another." (Marcia, 1966)

Marcia's work departs from Erikson's in a number of ways. For one thing, Marcia assumes that some sort of crisis, even if it is only a period of indecision, is necessary to achieve an identity, and that this crisis and its resolution are *conscious*. Thus, people who are classified as Foreclosures, even though they are clear about who they are, are not considered to be high in identity. Those classified as Identity Achievements and Moratoriums are considered higher in identity, while Foreclosures and Identity Diffusions are considered lower. In contrast to Marcia, Erikson has argued that while people may be aware of dealing with

identity issues, the process of identity formation is largely *unconscious*. Further, he does not insist that anyone who does not have a conscious crisis is a Foreclosure.

Marcia also assumes that the central issues for identity are occupation and ideology, and that the resolution of an identity crisis involves a clear commitment to a particular goal or set of values. For Erikson, however, identity touches a wide range of issues and may be different for different people. A person might be "committed" to an occupation and ideology, yet be struggling with sexual identity. Also, Erikson stresses that identity formation has a "dark and negative side which throughout life can remain an unruly part of the total identity" (1975, p. 20). Everyone, he argues, harbors a negative identity consisting of all the things the person wants not to be, or was warned against being in the course of growing up. In periods of crisis, the person may give up on his or her positive identity and allow the negative identity to emerge, like a Dr. Jekyll and Mr. Hyde. Identity, as we shall see in more detail later in this chapter, is an issue in many of the social problems of adolescence—delinquency, drinking and drugs, cults, teenage pregnancy.

Finally, Erikson's polarity of "identity" versus "identity confusion" does not precisely correspond to Marcia's four identity statuses. Erikson's theory deals with a continuum of mental health and pathology. Thus, identity is experienced as a sense of "psychosocial well-being—a feeling of being 'at home in one's body,' of 'knowing where one is going' " (1980, p. 127). At the opposite pole, extreme identity confusion is reflected in neurotic or psychotic symptoms. In the middle of the continuum are milder forms of identity confusion and the fluctuations of identity Erikson considers normal. Marcia (1980), on the other hand, is dealing with four different *styles* of identity, each of which may have a healthy or pathological aspect.

Although the work of Marcia and his associates differs from Erikson's notions, it does provide some useful empirical data on the experience of identity, particularly for American college students. There is little research information so far about identity processes in young people outside the college-going population. Actually, the decision about whether or not to go to college is a major issue for many young people, with important implications for identity. But identity in high school students has not been studied. Another limitation is that the identity status of women has been studied less than that of men.

Many studies explore the personality correlates of the different identity statuses. The evidence suggests that late-adolescent males with distinct identity styles differ in a number of other ways: Moratoriums rank the highest in anxiety, as expected from their "in-crisis" status, and Foreclosures rank the lowest (Marcia, 1966). Foreclosures are high in "authoritarian" values and are more likely to change their level of self-esteem according to what other people think of them (Marcia, 1967). In terms of moral reasoning, individuals classified as Foreclosures and Diffusions tend to give conventional responses, while those considered high in identity (Identity Achievement and Moratorium status) reason at the postconventional level (Podd, 1972).

Identity classification has also been related to intimacy, which agrees with Erikson's hypothesis that identity is a precursor to intimacy. One study found that young men in the two high identity statuses tended to have close, mutual relationships with women, while those in the two low identity statuses tended to have stereotyped, exploitative relationships. Identity Diffusion individuals have been found to be more isolated from peers of both sexes than those in other groups (Orlovsky, Marcia, & Lesser, 1973). In terms of interpersonal style, one study found Identity Diffusions to be withdrawn, feeling at odds with the world, and keeping strange hours. In contrast, Foreclosures led structured, happy lives. They studied hard and kept regular hours (Donovan, 1975). Other research (Jordan, 1971) found that Foreclosures seemed to be "participating in a love affair" with their parents, while Identity Diffusions felt rejected by and detached from their parents, and Moratorium and Identity Achievement individuals had ambivalent relations with theirs.

There is some question about whether identity status reflects different ongoing personality styles rather than a developmental process unique to adolescence (see Donovan, 1975). Nevertheless, some observers have looked at changes in identity status through the college years. In a series of studies (A. S. Waterman, Geary, & Waterman, 1974; Waterman & Waterman, 1971, 1972), freshman males classified into the four identity status groups were followed until the end of their senior year. During their freshman year, more than 75 percent of the students changed their identity status in one or both areas (occupation or ideology), including many who had been placed in the Identity Achievement status. The failure to find the Identity Achievers to be more stable than the others suggests that the experience of going to college results in considerable rethinking of goals and ideas.

Although the authors consider this a "regressive" change, it would have been a more unfortunate finding if it had turned out that the college experience had left young people in the same frame of mind as they were at the end of high school. Indeed, although many young people do use college as a means to some occupational goal, for many others it has traditionally served as a kind of moratorium period. During this "time out" from adult responsibilities, young people can explore new ideas from the intellectual smorgasbord offered in courses, take the "Joe College" route of football, fraternities, and parties, or follow other styles of college experience which may or may not be relevant for later life.

By the senior year, the number of young men who had achieved a firm sense of identity had increased. Yet there were also a considerable number who were still in the Identity Diffusion category (A. S. Waterman, Geary, & Waterman, 1974). Students who had been Identity Achievers as freshmen ranked as the most stable, while those who had been in the Moratorium status were most likely to change, lending support to the notion that Moratorium students are in a decisional crisis, trying to work out their identity and life plans.

Gender Differences in Identity

As mentioned earlier, most work on identity status has been on young men. The studies that have been done with women present a confused picture, and the implications of each status seem to differ by sex. One study found that in some ways the Foreclosure identity category seemed more "adaptive" for women in that they were higher in self-esteem than the Identity Achievers (Marcia & Friedman, 1970). But a later study contradicted this by finding that female Identity Achievers were higher in self-esteem and lower in anxiety than Foreclosure women (Schenkel & Marcia, 1972).

An extensive study of identity development during the college years by Ann Constantinople (1969) also revealed striking sex differences. Both men and women showed increased identity achievement from the freshman to the senior year. However, while the women seemed more mature than the men as they entered college, the men showed greater gains in maturity over the four college years. Only the men

showed consistent decreases in Identity Diffusion.

Traditionally, men have been expected to forge an identity and break away from their parents. In contrast, women have not been encouraged to "find themselves," but rather to find a husband and develop an identity as his wife. Thus, studies done in the late 1960s (Marcia & Friedman, 1970; Schenkel & Marcia, 1972) found that sexuality was an important focus of identity formation. Since there have been dramatic changes in standards of sexuality and sex role behavior over the past twenty years, these results may no longer be applicable to college women today. Indeed, a review of the literature on identity development in 1982 (Waterman, 1982) found more evidence of similarities than of differences between young women and men. (For a discussion on how self and identity are viewed across cultures, see the box on Self, Identity, and Narcissism.)

Sexual and Sex Role Identity

The acquisition of sexual identity is regarded by many theorists as the most pervasive and lasting aspect of psychological development. Being male or female, masculine or feminine, is a central part of how we think about ourselves and how others define and behave toward us. As we saw in an earlier chapter, gender identity—knowing whether one is a boy or girl—begins in rudimentary form in infancy, at around the time language develops. By age four, children are intensely interested in sex-typing, or presumed boy-girl differences in tastes and personality. Although sexual identity develops throughout the entire life span (Livson, 1981), adolescence is a critical period for the achievement of sexual identity and conceptions of self. During this period, young people must come to terms with the sexual maturation of their bodies, develop relationships with the opposite sex in general and with sexual partners in particular, and define their future goals in regard to work, marriage, and parenthood.

Self, Identity, and Narcissism

We tend to think that a preoccupation with self and identity is a phenomenon unique to the United States and other industrialized societies in the recent decades, that we have developed a "culture of narcissism." It is true that Americans have become more concerned with inner psychological realities in recent years (see Veroff, Douvan, & Kulka, 1981), but the new psychological-mindedness is just an elaboration of a theme that has been persistent in Western history (see box on p. 263 in Chapter 7). And Western culture, in turn, seems to have elaborated a trend found in all societies that have reached a certain level of "complexity."

What do anthropologists mean by *complexity*? Complex societies have occupational specialization, are divided into social classes, and are politically centralized. Children are not loaded with family economic responsibilities at an early age. In such societies, both children and adults tend to be more egocentric—seeking attention, dominance, and help from other people (Whiting & Whiting, 1973, 1975). Thus, as explained by Munroe and Munroe, "cultural complexity breeds an efficiency that reduces the need for children to contribute to the family, and the result is an orientation away from the family and towards the self" (1975, p. 145).

While recent critics of narcissism suggest that a heightened concern with self implies less concern with others, the cross-cultural evidence suggests the opposite. Munroe and Munroe observe that the capacity for deep empathy may depend on a strong sense of self; being sensitive to oneself may lead to more awareness of others. This is what Erikson maintained: that the capacity for intimacy is dependent on the earlier achievement of a sense of identity. Modern, Westernized societies not only develop an emphasis on selfhood and individuality, they also stress love, intimacy, and strong emotional bonds (Goode, 1963; Leichty, 1963; LeVine, 1973a, 1973b).

Societies that promote self-awareness sometimes also support various ways to lose the self through mystical experiences or asceticism. Mystical beliefs and practices, such as those of yoga, Vedanta, Taoism, Zen Buddhism, and Christian and Hebrew mysticism have appeared only in societies complex enough to be called great civilizations. They do not appear in simpler, traditional societies. It seems that one must have a highly developed sense of self-awareness before one can wish to lose the self in a union with the universe or the ALL. Perhaps this is why adolescence, the period of life when self-concern is at its height, is also the time when individuals are most likely to turn to traditional religions, cults, and political movements.

The process of sex-typing can be explained in part as the acquisition of a gender schema (Bem, 1981). Like the self schema, the gender schema is a knowledge structure, a network of assumptions and expectations regarding male-female differences; those activities and characteristics appropriate for each sex. Social schemas may be thought of as theories about the social world which enable us to process information quickly and to respond appropriately. The gender schema is especially central and powerful in our lives because it is so deeply rooted in the way we think about and judge ourselves.

It is odd that even though our maleness or femaleness is biologically given at birth, we do not take it for granted. Rather, we worry about it, try to prove our manhood or womanhood, fear that we do not live up to the standards prescribed for our sex. Our self-concept and self-esteem become hostages of our gender schemas (Bem, 1981).

During adolescence, the individual is evaluating his or her own adequacy as a person in terms of the gender schema—trying to match inner preferences and attitudes, personal attributes, and social skills with the model provided by the larger society. If inner inclinations and identity fail to match society's standards of masculinity or femininity, or proper sexual behavior, then working out some strategy of dealing with the discrepancy becomes a critical problem for the young person (P. Miller & Simon, 1980).

For many adolescents, defining themselves with regard to sexuality and sex roles is the most difficult, confusing, and anxious aspect of growing up, as well as one of the most pleasurable and exciting. The attitudes of society, parents, and male and female peers are inconsistent and often contradictory. Yet the stakes are very high. In the balance are alternative def-

initions of self: Am I moral or immoral? Attractive or ugly? Normal or deviant? Homosexual or heterosexual?

Both sex roles and sexual norms are influenced by historical and cultural changes. Certain historical periods have had freer attitudes toward sexuality, others have been restrictive. During war time, women have been recruited to do traditional men's jobs. With men going off to war, women may be less reluctant to restrain themselves sexually. In recent years, there have been dramatic changes in the traditional messages; we have had both a sexual revolution and a sex role revolution. The recency of these trends makes it particularly difficult to develop a perspective on realities. Studies published in the 1970s may be based on data collected in the 1960s and have as little relevance for the 1980s as the prices of those decades do to the cost of things now. There is also the opposite problem of exaggerating the uniformity of current trends. For example, while there has been a notable increase in premarital sexual behavior for both men and women, and attitudes toward premarital sexuality have become more liberal (Clayton & Bokemeier, 1980), there is still great variation in people's attitudes and behavior—according to social class, race, religion, region of the country, and so on. The same is true of trends in support of equality between the sexes.

Sex Roles and Identity Development in Adolescence

The changing role of women is one of the most striking and talked about events in recent times. There are two separate but related aspects of this change: the rise of the ideology of women's liberation or sex role equality, and the social movement that seeks to translate these goals into reality. A less noticed but equal influence in the changing role has been "the subtle revolution" (R. Smith, 1979), the dramatic increase of women's participation in the labor market since the 1950s. Many of the ideas that seemed extreme when they were first proposed by activists in the women's movement have become accepted by a majority of the American people (see Cherlin, 1981; Yankelovich, 1981). It appears that the massive participation of women in the work force made many of these proposed changes workable and acceptable. We do not have the space to look at this social change in any kind of detail. The purpose here is to understand the implication of these changes for adolescents, especially young women.

Traditionally, marriage and motherhood have dominated young women's plans for the future. The adolescent boy's search for identity centers around the question, "What will I do?" But for young women the question has been, "Whom will I marry?" He chooses, but she waits to be chosen. Thus, women have had what Glen Elder has called "contingent" lives, dominated by factors over which they may have little control:

> Depending on the man she marries, a young woman's occupational plans and preparations may be invalidated, modified, or receive the support needed for eventual fulfillment. Lacking control over this event, on which everything seems to hinge, most young women have been understandably reluctant to take their future careers seriously during the premarital years, or even until after the childbearing and rearing phases of marriage. (1974, p. 202)

Recognition of the contingency of their lives has traditionally developed early. Thus, attracting boys and dating become highly central concerns. A series of studies by Lerner and his associates (1976) have shown that self-concepts for adolescent girls were more closely tied to their perceptions of their own attractiveness than they were for adolescent boys. Overall, the two sexes did not differ in how well they thought of themselves—just in the basis for their self-esteem. Interestingly, there was no relation between a woman's actual appearance and her self-concept—the link was between how attractive she *thought* she was and her self-concept.

The emphasis on heterosexual relations introduces a greater disparity between childhood and adolescent sex roles for females than it does for males (Katz, 1979). During childhood, both boys and girls are encouraged to do well in school. As girls enter adolescence, the message often changes. Traditionally they were told that marriage was their main concern; doing well in school was less important. In fact, being too smart was not an asset in the marriage market. In a study of mid-life women, many of those interviewed recall their shocked surprise at this turnabout in parental messages (L. Rubin, 1979). Research on college students revealed that even young men who believed in equality for women wanted to feel smarter than the women in their lives. The women in the same study were willing to oblige by "acting dumb" (Komarovsky, 1973).

The messages of parents, peers, and the media have their effect; the academic performance of adolescent girls declines (Mullis, 1975). As various observers have pointed out, women confront a double bind—a catch-22—with regard to vocational choice: if they commit themselves to a career, they put their "femininity" into question and may disadvantage themselves in the marriage market. (Since women traditionally "marry up," each rise in a woman's education and occupational status reduces the number of men available to her as marriage partners.) If, on the other hand, they follow the traditional route, they must give up whatever occupational goals they have had and make their well-being and style of life dependent on a husband.

In recent years, the traditional message has changed, and young women's aspirations, particularly those of college women, have been influenced by the changes. Since the mid-1970s, fewer and fewer college women expect to be solely housewives and mothers or believe that women should confine themselves to the home. While only about one out of five college women, at least through the 1970s, was committed to a full-time, continuous career, the modal response changed from full-time homemaker to an interrupted career pattern—a career with time out during the children's early years (Huston-Stein & Higgens-Trenk, 1978).

Sexuality and Identity

The traditional models of male and female behavior assigned sexuality a very different place in the lives of the two sexes, especially before marriage. The double standard meant that sex was not only permissible for young males, it was something to brag about. In contrast, for girls, sexuality was something to avoid or keep hidden. Thus, sexuality was central to the young man's identity, while romance, love, and marriage were central to the young woman's. The chief goal held out for young women was success in the marriage marketplace, in which virginity was an important asset. "Going all the way" with a boy, even a steady boyfriend, might result in loss of the boyfriend, ostracism by other girls, and a reputation as a "loose woman" or a "bad girl."

The double standard placed girls in a dilemma. On the one hand, being attractive to boys and having dates was proof of feminine identity and it encouraged self-esteem. The practice of dating, an American cultural invention which began in the 1920s, allowed young people great freedom for sexual experimentation. On the other hand, there were the social dangers of going all the way—not to speak of the risk of getting pregnant. Thus, while young men had only sexual failure to fear, young women had to fear both failure and success (Gagnon & Henderson, 1975). One result of this dilemma was petting, a compromise form of sexual behavior which was the major form of sexual expression among the unmarried—particularly the middle classes—in the 1940s and 1950s.

The Sexual "Revolution"

Since the advent of the sexual revolution in the 1960s, researchers have documented the increase in the overall level of premarital intercourse and the diminished difference between the numbers of men and women engaging in this activity (Clayton & Bokemeier, 1980). Although studies produce varying figures, it seems clear that, as one study observed, the whole concept of "premarital sex" is becoming outmoded: "Young people are not scheduling marriage on their life agenda simply to gratify their sexual needs or in order to legalize their sexual relationships" (Sorenson, 1973, p. 341). Recent research has shown that by the age of 18, about half of all young men and women have experienced sexual intercourse (Brozan, 1985). Rates in other industrialized countries are similar.

The double standard is also becoming less prevalent. In fact, in the high school years, young women are now more likely to be sexually experienced than young men. One study followed the sexual experience of young people who were tenth, eleventh, and twelfth graders in 1972 through the succeeding four years (Jessor & Jessor, 1977). By the end of the study, the females in each grade exceeded the males in the level of sexual activity; for those who had been in the tenth grade at the start of the study, 21 percent of the males and 28 percent

of the females had had intercourse; the figures for the twelfth graders was 33 percent for males and 55 percent for females. The authors conclude that "the traditional male-female asymmetry in rates of premarital sexual activity may be in the process of disappearing" (p. 76). Further evidence for the declining significance of a girl's virginity is the finding that in the early 1970s, the virginity of a bride was important to only 23 percent of young men aged 16 to 19 (Sorenson, 1973, Table 103).

Although the increase in premarital sex and other aspects of the sexual revolution have alarmed many people, there is in fact more continuity with the past than is generally realized. The prescribed model of sexual behavior did not always fit reality. In 1953, Kinsey and his associates startled the world with their finding that half of all 5,940 white women in their sample had had intercourse before marriage. This produced a greater shock than Kinsey's earlier finding that 83 percent of men in his sample had had premarital intercourse because it shattered the myth that women are asexual until marriage.

In fact, the great revolution in premarital sexuality had occurred during the 1920s—after the upheaval of the First World War and the invention of dating—or unsupervised courtship. In 1938, Lewis Terman had predicted that no girl would enter marriage a virgin after 1940 if present trends continued. However, the incidence of premarital sex hit a plateau after the great change of the 1920s and did not rise again until the second wave of the sexual revolution in the 1960s. Part of the reason the 1960s came as such a shock was that the decade brought not only changes in behavior but final recognition that virginity was not the universal condition of women before marriage. Young women no longer had to hide their sexual experience from friends or potential husbands.

The changed behavior and attitudes do not reflect a breakdown of moral standards. Rather, they reflect a "new sexual morality" based less on conformity to stereotyped sex roles and more on openness and affection between the sexes (Conger, 1975). Few young people are promiscuous sexual adventurers

with multiple partners; rather, they tend to be involved with only one person, with whom they share a close love relationship (Sorenson, 1973). The new moral standard that is evolving has been termed "permissiveness with affection" (Reiss, 1967). Sex has become an acceptable part of affectionate male-female relationships; it is not acceptable if there is no affection between the partners. Thus, in comparison with their fathers and grandfathers, today's young men are less likely to have sex with prostitutes or with girls from a lower social class whom they would not consider proper marriage partners. (See the box on Teenage Sexuality in the 1980s.)

Despite the increasing permissiveness in behavior and attitudes, it is important to realize

Teenage Sexuality in the 1980s

Many people who grew up before the sexual revolution of the 1960s and 1970s assume that today's teenagers are extremely sophisticated about sexual matters and free of the inhibitions, guilt, and anxiety that plagued previous generations. Some adults are extremely critical of young people today, believing that most of them are amoral, hedonistic narcissists, obsessed with sex, drugs, and rock and roll. Other adults, with different values, believe that today's more open society, free of Victorian taboos, permits young people to be more comfortable and "natural" about their sexuality. Actually, neither of these views is accurate. According to the evidence from recent surveys and interviews, the reality is considerably more complex.

Despite the frankness of movies, advertising, television, rock lyrics, and the print media, teenagers still find it hard to discuss sex openly, particularly with their parents. Although many people argue that sex education should take place at home, not at school, almost half the teens in one recent national survey (45 percent) reported that their parents taught them nothing at all about sex (Coles & Stokes, 1985).

Where do teenagers get information about sex? School, the media, and siblings are sources of information, but much of it comes from friends. Yet teenagers are not entirely open with their peers either. Among friends, especially boys, discussions of sex are often marked by boasting, exaggeration, and even lying. Teens of both sexes are often reluctant to reveal doubts, worries, and questions lest they be thought "weird" or ignorant.

In general, despite the sexual and sex role revolutions, today's teens are similar in many ways to previous generations. Coles and Stokes (1985) found in a national survey that a huge majority—87 percent—planned to get married. These percentages were not affected by their parents' marital status or by their own sexual experience.

Interestingly, though, this generation of teens seems headed for some difficulty with sex roles in marriage; 32 percent of the boys thought it better for women to stay home while men pursue their careers, but only 20 percent of the girls agreed. Further, 82 percent of the girls believed that women should be able to do anything men do. All in all, the evidence suggests that for today's teens, sexuality is still full of uncertainty, still centered on concerns about morality and normality, and still tied to a search for intimacy.

---

the great diversity that exists among young people in different social classes, religions, ethnic groups, and regions of the country. Sexual standards are closely correlated with the liberal-conservative political dimension (Reiss & Miller, 1979). They have also been linked to Kohlberg-type levels of morality. One study found that subjects with lower levels of development on Kohlberg's dilemmas tended to choose the traditional double standard of sexual morality. Those with high levels of moral development chose permissiveness with affection, or nonexploitive permissiveness without affection (Jurich, 1976).

Becoming Sexual

Even though sexual standards have changed, having sexual intercourse for the first time remains a significant event in the lives of most young people. In fact, most teens plan this momentous occasion (Coles & Stokes, 1985). Making the transition from virgin to nonvirgin changes young people's perception of their selves, their bodies, their families, and society (Sorenson, 1973). For girls in particular, despite the decline of the double standard, "losing" one's virginity was still a significant turning point.

Once she has had her first sexual intercourse, a girl often feels differently about herself—not deprived, or bereft of her identity, but different *within* herself. She seldom feels raped or violated by the experience, although she may feel her first sex partner was insensitive. She does feel more mature and experienced, but in a mildly defensive sense. She sometimes feels the need to rationalize what she has done and to feel more sympathetic with girls who have also had their first sexual experience. . . . She is, as one girl told us, "now on the other side of the fence." (Sorenson, 1973, p. 190)

The study by Coles and Stokes (1985) found that girls were much more likely to express am-

bivalence after first intercourse. To some degree, the girls' feelings were based less on moral or emotional reservations than simply on physical discomfort: many girls find first intercourse painful.

A longitudinal study by Jessor and Jessor (1977) found that the transition from virginity to nonvirginity was part of an overall pattern of changes in young people's lives, a shift to a more adult or unconventional lifestyle. Thus, the high school and college students who became nonvirgins during the study valued independence, had loosened their ties to their families and were more reliant on friends, and had also engaged in other "unconventional" or adultlike behavior, such as using alcohol or marijuana.

Coles and Stokes (1985) report that teens

who intended to go on to college had lower rates of sexual activity than those who did not. The percentages reveal a striking reversal: 78 percent of those who did not plan to attend college were nonvirgins, while 77 percent of those who wanted to attend had not yet had intercourse. Moreover, those with lower grades at the time of the survey were more sexually active. Coles suggests that the high-achieving students were channeling or "sublimating" their sexual energy into school. The most likely explanation of these findings, though, is class differences—middle-class young people are more likely both to go on to college and to be less sexually active. It may also be that teens who find school unrewarding are likely to seek more gratification from sex. In any event, further analysis of the survey data, or additional research, is needed to explain these findings.

Unplanned Parenthood

The most troubling aspect of the sexual revolution is unplanned, unwed teenage pregnancy. Studies have estimated that about 31 to 39 percent of teenage girls will become pregnant if current rates persist (Senderowitz & Paxman, 1985). How is it that, in the age of widely available, effective contraception, so many girls have unplanned pregnancies? Part of the explanation is simple ignorance—about how one becomes pregnant, about how to get and use contraceptives. One recent study (Coles & Stokes, 1985) found that almost half the teens surveyed (45 percent) were unable to answer a relatively simple question about when a woman can get pregnant. The same survey revealed that only little over half the teenagers (55 percent) regularly use birth control. Those who know about contraceptive devices find them hard to get, and many fear that to be "prepared" would rob sex of its spontaneity.

Unfortunately, the social and psychological consequences for a teenager who gets pregnant and decides to keep her baby are often very difficult for both mother and child. She is likely to drop out of school, be unable to provide for herself and the child, and thus be dependent on either her family or the government. She may feel pushed into getting married to someone she would not have chosen as a permanent partner.

Teenage pregnancy is clearly a serious problem—for society, for the teenaged girl, and for the child who is born to another child. But there is a great deal of public misunderstanding of the issue. As Catherine Chilman (1982) notes, teenage parenthood is not a simple issue that can be understood apart from more fundamental problems in contemporary American society. When longitudinal data are analyzed to control for poverty and race, teen parenthood in itself may add little to the long-term burdens of being born poor and black. Further, the idea that there is an "epidemic" of unwed motherhood, and that this is a crisis in need of

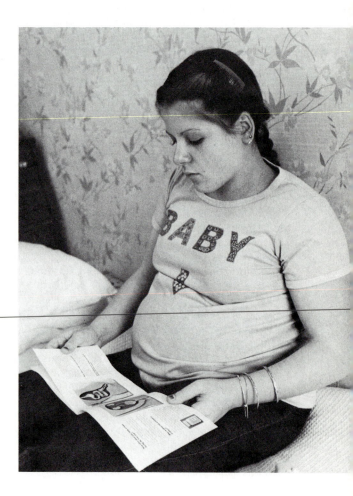

immediate and drastic government action, is misleading. As demographer Maris Vinovskis (1981) has pointed out, the rate of childbearing among young adolescents has actually remained constant over the past two decades—in spite of the great increase in adolescent sexual activity. (See the box on A Comparative Perspective on Teenage Pregnancy.)

Why then is there the perception of widespread teenage childbearing? Vinovskis lists several reasons. While the rate of teenage pregnancies has remained constant, the size of the teenage population has increased. So in abso-

lute terms, there are more teenage mothers in the population. Even more important, girls who get pregnant today act differently from their counterparts in the past. A teenage girl who became pregnant in the 1950s or 1960s, would be likely to do one of two things: get married or give up the baby for adoption. In recent years this pattern has changed drastically. The number of births legitimated by marriage declined from 65 percent in the early 1960s to 35 percent in the early 1970s. In other words, young people are no longer willing to accept early, unwanted marriages as an alter-

---

A Comparative Perspective on Teenage Pregnancy

Given the high rates of intercourse among teenagers, combined with a lack of knowledge and failure to use birth control, it is not surprising that teen pregnancy has become a major problem in recent years. It is surprising, however, that the United States leads all other industrialized countries in teenage pregnancies, births, and abortions (Brozan, 1985). The pregnancy rate for American girls aged 15 to 19 is 96 per 1,000, or almost 1 out of 10. This rate is more than double those in the next highest countries, England and Wales. A recent study sponsored by the Alan Guttmacher Institute and the Ford Foundation (Brozan, 1985) tried to find out why American girls are getting pregnant at rates unparalleled in countries that are similar to the United States in economic development and general cultural background.

The difference could not be explained by lower rates of sexual activity in the other countries: American teenagers are no more sexually active than their foreign peers. Nor is the difference due to higher abortion rates abroad: they are much higher here. The study found that by the time they are 18, 60 out of every 1,000 women in the United States have had an abortion. In contrast, the rates are 30 per 1,000 in Sweden, the next highest country in abortion use, and 7 per 1,000 in the Netherlands, which ranked lowest.

Our high teenage pregnancy rates cannot be explained by high fertility among black adolescents, many of whom live at levels of poverty unknown in Europe. The birth rate among white American teenagers alone is almost double that in the next closest country. Maternity and welfare benefits do not appear to promote teenage pregnancy either, because other countries provide much more generous support.

What, then, does account for the high rates of adolescent pregnancy here? The answer seems to lie in the peculiarly American combination of a liberalized sexual climate and a reluctance to help teenagers avoid pregnancy. In America, teenage sex is an intensely emotional issue and one that touches on deep religious feelings. Recently, conservative lawmakers have been stating that their goal is to prevent *sexual activity* and promote chastity among the young.

By contrast, in the European countries in the study, public policy is aimed at preventing teenage *pregnancy*. The countries with the lowest rates had easily accessible contraceptives for young people, with birth control devices offered free or at low cost, and with no required parental notification. These countries also had comprehensive sex education programs throughout their school systems.

native to having a child out of wedlock. The change in unwed mothers' decisions about what to do with their babies has been even more striking: a decade ago, more than 90 percent of babies born out of wedlock were given up for adoption; today, almost 90 percent are kept by the mother. As a result of these trends, the financial costs of teenage pregnancy for the general public have increased dramatically. The high costs of welfare payments to teenage mothers are one reason that government policy makers have come to be concerned about the problem.

While many in America prefer to denounce teenage sexuality and illegitimacy, it is hard to devise effective ways of dealing with them. Eliminating sex education or access to contraception is unlikely to reduce either sex or out-of-wedlock pregnancy. Controlling teenage sexuality would probably involve controlling adult sexuality also, and would require a great deal of government intrusion into private lives. As one study concludes,

> Teen-aged sexuality might recede if we could bring ourselves to accept greater censorship of movies, television, books and magazines, including the advertising therein . . . combined with greater restrictions on the daily movements of teen-agers, . . . a drastic reduction in unchaperoned social activities [and] . . . social sanctions against open displays of affection by young people, combined with the imposition of punishment in some form for those who stray from clearly marked "paths of righteousness." . . . For ourselves, we prefer to cope with the consequences of early sex as an aspect of an emancipated society, rather than pay the social costs its elimination would exact. (Zelnick, Kanter, & Ford, 1981, p. 182)

Vocational Choice and Identity

For both Piaget and Erikson, choosing an occupation is one of the major developmental is-

sues of adolescence. Yet vocational choice is one of the most underdeveloped research topics in developmental psychology (Vondracek & Lerner, 1982). Traditionally, becoming employed in a full-time job has been thought to be the borderline between adolescence and adulthood. Further, for contemporary Americans, the kind of work we do is a central part of our identity.

When we think about the topic of vocational choice, we are apt to form an image of a college student trying to pick a major, brooding about whether to be an engineer or a lawyer, deciding whether to go to work or graduate school. But that student, however agonizing the choices may seem at the time, is actually far along in the process of decision making.

Studies of the development of occupational identity trace its beginnings to childhood experience. One project (Ginzberg et al., 1951) divided occupational choice into three periods, the first of which, the fantasy stage, begins in early childhood and lasts until age 11 or so. At this age, children think they can enter any career, regardless of their own talents or the actual realities of pursuing such a career. During the tentative period, between 11 and 17, children become more realistic about their own abilities and the demands of particular occupations. Decisions are actually made about career plans in the third stage, the realistic choice period. This study found that women had a more difficult time making commitments, since they were not sure whether they would be married and what the effects of the future husband's career might be. In the decades since this study was done, however, young women have become more concerned about making commitments to a career. At the same time, the decision about what occupation to pursue is becoming more difficult for both men and women in the face of the shrinking job market and intense competition for high-level careers.

Today's adolescents represent a transitional generation in terms of vocational roles for men and women. Major changes in the American family have occurred over the course of their lifetimes and in the years preceding their births (see Vondracek & Lerner, 1982). Divorce rates

have risen, birth rates have dropped, and women have entered the workplace in massive numbers. Aside from the impact of these changes on the experience of growing up, they also have important implications for career planning. Young women no longer plan exclusively on marriage and motherhood as their sole lifetime career. The traditional sex role orientations are no longer adaptive; we are beginning to see greater similarity between the sexes in their vocational planning.

One study of occupational identity formation (Grotevant & Thorbecke, 1982) found that young men and women in their junior and senior years of high school had made equal progress toward achieving occupational identity. However, there were some male-female differences in concerns about work. Young women wanted to work hard and avoid competition; young men sought challenging tasks and were unconcerned about negative relationships with others.

Influences of Social Background

Ironically, the most fateful step in the process of choosing an occupation does not involve a real choice at all; rather, it is the social class one is born into. The socioeconomic level of the parents is the best predictor of the level the children will achieve (Blau & Duncan, 1967; Jencks, 1972). The family provides the child's first knowledge of the world of work; from parents, relatives, and friends, the child learns what kinds of jobs there are, what the opportunity structure is, what a person has to do to prepare for a particular job. In recent years, television has come to provide a significant proportion of the adolescents' knowledge about careers, especially about the kind of experiences and lifestyles that go along with particular occupations. These images may not be valid, but they appear to have more influence on decision making than factual information such as training prerequisites, opportunities, benefits, and risks.

At a more basic level, however, it is in the family that young people learn skills, personality traits, and certain attitudes toward self and the world that play a crucial role in occupational success. For example, poor and working-class families are apt to be more fatalistic than middle-class families; they are apt to agree with statements such as, "Getting a good job or promotion is largely a matter of luck—and 'who you know'—rather than hard work" (see Lefcourt, 1976). Such fatalism reflects the actual experiences of people at lower levels of the socioeconomic system. But such expectations can become self-fulfilling prophecies, discouraging children from trying hard.

Similarly, as the work of Kohn (1963) has shown, the way parents socialize their children reflects their own work experiences. Parents communicate to their children the skills, attitudes, and values most appropriate to their own workplace. Working-class families want their children to be neat, clean, obedient, and respectful toward authority—in other words, to conform to external standards. Middle-class parents emphasize such values as curiosity, self-expression, cooperation, and happiness. They are more concerned with inner feeling and motives than external conformity. Parents in both classes socialize their children for the worlds they know. Getting and keeping working-class jobs means going along with authority, whether it is the boss, the foreman, or the union leader. The higher up the occupational scale, the less important obedience becomes and the more the individuals are expected to know about how to get along with others and to control themselves.

Schooling is the crucial link between the parents' social class and the children. That is, the father's social class is the major determinant of the son's education, and it is in turn the amount of education the son has that influences the level of occupation he will pursue. If, however, the son manages to break this link and gets a better education than his father, then family background will play a lesser role in his future. With every step in his career, the influence of his father's background will fade still further. (These results apply only to whites. According to Blau and Duncan [1967], coming from a black family continues to be a disadvantage throughout the son's lifetime. These conclusions also seem equally applicable to daughters, but the major research has been done only on sons.)

It is harder to break the link between the parents' class background and the young person's future than Americans have traditionally believed. Research in recent years suggests that, by and large, the schools help to perpetuate such differences. In lower-class schools, teachers typically single out the few youngsters they think may have a chance to make it into middle-class society. Little is expected of the rest, except staying out of trouble. In response, many students defend their honor by rejecting the school and its ways. They treat the achieving students as outcasts and fools and take pride in breaking rules—smoking, drinking, cutting classes, and otherwise messing around—thus confirming the low expectations held for them. For those who do not take part in open rebellion, school becomes a boring wasteland, something to get through: "For the lower half of the school population—the general course, the voc-ed course, the yet to be certified losers with their low C grades—the high school is like a refugee camp, a camp for displaced persons waiting for something to happen" (Schrag, 1972, p. 360).

All of this is not to say that there is a completely closed vicious circle, with everyone's occupation completely determined by family background. Although the American dream may not be a valid image of everyone's experiences, many Americans are upwardly mobile. A majority of the sons of working-class fathers remain working class, but 37 percent do move into white-collar occupations (Blau & Duncan, 1967). Most upward mobility occurs in small steps. That is, the son of a factory worker becomes a foreman; the son of an insurance salesman becomes a doctor. Very few go from rags to riches. (The study did not include daughters.)

Historical Contexts

Apart from family background, the kind of career a young person has is strongly influenced by the historical period in which he or she comes of age and the kind of opportunities for education and employment available. Each succeeding cohort of adolescents in twentieth-century America has confronted a different opportunity structure.

Around the turn of the century, the occupational structure was like a pyramid. There were large numbers of low-level jobs, a smaller middle class, and a still narrower upper-middle class. Almost everyone went to elementary school, but only those with strong academic interests attended high school, and still fewer of those went on to college. During the depression, unemployment reached crisis proportions, not just for young people entering the labor force, but for many fathers and mothers with families to support. World War II ushered in an economic boom that persisted through the 1960s. Ironically, the cohort born during the Great Depression has been called the "lucky generation." Because the birth rate dropped dramatically after 1929, this was a relatively small cohort. They entered the labor market at a time of unprecedented opportunity in the late 1940s and early 1950s.

Their children, the baby boom generation—born between 1947 and 1964—faced a radically different set of conditions. The largest cohort in American history, the baby boomers have also been the most educated. During the postwar years, a high school education became the norm for everyone, and a college education came to be defined as the right of any person who wanted one. Between 1940 and 1980, the proportion of high school graduates among adults aged 25 to 29 rose from 38 percent to 86 percent (Hacker, 1983). By 1983, 38.9 percent of men and 30.5 percent of women aged 25 and over had attended college (U.S. Bureau of the Census, 1984).

Delinquency and Other Social Problems of Adolescence

When G. Stanley Hall wrote of adolescent storm and stress, heightened criminality was one of the major symptoms he had in mind. Hall believed that, along with the capacity for imagination and idealism, "criminogenic instincts" also arose with puberty. Later theorists put the blame for juvenile delinquency on bad neighborhoods and bad homes. Whatever the explanation, the problem of misbehaving youth has been a major social concern in America since the middle of the nineteenth century. The image of the teenager as a violent gang member or "rebel without a cause" is one of the stereotypes of American culture.

Rhetoric about the terrible state of American youth has been such a constant over the generations that it is sometimes hard to separate what is a serious problem from what is wild exaggeration. Yet juvenile crime does qualify as a truly worrisome social problem. Delinquents not only cause trouble in their adolescence, they also pose the threat of becoming persistent offenders as adults.

Delinquency includes a wide range of behavior, from serious crimes such as murder and assault to lesser crimes such as theft and acts that are considered crimes only because of age such as truancy, running away from home, or buying liquor. While only a relatively small proportion of adolescents commits serious crimes, over 80 percent confess on surveys to having committed one or more delinquent acts in the course of adolescence. Minor acts such as petty theft and smoking pot and more serious offenses such as assault and robbery rise in late childhood, reach a peak at around age 15 or 16, and then decline (Gold & Petronio, 1980; Greenberg, 1977).

The line between delinquency and nondelinquency is sometimes hard to draw; adolescents are often in a state of "drift" between conformity and misbehavior (Matza, 1964). A few years ago, a newspaper reported the story of a young man whose major interests in high school were "guns, bombs, and fires" (Theroux, 1980). He and his friends made powerful bombs which they set off in his backyard until one of them went off prematurely and injured his hand. On one occasion, they also skinned a tomcat and boiled its corpse, hoping to put the bones together to make a skeleton. Was this the prelude to a life of violent crime? Actually, the young man grew up to be a successful novelist and travel writer.

Although most young people grow out of whatever delinquent tendencies they may display as teenagers, the adolescent population accounts for a large proportion of crime in America. About 43 percent of all serious crimes are committed by persons under 18, and almost 20 percent by those under the age of 15

(Robertson, 1977). The stereotypical juvenile delinquent is a lower-class male, and in fact, the great majority of juveniles in the arrest statistics do fit that image. The vast majority of arrested juveniles are males, although there has been an increase in delinquency among girls in recent years.

Contrary to both the stereotype and the arrest statistics, however, delinquency, even when serious, is not confined to the lower class. Self-report studies have generally found no differences between classes, and some have found that middle-class adolescents are even more likely to commit crimes, including serious ones such as thefts and assaults.

Therefore, studies based on arrest statistics may be seriously misleading about the causes and consequences of delinquency. Juveniles who end up in jail or prison have been through several stages of selection. Overwhelmingly, as we will see, the evidence suggests that the social status of the offender determines whether an offense will lead to an arrest, an arrest to prosecution, a prosecution to conviction, and a conviction to imprisonment.

Labeling Theory

How does it happen that some young people come to be perceived as delinquents, while others, guilty of similar or worse offenses, are seen as high-spirited kids having fun? A sociological perspective called the **labeling theory** attempts to provide answers to such questions (H. Becker, 1963; Lemert, 1951, 1967). Briefly, the labeling theory argues that many people commit deviant acts from time to time, ranging from businessmen who cheat on their taxes to young people who try an illicit drug, shoplift a small item, or have a homosexual experience. Most such deviant behavior goes unnoticed. The individuals involved do not think of themselves as deviants, nor do other people. If, however, deviant acts are discovered and made public, the person is likely to be labeled as a "delinquent," a "crook," a "drug addict." Now the person is stigmatized by "normal" people. The deviant label dominates other people's

perception of the person. His or her biography may be reinterpreted as the past is searched for earlier "signs" of deviance. Eventually the person comes to identify with the label and other deviants who share it. Serving a term in reform school or prison makes it even more likely that the individual will take on a deviant identity and commit more such acts in the future. This response to the deviant label is called *secondary deviance*. The label has turned into a self-fulfilling prophecy.

While the labeling theory does not provide a complete explanation of deviance (Robertson, 1977), it does yield the important insight that only certain people and acts are labeled as deviant. Numerous empirical studies have shown that lower-class youths are more likely to get into trouble with the police than middle-class ones. In one study, two researchers spent nine months riding in police cars with officers from the juvenile bureau of a West Coast police department (Piliavan & Briar, 1964). Practically all of the incidents that came to the attention of the police were minor, and the officers were usually reluctant to make any arrests. However, if the youth in question was defiant or uncooperative, the police were likely to assume he was a "bad character" and arrest him. Style of dress and race also influenced the decision to arrest. Not surprisingly, white middle-class youths were least likely to be taken into custody.

A careful observational study by William Chambliss (1973) revealed a similar labeling process. Chambliss observed a middle-class gang he called the "Saints" and, in the same town, a lower-class one he called the "Roughnecks." The Saints were some of the most delinquent boys at their high school. They were constantly truant and engaged in drinking, wild driving, petty theft, and vandalism. One of their favorite forms of mischief was removing barricades and lanterns surrounding road repairs and watching motorists drive into the unprotected holes. Then they would erect the stolen barricades near a curve in the highway where oncoming drivers would crash into them. Despite these and many other forms of misbehavior, the Saints were perceived by the school, the police, and the community as a whole as bright, popular, good boys who occasionally sowed a wild oat or two. No one was aware of the extent of their delinquency.

The Roughnecks, by contrast, were about equal to the Saints in their delinquency, but were seen as tough young criminals who were headed for trouble. Over the period that Chambliss observed them, each member of the Roughnecks was arrested at least once, and several spent a night in jail.

Chambliss believes that teenagers like the Roughnecks are perceived and labeled as delinquent because they are visible, lower-class, nonmobile, and defiant. They not only looked like what delinquents are expected to look like, but "everyone" could observe their frequent fights, which were often with one another. Teenagers like the Saints, who established themselves as successful in school, and who were also from affluent homes, can be invisible when they misbehave. Chambliss concludes:

When it's time to leave adolescence, most will follow the expected path, settling into the ways of the middle class, remembering fondly the delinquent but unnoticed fling of their youth. The Roughnecks and others like them may turn around too. It is more likely that their noticeable deviance will have been so reinforced by police and community that their lives will be effectively channelled into careers consistent with their adolescent background. (1973, p. 31)

Delinquency and Identity

While the labeling theory illuminates part of the process by which some young people come to be recognized as delinquents, it does not explain why they commit delinquent acts in the first place. Nor does it explain why crime rises to a peak in the middle teens, then declines.

Many theorists believe that, to understand delinquency and the other characteristic problems of adolescence, it is necessary to look at both individual psychological issues and the place of adolescents in the larger society.

More than any other age, adolescence is a transitional period, a time of becoming something other than what one is or was. Neither adults nor children, adolescents are sometimes treated as one, sometimes the other. A classic sociological study of adolescence once called the age an "ill-defined no-man's land" (Hollingshead, 1949). Similarly, the psychologist Kurt Lewin (1939) believed that the "marginal" status of adolescents explained the typical difficulties of young people—not just delinquency, but shyness and emotional tension as well. David Greenberg (1977) also links delinquency and other problems to youths' position in modern industrial societies. He argues that any society that excludes young people from adult work and requires attendance at schools organized like ours is likely to have a significant amount of juvenile delinquency.

Greenberg points out that some kinds of delinquency are motivated by "rational" economic concerns. Many studies of delinquent gangs or individuals show that shoplifting and other forms of theft are instrumental activities—ways of getting desired goods such as clothes, records, food and drinks for parties. Adolescent theft is a response to the discrepancy between the high cost of teenage social life and the ability of teenagers to pay for it.

Other kinds of delinquency are not as "rationally" motivated. As Gold and Petronio (1980) indicate, the difficulties of finding a socially acceptable role identity seem to explain much of the data on adolescent delinquency. Erikson (1968) describes two different aspects of the task of constructing an identity. The young person must establish an ego identity, a core sense of being a coherent, continuing self. He or she must also establish a role identity— that is, find or establish a niche in society that fits one's interests, abilities, and values. The standard routes into adulthood are to attend college and prepare for a career, or to find a job or trade that does not require college skills.

(Traditionally, as we have seen, girls have had a more limited range of choices open to them; hence they have faced less uncertainty about their role identity than boys.)

Many young people are unable or unwilling to commit themselves to the available adult roles, and thus they rebel against the demands that they do so. Such adolescents may choose what Erikson has termed a "negative identity," that is, "an identity perversely based on all those identifications and roles which . . . had been presented to them as most undesirable" (1968, p. 197). Delinquent behavior peaks at about 15, the critical age for deciding whether or not to attend college. As one researcher explains, delinquency represents the need many adolescent males have to "repudiate, once and for all, the norms of the college-boy culture" (Cohen, 1955, p. 132). It is not only the response of lower-class youth to their failure in

While being rebellious is expected to a certain degree of all teenagers in American culture today, delinquency is a more effective negative identity for boys than for girls. Since delinquency expresses "macho" values such as toughness and daring, it can confirm a boy's sense of masculinity and boost his self-esteem. In contrast, girls confirm their femininity by being "good" and "nice" (see Ullian, 1984). Teenage boys who choose delinquent roles find an appreciative and supportive audience. Indeed, adult males may also try to confirm their masculine identities through risk-taking activities such as fast driving, gambling for high stakes, mountain climbing, sky diving (Goffman, 1974). For a 15-year-old boy, stealing the red flasher from a police car can be a "genuine bid for glory" (Gold & Petronio, 1980, p. 525).

In the end, the problems of adolescence reflect the society and culture in which young people come to maturity. Some scholars remind us that several generations ago, the muscles and energy of adolescents were once put to use to build this country, that teenaged immigrants came here in massive numbers because they could find jobs. They question the extreme emphasis on schooling as the only route to success, and whether even those who are suited for academic pursuits might not benefit at this particular stage of life from a chance to explore the world of adult work or do physical labor (Greenberg, 1977). Unfortunately, the economic situation of recent years has made the prospects of adolescents finding meaningful work even more remote than they have been in previous decades.

the role of student; it can also be the reaction of middle-class youth to failure or to what they perceive as excessive demands for achievement or conformity to arbitrary school rules.

Delinquency may be only one response an adolescent may make to problems of identity and self-esteem. Other common adolescent problems—drug abuse, alcoholism, pregnancy, joining a religious cult, or suicide—reflect different ways of responding to a similar set of concerns. (See the box on The "Epidemic" of Adolescent Suicide.)

The "Epidemic" of Adolescent Suicide

The death of a young person is always a tragedy. If that death is by suicide it takes an even greater emotional toll. Over the last several decades there has been a steep rise in suicide rates among young people. It is now the second leading cause of adolescent deaths, after accidents. More young people die from suicide than from cancer, heart disease, diabetes, pneumonia, and influenza together.

The most dramatic and highly publicized form of the problem is the cluster phenomenon—outbreaks of teenage suicide in some of the nation's most affluent suburbs. In 1983 and 1984, clusters of youthful suicides occurred in Westchester County, New York; Plano, Texas; and several other communities around the country. The rise in the suicide rate and the appearance of the cluster phenomenon have raised disturbing questions for parents, teachers, public officials, and for young people themselves.

Some of the basic facts are as follows:

- Suicide rates for youths between 15 and 24 have tripled in the last three decades. According to the National Center for Health Statistics, about 6,000 Americans in this age group killed themselves in 1983.
- Despite the rapid rise in youthful suicide, adolescents kill themselves less often than older people do. However, the rate difference between adults and adolescents has been shrinking in recent years. Further, young people have a greater "success" rate (Weiner, 1980).

    Almost the entire increase is due to the suicides of young males. Girls attempt suicide in far greater numbers, but boys are more successful in their attempts.
- Suicide rates for whites have been consistently higher than those for blacks, although the rates of both have converged in recent years.
- Traditionally, suicide rates at all ages have been higher in the affluent, industrialized countries than in underdeveloped ones, and higher among the middle class than among the poor (Alvarez, 1971).
- Rising youth suicide rates are found in many industrialized countries. America does not have the highest youth suicide rates: Japan, Czechoslovakia, and Hungary have that distinction (Holinger & D. Offer, 1981).
- Epidemics of youthful suicide have occurred in many times and places. The most famous took place in the early nineteenth century and was inspired by Goethe's novel, *The Sorrows of Young Werther*. The Romantic movement in literature at that time glorified youth, poetry, melancholy, suicide, and early death (Alvarez, 1971).
- Although the current rise in youthful suicide is disturbing, it should be kept in mind that the vast majority of adolescents do not kill themselves or even try to.

Why do they do it? Why does a teenager with "everything to live for" choose to die? Why does someone living in objectively miserable conditions, or suffering from some incurable disease, choose to live? Despite masses of statistics and numerous sociological and psychological theories, there are no simple answers. Some observers blame the current increase in adolescent suicide on changes in American society—rising divorce rates, inattentive parents, changing moral standards, increasing use of drugs and alcohol, the influence of television and the movies. Some have argued that the growing availability of guns in American homes makes it too easy for depressed adolescents to act out passing suicidal impulses. Doubtless, these factors play some role. But most experts acknowledge that the causes are complex; putting together the various correlates of youthful suicide does not explain a great deal of the variance. Or, to put it another way, there is a gap between general social and psychological explanations and the slow, hidden misery that leads a particular individual, at a particular moment, to decide that life is not worth living.

Despite the vast literature on suicide, research on the subject is beset with methodological difficulties. First, there are difficulties of definition. Some scholars include both attempted and successful suicides in their analyses, others consider only the latter. Then there are practical problems in defining a death as a suicide or an accident. Some police departments may not rule a death a suicide unless there is a suicide note. Doctors may try to protect the grieving family's feelings by labeling a young person's death an accident. Families themselves may try to cover up evidence of suicide. Finally, a person bent on suicide need not rely on guns or sleeping pills; many accidents and homicides are probably acts of self-destruction. For all these reasons, many experts believe the actual suicide rates are far higher than the official records show.

Research on suicide is further handicapped by having to rely most of the time on retrospective analysis. If the attempt has been successful, it is difficult to reconstruct the experiences that led to suicide. Because of grief and guilt, families may not be accurate informants. Then there is the problem of any retrospective analysis. As we mentioned in an earlier chapter, looking backward across someone's life from some known outcome, it is hard to avoid being influenced by knowledge of how the person's life ended. The tendency is to "rewrite" his or her life story to make it consistent with the tragic outcome (Garmezy, 1976).

But some suicides defy even retrospective analysis. Consider Anthony Caputo, one of the Westchester County cluster suicides (Weiss, 1984). Described by those who knew him as "a happy all-American guy," he seemed to have everything going for him. His family was wealthy and he was an A student at Fordham University. An accomplished guitarist who had cut a record with a rock group, Caputo was forming a new band. He had many friends, got along well with his family, did not use drugs, and rarely drank anything alcoholic.

Shortly before Caputo killed himself, he called several of his friends to say, "I can't take it any more"; none of them, however, recognized that he was in deep despair. Later they groped for reasons to explain his depression. Was he upset about a breakup with his girlfriend several months earlier, or about his band's progress, or because turning 20 "just freaked him out?" He was buried with his $1,500 guitar.

We will never know precisely why this "happy All-American guy" went up to the attic in his parents' home and hung himself. We do know that he must have been feeling unbearable misery and loneliness and that he could conceive of no other way to escape from that pain.

Clinicians have found that suggesting alternatives or ways to make the pain endurable often turns a young person away from suicide. When adolescents bent on suicide are prevented from carrying it out, they are almost always relieved and grateful. No matter how miserable they feel, the mood usually passes. Most suicidal adolescents are not firmly committed to ending their lives, but gamble that somebody will stop them or save them from death.

Unfortunately, though practically all suicidal teenagers declare their intention in one way or another, the people around them may not recognize their "cry for help." In retrospect, Arnold Caputo's statement that he could not take it any more was his cry for help. Sometimes the young person may say something like "I don't see any good reason to go on living." Sometimes the cry for help is indirect, as when a teenager gives away prized possessions or remarks, "This is the last time I'll see Boston."

In many instances, friends and family recognize the cry for help but avoid dealing with it. They fear if they mention the word "suicide," that may push the person over the brink. Friends may fear that saying anything will be disloyal or will get the young person in trouble. Experts generally agree that bringing the problem out into the open and talking it over helps rather than harms. They also recommend that someone seriously considering suicide should not be left alone. It is usually not very helpful to try to argue logically against suicide, to point out all the things he or she has to live for. It is better just to listen, to point out that many people feel the same way but are later glad they did not take their own lives, and that suicide is irrevocable. Most communities around the country have confidential, twenty-four-hour telephone hot lines for potential suicides or those who know someone who is considering suicide.

SUMMARY

1. Adolescent thought processes differ in many ways from those of younger children. Adolescents think about the past and the future, become absorbed in philosophical speculations about life and death and the meaning of things. They can also fall in love and imagine themselves as fictional characters.

2. Piaget considers such changes in adolescent thought reflective of an underlying cognitive change, the stage of formal operations. His research shows that adolescents can approach complex problems systematically, figure out logical consequences, and reflect on their own thought processes.

   Piaget's concept of formal operations has stimulated a great deal of research, which has in turn revealed some problems with his assumptions. Formal operational thought, as measured by Piaget's tasks, turns out *not* to be characteristic of most adolescents or even adults. At the same time, younger children show some signs of having the kinds of capacities that should not emerge until adolescence. Researchers have looked for other ways to conceptualize adolescent thought.

3. One of the more promising approaches is based on information processing models. Researchers using this approach attribute changes in adolescent thought, as well as earlier cognitive advances, to improvement in a variety of skills—attention, memory, strategies of memorizing and problem solving—as well as increased memory capacity.

4. The cognitive changes of adolescence transform the young person's emotional life. Erikson portrayed the central theme of adolescence as a search for identity. Identity may be viewed as a theory of the self that can make sense of various life events and goals and link the past, present, and future. The dangers of the period are premature closure, following family or cultural prescriptions without coming to grips with one's own inner feelings and needs; identity diffusion, being unable to work out any coherent identity; and negative identity, deliberately choosing to be what one's parents or oneself most fears and dislikes.

5. The quest for identity is not a universal human pattern. Young women do not appear to go through the stages of identity development that young men do. On the one hand, young women seem psychologically more mature than young men of the same age. On the other hand, it has traditionally been more difficult for young women to arrive at a clear-cut and coherent sense of self because their identity has usually depended on the men they marry.

   The question of identity, along with other aspects of the adolescent experience, is not universal across cultures, yet it is also not limited to the contemporary American scene. The issue of identity arises in complex societies where children are freed from the need to contribute to their family's economic survival. In such industrialized societies, all people, both children and adults, seem more aware of and concerned about themselves than people in simpler societies.

6. Identity also becomes consolidated in adolescence. In recent years, the process has been complicated by societywide changes in both sexual and sex role standards. Despite the sexual revolution, there is widespread ignorance about

sexual matters among adolescents. One result is a large number of teenage pregnancies and an increased percentage of adolescent unwed mothers who choose to keep and raise their children.

7. Important choices about vocational identity are formed in adolescence. Younger children often fantasize about possible careers, but the choices become much more realistic during the high school years. Family background, particularly one's parents' education and occupations, plays a large role in shaping the young person's occupational future. There is not as much upward mobility in America as is widely assumed.

8. Delinquency has been a major part of the "youth problem" which has persisted since the middle of the last century. The majority of adolescents admit to having committed some form of delinquency, usually minor. Through a process of selection and labeling, some young people, usually from the lower classes, come to be identified by the community and police as delinquents. The prevalence of delinquency over the adolescent period reflects the difficulties of achieving a role identity in contemporary society.

Key Terms

formal operations   **454–55**
identity   **461**
identity crisis   **461**
implicit psychology   **462**
labeling theory   **482**
metamemory   **460**
second-order thinking   **455**

CHAPTER 14

Adulthood and Aging

Grow old along with me. The best is yet to be.

—Robert Browning

The man who is a pessimist before forty-eight knows too much; the man who is an optimist after forty-eight knows too little.

—Mark Twain

There is no cure for birth and death save to enjoy the interval.

—Santayana

*U*ntil recently, developmental psychology could be described fairly accurately as the study of children and adolescents. Most developmental researchers believed in what Orville Brim (1976) has called the "mythical plateau of adulthood." Once past adolescence, a person's psychological nature was assumed to be set for life—or at least until the mental and physical deterioration of old age had set in.

Actually, the eighteenth- and nineteenth-century ancestors of developmental psychology took a different view. They saw psychological development as change over the entire life span, not confined to any specific age such as childhood (Baltes, 1979). And in the twentieth century, such theorists as Carl Jung, Charlotte Buhler, and Erik Erikson emphasized that development occurs throughout the whole course of adulthood. Despite these theories, however, developmental research continued to focus on child and adolescent development. The early years of life were a time of maximum psychological change and were believed to be a critical period for determining a person's cognitive and emotional future. Few researchers dealt with the possibility that psychological change could occur during adulthood; those who did assumed that any such change must be pathetic, foolish, and even pathological—a symptom of immaturity, or poor mental health (Labouvie-Vief, 1978).

Since the 1960s, however, there has been an explosion of research as well as popular writing on psychological development in adults. To judge by the number of books and newspaper and magazine articles on the subject, adulthood seems on its way to becoming as much a public obsession as childhood. We may now be leaving the "century of the child" and entering, as one scholar put it, the "century of the adult" (Graubard, 1978, p. vii).

More than just a new interest in adulthood is involved here: a new conception of adulthood has emerged. There is a recognition that Freud's famous definition of healthy adulthood—"to love and to work"—is not "a one-time accomplishment that settles the life course once and for all" (Swidler, 1980, p. 144). Where once the adult was supposed to be stable and unchanging, and change was pathological, a new adult ideal has emerged—that of continued growth and cognitive and emotional flexibility (Giele, 1980). What was once considered the adolescent "mode of experience" (Trow, 1978)—a mode of exploration, becoming, growth, and pain—has been extended across the adult years. A newspaper article entitled "Transition: How Adults Cope with Change" observed: "Adults don't stay put the way they used to. Everywhere you look, people are moving around, changing jobs, going back to school, getting divorced. Starting over, in short. At age 30, 40, 50, 60—there's no end to it" (*San Francisco Chronicle*, June 4, 1975, p. 36).

Currently, the nature and extent of change in adulthood is the subject of great controversy among psychologists and other social scientists. Is development in adulthood really like development in childhood? Is it correct to apply the term *development* at all to adults, even recognizing that the process may differ from that in children? Do adults pass through a regular series of psychological stages at particular ages? Another controversial issue concerns the stability or continuity of personality: do people

really change in adulthood, or do the seemingly dramatic outward changes only mask the essential sameness of the personality underneath?

Whatever the answers to these questions, it is clear that adulthood, both in reality and in psychological theory, is no longer what it was to previous generations. In this chapter, we examine first the reasons for the change and then the evidence that researchers have been gathering about the longest period of human life. We will examine physical, social, and psychological changes from early adulthood through old age.

Demography, Social Change, and the Discovery of Adulthood

One of the major reasons for the widespread interest in adulthood is that there are now more adults, proportionally, than ever before, and they are living longer than ever. Also, as mortality rates have declined across the life span, the birth rate has dropped from what it was before the twentieth century. Around the early 1900s, as demographer Peter Uhlenberg points out, 140 out of every 1,000 infants born would die in their first year. Now only 14 out of 1,000 die.

Also at the beginning of this century, the average life span was around 49. In 1982, it was 74.5 for all Americans, and it is still creeping upward (Figure 14.1). "The mortality decline in this century," Uhlenberg notes, "is greater than the total mortality decline that occurred during the 250 years preceding 1900" (1980, p. 313).

The most noticeable effect of changing death and birth rates is what has been termed "the graying of America," an increase in the average age of the population. In George Washington's time, when the first census was taken in 1790, the median age was 16, and only 20 percent of the population lived from birth to 70. Now more than 80 percent do so. By 1981, the median age passed 30. By 2030, it will approach

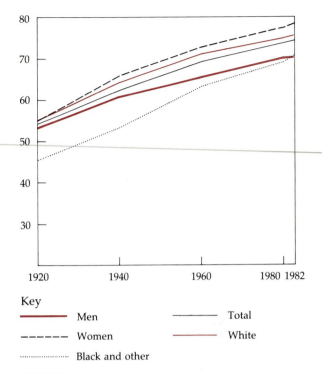

Key

——— Men	——— Total
- - - - Women	——— White
·········· Black and other	

FIGURE 14.1
An Increasing Life Span: Life Expectancy at Birth in the United States

Source: *Vital statistics of the United States*, annual, U.S. National Center for Health Statistics, Washington, D.C.: Government Printing Office.

40; one out of every six Americans will be over 65 (Mayer, 1977).

The kind of age distribution America had in George Washington's time is comparable to preindustrial or developing countries today. If we think of each succeeding age group piled on top of one another, as shown in Model Population 2 on p. 29 in Chapter 1, the form is triangular. Large numbers of children are born, but fewer and fewer survive as time advances. Advanced, industrial societies have what demographers call a stabilized age structure: all age groups are about the same size, until age 50 or so (see Model Population 1, p. 29).

Actual age distributions differ from the ideal model. Birth cohorts—people born in any particular year or period—vary in size. The baby boom generation creates a bulge in the population profile at every age it reaches. You can imagine it as an elephant passing through a boa constrictor. It overcrowded the schools during the 1960s and 1970s, raised unemployment in the 1980s, and will swell the ranks of the aged in the twenty-first century. Despite the variation in the size of different age groups, however, each will enjoy the extraordinary increase in life expectancy that has resulted from health, nutrition, and medical advances in this century.

Historical Perspectives on Declining Mortality

It is hard to appreciate what a novelty it is, historically speaking, for a majority of the population to live out a full life span. We know that since Biblical times the human life span has been defined as "three score and ten." We also know that writers through the ages have described the human life cycle, the most well known being Shakespeare's seven stages, beginning with the "infant, mewling and puking

in the nurse's arms," and ending with "second childishness and mere oblivion, sans teeth, sans eyes, sans taste, sans everything" (*As You Like It*, Act II, scene vii).

What is less familiar is how few people actually made it to the seventh stage in the past, or even to Shakespeare's fifth and sixth. The proportion of old people in the population has been completely transformed since the turn of the century, with the greatest change coming in the 1940s, 1950s and 1960s (Laslett, 1976).

As one writer recently observed, if someone from Shakespeare's time could return to England today, he or she would be as much surprised by the sight of large numbers of old people as by television. Before the twentieth century, most people did not experience the aging process and had little familiarity with it in others. People often became worn down, exhausted, and ravaged by disease when they were middle-aged, but it was unusual to see white hair, deep wrinkles, or the other changes in body and behavior that are so familiar to us today. This shortness of life is "one of the essential ways in which our forebears differed from us," notes Ronald Blythe. "Their knowledge of the destruction of the physical self was quite unlike anything we understand by hospital visits, or by simply walking down the street" (1979, p. 3).

Many of the most significant changes in modern life are due directly or indirectly to the profound changes in death rates that have occurred in the twentieth century. These range from the virtual disappearance of orphans and orphanages to birth control, the number of living grandparents children know, rising divorce rates, and the "empty nest" stage of married life.

The most direct yet subtle effect of the shift from high to low mortality rates is psychological. Until the early decades of this century, life had a precariousness we can scarcely understand today. It is true that we live with the possibility that nuclear holocaust could happen at any moment, and none of us is immune from disease or accidents. But except in time of war, we do not live with death as a pervasive, expectable part of daily life. Now it is a rare event. We see death as "naturally" occurring at the end of a long life, and it is unexpected if it occurs earlier (Katchadourian, 1978).

Most Americans do not experience death in their own nuclear families until their parents die when the children themselves are middle-aged. Mortality rates for specific ages show that since the nineteenth century death has been much more narrowly concentrated in older age groups than it ever had been (Keyfitz & Pfleger, 1968). In the past, death could occur at any age. Babies and young children were the most vulnerable, but in the days before anti-biotics, it was not unusual for young adults to die of tuberculosis, pneumonia, or other diseases or infections. Mozart died at 35, Schubert at 31, Keats at 25. A common theme in nineteenth-century literature was a young person dying "a beautiful death" (Ariès, 1981).

Peter Uhlenberg (1980) has developed measures for calculating the impact of mortality rates on the individual's family experience. He contrasted mortality rates prevalent in 1900 with those of 1976 and calculated how they would have affected individuals at various points in the life cycle. Thus, under 1900 mortality conditions, half of all parents would experience the death of a child; by 1976, only 6 percent would. More than half of all children in 1900 surviving to the age of 15 would have lost a parent or sibling. Now, children almost never experience the death of a close relative, except that of elderly grandparents. Today children are also far more likely to know their grandparents than their grandparents were to know their own—the probability of children at the age of 15 having three or more grandparents alive has increased from .17 to .55. These demographic facts suggest that statements about declining influence of grandparents in the lives of their grandchildren are wrong.

Changes in the Life Cycle

The decline in death rates since 1900 also has had a profound impact on marriage and the family life cycle. The demographic realities contrast sharply with nostalgic images of stable

families in past times. The young widow or widower was as common a figure on the social landscape as divorced people are today. The probability that a child would grow up in a "broken family" was greater than today, although then families were broken by death, and now by divorce. The change in mortality rates has contributed in several ways to the divorce rate.

The emergence of middle age as a distinct stage of the life course is also a product, in part, of the decline in mortality rates. The less likely children are to die in infancy or childhood, the more parents can plan the size of their families, and the fewer the number of children they have to have. Also, they can have their smaller number of children closer together. Today there are few families where sisters and brothers are ten, fifteen, or twenty years apart in age, as there were in the past.

These changes in fertility, combined with the lengthening of a life span, have made the "empty nest" stage a major part of the family life cycle. Meanwhile, the lengthening of the life span has meant that today's middle-aged people are much more likely than their counterparts in the past to have elderly parents to care for. In 1900, less than half of all couples in their fifties would have one or more living parents; in 1976, more than 86 percent had at least one, and half had two or more elderly parents (Uhlenberg, 1980). We have already noted that the death of elderly parents is the first encounter in their nuclear family that many middle-aged Americans have with mortality. Because of these demographic and other changes, middle age is now a more distinct period of life than it has been in the past.

Conceptions of Adulthood, Aging, and the Life Course

Although the social and demographic trends described above had developed over several decades, it is only since the 1960s that psychologists have concerned themselves with adulthood. Historian Winthrop Jordan (1978) points out that the concept of adulthood has only recently emerged in our culture. Adolescence and old age were "discovered" before adulthood. The difficulties of defining adulthood as a distinct period of life are illustrated in the work of G. Stanley Hall. At one point in his career, Hall saw all of life between puberty and old age as divided into two periods, adolescence and senescence: "The latter begins where the former ends (at about forty-five years of age) and . . . all we have thought characteristic of middle life consists only of the phenomena which are connected to the turn of the tide" (quoted in D. Ross, 1972).

The development of the study of adulthood fits Hall's image of two clearly defined but widely separated stages of life reaching toward one another. Both child development and gerontology have influenced thinking about adulthood. The stronger thrust toward studying adults came from gerontology. As that field progressed, it became clear that the physical, mental, and social changes of old age were hard to understand without knowledge of the earlier phases of adulthood.

The biopsychological models of aging connected rather neatly with *organismic* conceptions of child development. As we saw in an earlier chapter, organismic theories such as Werner's and Piaget's see development as a universal process built into the organism, tied to irreversible maturational forces (Reese & Overton, 1970). Looking at the whole life span from an organismic perspective, it is easy to think that the age curve of physical and mental functioning forms an upside-down U with a peak somewhere in the twenties. Social and personality functioning, according to the theory, inevitably changed with the loss of physical and mental powers. With age, people were assumed to become rigid, resistant to change, egocentric.

Approaches to Life Span Research

Researchers have become increasingly interested in social and personality change in adulthood and have moved away from the assumption that biological decline is the basic model for understanding those changes. There is, as mentioned earlier, no single approach to studying adulthood. Researchers have a variety of interests and use a variety of methods.

Some researchers theorized *stages* of adult life. Erik Erikson's eight stages (1950) were the forerunner of more recent accounts of adult stages such as those postulated by Daniel Levinson (1977) and popularized by Gail Sheehy in her best-selling book, *Passages* (1977). Other researchers, however, reject the idea that adults pass through particular stages at particular times in their lives. They argue that the kinds of issues that adults confront—issues of work, love, marriage and divorce, parenthood, life events—are not necessarily linked to any particular age or to any built-in changes in psychological structure. Rather, these critics argue, psychological change in adulthood derives from the specific conditions of individual's lives and the particular times and places in which they live out their lives (Baltes & Nesselroade, 1984; Dannefer, 1984a, 1984b). We will discuss the debate over personality development in adulthood later on in this chapter.

Life span developmental psychology takes a somewhat different approach. It assumes, as Baltes and Brim point out, that "behavior develops throughout life (from conception to death) and, moreover, that developmental processes, whatever their age location, can be better understood if they are seen in the context of the entire lifetime of individuals" (1979, p. xi). Thus, a researcher might take a concept or a process that has been studied at a particular age, such as attachment, and extend it over the entire life span, asking such questions as, What forms does attachment take in later childhood, in adulthood, and in old age? Similarly, researchers might look at memory, problem solving, or some other psychosocial process over an entire life. Life span researchers tend to give a great deal of attention to the interplay between individual development and social change.

Still another approach to adulthood is the **life course** perspective. It is concerned with the timing and sequencing of the major *events* of life: finishing school, moving away from home, getting married, starting work, having children, retiring. Scholars who use a life course approach have tended to be sociologists or historians, rather than psychologists (see Hareven, 1982). Instead of assuming that a person moves through a series of age-linked *stages*, the life course approach is more concerned with *transitions*. The life course approach recognizes that people can follow different, complicated pathways through life.

It postulates that people have several *careers*—a marital career, a work career, a parental career—which overlap and interact with each other. Life course researchers are less concerned with particular stages of life than they are with *when* people enter and leave particular roles, and how a change in one career—say marriage—affects changes in the others. For ex-

ample, how does early marriage or childbearing affect the rest of a woman's life course? Historians have discovered that there have been major changes since the last century in the ways people experience major life events and the sequence that the events follow. For instance, women today marry younger, have fewer children, and end childbearing earlier than they did a century ago. These changes have had a profound effect on women's labor force participation, consumer habits, and leisure time activities, as well as the quality of marriage.

Cohort Changes

Life course researchers are also sensitive to the ways generations differ from one another. As we noted earlier, a cohort is a group of people born in the same year, or who experience the same historical event at around the same age (Ryder, 1965). Thus, we can speak of the 1968 birth cohort, or the Vietnam War cohort. Popular writers often refer to cohorts more loosely as "the World War II generation" or "the '60s generation," not to mention the "baby boomers."

Cohorts differ in many ways. Matilda Riley (1976) has pointed out that "there is no pure process of aging": each generation differs from earlier and later ones because of various kinds of social changes such as in education, nutrition, and childrearing practices. People who

were 70 years old in 1980 had lived through a very different set of historical experiences than those who were 30 or 50 years old will have when they are 70. Because the septuagenarians were born in 1910, they witnessed World War I, the beginnings of radio, and the rise of the automobile and the movies. They also experienced the depth of the Great Depression just when they were starting out in work and marriage. Born at a time when life expectancy was around 50, they were among the first generation to survive en masse into old age. Raised at a time when very few parents were "child-centered" or knew about the psychology of child development, this cohort was taught the values of obedience, respect for authority, and unquestioning patriotism: my country, right or wrong.

In their thirties when World War II began,

the men of this cohort were eligible for the draft. After the war, they experienced the economic boom and the emergence of television. In their older years, they witnessed the space age, the sexual and sex role revolutions, the counterculture, the disillusionment with authority brought about by Watergate, Vietnam, and the resignation of a president. In contrast to younger people and future 70-year-olds, they are, on the whole, less educated, more rural, more working class, more immigrant.

Cohort differences complicate the work of the researcher trying to draw conclusions about adult development. A researcher who wants to trace the development of sexual behavior in people from 20 to 70 would not simply be able to ask people of different ages and make statements about how *individuals* change with age; each age group would represent a different cohort, which may have had different attitudes toward sex. Research designs have been worked out to untangle these issues, but the problem remains a tricky one in life span studies (see Baltes, Reese, & Nesselroade, 1977).

Paul Baltes and his colleagues (Baltes, Cornelius, & Nesselroade, 1979; Baltes & Willis, 1978) have attempted to account for the complexity of life span development by considering three major influences on individuals: age-graded, history-graded, and nonnormative (Figure 14.2).

- *Age-graded influences* refer to biological and social processes and events that are highly correlated with age. Thus, they depend on biological capacity or social norms. Age-graded influences are considered normative because they are similar for many individuals. Examples include puberty, menopause, entering first grade, retirement. Age-graded events constitute biological and social clocks for the adult life course.
- *History-graded influences* are the variety of ways in which living in a particular historical time shapes a person's life. Such historical influences can include wars, depressions, famines, immigration, as well as cultural factors such as ideologies. These

are also considered normative in that they affect most members of a particular cohort.
- *Nonnormative influences* are life events that are not tied to chronological age or historical period. They include illness, accidents, divorce, losing a job, winning a scholarship to college.

Constancy and Change

Another issue that has emerged from the study of life span development is that of constancy and change over the course of life. As we saw earlier, the assumption that personality remains stable has been the accepted doctrine in psychology for most of the past century. Freudians and behaviorists differed in basic ways about human nature, but they agreed that the experiences of infancy and early childhood have a strong and lasting effect on adulthood. Now life span scholars are challenging

---

FIGURE 14.2
The Nature of Life Span Development
Three basic determinants regulate the ontogenetic (age-graded), evolutionary (history-graded), and nonnormative influences on development.

Source: "Life-span developmental psychology: Some converging observations on history and theory" by P. B. Baltes, 1979, in P. B. Baltes & O. G. Brim, eds., *Life-span development and behavior*, vol. 2., New York: Academic Press.

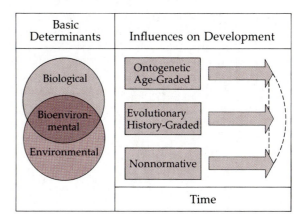

assumptions about personality stability and early childhood determinism (Brim & Kagan, 1980; Featherman, 1983).

Based on the analyses of several longitudinal studies, these scholars sum up the challenges to conventional thinking as follows:

1. Individuals have the capacity to change across the entire life span.
2. Infant and early childhood experience does not necessarily determine the behavior of the adolescent and adult.
3. Individuals are agents in their own development.

A person's life history results from the interaction of biological, psychological, social, and historical events, and the person's own responses to these influences and events.

The proponents of stability argue that, underneath the seeming changes, people are still basically the same—that, in a sense, change is an illusion. They believe that the most central and basic dimensions of personality, including the ones that make up a person's basic social and emotional style, remain stable throughout life. Thus, the anxious person, who is afraid of rejection in high school and of economic reces-

sion in adulthood, will probably be afraid of illness and death in old age (Costa & McCrae, 1980, p. 90).

Evidence for both stability and continuity can be found. Like the optimist and the pessimist looking at a half-filled (or half-empty) glass, researchers emphasize one or the other according to their theoretical or gut-level preferences. Some people seem to change little, others a great deal over the course of life. Some aspects of personality may be more stable, others more flexible. The interesting task for researchers is to find out the conditions under which people remain the same or change; stability needs as much explanation as change.

Ultimately, we are all both stable and changing. There is a core of stability in that we always live in the same body—we are always born in a particular time and place to a particular set of parents and, except in cases of mental illness or amnesia, are always attached to the same stream of memories, always the same "I." On the other hand, our body and our social roles change over the course of life. As John Clausen has noted, the natural state of the person is to be in the process of becoming different while remaining in many ways the same (in Brim, 1976, p. 246).

Physical Changes in Adulthood

Aging is, first of all, a bodily process. The innermost recesses of our minds may not recognize time, yet our bodies are constantly changing. We judge a person's age by how they look. An "old" person is someone we identify as old on the basis of appearance—white hair, wrinkled skin, bent-over posture, slow and stiff movements. Youth and middle age have their own stereotypes. But though physical changes are universal, individuals age differently. As Sharon Curtin notes,

> You see men of eighty still vital and tall and straight as oaks; you see men of fifty reduced to gray shadows in the human landscape. The cellular clock differs for

each one of us, and is profoundly affected by our own life experiences, our heredity, and perhaps most importantly, by the concepts of aging encountered in society and in oneself. (1972, p. 17)

There is room here only for a very brief look at some of the major physical changes involved in the aging process. These changes are extremely complex, involving the reproduction and function of cells, physiological changes such as hormone and sugar levels in the blood, as well as changes in organ systems such as the central nervous system, the heart and circulatory system, the skeletal and muscular systems. Further, there are complicated interactions between physical health, functional ability—the kinds of things a person can or cannot do—and lifestyle, such as diet, exercise, cigarette smoking, and stress (Fries & Crapo, 1981).

Individual and Social Variation

A person's chronological age may be an inaccurate measure of how he or she looks, feels, acts, and even functions physiologically. Even with his cancer surgery in the summer of 1985, President Reagan does not fit the stereotyped image of a man in his seventies. Some researchers have been trying to find functional-age measurements that determine how "old" a person is medically (Fozard & Popkin, 1978). A man of 50 who exercises regularly may have the muscle tone and cardiac functioning of a much younger man, while another 50-year-old who is overweight, smokes, and never exercises may be, physiologically speaking, in old age already.

There are such significant group and individual differences in the physical changes of adulthood that it is difficult to generalize. Not only do the two sexes differ in physiological aging, but there are social class and cohort differences as well. Women tend to live longer, by almost eight years, and they have fewer heart attacks than men.

Over the past 100 years people all around the world have increased in height and weight,

probably because of better nutrition and standards of health. These same factors may be related to the trend toward earlier menstruation, later onset of menopause, and other changes as well. Because of these cohort changes, it is difficult to use current cohorts of old people as models of aging in general. Yet most studies of physical change in adulthood are cross-sectional. Cross-sequential research studies that followed different cohorts through time to take account of cohort differences would be extremely useful.

Social class differences have an important influence on age changes in both health and appearance. In general, the lower in the socioeconomic hierarchy a person is, the earlier he or she ages. People with more time, money, and access to medical and dental care can look and feel youthful longer than can people with fewer of these resources. A 35-year-old coal miner's wife in Appalachia with more children than teeth may look and feel like an old woman. Her middle-class suburban counterpart may look ten years younger than her real age. An ethnographic study of elderly in one southern California town found that age in itself had little meaning apart from other life circumstances. One group of people in their seventies were tanned and fit and played tennis every day. Another group, much poorer in health and pocketbook, passed their time languishing in a downtown senior center (Fontana, 1977).

Age Changes in Physiological Function

Physically, if not psychologically, adulthood does fit the model of a long, stable plateau. Most changes are gradual. In fact, some of the changes that become apparent in middle age have been in process since childhood, such as the build-up of fat in the arteries. Eyesight and hearing begin to decline from the age of 20 (Timiras, 1972).

While we divide adulthood into distinct psychological and social phases, physiologically it is a time of slow but steady decline. Nathan Shock (1977) has shown that for many of our

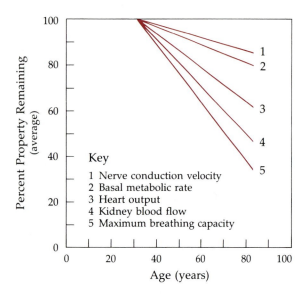

FIGURE 14.3
The Decline of Organ Function
Organ function declines in a linear manner with increasing age.

Source: "Discussion on mortality and measurement of aging" by N. W. Shock, 1960, in B. L. Strehler et al., eds., *The biology of aging: A symposium*, Washington, D.C.: American Institute of Biological Sciences.

major organ systems, the decline comes close to being a straight line (Figure 14.3). However, because the capacity of our organs is much greater than we need for ordinary functioning, we seldom notice these losses.

Physical functioning reaches its peak level in early adulthood. Roughly between the ages of 18 and 30, strength, endurance, agility, coordination, and speed of response are at their best. People generally have less concern about health at this age than at any other. Physically, women are in prime condition for having a first baby during these years. Most Olympic athletes are in this age group, particularly those who compete in events demanding extremes of agility or speed, such as jumping or short-distance running.

After the peak of early adulthood, changes in physical condition are gradual. Middle age is hard to define socially and in terms of chrono-

logical age. It is equally difficult to point to the physical onset of middle age. The thirties may be regarded as a turning point because there is some slackening of abilities and the first signs of aging begin to appear (Marshall, 1968). By the age of 40, the time it takes to react to a sudden stimulus has begun to increase because of the aging of the brain. People in their thirties may notice they are beginning to have trouble reading small print; this change, which usually creates the need for reading glasses or bifocals, is caused by a loss of elasticity in the eye.

Some athletes continue their careers well into their thirties, but those whose specialties involve speed and agility realize that they are past their prime. In contrast, strength and endurance are at peak levels during the thirties, and over-30 athletes do well at such events as long-distance running, walking, and weight lifting.

Some time in their thirties or forties, most people find they have to start paying attention to their bodies in ways that they did not have to before. Staying up to all hours of the night takes a greater toll than it did earlier. Most people find they have to control their diets to keep from gaining weight. In middle age, there is a redistribution of fat in the body and a tendency for muscle to turn to fat. In adolescence, body fat is only 10 percent of body weight, but in middle age it is 20 percent (Troll, 1975).

Between 40 and 60, the biological decline from the peak of adulthood becomes clearer, although there are extreme individual differences in the rate and appearance of aging. Muscular strength declines during the forties; men in their late fifties can perform only about 60 percent of what 40-year-olds can do (Marshall, 1968). Speed of reaction slows down further, so that men in their fifties and sixties have trouble with jobs demanding either heavy labor or a fast pace of work, such as on an assembly line. Of course, in occupations that do not demand physical exertion, individuals between 40 and 60 are usually at the peak of their careers.

Menopause

Although middle age changes men's physiology in a variety of ways, there is no dramatic event for them comparable to menopause in women. Between the ages of 45 and 55, women's menstrual periods stop, and in some women hormonal imbalances can create uncomfortable symptoms such as hot flashes. Menopause, called "the climacterium" in medicine, or "the change of life" in popular terms, was once regarded by social scientists and medical authorities as a major crisis, an event of overwhelming significance in a woman's life. Today it is considered just one of the events of middle age, which may have less of an impact on a woman's social and psychological well-being than does her work, the state of her marriage, or the emptying of the nest.

Bernice Neugarten and her associates (1963) found that younger women were more worried about the prospect of going through menopause than were women who were living through it or were past it. Three-quarters of women who had experienced menopause felt it did not change them in an important way, although half of them had found it an unpleasant experience. The other half said that menopause had no effects on appearance, health, emotional well-being, or sexual relations. More recently, in a study of over 700 Japanese and American women, 75 percent reported none of the symptoms usually associated with menopause (Goodman, Stewart, & Gilbert, 1977).

Many of the changes that come with age, such as menopause, are private events. For both men and women, the most significant signs of aging are ones that are visible to other people—gray hair, baldness, wrinkles, dentures, bifocals, thickened waistlines, stiff joints. It is these changes that are likely to influence how old a person feels and how other people act toward him or her. Yet some of these changes can be controlled and even reversed. While eyesight, hearing, or the condition of one's teeth rarely improve with age, weight, body shape, and general health can be improved. In a study of women between the ages of 33 and 56, 20 percent reported improvements in such physical symptoms of aging (Rossi, 1980).

Physical Change in Old Age

The health and strength of individuals over 65 varies enormously. Nevertheless, in the last decades of life bodily changes become a major concern. They affect social and psychological functioning in important ways and in turn are influenced by them. Old age is a time when chronic diseases, which may have existed for several years without symptoms, begin to appear. The major ones of old age are arthritis, cancer, heart disease, and high blood pressure (see Figure 14.4). Having a chronic condition makes one susceptible to infectious diseases, such as pneumonia and flu. In addition, even old people in fairly good health experience the

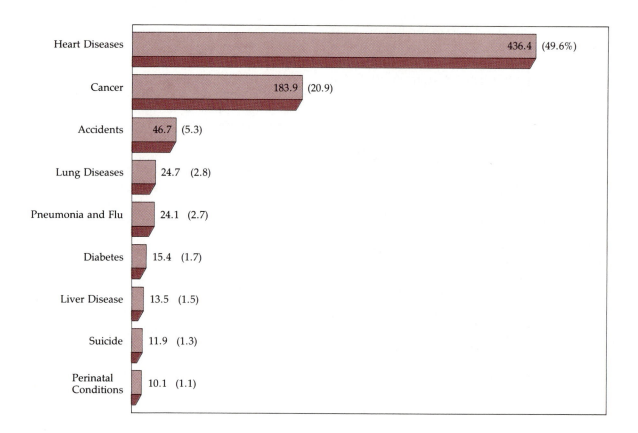

Heart Diseases	436.4 (49.6%)
Cancer	183.9 (20.9)
Accidents	46.7 (5.3)
Lung Diseases	24.7 (2.8)
Pneumonia and Flu	24.1 (2.7)
Diabetes	15.4 (1.7)
Liver Disease	13.5 (1.5)
Suicide	11.9 (1.3)
Perinatal Conditions	10.1 (1.1)

general diminishing of functioning associated with age: declines in energy, muscular strength, and speed of response, impaired sight and hearing, difficulty in adapting to extreme cold or heat.

Central Nervous System Changes

It is a common observation that old people are slower than younger and middle-aged adults in a wide range of activities. This general slowing is documented in a variety of studies showing age differences on tests of reaction time and other tasks where speed is measured. There is considerable evidence that this decline in speed is a function of changes in the brain and nervous system. The speed at which impulses move along nerve fibers shows a gradual but steady decrease after the age of 30 (F. E. Bloom, Lazerson, & Hofstader, 1985), which supports the pattern found in other organ sys-

FIGURE 14.4
The Leading Causes of Death
Total crude death rate per 100,000, by cause, in 1980. The figures in parentheses indicate percentage of the total number of deaths in that year. Notice how heart disease and cancer far outstrip the other leading causes of death.

Source: *Vital statistics of the United States*, annual, U.S. National Center for Health Statistics, Washington, D.C.: Government Printing Office.

tems. Disease, especially of the heart and circulatory system, can accelerate these brain and nervous system changes, but the latter seem to occur independently of illness as a part of normal aging. The actual rate of decline varies markedly from person to person.

There is also evidence that the slowing of behavior can be modified to some extent. One

live into their seventies and eighties, greater percentages will develop Alzheimer's—or, as it is referred to by neurologists, senile dementia of the Alzheimer's type or SDAT.

The disease produces progressive psychological deterioration. It eventually leads to profound intellectual decline, including confusion and loss of memory. Personality changes occur also; the person may become abusive and hostile to loved ones. Family members often feel the old person has been transformed into a stranger, and due to memory loss, the victim of Alzheimer's eventually cannot recognize anyone.

The brains of people with Alzheimer's disease show what seem to be exaggerations of the normal aging process. Microscopic examination of the cortex reveals tangles of nerve fibers and plaques consisting of accumulations of cellular debris. The brains of Alzheimer victims also suffer from a sharp decline in a chemical that is needed for communication among

study showed that older adults could increase their speed of response with practice (Hoyer, Labouvie, & Baltes, 1973). Also, to a certain extent, older adults may make up for the loss of speed with greater accuracy (Rabbit & Birren, 1967). There is even evidence that persistent exercise can postpone the decline in brain functioning that leads to psychomotor slowness (Spirduso, 1980).

Alzheimer's Disease

Alzheimer's disease, a form of senility, is a disorder of the aging brain that is now approaching epidemic proportions. By the end of the twentieth century, it may be the most prevalent neurological disorder of all time (F. E. Bloom, Lazerson, & Hofstader, 1985). It is an ironic by-product of improvements in the health of the general population and the extension of the expectable life span; as more people

nerve cells. This finding may lead to a treatment for the disorder. As of now, however, there is no treatment or cure, and the cause remains unknown. While Alzheimer's disease is becoming a major health problem, it should be kept in mind that it afflicts only a minority—about 10 or 15 percent—of the population over 65.

Senility is not the inevitable outcome of long life, even if one lives to be 80 or 90. Some disorders of the brain are even reversible. Unfortunately, as Robert Butler (1975) points out, many old people are diagnosed as "senile" when in fact they are suffering from physical and emotional problems that can be treated.

Separating Aging from Disease

Suppose cures were found for every known disease. No one would die from cancer, heart disorders, or any other ailment. How long would we live? The surprising answer is that we would not have longer life spans than earlier generations have had. The popular notion that the human life span has been extended in recent years is misleading. **Life expectancy** has increased, not the maximum amount of time it is possible for a human being to live (see box and Figures 14.5 and 14.6 on Survival Curves). In spite of all the medical advances that have enabled masses of people to live into old age, the maximum life span has not increased since Biblical times.

Each species of animal has a characteristic life span that appears to be programmed into its genes. The life *span* is the age at which the average individual would die if there were no diseases or accidents; for humans, this is about 85 and has been constant for centuries (Fries & Crapo, 1981). The maximum amount of time it is possible for a human to live—the *maximum life potential* (MLP) of our species—is about 115 years. Despite claims of some individuals that they are 137 or 167, only five persons have been confirmed as living beyond 112. The oldest of these was a 114-year-old Japanese man.

Scientists do not agree on a theory of aging—that is, what causes people to grow old and

Survival Curves

Survival curves plot the percentage of a given population that survives at succeeding ages (Figure 14.5). For animal populations in the wild and human populations in "uncivilized" environments, the curve marks a steady decline over time; death is as likely to occur at one age as at any other. For civilized, human populations, the curve bends upward to the right, indicating that people are surviving until later ages. Note, however, that all the curves meet at the same place: no matter how many people survive until old age, very few live into their nineties.

Our own society is approaching the rectangular curve (Figure 14.6). The dip after birth represents infant mortality, much of which is irreducible. Then there is a slow decline until age 70. After 75, the curve turns down sharply as the population reaches the natural limit of the human life span. Most gerontologists believe that this limit can never be extended, but that it is possible through careful attention to diet, exercise, and life style for much of the population to maintain a youthful level of health and vitality until very late in life.

eventually die. A number of different hypotheses have been proposed, though it is likely that several causes of aging exist, not just one (Shock, 1977). Theories that aging is programmed into the body compete with those which hold that aging results from the wearing out of the body through time. Hypotheses also differ as to whether aging is a process that occurs primarily in the cells or at the organ system level—the heart and circulatory system, the central nervous system, and so forth. (In fact, while most researchers believe that the human life span is fixed genetically and can never be altered, a small minority argues that it may be possible to alter the aging process it-

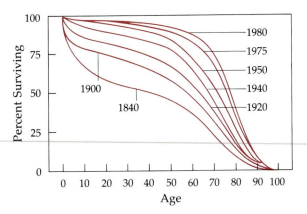

FIGURE 14.5
Survival Curves
Sequential survival curves in the United States from 1840 to 1980.

Source: U.S. Bureau of Health Statistics.

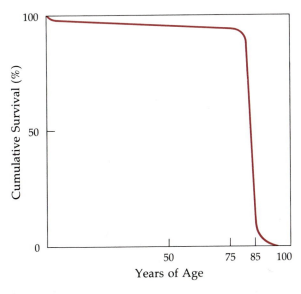

FIGURE 14.6
The Rectangular Survival Curve
Death rates in industrial societies are minimal until people reach their seventies, at which time the rates increase so rapidly that the survival curve almost forms a rectangle.

Source: *Vitality and aging* by J. F. Fries & L. M. Crapo, 1981, San Francisco: W. H. Freeman.

self and thereby extend the human life span to 150 or 200 years [Walford, 1983]).

The most widely accepted theory of aging emphasizes mechanisms in the cell that have a finite life span. The observations of Leonard Hayflick (1980) are central to the present understanding of the aging process. In a series of landmark studies, Hayflick discovered that there is a kind of genetic clock ticking away inside every cell. He found that cells grown in test tubes from human fetuses have a precisely limited life span: they divide about fifty times and then stop. If frozen after twenty doublings, the cells seemed to "remember" that they had thirty more to go when thawed. Cells from people of various ages doubled in inverse relation to their age; the older the donor, the fewer the doublings.

The maximum number of times a cell can divide has come to be known as the **Hayflick limit.** As cells approach this limit, they take on the characteristics of what have been commonly recognized as old cells. Thus, while Hayflick's observations do not serve as a direct or complete explanation of aging, they are currently regarded as a model of aging in animals and humans.

Most gerontologists who accept the Hayflick limit are not working toward an extension of the human life span, rather at the "compression of morbidity"; that is, their aim is to maintain health and vitality for as long as possible, and thus minimize the period of senescence just before death. Lewis Thomas (1979) has suggested, as a metaphor for this view of aging and death, the wonderful "one hoss shay" in Oliver Wendell Holmes's poem. None of the shay's parts ever wore out, but one day "it went to pieces all at once—/all at once and nothing first—/Just as bubbles do when they burst."

An important study of the differences between aging and disease was carried out by Birren and his associates (1963). These researchers studied forty-seven very healthy men between the ages of 65 and 91. The good health of these men had been established in clinical examinations. Yet more extended analysis revealed that the group actually consisted of two subgroups. In one subgroup, no signs of disease appeared even after intensive physical exams. In the other group, intensive examination revealed mild disease conditions that had not given rise to any symptoms.

A major finding was that even a mild degree of disease can have important consequences on a wide range of functioning. For example, the optimally healthy old men did not differ from much younger men in blood flow to the brain, a factor that may influence the efficiency of brain functioning. Even in this group, however, there was some evidence of aging. There were significant differences between the optimally healthy and those with mild symptoms of disease on this measure. In general, the electrical activity of the brain slowed with age, as measured by the EEG and correlated with speed on psychological tests and reaction time measures.

A follow-up study of the same men eleven years later (Granick & Patterson, 1971) revealed that most (63 percent) of the very healthy group survived, but only 30 percent of the less healthy group did so. The study also revealed the importance of psychological and social factors in mortality. A lifestyle that was both orderly and gratifying, and did not include smoking cigarettes, was 80 percent more likely to produce longevity.

We should not conclude this very abbreviated review of the bodily changes of aging without noting that, despite the physical declines in old age, some older people can outperform younger people. The pianist Arthur Rubinstein, who lived into his nineties, remained a master of the eighty-eight-key piano, manipulating millions of notes in the course of a recital. A short time ago there were news stories of an 80-year-old woman who regularly runs marathons. In a television interview, she reported she took up running at the age of 72 because her doctor had recommended exercise. She had not been a runner earlier in her life, she said, because in those days "women weren't supposed to do such things."

In sum, then, we should not generalize too broadly about the physical changes of adulthood and aging. There are great individual, group, and cohort differences. The cohorts who are old now did not enjoy optimal health care and nutrition in their early years. On the other hand, recent cohorts of younger people have been exposed more to environmental pollution, radiation, and dietary changes which have been decried by nutritional experts—the kind of highly processed, chemically treated, nutritionally poor diet no other humans have ever eaten. Future generations of old people are likely to differ in many ways from today's senior citizens, physically as well as socially and psychologically.

Cognitive Changes in Adulthood

Until recently, the fate of the mind in adulthood was believed to parallel that of the body. Psychologists took it for granted that intelligence, like muscular strength, reaches an early peak and then fades. Paradoxically, the concept of IQ constancy was applied to children, while a very different concept was applied to adults (Eichorn, Hunt, & Honzik, 1981). As intelligence went, so also went learning, memory, and creativity. This *irreversible decrement* model (Shaie, 1979), which places the onset of senility somewhere around the age of 30, seemed to be the undeniable conclusion from many research findings. There is evidence, for example, that the brain begins to lose weight before the age of 30, due to the loss or degeneration of brain cells. Studies of creativity and intellectual productivity appeared to show that the most important contributions to science, art, and literature are made in young adulthood and fall off sharply after middle age (Lehman, 1953). Finally, a large body of studies documented the poor performance of older people on IQ tests, as well as tests of learning, memory, problem solving, and perception.

In the last few years, however, this view has been considerably revised. The irreversible decrement model no longer seems valid. Many kinds of intellectual skills remain stable well into old age, decrements can be compensated

The picture began to change, though, as longitudinal data became available. A number of studies reexamined people who had been tested years before, and a summary of the results (Botwinick, 1977) showed that performance on IQ tests increases at least until age 50 or 60 and during the seventies and eighties declines modestly. It now seems clear that a large part of the difference between the two kinds of studies—cross-sectional and longitudinal—was caused by cohort differences, especially differences in education. Over the course of this century, the level of education has been rising. Thus, the early cross-sectional studies compared people who not only differed in age but educational level.

But longitudinal studies have their own problems: they may overestimate the level of intelligence of older people. As explained in an earlier chapter, when a study goes on over a long period of time, some people inevitably drop out. The dropouts are usually not a random sample of the whole original group, but rather tend to be those who scored low in the first place (Schaie, Labouvie, & Barrett, 1973). The scores of those who remain, therefore, are likely to be higher than those of the original sample who did not show up for later testings.

While the early decline model of intelligence suggested by cross-sectional studies is clearly wrong, the question of how age affects cognitive functioning is not clear. Much remains to be learned about the kinds of ability that remain stable or even improve across adulthood versus those that decline. Also, researchers are trying to devise ways of untangling the age changes from cohort differences as well as from environmental or cultural changes that may affect people of all ages. This is an active and sometimes hotly debated area of research.

for, and some intellectual functions may even improve from early to later adulthood.

How did this drastic revision of earlier data come about? The earlier researchers had not distinguished between age *differences* and age *changes*. That is, they assumed that by comparing the scores of young, middle-aged, and older adults, they would thereby have a true picture of the course of individual intellectual development. For example, H. E. Jones and Conrad published a classic study in 1933 which compared the performances of 1,000 10- to 60-year-olds from New England villages on the Army Alpha, an IQ test used in World War I. Scores were highest among the 18- to 21-year-olds and declined progressively among the older groups. At around the same time, the Wechsler-Bellevue intelligence test was being developed and was given to large numbers of people in order to standardize scores. Here, too, older groups scored progressively worse than younger ones.

Fluid versus Crystallized Intelligence

While many studies look at overall test scores, some researchers have examined the fate of specific mental abilities over time. An important model of adult intellectual development is based on the hypothesis that there are two broad types of intelligence, fluid and crystallized (Horn & Donaldson, 1976). **Crystallized intelligence** consists of abilities based on prior information or experience. Prime examples are tests of vocabulary or general information and some of reasoning. These abilities are the least likely to decline and may even improve almost to the end of life. **Fluid intelligence,** by contrast, refers to abilities that do not make use of prior information. Rather, it manipulates new information to solve problems. Examples are repeating a series of numbers in reverse order, or figuring out how to reproduce block designs. Fluid intelligence, according to the theory, parallels the growth and decline of the physical organism (Figure 14.7).

The theory of fluid versus crystallized intelligence has been influential, but it is also controversial. The evidence for the theory rests on cross-sectional designs—comparing people of different ages. We have seen why age *differences* cannot be taken at face value as evidence for age *changes*, or how individuals change with age (Schaie, 1979). A more fundamental criticism has been directed at the very attempt to develop a theory of adult intelligence that assumes there is some universal process of intellectual decline based on the physical deterioration of aging (Baltes & Willis, 1979). According to these researchers, trends in intellectual ability vary too much across individuals and cohorts to make global statements about how and when mental abilities decline with age. They also point to evidence that fluid intelligence is not as immune from the effects of experience, education, and motivation as it was originally thought to be.

Further, the critics of the notion of universal decline also point to the likelihood that there is more *plasticity* of intelligence in adulthood and old age than is usually believed (Baltes & Schaie, 1976). A number of studies have tried to identify factors that might be causing older adults to perform less well than younger adults. For example, older adults may not be as test-wise or familiar as younger people with the kinds of tasks presented by researchers, but their intellectual performance can be improved through training (Labouvie-Vief &

Gonda, 1976; Plemons, Willis, & Baltes, 1978). Hearing loss is also associated with lowered cognitive performance in both young and old (Granick, Kleban, & Weiss, 1976; Hine, 1970), but of course is more prevalent among the old.

Schaie's Sequential Research

To untangle the effects of age and cohort differences on various kinds of intellectual functioning, K. Warner Schaie (1965) has carried out an extensive program of research. He has devised a number of sequential research designs to overcome some of the problems of cross-sectional and longitudinal research. In one study (Schaie, Labouvie, & Buesch, 1973), three independent cross-sectional samples were compared: groups ranging in age from 21 to 81 were tested in 1956, 1963, and 1970. The results showed that people of the same age had different scores, depending on which cohort they were from. For example, people who were 60 in 1970 performed better than those who were 60 in 1956. This analysis also showed the importance of cohort differences. Over a fourteen-year period, scores for the first three

cohorts remained fairly stable. The fourth cohort dropped and then increased, while the three oldest cohorts declined linearly.

While the above study involved different individuals, in later studies Schaie and his associates tested the same individuals from different cohorts a number of times. This research followed a *cohort-sequential* design. Repeated measures on the same individuals revealed great differences in the ways intellectual functioning changes with age. Not only do cohort differences make it difficult to make general statements about normative age changes, but individual variation is so great that it is difficult to generalize about cohort effects.

At present, researchers disagree about how useful the concept of fluid versus crystallized intelligence is, how great the impact of cohort differences on intelligence is, and how early and how much fluid intelligence declines with age. Nevertheless, most researchers in the field would probably concur that intellectual abilities do not necessarily decline after early adulthood; some may improve, some may decline, others may remain stable. Further, the pattern of intellectual change in adulthood varies from one person to the next. Global statements based on age alone are bound to be wrong; and being born in one historical era rather than another has a large impact on intellectual performance.

For most individuals, age will eventually cause a decline on tasks involving speed of response, such as naming in three minutes all the words one can think of beginning with a certain letter. Also, people with heart and circulatory problems and those living in deprived environments may show decrements beginning in their late fifties or early sixties (Schaie, 1979).

Beyond all these issues is the question of the significance of whatever age trends may be found in the research literature. A decline in some performance may be statistically significant yet may make little practical difference in how a person performs in everyday life. The older person's slower speed of reaction and information processing may have little impact on actual decision making, and can often be more than compensated for by the older person's

judgment and experience. As Schaie observes, "Aging is *not* synonymous with intellectual incompetence. It is only as the 80's are reached that age-related decrement becomes evident in many persons, and even then to a lesser extent than previous literature has led us to believe" (1981, p. 211).

Finally, there are some limitations in the research on adult cognitive development. As we have mentioned earlier, all of the people who appear as subjects in the literature on gerontology were born before or around the turn of the century. No one has ever tested a 70-year-old born after 1920! Further, psychologists have tended to emphasize cognitive variables that emerge in childhood and to measure them with tests originally designed to differentiate among school children. Few have attempted to identify and work with variables and tasks that might be more relevant for adults. Recently, however, some researchers have been trying to identify aspects of cognitive performance that might improve over the life span. One quality that has traditionally been associated with maturity is wisdom. Vivian Clayton and others (Clayton, 1975; Clayton & Birren, 1980) have explored the meaning of wisdom to people of various ages and attempted to relate the concept of theories of cognitive, moral, and personality development. In the future, as the graying of America increases still further, we may see more of an adult-centered approach to cognitive development across the life span.

Social and Personality Changes in Adulthood: Stages and Transitions

Until very recently, personality changes across adulthood were believed to follow the same course of stability followed by inevitable physical and intellectual decline; early and middle adulthood were a long plateau of personality sameness, then as people aged, their personalities became more rigid, dogmatic, and egocentric (Labouvie-Vief, 1978). Eventually, according to a theory that was once enormously

FIGURE 14.7
Sample Test Items Marking Fluid and Crystallized Intelligence

Secondary Ability	Primary Ability	Directions/Items
Fluid	Induction	Each problem has five groups of letters with four letters in each group. Four of the groups of letters are alike in some way. You are to find the rule that makes these four groups alike. The fifth group is different from them and will not fit the rule.*
		1. NOPQ DEFL ABCD HIJK UVWX
		2. NLIK PLIK QLIK THIK VLIK
		3. VEBT XGDV ZIFX KXVH MZXJ
Fluid	Visualization	Below is a geometric figure. Beneath the figure are several problems. Each problem consists of a row of five shaded pieces. Your task is to decide which of the five shaded pieces when put together will make the complete figure. Any number of shaded pieces from 2 to 5 may be used to make the complete figure. Each piece may be turned around to any position but it cannot be turned over.†

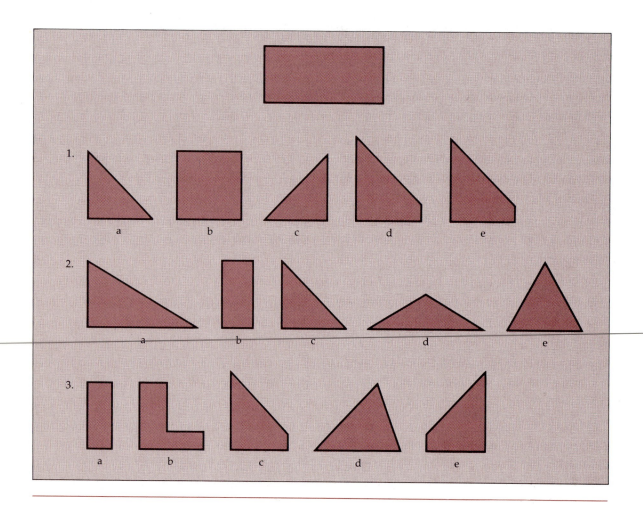

Secondary Ability	Primary Ability	Directions/Items
Crystallized	Verbal meaning	Choose one of the four words in the right-hand box which has the same meaning or nearly the same meaning as the word in the left-hand box.‡

attempt	run try hate stop
pecuniary	trifling unusual involving money esthetic
germane	microbe contagious relevant different

Secondary Ability	Primary Ability	Directions/Items
Crystallized	Mechanical knowledge	Complete each of the statements by selecting the correct alternative or answer.§

1. The process of heating two pieces of heavy metal so hot that they will fuse (melt together) is known as
   riveting
   soldering
   welding
   forging
2. A paint sprayer functions in exactly the same way as a
   centrifugal water pump
   carbon-dioxide fire extinguisher
   perfume atomizer
   vacuum cleaner
3. The tool used to rotate a cylindrical object such as a water pipe is a
   Stillson wrench
   open-end wrench
   box-end wrench
   socket wrench

Answers: Induction: 1. DEFL, 2. THIK, 3. VEBT
      Visualization: 1. a, c, d, e 2. a, d, e 3. b, c, e
      Verbal meaning: 1. try, 2. involving money, 3. relevant
      Mechanical knowledge: 1. welding, 2. perfume atomizer, 3. Stillson wrench
*Letter Sets Test, I-J; Educational Testing Service, 1962, 1976.
†Form Board Test, VZ-1; Educational Testing Service, 1962, 1976.
‡Vocabulary Test, V-5; Educational Testing Service, 1962, 1976.
§Mechanical Information Test, MK-2; Educational Testing Service, 1962 (test no longer in print).

Sources: *Manual for kit of factor-referenced cognitive tests* by R. B. Ekstrom et al., 1976, Princeton, N.J.: Educational Testing Service; *Kit of reference tests for cognitive factors* by J. W. French, R. B. Ekstrom, & L. A. Price, 1963, Princeton, N.J.: Educational Testing Service.

influential, *disengagement* occurs: the older person gradually withdraws from the world of people and social activities (Cummings & Henry, 1961). Disengagement was viewed at first as a natural and healthy way of aging—the inevitable response of a weakening organism to the pressures of ordinary social life.

In recent years, however, a much more complex and less pessimistic model of adulthood has emerged. There is no general theory of adult development, but a number of interesting new approaches are being formulated. Currently, there are two contrasting models to the recent work on adult development: the normative crisis and the social timetable.

The Normative Crisis Model

The *normative crisis* model was popularized in Gail Sheehy's best-selling book, *Passages* (1977), as well as by the writings of Roger Gould (1978) and Daniel Levinson (1978), on whose work Sheehy's book was based. It was this group of writers that helped to make the term **midlife crisis** a household word.

The crisis model of adult development is rooted in Erikson's theory of the life cycle, although he did not explicitly describe a midlife crisis. Erikson, as we have seen, has argued that human development across the life span is like the growth of an embryo: each developmental task has a particular "time of special ascendancy" (1959, p. 52). The life course consists of a series of developmental crises because each new task involves a radical change in the person's perspective. If the crisis is avoided or unresolved, the person's future development is impaired. Thus, the adolescent must resolve his or her identity crisis in order to deal with the stage of intimacy versus isolation (refer back to Figure 3.2 on p. 92). Erikson has not elaborated the later stages of the life cycle in anything like the length and detail with which he has written about adolescence. Nor has he specified the ages for each stage. It is generally assumed, however, that the sixth stage, intimacy versus isolation, centers on early adulthood; the seventh, generativity versus self-

absorption, represents the middle years; while integrity versus despair, the eighth, is the crisis of old age.

Recent writings about the stages of adulthood are based on Erikson's ideas, especially the notion of crisis as a built-in part of adult development. All of these writers—Gould, Levinson, Sheehy, Vaillant—see the middle years as a watershed period of life during which a person reevaluates his or her entire past and sense of self, enters a crisis, and emerges with a new identity.

These theorists see the sense of identity a person forms after adolescence as only a provisional one, a set of stereotyped roles formed in response to pressures of family, peers, and society. Later, these choices of who and what one is may falter as youth fades. Beginning in the thirties, people may feel trapped in the careers and lifestyles they had chosen earlier. George Vaillant, based on his studies of the lives of men from an elite university, claims that the forties bring a return of the storm and stress of adolescence:

> As adolescence is a period for acknowledging parental flaws and discovering the truth about childhood, so the forties are a time for reassessing and reordering the truth about adolescence and young adulthood.
>
> At age 40—give or take a decade—men leave the compulsive, unreflective busywork of their occupational apprenticeships, and once more become explorers of the world within. (1977, p. 220)

These writers believe that every individual must pass through a midlife crisis, and that failure to do so will have dire consequences later in life. For example, Sheehy writes:

> If one has refused to budge through the mid-life transition, the sense of staleness will calcify into resignation. One by one, the safety and supports will be withdrawn from the person who is standing still. Parents will become children; children will become strangers; a mate will grow

away or go away; the career will become just a job—and each of these events will become an abandonment. The crisis will probably emerge again around 50. (1976, p. 46)

But the crisis view of adulthood is not pessimistic. It assumes crises are a normal and predictable part of development; faced bravely, they bring new mastery and growth. As Sheehy puts it, "when we enter mid-life, we also have the opportunity for true adulthood, whereupon we proceed either to wither inside our husks or to regather and re-pot ourselves for the flowering into our full authenticity" (1976, p. 49).

The idea of stages in adult development has become widely popular. People over 30 talk about their midlife crisis the way college students talk about their identity crisis. In fact, some critics have wondered whether there is any difference between the two: "Is the mid-life crisis, if it exists, more than a warmed over identity crisis? If it is not, in what ways is it different, and why does it occur in the middle years?" (Perun & Bielby, 1979, p. 294).

Like storm and stress theories of adolescence, the concept of the midlife crisis seems to reflect the experience of the more advantaged educational and occupational groups. The observations that led to the concept were made by psychologists and psychoanalysts working with upper-middle-class and professional individuals (Giele, 1980). It is these kinds of people who are most likely to engage in the kind of introspective stocktaking that is the core of the concept of midlife crisis. Also, people with less education and fewer economic resources have fewer options for charting new directions for their lives in their middle years. Among lower-middle-class and blue-collar families, life is dominated by making ends meet, dealing with everyday events, and coping with unexpected crises.

Some researchers are dissatisfied with stage models of adult development. They criticize the vague way that such concepts as "stage," "development," and "crisis" are used by the stage theorists. For example, John Flavell (1970)

has argued that a developmental psychology of adulthood, to merit the name, would have to show the major changes, the directionality, and the cross-individual commonality typical of developmental change in childhood and adolescence. In addition, most researchers in child development reject the notion that age in itself causes developmental change: they do not say a child does X "because" he or she is 4 or 8 or 13; rather, they view age as a surrogate for other variables or processes (Wohlwell, 1973).

Stage theorists, however, talk about age as if it were a cause. Above all, critics point to a lack of evidence that there are in fact "normative" crises that each and every individual must pass through in an orderly sequence and at a specific age. As we saw in an earlier chapter, the concept of adolescence as a time of storm and stress has itself been considerably modified if not rejected entirely by most researchers in adolescent development. Brim suggests that the field of adult development resembles the field of child development some fifty years ago: "Like child development then, it is in real danger from pop culture renderings of "life stages," from the public seizing on the idea of age-linked stages of development, such as 'male mid-life crisis' just as it seizes on astrology and tea-leaf reading" (1976, p. 7).

The Social Timetable Model

The other approach to adult development, the *social timetable* model, has a radically different view of the life course. The central idea here is that a person's life is paced and regulated by timetables embedded in the larger society:

> There exists a socially prescribed timetable for the ordering of major life events; a time of the life span when men and women are expected to marry, a time to raise children, a time to retire. This normative pattern is adhered to, more or less consistently, by most persons within a given social group. (Neugarten, 1970, pp. 71–72)

Neugarten and others in this tradition postulate that because of the timetable prescribed by society, and internalized into the self, people have a concept of an "average expectable life cycle" (R. Butler, 1968). They know what changes life has in store, and are not unduly upset by them, *provided the changes occur on time*. Crises only occur when events are off schedule or unanticipated: the death of an elderly parent is a sad, but not extremely traumatic event; the death of a child is devastating. Unexpected events such as losing a job, having an accident, or becoming seriously ill can also lead to crisis.

Thus, according to this view, there is no grand, built-in plan for adult development. Society provides a predictable timetable for life changes. Crises may occur, but these do not alter a person's sense of identity or the course of a life. And they are not caused by some built-in growth process. Rather, they occur in response to changes in a person's body, career, and family life.

Although midlife does not, in this theory, bring a replay of adolescent turbulence, people do gradually shift their self-concepts as they cope with the complex of changes that occur in their bodies, careers, and families. Neugarten (1968) presents evidence that people change their perspective of time in midlife; they think about their lives in terms of "time left to live" rather than "time since birth." Along with this shift in time perspective, middle-aged men and women become more introspective and reflective about themselves and their lives. Thus, while Neugarten does present evidence showing marked psychological changes in middle age, such changes do not arise in response to some built-in developmental force or to "internal voices that have been mute for years now clamor(ing) to be heard" (Levinson, 1978, p. 200).

An Examination of the Models

While each of the two approaches supplies insight into the psychology of adulthood, each has its limitations and leaves many questions unanswered. A key difference between the two models is the relation between developing individuals and their social context. Like organismic theories of child development, the crisis model of adulthood takes place in what Riegel (1973) has called a "sociocultural vacuum." Yet most writers in the crisis school are not describing changes in internal psychological structures or modes of information processing, nor is there evidence that there is a cognitive change in adulthood comparable, say, to the adolescent shift to more abstract, formal modes of thought (Haan, 1981). Much of what they describe has to do with people's reactions to biological and social changes, such as the change in appearance or health, the children leaving home, parents getting old.

While the crisis model ignores social reality, the timing-of-events model takes an "oversocialized" view of adults (Wrong, 1968). It portrays adults as passively internalizing whatever the social norms happen to be. The passive organism model of human behavior has been largely rejected in child psychology and even in animal psychology; hence it seems scarcely appropriate as a model for human adults. As Atchley (1975) has pointed out, age norms are problematic, not given; they vary from place to place as well as by social class, race, ethnicity, and sex. Some age norms are prescribed by law—the ages at which one can drink, drive, or vote, and, at the other end of the life span, the age at which one can collect Social Security. Some norms are based on strong custom—for instance, that men should marry women younger than themselves—other norms may be quite flexible and may be interpreted and applied in various ways. There is surprisingly little research on age norms—the major study being published in 1965 (Neugarten, Moore, & Lowe), which reported data now two decades old.

In recent years, there have been great changes in age norms. Bernice Neugarten herself has suggested that we may be becoming an "age irrelevant society":

> Ours seems to be a society that has become accustomed to 70-year-old students, 30-year-old college presidents, 22-year-old mayors, 35-year-old grandmothers, 50-year-old retirees, 65-year-old fathers of preschoolers, 60-year-olds and 30-year-olds wearing the same clothing styles, and 85-year-old parents caring for 65-year-old offspring.
> (Neugarten & Hagestad, 1976, p. 52)

While the timetable model sees individuals as internalizing age norms smoothly, a very different view of the social meaning of growing up and aging is found in the age stratification model (Foner & Kertzer, 1978). The conception here is that society is divided into age groups in much the same way that it is divided into social class groups. Within a given society, children, young people, the middle-aged, and the elderly are set apart from one another in a variety of ways; they have a different relation to work, play, marriage. They differ in styles of dress, as well as in power and prestige. According to this view, conflicts and tensions *between* age groups are inevitable as each group struggles to protect its own interests against the others.

However, the age stratification system differs from the class system in that everybody experiences mobility—everybody ages. A person moving from one age stratum to the next may experience as much tension and strain as someone who moves from one class to another. In this view, a person moving from childhood to middle adulthood to old age would be moving from rags to riches to rags again—considering the general privileges and power of the various age groups in our society. As Riley notes, "The degree of strain engendered by such transitions depends upon diverse social conditions—upon the continuity or discontinuity in the role sequences . . . upon how fully institutionalized a role may be . . . or upon how effectively people are trained or socialized at every stage of life" (quoted in Quadagno, 1980, pp. 93–94).

Images and Models of the Life Course

For all of the versions of adult development and alternative visions of the life course, there is as yet no widely accepted, integrated theory of the life course. As John Clausen (1972) has suggested, it may be unrealistic to think there could be a theory of something as complex as the life course. A person's "life course" contains all of his or her experience from birth to death. The human life course is unique—no single person's life is exactly like any other—and yet it is universal; every life course tells the same basic story: a person is born, lives a number of years, and dies. In addition to being both universal and uniquely individual, the life course varies by time and place, social group and sex.

Recently, some researchers have tried to suggest models and metaphors for the life course that deal with this complexity. Rejecting the notion that the life course can be divided into a series of global stages based on chronological age, these researchers describe it as moving along a number of distinct but interlocking pathways. A person has one life to live, but that life is made up of several different kinds of "careers"—our body's career through growth and aging, health and sickness; our family career, as we progress through the family cycle; our work career.

Robert Atchley (1975) has charted several of these dimensions of the life course, along with the approximate ages at which they occur (Figure 14.8). He observes that the timing of any given life event can vary widely. Moreover, people can be at widely discrepant places on the various timelines; a 55-year-old man can be thinking about retiring at the same time that he is becoming a father for the first time. A 39-

year-old woman can be a college freshman at the same time that she is in the "empty nest" stage of the family cycle.

FIGURE 14.8
A Developmental Timeline
The relationships between the life course, occupational cycle, the family cycle, and the economic cycle are shown according to chronological age. An individual's development may vary considerably from this model.

Source: "The life course, age grading, and age-linked demands for decision making" by R. C. Atchley, 1975, in N. Datan & L. Ginsberg, eds., *Life-span developmental psychology: Normative life crises*, New York: Academic Press.

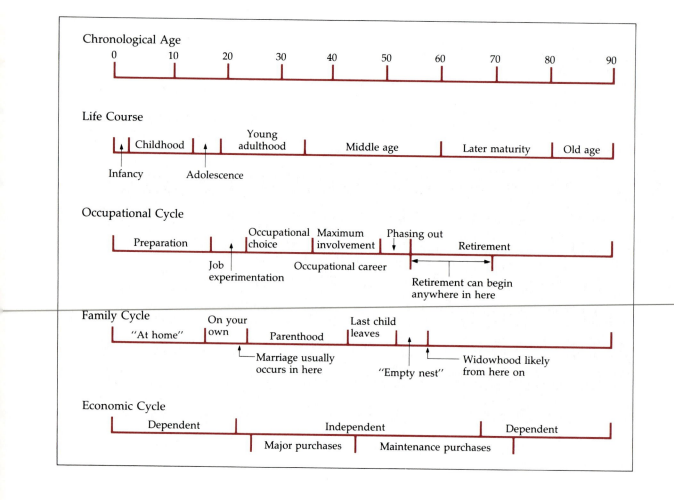

Another theorist, Harold Wilensky (1981), also sees the life course as a set of interlocking cycles of family life, work, consumer behavior, and social participation. Wilensky presents evidence showing that satisfaction over the life span results from the interaction of these various strands of behavior. Thus, maximum tension or low morale occur at points of "life cycle squeeze"—couples with preschool children; older couples, especially the prematurely retired; and solitary survivors. Perhaps the best metaphor for the life course is the musical one suggested by Riegel (1977). He compares the life course to a polyphonic musical composition in which there are various sequences of sound or melodies. Sometimes the themes are in harmony, but more often they are in discord.

Looking within each strand of the life course, researchers are now seeing more complexity than in the past. The family life cycle, or a person's working life, is not an inevitable, regular sequence of events, but rather a series of choices; each choice leads to further choices and closes off whole areas of experience. For example, becoming a lawyer is the outcome of a series of decisions: choosing an academic track in high school, going to college, choosing to work hard enough to qualify for admission to law school, dedicating effort and time to law school work, and studying to pass the bar. Becoming an unwed mother is also the outcome

A Vietnamese refugee family.

between psychologists, sociologists, anthropologists, historians, and demographers. Powerful new statistical techniques make it possible to describe and analyze the life course of a large population in ways that would have been impossible a few years ago.

And yet, as James Olney (1980) has pointed out, the *life course* is very different from a particular individual's *life history,* and very different indeed from our own lives. Olney contrasts biography with autobiography. There is a tremendous difference, he points out, between the story of a person's life told from the outside and from the inside. The inner view differs from even the most detailed biography of a life. Our own experience, as we live it, is not a matter of norms, stages, statistics, or curves on a graph. Nor do we live our lives as a matter of cause and effect—making a particular choice as adults because this or that event happened to us in childhood. But we do not necessarily have a clearer or more accurate view of our lives than an observer would. The views from inside and outside are simply that, different perspectives on the same complex reality. As students of human development, we need both views. We should not forget that behind the norms and statistics are individuals immersed in their own particular lives. But the study of human development can also broaden our understanding of our own and others' lives.

of a series of decisions: deciding to have premarital sex, deciding not to use contraceptives, deciding not to have an abortion (Furstenberg, 1976).

Recent studies of the life course are some of the most exciting developments in the social sciences. There is a new and lively interaction

SUMMARY

1. In recent years, developmental psychology has come to include the entire life span, not just children and adolescents. Part of the reason for this new interest in adulthood comes from changes in the life span and the distribution of ages in the population. America and other modern societies are "graying" as people live longer and birth rates drop. Further, in modern societies, people experience stages in the life span that did not exist in generations past—such as the "empty nest" period and retirement.

2. Both popular and scientific conceptions of adulthood have changed. Adulthood used to be thought of either as a "mythical plateau," a time of changelessness through several decades until the decline and deterioration of old age; or as mental and physical functioning peaking in the twenties, with steady decline after that point. More recently, researchers have come to realize that social and personality changes can occur across the life span. Biological decline is no longer taken for granted as the model for understanding change in adulthood.

3. Currently, there are a variety of theoretical and research approaches to life span development. Some researchers, influenced by Erikson, postulate a series of developmental stages occurring universally and at particular ages across the life cycle. These *life stage* theorists, who include Roger Gould, Daniel Levinson, and Gail Sheehy, believe that a midlife crisis is an inevitable part of the human life cycle. Other researchers are critical of the stage model of adulthood; they point out that the so-called stages of adult life are not comparable to the changes of childhood. Further, research has not documented the existence of such stages as midlife crisis across representative samples of the population.

   Researchers in the *life course* perspective focus on the timing and sequencing of major life transitions, such as finishing school, starting work, getting married, having children. They have discovered that different cohorts—people born at different times—have different patterns of these life transitions. Further, cohorts differ in a host of ways, depending on social, political, economic, and cultural changes in the society as a whole. As a result of these cohort changes, there is no single pattern or pure process of aging that is uninfluenced by a changing social context.

4. The bodily changes across adulthood are the most obvious signs of advancing age. Physical functioning reaches a peak in the twenties and begins to decline in the thirties. However, there is tremendous individual variation in physical aging; a person can be physically "older" or "younger" than his or her chronological age. Physical aging is also influenced by general health, diet, exercise, and so on.

5. Intellectual functioning in adults is currently the subject of much research as well as controversy. It used to be thought that intelligence declined markedly with age. Then researchers learned that this observed decline was an artifact of the cross-sectional method used to assess IQ. Older generations were less educated, and hence performed less well than younger ones. Longitudinal studies have revealed that IQ can actually rise through the middle years. The nature and degree of intellectual decline in old age is currently being debated. John Horn and his associates claim that *crystallized* intelligence—stored knowledge—remains high, but that *fluid* intelligence, involving the manipulation of new information, declines markedly with age. K. Warner Schaie and his associates dispute the extent and uniformity of intellectual decline in old age. Recently, researchers have discovered ways of compensating for the intellectual inefficiencies of old age.

6. There is as yet no widely accepted, integrated theory of the life course. Nevertheless, the study of human development across the life span is one of the most exciting areas of research in the social sciences. Researchers from many different fields are contributing new methods and findings.

Key Terms

crystallized intelligence **510**
fluid intelligence **510**
Hayflick limit **507**

life course **497**
life expectancy **506**
midlife crisis **514**

Glossary

accommodation   Adaptation to external reality by changing the self. A term used by Piaget to describe the process by which new information changes old schemes.

adolescence   The period of transition from childhood dependence and immaturity to the greater maturity and independence of adulthood. The period starts with puberty and roughly spans ages 12 to 21 in girls and 13 to 22 in boys. During this period, major changes occur at varying rates in sexual characteristics, body image, sexual interest, social roles, and intellectual development.

affordances   The functional properties of objects encountered by an organism in its own environment; e.g., a cave affords shelter, a branch affords support to a bird. A term used by J. J. Gibson.

anorexia nervosa   A persistent refusal of food, often accompanied by amenorrhea, vomiting, severe weight loss. The condition occurs most frequently in adolescent girls.

assimilation   Responding in a familiar, habitual way to a new situation. In Piaget's theory, the process of fitting new information into old schemes.

attachment   A close emotional relationship between two persons, characterized by mutual affection and a desire to maintain proximity. Bowlby uses the term in a narrower sense to refer to the infant's tie to the mother or other attachment figure as a source of security, especially when under stress.

attachment-in-the-making   Bowlby's term for the second stage of attachment. The period in infancy when the child can discriminate between strangers and familiar people, but does not show strong preferences. See **preattachment**, **clear-cut attachment**, **goal-corrected partnership**.

autistic, autism   A retreat from reality into a private world of fantasies, thoughts, and, in extreme cases, delusions and hallucinations. The autistic person is turned inward, a "shut-in" personality, completely preoccupied with his or her own needs and wishes, which are gratified largely or wholly in imagination.

autonomic nervous system   The part of the nervous system that governs involuntary actions and produces bodily response to emotional arousal.

behaviorism   A school of psychology founded by John B. Watson and based on the premise that only overt behavior should be studied, without reference to consciousness or mental processes.

blastocyst   The stage of the fertilized egg in which a layer of cells surrounds a fluid-filled cavity. See **embryo**, **fetus**.

bonding   A close attachment, or affiliation, between individuals. Recently used in a narrower sense to refer to the process of a mother and infant becoming attached in the hours after birth.

bulimia   An eating disorder involving repeated episodes of uncontrolled consumption of large quantities of food and drink in a short time followed by a depressed mood and self-deprecation, and in many cases attempts to lose weight by dieting or vomiting.

case study   An intensive study of one individual.

centeredness   According to Piaget, the tendency of the young child to focus on one particular aspect of a situation and ignore other relevant aspects.

centering   See **centeredness**.

chromosome   A ribbon of DNA in a cell's nucleus on which genes are strung like beads.

classical conditioning   A change of behavior so that what was once a neutral or natural stimulus takes on a new significance. See **instrumental conditioning**.

classification   The process of sorting objects into mutually exclusive categories.

clear-cut attachment   Bowlby's term for the third stage of attachment. The period from seven months into the second year when the infant shows strong preference for attachment figures. See **preattachment, attachment-in-the-making, goal-corrected partnership**.

cognitive-developmental model   General term for the model of development used by Piaget and his followers.

cohort   A group of people born at any specific time (e.g., the baby boomer generation).

concrete operational, concrete operations   Third Piagetian stage of development, lasting from approximately ages 7 to 11, in which a child acquires the ability to perform certain actions mentally ("operations"), to think more logically about real objects and experiences. See **sensorimotor, preoperational, formal operations, operational thought**.

conservation   Piaget's term for the awareness that physical qualities do not change in amount when they are altered in appearance.

contingency   A dependency relationship between events; the occurrence of one event is dependent on the occurrence of a prior event.

contingent   A dependent relationship between events, as between response and reward.

control group   A group of subjects in a study to whom no independent variables are introduced. It is used as a basis of comparison for the experimental group, which has the same makeup as the control group. See **experimental group**.

conventional level   Kohlberg's second and intermediate level of moral reasoning, characterized by identification with and conformity to the moral rules of family and society. See **preconventional level, postconventional level**.

convergent thinking   An aspect of critical thinking characterized by the search for a problem's best answer. The task is one of analyzing the alternatives to determine the most logical answer. See **divergent thinking**.

correlation   A statistical technique that indicates whether certain scores on one variable of a study will go along with the same scores on another variable.

cross-model association   The coordination of sensory inputs involving some combination of visual, auditory, and/or tactile stimulation.

cross-section   A representative sample. In the context of Chapter 2, a cross-sectional study is research done on people of several different ages.

cross-sequential   A research method that combines cross-sectional and longitudinal approaches, that is, a cross-section of ages followed over time.

crystallized intelligence   The ability to understand relations or solve problems that depend on knowledge acquired from schooling and other cultural influences.

deep structure   In linguistics, it is the meaning of a sentence; the grammatical relationship inherent in the words of a sentence that is not immediately apparent from the formal order of the words alone.

dependent variable   The outcome of an experiment, the change that results from the manipulation of the experimenter. See **independent variable**.

discrepancy   The difference between a stimulus and an existing schema. Moderate discrepancies attract more attention than either identical stimulus.

dishabituation   In studies of infant attention, the tendency to respond once again when a repeated stimulus changes. See **habituation**.

displacement   The property of language that makes it possible to refer to absent events and objects.

divergent thinking   An aspect of creative thinking characterized by the formulation of alternative solutions to problems. The task is to generate answers, rather than to analyze solutions logically that have already been formulated. See **convergent thinking**.

DNA   Abbreviation for deoxyribonucleic acid. The molecular basis for heredity; the determinant of growth and development of all living things.

dominance   The property of one of a pair of traits that suppresses the other. See **recessiveness**.

ecological validity   Direct relevance to real life.

ego   Freud's term that represents reason and common sense; the part of the personality recognized as the "I." See **id, superego**.

embryo   The fertilized egg that has divided into the blastocyst and implanted itself in the endometrium of the uterus. See **blastocyst, fetus**.

embryonic stage   The second period of fetal development, lasting about six weeks and covering the time when the blastocyst has implanted itself in the endometrium—forming the embryo—to when the embryo takes on a recognizable human form. See **germinal stage, fetal stage**.

epigenesis   A historical theory of development which held that an outside force exerted itself upon a formless substance to transform the substance into a recognizable shape. See **preformationism**.

ethologist   One who studies the relationship between an animal species and its total environment.

experience pattern   Escalona's term for the combination of child, parent, and environmental qualities and events that shape each child's development.

experimental group   The group that has its variables manipulated in an experiment. See **control group**.

experimental method   A method of study in which the researcher manipulates the variables. See **nonexperimental method**.

fetal stage   The third and final stage of prenatal development, lasting from the beginning of the third month in utero until birth. During this period, the fetus's skeleton calcifies, the organs are refined, and the fetus grows in size and weight. See **germinal stage**, **embryonic stage**.

fetus   The developing human from the eighth week to ninth month in utero. See **blastocyst**, **embryo**.

field experiment   An experimental method applied to a real-life setting.

five to seven shift   The period of striking progress in all aspects of a child's development between ages five to seven. Some of the changes are a decline in egocentrism, the ability to adopt the perspective of others, and vastly improved competence in communication.

fluid intelligence   The ability to perceive relations and solve relational problems of the type that are not taught and are relatively free of cultural influences.

formal operations   The fourth Piagetian stage of development, about age 11 or 12, in which the individual begins to think more rationally and systematically about abstract concepts and hypothetical events. Reason is freed from dependence on actual objects: the adolescent can think about thinking. See **sensorimotor, preoperations, concrete operations, operational thought**.

gender identity   A person's basic identification as either a boy or a girl. This is not to be confused with ''masculine'' or ''feminine'' actions or with sex-object preference.

genotype   The genetic makeup of an individual. See **phenotype**.

germinal stage   The first stage of prenatal development, lasting from fertilization of the egg until the many-celled egg, or blastocyst, implants itself in the endometrium of the uterus. See **embryonic stage**, **fetal stage**.

goal-corrected partnership   According to Bowlby, the fourth stage of attachment, when the child realizes the parent is a person with her or his own goals and motives. See **preattachment, attachment-in-the-making, clear-cut attachment**.

goodness of fit   A term used to describe how well a child's temperament fits with his or her parents' expectations and the environment.

habituation   The process of growing accustomed to a situation or pattern of behavior. The organism eventually stops responding to a stimulus that is repeated over and over. See **dishabituation**.

Hayflick limit   The limit on the number of times a cell can divide.

heritability   The capacity to be inherited; an estimate, based on a sample of individuals, of the relative contribution of genetics to a given trait or function.

holophrase   A single-word utterance that represents an entire sentence's meaning (e.g., ''Mama,'' ''Milk''). Spoken by children 18 months or younger.

hypothesis   A proposition that must be tested or proved.

id   Freudian concept of that portion of the personality that represents blind impulse and energy and operates according to the pleasure principle. See **ego, superego**.

identification   A psychological process in which a person assimilates aspects of another person to the self. To psychoanalysts, it transforms the person in many ways; personality is formed through a series of identifications.

identity   The sense of personal continuity and sameness, of knowing who and what one is psychologically and in relation to other people and society.

identity crisis   Defined by Erikson as an anxiety state experienced primarily by adolescents who find it difficult to establish a clearly defined personal identity and a consistent role in society.

implicit psychology   Commonsense, often unspoken beliefs held by the average person about psychological functioning.

imprinting   The instinctive process by which animals—most commonly birds—follow and become attached to whatever object is close to them at a critical time shortly after birth.

independent variable   The stimulus or situation in an experiment that the researcher manipulates; the variable that is ''causing'' an effect. See **dependent variable**.

instrumental conditioning   The behaviorist theory that voluntary behavior followed by a reward tends to be repeated; behavior will not be repeated if unrewarded over a period of time. See **classical conditioning**.

interactional model   According to Sameroff, a model of development that combines personal *and* environmental features to explain a child's development. See **main effects model, transactional model**.

invariant   The quality of remaining constant under varying conditions.

labeling theory   The view that a label may have a significant effect on behavior. E.g., describing an individual as deviant tends to become an automatic, self-fulfilling prophecy that may result in mental disorder or delinquency.

Language Acquisition Device (LAD)   A set of linguistic processing skills that nativists (e.g., Chomsky) believe to be innate; presumably the LAD enables a child to infer the rules governing other's speech and then to use these rules to produce language.

law of large numbers   The likelihood that, the greater the sample taken in a study, the greater accuracy of the results.

libido   Freudian term for sexual energy.

life course   The individual's life as a whole, especially in relation to major points of transition, such as entering school, leaving home, getting married, starting a career, becoming a parent, retiring, etc.

life expectancy   The average number of years a person can expect to live, based on age, sex, nationality, etc.

life history   A case study of a large portion of a person's life course.

life span   The precise length of an individual's life or the typical duration in the life of a species.

longitudinal   A type of study that gains information on subjects by following them over a long period of time.

main effects model   According to Sameroff, a model of development that sees either the environment *or* the child's traits as the major influence on development. See **interactional model, transactional model**.

maternal deprivation   A lack of adequate affection, care, and stimulation from the mother or mother substitute, particularly during infancy. Often occurs in disturbed families and in institutions and may have detrimental effects on aspects of the child's personality and emotional and intellectual development. It may lay the basis for severe mental disorder.

meiosis   A stage in the production of ova and spermatozoa in which each daughter cell contains only one of each pair of chromosomes from the original diploid set in the parental gonads. During fertilization, the ova and spermatozoa fuse to restore the double set of chromosomes within the nucleus of the newly formed zygote. See **mitosis**.

menarche   A girl's first menstrual period.

metacognition   Thinking about thinking.

metamemory   One's knowledge about memory and memory processes.

midlife crisis   A psychological crisis occurring during the middle years, roughly 45 to 60. Frequently mentioned traumatic events for women are menopause and the departure of children from the home; and for men, health problems, sexual concerns, and career troubles.

mitosis   The process by which a body cell reproduces by dividing into two daughter cells, each having the same number and kinds of chromosomes. See **meiosis**.

moral judgment   The beliefs an individual applies in discriminating between right and wrong; the attitudes that comprise a person's moral orientation whether or not they govern behavior in each situation.

morpheme   The smallest meaningful units of language. These include words and grammatical markers such as prefixes, suffixes, and verb-tense modifiers.

nativist   The nature side of the nature-nurture debate; the belief that individual differences in personality are due to constitutional and genetic factors.

natural experiment   An experiment in which the subjects are exposed to unusual conditions that are not manipulated by the researcher.

naturalistic   A method of study that observes and describes behavior in its natural context.

noncontingent   Term referring to a lack of relationship between events.

nonexperimental method   A method of study in which the researcher randomizes the variables so they will not have an effect on the outcome. See **experimental method**.

object permanence   The knowledge that an object continues to exist when it is out of sight. A term used by Piaget.

Oedipal conflict   Freud's term for the stage a four- or five-year-old boy goes through in developing a sexual identity as well as a conscience and a set of ideals for the self. Simply put, a boy's love for his mother is offset by fear of his father's revenge.

Terrified that his father will castrate him, the boy renounces his desire for his mother and identifies with his father.

operation, operations   According to Piaget, mental manipulations of information, such as adding, subtracting, reversing, ordering, etc.

operational thought   Piaget's term for the most advanced stage of cognitive development. During this stage, the individual can manipulate and transform information systematically and logically. See **sensorimotor**, **preoperational**, **concrete operational**, **formal operations**.

personality perception   The process of forming impressions of other people's personal qualities.

phenotype   The physical characteristics of an individual. See **genotype**.

phoneme   The basic units of sound that are used in a spoken language.

phonology   The sound system of a language and the rules for combining these sounds to produce meaningful units of speech.

placenta   An organ, formed from the lining of the uterus with the membranes of the fetus. It provides for the nourishment of the fetus and the elimination of metabolic wastes.

postconventional level   Kohlberg's third and highest level of moral reasoning characterized by commitment to valid moral principles sustained independently of any identification with family, group, or country. See **preconventional level**, **conventional level**.

postterm   A birth that occurs more than 293 days, or 42 weeks, after the onset of the mother's last menstrual period. See **term**, **preterm**.

pragmatics   Principles that underlie the effective and appropriate use of language in social contexts.

preattachment   According to Bowlby, the first stage of attachment: a phase in infancy before the child can discriminate between familiar and unfamiliar people. See **attachment-in-the-making**, **clear-cut attachment**, **goal-corrected partnership**.

preconventional level   Kohlberg's first level of moral reasoning characteristic of children and marked by obedience, unquestioning acceptance of parent's moral definitions, and evaluation of an act's material consequences only. See **conventional level**, **postconventional level**.

preformationism   A historical theory of development which held that miniature replicas of the adult organism were contained in the germ cells. See **epigenesis**.

preoperational, preoperations   The second Piagetian stage of development, taking place from about 18 months to 7 years of age, in which the child learns to use language, symbols, and mental imagery. See **sensorimotor**, **concrete operational**, **formal operations**, **operational thought**.

preterm   A birth that occurs fewer than 259 days after the onset of the mother's last mentrual period. See **term**, **postterm**.

primary circular reaction   Piaget's term for an early repetitive action centered on the infant's own body, i. e., discovered by chance and performed over and over, such as grasping, kicking, vocalizing. It indicates a primitive link between goal and action. See **secondary circular reaction**, **tertiary circular reaction**.

primary process   Freudian theory of the type of thinking that is found in dreams and hallucinations. It is visual and blurs the distinction between real and unreal, past and present. See **secondary process**.

productivity   In the context of Chapter 8, the ability to combine individual words to produce an unlimited number of sentences.

protoconversation   The back-and-forth vocalizing between infants and parents that paves the way for language use.

psychosexual theory   Descriptive term for Freud's developmental theory which states that the driving force in a child's development is sexual energy. See **psychosocial theory**.

psychosocial theory   The type of developmental theory, such as that espoused by Erikson, that defines a child's development as the process of social interaction between the child and his or her parents (or other emotionally significant people). See **psychosexual theory**.

puberty   The point at which a person reaches sexual maturity and is physically capable of fathering or conceiving a child.

recessiveness   The property of one of a pair of traits that is dominated by the other of the pair. See **dominance**.

releasor stimulus   An event or action that evokes a particular behavior in all members of a species.

role taking   The ability to take the role or viewpoint of another person. It is an essential process in cognitive and social development.

schema   The psychological term for mental representation of experience. The plural is sometimes called schemata. See **scheme**.

scheme   A Piagetian term for an infant's concepts in the sensorimotor period. These are action patterns—sucking, grasping—as well as the inner, mental basis for the action. See **schema**.

secondary circular reaction   Piaget's term for a repetitive action that signifies the infant's aim of making things happen. The infant engages in actions that have yielded results in the past but is not able to coordinate them to meet the requirements of a new situation. See **primary circular reaction**, **tertiary circular reaction**.

secondary process   Freudian term for the type of thinking that is based on logic and reason, and thus makes the distinction between real and not real, past and present. It becomes the normal, waking mode of thought after infancy. See **primary process**.

second-order thinking   A feature of Piaget's formal operations. The ability to manipulate representations of reality, e.g., to understand proportions and analogies. See **formal operations**.

secular trend   The main trend or direction of a time series, as distinguished from temporary or seasonal variations.

self   The person as seen from his or her own point of view; most psychologists accept William James's distinction between two aspects of the self—the "I" (the subjective awareness of self) and the "Me" (the self-concept; the self as it might be viewed by another person).

semanticity   One of the three formal properties of language. The learning of meanings of words and the process of communicating meaning through language.

semantics   The meaning of words and sentences.

sensorimotor   First Piagetian stage in cognitive development of the child, lasting from birth to about 18 months. The infant learns to combine and coordinate certain elementary schemas and thus becomes increasingly organized, purposeful, and intelligent. See **preoperational**, **concrete operational**, **formal operations**, **operational thought**.

separation anxiety   A wary or fretful reaction that infants often display when separated from their attachment figures.

seriation   A cognitive operation that allows one to order a set of stimuli along a quantifiable dimension such as height or weight.

significance   The fact that a particular finding in a study is unlikely to have happened by chance.

social cognition   The ability to understand the thoughts, feelings, motives, and intentions of oneself and other people.

social learning model   An approach to the study of behavior in which behavior is assumed to be developed and regulated (1) by external stimulus events, such as the influence of other individuals; (2) by external reinforcement, such as praise, blame, and rewards; and, most important (3) by the effects of cognitive processes, such as thinking and judgment, on the individual's behavior and on the environment that influences him or her.

social learning theory   Modern psychological theory which questions how behavior is acquired in the first place.

socialization   Acquisition of roles, behavior, and attitudes expected of the individual in society.

stimulus-response (S-R)   A learning theory based on behaviorism.

strange situation   Laboratory test devised by Mary Ainsworth to assess a child's attachment to a parent.

stranger anxiety   A wary or fretful reaction that infants often display when approached by an unfamiliar person.

structure dependence   The property of language that makes meaning dependent on word order or some other structural feature.

superego   Freudian term for the part of the personality that watches and judges the ego; it represents the rules and standards of adult society as they are transmitted by parents. See **ego**, **id**.

surface structure   The linear relationship between the words of a sentence, i.e., the relationship that is merely formal or grammatically consistent. It may not reveal the underlying grammatical structure.

syllogism   A form of reasoning in which a major and a minor premise yield a conclusion that is true only if the two premises are true (e.g., If A is greater than B and B is greater than C, then A is greater than C).

symbiotic   Term used by Mahler and others to refer to a stage in early infancy when the infant sees no separation between self and mother.

symbol(s)   Any object, figure, or image that represents something else.

syntax   The structure of language; the rules specifying how words and grammatical markers are to be combined to produce meaningful sentences.

temperament   The individual's general style of behavior; includes energy and activity levels, emotionality, intensity and tempo of response, quality of mood, sociability, etc.

term   The length of the normal pregnancy or gestation period. The average term in humans is 40

weeks, or 280 days, measured from the first day of the last menstrual period, but a range of 259 to 293 days is considered normal. See **preterm**, **postterm**.

tertiary circular reaction   Piaget's term for an infant's action, usually emerging near the beginning of the second year, that creatively alters former schemes to fit the requirements of new situations. See **primary circular reaction**, **secondary circular reaction**.

transactional model   According to Sameroff, a model of development that views both the child and the environment as constantly *changing*, active influences on one another. See **interactional model**, **main effects model**.

transitivity   (1) An illusory transfer of symptoms or other characteristics to other people, e.g., a schizophrenic patient's belief that other persons are also experiencing his hallucinations, are also being persecuted, or are also lacking a stomach or another internal organ; (2) The ability to recognize relations among elements in a serial order.

transsexual   A man or woman who believes that he or she is psychologically a member of the opposite sex and anatomically in the ''wrong'' body.

unconscious   In psychoanalytic theory, the part of the mind that contains memories, emotional conflicts, wishes, and repressed impulses that are not directly accessible to awareness, but which have dynamic effects on thought and behavior.

variables   The elements in an experiment that are allowed to change. See **dependent variable**, **independent variable**.

zygote   A single cell formed at conception from the union of a sperm and an ovum. See **blastocyst**.

References

Able, T. E., & Jaffe, N. F. (1950). Cultural background of female puberty. *American Journal of Psychotherapy, 4,* 90–113.

Adams, G. R. (1977). Physical attractiveness research: Toward a developmental social psychology of beauty. *Human Development, 20,* 217–239.

Adelson, J. (1979). Adolescence and the generalization group. *Psychology Today, 12*(9), 33–37.

Ahrens, R. (1954). Beitrage zur eintwicklung des physiognomie—und mimikerkennes. *Zeitschrift für Experimentelle und Angewandte Psychologie, 2,* 412–494, 599–633.

Ainsworth, M.D.S. (1963). The development of mother-infant interaction among the Ganda. In B. M. Foss (Ed.), *Determinants of infant behavior* (Vol. 4). London: Methuen.

Ainsworth, M.D.S. (1967). *Infancy in Uganda: Infant care and the growth of love.* Baltimore: Johns Hopkins University Press.

Ainsworth, M.D.S. (1973). The development of infant-mother attachment. In B. M. Caldwell & H. N. Ricciuti (Eds.), *Review of child development research* (Vol. 3, pp. 1–94). Chicago: University of Chicago Press.

Ainsworth, M.D.S. (1982). Attachment: retrospect and prospect. In C. M. Parkes & J. Stevenson-Hinde (Eds.), *The place of attachment in human behavior.* New York: Basic Books.

Ainsworth, M.D.S., & Bell, S. M. (1970). Attachment, exploration, and separation: Illustrated by the behavior of one-year-olds in a strange situation. *Child Development, 41,* 49–67.

Ainsworth, M.D.S., Bell, S. M., & Stayton, D. J. (1971). Individual differences in strange-situation behavior in one-year-olds. In H. R. Schaffer (Ed.), *The origins of human social relations.* London: Academic Press.

Ainsworth, M.D.S., Blehar, M., Waters, E., & Wall, S. (1978). *Patterns of attachment.* Hillsdale, NJ: Erlbaum.

Ainsworth, M.D.S., & Wittig, B. A. (1969). Attachment and exploratory behavior of one-year-olds in a strange situation. In B. M. Foss (Ed.), *Determinants of infant behaviour* (Vol. 4). London: Methuen.

Alexander, B. K., & Harlow, H. F. (1965). Social behaviors in juvenile rhesus monkeys subjected to different rearing conditions during the first 6 months of life. *Zoologische Jarbucher Psysiologie, 60,* 167–174.

Allen, V. C. (1976). *Children as teachers: Theory and research on tutoring.* New York: Academic Press.

Allport, G. W. (1937). *Personality: A psychological interpretation.* New York: Holt, Rinehart & Winston.

Allred, G. H., Harper, J. M., & Wadham, R. A. (1984). Physics and the behavioral sciences. In R. J. Corsini (Ed.), *Encyclopedia of psychology* (Vol. 3). New York: Wiley.

Alvarez, A. (1971). *The savage God: A study of suicide.* New York: Random House.

Amsterdam, B. K. (1972). Mirror self-image reactions before age two. *Developmental Psychology, 5,* 297–305.

Anastasi, A. (1958). Heredity, environment and the question "How?" *Psychological Review, 65,* 197–208.

Anglin, J. (1977). *Word, object, and conceptual development.* New York: Norton.

Annis, L. F. (1978). *The child before birth.* Ithaca, NY: Cornell University Press.

Antinucci, F., & Parisi, D. (1973). Early language acquisition: A model and some data. In C. A. Ferguson & D. I. Slobin (Eds.), *Studies of child language development* (pp. 607–619). New York: Holt, Rinehart & Winston.

Antonucci, T. (1976). Attachment: A life-span concept. *Human Development, 19,* 135–142.

Antonucci, T., Tamir, L. M., & Dubnoff, S. (1980). Mental health across the family life cycle. In K. W. Back (Ed.), *Life course: Integrative theories and exemplary populations* (AAAS

Selected Symposium 41). Boulder, CO: Westview Press for the American Association for the Advancement of Science.

Appel, A., Jr. (1983). *Signs of life*. New York: Knopf.

Archer, D., Iritani, B., Kimes, D. D., & Barrios, M. (1983). Face-ism: Five studies of sex differences in facial prominence. *Journal of Personality and Social Psychology, 45,* 725–735.

Arend, R., Gove, F., & Sroufe, L. A. (1981). Continuity of individual adaptation from infancy to kindergarten: A predictive study of ego-resiliency and curiosity in preschoolers. *Child Development, 50,* 950–959.

Argyle, M. (1972). *The psychology of interpersonal behavior*. London: Penguin.

Argyle, M., & Furnham, A. (1983). Sources of satisfaction and conflict in long-term relationships. *Journal of Marriage and the Family, 45*(3), 481–493.

Ariès, P. (1962). *Centuries of childhood: A social history of family life* (R. Baldick, Trans.). New York: Vintage Books. (Originally published 1960)

Ariès, P. (1981). *The hour of our death*. New York: Knopf.

Aronson, E., & Rosenbloom, S. (1971). Space perception in early infancy: Perception with a common auditory-visual space. *Science, 172,* 1161–1163.

Asher, S. R., & Hymel, S. (1981). Children's social competence in peer relations: Sociometric and behavioral assessments. In J. D. Wine & M. D. Singe (Eds.), *Social competence*. New York: Guilford Press.

Aslin, R. N., Pisoni, D. B., & Jusczyk, P. W. (1983). Auditory development and speech perception in infancy. In P. H. Mussen (Ed.), *Handbook of child psychology: Vol. 2. Infancy and developmental psychobiology* (pp. 573–687). New York: Wiley.

Atchley, R. (1975). The life course, age grading, and age-linked demands for decision making. In N. Datan & L. H. Ginsberg (Eds.), *Life-span developmental psychology: Normative life crises* (pp. 261–278). New York: Academic Press.

Babson, S. G., & Benson, R. C. (1971). *Management of high risk pregnancy and intensive care of the neonate*. St. Louis: C. V. Mosby.

Babson, S. G., Pernoll, M. L., Benda, G. I., & Simpson, K. (1980). *Diagnosis and management of the fetus and neonate at risk: A guide for team care* (4th ed.). St. Louis: C. V. Mosby.

Back, K. (1980). *Life course: Integrative theories and exemplary populations* (AAAS Selected Symposium 41). Boulder, CO: Westview Press for the American Association for the Advancement of Science.

Bakan, D. (1971). Adolescence in America: From ideal to social fact. *Daedalus, 100,* 979–995.

Baldwin, A. (1968). *Theories of development*. New York: Wiley.

Baldwin, J. M. (1895). *Mental development and the child and the race, method and processes*. New York: Macmillan.

Baldwin, J. M. (1906). *Social and ethical interpretations of mental development*. New York: Macmillan.

Baltes, P. B. (1979). Life-span developmental psychology: Some converging observations on history and theory. In P. B. Baltes & O. G. Brim, Jr. (Eds.), *Life-span development and behavior* (Vol. 2). New York: Academic Press.

Baltes, P. B., & Brim, O. G., Jr. (Eds.). (1978–1983). *Life-span development and behavior* (Vols. 1–5). New York: Academic Press.

Baltes, P. B., Cornelius, S. W., & Nesselroade, J. R. (1979). Cohort effects in developmental psychology. In J. R. Nesselroade & P. B. Baltes (Eds.), *Longitudinal research in the study of behavior and development*. New York: Academic Press.

Baltes, P. B., & Nesselroade, J. R. (1984). Paradigm lost and paradigm regained: Critique of Dannefer's portrayal of life-span developmental psychology. *American Sociological Review, 49*(6), 841–847.

Baltes, P. B., Reese, H. W., & Nesselroade, J. R. (1977). *Life-span developmental psychology: An introduction to research methods*. Monterey, CA: Brooks/Cole.

Baltes, P. B., & Schaie, K. W. (1976). On the plasticity of intelligence in adulthood and old age: Where Horn and Donaldson fail. *American Psychologist, 31,* 720–725.

Baltes, P. B., & Willis, S. L. (1977). Toward psychological theories of aging and development. In J. E. Birren & K. W. Schaie (Eds.), *Handbook of the psychology of aging*, Belmont, CA: Wadsworth.

Baltes, P. B., & Willis, S. L. (1979). Life-span developmental psychology, cognitive functioning and social policy. In M. W. Riley (Ed.), *Aging and birth to death: Interdisciplinary perspectives* (AAAS Selected Symposium 30, pp. 15–46). Boulder, CO: Westview Press for the American Association for the Advancement of Science.

Bandura, A. (1969). Social-learning theory of identificatory processes. In D. A. Goslin (Ed.), *Handbook of socialization theory and research*. Chicago: Rand McNally.

Bandura, A., Ross, D., & Ross, S. A. (1963). Imitation of film-mediated aggressive models. *Journal of Abnormal and Social Psychology, 66,* 3–11.

Bandura, A., & Walters, R. H. (1963). *Social learning and personality development*. New York: Holt, Rinehart & Winston.

Banks, M. S. (1980). The development of visual accommodation during early infancy. *Child Development, 51*, 646–666.

Banks, M. S., & Salapatek, P. (1983). Infant visual perception. In P. H. Mussen (Ed.), *Handbook of child psychology: Vol. 2. Infancy and developmental psychobiology* (4th ed.). New York: Wiley.

Bannister, D., & Agnew, J. (1977). The child's construing of self. In J. K. Cole & A. W. Landfield (Eds.), *Nebraska Symposium on Motivation 1976* (Vol. 24). Lincoln: University of Nebraska Press.

Barker, R. G. (1968). *Ecological psychology: Concepts and methods for studying the environment of human behavior*. Stanford: Stanford University Press.

Barker, R. G., et al. (1966). *One boy's day*. Hamden, CT: Shoe String Press. (Reprint of 1951 edition)

Bates, E., (1976). *Language and context: The acquisition of pragmatics*. New York: Academic Press.

Bates, E., Benigni, L., Bretherton, I., Camaioni, L., & Volterra, V. (1977). From gesture to the first word: On cognitive and social prerequisites. In M. Lewis & L. Rosenblum (Eds.), *Interaction, conservation and the development of language* (pp. 247–307). New York: Wiley.

Bates, J. E. (1980). The concept of difficult temperament. *Merrill-Palmer Quarterly, 26*, 299–319.

Bauer, D. H. (1976). An exploratory study of developmental changes in children's fears. *Journal of Child Psychology and Psychiatry, 117*, 69–74.

Baumrind, D. (1971). Current patterns of parental authority. *Developmental Psychology Monograph, 4*(1, Pt. 2), 79–103.

Baumrind, D. (1973). The development of instrumental competence through socialization. In A. D. Pick (Ed.), *Minnesota Symposia on Child Psychology* (Vol. 7). Minneapolis: University of Minnesota Press.

Baumrind, D. (in press). Sex differences in moral reasoning: Response to Walker's (1984) conclusion that there are none. *Child Development*.

Becker, E. (1973). *The denial of death*. New York: Free Press.

Becker, H. (1963). *Outsiders: Studies in the sociology of deviance*. New York: Free Press.

Becker, W. C. (1964). Consequences of different kinds of parental discipline. In M. L. Hoffman & L. W. Hoffman (Eds.), *Review of child development research* (Vol. 1). New York: Russell Sage Foundation.

Beckwith, L. (1979). Prediction of emotional and social behavior. In J. D. Osofsky (Ed.), *Handbook of infant development* (pp. 707–741). New York: Wiley.

Bell, A., & Weinberg, M. (1978). *Homosexualities: A study of diversity among men and women*. New York: Simon & Schuster.

Bell, R. Q. (1968). A reinterpretation of the direction of effects in studies of socialization. *Psychological Review, 75*, 81–95.

Bell, R. Q. (1974). Contributions of human infants to caregiving and social interaction. In M. Lewis & L. A. Rosenblum (Eds.), *The effect of the infant on its caregiver*. New York: Wiley.

Bell, R. Q. (1977). Human infant—effects in the first year. In R. Q. Bell & L. V. Harper (Eds.), *Child effects on adults* (pp. 122–148). Hillsdale, NJ: Erlbaum.

Bell, R. Q. (1979). Parent, child, and reciprocal influences. *American Psychologist, 34*, 821–826.

Bell, R. Q., & Harper, L. V. (1977). *Child effects on adults*. Hillsdale, NJ: Erlbaum.

Bell, S. M., & Ainsworth, M.D.S. (1972). Infant crying and maternal responsiveness. *Child Development, 43*, 1171–1190.

Bellah, R. N., Madsen, R., Sullivan, W. H., Swidler, A., & Tipton, S. A. (1985). *Habits of the heart*. Berkeley: University of California Press.

Belmont, N. (1976). Levana: Or how to raise up children. In R. Forster & O. Ranum (Trans. and Eds.), *Family and society*. Baltimore: Johns Hopkins University Press.

Bem, D., & Funder, D. (1978). Predicting more of the people more of the time: Assessing the personality of situations. *Psychological Review, 85*, 485–501.

Bem, S. L. (1981). Gender scheme theory: A cognitive account of sex typing. *Psychological Review, 88*, 354–364.

Benedict, R. (1938). Continuities and discontinuities in cultural conditioning. *Psychiatry, 1*, 161–167.

Berg, M., & Medrich, E. A. (1977). Children in five neighborhoods: Working paper. (Children's Time Study, Schools of Law and Education, University of California, Berkeley)

Berg, M., & Medrich, E. A. (1980). Children in four neighborhoods: The physical environment and its effect on play and play patterns. *Environment and Behavior, 12*(3), 320–348.

Berger, K. S. (1980). *The developing person*. New York: Worth.

Bergler, E. (1964). *Parents not guilty of their children's neuroses*. New York: Liveright.

Berlyne, D. E. (1960). *Conflict, arousal and curiosity*. New York: McGraw-Hill.

Bernard, J. (1982). *The future of marriage.* New Haven: Yale University Press.

Bernstein, A. C., & Cowan, P. A. (1975). Children's concepts of how people get babies. *Child Development, 46,* 77–91.

Bernstein, B. (1975). *Class, codes, and control: Vol. 3. Towards a theory of educational transmissions.* London: Routledge & Kegan Paul.

Berry, D. S., & McArthur, L. Z. (1985). Some components and consequences of a baby face. *Journal of Personality and Social Psychology, 48,* 312–323.

Berry, J. W., & Dasen, P. (Eds.). (1974). *Culture and cognition: Readings in cross-cultural psychology.* London: Methuen.

Berscheid, E. (1983). Emotion. In H. H. Kelley, E. Berscheid, A. Christensen, J. H. Harvey, T. L. Huston, G. Levinger, E. McClintock, L. A. Peplau, & D. R. Peterson (Eds.), *Close relationships.* New York: W. H. Freeman.

Berscheid, E., & Walster, E. (1974). Physical attractiveness. In L. Berkowitz (Ed.), *Advances in experimental social psychology* (Vol. 7). New York: Academic Press.

Berscheid, E., Walster, E., Dion, E., & Walster, G. W. (1971). Physical attractiveness and dating choice: A test of the matching hypothesis. *Journal of Experimental Social Psychology, 7,* 173–189.

Birren, J. E., Butler, R. N., Greenhouse, S. W., Sokoloff, L., & Yarrow, M. R. (Eds.). (1963). *Human aging: A biological and behavioral study* (Publication No. HSM 71–9051). Washington, DC: Government Printing Office.

Blakemore, C. (1977). *Mechanics of the mind.* New York: Cambridge University Press.

Blasi, A. (1983). The self and cognition: The roles of the self in the acquisition of knowledge, and the role of cognition in the development of the self. In B. Lee & G. G. Noam (Eds.), *Developmental approaches to the self.* New York: Plenum Press.

Blau, P. M., & Duncan, G. D. (1967). *The American occupational structure.* New York: Wiley.

Block, J. (1961). *The Q-sort method in personality assessment and psychiatric research.* Springfield, IL: Charles C. Thomas.

Block, J., & Haan, N. (1971). *Lives through time.* Berkeley: Bancroft Books.

Bloom, B. (1964). *Stability and change in human characteristics.* New York: Wiley.

Bloom, F. E., Lazerson, A., & Hofstadter, L. (1985). *Brain, mind, and behavior.* New York: W. H. Freeman.

Bloom, L. (1973). *One word at a time: The use of single word utterances before syntax.* The Hague: Mouton.

Bloom, L., Lightbown, P., & Hood, L. (1975). Structure and variation in child language. *Monographs of the Society for Research in Child Development, 40*(Serial No. 160).

Blos, P. (1962). *On adolescence: A psychoanalytic interpretation.* New York: Free Press.

Blythe, R. (1979). *The view in winter: Reflections on old age.* New York: Harcourt Brace Jovanovich.

Bodmer, W. F., & Cavalli-Sforza, L. L. (1976). *Genetics, evolution, and man.* San Francisco: W. H. Freeman.

Borke, H. (1975). Piaget's mountains revisited: Changes in the egocentric landscape. *Developmental Psychology, 11*(2), 240–243.

Borke, H. (1978). Piaget's view of social interaction and the theoretical construct of empathy. In L. Siegel & C. J. Brainerd (Eds.), *Alternatives to Piaget: Critical essays on the theory* (pp. 29–42). New York: Academic Press.

Bornstein, M. H. (1975). Qualities of color vision in infancy. *Journal of Experimental Child Psychology, 19,* 401–419.

Botwinick, J. (1977). Intelligence and aging. In J. E. Birren & K. W. Schaie (Eds.), *Handbook of the psychology of aging.* New York: Van Nostrand Reinhold.

Bower, T.G.R. (1977). *A primer of infant development.* San Francisco: W. H. Freeman.

Bowlby, J. (1951). *Maternal care and mental health* (World Health Organization Monograph Series No. 2). Geneva: World Health Organization. (Reprinted by Schocken Books 1966)

Bowlby, J. (1952). *Maternal care and mental health.* Report for the World Health Organization, Geneva. (Reprinted by Schocken Books 1966)

Bowlby, J. (1958). The nature of the child's tie to his mother. *International Journal of Psychoanalysis, 39,* 350–373.

Bowlby, J. (1960). Separation anxiety. *International Journal of Psychoanalysis, 41,* 89–113.

Bowlby, J. (1969). *Attachment: Attachment and loss* (Vol. 1). New York: Basic Books.

Bowlby, J. (1973). *Separation: Anxiety and anger* (Vol. 2). New York: Basic Books.

Bowlby, J. (1977). The making and breaking of affectional bonds. *British Journal of Psychiatry, 130,* 421–431.

Bowlby, J. (1980). *Loss: Sadness and depression* (Vol. 3). New York: Basic Books.

Bowlby, J. (1982). Attachment and loss: Retrospect and prospect. *American Journal of Orthopsychiatry, 52*(4), 664–678.

Brainerd, C. J. (1978). *Piaget's theory of intelligence.* Englewood Cliffs, NJ: Prentice-Hall.

Branigan, G. (1977). *Some early constraints on word combinations.* Unpublished doctoral dissertation, Boston University.

Breitmayer, B. J., & Ricciuti, H. N. (1983). *Impact of neonatal temperament on care-giver behavior.* Paper presented at the biennial meeting, Society for Research in Child Development.

Breland, K., & Breland, M. (1961). The misbehavior of organisms. *American Psychologist, 16,* 681–684.

Bretherton, I. (in press). Attachment theory: Retrospect and prospect. *Monographs of the Society for Research in Child Development.*

Bretherton, I., & Bates, E. (1979). The emergence of intentional communication. In I. C. Uzgiris (Ed.), *New directions for child development: No. 4. Social interaction and communication during infancy* (pp. 81–100). San Francisco: Jossey-Bass.

Brim, O. G., Jr. (1976). Life-span development of the theory of oneself: Implications for child development. In H. Reese (Ed.), *Advances in child development and behavior* (Vol. 2, pp. 241–251). New York: Academic Press.

Brim, O. G., & Kagan, J. (1980). *Constancy and change in human development.* Cambridge, MA: Harvard University Press.

Brody, J. E. (1983, April 1). Bonding at birth. *San Francisco Chronicle,* p. 25.

Bronfenbrenner, U. (1958). Socialization and social class through time and space. In E. E. Maccoby, T. M. Newcomb, & E. L. Hartley (Eds.), *Readings in social psychology.* New York: Holt, Rinehart & Winston.

Bronfenbrenner, U. (1974). Developmental research, public policy and the ecology of childhood. *Child Development, 45,* 1–5.

Bronfenbrenner, U. (1979). *The ecology of human development: Experiments by nature and design.* Cambridge, MA: Harvard University Press.

Bronfenbrenner, U. (Ed.) (with M. A. Mahoney). (1972). *Influences on human development.* Hillsdale, IL: Dryden Press.

Bronowski, J. (1973). *The ascent of man.* Boston: Little, Brown.

Bronowski, J. (1978). *The origins of knowledge and imagination.* New Haven: Yale University Press.

Bronson, G. (1974). The postnatal growth of visual capacity. *Child Development, 45,* 873–890.

Bronson, W. C. (1966). Early antecedents of emotional expressiveness and reactivity-control. *Child Development, 37,* 793–810.

Brooks-Gunn, J., Ruble, D. N., & Clarke, E. (1977). College women's attitudes and expectations concerning menstrual-related changes. *Psychosomatic Medicine, 39,* 288–298.

Broughton, J. M. (1978). Development of concepts of self, mind, reality, and knowledge. In W. Damon (Ed.), *New directions for child development: Social cognition* (No. 1, pp. 75–100). San Francisco: Jossey-Bass.

Broughton, J. M. (1983). The cognitive-developmental theory of adolescent self and identity. In B. Lee & G. G. Noam (Eds.), *Developmental approaches to the self* (pp. 215–266). New York: Plenum Press.

Broughton, J. M., & Riegel, K. F. (1977). Developmental psychology and the self. *Annals of the New York Academy of the Sciences, 291,* 149–167.

Brown, A. L., & Deloache, J. S. (1978). Skills, plans, and self-regulation. In R. S. Siegler (Ed.), *Children's thinking: What develops?* (pp. 3–35). Hillsdale, NJ: Erlbaum.

Brown, R. (1958). *Words and things.* New York: Free Press.

Brown, R. (1965). *Social psychology.* New York: Free Press.

Brown, R. (1973). *A first language: The early stages.* Cambridge, MA: Harvard University Press.

Brown, R. (1975). See chapters 5, 6, 9, 11, 12, and 13 in R. Brown & R. J. Herrnstein (Eds.), *Psychology.* Boston: Little, Brown.

Brown, R., Cazden, C. B., & Bellugi, U. (1969). The child's grammar from 1 to 3. In J. S. Hill (Ed.), *Minnesota Symposia on Child Psychology,* (Vol. 2, pp. 28–73). Minneapolis: University of Minnesota Press.

Brown, R., & Hanlon C. (1970). Deviational complexity and order of acquisition in child speech. In J. R. Hayes (Ed.), *Cognition and the development of language,* pp. 11–53. New York: Wiley.

Brown, R., & Herrnstein, R. J. (1975). *Psychology.* Boston: Little, Brown.

Brozan, N. (1985, March 13). U.S. leads industrialized nations in teen-age births and abortions. *New York Times,* p. 1.

Bruner, J. S. (1966). On the conservation of liquids. In J. S. Bruner, R. R. Olver, & P. M. Greenfield (Eds.), *Studies in cognitive growth.* New York: Wiley.

Bruner, J. S. (1978a). Berlyne Memorial Lecture: Acquiring the uses of language. *Canadian Journal of Psychology, 32*(4), 204–218.

Bruner, J. S. (1978b). Learning how to do things with words. In J. S. Bruner & A. Garton (Eds.), *Human growth and development* (Wolfson College Lectures, 1976). Oxford: Oxford University Press.

Bruner, J. S. (1983). *In search of mind: Essays in autobiography.* New York: Harper & Row.

Bruner, J. S., & Koslowski, B. (1972). Visually preadapted constituents of manipulatory action. *Perception, 1,* 3–15.

Bruner, J. S., Olver, R. R., & Greenfield, P. M. (1966). *Studies in cognitive growth.* New York: Wiley.

Bryant, P. (1974). *Perception and understanding in young children: An experimental approach.* New York: Basic Books.

Bullowa, M. (1979). Infants as conversational partners. In T. Myers (Ed.), *The development of conversation and discourse* (pp. 44–60). Edinburgh: Edinburgh University Press.

Burt, C. W. (1958). The inheritance of mental ability. *American Psychologist, 13,* 1–15.

Burt, C. W. (1966). The genetic determination of differences in intelligence: A study of monozygotic twins reared together and apart. *British Journal of Psychology, 57,* 137–153.

Buss, A. H., & Plomin, R. (1975). *A temperament theory of personality development.* New York: Wiley.

Buss, A. H., Plomin R., & Willerman, L. (1973). The inheritance of temperaments. *Journal of Personality, 41,* 513–524.

Buss, D. M. (1981). Predicting parent-child interactions from children's activity. *Developmental Psychology, 17*(1), 59–65.

Butler, R. A. (1958). The differential effect of visual and auditory incentives on the performance of monkeys. *American Journal of Psychology, 71,* 591–593.

Butler, R. N. (1968). The life review: An interpretation of reminiscence in the aged. In B. L. Neugarten (Ed.), *Middle age and aging.* Chicago: University of Chicago Press.

Butler, R. N. (1975). *Why survive? Being old in America.* New York: Harper & Row.

Butterfield, E. L., & Siperstein, G. N. (1972). Influence of contingent auditory stimulation upon non-nutritional suckle. In J. Bosma (Ed.), *Oral sensation and perception: The mouth of the infant.* Springfield, IL: Charles C. Thomas.

Butterworth, G. (1981, August). *Structure of the mind in human infancy.* Paper presented at the meeting of the International Society for the Study of Behavioral Development, Toronto.

Cairns, R. B., & Johnson, D. L. (1965). The development of interspecies social preferences. *Psychonomic Science, 2,* 337–338.

Cairns, R. B., & Valsiner, J. (1984). Child psychology. In M. R. Rosenzweig & L. W. Porter (Eds.), *Annual Review of Psychology, 35,* 553–577.

Caldwell, B. M. (1964). The effects of infant care. In M. L. Hoffman & L. W. Hoffman (Eds.), *Review of child development research* (Vol. 1). New York: Russell Sage Foundation.

Campbell, D. T., & Fiske, D. W. (1959). Convergent and discriminant validation by the multitrait-multimethod matrix. *Psychological Bulletin, 56,* 81–105.

Campos, J. J., Barrett, K. C., Lamb, M. E., Goldsmith, H. H., & Stenberg, C. (1983). Socioemotional development. In P. H. Mussen (Ed.), *Handbook of child psychology* (Vol. 2, pp. 783–915). New York: Wiley.

Campos, J. J., Hiatt, S., Ramsay, D., Henderson, C., & Svejda, M. (1978). The emergence of fear of heights. In M. Lewis & L. Rosenblum (Eds.), *The development of affect.* New York: Plenum Press.

Campos, J. J., Langer, A., & Krowitz, A. (1970). Cardiac responses on the visual cliff in prelocomotor human infants. *Science, 170,* 196–197.

Campos, J. J., & Maffei, L. (1970). The emergence of fear on the visual cliff. In M. Lewis & L. Rosenblum (Eds.), *The origins of affect.* New York: Plenum Press.

Carey, W. B. (1970). A simplified method for measuring infant temperament. *Journal of Pediatrics, 77,* 188–194.

Carey, W. B. (1982). Validity of parental assessment of development and behavior. *American Journal of Diseases of Children, 136,* 97–99.

Carey, W. B. (in press). The validity of temperament assessments. In T. B. Brazelton & H. Als (Eds.), *Behavioral assessment of newborn and young infants.* Hillsdale, NJ: Erlbaum.

Carmichael, L. (1970). The onset and early development of behavior. In P. H. Mussen (Ed.), *Carmichael's manual of child psychology* (Vol. 1). New York: Wiley.

Caron, A. J., & Caron, R. F. (1982). Cognitive development in early infancy. In T. M. Field, A. Huston, H. C. Quay, L. Troll, & G. E. Finley (Eds.), *Review of human development.* New York: Wiley.

Caron, A. J., Caron, R. F., Caldwell, R. C., & Weiss, S. J. (1973). Infant perception of the structural properties of the face. *Developmental Psychology, 9,* 385–399.

Carter, A. (1979). The disappearance schema. In E. Keenan (Ed.), *Studies in developmental pragmatics.* New York: Academic Press.

Case, R. (1978). Intellectual development from birth to adulthood: A neo-Piagetian interpretation. In R. S. Siegler (Ed.), *Children's thinking: What develops?* Hillsdale, NJ: Erlbaum.

Cavalli-Sforza, L. L. (1974). Genetics of human populations. *Scientific American, 231*(3), 181–189.

Cavalli-Sforza, L. L., & Bodmer, W. F. (1978). *The genetics of human populations.* San Francisco: W. H. Freeman.

Cazden, C. (1965). *Environmental assistance to the child's acquisition of grammar.* Unpublished doctoral dissertation, Harvard University.

Chambliss, W. J. (1973). The saints and the roughnecks. *Society, 11,* 24–31.

Charlesworth, W. R. (1969). The role of surprise in cognitive development. In D. Elkind & J. H. Flavell (Eds.), *Studies in cognitive development* (pp. 257–314). New York: Oxford University Press.

Chein, I. (1972). *The science of behavior and the image of man.* New York: Basic Books.

Chen, E. (1979, December). Twins reared apart: A living lab. *New York Times Magazine,* p. 110.

Cherlin, A. (1981). *Marriage, divorce, remarriage: Changing patterns in the post-war United States.* Cambridge, MA: Harvard University Press.

Chernin, K. (1981). *The obsession: Reflections on the tyranny of slenderness.* New York: Harper & Row.

Chevalier-Skolnikoff, S. (1977). A Piagetian model for describing and comparing socialization in monkey, ape, and human infants. In S. Chevalier-Skolnikoff & F. E. Poirier (Eds.), *Primate bio-social development: Biological, social, and ecological determinants.* New York: Garland.

Chi, M.T.H. (1978). Knowledge structures and memory development. In R. S. Siegler (Ed.), *Children's thinking: What develops?* (pp. 73–96). Hillsdale, NJ: Erlbaum.

Child, I. L. (1984). Primitive mentality. In R. J. Corsini (Ed.), *Encyclopedia of psychology* (Vol. 3, p. 70). New York: Wiley, Interscience.

Childers, P., & Wimmer, M. (1971). The concept of death in early childhood. *Child Development, 42,* 1299–1301.

Chilman, C. S. (1982). Adolescent childbearing in the United States: Apparent causes and consequences. In T. M. Field, A. Huston, H. C. Quay, L. Troll, & G. E. Finley (Eds.), *Review of human development* (pp. 418–431). New York: Wiley.

Chodorow, N. (1974). Family structure and feminine personality. In M. Z. Rosaldo & L. Lamphere (Eds.), *Woman, culture and society.* Stanford: Stanford University Press.

Chodorow, N. (1978). *The reproduction of mothering: Psychoanalysis and the sociology of gender.* Berkeley: University of California Press.

Chomsky, C. (1969). *The acquisition of syntax in children from five to ten.* Cambridge, MA: MIT Press.

Chomsky, N. (1957). *Syntactic structures.* The Hague: Mouton.

Chomsky, N. (1959). A review of B. F. Skinner's *Verbal behavior. Language, 35,* 26–58.

Chomsky, N. (1965). *Aspects of a theory of syntax.* Cambridge, MA: MIT Press.

Chomsky, N. (1966). *Cartesian linguistics.* New York: Harper & Row.

Chomsky, N. (1968). *Language and mind.* New York: Harcourt, Brace & World.

Chomsky, N. (1975). *Reflections on language.* New York: Pantheon.

Chomsky, N. (1980). Initial states and steady states: The linguistic approach. In M. Piatelli-Palmarini (Ed.), *Language and learning: The debate between Jean Piaget and Noam Chomsky* (pp. 107–130). Cambridge, MA: Harvard University Press.

Chukovski, K. (1966). *From two to five* (M. Morton, Ed. & Trans.). Berkeley: University of California Press.

Church, J. (1968). *Three babies: Biographies of cognitive development.* New York: Vintage Books.

Churchland, P. M. (1984). *Matter and consciousness: A contemporary introduction to the philosophy of mind.* Cambridge, MA: MIT Press, Bradford.

Clark, E. V. (1973). What's in a word? On the child's acquisition of semantics in his first language. In T. E. Moore (Ed.), *Cognitive development and the acquisition of language.* New York: Academic Press.

Clark, H. H., & Clark, E. V. (1977). *Psychology and language.* New York: Harcourt Brace Jovanovich.

Clarke, A. M., & Clarke, A.D.B. (Eds.). (1976). *Early experience: Myth and evidence.* New York: Free Press.

Clarke-Stewart, A. (1982). *Daycare.* Cambridge, MA: Harvard University Press.

Clausen, J. (1972). The life course of individuals. In M. W. Riley, J. Johnson, & A. Foner (Eds.), *Aging and society: A sociology of age stratification* (Vol. 3, pp. 457–514). New York: Russell Sage Foundation.

Clayton, R. R., & Bokemeier, J. L. (1980. Premarital sex in the seventies. *Journal of Marriage and the Family, 42*(4), 759–775.

Clayton V. P. (1975). Erikson's theory of human development as it applies to the aged: Wisdom as contradictive cognition. *Human Development, 18,* 119–128.

Clayton, V. P., & Birren, J. E. (1980). The development of wisdom across the life span: A reexamination of an ancient topic. In P. B. Baltes & O. G. Brim, Jr. (Eds.), *Life-span development and behavior* (Vol. 3, pp. 103–135). New York: Academic Press.

Cohen, A. K. (1955). *Delinquent boys.* New York: Free Press.

Cohen, L. B., DeLoache, J. S., & Strauss, M. S. (1979). Infant visual perception. In J. D. Osofsky (Ed.), *Handbook of infant development.* New York: Wiley.

Cohen, S. E. (1974). Developmental differences in infants' attentional responses to face-voice incongruity of mother and stranger. *Child Development, 45,* 1155–1158.

Cohler, B. J. (1982). Personal narrative and the life course. In P. B. Baltes & O. G. Brim, Jr. (Eds.), *Life-span development and behavior* (Vol. 4, pp. 205–241). New York: Academic Press.

Coie, J. D., & Dodge, K. A. (1983). Continuities and changes in children's social status: A five-year longitudinal study. *Merrill-Palmer Quarterly, 29,* 261–282.

Colby, A., & Damon, W. (1983). Listening to a different voice: A review of Gilligan's *In a different voice. Merrill-Palmer Quarterly, 29,* 473–481.

Colby, A., Kohlberg, L., Gibbs, J., Candee, D., Spelcher-Dubin, B., Hewer, A., Kauffman, K., & Power, C. (1983). *The measurement of moral judgement: Standard issue scoring manual.* New York: Cambridge University Press.

Cole, M., Gay, J., Glick, J. A., & Sharp, D. W. (1971). *The cultural context of learning and thinking.* New York: Basic Books.

Coles, R. (1967). *Children of crisis: A study of courage and fear.* Boston: Little, Brown.

Coles, R. (1985). A psychological perspective. In R. Coles & G. Stokes, *Sex and the American teenager* (pp. 1–32). New York: Harper & Row, Colophon Books.

Coles, R., & Stokes, G. (1985). *Sex and the American teenager.* New York: Harper & Row, Colophon Books.

Comstock, G., Chaffee, S., Katzman, N., McCombs, M., & Roberts, D. (1978). *Television and human behavior.* New York: Columbia University Press.

Condon, W. S. (1975). Speech makes babies move. In R. Lewin (Ed.), *Child alive!* (pp. 75–85). Garden City, NY: Anchor Books.

Condon, W. S. (1977). A primary phase in the organization of infant responding behavior. In H. R. Schaffer, *Studies in mother-infant interaction* (pp. 153–176). New York: Academic Press. (Proceedings of the Loch Lomond Symposium, Ross Priory, University of Strathclyde)

Condon, W. S., & Sander, L. W. (1974). Neonate movement is synchronized with adult speech: International participation and language acquisition. *Science, 183,* 99–101.

Conel, J. L. (1939–1963). *The postnatal development of the human cerebral cortex* (Vols. 1–7). Cambridge, MA: Harvard University Press.

Conger, J. J. (1975). Sexual attitudes and behavior of contemporary adolescents. In J. J. Conger (Ed.), *Contemporary issues in adolescent development* (pp. 221–230). New York: Harper & Row.

Connell, J. P., & Goldsmith, H. H. (1982). A structural modeling approach to the study of attachment and strange situation behaviors. In R. Emde & R. Harmon (Eds.), *Attachment and affiliative systems: Neurological and psychobiological aspects.* New York: Plenum Press.

Constantinople, A. (1969). An Eriksonian measure of personality development in college students. *Developmental Psychology, 1,* 357–372.

Cooley, C. H. (1902). *Human nature and the social order.* New York: Scribner.

Coopersmith, S. (1967). *The antecedents of self-esteem.* San Francisco: W. H. Freeman.

Corder-Bolz, C. R. (1980). Mediation: The role of significant others. *Journal of Communication, 30,* 106–118.

Cordiera, G., McGraw, K., & Drabman, R. (1979). Doctor or nurse: Children's perceptions of sex typed occupations. *Child Development, 50,* 590–593.

Corter, C., Trehub, S., Boukydis, C., Ford, L., Celhoffer, L., & Minde, K. (1978). Nurses' judgments of the attractiveness of premature infants. *Infant Behavior and Development, 1,* 373–380.

Cortese, A. J. (1984). Standard issue scoring of moral reasoning: A critique. *Merrill-Palmer Quarterly, 30,* 227–246.

Costa, P. T., Jr., & McCrae, R. R. (1980). Still stable after all these years: Personality as a key to some issues in adulthood and old age. In P. B. Baltes & O. G. Brim, Jr. (Eds.), *Life-span development and behavior* (Vol. 3, pp. 65–102). New York: Academic Press.

Cottle, T. J. (1972). The connections of adolescence. In J. Kagan & R. Coles (Eds.), *Twelve to sixteen: Early adolescence.* New York: Norton.

Coveney, P. (1967). *The image of childhood.* Baltimore: Penguin.

Cowan, P. A. (1978). *Piaget with feeling: Cognitive, social, and emotional dimensions.* New York: Holt, Rinehart & Winston.

Cowen, E. L., Pederson, A., Babijian, H., Izzo, L. D., & Trost, M. A. (1973). Long-term follow-up of early detected vulnerable children. *Journal of Consulting and Clinical Psychology, 41,* 438–446.

Crick, F.H.C. (1977). Developmental biology. In R. Duncan & M. Weston-Smith (Eds.), *The encyclopedia of ignorance: Life sciences and earth sciences* (pp. 299–304). New York: Pergamon Press.

Cromer, R. F. (1974). The development of language and cognition: The cognition hypothesis. In B. Foss (Ed.), *New perspectives in child development.* Harmondsworth, England: Penguin Books.

Cuber, J. F., & Harroff, P. (1965). *Sex and the significant Americans.* Baltimore: Penguin.

Cummings, E., & Henry, W. E. (1961). *Growing old: The process of disengagement.* New York: Basic Books.

Curtin, S. R. (1972). *Nobody ever died of old age.* Boston: Little, Brown.

Curtiss, S. (1977). *Genie: A linguistic study of a modern-day wild child.* New York: Academic Press.

Damon, W. (1977). *The social world of the child.* San Francisco: Jossey-Bass.

Damon, W., & Hart, D. (1982). The development of self-understanding from childhood to adolescence. *Child Development, 53,* 841–864.

Dannefer, D. (1984a). Adult development and social theory: A paradigmatic reappraisal. *American Sociological Review, 49,* 100–116.

Dannefer, D. (1984b). The role of the social in life-span developmental psychology, past and future: Rejoinder to Baltes and Nesselroade. *American Sociological Review, 49*(6), 847–850.

Danner, F. W., & Day, M. C. (1977). Eliciting formal operations. *Child Development, 48,* 1600–1607.

Danziger, K. (1971). *Socialization.* Harmondsworth, England: Penguin.

Darwin, C. (1859). *On the origin of species.* London: John Murray.

Darwin, C. (1871). *The descent of man.* London: John Murray.

Darwin, C. (1975). *The expression of the emotions in man and animals.* Chicago: University of Chicago Press. (Originally published 1872)

Darwin, C. (1877). A biographical sketch of an infant. *Mind, 2,* 285–294.

Dasen, P. R. (1972). Cross-cultural Piagetian research: A summary. *Journal of Cross-Cultural Psychology, 3*(1), 29–39.

Davenport, R. K., & Rogers, C. M. (1970). Intermodal equivalence of stimuli in apes. *Science, 168,* 279–280.

Davis, K. (1947). Final note on a case of extreme isolation. *American Journal of Sociology, 50,* 432–437.

Davis, K. (1972). The American family in relation to demographic change. In C. F. Westapp & R. Parke, Jr. (Eds.), *Commission on population growth and the American future: Research Report 1. Demographic and social aspects of population growth* (pp. 246–247). Washington, DC: Government Printing Office.

Davison, G. C. (1973). Counter-control in behavior modification. In L. A. Hamerlynck, L. C. Handy, & E. J. Marsh (Eds.), *Behavior change: Methodology, concepts, and practice.* Champaign, IL: Research Press.

DeCasper, A. J., & Fifer, W. P. (1980). Of human bonding: Newborns prefer their mother's voices. *Science, 208,* 1174–1176.

De Fries, J. C., Corley, R. P., Johnson, R. C., Vandenberg, S. G., & Wilson, J. R. (1982). Sex-by-generation interactions in the Hawaii family study of cognition. *Behavior Genetics, 12,* 223–230.

Demos, J., & Demos, V. (1969). Adolescence in historical perspective. *Journal of Marriage and the Family, 31,* 632–638.

Dennis, W. (1960). Causes of retardation among institutional children: Iran. *Journal of Genetic Psychology, 96,* 47–59.

Dennis, W. (1973). *Children of the crèche.* New York: Appleton-Century-Crofts.

Dennis, W. (Ed.). (1972). *Readings in the history of psychology.* New York: Appleton-Century-Crofts.

Derryberry, D., & Rothbart, M. K. (1984). Emotion, attention, and temperament. In C. E. Izard, J. Kagan, & R. B. Zajonc (Eds.), *Emotions, cognition, and behavior.* New York: Cambridge University Press.

Desmond, A. J. (1979). *The ape's reflexion.* New York: Dial Press, James Wade.

de Villiers, P. A., & de Villiers, J. C. (1979). *Early childhood.* Cambridge, MA: Harvard University Press.

De Vries, R. (1969). Constancy of generic identity in the years three to six. *Monographs of the Society for Research in Child Development, 34*(Serial No. 127).

De Vries, R. (1970). The development of role-taking as reflected by the behavior of bright, average and retarded children in a vocal guessing game. *Child Development, 41,* 759–770.

Dion, K. K. (1972). Physical attractiveness and evaluations of children's transgressions. *Journal of Personality and Social Psychology, 24,* 207–213.

Dion, K., & Berscheid, E. (1974). Physical attractiveness and peer perception among children. *Sociometry, 37,* 1–12.

Dirks, J., & Gibson, E. (1977). Infants' perception of similarity between live people and their photographs. *Child Development, 48,* 124–130.

Dixon, J. C. (1957). Development of self-recognition. *Journal of Genetic Psychology, 91,* 251–256.

Dobbing, J. (1974). Fetal and postnatal growth and development of the human brain. *Annals of Human Biology, 2,* 88.

Dobbing, J., & Sands, J. (1973). Quantitative growth and development of the human brain. *Archives of Disease in Childhood, 48,* 757–767.

Dobson, V., & Teller, D. Y. (1978). Visual acuity in human infants: A review and comparison of behavioral and electrophysiological studies. *Vision Research, 18,* 1469–1483.

Dollard, J., & Miller, N. E. (1950). *Personality and psychotherapy: An analysis in terms of learning, thinking, and culture.* New York: McGraw-Hill.

Donaldson, M. C. (1978). *Children's minds.* New York: Norton.

Donovan, J. M. (1975). Identity status and interpersonal style. *Journal of Youth and Adolescence, 4*(1), 37–55.

Douglas, J. W., Ross, J. M., & Simpson, H. R. (1968). *All our future: A longitudinal study of secondary education.* London: Peter Davies.

Drabman, R. S., Robertson, S. J., Patterson, J. N., Jarvie, G., Hammer, D., & Cordua, G. (1981). Children's perception of media portrayed sex roles. *Sex Roles, 7*(4), 379–389.

Dreyfus, H. (1979). *What computers can't do: The limits of artificial intelligence.* New York: Harper & Row.

Dubin, R., & Dubin, E. R. (1965). Children's social perceptions: A review of research. *Child Development, 36,* 809–838.

Duncan, S. D., Jr. (1975). Interaction units speaking turns in dyadic, face-to-face conversation. In A. Kendon, R. M. Harris, & M. R. Key (Eds.), *Organization of behavior in face-to-face interaction.* The Hague: Mouton.

Dunn, J. (1975). Patterns of early interaction: Continuities and consequences. In H. R. Schaffer (Ed.), *Studies in mother-infant interaction.* London: Academic Press.

Dunn, J. (1980). Individual differences in temperament. In M. Rutter (Ed.), *Developmental psychiatry.* London: William Heinemann.

Dunn, J., & Kendrick, C. (1980). Studying temperament and parent-child interaction: Comparison of interview and direct observation. *Developmental Medicine and Child Neurology, 22,* 484–496.

Dunn, J., Kendrick, C., & MacNamee, R. (1981). The reaction of first-born children to the birth of a sibling: Mothers' reports. *Journal of Child Psychology and Psychiatry, 22,* 1–18.

Eagle, M. (1984). *Recent developments in psychoanalysis.* New York: McGraw-Hill.

Eichorn, D. H. (1981). Samples and procedures. In D. H. Eichorn, J. A. Clausen, N. Haan, M. P. Honzik, & P. H. Mussen (Eds.), *Present and past in middle life* (pp. 33–51). New York: Academic Press.

Eichorn, D. H., Hunt, J. V., & Honzik, M. P. (1981). Experience, personality, and IQ: Adolescence to middle age. In D. H. Eichorn, J. A. Clausen, N. Haan, M. P. Honzik, & P. H. Mussen (Eds.), *Present and past in middle life* (pp. 89–116). New York: Academic Press.

Eimas, P. D. (1975). Speech perception in early infancy. In L. B. Cohen & P. Salapatek (Eds.), *Infant perception: From sensation to cognition* (Vol. 2). New York: Academic Press.

Eimas, P. D., Siqueland, E., Jusczyk, P., & Vigorito, J. (1971). Speech perception in infants. *Science, 171,* 303–306.

Ekman, P. (Ed.). (1982). *Emotion in the human face.* New York: Cambridge University Press.

Ekstrom, R. B., French, J. W., Harman, H. H., & Derman, D. (1976). *Manual for kit of factor-referenced cognitive tests.* Princeton, NJ: Educational Testing Service.

Elder, G. H., Jr. (1974). *Children of the Great Depression.* Chicago: University of Chicago Press.

Elder, G. H., Jr. (1975a). Adolescence in the life cycle: An introduction. In S. E. Dragastin & G. H. Elder (Eds.), *Adolescence in the life cycle: Psychological change and social context* (pp. 1–22). New York: Wiley.

Elder, G. H., Jr. (1975b). Age differentiation and the life course. In A. Inkeles (Ed.), *Annual Review of Sociology, 1,* 165–190.

Elder, G. H., Jr. (1978). Family history and the life course. In T. Hareven (Ed.), *Transitions: The family and the life course in historical perspective* (pp. 17–64). New York: Academic Press.

Elkind, D. (1974). *Children and adolescents: Interpretive essays on Jean Piaget* (2nd ed.). New York: Oxford University Press.

Elkind, D. (1981). *The hurried child.* Reading, MA: Addison-Wesley.

Emde, R. N. (1983). The pre-representational self and its affective core. *Psychoanalytic Study of the Child, 38,* 165–192.

Emde, R. N., Gaensbauer, T. J., & Harmon, R. J. (1976). Emotional expression in infancy: A biobehavioral study. *Psychological Issues, 10*(1, Monograph 37).

Emde, R. N., & Harmon, R. J. (1984). *Continuities and discontinuities in development.* New York: Plenum Press.

Emmerich, W. (1959). Parental identification in young children. *Genetic Psychology Monographs, 60,* 257–308.

Emmerich, W. (1968). Personality development and concepts of structure. *Child Development, 39,* 671–690.

Endler, N. S. (1983). Interactionism: A personality model but not yet a theory. In R. A. Dienstbieri (Ed.), *Nebraska Symposium on Motivation (1982).* Lincoln: University of Nebraska Press.

Epstein, S. (1973). The self-concept revisited or a theory of a theory. *American Psychologist, 28,* 405–416.

Epstein, S. (1979). The stability of behavior: Pt. 1. On predicting most of the people much of the time. *Journal of Personality and Social Psychology, 37,* 1097–1126.

Erikson, E. H. (1950). *Childhood and society.* New York: Norton.

Erikson, E. H. (1959). Identity and the life cycle. *Psychological Issues, 1*(1), 1–164.

Erikson, E. H. (1968). *Identity, youth, and crisis.* New York: Norton.

Erikson, E. H. (1975). *Life history and the historical moment.* New York: Norton.

Erikson, E. H. (1980). *Identity and the life cycle.* New York: Norton.

Erikson, E. H. (1984). Reflections on the last stage—and the first. In A. J. Solnit et al. (Eds.), *The psychoanalytic study of the child* (Vol. 39). New Haven: Yale University Press.

Ervin-Tripp, S. M. (1964). Imitation and structural change in children's language. In E. H. Lenneberg (Ed.), *New directions in the study of language* (pp. 163–189). Cambridge, MA: MIT Press.

Ervin-Tripp, S. M. (1976a). *Turn-taking in children.* Paper presented at University of Michigan.

Ervin-Tripp, S. M. (1976b). Language development. *Catalogue of Selected Documents in Psychology, 6,* 95.

Ervin-Tripp, S. M., & Mitchell-Kernan, C. (1977). *Child discourse.* New York: Academic Press.

Escalona, S. K. (1963). Patterns of infantile experience and the developmental process. *Psychoanalytic Study of the Child, 18,* 197–244.

Estes, W. K. (1977). Reinforcement in human behavior. In I. L. Janis (Ed.), *Current trends in psychology* (pp. 135–141). Los Altos, CA: William Kaufmann.

Eyferth, K. (1961). Leistungen verschiedener gruppen von besatzungskindern in Hamburg-Wechsler intelligenztest für kinder (HAWIK). *Archiv für die Gesamte Psychologie, 113,* 222–241.

Fagan, J. F. (1973). Infants' delayed recognition, memory and forgetting. *Journal of Experimental Child Psychology, 16,* 424–450.

Fagan, J. F. (1979). The origins of facial pattern recognition. In M. H. Bornstein & W. Kessen (Eds.), *Psychological development from infancy: Image to intention.* Hillsdale, NJ: Erlbaum.

Fantz, R. L. (1961). The origin of form perception. *Science, 204,* 66–72.

Fantz, R. L. (1963). Pattern vision in newborn infants. *Science, 140,* 296–297.

Fantz, R. L. (1965). Visual perception from birth as shown by pattern selectivity. In H. E. Whipple (Ed.), *New issues in infant development. Annals of New York Academy of Science, 118,* 793–814.

Farber, S. L. (1981). *Identical twins reared apart.* New York: Basic Books.

Faust, M. S. (1960). Developmental maturity as a determinant in prestige of adolescent girls. *Child Development, 31,* 173–186.

Featherman, D. L. (1983). The life-span perspective in social science research. In P. B. Baltes & O. G. Brim (Eds.), *Life-span development and behavior* (Vol. 5, pp. 1–59). New York: Academic Press.

Feffer, M. H., & Gourevitch, V. (1960). Cognitive aspects of role-taking in children. *Journal of Personality, 28,* 383–396.

Feldman, S. S. (1977). The bonding bind: Review of M. H. Klaus and J. H. Kennell, *Maternal infant bonding: The impact of early separation or loss on family development. Contemporary Psychology, 22,* 486–487.

Feldman, H., Goldin-Meadow, S., & Gleitman, L. (1978). Beyond Herodotus: The creation of language by linguistically deprived deaf children. In A. Lock (Ed.), *Action, symbol, and gesture: The emergence of language.* New York: Academic Press.

Fillmore, C. J. (1968). The case for case. In E. Bach & R. T. Harms (Eds.), *Universals in linguistic theory.* New York: Holt, Rinehart & Winston.

Finger, J. A., & Silverman, M. (1966). Changes in academic performance in junior high school. *Personnel and Guidance Journal, 45*(2), 157–164.

Fisher, K. W. (1980). A theory of cognitive development: Control and construction of hierarchies of skills. *Psychological Review, 87,* 477–531.

Fisher, K. W., & Watson, M. W. (1981). Explaining the Oedipus conflict. In *Cognitive development* (New directions for child development, No. 12). San Francisco: Jossey-Bass.

Flandrin, J. L. (1979). *Families in former times: Kinship, household, and sexuality.* Cambridge: Cambridge University Press.

Flapan, D. (1968). *Children's understanding of social interaction.* New York: Teachers College Press.

Flavell, J. (1963). *The developmental psychology of Jean Piaget.* Princeton, NJ: Van Nostrand.

Flavell, J. (1968). *The development of role-taking and communication skills in children.* New York: Wiley.

Flavell, J. (1970). Concept development. In P. H. Mussen (Ed.), *Carmichael's manual of child psychology* (3rd ed.). New York: Wiley.

Flavell, J. (1974). The development of inferences about others. In T. Mischel (Ed.), *Understanding other persons.* Oxford: Blackwell, Basel & Mott.

Flavell, J. (1977). *Cognitive development.* Englewood Cliffs, NJ: Prentice-Hall.

Flavell, J. H., Botkin, P. T., Fry, C. L., Jr., Wright, J., & Jarvis, P. (1968). *The development of role-taking and communication skills in young children.* New York: Wiley.

Flavell, J. H., Shipstead, S. G., & Croft, K. (1978). *What young children think you see when their eyes are closed.* Unpublished manuscript, Stanford University.

Fodor, J. A., Bever, T. G., & Garrett, M. F. (1974). *The psychology of language: An introduction to psycholinguistics and generative grammar.* New York: McGraw-Hill.

Fogelson, R. D. (1982). Person, self, and identity: Some anthropological retrospects, circumspects, and prospects. In B. Lee & K. Smith (Eds.), *Psychosocial theories of the self* (pp. 67–109). New York: Plenum Press.

Foner, A., & Kertzer, D. (1978). Transitions over the life course: Lessons from age-set societies. *American Journal of Sociology, 83,* 1081–1104.

Fontana, A. (1977). *The last frontier: The social meaning of growing old.* Beverly Hills: Sage.

Fortes, M. (1970). Social and psychological aspects of education in Taleland. In J. Middleton (Ed.), *From child to adult* (pp. 14–74). Garden City, NY: Natural History Press.

Fowler, W. (1962). *The development of scientific method.* Oxford: Pergamon Press.

Fozard, J. L., & Popkin, S. J. (1978). Optimizing adult development: Ends and means of an applied psychology of aging. *American Psychologist, 33,* 975–989.

Fraiberg, S. (1959). *The magic years: Understanding and handling the problems of early childhood.* New York: Scribners.

Fraiberg, S. (1974). Blind infants and their mothers: An examination of the sign system. In M. Lewis & L. A. Rosenblum (Eds.), *The effect of the infant on its caregiver* (pp. 215–232). New York: Wiley.

Fraiberg, S. (1977). *Insights from the blind.* New York: Basic Books.

Framo, J. L. (1972). *Family interaction: A dialogue between family researchers and family therapists.* New York: Springer.

Frank, A. (1972). *Diary of Ann Frank.* (B. M. Mooyaart-Doubleday, Trans.). New York: Pocket Books.

Frazier, A., & Lisonbee, A. K. (1971). Adolescent concerns with physique. In R. E. Muuss (Ed.), *Adolescent behavior and society: A book of readings.* New York: Random House.

Frazier, T. M., Davis, G. H., Goldstein, H., & Goldberg, I. (1961). Cigarette smoking: A prospective study. *American Journal of Obstetrics and Gynecology, 81,* 988–996.

Freedman, D. G. (1964). Smiling in blind infants and the issue of innate vs. acquired. *Journal of Child Psychology and Psychiatry, 5,* 171–184.

Freedman, J. L. (1984). Effect of television violence on aggressiveness. *Psychological Bulletin, 96*(2), 227–246.

French, J. W., Ekstrom, R. B., & Price, L. A. (1963). *Kit of reference tests for cognitive factors.* Princeton, NJ: Educational Testing Service.

Freud, A. (1936). *The ego and the mechanisms of defense.* New York: Norton.

Freud, A. (1969). Adolescence as a developmental disturbance. In G. Kaplan & S. Lebovici (Eds.), *Adolescence: Psychological perspectives.* New York: Basic Books.

Freud, A., & Dann, S. (1951). An experiment in group upbringing. *Psychoanalytic Study of the Child, 6,* 127–168.

Freud, S. (1920). *The standard edition of the complete psychological works of Sigmund Freud.* London: Hogarth Press.

Freud, S. (1938). *An outline of psychoanalysis.* London: Hogarth Press.

Freud, S. (1955). *Beyond the pleasure principle. Standard Edition.* London: Hogarth Press. (Originally published 1909)

Fries, J. F., & Crapo, L. M. (1981). *Vitality and aging.* San Francisco: W. H. Freeman.

Frodi, A. M., Lamb, M. E., Leavitt, L. A., Donovan, W. L., Neff, C., & Sherry, D. (1978). Fathers' and mothers' responses to the faces and cries of normal and premature infants. *Developmental Psychology, 14,* 490–498.

Fromm, E. (1970). *The crisis of psychoanalysis.* New York: Holt, Rinehart & Winston.

Fuchs, V. (1983). *How we live: An economic perspective on Americans from birth to death.* Cambridge, MA: Harvard University Press.

Furman, W., Rake, D. F., & Hartup, W. W. (1979). Rehabilitation of socially withdrawn children through mixed-age and same-age socialization. *Child Development, 50,* 912–922.

Furstenberg, F. (1976). *Unplanned parenthood: The social consequences of teenage childbearing.* New York: Free Press.

Furth, H. G. (1966). *Thinking without language: Psychological implications of deafness.* New York: Free Press.

Gaensbauer, T. J., Connell, J. P., & Shultz, L. (1983). Emotion and attachment: Interrelationships in a structured laboratory paradigm. *Developmental Psychology, 19*(6), 815–831.

Gagnon, J. H. (1974). Scripts and the coordination of sexual conduct. In J. K. Cole & R. Deinstbrier (Eds.), *Nebraska Symposium on Motivation* (Vol. 21). Lincoln: University of Nebraska Press.

Gagnon, J. H., & Henderson, B. (1975). *Human sexuality: An age of ambiguity* (MagaBack Social Issues Series, No. 1). Boston: Little, Brown, Educational Associates.

Gagnon, J. H., & Simon, W. (1973). *Sexual conduct.* Chicago: Aldine.

Galenson, E. (1979). Development from one to two years. In J. D. Noshpritz (Ed.), *Basic handbook of child psychiatry* (Vol. 1). New York: Basic Books.

Gallagher, J. M., & Wright, R. J. (1979). Piaget and the study of analogy: Structural analysis of items. In J. Magary (Ed.), *Piaget and the helping professions* (Vol. 8). Los Angeles: University of Southern California Press.

Gallup, G. G., Jr. (1970). Chimpanzees: Self-recognition. *Science, 167,* 86–87.

Gallup, G. G., Jr. (1975). Towards an operational definition of self-awareness. In R. H. Tuttle (Ed.), *Socioecology and psychology of primates.* The Hague: Mouton.

Gallup, G. G., Jr. (1977). Absence of self-recognition in a monkey *(Macaca fascicularis)* following prolonged exposure to a mirror. *Developmental Psychobiology, 10,* 281–284.

Gallup, G. G., Jr. (1979). Self-recognition in chimpanzees and man: A developmental and comparative perspective. In M. Lewis & L. A. Rosenblum (Eds.), *The child and its family.* New York: Plenum Press.

Gallup, G. G., Jr., McClure, M. K., Hill, S. D., & Bundy, R. A. (1971). Capacity for self-recognition in differentially reared chimpanzees. *Psychological Record, 21,* 69–74.

Gallup, G. G., Jr., Wallnau, L. B., & Suarez, S. D. (1978, November). *An attempt to assess self-recognition in mother-infant rhesus monkey pairs.* Paper presented to the Psychonomic Society, San Antonio.

Garcia Coll, C. T., Kagan, J., & Resnick, J. S. (1984). Behavioral inhibitions in young children. *Child Development, 55,* 1005–1019.

Gardner, B. T., & Gardner, R. A. (1980). Two comparative psychologists look at language acquisition. In K. E. Nelson (Ed.), *Children's language* (Vol. 2). New York: Gardner Press.

Gardner, R. A., & Gardner, B. T. (1969). Teaching sign language to a chimpanzee. *Science, 165,* 664–672.

Gardner, R. A., & Gardner, B. T. (1978). Comparative psychology and language acquisition. *Annals of the New York Academy of Science, 309,* 37–76.

Garfinkel, R., & Thorndike, R. L. (1976). Binet item difficulty then and now. *Child Development, 47,* 959–965.

Garmezy, N. (1976). *Vulnerable and invulnerable children: Theory, research, and intervention* (Journal Supplement Abstract Service, No. MS. 1337). Washington, DC: American Psychological Association.

Garmezy, N. (1981). Children under stress: Perspectives on antecedents and correlates of vulnerability and resistance to psychopathology. In A. I. Rabin, J. Aronoff, A. M. Barclay, & R. A. Zucker (Eds.), *Further explorations in personality* (pp. 196–269). New York: Wiley, Interscience.

Garmezy, N. (1983). Stressors of childhood. In N. Garmezy & M. Rutter (Eds.), *Stress, coping, and development in children* (pp. 43–84). New York: McGraw-Hill.

Garvey, C. (1974). Some properties of social play. *Merrill-Palmer Quarterly, 20,* 163–180.

Garvey, C. (1977). *Play.* Cambridge, MA: Harvard University Press.

Gay, J., & Cole, M. (1967). *The new mathematics and an old culture.* New York: Holt, Rinehart & Winston.

Geertz, C. (1965). The impact of the concept of culture on the concept of man. In J. R. Platt (Ed.), *New views of the nature of man* (pp. 93–118). Chicago: University of Chicago Press.

Geertz, C. (1973). Person time and conduct in Bali. In C. Geertz (Ed.), *The interpretation of cultures: Selected essays.* New York: Basic Books.

Gelman, R. (1972). The nature and development of early number concepts. In H. W. Reese (Ed.), *Advances in child development and behavior* (Vol. 7). New York: Academic Press.

Gelman, R. (1978). Cognitive development. *Annual Review of Psychology, 29,* 297–332.

Gelman, R. (1979). Preschool thought. *American Psychologist, 34,* 900–905.

Gelman, R., & Baillargeon, R. (1983). A review of Piagetian concepts. In P. Mussen (Ed.), *Handbook of child development: Vol. 3. Cognitive development.* New York: Wiley.

Gerbner, G., Gross, L., Eleey, M. F., Jackson-Beeck, M., Jeffries-Fox, S., & Signorielli, N. (1977). TV violence profile: Pt. 8. The highlights. *Journal of Communication, 27*(2), 171–180.

Gerbner, G., Gross, L., Morgan, M., & Signorielli, N. (1980). The "Mainstreaming" of America: Violence profile no. 11. *Journal of Communication, 30*(3), 10–29.

Gergen, K. J. (1980). The emerging crisis in life-span developmental theory. In P. B. Baltes & O. G. Brim, Jr. (Eds.), *Life-span development and behavior* (Vol. 3, pp. 31–63). New York: Academic Press.

Gergen, K. M., Greenberg, M., & Willis, R. (1981). *Social exchange.* New York: Plenum Press.

Geschwind, N. (1964). The development of the brain and the evolution of language. In C. Stuart (Ed.), *Monograph Series on Language and Linguistics* (pp. 155–169). Washington, DC: Georgetown University Press.

Geschwind, N. (1972). Language and the brain. *Scientific American, 226*(4), 76–83.

Geschwind, N. (1979). Specializations of the human brain. In Scientific American staff (Eds.), *The brain* (pp. 108–117). San Francisco: W. H. Freeman.

Gesell, A. (1928). *Infancy and human growth.* New York: Macmillan.

Gesell, A. (1943). *Infant and child in the culture of today.* New York: Harper.

Gesell, A., & Ilg, F. L. (1949). *Child development.* New York: Harper.

Gewertz, J. L., & Boyd, E. F. (1977). Does maternal responding imply reduced infant crying? A critique of the 1972 Bell and Ainsworth report. *Child Development, 48,* 1200–1207.

Gibbs, J. C. (1978). Kohlberg's moral stage theory: A Piagetian revision. *Human Development, 22*(2), 89–112.

Gibson, E. J. (1969). *Principles of perceptual learning and development.* New York: Appleton-Century-Crofts.

Gibson, E. J., & Spelke, E. (1983). The development of perception. In P. H. Mussen (Ed.), *Handbook of child psychology* (Vol. 3). New York: Wiley.

Gibson, J. J. (1966). *The senses considered as perceptual systems.* Boston: Houghton Mifflin.

Gibson, J. J. (1977). The theory of affordances. In R. Shaw & J. Bransford (Eds.), *Perceiving, acting, and knowing.* Hillsdale, NJ: Erlbaum.

Giele, J. Z. (1980). Adulthood as transcendence of age and sex. In N. J. Smelser & E. H. Erikson (Eds.), *Themes of work and love in adulthood* (pp. 151–173). Cambridge, MA: Harvard University Press.

Gilbert, S. (1979, Fall). Hunger pains. *University Publishing.*

Gilford, R., & Bengston, V. (1979). Measuring marital satisfaction in three generations: Positive and negative dimensions. *Journal of Marriage and the Family, 41,* 387–398.

Gill, M. M. (1967). The primary process. In R. R. Holt (Ed.), *Motives and thoughts: Psychoanalytic essays in honor of David Rapaport* (Psychological Issues Monographs, 18–19, pp. 260–298).

Gilligan, C. (1982). *In a different voice.* Cambridge, MA: Harvard University Press.

Ginsburg, H., & Opper, S. (1979). *Piaget's theory of intellectual development* (2nd ed.). Englewood Cliffs, NJ: Prentice-Hall.

Ginzberg, E., Ginsburg, S. W., Axelrod, S., & Herma, J. L. (1951). *Occupational choice.* New York: Columbia University Press.

Gitlin, T. (1983). *Inside prime time.* New York: Pantheon.

Gleitman, L. R., & Wanner, E. (1984). Current issues in language learning. In M. H. Bornstein & M. E. Lamb (Eds.), *Developmental psychology: An advanced textbook* (pp. 181–240). Hillsdale, NJ: Erlbaum.

Glenn, N. D. (1975). The contribution of marriage to the psychological well-being of males and females. *Journal of Marriage and the Family, 37,* 594–600.

Glucksberg, S., Kraus, R. M., & Higgens, T. (1975). The development of communication skills in children. In F. Horowitz (Ed.), *Review of child development research* (Vol. 4). Chicago: University of Chicago Press.

Goertzel, V., & Goertzel, M. G. (1962). *Cradles of eminence.* Boston: Little, Brown.

Goffman, E. (1974). *Frame analysis.* New York: Harper & Row.

Gold, M., & Douvan, E. (Eds.). (1969). *Adolescent development: Readings in research and theory.* Boston: Allyn & Bacon.

Gold, M., & Petronio, R. J. (1980). Delinquent behavior in adolescence. In J. Adelson (Ed.), *Handbook of adolescent psychology* (pp. 495–535). New York: Wiley.

Goldin-Meadow, S. (1982). The resilience of recursion: A study of a communication system developed without a conventional language model. In L. R. Gleitman & E. Wanner (Eds.), *Language acquisition: The state of the art.* New York: Cambridge University Press.

Goldin-Meadow, S., & Mylander, C. (1984). Gestural communication in deaf children: The effects and noneffects of parental input on early language development. *Monographs of the Society for Research in Child Development, 49* (3–4, Serial No. 207).

Goldsmith, H. H., & Campos, J. J. (1982). Toward a theory of infant temperament. In R. N. Emde & R. Harmon (Eds.), *The development of attachment and affiliative systems: Psychobiological aspects.* New York: Plenum Press.

Goldsmith, H. H., & Gottesman, I. I. (1981). Origins of variation in behavioral style: A longitudinal study of temperament in young twins. *Child Development, 52,* 91–103.

Golomb, C., & Cornelius, C. B. (1977). Symbolic play and its cognitive significance. *Developmental Psychology, 13*(3), 246–252.

Goode, W. J. (1963). *World revolution and family patterns.* New York: Free Press.

Goode, W. J. (1971). Force and violence in the family. *Journal of Marriage and the Family, 33*(4), 624–636.

Goodman, J. F. (1979). ''Ignorance'' versus ''stupidity''—The basic disagreement. *School Psychology Digest, 8,* 47–62.

Goodman, M. E. (1970). *The culture of childhood: Child's eye views of society and culture.* New York: Teachers College Press.

Goodman, M. J., Stewart, G. J., & Gilbert, F., Jr. (1977). A study of certain medical and physiological variables among Caucasian and

Japanese women living in Hawaii. *Journal of Gerontology, 32*(3), 291–298.

Goody, J. (1977). *The domestication of the savage mind.* Cambridge: Cambridge University Press.

Goody, J., & Watt, I. (1963). The consequences of literacy. In J. Goody (Ed.), *Literacy in traditional societies.* Cambridge: Cambridge University Press.

Gopnik, A., & Meltzoff, A. N. (1984). Semantic and cognitive development in 15 to 21 month old children. *Journal of Child Language, 11,* 495–513.

Gordimer, N. (1979). *Burger's daughter.* New York: Viking.

Gottlieb, G. (1976). The roles of experience in the development of behavior and the nervous system. In G. Gottlieb (Ed.), *Studies on the development of behavior and the nervous system: Vol. 3. Neural and behavioral specificity.* New York: Academic Press.

Gottman, J., Gonzo, J., & Rasmussen, B. (1975). Social interaction, social competence, and friendship in children. *Child Development, 46,* 709–718.

Gouin-Decarie, T. (1965). *Intelligence and affectivity in early childhood.* New York: International Universities Press.

Gouin-Decarie, T. (1969). A study of the mental and emotional development of the Thalidomide child. In B. M. Foss (Ed.), *Determinants of infant behavior* (Vol. 4). London: Methuen.

Gould, R. L. (1978). *Transformations: Growth and change in adult life.* New York: Simon & Schuster.

Gould, R. L. (1981). *The mismeasure of man.* New York: Norton.

Gould, S. J. (1977). *Ontogeny and phylogeny.* Cambridge, MA: Harvard University Press, Belknap Press.

Graham, P., Rutter, M., & George, S. (1973). Temperamental characteristics as predictors of behavior disorders in children. *American Journal of Orthopsychiatry, 43,* 328–339.

Granick, S., Kleban, M. H., & Weiss, A. D. (1976). Relationships between hearing loss and cognition in normally hearing aged persons. *Journal of Gerontology, 31,* 434–440.

Granick, S., & Patterson, R. D. (Eds.). (1971). *Human aging II: An eleven-year followup biomedical and behavioral study.* Washington, DC: Government Printing Office.

Graubard, S. R. (1978). Preface. In E. H. Erikson (Ed.), *Adulthood.* New York: Norton.

Graves, S. B. (1976). Television and its impact on the cognitive and affective development of minority children. In G. L. Berry & C. Mitchell-Kernan (Eds.), *Television and the socialization of the minority child.* New York: Academic Press.

Graves, Z., & Glick, J. (1978). The effect of context on mother-child intervention: A progress report. *Quarterly Newsletter of the Institute of Comparative Human Development, 2,* 41–46.

Green, R. (1978). Sexual identity of 37 children raised by homosexual or transsexual parents. *American Journal of Psychiatry, 135*(6), 692–697.

Greenberg, D. (1977). Delinquency and the age structure of society. *Contemporary Crises, 1,* 189–223.

Greenberg, J. R., & Mitchell, S. A. (1983). *Object relations in psychoanalytic theory.* Cambridge, MA: Harvard University Press.

Greenfield, P. M. (1966). On culture and conservation. In J. S. Bruner, R. P. Olver, & P. M. Greenfield (Eds.), *Studies in cognitive growth.* New York: Wiley.

Greenfield, P. M. (1984). *Mind and media: The effects of television, video games, and computers.* Cambridge, MA: Harvard University Press.

Greenfield, P. M., & Smith, J. H. (1976). *The structure of communication in early language development.* New York: Academic Press.

Grice, H. P. (1975). Logic and conversation (published in part). In P. Cole & J. L. Morgan (Eds.), *Syntax and semantics: Vol. 3. Speech acts* (pp. 41–58). New York: Seminar Press.

Grieve, R., & Hoogenrand, R. (1979). First words. In P. Fletcher & M. Garman (Eds.), *Language acquisition* (pp. 93–104). Cambridge: Cambridge University Press.

Grinder, R. E. (1969). The concept of adolescence in the genetic psychology of G. Stanley Hall. *Child Development, 40,* 355–366.

Groos, K. (1901). *The play of man* (E. L. Baldwin, Trans.). New York: Appleton.

Grossman, E. E., & Grossman, K. (1984). Discovery and proof in attachment research. *Behavioral and Brain Sciences, 7,* 154–155.

Grossman, E. E., Grossman, K., Huber, F., & Wartner, U. (1981). German children's behavior towards their mothers at 12 months and their fathers at 18 months in Ainsworth's strange situation. *International Journal of Behavioral Development, 4,* 157–181.

Grotevant, H. D., & Thorbecke, W. L. (1982). Sex differences in styles of occupational identity formation in late adolescence. *Developmental Psychology, 18*(3), 396–405.

Grubb, N., & Lazerson, M. (1982). *Broken promises.* New York: Basic Books.

Guardo, C. J., & Bohan, J. B. (1971). Development of a sense of self-identity in children. *Child Development, 42,* 1909–1921.

Guilford, J. P. (1967). *The nature of human intelligence.* New York: McGraw-Hill.

Guttmacher, A. F. (1973). *Pregnancy, birth and family planning.* New York: Viking.

Haan, N. (1981). Common dimensions of personality development: Early adolescence to middle life. In D. H. Eichorn, J. A. Clausen, N. Haan, M. P. Honzik, & P. H. Mussen (Eds.), *Present and past in middle life.* New York: Academic Press.

Haan, N., Smith, M. B., & Block, J. H. (1968). The moral reasoning in young adults: Political-social behavior, family background, and personality correlates. *Journal of Personality and Social Psychology, 10,* 183–201.

Hacker, A. (1983). *A statistical portrait of the American people.* New York: Viking.

Hagen, J., & Hale, G. (1973). The development of attention in children. In A. D. Pick (Ed.), *Minnesota Symposia on Child Psychology* (Vol. 7). Minneapolis: University of Minnesota Press.

Haith, M. M. (1980). *Rules newborns look by.* Hillsdale, NJ: Erlbaum.

Haith, M. M., Bergman, T., & Moore, M. J. (1977). Eye contact and face scanning in early infancy. *Science, 198,* 853–855.

Hall, E. (1984, December). A sense of control: Conversation with Judith Rodin. *Psychology Today,* 38–45.

Hall, G. S. (1891). Notes on the study of infants. *Pedagogical Seminary, 1,* 127–138.

Hall, G. S. (1896). The first five-hundred days of a child's life. *Child Study Monographs, 97*(2), 330–342, 394–407, 458–473, 522–537, 586–608.

Hall, G. S. (1904). *Adolescence: Its psychology and its relations to physiology, anthropology, sociology, sex, crime, religion and education.* New York: Appleton.

Hall, V. C., & Kingsley, R. C. (1968). Conservation and equilibration theory. *Journal of Genetic Psychology, 113,* 195–213.

Halliday, M.A.K. (1975). *Learning how to mean: Explorations in the development of language.* London: Edward Arnold.

Hallowell, A. I. (1971). *Culture and experience* (2nd ed.). Philadelphia: University of Pennsylvania Press.

Halmi, K. A. (1978). Anorexia nervosa: Recent investigations. *Annual Review of Medicine, 29,* 37–149.

Halverson, H. M. (1931). An experimental study of prehension in infants by means of systematic cinema records. *Genetic Psychology Monographs, 10,* 107–286.

Hamburg, B. (1974). Early adolescence: A specific and stressful stage of the life cycle. In G. Coelho, D. A. Hamburg, & J. E. Adams (Eds.), *Coping and adaption.* New York: Basic Books.

Hamburger, J. (1978). *Discovering the individual.* New York: Norton.

Handel, G. (Ed.). (1985). *The psychosocial interior of the family* (2nd ed.). New York: Aldine.

Hanson, D. A., & Johnson, V. A. (1985). *Strategies of active non-learning: Evading and dissembling in the classroom.* Paper delivered at the American Education Research Association, Chicago.

Hansson, R. O., Jones, W. H., & Carpenter, B. N. (1984). Relational competence and social support. In P. Shaver (Ed.), *Review of personality and social psychology: Emotions, relationships, and health* (Vol. 5, pp. 265–284). Beverly Hills Sage.

Hareven, T. K. (1978). The last stage: Historical adulthood and old age. In E. H. Erikson (Ed.), *Adulthood* (pp. 201–216). New York: Norton.

Hareven, T. K. (1982). The life course and aging in historical perspective. In T. K. Hareven & K. J. Adams (Eds.), *Aging and life course transitions: An interdisciplinary perspective* (pp. 1–26). New York: Guilford Press.

Hareven, T. K., & Adams, K. J. (Eds.). (1982). *Aging and life course transitions: An interdisciplinary perspective.* New York: Guilford Press.

Harlow, H. F. (1950). Learning and satiation of response in intrinsically motivated complex puzzle performance by monkeys. *Journal of Comparative Physiology and Psychology, 43,* 289–294.

Harlow, H. F. (1958). The nature of love. *American Psychologist, 13,* 673–685.

Harlow, H. F. (1962). Heterosexual affectional system in monkeys. *American Psychologist, 17,* 1–9.

Harlow H. F., & Harlow, M. K. (1965). The affectional systems. In A. M. Schrier, H. F. Harlow, & F. Stollnitz (Eds.), *Behavior of non-human primates* (Vol. 2, pp. 287–334). New York: Academic Press.

Harlow, H. F., & Harlow, M. K. (1966). Learning to love. *American Scientist, 54,* 244–272.

Harlow, H. F., & Harlow, M. K. (1969). Effects of various mother-infant relationships on rhesus monkey behaviors. In B. M. Foss (Ed.), *Determinants of infant behavior* (Vol. 4). London: Methuen.

Harlow, H. F., Harlow, M. K., & Suomi, S. J. (1971). From thought to therapy: Lessons from a primate laboratory. *American Scientist, 59,* 538–649.

Harlow, H. F., & Zimmerman, R. R. (1959). Affectional responses in the infant monkey. *Science, 130,* 431–432.

Harré, R. (1976). Living up to a name. In R. Harré (Ed.), *Personality* (pp. 44–60). Oxford: Basil Blackwell.

Harris, B. (1979). Whatever happened to Little Albert? *American Psychologist, 34,* 151–160.

Harris, L. P. (1977). Self-recognition among institutionalized, profoundly retarded males: A replication. *Bulletin of the Psychonomic Society, 9,* 43–44.

Harris, M. (1968). *The rise of anthropological theory.* New York: Crowell.

Harris, P. L. (1983). Infant cognition. In P. H. Mussen (Ed.), *Handbook of child psychology: Vol. 2. Infancy and developmental psychobiology* (4th ed.). New York: Wiley.

Harter, S. (1983). Developmental perspectives on the self-system. In P. H. Mussen (Ed.), *Handbook of child psychology: Vol. 4. Socialization, personality, and social development* (pp. 275–385). New York: Wiley.

Hartshorne, H., & May, M. (1928). *Studies in the nature of character: Vol. 1. Studies in deceit.* New York: Macmillan.

Hartup, W. W. (1970). Peer interaction and social organization. In P. H. Mussen (Ed.), *Carmichael's manual of child psychology* (Vol. 2). New York: Wiley.

Hartup, W. W. (1976). Peer interaction and the behavioral development of the individual child. In E. Schopler & R. J. Reichler (Eds.), *Psychopathology and child development.* New York: Plenum Press.

Hartup, W. W. (1979). The social worlds of childhood. *American Psychologist, 34*(10), 944–950.

Hartup, W. W. (1983). Peer relations. In P. H. Mussen (Ed.), *Handbook of child psychology: Vol. 4. Socialization, personality, and social development* (pp. 103–196). New York: Wiley.

Hartup, W. W., & Lempers, J. (1973). A problem in life-span development: The interactional analysis of family attachment. In P. Baltes & K. W. Schaie (Eds.), *Life-span developmental psychology: Personality and socialization.* New York: Academic Press.

Hayes, C. (1951). *The ape in our house.* New York: Harper.

Hayflick, L. (1980). The cell biology of human aging. *Scientific American, 242,* 58–65.

Hearnshaw, L. S. (1979). *Cyril Burt: Psychologist.* New York: Vintage Books.

Hebb, D. O. (1980). *Essay on mind.* Hillsdale, NJ: Erlbaum.

Heider, F. (1958). *The psychology of interpersonal relations.* New York: Wiley.

Henderson, S. (1982). The significance of social relationships in the etiology of neurosis. In C. M. Parkes & J. Stevenson-Hinde (Eds.), *The place of attachment in human behavior.* New York: Basic Books.

Henle, M. (1962). On the relation between logic and thinking. *Psychological Review, 69,* 366–378.

Henry, J. (1963). *Culture against man.* New York: Vintage Books.

Hicks, M. W., & Platt, M. (1970). Marital happiness and stability. *Journal of Marriage and the Family, 32,* 553–574.

Hilgard, E. R. (1980). Consciousness in contemporary psychology. *Annual Review of Psychology, 31.*

Hill, S. D., Bundy, R. A., Gallup, G. G., Jr., & McClure, M. K. (1970). Responsiveness of young nursery-reared chimpanzees to mirrors. *Proceedings of the Louisiana Academy of Sciences, 33,* 77–82.

Himmelweit, H. T., Oppenheim, A. N., & Vince, P. (1958). *Television and the child: An empirical study of the effect of television on the young.* London: Oxford University Press.

Hinde, R. A. (1979). *Towards understanding relationships.* London: Academic Press.

Hinde, R. A. (1982). Attachment: Some conceptual and biological issues. In C. M. Parkes & J. Stevenson-Hinde (Eds.), *The place of attachment in human behavior.* New York: Basic Books.

Hinde, R. A., & Stevenson-Hinde, J. (Eds.), (1973). *Constraints on learning: Limitations and predispositions.* New York: Academic Press. (Based on a conference sponsored at St. John's College, Cambridge, England)

Hine, W. D. (1970). The abilities of partially hearing children. *British Journal of Educational Psychology, 40,* 171–178.

Hirsch, J. (1970). Behavior-genetic analysis and its biosocial consequences. *Seminars in Psychiatry, 2,* 89–105.

Hockett, C. F. (1960). The origin of speech. In Scientific American staff (Eds.), *Human communication: Language and its psychobiological bases* (pp. 7–12). San Francisco: W. H. Freeman.

Hockett, C. F. (1963). The problem of universals in language. In J. H. Greenberg (Ed.), *Universals of language.* Cambridge, MA: MIT Press.

Hockett, C. F. (1982). The origin of speech. In S.-Y. Wang (Ed.), *Human communication.* San Francisco: W. H. Freeman.

Hoffman, M. L., & Saltzstein, H. D. (1967). Parent discipline and the child's moral development. *Journal of Personality and Social Psychology, 5,* 45–57.

Hogan, R. (1980). The gifted adolescent. In J. Adelson (Ed.), *The handbook of adolescent psychology* (pp. 536–559). New York: Wiley.

Holinger, P. C., & Offer, D. (1981). Perspectives on suicide in adolescence. In R. G. Simmons (Ed.), *Research in community and mental health* (Vol. 2, pp. 139–157). Greenwich, CN: JAI Press.

Hollingshead, A. B. (1949). *Elmtown's youth.* New York: Viking.

Holt, R. R. (1977). Freud's theory of the primary process: Present status. In T. Shapiro (Ed.), *Psychoanalysis and contemporary science: An annual of integrative and interdisciplinary studies* (Vol. 5, pp. 61–99). New York: International Universities Press.

Homans, G. (1974). *Human behavior: Its elementary forms.* New York: Harcourt Brace Jovanovich.

Honzik, M. P., Macfarlane, J. W., & Allen, L. (1948). The stability of mental test performance between two and eighteen years. *Journal of Experimental Education, 4,* 309–324.

Hooker, E. (1965). Gender identity in male homosexuals. In J. Money (Ed.), *Sex research.* New York: Holt, Rinehart & Winston.

Horn, J. L., & Donaldson, G. (1976). On the myth of intellectual decline in adulthood. *American Psychologist, 31,* 701–719.

Howe, S. G. (1972). The education of Laura Bridgeman. In W. Dennis (Ed.), *Historical readings in developmental psychology* (pp. 62–67). New York: Appleton-Century-Crofts.

Hoyer, F. W., Labouvie, G., & Baltes, T. (1973). Modification of response speed in intellectual performance in the elderly. *Human Development, 16,* 233–242.

Hubel, D. H., & Wiesel, T. N. (1965). Binocular interaction in striate cortex kittens reared with artificial squint. *Journal of Neurophysiology, 28,* 1041–1059.

Hughes, M. (1975). *Egocentrism in pre-school children.* Unpublished doctoral dissertation, Edinburgh University.

Hunt, D. (1970). *Parents and children in history: The psychology of family life in early modern France.* New York: Basic Books.

Hunt, J. M. (1961). *Intelligence and experience.* New York: Ronald Press.

Hunt, J. M. (1965). Intrinsic motivation and its role in psychological development. In D. Levine (ed.), *Nebraska Symposium on Motivation* (Vol. 13). Lincoln: University of Nebraska Press.

Hunt, M. (1982). *The universe within: A new science explores the human mind.* New York: Simon & Schuster.

Huston, A., & Wright, J. C. (1982). Effects of communications media on children. In C. B. Kopp & J. B. Krakow (Eds.), *The child: Development in a social context* (pp. 576–629). Reading, MA: Addison-Wesley.

Huston-Stein, A., & Higgens-Trenk, A. (1978). Development of females from childhood through adulthood: Career and feminine role orientations. In P. B. Baltes (Ed.), *Life-span development and behavior* (Vol. 1, pp. 258–296). New York: Academic Press.

Huttenlocher, J. E. (1974). The origins of language comprehension. In R. L. Solso (Ed.), *Theories in cognitive psychology: The Loyola Symposium* (pp. 331–368). Hillsdale, NJ: Erlbaum.

Inhelder, B., & Piaget, J. (1958). *The growth of logical thinking from childhood to adolescence.* New York: Basic Books.

Inhelder, B., & Piaget, J. (1964). *The early growth of logic in the child* (E. A. Lunzer & D. Papert, Trans.). New York: Harper & Row.

Isaac, G. (1978). The foodsharing behavior of proto-human hominids. *Scientific American, 238*(4), 90–108.

Isaacs, S. (1966). *Intellectual growth in young children.* New York: Schocken.

Isotoma, Z. M. (1975). The development of voluntary memory in children of pre-school age. *Soviet Psychology, 13*(4), 5–64.

Izard, C. E. (1977). *Human emotions.* New York: Plenum Press.

Izard, C. E., Kagan, J., & Zajonc, R. B. (1984). *Emotions, cognition, and behavior.* New York: Cambridge University Press.

Jacobs, D. (1982). *But we need the eggs: The magic of Woody Allen.* New York: St. Martin's Press.

Jacobson, D. (1966). Riddles of existence. In E. Blischen (Ed.), *The world of children.* London: Paul Hamlyn.

Jacobson, S. W., & Kagan, J. (1979). Interpreting "imitative" responses in early infancy. *Science, 205,* 215–217.

Jaffe, J., & Feldstein, S. (1970). *Rhythms of dialogue.* New York: Academic Press.

James, W. (1890). *Principles of psychology* (Vol. 1). New York: Holt. (Reprinted 1983, Cambridge, MA: Harvard University Press)

Jaynes, J. (1977). *The origin of consciousness in the breakdown of the bicameral mind.* Boston: Houghton Mifflin.

Jencks, C. (1972). *Inequality: A reassessment of the effect of family and schooling in America.* New York: Basic Books.

Jensen, A. R. (1969). How much can we boost IQ and scholastic achievement? *Harvard Educational Review, 39,* 1–123.

Jensen, A. R. (1980). *Bias in mental testing.* New York: Free Press.

Jerison, H. J. (1982). The evolution of consciousness. In Sir J. Eccles (Ed.), *Mind and brain: The many-faceted problems* (pp. 13–27). Washington, DC: Paragon House.

Jersild, A. T., & Holmes, F. B. (1935). Children's fears. *Child Development Monographs.* New York: Teachers College Press.

Jessor, R., & Jessor, S. L. (1977). *Problem behavior and psychosocial development.* New York: Academic Press.

Joffe, L. S., & Vaughn, B. E. (1982). Infant-mother attachment: Theory, assessment and implications for development. In B. B. Wolman (Ed.), *Handbook of developmental psychology.* Englewood Cliffs, NJ: Prentice-Hall.

Johnson, M. (1963). Sex role learning in the nuclear family. *Child Development, 34,* 319–333.

Johnston, J., & Ettema, J. (1982). *Positive images: Breaking stereotypes with children's television.* Beverly Hills: Sage.

Jones, H. E. (1949). Adolescence in our society. In *The family in a democratic society.* Anniversary papers of the Community Service Society of New York. New York: Columbia University Press.

Jones, H. E., & Conrad, H. S. (1933). The growth and decline of intelligence. *Genetic Psychology Monographs, 13*(3), 239–298.

Jones, K. L., & Smith, D. W. (1973). Recognition of the fetal alcohol syndrome in early infancy. *Lancet, 2,* 999–1001.

Jones, M. C. (1965). Psychological correlates of somatic development. *Child Development, 36,* 899–911.

Jordan, D. (1971). *Parental antecedents and personality characteristics of ego identity statuses.* Unpublished doctoral dissertation, State University of New York, Buffalo.

Jordan, W. J. (1978). Searching for adulthood in America. In E. H. Erikson (Ed.), *Adulthood* (pp. 189–200). New York: Norton.

Josselson, R. (1980). Ego development in adolescence. In J. Adelson (Ed.), *Handbook of adolescent psychology* (pp. 188–210). New York: Wiley.

Jurich, A. P. (1976). *Moral development in the adolescent years.* Department of Family and Child Development, Kansas State University.

Kaestle, C. F., & Vinovskis, M. A. (1978). From apron strings to ABC's: Parents, children and schooling in nineteenth-century Massachusetts. In J. Demos & S. S. Boocock (Eds.), *Turning points: Historical and sociological essays on the family* (pp. 539–580). Chicago: University of Chicago Press.

Kagan, J. (1967). On the need for relativism. *American Psychologist, 22*(2), 131–142.

Kagan, J. (1970). The determinants of attention in the infant. *American Scientist, 58,* 298–306.

Kagan, J. (1971). *Change and continuity in infancy.* New York: Wiley.

Kagan, J. (1972). Motives and development. *Journal of Personality and Social Psychology, 22,* 51–66.

Kagan, J. (1976). Emergent themes in human development. *American Scientist, 64,* 186–196.

Kagan, J. (1978). *The growth of the child: Reflections on human development.* New York: Norton.

Kagan, J. (1980). Perspectives on continuity. In O. G. Brim, Jr., & J. Kagan (Eds.), *Constancy and change in human development* (pp. 26–74). Cambridge, MA: Harvard University Press.

Kagan, J. (1981). *The second year: The emergence of self-awareness.* Cambridge, MA: Harvard University Press.

Kagan, J. (1982a). The construct of difficult temperament: A reply to Thomas, Chess, and Korn. *Merrill-Palmer Quarterly, 28,* 21–24.

Kagan, J. (1982b). *Psychological research on the human infant: An evaluative summary.* New York: Grant Foundation.

Kagan, J. (1984). *The nature of the child.* New York: Basic Books.

Kagan, J., Kearsley, R. B., & Zelazo, P. R. (1978). *Infancy: Its place in human development.* Cambridge, MA: Harvard University Press.

Kagan, J., & Lewis, M. (1965). Studies of attention in the human infant. *Merrill-Palmer Quarterly, 11,* 95–127.

Kagan, J., & Moss, H. (1983). *Birth to maturity* (2nd ed.). New Haven: Yale University Press.

Kahneman, D., Slovic, P., & Tversky, A. (Eds.). (1982). *Judgment under uncertainty: Heuristics and biases.* Cambridge: Cambridge University Press.

Kail, R. V. (1979). *The development of memory in children.* San Francisco: W. H. Freeman.

Kamin, L. J. (1974). *The science and politics of IQ.* Hillsdale, NJ: Erlbaum.

Karniol, R. (1978). Children's use of intention cues in evaluating behavior. *Psychological Bulletin, 85*(1), 76–85.

Katchadourian, H. A. (1978). Medical perspectives on adulthood. In E. H. Erikson (Ed.), *Adulthood* (pp. 33–60). New York: Norton.

Katz, P. A. (1979). The development of female identity. *Sex Roles, 5,* 155–178.

Kavanaugh, J. L. (1967). Behavior of captive white footed mice. *Science, 155,* 1623–1639.

Keating, D. P. (1980). Thinking processes in adolescence. In J. Adelson (Ed.), *Handbook of adolescent psychology* (pp. 211–246). New York: Wiley.

Kegan, R. (1982). *The evolving self: Problem and process in human development.* Cambridge, MA: Harvard University Press.

Keller, H. (1917). *The story of my life: With her letters (1887–1901).* New York: Doubleday.

Kelly, G. A. (1955). *Theory of personality: The psychology of personal constructs.* New York: Norton.

Kendon, A. (1967). Some functions of gaze direction in social interaction. *Acta Psychologica, 26,* 22–63.

Keniston, K. (1971). *Youth and dissent.* New York: Harcourt Brace Jovanovich.

Kennell, J. H., Trouse, M. A., & Klaus, M. H. (1975). Evidence for a sensitive period in the human mother. In *CIBA Foundation Symposium 33.* Amsterdam: Elsevier.

Kenny, D. A. (1979). *Correlation and causality*. New York: Wiley.

Kessen, W. (1965). *The child*. New York: Wiley.

Kessen, W. (1966). Questions for a theory of cognitive development. In H. W. Stevenson (Ed.), *Concept of development. Monographs of the Society for Research in Child Development, 31*(5, Serial No. 107).

Kessen, W., Haith, M. M., & Salapatek, P. H. (1970). Human infancy: A bibliography and guide. In P. H. Mussen (Ed.), *Carmichael's manual of child psychology* (3rd ed., Vol. 1, pp. 287–360). New York: Wiley.

Kett, J. F. (1971). Adolescence and youth in nineteenth-century America. *Journal of Interdisciplinary History, 2*, 283.

Kett, J. F. (1977). *Rites of passage: Adolescence in America, 1790 to the present*. New York: Basic Books.

Keyfitz, N., & Pfleger, W. (1968). *World population: An analysis of vital data*. Chicago: University of Chicago Press.

Kimmel, D. C. (1974). *Adulthood and aging*. New York: Wiley.

Kinsbourne, M., & Hiscock, M. (1983). The normal and deviant development of functional lateralization of the brain. In P. H. Mussen (Ed.), *Handbook of child psychology* (Vol. 2, pp. 157–280). New York: Wiley.

Kinsey, A. C., Pomeroy, W. B., & Martin, C. E. (1948). *Sexual behavior in the human male*. Philadelphia: W. B. Saunders.

Klaus, M., & Kennell, J. (1976). *Maternal-infant bonding*. St. Louis: C. V. Mosby.

Klein, M. (1981). On Mahler's autistic and symbiotic phases. *Psychoanalysis and Contemporary Thought, 4*(1), 69–105.

Klima, E., & Bellugi, U. (1973). Teaching apes to communicate. In G. A. Miller (Ed.), *Communication, language, and meaning*. New York: Basic Books.

Kluckhohn, C., & Murray, H. A. (Eds.). (1948). *Personality in nature, society and culture*. New York: Knopf.

Knudtson, F. W. (1976). Life-span attachment: Complexities, questions, and considerations. *Human Development, 19*, 182–196.

Kochman, T. (1972). Black American speech events and a language program for the classroom. In C. B. Cazden, V. P. John, & D. Hymes (Eds.), *Functions of language in the classroom* (pp. 211–261). New York: Teachers College Press.

Koff, E., Rierdan, J., & Silverstone, E. (1978). Changes in representation of body image as a function of menarcheal status. *Developmental Psychology, 14*(6), 635–642.

Kohlberg, L. (1963). The development of children's orientations toward a moral order: Pt. 1. Sequence in the development of moral thought. *Vita Humana, 6*, 11–33.

Kohlberg, L. (1966). A cognitive-developmental analysis of children's sex-role concepts and attitudes. In E. E. Maccoby (Ed.), *The development of sex differences*. Stanford: Stanford University Press.

Kohlberg, L. (1969). Stage and sequence: The cognitive-developmental approach to socialization. In A. Goslin (Ed.), *Handbook of socialization theory and research*. Chicago: Rand McNally.

Kohlberg, L. (1983). *The philosophy of moral development*. New York: Harper & Row.

Kohlberg, L. (1984). *The psychology of moral development* (Vol. 2). New York: Harper & Row.

Kohlberg, L., & De Vries, R. (1983). *Developmental psychology in early education*. New York: Longman.

Kohlberg, L., Lacrosse, O. J., & Ricks, O. (1971). The predictability of adult mental health from childhood behavior. In B. Wolman (Ed.), *Manual of child psychopathology*. New York: McGraw-Hill.

Kohn, M. L. (1963). Social class and parent-child relationships. *American Journal of Sociology, 68*, 471–480.

Kohut, H. (1973). Thoughts on narcissism and narcissistic rage. *Psychoanalytic Study of the Child, 27*, 360–401.

Kohut, H. (1977). *The restoration of the self*. New York: International Universities Press.

Komarovsky, M. (1973). Cultural contradictions and sex roles: The masculine case. In A. S. Skolnick & J. H. Skolnick (Eds.), *Family in transition* (pp. 190–218). Boston: Little, Brown.

Konner, M. J. (1977). Infancy among the Kalahari Desert sun. In P. H. Leiderman, S. R. Tulkin, & A. Rosenfeld (Eds.), *Culture and infancy*. New York: Academic Press.

Korner, A. F. (1973). Individual differences at birth: Implications for early experience and later development. In J. C. Westman (Ed.), *Individual differences in children* (pp. 69–82). New York: Wiley.

Kuhl, P. K. (1978). Predispositions for the perception of speech-sound categories: A species-specific phenomenon? In F. D. Minifie & L. L. Lloyd (Eds.), *Communicative and cognitive abilities: Early behavioral assessment*. Baltimore: University Park Press.

Kuhn, D. (1984). Cognitive development. In M. H. Bornstein & M. E. Lamb (Eds.), *Developmental psychology: An advanced textbook* (pp. 133–180). Hillsdale, NJ: Erlbaum.

Kuhn, T. (1962). *The structure of scientific revolutions*. Chicago: University of Chicago Press.

Kulka, R. A., & Weingarten, H. (1979, August). *The long-term effects of parental divorce in childhood on adult adjustment: A twenty-year study.* Paper presented at the meeting of the American Sociological Association, Boston.

Kurdek, L. A. (1977). Structural components and intellectual correlates of cognitive perspective taking in first- through fourth-grade children. *Child Development, 48,* 1503–1511.

Kurtines, W., & Greif, E. B. (1974). The development of moral thought: Review and evaluation of Kohlberg's approach. *Psychological Bulletin, 81*(8), 453–470.

Laboratory of Comparative Human Cognition (1983). Culture and cognitive development. In P. H. Mussen (Ed.), *Handbook of child psychology: Vol. 1. History, theory and methods* (4th ed., pp. 295–356). New York: Wiley.

Labouvie-Vief, G. (1978). Adult cognitive development: In search of alternative interpretations. *Merrill-Palmer Quarterly, 23,* 227–263.

Labouvie-Vief, G., & Gonda, J. N. (1976). Cognitive strategy training and intellectual performance in the elderly. *Journal of Gerontology, 31,* 327–332.

Labov, W. (1972). *Language in the inner city: Studies in the black vernacular.* Philadelphia: University of Pennsylvania Press.

Lacan, J. (1936/1977). The mirror-stage as formative of the function of the I as revealed in psychoanalytic experience. In J. Lacan (Ed.), *Ecrits: A selection* (A. Shendan, Trans.). New York: Norton.

Lacey, J. I., & Lacey, B. C. (1970). Some autonomic and central nervous system relationships. In P. Black (Ed.), *Physiological correlates of emotion.* New York: Academic Press.

La Farge, P. (1972). An uptight adolescence. In J. Kagan & R. Coles (Eds.), *Twelve to sixteen: Early adolescence.* New York: Norton.

Laing, R. D. (1969). *The divided self.* New York: Pantheon.

Laing, R. D. (1970). *The self and others.* New York: Pantheon.

Lamb, M. E. (1979). The effects of the social context on dyadic social interaction. In M. E. Lamb, S. J. Suomi, & G. R. Stephenson (Eds.), *Social interaction analysis.* Madison: University of Wisconsin Press.

Lamb, M. E. (1981). The development of father-infant relationships. In M. E. Lamb (Ed.), *The role of the father in child development.* New York: Wiley.

Lamb, M. E., & Hwang, C. P. (1982). Maternal attachment and mother-neonate bonding: A critical review. In M. E. Lamb & A. L. Brown (Eds.), *Advances in developmental psychology* (Vol. 2). Hillsdale, NJ: Erlbaum.

Lamb, M. E., Thompson, R. A., Gardner, W. P., Charnov, E. L., & Estes, D. (1984). Security of infantile attachment as assessed in the "Strange Situation": Its study and biological interpretation. *Behavioral and Brain Sciences, 7,* 127–154.

Lancaster, J. B. (1975). *Primate behavior and the emergence of human culture.* New York: Holt, Rinehart & Winston.

Lane, H. (1976). *The wild boy of Aveyron.* Cambridge, MA: Harvard University Press.

Langer, W. L. (1972). Checks on population growth: 1750–1850. *Scientific American, 226,* 93–100.

Langlois, J. H. (in press). From the eye of the beholder to behavioral reality: The development of social behaviors and social relations as a function of physical attractiveness. In C. P. Herman (Ed.), *Physical appearance, stigma, and social behavior: The Ontario Symposium on Personality and Social Psychology.* New York: Erlbaum.

Langlois, J. H., & Downs, A. C. (1979). Peer relations as a function of physical attractiveness: The eye of the beholder or behavioral reality? *Child Development, 50,* 409–418.

Langlois, J. H., & Stephan, C. W. (1981). Beauty and the beast: The role of physical attractiveness in the development of peer relations and social behavior. In S. S. Brehm, S. M. Kassin, & F. Y. Gibbons (Eds.), *Developmental social psychology.* New York: Academic Press.

Laslett, P. (1976). Societal development and aging. In R. H. Binstock & E. Shanas (Eds.), *Handbook of aging and the social sciences* (pp. 87–116). New York: Van Nostrand Reinhold.

Laurendeau, M., & Pinard, A. (1970). *Development of the concept of space in the child.* New York: International Universities Press.

Leboyer, F. (1975). *Birth without violence.* New York: Knopf.

Lefcourt, H. M. (1973). The function of the illusions of control and freedom. *American Psychologist, 28,* 417–425.

Lefcourt, H. M. (1976). *Locus of control: Current trends in theory and research.* Hillsdale, NJ: Erlbaum.

Lehman, H. C. (1953). *Age and achievement.* Princeton: Princeton University Press.

Leichty, M. M. (1963). Family attitudes and self concepts in Vietnamese and U.S. children. *American Journal of Orthopsychiatry, 33,* 38–50.

Lemert, E. M. (1951). *Social pathology.* New York: McGraw-Hill.

Lemert, E. M. (1967). *Human deviance, social problems, and social control.* Englewood Cliffs, NJ: Prentice-Hall.

Lempers, J. D. (1976). *Production of pointing: Comprehension of pointing and understanding of looking behavior in young children.* Doctoral dissertation, University of Minnesota, Minneapolis.

Lempers, J. D., Flavell, E. R., & Flavell, J. H. (1977). The development in very young children of tacit knowledge concerning visual perception. *Genetic Psychology Monographs, 95,* 3–53.

Lenneberg, E. H. (1973). Biological aspects of language. In G. A. Miller (Ed.), *Communication, language, and meaning: Psychological perspectives* (pp. 49–60). New York: Basic Books.

Lerner, J. V., & Lerner, R. M. (1983). Temperament and adaptation across life: Theoretical and empirical issues. In P. B. Baltes & O. G. Brim, Jr. (Eds.), *Life-span development and behavior* (Vol. 5, pp. 197–231). New York: Academic Press.

Lerner, R. M., Orlos, J. B., & Knapp, J. R. (1976). Physical attractiveness, physical effectiveness, and self-concept in late adolescents. *Adolescence, 11,* 313–326.

Lerner, R. M., & Ryff, C. D. (1978). Implementation of the life-span view of human development: The sample case of attachment. In P. B. Baltes (Ed.), *Life-span development and behavior* (Vol. 1). New York: Academic Press.

Lerner, R. M., Spanier, G. B., & Belsky, J. (1982). The child in the family. In C. B. Kopp & J. B. Krakow (Eds.), *The child: Development in a social context* (pp. 393–455). Reading, MA: Addison-Wesley.

Leung, E., & Rheingold, H. (1981). Development of pointing as a social gesture. *Developmental Psychology, 17,* 215–220.

Lever, J. (1976). Sex differences in the games children play. *Social Problems, 23*(4), 478–487.

Lever, J. (1978). Sex differences in the complexity of children's play and games. *American Sociological Review, 43,* 471–483.

LeVine, R. A. (1973a). *Culture, behavior, and personality.* Chicago: Aldine.

LeVine, R. A. (1973b). Patterns of personality in Africa. *Ethos, 1,* 123–152.

Levinson, D. J. (1977). Mid-life transition period in adult psychosocial development. *Psychiatry, 40,* 99–112.

Levinson, D. J. (1978). *The seasons of a man's life.* New York: Ballantine.

Lévy-Bruhl, L. (1923). *Primitive mentality.* London: Allen & Unwin.

Lewin, K. (1939). Field theory and experiment in social psychology: Concepts and methods. *American Journal of Sociology, 44,* 868–897.

Lewis, M. (1982). The social network systems model: Toward a theory of social development. In T. M. Field, A. Huston, H. C. Quay, L. Troll, & G. E. Finley (Eds.), *Review of human development.* New York: Wiley.

Lewis, M., & Brooks-Gunn, J. (1978). Self-knowledge and emotional development. In M. Lewis and L. Rosenblum (Eds.), *The development of affect.* New York: Plenum Press.

Lewis, M., & Brooks-Gunn, J. (1979). *Social cognition and the acquisition of self.* New York: Plenum Press.

Lewis, M., Feiring, C., McGuffog, C., & Jaskir, J. (1984). Predicting psychopathology in six year olds for early social relations. *Child Development, 55*(1), 123–136.

Lewis, M., & Schaeffer, S. (1981). Peer behavior and mother-infant interaction in maltreated children. In M. Lewis & L. Rosenblum (Eds.), *The uncommon child: The genesis of behavior* (Vol. 3). New York: Plenum Press.

Lewis, M., Young, G., Brooks, J., & Michalson, L. (1975). The beginning of friendship. In M. Lewis & L. Rosenblum (Eds.), *Friendship and peer relations: The origins of behavior* (Vol. 4). New York: Wiley.

Lewontin, R. C. (1982). *Human diversity.* San Francisco: W. H. Freeman.

Lewontin, R. C., Rose, S., & Kamin, L. J. (1984). *Not in our genes: Biology, ideology, and human nature.* New York: Pantheon.

Liben, L. S., & Signoriella, M. L. (1980). Gender-related schemata and constructive memory in children. *Child Development, 5,* 11–18.

Lidz, T. (1976). *The person.* New York: Basic Books.

Lieberman, P. (1975). The evolution of speech and language. In J. F. Kavanagh & J. E. Cutting (Eds.), *The role of speech in language* (pp. 83–106). Cambridge, MA: MIT Press.

Liebert, R. M., & Poulos, R. W. (1975). Television and personality development: The socializing effects of an entertainment medium. In A. Davids (Ed.), *Child personality and psychopathology: Current topics* (Vol. 2). New York: Wiley.

Lipsitt, L. P. (1977). The study of sensory and learning processes in the newborn. *Symposium on Neonatal Neurology: Clinics in Perinatalogy, 4,* 163–186.

Lipsitt, L. P., Engen, T., & Kaye, H. (1963). Developmental changes in the olfactory threshold of the neonate. *Child Development, 34,* 371–376.

Lipsitt, L. P., & Levy, N. (1959). Pain threshold in the neoprimate. *Child Development, 30,* 547–554.

Livesley, W. J., & Bromley, D. B. (1973). *Person perception in childhood and adolescence.* London: Wiley.

Livson, F. B. (1981). Paths to psychological health in the middle years: Sex differences. In D. H. Eichorn, N. Haan, J. A. Clausen, M. P. Honzik, & P. H. Mussen (Eds.), *Present and past in middle life* (pp. 195–221). New York: Academic Press.

Livson, N., & Peskin, H. (1980). Perspectives on adolescence from longitudinal research. In J. Adelson (Ed.), *Handbook of adolescent psychology* (pp. 47–98). New York: Wiley.

Lorenz, K. Z. (1956). Comparative behaviorology. In J. M. Tanner & B. Inhelder (Eds.), *Discussions on child development* (Vol. 1). London: Tavistock.

Lowenthal, M. F., & Haven, C. (1968). Interaction and adaptation: Intimacy as a critical variable. *American Sociological Review, 33,* 20–30.

Lowenthal, M. F., Thurnher, M., & Chiriboga, D. (1976). *Four stages of life.* San Francisco: Jossey-Bass.

Lowenthal, M. F., & Weiss, L. (1976). Intimacy and crises in adulthood. *Counseling Psychologist, 6,* 10–15.

Luckmann, T. (1979). Personal identity as an evolutionary and historical problem. In M. von Cranach, K. Foppa, W. Lepenies, & D. Ploog (Eds.), *Human ethology: Claims and limits of a new discipline* (pp. 56–74). Cambridge: Cambridge University Press.

Luria, A. (1976). *Cognitive development.* Cambridge, MA: Harvard University Press.

Lyle, J., & Hoffman, H. (1972). Children's use of television and other media. In E. A. Rubinstein, G. A. Comstock, & J. P. Murray (Eds.), *Television and social behavior: Vol. 4. Television in day-to-day life: Patterns of use.* Washington, DC: Government Printing Office.

Maccoby, E. E. (1980). *Social development.* New York: Wiley.

Maccoby, E. E., & Jacklin, C. (1974). *The psychology of sex differences.* Stanford: Stanford University Press.

MacDonald, G. W. (1981). Structural exchange and marital interaction. *Journal of Marriage and the Family, 43,* 825–839.

Macfarlane, A. (1977). *The psychology of childbirth.* Cambridge, MA: Harvard University Press.

Macfarlane, J. W. (1938). Studies in child guidance: Vol. 1. Methodology of data collection and organization. *Monographs of the Society for Research in Child Development,* Vol. 3 (6).

Macfarlane, J. W. (1958). The significance of early and later maturation in individual cases. In *Physical and Behavioral Growth, Report of the 26th Ross Pediatrics Research Conference,* pp. 69–78. Department of Pediatrics, University of California School of Medicine, San Francisco, October 30–31, 1957.

Macfarlane, J. W. (1963). From infancy to adulthood. *Childhood Education, 39,* 336–342.

Macfarlane, J. W. (1964). Perspectives on personality consistency and change from the Guidance Study. *Vita Humana, 7,* 115–126.

Mackenzie, B. (1984). Explaining race differences in IQ: The logic, the methodology, the evidence. *American Psychologist, 39*(11), 1214–1233.

Mackintosh, N. J. (1980). Book review of *Cyril Burt: Psychologist* by J. S. Hearnshaw. *British Journal of Psychology, 71,* 174–175.

Macnamara, J. (1972). Cognitive bases of language learning in infants. *Psychological Review, 79,* 1–13.

Mahler, M. S. (1968). *On human symbiosis and the vicissitudes of individuation.* New York: International Universities Press.

Mahler, M. S., Pine, F., & Bergman, A. (1975). *The psychological birth of the human infant.* New York: Basic Books.

Main, M. (1981). Avoidance in the service of attachment: A working paper. In K. Immelmann, G. Barlow, L. Petrinovich, & M. Main (Eds.), *Behavioral development: The Bielefeld interdisciplinary project* (pp. 651–693). New York: Cambridge University Press.

Main, M., Kaplan, N., & Cassidy, J. (1985). Security in infancy, childhood, and adulthood: A move to the level of representation. In I. Bretherton & E. Waters (Eds.), *Growing points of attachment: Theory and research. Monographs for the Society for Research in Child Development, 50* (Serial No. 209, Nos. 1–2), 66–104.

Main, M., & Weston, D. (1981). The quality of the toddler's relationship to mother and father: Related to conflict behavior and the readiness to establish new relationships. *Child Development, 52,* 932–940.

Main, M., & Weston, D. (1982). Avoidance of the attachment figure in infancy: Descriptions and interpretations. In C. M. Parkes & J. Stevenson-Hinde (Eds.), *The place of attachment in human behavior.* New York: Basic Books.

Mandler, J. M. (1983). Representations. In P. H. Mussen (Ed.), *Handbook of child psychology: Vol. 3. Cognitive Development* (pp. 420–494). New York: Wiley.

Marcia, J. E. (1966). Development and validation of ego identity status. *Journal of Personality and Social Psychology, 3*(5), 551–558.

Marcia, J. E. (1967). Ego identity status: Relationship to change in self-esteem, "general maladjustment," and authoritarianism. *Journal of Personality, 35*(1), 119–133.

Marcia, J. E. (1980). Identity to adolescence. In J. Adelson (Ed.), *Handbook of adolescent psychology* (pp. 159–187). New York: Wiley.

Marcia, J. E., & Friedman, M. L. (1970). Ego identity in college women. *Journal of Personality, 38*(2), 249–263.

Marks, F. R. (1975). Detours on the road to maturity: A view of the legal conception of growing up and letting go. *Law and Contemporary Problems, 39*, 78–92.

Markus, H. (1977). Self-schemata and processing information about the self. *Journal of Personality and Social Psychology, 35*(2), 63–78.

Markus, H. (1980). The self in thought and memory. In D. M. Wegner & R. R. Vallacher (Eds.), *The self in social psychology*. New York: Oxford University Press.

Marshall, W. A. (1968). *Development of the brain*. Edinburgh: Oliver & Boyd.

Marvin, R. S. (1974). *Aspects of the preschool child's changing conceptions of his mother*. Unpublished manuscript, University of Virginia.

Masangkay, Z. S., McCluskey, K. A., McIntyre, C. W., Simi-Knight, J., Vaughn, B. E., & Flavell, J. H. (1974). The early development of inferences about the visual percepts of others. *Child Development, 45*, 357–366.

Masson, J. (1984). *Assault on truth*. New York: Farrar, Straus & Giroux.

Masters, J. C., Ford, M. E., Arend, R., Grotevant, H. D., & Clark L. V. (1979). Modeling and labeling as integrated determinants of children's sex-typed initiative behavior. *Child Development, 50*, 364–371.

Masters, J. C., & Wilkinson, A. (1976). Consensual and discriminative stereotypy of sex-type judgments by parents and children. *Child Development, 47*, 208–217.

Matas, L., Arend, R., & Sroufe, L. A. (1978). Continuity of adaptation in the second year: The relationship between quality of attachment and alter competence. *Child Development, 49*, 547–556.

Matza, D. (1964). *Delinquency and drift*. New York: Wiley.

Mauss, M. (1979). *Sociology and psychology: Essays*. London: Routledge & Kegan Paul. (Originally published 1950)

Mayer, A. J. (1977, February 28). The graying of America. *Newsweek*.

McCall, R. B. (1977). Challenges to a science of developmental psychology. *Child Development, 48*, 333–334.

McCall, R. B. (1979). The development of intellectual functioning in infancy and the prediction of later IQ. In J. D. Osofsky (Ed.), *Handbook of infant development* (pp. 704–741). New York: Wiley.

McCall, R. B., Appelbaum, M. I., & Hogarty, P. S. (1973). Developmental changes in mental performance. *Monographs of the Society for Research in Child Development, 38*(3, Serial No. 150), 1–84.

McCall, R. B., Eichorn, D. H., & Hogarty, P. S. (1977). Transitions in early mental development. *Monographs of the Society for Research in Child Development, 42*(3, Serial No. 171).

McCullers, J. (1969). G. Stanley Hall's conception of mental development and some indications of its influence on developmental psychology. *American Psychologist, 24*(12), 1109–1114.

McNeill, D. (1966). Semiotic extension. In R. L. Solso (Ed.), *Information processing and cognition: The Loyola Symposium* (pp. 351–380). Hillsdale, NJ: Erlbaum.

Mead, G. H. (1934). *Mind, self, and society*. Chicago: University of Chicago Press.

Mead, M. (1970). *Culture and commitment*. Garden City, NY: Doubleday, Natural History Press.

Medrich, E. A., Roizen, J. A., Rubin, V., & Buckley, S. (1982). *The serious business of growing up*. Berkeley: University of California Press.

Mehler, J., Bertoncini, J., Barriere, M., & Jassik-Gerschenfeld, D. (1978). Infant recognition of mother's voice. *Perception, 7*, 491–497.

Mellar, W. S. (1974). The role of visual holding cues in the simultanizing strategy in infant operant learning. *British Journal of Psychology, 65*, 505–518.

Meltzoff, A. N., & Moore, M. K. (1977). Imitation of facial and manual gestures by human neonates. *Science, 198*, 800–802.

Menyuk, P. (1971). *The acquisition and development of language*. Englewood Cliffs, NJ: Prentice-Hall.

Merleau-Ponty, M. (1964). *The primacy of perception*. Evanston, IL: Northwestern University Press.

Millar, W. S. (1976). Operant acquisition of social behavior in infancy: Basic problems and constraints. In H. W. Reese (Ed.), *Advances in child development and behavior* (Vol. 11). New York: Academic Press.

Miller, G. (1977). *Spontaneous apprentices: Children and language*. New York: Seabury Press.

Miller, J. (1978). *The body in question*. New York: Random House.

Miller, P. Y., & Simon, W. (1980). The development of sexuality in adolescence. In J. Adelson (Ed.), *Handbook of adolescent psychology* (pp. 383–407). New York: Wiley.

Milne, A. A. (1939). *Autobiography*. New York: Dutton.

Minuchin, S., Rosman, B. L., & Barker, L. (1978). *Psychosomatic families: Anorexia nervosa in context*. Cambridge, MA: Harvard University Press.

Mischel, T. (Ed.). (1977). *The self: Psychological and philosophical issues*. Oxford: Basil Blackwell.

Mischel, W. (1968). *Personality and assessment.* New York: Wiley.

Mischel, W., & Moore, B. (1973). Effects of attention to symbolically presented rewards upon self-control. *Journal of Personality and Social Psychology, 28*(2), 172–179.

Mischel, W., & Peake, P. K. (1983). Analyzing the construction of consistency in personality. In M. M. Page (Ed.), *Nebraska Symposium on Motivation (1982)* (pp. 233–262). Lincoln: University of Nebraska Press.

Miyake, K., Chen, S-J., & Campos, J. J. (1985). Infant temperament, mother's mode of interaction, and attachment in Japan: An interim report. In I. Bretherton & E. Waters (Eds.), *Growing points of attachment theory and research. Monographs of the Society for Research in Child Development, 50*(Serial No. 209, Nos. 1–2), 276–297.

Miyake, K., Chen, S-J., Ujiie, T., Tajima, N., Satoh, K., & Takahaski, K. (1981–1982). Infant's temperamental disposition, mother's mode of interaction, quality of attachment, and infant's receptivity to socialization. In *Faculty of Education Annual Report,* Research and Clinical Center of Child Development, Hokkaido University, Sapporo, Japan.

Monetmeyer, R., & Eisen, M. (1977). The development of self-conceptions from childhood to adolescence. *Developmental Psychology, 13*(4), 314–319.

Money, J. (1961). Sex hormones and other variables in human eroticism. In W. C. Young (Ed.), *Sex and internal secretions.* Baltimore: Williams & Wilkins.

Money, J., & Ehrhardt, A. (1972). *Man and woman, boy and girl.* Baltimore: John Hopkins University Press.

Montaigne, M. (1952). *The Essays: The great books of the Western world* (Vol. 25). Chicago: Encyclopedia Brittanica. (Originally published 1580–1588)

Montessori, M. (1973). *The Montessori method.* Cambridge, MA: Robert Bentley.

Morris, J. (1974). *Conundrum.* New York: Harcourt Brace Jovanovich.

Mortimer, J. T., Finch, M. I., & Kumka, I. (1982). Persistence and change in development: The multidimensional self-concept. In P. B. Baltes & O. G. Brim, Jr. (Eds.), *Life-span development and behavior.* New York: Academic Press.

Moss, H. A., & Robson, K. S. (1968). Maternal influences in early social visual behavior. *Child Development, 39,* 401–498.

Moss, H. A., & Susman, E. J. (1980). Longitudinal study of personality development. In O. G. Brim, Jr., & J. Kagan (Eds.), *Constancy and change in human development* (pp. 530–595). Cambridge, MA: Harvard University Press.

Mountcastle, V. B. (1975). The view from within: Pathways to the study of perception. *Johns Hopkins Medical Journal, 136,* 109–131.

Mueller, E., & Lucas, T. (1975). A developmental analysis of peer interaction among toddlers. In M. Lewis & L. Rosenblum (Eds.), *Peer relations and friendship.* New York: Wiley.

Mullis, I.V.S. (1975). *Educational achievement and sex discrimination.* Paper prepared for the National Assessment of Education Progress Project. Denver, CO: Education Commission of the States.

Munroe, R. L., & Munroe, R. H. (1975). *Cross-cultural human development.* Monterey, CA: Brooks/Cole.

Mussen, P. H. (1970). *Manual of child psychology* (3rd ed., Vol. 1). New York: Wiley.

Mussen, P. H. (1983). *Handbook of child psychology* (Vols. 1–4). New York: Wiley.

Myrdal, J. (1968). *Confessions of a disloyal European.* New York: Pantheon.

Nagel, E., & Newman, J. R. (1958). *Godel's proof.* New York: New York University Press.

Neimark, E. D. (1975). Longitudinal development of formal operations thought. *Genetic Psychology Monographs, 91,* 171–225.

Neimark, E. D. (1979). Current status of formal operations research. *Human Development, 22,* 60–67.

Neimark, E. D., & Lewis, N. (1967). The development of logical problem solving strategies. *Child Development, 38,* 107–117.

Neisser, U. (1976). *Cognition and reality.* San Francisco: W. H. Freeman.

Nelson, K. (1973). Structure and strategy in learning to talk. *Monographs of the Society for Research in Child Development, 38* (Serial No. 149), 1–138.

Nelson, K. (1981). Social cognition in a script framework. In J. H. Flavell & L. Ross (Eds.), *Social cognitive development.* New York: Cambridge University Press.

Neugarten, B. L. (1968). Adult personality: Toward a psychology of the life cycle. In B. L. Neugarten (Ed.), *Middle age and aging.* Chicago: University of Chicago Press.

Neugarten, B. L. (1970). Dynamics of transition of middle age to old age. *Journal of Geriatric Psychology, 4,* 71–87.

Neugarten, B. L. (1974, September). Age groups in American society and the rise of the young old. *Annals of the American Academy of Science, 187–* 198.

Neugarten, B. L., & Hagestad, G. O. (1976). Age and the life course. In R. H. Binstock & E. Shanas (Eds.), *Handbook of aging and the social sciences* (pp. 35–55). New York: Van Nostrand Reinhold.

Neugarten, B. L., Havighurst, R. J., & Tobin, S. S. (1968). Personality and patterns of aging. In B. L. Neugarten (Ed.), *Middle age and aging.* Chicago: University of Chicago Press.

Neugarten, B. L., Moore, J. W., & Lowe, J. C. (1965). Age norms, age constraints, and adult socialization. *American Journal of Sociology, 70*(6), 710–716.

Neugarten, B. L., Wood, V., Krames, R. J., & Loomis, B. (1963). Women's attitudes toward the menopause. *Vita Humana, 6,* 140–151.

New York Times. (1978, May 7). Age population up 18% in 7 years.

New York Times. (1984, December 15). Experts describe "epidemic" of teen-age suicides.

Newport, E. L., Gleitman, H., & Gleitman, L. R. (1977). Mother, I'd rather do it myself: Some effects and non-effects of maternal speech style. In C. E. Snow & C. A. Furguson (Eds.), *Talking to children: Language input and acquisition* (pp. 109–150). Cambridge: Cambridge University Press.

Newson, J., & Newson, E. (1974). Cultural aspects of childrearing in the English-speaking world. In M.P.M. Richards (Ed.), *The integration of the child into a social world.* London: Cambridge University Press.

Newson, J., & Newson, E. (1976). *Seven years old in the home environment.* New York: Wiley.

Newson, J., & Newson, E. (1977). *Perspectives on school at seven years old.* Edison, NJ: Allen & Unwin.

Nguyen, M. L., Meyer, K. K., & Winick, M. (1977). Early malnutrition and "late" adoption: A study of their effects on the development of Korean orphans adopted into American families. *American Journal of Clinical Nutrition, 30,* 1734–1739.

Nijhuis, J. G., Prechtl, H. F., Martin, C. B., & Bots, R. S. (1982). Are there behavioral states in the human fetus? *Early Human Development, 6*(2), 177–195.

Niswander, K. R., & Gordon, M. (Eds.). (1972). *The women and their pregnancies: The collaborative perinatal study of the National Institute of Neurological Diseases and Stroke.* Washington, DC: NIH, Government Printing Office.

Noble, G. (1975). *Children in front of the small screen.* Beverly Hills: Sage.

Norman, D. (1980). Twelve issues for cognitive science. *Cognitive Science, 4,* 1–32.

Novak, M. A., & Harlow, H. F. (1975). Social recovery of monkeys isolated for the first years of life: Pt. 1. Rehabilitation and therapy. *Developmental Psychology, 11,* 453–465.

Nuttin, J., & Greenwald, A. G. (1968). *Reward and punishment in human learning.* New York: Academic Press.

Oatley, K., & Bolton, W. (1985). A social-cognitive theory of depression in reaction to life events. *Psychological Review, 92*(3), 372–388.

O'Connor, P., & Brown, G. W. (1984). Supportive relationships: Fact or fantasy? *Journal of Social and Personal Relationships, 1*(2), 159–175.

Offer, D. (1969). *The psychological world of the teenager.* New York: Basic Books.

Offer, D., & Offer, J. B. (1975). *From teenage to young manhood.* New York: Basic Books.

Olney, J. (1980). Biography, autobiography and the life course. In K. W. Back (Ed.), *Life course: Integrative theories and exemplary populations* (AAAS Selected Symposium 41). Boulder, CO: Westview Press for the American Association for the Advancement of Science.

Olson, D. R. (1977). From utterance to text: The bias of language in speech and writing. *Harvard Educational Review, 47,* 257–281.

Olson, G. M., & Sherman, T. (1983). A conceptual framework for the study of infant mental processes. In L. P. Lipsitt (Ed.), *Advances in infancy research* (Vol. 3). Norwood, NJ: Ablex.

Opie, I., & Opie, P. (1959). *The lore and language of school children.* Oxford: Oxford University Press.

Orbach, J., Traub, A. C., & Olson, R. (1966). Psychophysical studies of body-image: Pt. 2. Normative data on the adjustable body-distorting mirror. *Archives of General Psychiatry, 14,* 41–47.

Orlovsky, J. L., Marcia, J. E., & Lesser, I. M. (1973). Ego identity status and the intimacy vs. isolation crisis of young adulthood. *Journal of Personality and Social Psychology, 27*(2), 211–219.

Osgood, C. E., & Bock, J. K. (1977). Salience and sentencing: Some production principles. In S. Rosenberg (Ed.), *Sentence production: Development in research and theory.* Hillsdale, NJ: Erlbaum.

Papousek, H., & Papousek, M. (1979). Early ontogeny of human social interaction: Its biological roots and dimensions. In M. Von Cranach, K. Foppa, W. Lepenies, & D. Ploog (Eds.), *Human ethology.* London: Cambridge University Press.

Parke, R. D. (1978). Children's home environments: Social and cognitive effects. In I. Altman & J. F. Wohlwill (Eds.), *Children and the environment.* New York: Plenum Press.

Parke, R. D., & Asher, S. R. (1983). Social and personality development. In M. R. Rosenzweig & L. W. Porter (Eds.), *Annual Review of Psychology, 34*, 465–509.

Parkes, C. M., & Stevenson-Hinde, J. (Eds.). (1982). *The place of attachment in human behavior.* New York: Basic Books.

Parsons, C. (1960). Inhelder and Piaget's "The growth of logical thinking": Pt. 2. A logician's viewpoint. *British Journal of Psychology, 51*, 75–84.

Parten, M. B. (1932). Social participation among preschool children. *Journal of Abnormal Social Psychology, 27*, 243–269.

Pasamanick, B., & Knobloch, H. (1961). Epidemiologic studies on the complications of pregnancy and the birth process. In G. Kaplan (Ed.), *Prevention of mental disorders in children.* New York: Basic Books.

Pasamanick, B., & Knobloch, H. (1966). Retrospective studies on the epidemiology of reproductive casualty: Old and new. *Merrill-Palmer Quarterly, 12*, 7–26.

Pascual-Leone, J. (1970). A mathematical model for the transition rule in Piaget's developmental stages. *Acta Psychologica, 32*, 301–345.

Patterson, F. (1978, October). Conversations with a gorilla. *National Geographic, 154*, 438.

Patterson, G. R. (1976). *Living with children.* Champaign, IL: Research Press.

Patterson, G. R. (1982). *Coercive family process.* Eugene, OR: Castalia Press.

Patterson, G. R., & Cobb, J. A. (1971). A dyadic analysis of "aggressive" behavior. In J. P. Hill (Ed.), *Minnesota Symposium on Child Psychology* (Vol. 5). Minneapolis: University of Minnesota Press.

Patterson, G. R., & Fagot, B. I. (1967). Selective responsiveness to social reinforcers and deviant behavior in children. *Psychological Record, 17*(3), 369–378.

Patterson, G. R., Littman, R. A., & Bricker, W. (1967). Assertive behavior in children: A step toward a theory of aggression. *Monographs of the Society for Research in Child Development, 32*(5, Serial No. 113).

Pearlin, L. I. (1971). *Class context and family relations: A cross-national study.* Boston: Little, Brown.

Peevers, B. H., & Secord, P. F. (1973). Developmental changes in attribution of descriptive concepts to persons. *Journal of Personality and Social Psychology, 27*, 120–128.

Pelled, N. (1964). On the formation of object relations and identifications of the kibbutz child. *Israel Ann. Psychiatry, 2*, 144–161.

Peracchio, A. (1983, November 16). Surgery or death? "Baby Doe" rights questioned. *The Daily Californian.*

Perlmutter, M. (1978). What is memory aging the aging of? *Developmental Psychology, 14*,(4).

Perlmutter, M., & Angrist-Myers, N. (1979). The development of recall in 2 to 4 year-old children. *Developmental Psychology, 15*(1), 73–83.

Perun, P. J., & Bielby, D. D. (1979). Midlife: A discussion of competing models. *Research on Aging, 1*, 275–300.

Peskin, H. (1967). Pubertal onset and ego functioning: A psychoanalytic approach. *Journal of Abnormal Psychology, 72*, 1–15.

Peskin, H. (1973). Influence of the developmental schedule of puberty on learning and ego functioning. *Journal of Youth and Adolescence, 2*, 343–350.

Peter, L. J. (1977). *Peter's quotations: Ideas for our time.* New York: Morrow.

Peterfreund, E. (1978). Some critical comments on psychoanalytic conceptualizations of infancy. *International Journal of Psychoanalysis, 59*, 427–441.

Petrie, A. (1978). *Individuality in pain and suffering.* Chicago: University of Chicago Press.

Piaget, J. (1927–1928). La première année de l'enfant. *British Journal of Psychology, 18*, 97–120. Paper read before the British Psychological Society, October 1927 and January 1928.

Piaget, J. (1928). *Judgment and reasoning in the child* (M. Warden, Trans.). New York: Harcourt, Brace.

Piaget, J. (1952). *The origins of intelligence in children* (M. Cook, Trans.). New York: International Universities Press. (Originally published in French in 1936)

Piaget, J. (1954). *The construction of reality in the child* (M. Cook, Trans.). New York: Basic Books. (Originally published in French in 1936)

Piaget, J. (1962). *Play, dreams, and imitation in childhood* (C. Gattegno & F. M. Hodgson, Trans.). New York: Norton. (Originally published in French in 1945, translated 1951)

Piaget, J. (1967). Cognitions and conservations: Two views. *Contemporary Psychology, 12*, 530–533.

Piaget, J. (1970). Piaget's theory. In P. H. Mussen (Ed.), *Manual of child psychology* (Vol. 9, pp. 703–732). New York: Wiley.

Piaget, J. (1972). Intellectual evolution from adolescence to adulthood. *Human Development, 15*, 1–12.

Piaget, J. (1977). *The development of thought: Equilibration of cognitive structures.* New York: Viking.

Piaget, J. (1980). *Experiments in contradiction.* Chicago: University of Chicago Press.

Piaget, J., & Inhelder, B. (1956). *The child's conception of space* (F. J. Langdon & J. L. Lunzer, Trans.). Atlantic Highlands, NJ: Humanities Press.

Piaget, J., & Inhelder, B. (1958). *The growth of logical thinking from childhood to adolescence: An essay on the construction of formal operational structures* (A. Parsons & S. Milgram, Trans.). New York: Basic Books. (Originally published in French in 1955)

Piaget, J., & Inhelder, B. (1966/1971). *Mental imagery in the child: A study of the development of imaginal representation* (P. A. Chilton, Trans.). New York: Basic Books.

Piaget, J., & Inhelder, B. (1969). *The psychology of the child* (H. Weaver, Trans.). New York: Basic Books. (Originally published in French in 1966)

Piel, G., Flanagan, D., Bello, F., & Morrison, P. (Eds.). (1979). *The brain.* San Francisco: W. H. Freeman.

Piliavin, I., & Briar, S. (1964). Police encounters with juveniles. *American Journal of Sociology, 70,* 206–214.

Pitts, J. (1968). The family and peer groups. In N. W. Bell & E. F. Vogel (Eds.), *A modern introduction to the family.* New York: Free Press.

Plemons, J. K., Willis, S. L., & Baltes, P. B. (1978). Modifiability of fluid intelligence in aging: A short-term longitudinal training approach. *Journal of Gerontology, 33,* 224–231.

Plomin, R. (1982). The difficulty concept of temperament: A response to Thomas, Chess, and Korn. *Merrill-Palmer Quarterly, 28,* 25–34.

Plumb, J. H. (1972). The great change in children. *Intellectual Digest, 2,* 82–84.

Podd, M. H. (1972). Ego identity status and morality: The relationship between two developmental constructs. *Developmental Psychology, 6,* 497–507.

Poincaré, J. (1952). *Science and hypothesis.* New York: Dover. (Originally published 1908)

Popper, K. (1972). *Objective knowledge: An evolutionary approach.* Oxford: Oxford University Press.

Popper, K. R., & Eccles, J. C. (1977). *The self and its brain.* New York: Springer Verlag.

Pratt, M. W., Golding, G., & Hunter, W. J. (1984). Does morality have a gender? Sex, sex role, and moral judgment relationships across the adult lifespan. *Merrill-Palmer Quarterly, 30,* 321–340.

Preyer, W. (1883). *The mind of the child: Pt. 1. The senses and the will.* New York: Appleton.

Preyer, W. (1889). *The mind of the child: Pt. 2. The development of the intellect.* New York: Appleton.

Price-Williams, D., Gordon, W., & Ramirez, M. (1969). Skill and conservation: Study of pottery-making children. *Developmental Psychology, 1,* 769.

Quadagno, J. S. (Ed.). (1980). *Aging, the individual and society: Readings in social gerontology.* New York: St. Martin's Press.

Rabbitt, P., & Birren, J. E. (1967). Age and responses to sequences of repetitive and interruptive signals. *Journal of Gerontology, 22,* 143–150.

Rabinowicz, T. (1979). The differentiated maturation of the human cerebral cortex. In F. Faulkner & J. M. Tanner (Eds.), *Human growth* (Vol. 3). New York: Plenum Press.

Rainwater, L. (1977). *What money buys: Inequality and the racial meanings of income.* New York: Basic Books.

Rank, O. (1971). *The double: A psychoanalytic study* (H. Tucker, Jr., Trans. & Ed.). Chapel Hill: University of North Carolina Press.

Reedy, M. N., Birren, J. E., Schaie, K. W. (1981). Age and sex differences in satisfying love relationships across the adult life span. *Human Development, 24,* 52–66.

Reese, W. H., & Overton, W. F. (1970). Models of development and theories of development. In L. R. Goulet & P. B. Baltes (Eds.), *Life-span developmental psychology: Research and theory.* New York: Academic Press.

Reis, H. T. (1982). An introduction to the use of structural equations: Prospects and problems. In L. Wheeler (Ed.), *Review of Personality and Social Psychology* (Vol. 1, pp. 255–287). Beverly Hills: Sage.

Rest, J. (1983). Moral development. In P. H. Mussen (Ed.), *Handbook of child psychology* (4th ed., Vol. 3). New York: Wiley.

Rheingold, H. L., & Cook, K. V. (1975). The contents of boys' and girls' rooms as an index of parents' behavior. *Child Development, 46,* 459–463.

Rheingold, H. L., & Eckerman, C. O. (1970). The infant separates himself from his mother. *Science, 168,* 78–83.

Rice, M. L., Huston, A. C., & Wright, J. C. (1982). The forms of television: Effects on children's attention, comprehension, and social behavior. In D. Pearl, L. Bouthilet, & J. Lazar (Eds.), *Television and behavior: Ten years of scientific progress and implications for the eighties: Vol. 2. Technical reviews.* Rockville, MD: National Institute of Mental Health.

Riegel, K. F. (1973). An epitaph for a paradigm. *Human Development, 16,* 1–3.

Riegel, K. F. (1975). Adult life crisis: A dialectic interpretation of development. In N. Datan & L. Ginsberg (Eds.), *Life-span developmental psychology: Normative life crises.* New York: Academic Press.

Riegel, K. F. (1976). The dialectic of human development. *American Psychologist, 31,* 689–700.

Riegel, K. F. (1977). Past and future trends in gerontology. *Gerontologist, 17,* 105–113.

Riegel, K. F., & Meacham, J. A. (1976). *The developing individual in a changing world* (Vol. 1). Chicago: Aldine.

Riley, D. (1983). *War in the nursery: Theories of the child and mother.* London: Virago.

Riley, M. A., Johnson, M., & Foner, A. (1972). *Aging and Society: A sociology of age stratification* (Vol. 3). New York: Russell Sage Foundation.

Riley, M. W. (1976). Age strata in social systems. In R. H. Binstock & E. Shanas (Eds.), *Handbook of aging and the social sciences.* New York: Van Nostrand Reinhold.

Rist, R. (1973). *The urban school: A factory for failure.* Cambridge, MA: MIT Press.

Robertson, J. (1977). *Sociology.* New York: Worth.

Robertson, J., & Bowlby, J. (1952). Responses of young children to separation from their mother: Pt. 2. Observations of the sequences of response of children aged 16 to 24 months during the course of separation. *Courrier du Centre International de L'Enfance, 2,* 131–142.

Robertson, J., & Robertson, J. (1971). Young children in brief separation: A fresh look. *Psychoanalytic Study of the Child, 26,* 264–315.

Robson, K. S., & Moss, H. A. (1970). Patterns and determinants of maternal attachment. *Journal of Pediatrics, 77,* 976.

Roche, A. F. (Ed.). (1979). Secular trends in human growth, maturation, and development. *Monographs of the Society for Research in Child Development, 44*(3–4, Serial No. 179).

Roethke, T. (1957). *Word for the wind.* London: Secker & Warburg.

Roff, M. (1961). Childhood social interactions and young adult bad conduct. *Journal of Abnormal and Social Psychology, 63*(2), 333–337.

Rogoff, B., Sellers, M. J., Pirrotta, S., Fox, N., & White, S. H. (1976). Age of assignment of roles and responsibilities to children: A cross-cultural survey. In A. Skolnick (Ed.), *Rethinking childhood: Perspectives on development and society,* (pp. 249–268). Boston: Little, Brown.

Rook, K. S. (1984). Promoting social bonding: Strategies for helping the lonely and socially isolated. *American Psychologist, 39*(12), 1389–1407.

Rook, K. S. (1985). Research on social support, loneliness, and social isolation: Toward an integration. In P. Shaver (Ed.), *Review of personality and social psychology: Emotions, relationships, and health* (Vol. 5, pp. 239–264). Beverly Hills: Sage.

Rosaldo, M. Z. (1984).Toward an anthropology of self and feeling. In R. A. Schweder & R. A. LeVine (Eds.), *Culture theory: Essays on mind, self, and emotion* (pp. 137–157). Cambridge: Cambridge University Press.

Rosch, E. (1975). Cognitive representation of semantic categories. *Journal of Experimental Psychology, 104,* 192–233.

Rosch, E. H., Mervis, C. B., Gray, W. D., Johnson, D. M., & Boyes-Braem, P. (1976). Basic objects in natural categories. *Cognitive Psychology, 8,* 382–439.

Rosenberg, M. (1979). *Conceiving the self.* New York: Basic Books.

Rosenblum, L. A. (1971). Infant attachment in monkeys. In R. Schaffer (Ed.), *The origins of human social relations* (pp. 85–113). New York: Academic Press.

Rosenblum, L. A., & Kaufman, I. C. (1968). Variations in infant development and response to maternal loss in infants. *American Journal of Orthopsychiatry, 38,* 418–426.

Rosenthal, R., & Rubin, D. B. (1980). Summarizing 345 studies of interpersonal expectancy effects. In R. Rosenthal (Ed.), *Quantitative assessment of research domains: New directions for methodology of social and behavioral sciences* (Vol. 5). San Francisco: Jossey-Bass.

Rosenzweig, M. R., & Bennett, E. L. (1977). Effects of environmental enrichment or impoverishment on learning and on brain values in rodents. In B. P. Oliverio (Ed.), *Genetics, environment, and intelligence.* Amsterdam: Elsevier/North-Holland.

Rosenzweig, M. R., & Bennett, E. L. (1978). Experimental influences on brain anatomy and brain chemistry in rodents. In G. Gottlieb (Ed.), *Studies on the development of behavior and the nervous system: Vol. 4. Early influences* (pp. 289–327). New York: Academic Press.

Rosenzweig, M. R., & Leiman, A. L. (1982). *Physiological psychology.* Lexington, MA: D. C. Heath.

Ross, D. (1972). *G. Stanley Hall: The psychologist as prophet.* Chicago: University of Chicago Press.

Ross, G. S. (1980). Categorization in one- to two-year-olds. *Developmental Psychology, 16,* 391–396.

Rossi, A. S. (1968). Transition to parenthood. *Journal of Marriage and the Family, 30,* 26–39.

Rossi, A. S. (1980). Aging and parenthood in the middle years. In P. B. Baltes & O. G. Brim, Jr. (Eds.), *Life-span development and behavior* (Vol. 3., pp. 137–205). New York: Academic Press.

Rothbart, M. K., & Derryberry, D. (1981). Development of individual differences in temperament. In M. E. Lamb & A. L. Brown (Eds.), *Advances in developmental psychology* (Vol. 1). Hillsdale, NJ: Erlbaum.

Rotman, B. (1977). *Jean Piaget: Psychologist of the real*. Ithaca, NY: Cornell University Press.

Rubenstein, J. L., & Hawes, C. (1979). Caregiving and infant behavior in day care and in homes. *Developmental Psychology, 15*, 1–24.

Rubin, J. Z., Provenzano, F. J., & Luria, Z. (1974). The eye of the beholder: Parents' views on sex of newborns. *American Journal of Orthopsychiatry, 44*, 512–519.

Rubin, K. H., Fein, G. G., & Vandenberg, B. (1983). Play. In P. Mussen (Ed.), *Handbook of child psychology*. New York: Wiley.

Rubin, K. H., Maioni, T. L., & Hornung, M. (1976). Free play behaviors in middle and lower class preschoolers: Parten and Piaget revisited. *Child Development, 47*, 414–419.

Rubin, K. H., & Pepler, D. J. (1983). A neo-Piagetian perspective of children's play. *Journal of Contemporary Educational Psychology*.

Rubin, L. B. (1976). *Worlds of pain*. New York: Basic Books.

Rubin, L. B. (1979). *Women of a certain age*. New York: Harper & Row.

Rubin, L. B. (1985). *Just friends: The role of friendship in our lives*. New York: Harper & Row.

Rubin, Z. (1980). *Children's friendships*. Cambridge, MA: Harvard University Press.

Rumbaugh, D. M., & Gill, T. W. (1976). The mastery of language-type skills by the chimpanzee. In S. Harnad, H. Steklis, & S. Lancaster (Eds.), *Origins and evolutions of language and speech* (pp. 562–578). New York: N.Y. Academy of Sciences.

Runyan, W. M. (1978). The life course as a theoretical orientation: Sequences of person-environment interaction. *Journal of Personality, 46*, 552–558.

Runyan, W. M. (1980). A stage-state analysis of the life course. *Journal of Personality and Social Psychology, 38*, 951–962.

Runyan, W. M. (1982). *Life histories and psychobiography*. New York: Oxford University Press.

Russell, M. J. (1976). Human olfactory communication. *Nature, 260*, 520–522.

Rutter, M. (1979). Maternal deprivation, 1972–1978: New findings, new concepts, new approaches. *Child Development, 50*, 283–305.

Rutter, M. (1980). The long-term effects of early experience. *Developmental Medicine and Child Neurology, 22*, 800–815.

Rutter, M. (1981). *Maternal deprivation reassessed*. New York: Penguin.

Rutter, M. (1983). Stress, coping and development: Some issues and questions. In M. Rutter & N. Garmezy (Eds.), *Stress, coping and development* (pp. 1–41). New York: McGraw-Hill.

Rutter, M., Birch, H. G., Thomas, A., & Chess, S. (1964). Temperamental characteristics in infancy and the later development of behavioral disorders. *British Journal of Psychiatry, 110*, 651–661.

Rutter, M., Tizard, J., & Whitmore, K. (1970/1981). *Education, health and behavior*. Huntington, NY: Krieger.

Rycroft, C. (1973). *Dictionary of psychoanalysis*. New York: Penguin.

Ryder, N. B. (1965). The cohort as a concept in the study of social change. *American Sociological Review, 30*, 843–861.

Ryle, G. (1971). *Collected papers* (Vol. 2). New York: Barnes & Noble.

Sacks, H., Schegloff, E. A., & Jefferson, G. (1974). A simplest systematics for the organization of turn-taking in conversation. *Language, 50*, 696–735.

Sagi, A., Lamb, M. E., Estes, D., Shoham, R., Lewkowicz, K. S., & Dvir, R. (1982). *Security of infant-adult attachment among kibbutz-reared infants*. Paper presented at the meeting of the International Conference on Infant Studies, Austin, Texas.

Sagi, A., Lamb, M. E., Lewkowicz, K. S., Shoham, R., Dvir, R., & Estes, D. (1985). Security of infant-mother, -father, and -metapelet attachments among kibbutz-reared Israeli children. In I. Bretherton & E. Waters (Eds.), *Growing points of attachment: Theory and research. Monographs of the Society for Research in Child Development, 50*(Serial No. 209, Nos. 1–2).

Salapatek, P. (1975). Pattern perception in early infancy. In L. B. Cohen & P. Salapatek (Eds.), *Infant perception: From sensation to cognition: Vol. 1. Basic visual processes*. New York: Academic Press.

Salomon, G. (1979). *Interaction of media, cognition, and learning*. San Francisco: Jossey-Bass.

Salomon, G., & Cohen, A. A. (1977). Television formats, mastery of mental skills, and the acquisition of knowledge. *Journal of Educational Psychology, 69*, 612–619.

Salter, A. (1949). *Conditioned reflex therapy: The direct approach to the reconstruction of personality*. New York: Farrar, Straus.

Sameroff, A. J. (1975). Early influences on development: Fact or fancy. *Merrill-Palmer Quarterly, 21*, 267–294.

Sameroff, A. J., & Cavanaugh, P. J. (1979). Learning in infancy: A developmental perspective. In J. Osofsky (Ed.), *Handbook of infant development*. New York: Wiley.

Sameroff, A. J., & Chandler, M. J. (1975). Reproductive risk and the continuum of caretaking casualty. In F. D. Horowitz (Ed.), E. M. Hetherington, S. Scarr-Salapatek, & G. M. Siegel (Assoc. Eds.), *Review of child development research* (Vol. 4, pp. 187–244). Chicago: University of Chicago Press.

Samuels, C. (in press). Bases for the development of self in infancy. *Human Development.*

San Francisco Chronicle. (1975, June). Transition: How adults cope with changes.

Sarbin, T. R. (1968). A preface to a psychological analysis of the self. In C. Gordon & K. J. Gergen (Eds.), *The self in social interaction.* New York: Wiley.

Savage-Rumbaugh, E. S. (1979). Symbolic communication: Its origins and early development in the chimpanzee. In E. Wolf (Ed.), *New directions for child development: No. 3. Early symbolization* (pp. 1–15). San Francisco: Jossey-Bass.

Savage-Rumbaugh, E. S., & Rumbaugh, D. M. (1978). Symbolization, language, and chimpanzees: A theoretical reevaluation based on initial language acquisition processes in four young *pan troglodytes. Brain and Language,* 6(3), 265–300.

Savage-Rumbaugh, E. S., Rumbaugh, D. M., & Boysen, S. (1978). Symbolic communication between two chimpanzees. *Science, 201,* 641–644.

Savage-Rumbaugh, E. S., Rumbaugh, D. M., & Boysen, S. (1981). Do apes use language? *American Scientist, 68,* 49–61.

Scaife, M., & Bruner, J. S. (1975). The capacity for joint visual attention in the infant. *Nature, 253,* 265–266.

Scanlon, J. V. (1975). Self-reported behavior and attitudes of youth, 12–17 years. *Vital and Health Statistics* (Series 11, No. 147). Washington, DC: Government Printing Office.

Scarr, S. (1984). *Mother care/Other care.* New York: Basic Books.

Scarr, S., & Weinberg, R. A. (1976). IQ test performance of black children adopted by white families. *American Psychologist, 31,* 726–739.

Schafer, R. (1976). *A new language for psychoanalysis.* New Haven: Yale University Press.

Schafer, R. (1978). *Language and insight.* New Haven: Yale University Press.

Schaffer, H. R. (1971). *The growth of sociability.* Baltimore: Penguin.

Schaffer, H. R. (1977). *Studies in mother-infant interaction.* New York: Academic Press.

Schaffer, H. R. (1979). Acquiring the concept of the dialogue. In M. H. Bornstein & W. Kessen (Eds.), *Psychological development from infancy: Image to intention.* Hillsdale, NJ: Erlbaum.

Schaffer, H. R. (1983). Review of F. N. Emde and R. J. Harmon (Eds.), *The development of attachment and affiliative systems. Contemporary Psychology, 28,* 268.

Schaffer, H. R., & Emerson, P. E. (1964). The development of social attachments in infancy. *Monographs of the Society for Research in Child Development,* 29(Serial No. 3).

Schaie, K. W. (1965). A general model for the study of developmental problems. *Psychological Bulletin, 64,* 92–107.

Schaie, K. W. (1979). The primary mental abilities in adulthood: An exploration in the development of psychometric intelligence. In P. B. Baltes & O. G. Brim, Jr. (Eds.), *Life-span development and behavior* (Vol. 2). New York: Academic Press.

Schaie, K. W. (1981). The Seattle Longitudinal Study: A twenty-one year exploration of psychometric intelligence in adulthood. In K. W. Schaie (Ed.), *Longitudinal studies of adult psychological development.* New York: Guilford Press.

Schaie, K. W., Labouvie, G. F., & Barrett, T. J. (1973). Selective attrition effects in a fourteen-year study of adult intelligence. *Journal of Gerontology, 28,* 328–334.

Schaie, K. W., Labouvie, G. F., & Buesch, B. U. (1973). Generational and cohort-specific differences in adult cognitive functioning: A fourteen-year study of independent samples. *Developmental Psychology, 9,* 151–166.

Schank, R., & Albelson, R. (1977). *Scripts, plans, goals and understanding.* Hillsdale, NJ: Erlbaum.

Schantz, C. U. (1983). Social cognition. In P. H. Mussen (Ed.), *Handbook of child psychology: Vol. 3. Cognitive development* (pp. 495–555). New York: Wiley.

Scheibe, K. E. (1985). Historical perspectives on the presented self. In B. R. Schlenker (Ed.), *The self and social life* (pp. 33–64). New York: McGraw-Hill.

Schenkel, S., & Marcia, J. E. (1972). Attitudes toward premarital intercourse in determining ego identity status in college women. *Journal of Personality, 40,* 472–482.

Schilder, P. (1950). *The image and appearance of the human body.* New York: International Universities Press. (Originally published 1935)

Schlenker, B. R. (1985). Identity and self-identification. In B. R. Schlenker (Ed.), *The self and social life* (pp. 65–99). New York: McGraw-Hill.

Schor, R. E. (1959). Hypnosis and the concept of the generalized reality orientation. *American Journal of Psychotherapy, 13,* 582–602.

Schrag, P. (1972). Growing up on Mechanic Street. In T. J. Cottle (Ed.), *The prospect of youth.* Boston: Little, Brown.

Schramm, W., Lyle, J., & Parker, E. B. (1961). *Television in the lives of our children.* Stanford: Stanford University Press.

Schumm, W. R., Jurich, A. P., Bollman, S. R., & Bugaighis, A. (1985). His and her marriage revisited. *Journal of Family Issues, 6*(2), 221–227.

Schweder, R. A., & LeVine, R. A. (Eds.). (1984). *Culture theory: Essays on mind, self and emotion.* Cambridge: Cambridge University Press.

Scollen, R. T. (1974). *One child's language from one to two: The origins of construction.* University of Hawaii Working Papers in Linguistics.

Scribner, S., & Cole, M. (1973). Cognitive consequences of formal and informal education. *Science, 182,* 553–559.

Scribner, S., & Cole, M. (1978). Unpackaging literacy. *Social Science Information, 17,* 19–40.

Sears, R. R. (1977). Sources of life satisfactions of the Terman gifted men. *American Psychologist, 32,* 119–128.

Seashore, M., Leifer, A., Barnett, C., & Leiderman, P. (1973). The effects of denial of early mother-infant interaction on maternal self-confidence. *Journal of Personality and Social Psychology, 26*(3), 369–378.

Sebeok, T. A., & Rosenthal, R. (Eds.). (1981). *The clever Hans phenomenon: Communication with horses, whales, apes and people.* New York: New York Academy of Sciences.

Sebeok, T. A., & Umiker-Sebeok, D. J. (1980). *Speaking of apes: A critical anthology of two-way communication with man.* New York: Plenum Press.

Secord, P. F., & Peevers, B. H. (1974). The development and attribution of person. In T. Mischel, *Understanding other persons* (pp. 117–142). Oxford: Basil Blackwell.

Seligman, M.E.P. (1970). On the generality of the laws of learning. *Psychological Review, 77,* 406–418.

Seligman, M.E.P. (1975). *Helplessness: On depression, development, and death.* San Francisco: W. H. Freeman.

Sellitz, C., Wrightsman, L., & Cooke, S. (1976). *Research methods in social relations.* New York: Holt, Rinehart & Winston.

Selman, R. L. (1976). Social-cognitive understanding: A guide to educational and clinical practice. In T. Lickona (Ed.), *Moral development and moral behavior: Theory, research and social issues.* New York: Holt, Rinehart & Winston.

Selman, R. L. (1980). *The growth of interpersonal understanding.* New York: Academic Press.

Selman, R. L., & Byrne, D. F. (1974). A structural developmental analysis of levels of role taking in middle childhood. *Child Development, 45,* 803–806.

Senderowitz, J., & Paxman, J. M. (1985). Adolescent fertility: World-wide concerns. *Population Bulletin, 40*(2). Washington, DC: Population Reference Bureau.

Sennett, R., & Cobb, J. (1974). *The hidden injuries of class.* New York: Random House.

Sexton, P. C. (1967). *The American school: A sociological analysis.* Englewood Cliffs, NJ: Prentice-Hall.

Sharp, D., Cole, M., & Lave, C. (1979). Education and cognitive development: The evidence from experimental research. *Monographs of the Society for Research in Child Development, 44* (1–2, Serial No. 178).

Shattuck, R. (1980). *The forbidden experiment.* New York: Farrar, Straus & Giroux.

Shatz, M. (1982). On mechanisms of language acquisition: Can features of the communicative environment account for development? In E. Wanner & L. R. Gleitman (Eds.), *Language acquisition: The state of the art.* Cambridge: Cambridge University Press.

Shatz, M., & Gelman, R. (1973). The development of communication skills: Modifications in the speech of young children as a function of listener. *Monographs of the Society for Research in Child Development, 38* (5, Serial No. 152).

Shaver, P. (Ed.). (1984). *Review of personality and social psychology: Emotions, relationships, and health.* Beverly Hills: Sage.

Shaver, P., & Rubinstein, C. (1980). Childhood attachment experience and adult loneliness. In L. Wheeler (Ed.), *Review of personality and social psychology* (Vol. 1, pp. 42–73). Beverly Hills: Sage.

Sheehy, G. (1977). *Passages.* New York: Bantam.

Shipman, G. (1971). The psychodynamics of sex education. In R. E. Muuss (Ed.), *Adolescent behavior and society: A book of readings.* New York: Random House.

Shock, N. (1960). Discussion on mortality and measurement of aging. In B. L. Strehler et al. (Eds.), *The biology of aging: A symposium.* Washington, DC: American Institute of Biological Sciences.

Shock, N. (1977). Systems integration. In L. Hayflick & C. E. Finch (Eds.), *Handbook of the biology of aging* (pp. 639–665). New York: Van Nostrand Reinhold.

Shuey, H. (1934). Recent trends in science and the development of modern topology. *Psychological Review, 41,* 207–235.

Siegel, O. (1982). Personality development in adolescence. In B. B. Wolman (Ed.), *Handbook of developmental psychology* (pp. 537–548). Englewood Cliffs, NJ: Prentice-Hall.

Siegler, R. S. (1978). The origins of scientific reasoning. In R. S. Siegler (Ed.), *Children's thinking: What develops?* Hillsdale, NJ: Erlbaum.

Simmons, R. G., Blyth, D. A., Van Cleave, E. F., & Busch, D. M. (1979). Entry into early adolescence: The impact of school structure, puberty, and early dating on self-esteem. *American Sociological Review, 44*(6), 948–967.

Simon, H. A. (1975). The function equivalence of problem-solving skills. *Cognitive Psychology, 7,* 268–288.

Simpson, E. L. (1974). Moral development research: A case study of scientific cultural bias. *Human Development, 17*(2), 81–106.

Sinclair-de-Zwart, H. (1967). *Acquisition du langage et dévèloppement de la pensée.* Paris: Dunod.

Singer, J. L. (1973). *The child's world of make-believe.* New York: Academic Press.

Singer, J. L. (1978). Experimental studies of daydreaming and the stream of thought. In K. S. Pope & J. L. Singer (Eds.), *The stream of consciousness* (pp. 187–223). New York: Plenum Press.

Siqueland, E. R. (1968). Reinforcement patterns and extinction inhuman newborns. *Journal of Experimental Child Psychology, 6,* 431–442.

Siqueland, E. R., & Lipsitt, J. P. (1966). Conditioned head-turning in human newborns. *Journal of Experimental Child Psychology, 3,* 356–376.

Skinner, B. F. (1938). *The behavior of organisms.* New York: Appleton-Century-Crofts.

Skinner, B. F. (1953). *Science and human behavior.* New York: Macmillan.

Skinner, B. F. (1957). *Verbal behavior.* New York: Appleton-Century-Crofts.

Skodak, M., & Skeels, H. M. (1949). A final follow-up study of 100 adopted children. *Journal of Genetic Psychology, 75,* 85–125.

Skolnick, A. (1981). Married lives: Longitudinal perspectives on marriage. In D. H. Eichorn, J. A. Clausen, N. Haan, M. P. Honzik, & P. H. Mussen (Eds.), *Present and past in middle life* (pp. 269–298). New York: Academic Press.

Skolnick, A. (in press). Early attachment and personal relationships across the life course. In R. Lerner & D. Featherman, (Eds.), *Life-span development and behavior* (Vol. 7). Hillsdale, NJ: Erlbaum.

Slobin, D. I. (1979). *Psycholinguistics* (2nd ed.). Glenview, IL: Scott, Foresman.

Slobin, D. I. (1982). Universal and particular in the acquisition of language. In L. Gleitman & E. Wanner (Eds.), *Language acquisition: The state of the art.* New York: Cambridge University Press.

Smedslund, J. (1961). The acquisition of conservation of substance and weight in children: Pt. 3. Extinction of conservation of weight acquired "normally" by means of empirical controls on a balance; Pt. 5. Practice in conflict situations without external reinforcement. *Scandinavian Journal of Psychology, 2,* 85–87, 156–160.

Smelser, N., & Erikson, E. H. (Eds.). (1980). *Themes of work and love in adulthood.* Cambridge, MA: Harvard University Press.

Smilansky, S. (1968). *The effects of sociodramatic play on disadvantaged pre-school children.* New York: Wiley.

Smith, A. (1966). Certain hypothesized hemispheric differences in language and visual functions in human adults. *Cortex, 2,* 109–126.

Smith, A. (1984). *The mind.* New York: Viking.

Smith, A., & Sugar, O. (1975). Development of above normal language and intelligence 21 years after hemispherectomy. *Neurology, 25,* 813–818.

Smith, D. W. (1977). *Growth and its disorders.* Philadelphia: W. B. Saunders.

Smith, M. B. (1968). Toward a conception of the competent self. In J. Clausen (Ed.), *Socialization and society* (Vol. 7, pp. 273–289). Boston: Little, Brown.

Smith, M. B. (1978). Perspectives on selfhood. *American Psychologist, 33*(12), 1053–1063.

Smith, R. E. (1979). *The subtle revolution: Women at work.* Washington, DC: The Urban Institute.

Snarey, J. R. (1985). Cross-cultural universality of social-moral development: A critical review of Kohlbergian research. *Psychological Bulletin, 97,* 202–232.

Snell, B. (1960). *The discovery of mind.* Cambridge, MA: Harvard University Press.

Snow, C. E. (1977). The development of conversation between mothers and babies. *Journal of Child Language, 4,* 1–22.

Snow, C. E., & Ferguson, C. A. (Eds.). (1977). *Talking to children: Language input and acquisition.* Cambridge: Cambridge University Press.

Sokolov, E. N. (1963). *Perception and the conditioned reflex.* New York: Macmillan.

Solomon, R. L., & Turner, L. H. (1962). Discriminative classical conditioning in dogs paralyzed by Curare can later control discriminative avoidance responses in the normal state. *Psychological Review, 69,* 202–219.

Sontag, L. W. (1966). Implications of fetal behavior and environment for adult personalities. *Annals of the New York Academy of Sciences, 134,* 782–786.

Sorell, G. T., & Nowak, C. A. (1981). The role of physical attractiveness as a contributor to human development. In R. M. Lerner & N. A. Busch-Rossenagel (Eds.), *Individuals as producers of their own development.* New York: Basic Books.

Sorenson, R. C. (1973). *Adolescent sexuality in contemporary America (The Sorensen Report).* New York: World.

Spanier, G., & Lewis, R. A. (1980). Marital quality: A review of the seventies. *Journal of Marriage and the Family, 42,* 825–840.

Spelke, E. S., & Owsley, C. J. (1979). Intermodal exploration and knowledge in infancy. *Infant Behavior and Development, 2,* 13–27.

Spelke, E. S. (1979). Perceiving bimodally specified events in infancy. *Developmental Psychology, 15,* 626–636.

Spelt, D. K. (1948). The conditioning of the human fetus in utero. *Journal of Experimental Psychology, 38,* 338–346.

Spencer, H. (1873). *Principles of psychology* (3rd ed., Vol. 2). New York: Appleton.

Spirduso, W. W. (1980). Physical fitness, aging, and psychomotor speed. *Journal of Gerontology, 35,* 850–865.

Spiro, M. E. (1954). Is the family universal? *American Anthropologist, 56,* 840–846.

Spitz, R. (1945). Hospitalism: An inquiry into the genesis of psychiatric conditions in early childhood. In R. S. Eissler (Ed.), *Psychoanalytic study of the child.* New Haven: Yale University Press.

Spitz, R. (1965). *The first year of life.* New York: International Universities Press.

Spitzer, R. L., Skodol, A. E., Gibbon, M., & Williams, J.B.W. (1983). *Psychopathology: A casebook.* New York: McGraw-Hill.

Springer, S. P., & Deutsch, G. (1981). *Left brain, right brain.* San Francisco: W. H. Freeman.

Stacey, N., Deardon, R., Pill, R., & Robinson, D. (1970). *Hospitals, children and their families: The report of a pilot study.* London: Routledge & Kegan Paul.

Stearns, P. (1980). Modernization and social history: Some suggestions and a muted cheer. *Journal of Social History, 17*(2), 189–209.

Stein, A. H., & Friedrich, L. K. (1975). The effects of television content on young children. In A. D. Pick (Ed.), *Minnesota Symposium of Child Psychology* (Vol. 9, pp. 78–105). Minneapolis: University of Minnesota Press.

Steinberg, B. M., & Dunn, L. A. (1976). Conservation competence and performance in Chiapas. *Human Development, 19,* 14–25.

Stephens, W. N. (1963). *The family in cross-cultural perspective.* New York: Holt, Rinehart, & Winston.

Stern, D. (1974). Mother and infant at play: The dyadic interaction involving facial, vocal, and gaze behaviors. In M. Lewis & L. A. Rosenblum (Eds.), *The effect of the infant upon the caregiver.* New York: Wiley.

Stern, D. (1977). *The first relationship: Infant and mother.* Cambridge, MA: Harvard University Press.

Stern, D. N. (1983). The early development of schemas of self, other, and "self with other." In J. D. Lichtenberg & S. Kaplan (Eds.), *Reflections on self psychology,* (pp. 49–84). Hillsdale, NJ: Erlbaum.

Sternberg, R. J., & Nigro, G. (1980). Developmental patterns in the solution of verbal analogies. *Child Development, 51,* 27–38.

Sternberg, R. J., & Powell, J. S. (1983). The development of intelligence. In P. H. Mussen (Ed.), *Handbook of child psychology* (Vol. 3, pp. 341–415). New York: Wiley.

Sternberg, R. J., & Rifkin, B. (1979). The development of analogical reasoning processes. *Journal of Experimental Child Psychology, 27,* 195–232.

Stevens, K. N. (1975). The potential role of property detectors in the perception of consonants. In C.G.M. Fant & M.A.A. Tatham (Eds.), *Auditory analysis and perception of speech.* New York: Academic Press.

Stevenson, H. W., Parker, T., Wilkinson, A., Bonnevaux, B., & Gonzalez, M. (1978). Schooling, environment and cognitive development: A cross-cultural study. *Monographs of the Society for Research in Child Development, 43* (Serial No. 175).

Stolz, H. R., & Stolz, L. M. (1951). *Somatic development of adolescent boys.* New York: Macmillan.

Stone, L. (1977). *The family, sex and marriage in England, 1500–1800.* New York: Harper & Row.

Strauss, M. S. (1979). Abstraction of prototypical information by adults and 10-month-old infants. *Journal of Experimental Psychology: Human Learning and Memory, 5,* 618–632.

Strauss, M. S., & Curtis, L. E. (1981). *Infant perception of patterns differing in goodness of form* Paper presented at the meeting of the Society for Research in Child Development, Boston.

Strehler, B. L., Ebert, J., Glass, H., & Schock, N. (Eds.). (1960). *The biology of aging.* Washington, DC: American Institute of Biological Sciences. (A symposium held at Galtenburg under sponsorship of AIBS and with support of NSF)

Struhsaker, T. T. (1967). Auditory communication among vervet monkeys (ceropithecusa ethiops). In S. A. Altmann (Ed.), *Social communication among primates* (pp. 281–324). Chicago: University of Chicago Press.

Sugarman, S. (1979). *Scheme, order and outcome: The development of classification in children's early block play.* Doctoral dissertation, University of California, Berkeley.

Sullivan, H. S. (1953). *The interpersonal theory of psychiatry.* New York: Norton.

Sunley, R. (1955). Early nineteenth-century American literature on child rearing. In M. Mead & M. Wolfenstein (Eds.), *Childhood in contemporary cultures* (pp. 50–167). Chicago: University of Chicago Press.

Suomi, S. J. (1982). Biological foundations and developmental psychobiology. In C. B. Kopp & J. B. Krakow (Eds.), *The child: Development in a social context* (pp. 42–91). Reading, MA: Addison-Wesley.

Super, C. M., & Harkness, S. (1982). The development of affect in infancy and early childhood. In D. A. Wagner & H. W. Stevenson (Eds.), *Cultural perspectives on child development* (pp. 1–19). San Francisco: W. H. Freeman.

Surber, C. F. (1977). Developmental processes in social inference: A verging of intentions and consequences in moral judgment. *Developmental Psychology, 13*, 654–665.

Sussman, G. D. (1982). *Selling mothers' milk: The wet-nursing business in France, 1715–1914.* Urbana: University of Illinois Press.

Sutton-Smith, B. (1980). Piaget on play: A critique. *Psychological Review, 73*, 104–110.

Svejda, M., Campos, J., & Emde, R. N. (1980). Mother-infant "bonding": Failure to generalize. *Child Development, 51*, 775–780.

Svejda, M., Pannabecker, B., & Emde, R. N. (1982). Parent-to-infant attachment: A critique of the early "bonding" model. In R. N. Emde & R. J. Harmon (Eds.), *The development of attachment and affiliative systems: Psychological aspects.* New York: Plenum Press.

Swidler, A. (1980). Love and adulthood in American culture. In N. Smelser & E. H. Erikson (Eds.), *Themes of work and love in adulthood.* Cambridge, MA: Harvard University Press.

Tanner, J. M. (1970). Physical growth. In P. H. Mussen (Ed.), *Carmichael's manual of child psychology* (Vol. 1, pp. 77–155). New York: Wiley.

Tanner, J. M. (1972). Human growth hormone. *Nature, 237*, 431–437.

Tanner, J. M. (1974). Variability of growth and maturity in newborn infants. In M. Lewis & L. A. Rosenblum (Eds.), *The effect of the infant on its caregiver.* New York: Wiley.

Tanner, J. M. (1978). *Fetus into man: Physical growth from conception to maturity.* Cambridge, MA: Harvard University Press.

Tanner, J. M., & Inhelder, B. (Eds.). (1956). *Discussions on child development* (Vol. 4). London: Tavistock.

Tanner, J. M., & Whitehouse, R. H. (1976). Clinical longitudinal standards for height, weight, height velocity, weight velocity and the stages of puberty. *Archives of Disease in Childhood, 51*, 170–179.

Terrace, H. S. (1985). In the beginning was the "name." *American Psychologist, 40*, 1011–1028.

Terrace, H. S., & Bever, T. G. (1976). What might be learned from studying language in the chimpanzee? The importance of symbolizing oneself. *Annals of the New York Academy of Science, 280*, 586.

Theroux, T. (1980, September 14). The great class reunion bazaar. *New York Times Magazine*, pp. 88ff.

Thomas, A., & Chess, S. (1977). *Temperament and development.* New York: Brunner/Mazel.

Thomas, A., & Chess, S. (1980). *The dynamics of psychological development.* New York: Brunner/Mazel.

Thomas, A., Chess, S., & Birch, H. G. (1968). *Temperament and behavior disorders in children.* New York: New York University Press.

Thomas, A., Chess, S., & Birch, H. G. (1970). The origin of personality. *Scientific American, 223*(2).

Thomas, A., Chess, S., Birch, H. G., Hertzig, M. E., & Korn, S. (1983). *Behavioral individuality in early childhood.* New York: New York University Press.

Thomas, A., Chess, S., & Korn, S. (1982). The reality of difficult temperament. *Merrill-Palmer Quarterly, 28*(1), 1–20.

Thomas, L. (1979). The deacon's masterpiece. In L. Thomas (Ed.), *The Medusa and the snail* (pp. 130–136). New York: Viking.

Thomas, L. (1982, March 14). The art of teaching science. *New York Times Magazine*, 98ff.

Thomas, L. (1983). *Late night thoughts on listening to Mahler's Ninth Symphony.* Toronto: Bantam.

Thompson, R. A., Lamb, M. E., & Estes, D. (1982). Stability of infant-mother attachment and its relationship to changing life circumstances in an unselected middle class sample. *Child Development, 53*, 144–148.

Thompson, W. R., & Melzack, R. (1956). Early environment. *Scientific American, 194*(1), 38–42.

Thurstone, L. (1938). Primary mental abilities. *Psychometric Monographs* (No. 1). Chicago: University of Chicago Press.

Timiras, P. S. (1972). *Developmental physiology and aging.* New York: Macmillan.

Tizard, B., & Hodges, J. (1978). The effect of institutional rearing on the development of eight-year-old children. *Journal of Child Psychology and Psychiatry, 19*, 99–118.

Tizard, B., & Rees, J. (1974). A comparison of the effects of adoption, restoration to the natural mother, and continued institutionalization on the cognitive development of four-year-old children. *Child Development, 45*(1), 92–99.

Tizard, B., & Rees, J. (1975). The effect of early institutional rearing on the behavior problems and affectional relationships of four-year-old children. *Journal of Child Psychology and Psychiatry and Allied Disciplines, 16*(1), 61–73.

Tizard, J. (1974). Early malnutrition, growth and mental development. *British Medical Bulletin, 30,* 169–174.

Tizard, J., & Tizard, B. (1974). The institution as an environment for development. In M.P.M. Richards (Ed.), *The integration of a child into a social world* (pp. 137–152). Cambridge: Cambridge University Press.

Tomkins, S. S. (1962). *Affect, imagery, consciousness* (Vols. 1 & 2). New York: Springer.

Trabasso, T. (1975). Representation, memory and reasoning: How do we make transitive inferences? In A. D. Pick (Ed.), *Minnesota Symposium on Child Psychology* (Vol. 9). Minneapolis: University of Minnesota Press.

Tracy, F., & Stimpfl, J. (1909). *The psychology of childhood* (7th ed.). Boston: D. C. Heath.

Traub, A. C., & Orbach, J. (1964). Psychophysical studies of body-image: The adjustable body-distorting mirror. *Archives of General Psychiatry, 11,* 53–66.

Trexler, R. C. (1973). Infanticide in Florence: New sources and first results. *History of Childhood Quarterly, 1*(1), 98–116.

Trilling, L. (1972). *Sincerity and authenticity.* Cambridge, MA: Harvard University Press.

Trivers, R. L. (1974). Parent-offspring conflict. *American Zoologist, 14,* 249–264.

Troll, L. (1975). *Development in early and middle adulthood.* Monterey, CA: Brooks/Cole.

Trow, G.W.S., Jr. (1978, May 29). Profile of Ahmet Ertegun. *New Yorker.*

Tulkin S. R., & Konner, M. J. (1973). Alternative conceptions of intellectual functioning. *Human Development, 16,* 33–52.

Turiel, E. (1983). *The development of social knowledge: Morality and convention.* Cambridge: Cambridge University Press.

Tversky, A., & Kahneman, D. (1971). Belief in the law of small numbers. *Psychological Bulletin, 2,* 105–110.

Tyler, L. E. (1978). *Individuality: Human possibilities and personal choice in the psychological development of men and women.* San Francisco: Jossey-Bass.

Uhlenberg, P. (1980). Death and the family. *Journal of Family History, 5*(3), 313–320.

Ullian, D. (1984). Why girls are good: A constructivist view. *American Journal of Orthopsychiatry, 54*(1), 71–82.

UNICEF. (1983). The state of the world's children, 1984. Oxford University Press.

U.S. National Center for Health Statistics (annual). *Vital Statistics of the U.S.*

Utall, W. R. (1978). *The psychology of mind.* Hillsdale, NJ: Erlbaum.

Vaillant, G. E. (1977). *Adaptation to life.* Boston: Little, Brown.

Van Gennep, A. (1961). *Rites of passage* (M. B. Vizedon & G. L. Caffee, Trans.). Chicago: University of Chicago Press.

Van Lawick-Goodall, J. (1972). *In the shadow of man.* New York: Dell.

Vaughn, B., Egeland, B., Sroufe, L. A., & Waters, E. (1979). Individual differences in infant-mother attachment at twelve and eighteen months: Stability and change in families under stress. *Child Development, 50,* 971–975.

Vaughn, B., Gove, F., & Egeland, B. (1980). The relationship between out-of-home care and the quality of infant-mother attachment in an economically disadvantaged sample. *Child Development, 51,* 1203–1214.

Veroff, J., Douvan, G., & Kulka, R. A. (1981). *The inner American: A self-portrait from 1957 to 1976.* New York: Basic Books.

Vinovskis, M. A. (1981, Summer). An "epidemic" of adolescent pregnancy? *Journal of Family History, 6,* 205–230.

Vondracek, F. W., & Lerner, R. M. (1982). Vocational role development in adolescence. In B. Wolman (Ed.), *Handbook of developmental psychology* (pp. 602–614). Englewood Cliffs, NJ: Prentice-Hall.

Von Senden, M. (1960). *Space and sight.* (P. Heath, Trans.). New York: Free Press.

Vygotsky, L. S. (1962). *Thought and language.* Cambridge, MA: MIT Press.

Vygotsky, L. S. (1978). *Mind in society: The development of higher psychological processes.* Cambridge, MA: Harvard University Press.

Wachtel, P. (1977). *Psychoanalysis and behavior therapy: Toward an integration.* New York: Basic Books.

Waddington, C. H. (1966). *Principles of development and differentiation.* New York: Macmillan.

Wade, N. (1976). IQ and heredity: Suspicion of fraud beclouds classic experiment. *Science, 194,* 916–919.

Walford, R. L. (1983). *Maximum life span.* New York: Avon Books.

Walker, L. (1984). Sex differences in the development of moral reasoning: A critical review of the literature. *Child Development, 55*(3), 677–691.

Wallon, H. (1949). *Les origines du caractère chez l'enfant: Les Précludes du sentiment de personalité* (2nd ed.). Paris: Presses Universitaires de France.

Wallston, B. S., DeVellis, B. M., & DeVellis, R. F. (1983). Social support and physical health. *Health Psychology, 2,* 367–391.

Washburn, S. L. (1978). Human behavior and the behavior of the other animals. *American Psychologist, 33*(5), 405–418.

Washburn, S. L., & DeVore, I. (1961). In S. L. Washburn (Ed.), *Social life of early man.* Chicago: Aldine.

Washburn, S. L., & Howell, F. C. (1960). Human evolution and culture. In S. Tax, *The evolution of man* (Vol. 2). Chicago: University of Chicago Press.

Waterman, A. S. (1982). Identity development from adolescence to adulthood: An extension of theory and a review of research. *Developmental Psychology, 18*(3), 341–358.

Waterman, A. S., Geary, P. S., & Waterman, C. K. (1974). A longitudinal study of changes in ego identity status from the freshman to the senior year at college. *Developmental Psychology, 10,* 387–392.

Waterman, A. S., & Waterman, C. K. (1971). A longitudinal study of changes in ego identity status during the freshman year at college. *Developmental Psychology, 5,* 167–173.

Waterman, A. S., & Waterman, C. K. (1972). The relationship between freshman ego identity status and subsequent academic behavior: A test of the predictive validity of Marcia's categorization system for identity status. *Developmental Psychology, 6*(1), 179.

Waters, E. (1978). The reliability and stability of individual differences in infant-mother attachment. *Child Development, 49,* 483–494.

Waters, E. (1980). Traits, relationships and behavioral systems: The attachment construct and the organization of behavior and development. In K. Immelman, E. Barlow, M. Main, & L. Petrinovich (Eds.), *Development of behavior.* New York: Cambridge University Press.

Waters, E., & Deane, D. (1982). Infant-mother attachment: Theories, models, recent data, and some tasks for comparative developmental analysis. In L. W. Hoffman, R. Gandelman, & H. R. Schiffman (Eds.), *Parenting: Its causes and consequences.* Hillsdale, NJ: Erlbaum.

Waters, E., & Noyes, D. M. (1983–1984). Psychological parenting vs. attachment theory: The child's best interests and the risks in doing the right things for the wrong reasons. *New York University Review of Law and Social Changes, 12*(3), 505–515.

Waters, E., Wipman, J., & Sroufe, L. A. (1979). Attachment, positive affect, and competence in the peer group: Two studies in construct validation. *Child Development, 50,* 821–829.

Watson, J. B. (1913). Psychology as the behaviorist views it. *Psychological Review, 20,* 158–177.

Watson, J. B. (1950). *Behaviorism.* New York: Norton.

Watson, J. B., & Rayner, R. A. (1920). Conditioned emotional reactions. *Journal of Experimental Psychology, 3,* 1–14.

Watson, J. D., & Crick, F.H.C. (1953). Molecular structure of nucleic acids. *Nature, 171,* 737–738.

Watson, J. S. (1966). The development and generalization of "contingency awareness" in early infancy: Some hypotheses. *Merrill-Palmer Quarterly, 12,* 123–135.

Watson, J. S. (1972). Smiling, cooing, and "the game." *Merrill-Palmer Quarterly, 18,* 323–339.

Watson, J. S. (1979). Perception of contingency as a determinant of social responsiveness. In E. Thomas (Ed.), *The origins of social responsiveness.* Hillsdale, NJ: Erlbaum.

Watson, J. S. (1983). Contingency perception in early social development. Unpublished paper. Berkeley: University of California.

Watson, M. W. (1981). The development of social roles: A sequence of social-cognitive development. In K. W. Fisher (Ed.), *New directions for child development: Cognitive development* (pp. 33–41). San Francisco: Jossey-Bass.

Webb, E. J., Campbell, D. T., Schwartz, R. D., & Sechrest, L. (1966). *Unobtrusive measures: A survey of non-reactive research in social science.* Chicago: Rand McNally.

Webster's Ninth New Collegiate Dictionary. (1984). Springfield, MA: Merriam-Webster.

Wechsler, D. (1955). *Manual for the Wechsler Adult Intelligence Scale.* New York: Psychological Corporation.

Wegner, D. M., & Wallacher, R. R. (Eds.). (1977). *The self in social psychology.* New York: Oxford University Press.

Weideger, P. (1975). *Menstruation and menopause.* New York: Knopf.

Weiner, I. B. (1980). Psychopathology in adolescence. In J. Adelson (Ed.), *Handbook of adolescent psychology* (pp. 447–471). New York: Wiley.

Weiss, M. J. (1984, June). The riddle of teenage suicide. *Ladies Home Journal,* 54.

Weiss, R. (1982). Attachment in adult life. In C. M. Parkes & J. Stevenson-Hinde (Eds.), *The place of attachment in human behavior.* New York: Basic Books.

Weiss, R. (n.d.). *The social ties of children: Nature and development as inferred from observations of adult social ties.* Unpublished paper.

Weiss, R. S. (1973). *Loneliness: The experience of social and emotional isolation.* New York: Basic Books.

Werner, E. E., & Smith, R. S. (1977). *Kauai's children come of age.* Honolulu: University of Hawaii Press.

Werner, E. E., & Smith, R. S. (1982). *Vulnerable but invincible: A study of resilient children.* New York: McGraw-Hill.

Werner, H. (1957). The concept of development from a comparative and organismic point of view. In D. B. Harris (Ed.), *The concept of development*. Minneapolis: University of Minnesota Press.

Werner, H., & Kaplan, B. (1963). *Symbol formation*. New York: Wiley.

Wertheimer, M. (1945). *Productive thinking*. Chicago: University of Chicago Press.

Wertheimer, M. (1961). Psychomotor coordination of auditory and visual space at birth. *Science, 134,* 1692.

Whitaker, C. (1972). Quoted in J. L. Framo (Ed.), *Family interaction: A dialogue between family researchers and family therapists*. New York: Springer.

White, B. L., Castle, P., & Held, R. (1964). Observation on the development of visually directed reaching. *Child Development, 35,* 349–364.

White, B. L., & Held, R. (1966). Plasticity of sensory-motor development in the human infant. In J. F. Rosenblith & W. Allinsmith (Eds.), *The causes of behavior*. Boston: Allyn & Bacon.

White, L. (1978). Science and the sense of self: The medieval background of a modern confrontation. *Daedalus, 107*(2), 47–59.

White, R. W. (1960). Competence and the psychosexual stages of development. In M. Jones (Ed.), *Nebraska Symposium on Motivation* (pp. 97–141). Lincoln: University of Nebraska Press.

White, R. W. (1963). Ego and reality in psychoanalytic theory: A proposal regarding independent ego energies. *Psychological Issues, 3*(3), Monograph 11. New York: International Universities Press.

White, R. W. (Ed.). (1966). *The study of lives*. New York: Atherton.

White, S. (1965). Evidence for a hierarchical arrangement of learning processes. In L. P. Lipsitt & C. C. Spiker (Eds.), *Advances in child development and behavior* (pp. 184–220). New York: Academic Press.

White, S. (1970). The learning theory approach. In P. Mussen (Ed.), *Carmichael's manual of child psychology* (Vol. 1, pp. 657–702). New York: Wiley.

White, S. (1975). *Speculations on the future fate of early childhood education*. Paper presented at the American Education Research Association, Washington, DC.

White, S. (1976). The active organism in theoretical behavior. *Human Development, 19,* 99–107.

Whiting, B. B., & Whiting, J.W.M. (1975). *Children in six cultures: A psycho-cultural analysis*. Cambridge, MA: Harvard University Press.

Whiting, J.W.M., & Whiting, B. B. (1973). Altruistic and egoistic behavior in six cultures. In L. Nader & T. W. Maretzki (Eds.), *Cultural illness and health: Essays in human adaptation*. Washington, DC: American Anthropological Association.

Wiesel, T. N., & Hubel, D. H. (1965). Extent of recovery from the effects of visual deprivation in kittens. *Journal of Neurophysiology, 28,* 1060–1072.

Wilensky, H. L. (1981). Family life cycle, work and the quality of life: Reflections on the roots of happiness, despair and indifference in modern society. In B. Gardell & G. Johansson (Eds.), *A working life: A social science contribution to work reform* (pp. 235–265). New York: Wiley.

Willerman, L., Broman, C. H., & Fiedler, M. (1970). Infant development, preschool IQ, and social class. *Child Development, 170,* 1329–1331.

Williams, R. J. (1956). *Biochemical individuality*. Los Angeles: Cancer Control Society.

Williams, R. J. (1976). On your startling biochemical individuality. *Executive Health, 12*(8).

Wilson, E. O. (1975). *Sociobiology: The new synthesis*. Cambridge, MA: Harvard University Press.

Wilson, E. O. (1978). *On human nature*. Cambridge, MA: Harvard University Press.

Winick, M., Meyer, N. K., & Harris, R. C. (1975). Malnutrition and environmental enrichment by early adoption. *Science, 190,* 1173–1175.

Winn, M. (1978). *The plug-in drug*. New York: Viking.

Winnicott, D. W. (1965). *The maturation processes and the facilitating environment*. New York: International Universities Press.

Wohlwell, J. F. (1973). *The study of behavioral development*. New York: Academic Press.

Wolf, K. M. (1967). *The origins of individuality*. Unpublished paper, Yale University.

Wolfenstein, M. (1954). *Children's humor: A psychological analysis*. Glencoe, IL: Free Press.

Wolfenstein, M. (1955). French parents take their children to the park. In M. Mead & M. Wolfenstein (Eds.), *Childhood in contemporary cultures* (pp. 169–178). Chicago: University of Chicago Press.

Wolfenstein, M. (1978). *Children's humor*. Bloomington: Indiana University Press.

Wolff, P. H. (1960). The developmental psychologies of Jean Piaget and psychoanalysis. *Psychological Issues, 2*(1), Monograph 5.

Wolff, P. H. (1963). Developmental and motivational concepts in Piaget's sensorimotor theory of intelligence. *Journal of the American Academy of Child Psychology, 2,* 225–243.

Wolpe, J., & Rachman, S. (1960). Psychoanalytic "evidence": A critique based on Freud's case of Little Hans. *Journal of Nervous and Mental Disease, 131,* 135–147.

Woodruff, D. S. (1978). Brain electrical activity and behavior relationships over the life span. In P. B. Baltes & O. G. Brim, Jr. (Eds.), *Life-span development and behavior* (Vol. 1, pp. 111–179). New York: Academic Press.

Woods, B. T., & Teuber, H. L. (1978). Changing patterns of childhood aphasia. *Annals of Neurology, 3,* 273–280.

Wrigley, E. A. (1972). The process of modernization and the industrial revolution in England. *Journal of Interdisciplinary History, 3*(2), 225–260.

Wrong, D. (1961). The oversocialized conception of man in modern sociology. *American Sociological Review, 26,* 183–193.

Yakovlev, T. I., & Lecours, A. R. (1967). The myelogenetic cycles of regional maturation of the brain. In A. Minkowski (Ed.), *Regional development of the brain in early life.* Oxford: Basil Blackwell.

Yando, R., Seitz, V., & Ziegler, E. (1979). *Intellectual and personality characteristics of children: Social-class and ethnic-group differences.* Hillsdale, NJ: Erlbaum.

Yankelovich, D. (1981). *New rules.* New York: Random House.

Youniss, J. (1980). *Parents and peers in social development: A Sullivan-Piaget perspective.* Chicago: University of Chicago Press.

Zahn-Waxler, C., Radke-Yarrow, M., & King, R. A. (1979). Child-rearing and children's prosocial initiations toward victims of distress. *Child Development, 50,* 319–330.

Zelnick, M., Kanter, J. F., & Ford, K. (1981). Sex and pregnancy in adolescence. In *Sage Library of Social Research* (Vol. 133). Beverly Hills: Sage.

Copyrights and Acknowledgments

Chapter 2

Page 36 Peter Arnold, Inc., photo by George Roos.   **39** (top) Black Star, photo by Yves Debraine; (bottom) Monkmeyer Press Photo Service, photo by Mimi Forsyth.   **41** From the infant laboratories of Professor Einar R. Siqueland, Brown University.   **42** Archive Pictures, photo by Abigail Heyman.   **47** John and Laura Hawkins.   **50** (left) Texas Stock Photos, photo by Michael D. Sullivan; (upper right) Trinity Photos, photo by R. Meier; (lower right) Jim West.   **51** Nina Leen, *Life* Magazine © 1964 Time Inc.   **52** Universal Press Syndicate.   **56** Photos courtesy of Vivian Dixon, Houston, TX.   **58** Culver Pictures.   **59** (left) UPI/Bettmann Newsphotos; (right) Black Star, © James Kemp.   **63** Photo Researchers, photo by Ed Lattau.

Chapter 3

Page 66 Jeroboam, photo by Ken Graves.   **71** Strix Pix.   **73** © Academy of Motion Picture Arts and Sciences.   **76** Culver Pictures.   **78** Sovfoto.   **82** Monkmeyer Press Photo Service, photo by Mimi Forsyth.   **84** National Library of Medicine.   **87** With the compliments of the Austrian Press and Information Service.   **91** Courtesy of the Harvard University News Office.   **94** Courtesy of the William Alanson White Psychiatric Foundation, Inc.   **96** Black Star, photo by Yves Debraine.   **101** Monkmeyer Press Photo Service, photo by Bill Anderson.

Part II

Page 108 Jeroboam, photo by Suzanne Arms.

Chapter 4

Page 110 Jeroboam, photo by Suzanne Arms.   **119** Culver Pictures.   **120** Bettmann Archives/BBC Hulton Picture Library.   **123** (left) Strix Pix; (right) Archive Pictures, photo by Charles Harbutt.   **132** UPI/Bettmann Newsphotos.   **133** Photo Researchers, photo © Robert Goldstein 1982.   **137** (upper) Jeroboam, photo by Suzanne Arms; (lower) Stock Boston, photo © Jean-Claude Lejeune.   **140** Stephen McBrady.   **142** Archive Pictures, photos by Michael O'Brien.

Chapter 5

Page 148 Peter Aitken.   **152** Richard Hutchings.   **154** (upper) Richard Hutchings; (lower) Stephen McBrady.   **156** Strix Pix.   **167** Barbara Gannon.   **179** Monkmeyer Photo Press Service, photos by Zimbel.   **180** Richard Hutchings.   **183** Jean Shapiro.   **184** John and Laura Hawkins.   **187** Stock Boston, photo by Peter Menzel.

Chapter 6

Page 190 Jean-Claude Lejeune.   **194** © Continental Pictures.   **201** (left) From *La Deportation* (L'academie des Sciences Morales et Politiques, 1968), photo courtesy of the Simon Wiesenthal Center Library; (right) from *The Murders at Bullenhuser Damm* by Gunther Schwarberg, © 1984 National Jewish Resource Center. By permission of Indiana University Press, photo courtesy of the Simon Wiesenthal Center Library.   **204** Everett Waters.   **205** Strix Pix.   **206** Jean Shapiro.   **218** Photo Researchers, photo by Erika Stone.

Part III

Page 234 Stephen McBrady.

Chapter 7

Page 236 Stock Boston, photo © Elizabeth Crews.   **240** By permission of the Houghton Library, Harvard University.   **243** (left) State University of New York at Albany; (right) photo courtesy of Gordon Gallup, Jr.   **246** Stephen McBrady.   **249** Maria Karras.   **252** (two upper left, middle, two lower) Jean Shapiro; (upper right) Stock Boston, photo by George Cohen; (middle left) World Health Organization, photo by Chevalier; (middle right) Stock Boston, photo by Frank Siteman.   **253** The Margaret S. Mahler Psychiatric Research Foundation.   **254** (left) Nawrocki Stock Photos, photo by Jim Wright; (right) Monkmeyer Press Service Photos, photo by Mimi Forsyth.   **257** Stock Boston, photo by Jean-Claude Lejeune.

Chapter 8

Page 268 Nawrocki Stock Photos, photo by Jim Whitmer.   **270** Perkins School for the Blind.   **271** © American Academy of Motion Picture Arts and Sciences.   **272** American Foundation for the Blind.   **277** Massachusetts Institute of Technology.   **282** Joanne Meldrum.   **285** Nawrocki Stock Photos, © William S. Nawrocki.   **287** Stock Boston, photo by Daniel S. Brody.   **288** Strix Pix.   **289** Stock Boston, photo by Jean-Claude Lejeune.   **291** Stock Boston, photo by Elizabeth Crews.   **293** Stock Boston, photo by Christopher Morrow.   **296** Strix Pix.   **301** Animals, Animals, © Stewart D. Halperin.   **303** H. S. Terrace, Columbia University.

Chapter 9

Page 308 Jean-Claude Lejeune.   **310** © Academy of Motion Picture Arts and Sciences.   **312** Strix Pix.   **317** AP/Wide World Photos.   **318** Stock Boston, photo by Elizabeth Crews.   **319** Peter Glass.   **322** Helen Borke.   **327** Texas Stock Photos, photo by Bob Daemmrich.   **329** Stock Boston, photo by Owen Franken.   **330** (left) Photo Researchers, photo by Alice Kandell; (right) Barbara Kirk Baker.   **332** (left) Derek Bayes, *Life* Magazine © Time Inc.; (right) Henry Grossman, *People* Weekly, © 1974 Time Inc.   **335** (left) Courtesy of Dr. John Money from J. Money and A. A. Ehrhardt, *Man and Woman, Boy and Girl*, Baltimore: Johns Hopkins University Press, 1973; (right) M. I. New and R. L. Levine, "Congenital adrenal hyperplasia" in *Advances in Human Genetics*, Vol. 4 by H. Harris and K. Hirschhorn (eds.), New York: Plenum Press, 1973.   **337** Stock Boston, photo by Frances Cox.   **339** Photo Researchers, photo by Michael Hayman.   **341** Stock Boston, photo by Elizabeth Crews.   **343** Photo Researchers, photo by Myron Papiz.   **345** (left) Stock Boston, photo by Jean-Claude Lejeune; (right) Stock Boston, photo by James R. Holland.   **346** (top) Jean Shapiro; (bottom) Stock Boston, photo by Michael Hayman.

Part IV

Page 350 Nawrocki Stock Photos, photo by Jim Wright.

Chapter 10

Page 352 Strix Pix.   **355** Courtesy of Sheldon White.   **356** Roger W. Neal.   **357** Jeroboam, photo by Budd Gray.   **360** Courtesy of Jerome Bruner, photo by Stanley Seligson.   **362** Strix Pix.   **363** Thomas Judd.   **370** (left) Stock Boston, photo by Richard Balzar; (right) Stock Boston, photo by Cary Wolinsky.   **371** Martin R. Jones.   **375** Brown Brothers.   **377** Stock Boston, photo by Elizabeth Crews.   **383** Tom Lagace.

Chapter 11

Page 386 Nawrocki Stock Photos, photo by Jim Wright.
391 © Academy of Motion Picture Arts and Sciences.
400 Texas Stock Photos, photo by Michael D. Sullivan.
402 Marilyn Sanders. **403** Texas Stock Photos, photo by
David E. Kennedy. **405** Photo source unknown.
406 Archive Pictures, photo by Earl Dotter. **409** (left)
Nawrocki Stock Photos, photo by Jim Wright; (right) Stock
Boston, photo by Peter Menzel. **410** Courtesy of Family
Communications, Inc. **413** Marshall Berman. **416** Strix
Pix. **417** Strix Pix. **419** Archive Pictures, photo by
Abigail Heyman.

Chapter 12

Page 426 Archive Pictures, photo by Bill Burke. **428** Archive Pictures, photo by Charles Harbutt. **430** Strix Pix.
436 Strix Pix. **439** Stock Boston, photo by Michael Hayman.
441 Archive Pictures, photo by Earl Dotter. **442** From *Case
Studies in Behavior Modification*, by Leonard P. Ullmann
and Leonard Krasner (eds.), New York: Holt, Rinehart and
Winston, 1965. **444** Texas Stock Photos, photo by Michael
D. Sullivan. **445** Archive Pictures, photo by Mary Ellen
Mark. **446** (top) Strix Pix; (bottom) AP/Wide World Photos. **447** Printed by permission of the Estate of Norman
Rockwell, copyright © 1954 Estate of Norman Rockwell.
449 Jean-Claude Lejeune.

Part V

Page 450 Photo supplied by the author.

Chapter 13

Page 452 Photo supplied by the author. **461** Monkmeyer
Press Photo Service, photo by Paul Conklin. **462** Archive
Pictures, photo by Abigail Heyman. **463** Jeroboam, photo
by Jane Scherr. **464** Photos supplied by the author.
465 Nawrocki Stock Photos, photo by Jim Whitmer. **469** Archive Pictures, photo by Abigail Heyman. **471** Bob Combs.
472 Library of Congress. **474** (left) Photo Researchers,
photo by Chester Higgins, Jr.; (right) Stock Boston.
475 Photo Researchers, photo by Erika Stone. **478** Stock
Boston, photo by Frank Siteman. **479** Archive Pictures,
photo by Joan Lipton. **481** Texas Stock Photos, photo
by Bob Daemmrich. **483** Texas Stock Photos, photo by
Michael D. Sullivan. **484** Jim West. **485** Jeroboam, photo
by Michael Payne. **487** Texas Stock Photos, photo by
David E. Kennedy.

Chapter 14

Page 490 Stock Boston, photo by Tom Cheek. **492** National
Archives. **494** Texas Stock Photos, photo by Bob
Daemmrich. **495** Strix Pix. **497** John and Laura
Hawkins. **498** Monkmeyer Press Photos, photo by Sam
Falk. **500** Texas Stock Photos, photo by Michael D. Sullivan.
502 Jean-Claude Lejeune. **505** (top) Strix Pix; (bottom)
Roger W. Neal. **509** Dale G. Folstad. **510** Texas Stock
Photos, photo by Ralph Barrera. **515** Texas Stock Photos,
photo by Michael D. Sullivan. **519** Archive Pictures, photo
by Rebecca Chao. **520** Jeroboam, photo by Bruce Kliewe.

Color Sections

First Color Insert

Page 1 Drs. Michael E. Phelps/John C. Mazziotta, UCLA
(Medicine). **2** (all) © Donald Yeager, 1973, 1977, 1984,
1985. **3** (left and upper right) © Donald Yeager, 1973, 1977,
1984, 1985; (lower right) Jeroboam, photo by Evan Johnson.
4 (upper) Jeroboam, photo by Evan Johnson; (lower left)
Westlight, photo by Chuck O'Rear; (lower right) Magnum
Photos, photo by Eve Arnold.

Second Color Insert

Page 1 Culver Pictures, Inc. **2** (left) Jeroboam, photo by
Kent Reno; (upper right) Peter Arnold, Inc., photo by
Jacques Jangoux; (lower right) Jeroboam, photo by Kit
Hedman. **3** (upper) John Running; (lower) Jeroboam,
photo by Kit Hedman. **4** (upper) Zev Radovan, Jerusalem;
(lower) Jean Shapiro.

Third Color Insert

Page 1 Zev Radovan, Jerusalem. **2** Texas Stock Photos,
photos by Bob Daemmrich. **3** Richard Hutchings.
4 Richard Hutchings.

Fourth Color Insert

Page 1 (upper left) Jeroboam, photo by Jorge Ianiszewski;
(upper right) Westlight, photo by Craig Aurness; (middle
left) Magnum Photos, photo by Tony Ray Jones; (middle
right) Magnum Photos, photo by C. Steele-Perkins; (lower)
Magnum Photos, photo by Paul Fusco. **2** (upper left)
Photo Researchers, photo by Sam Brooks; (upper right)
Magnum Photos, photo by C. Steele-Perkins; (middle)
Photo Researchers, photo by Tomas D. W. Friedmann;
(lower) Photo Researchers, photo by Diane Rawson.
3 (upper left) Magnum Photos, photo by C. Steele-Perkins;
(upper right) Photo Researchers, photo by Hamilton
Wright; (lower left) Photo Researchers, photo by George
Holton; (middle) Jeroboam, Rocky Weldon; (middle right)
Photo courtesy of Joan and Skip Ennis, New York. **4** (upper
right) © Courtesy of Joan Collins; (upper left) drawing by
Helen E. Hokinson, © 1948, 1976 The *New Yorker* Magazine,
Inc.; (lower left) drawing by Whitney Darrow, Jr., © 1947,
1975 The *New Yorker* Magazine, Inc.; (lower right) AP/Wide
World Photos, photo by Pete Souza, The White House.

Cover

(Middle) Nick Pavloff; (lower left) Nawrocki Stock Photos,
photo by W. R. Miller; (lower middle) Nick Pavloff; (lower
right) John Running.

Index